NEW ORLEANS JAZZ, MAHALIA JACKSON AND THE PHILOSOPHY OF ART

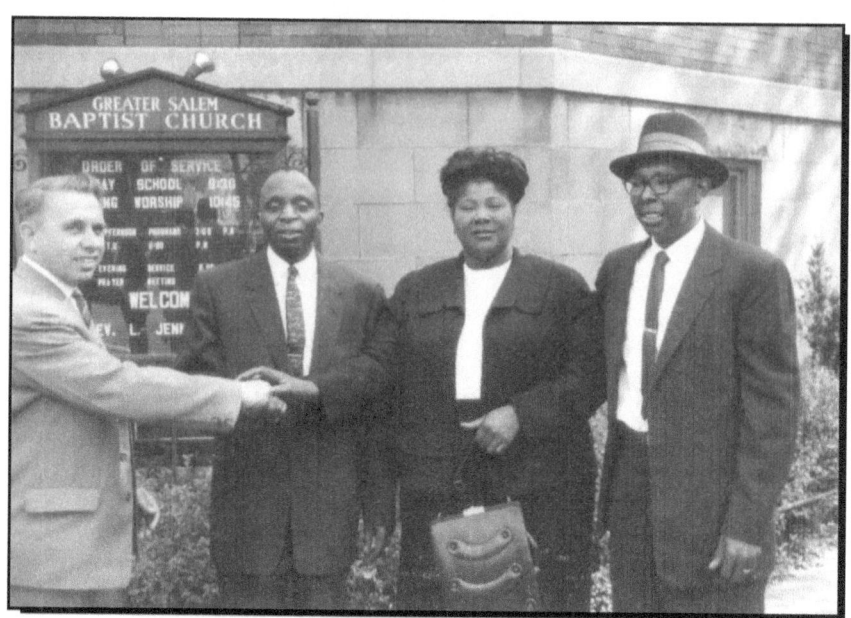

Hans Rookmaaker meets Mahalia Jackson at the Greater Salem Baptist Church in Chicago, 1961.

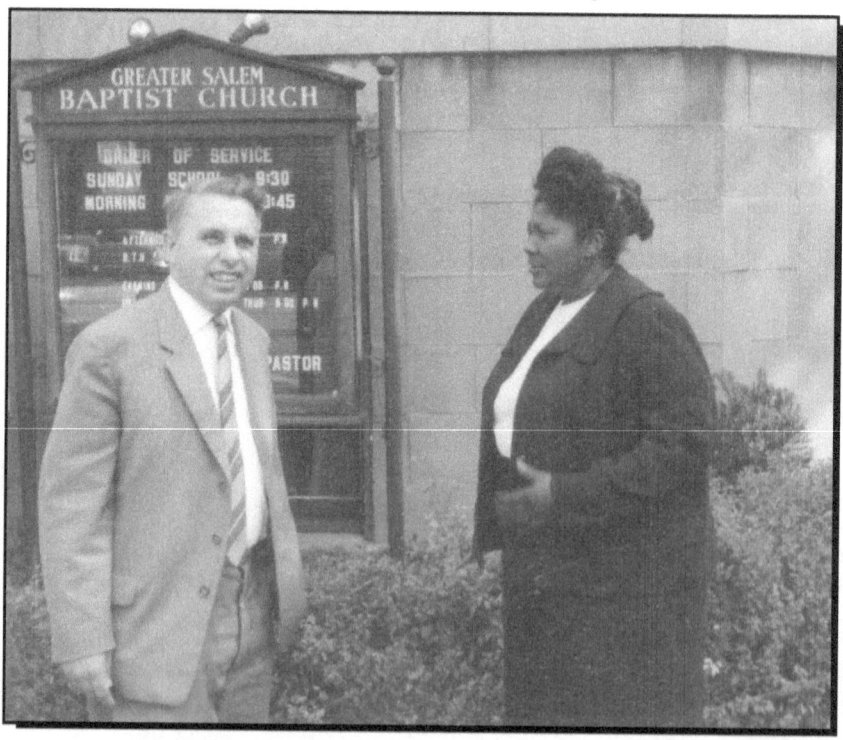

NEW ORLEANS JAZZ, MAHALIA JACKSON AND THE PHILOSOPHY OF ART

The Complete Works of
Hans R. Rookmaaker

Volume 2

Edited by
Marleen Hengelaar-Rookmaaker

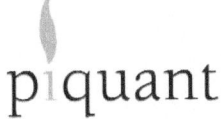

Copyright © 2002 by Marleen Hengelaar-Rookmaaker

This edition copyright © 2021 by Piquant Editions in the UK

Piquant Editions
Website: www.piquanteditions.com

First edition 2002
Paperback edition 2021

ISBN for this volume: 978-1-909281-81-3

The right of Marleen Hengelaar-Rookmaaker to be identified as author of this work has been asserted by her in accordance with the Copyright, Designs and Patents Act, 1988.

All Rights Reserved. No part of this publication may be reproduced, stored in a retrieval system or transmitted, in any form or by any means, electronic, mechanical, photocopying, recording or otherwise, without the prior written permission of the publisher or the Copyright Licensing Agency.

Jazz, Blues en Spirituals, copyright ©1959 by H.R. Rookmaaker
(Wageningen: Zomer en Keunings); copyright © 2000 by
Marleen Hengelaar-Rookmaaker
Articles on philosophy and aesthetics, and various articles on music:
copyright © by H.R. Rookmaaker; copyright © 2000 by
Marleen Hengelaar-Rookmaaker

British Library Cataloguing-in-Publication Data
A catalogue record of this book is available in the UK from the British Library.

ISBN 978-1-909281-81-3

Cover art: Marc de Klijn, detail from
Monuments in the (pre)history of modern art (2000)
Cover design: Jonathan Kearney

Piquant Editions actively supports theological dialogue and an author's right to publish but does not necessarily endorse the individual views and opinions set forth here or in works referenced within this publication, nor guarantee technical and grammatical correctness. The publishers do not accept any responsibility or liability to persons or property as a consequence of the reading, use or interpretation of its published content.

Overview Contents for the Six Volumes of the Complete Works of Hans Rookmaaker

The contents of volumes 1 to 6 have been organized partly chronologically and partly thematically. Most of the writings compiled in volumes 1 and 2 date from before 1960, while most of the materials brought together in volumes 3 to 6 were written after 1960. Each of the volumes contains one or more books as well as articles. Two books, previously published in Dutch only, appear in English for the first time: *Jazz, Blues and Spirituals* (1960) and *Art and Entertainment* (1962). In addition, roughly a thousand pages of Dutch articles have been translated into English: exhibition and music reviews; many short articles on art, music, and Christianity and culture written for Christian periodicals; articles that are scholarly and art-historical; and articles that are long and philosophical like the ones for *Philosophia Reformata*. Also included are the lectures given at l'Abri and Westminster Seminary. The two series of lectures, on 'God's Hand in History' and 'Revelation', have been integrated by Colin Duriez into one unit entitled 'God's Hand in History'.

Volume 1: ART, ARTISTS AND GAUGUIN

- Foreword by Jeremy Begbie
- Scholarly introduction by Graham Birtwistle
- Gauguin and Nineteenth-Century Art Theory (*Synthetist Art Theories*)
- Rookmaaker as art critic (1949–1956): exhibition reviews

Volume 2: NEW ORLEANS JAZZ, MAHALIA JACKSON AND THE PHILOSOPHY OF ART

- Philosophy and aesthetics: articles on style, world view, philosophy of art and education
- *Jazz, Blues and Spirituals*
- Music articles: African-American music, blues, spirituals and gospel, jazz, rock, and classical music

**Volume 3: THE CREATIVE GIFT, DÜRER, DADA AND
DESOLATION ROW**

- *Art and Entertainment*
- *The Creative Gift*
- Articles on history, faith and culture, faith and lifestyle, and faith and scholarship

**Volume 4: WESTERN ART AND THE MEANDERINGS
OF A CULTURE**

- Articles on Western art from the Middle Ages until the nineteenth century: themes and motifs, general reflections on art, plus an unfinished manuscript
- *Art Needs No Justification*
- Art and the Christian: articles, letters, and the Westminster discussion sessions 'Comments on Art and Culture'
- Miscellaneous articles and exhibition reviews

Volume 5: MODERN ART AND THE DEATH OF A CULTURE

- *Modern Art and the Death of a Culture*
- *Art and the Public Today*
- Articles on twentieth-century artists and streams, modern art, and the question: Do we need to be modern in order to be contemporary?
- Reviews of books on modern art and reviews of expositions of twentieth-century sculpture

Volume 6: OUR CALLING AND GOD'S HAND IN HISTORY

- Biography of Hans Rookmaaker by Laurel Gasque
- Interviews
- 'God's Hand in History' and the l'Abri lectures
- Indexes to all six volumes of the *Complete Works*

Contents of Volume 2

List of Photographs	xi
Acknowledgments	xii

Part I: Philosophy and Aesthetics

The Basic principles of the Philosophy of the Cosmonomic Idea	3

1 Basic principles (3); 2 The Philosophy of the Cosmonomic Idea (5); 3 How is reality constructed? (6); 4 What is the use of philosophy? (8)

What the Philosophy of the Cosmonomic Idea has Meant to Me	10
The Philosophy of Unbelievers	13

1 Philosophy and the human heart (13); 2 Philosophy and the world order (16)

Book Review: Dr J. Stellingwerff, *Origin and Future of Creative Man*	21
Sketch for an Aesthetic Theory based on the Philosophy of the Cosmonomic Idea	24

General introduction (24);1 Aesthetic theory (25); 2A The science of art, general (56); 2B The science of art, applied to music (63); Epilogue (77)

Style and World View	80

1 What is style? (80); 2 Who influences style? (81); 3 The influences of style on art (82); 4 Style and world view in the twentieth century (84); 5 Style and Christian art (87)

The Aesthetic Sphere and Disclosure	89
Science, Aesthetics and Art	93

Science (93); Aesthetics (99); Art (107)

The Iconic Function	114
Norms for Art and Art Education?	116

The problem of our time (116); Norms for art (118); Beyond words and proof (120); We all use norms (121); Historicism (122); Subjectivism (124); Aestheticism (125); The fear of the future generations (126); Art is difficult (127); The structure of a work of art (127); Art and world view (129); Reality is not static (130); Judging art (131); Conclusions (134)

Art, Aesthetics, and Beauty	138

Art (138); Aesthetics (140); Beauty (142)

Art, Philosophy and our View of Reality	144

We see what we know *(145)*; Against subjectivism *(146)*; Three examples *(144)*

Book Review: Calvin G. Seerveld, *A Turnabout in Aesthetics to Understanding*   151

Part II: Jazz, Blues and Spirituals

Preface by Hans Rookmaaker to the First Edition   157

Acknowledgments to the First Edition   158

1 Origins   159

African music (159); White folk music (160); African music in South America (161); African-American work songs in the USA (162); Children's songs/nursery rhymes (164); The first of the African-American Christian songs in North America (167); The origin of the true Negro spiritual (169)

2 Nineteenth Century: Development   172

The development of the spirituals in the nineteenth century (172); The origin of the westernized spiritual (175); The background to the true spiritual (178); Secular folk songs during the age of slavery (179); Minstrel shows (181); Secular hollers (181); The origin of the blues (184); The background to the blues (188); The blues as sung by Ma Rainey et al. (190); The first brass band music (193); String bands (194); Ragtime (195)

3 Twentieth Century: pre-World War I   197

New Orleans around 1900 (197); Black music in New Orleans (199); Brass bands in New Orleans (201); Jelly Roll Morton in New Orleans (201); The development of early jazz (204); Early white jazz (207); Handy's blues (208)

4 The 1920s   211

Post-1918 New Orleans music in Chicago: King Oliver (211); Post-1918 New Orleans music in Chicago: other bands, Morton (217); White jazz in Chicago (218); The development of jazz on the white scene (220); Black folk songs in the 1920s (223); Church music in the 1920s (225); Origin of the commercial spirituals (229); The blues of Bessie Smith (230); Folk blues in the 1920s (231); Piano folk music (233); Jug bands (234); Jelly Roll Morton's jazz in 1926 (235); White Chicago jazz (237); Armstrong's Hot Five and Hot Seven (240); The development of new African-American jazz after about 1927 (243); The later jazz of Oliver and Williams (244); Morton's later developments (246); The development of jazz in New Orleans in the 1920s (248); The entrance and development of Ellington (249)

5 The 1930s   254
  Jazz in Kansas City around 1930 (254); Blind Willie Johnson (254); The commercialization and development of jazz (256); Beginning to look to the past (258); The emergence of the study of folk music: Leadbelly (259); Gershwin's opera (262); Jelly Roll Morton's recordings for the Library of Congress (264); The collection of jazz records and the study of the history of jazz (265); Spirituals in the 1930s: Rosetta Tharpe (266); Blues after 1935 (268); The birth of swing (269); The swing of Basie and co. (271)

6 The 1940s   273
  The birth of modern jazz (273); The rediscovery of New Orleans jazz (279); White revival and Dixieland jazz (283); Commercial spirituals since approximately 1940 (286); New church choral song (287); Black folk music after about 1940 (290); Blues and spirituals among the working class after about 1940 (291)

7 The 1950s and Beyond   293
  Jazz in the 1950s (293); The development of modern jazz (295); Swing ad absurdum (299); The problem of jazz in our world (300); Tragedy threatens in the development of gospel songs (304); Spiritual solos: Mahalia Jackson (306)

Selected Bibliography to the First Edition   310
Updated Discography and Resources   312

Part III: Music Articles

African and African-American music   317
  African music as it really is: disenchantment and confirmation of a romantic dream (317); From Eliza to Odetta (318); American folk music at its best (322)

Blues   325
  Poetic fiction in the blues (325); Blind Lemon Jefferson (326); Ida Cox (328); Folk songs of black Americans (330); African-American music as a source of beauty and historical information (331); Hollerin' and cryin' the blues (333); Nothin' but the blues (336)

Spirituals and Gospel   338
  Let's sing the old Dr Watts: a chapter in the history of Negro spirituals (338); The Negro spiritual in church (345); Spirituals in concert form (347); Voices of victory (349); Two church services in Harlem (351); The African-American church service in the USA (352); Visiting Mahalia Jackson (353); USA 1961 (356)

Jazz 359

> *Listening to jazz (359); 'Jazz', jazz and classical (362); Original Dixieland jazz band (367); Jelly Roll Morton (369); Ory's Creole trombone (370); Jazz on the riverboats (372); A New Orleans suite (373); Johnny Dodds: a great and modest musician (375)*

Rock 377

> *The background to modern music: an interview (377)*

Classical Music 382

> *Old music (382); Bach and Mozart (383)*

Notes to Volume 2 385

List of Photographs

1. A manuscript edition of minstrel music.
2. A glimpse of a black village in the South.
3. A chain gang.
4. A typical wooden church common to the rural South.
5. People going to church in their Sunday best.
6. A glimpse of the congregation during a service.
7. Front page of an issue of one of Scott Joplin's ragtimes.
8. Jack Wimes, a euphonium player in one of the brass bands.
9. Scott and Celeste Dunbar.
10. One of the first jazz-bands in New Orleans, the Superior Band, with Buddy Johnson, Bunk Johnson, Big Eye Louis Nelson, and Billy Marrero, Walter Brundy, Peter Bocage, Richard Payne.
11. The famous King Oliver's Creole Jazz Band, featuring Babe Dodds, Honoré Dutrey, Bill Johnson, Louis Armstrong, Johnny Dodds, Lilian Hardin, King Oliver.
12. Kid Ory's band, with Minor Hall, Kid Ory, Mutt Carey, Fred Washington, Dink Johnson.
13. Kid Ory and his band after 1945, with Minor Hall, drums; Kid Ory, trombone; Lloyd Glenn, piano; John Buckner, trumpet; Joe Darensbourg, clarinet; Ed Garland, double bass.
14. A typical jug band, showing a guitar, a jug and a washboard, with Philip Ramsay Sr.:, Mozelle Moore, Philip Ramsay Jr.
15. A Race record sleeve.
16. Bessie Smith.
17. Gertrude 'Ma' Rainey.
18. Jelly Roll Morton.
19. Bunk Johnson.
20. Babe Dodds.
21. The Lewis-Robinson Band, featuring George Lewis on clarinet and Jim Robinson on trombone.
22. A jam session with Dizzy Gillespie.
23. The Spirit of Memphis Quartet, showing Jet Bledsoe (lead), Fred Howard (baritone), Earl Malone (bass) and below from left to right, Silas Steele (lead) and Robert Reed (tenor).
24. The Dixie Hummingbirds.
25. Doc Reed.
26. The Starlight Gospel Singers.
27. Sister Rosetta Tharpe.
28. A storefront church in one of the big cities of the North.
29. Mahalia Jackson during a performance.
30. Georgia Peach (Clara Gholson Brock).

Acknowledgments

A major word of thanks is due to the translators G. Bromiley, Edith Reitsema and Alida L. Sewell. Only three articles in this volume were written in English, all the rest had to be translated. Thanks to their commitment this volume became a reality. I am especially grateful that Don Morton joined the translation team at just the right time. His expertise in translating Dooyeweerdian materials and careful proofreading proved indispensable. I would also like to thank Ate van Delden, Ric Ashley, Jan Ophuis of the Nederlands Jazz Archief and Rien Wisse and Wim Verbei of the blues magazine *Block* for their suggestions and help in putting together a list of recommended CDs for the updated discography (p.311).

Marleen Hengelaar-Rookmaaker
Ommen, The Netherlands

Part I

PHILOSOPHY AND AESTHETICS

The Basic Principles of the Philosophy of the Cosmonomic Idea[1]

1 Basic principles

When a person repents and turns to the living God and is born again, this can and may not be an abstract event with meaning only for his or her faith and emotional life. No, the new person, born again, stands in the midst of this world. She or he has now become a shoot of the olive tree (Romans 11:17), a member of the body of which Christ is the Head (1 Corinthians 12:12 ff.), and this shoot shall bring forth fruit (John 15:5). God takes hold of that person in the heart of his or her existence, of his or her personality. Not merely a part of such a person's humanity is converted, not just a soul and a faith function considered separately from the rest, but the whole flesh-and-blood person, who believes, feels, loves, thinks, speaks, and judges things to be beautiful or ugly. The born-again person becomes a servant, a slave of the Lord in every area of life, with all the talents and potential that the Lord gives her or him.

That is how the early Christians approached scholarship, amongst other things. Unfortunately they did not break sufficiently with the late Greek (Hellenistic) views of their time. And we should not be too judgmental about that for, even twenty centuries later, many people are still unable to see the difference despite an accumulated wealth of insight into the word of God. Especially the Alexandrian scholar Philo, a Jew who gave allegorical explanations of the Old Testament, enjoyed much influence. And this remained the dominant tone, despite the fact that during the time of the Church Fathers we continue to hear the prophetic confession of God's will, way and truth.

And ever since, Christian scholars have remained tied to the wisdom of the Greeks, which was actually the wisdom of the world. That is how it was with Scholasticism, where an attempt was made to syncretize a Christian nucleus with the teachings of Aristotle. Calvin pointed out the mistake of doing so, in the light of the Scripture: 'Have nothing to do with the fruitless deeds of darkness, but rather expose them' (Ephesians 5:11, c.f. also Colossians 2:8). After Calvin, Protestant scholars again began to give a listening ear to the teaching (philosophies) of the time. By the grace of God, Groen van Prinsterer and, later, Abraham Kuyper again saw the large chasm between Christendom and the world, and hence also between Christian scholarship and worldly scholarship. For the 'worldly person' wants to be lord and master, autonomous, restricted by nothing outside of self. Such a person wants to build a world out of his or her own thinking, control nature in order to reveal his or her own mastery, and is in the first place concerned with the greatness of humankind, wanting to claim the very sovereignty that rightly belongs to God. The truly Christian scholar, by contrast, will want to study God's works in humility before the One who created her or him, the world, the universe and all that is in it, in obedience to his word, in order to give glory and honour to God. And that is why Christian scholars, no matter how much they adopted 'worldly wisdom', have always had God's creation as their given starting point. They have never wanted to put themselves in the place of the Creator, but have always seen their task in the scientific investigation of the concrete, created reality, as they know it from experience in the light of God's word.

Are we saying that a non-Christian cannot know reality? Calvin's word is valid here. He wrote that a man knows the world insofar as he knows himself, and that he knows himself insofar as he knows God. What is the situation? Apostate human beings have blinded themselves to the transcendent God, who is beyond time. But human beings have been constructed in such a way by God that they have to choose a god for themselves. Once a person no longer knows God, he or she knows only temporal reality. That is why such persons will choose temporal things, immanent ones, to make into their god. They put something immanent in the place of the One who is transcendent, beyond time.

And that something is always a part of reality that has been abstracted from reality. To abstract something means to disconnect in theoretical thought a piece from the cohesion of temporal reality. For example, if you do that with the psychic function it will lead to psychologism, as in Romanticism. In the case of the logical function, it will turn into *reine Vernunft*, pure thinking (as expounded by Kant and many others). This process can also be applied to the physical function (as in the extremely consistent materialists), the biotic function (as in vitalism, e.g. Bergson), the historical function (historicism, as that of Spengler in his book 'The Decline of the West', *Untergang des Abendlandes*), the economic function (as in Marx and others). This is where people bend the knee in front of an abstraction, made by themselves, while transgressing the Second Commandment of God. Even though it is not a wooden or stone image, it is a human-made product. As soon as they accept such abstractions as absolute, they no longer know reality (c.f. Ephesians 4:18). Only the one (abstracted) function then constitutes reality for them. We can see this with the positivists, who absolutized the laws of nature as if they were the origin of life and its creator. They made the laws to be god. They said that the rainbow did not exist, and it is true that we can neither grasp nor weigh the rainbow, which is not a material thing. But does that make it any less real?

Christian philosophers should, however, not absolutize one of the aspects of reality, because they know the true God. They do not pull reality askew and so they alone can come to a true insight regarding reality, by the light of God's word. And if as Christian philosophers we humbly do our task in the scholarly arena, in subjection to him, praying that he will assist us with his Spirit in the work to which he has called us, as obedient and yet unworthy servants (Luke 17:10), we may be assured that our work will bear fruit (1 Corinthians 15:58).

Professors Dooyeweerd and Vollenhoven have, by God's grace, been able to continue to work in the direction set out by Dr Kuyper to find the way to a Christian philosophy.

2 The Philosophy of the Cosmonomic Idea

In the first article we explained that a Christian philosophy is not only a necessity but also the view that should be natural for us Christians.

This time we will consider something of the work of Professors Dooyeweerd and Vollenhoven on the Philosophy of the Cosmonomic Idea.

This philosophy starts by refuting the point of view basic to the worldly philosophies, namely that scholarship is supposed to be neutral, not influenced by the faith of the scholar. This 'neutrality-postulate' is the first bastion or stronghold to be besieged and taken. It shows that every philosophy starts from religious presuppositions. For it is always people who are philosophically active; every human action flows from the heart, where we have chosen for or against God, for or against Christ. This religious choice of position, in the heart of our existence, of our being, is concretized in our world view, which comes to expression in all our actions, thinking, believing, and therefore also in our philosophical and scholarly work.

In the first article we pointed out how apostasy from God results in humans no longer being able to know reality as it is. They continually tear reality apart by placing one part above the rest, one aspect over the others. Only the Christian can see and recognize that human being, and therefore temporal reality as well, has been given a number of functions by God. These functions are very different in character and yet they cohere. They are also called 'law spheres'. They are the various aspects by which reality presents itself to us. Professor Dooyeweerd distinguishes fourteen law spheres: the spheres of number and of space; the physical sphere and the biotic (life) sphere; the psychic, logical, historical, and linguistic (i.e. of symbolic meaning, of language) spheres; the social and economic spheres; the sphere of aesthetic function, and the spheres of law, love, and faith. These spheres are created by God and are in a particular relationship, with a certain coherence, according to the so-called cosmic law order. The one presupposes the other. For example, a person cannot feel, see or hear (psychological function) if she or he does not live (biotic function). And the latter would be impossible if he or she did not have a material body. And how could humans form or make something (historical function), if they could not think (logical function)? And how could a language exist, if humans could not give form to the language? And how could we relate (social function), if we could not speak with one another? And without social relationships economic life would cease to be possible.

Every one of those law spheres enjoys sphere sovereignty, which means the laws that are valid within that sphere are not valid as such in another sphere. A physical law (e.g. of causality) is not as such applicable to the area of jurisprudence or aesthetics. And yet the various spheres are not independent of one another. The laws of the one can appear in the other, but then they receive a completely new meaning. Thus there is a juridical causality, whereby a physical law 'returns' in the juridical function. We see this operate, for example, if I were to torch a house. It calls for prosecution in a juridically causal manner. But it is and remains something that belongs to the sphere of jurisprudence. For the actual physical causality (the fact that I used a match, which I put into contact with some paper drenched in oil, causing a chemical reaction, and so on) is of no interest as such to the judge; he is interested in the juridical consequences of this action, which was the juridical cause.

In respect of each of the law spheres we can make a distinction between the law side and the subject side. Every human being is a subject in relation to the various spheres and is subjected to them. If that were not the case, then humans would have no law to determine them and they would sink into nothingness. For example, if no laws were given for thinking or for aesthetics, a person simply could not think, could not find something beautiful or ugly. Everything created is limited and determined by the law (in its various aspects), while only the Creator, of both law and the subject, precisely as Creator and Lawgiver, is not determined by a law. We can make a further distinction between the laws of nature and the norms or rules that determine proper behaviour. If I let go of a stone, it must fall. It is subject to the laws of nature, in this case gravity. But all the law spheres above the psychic sphere are normative; they indicate how things ought to be, but human beings can subjectively choose not to obey these norms. I can think illogically (i.e. at variance with the laws of thinking), I can make something ugly (at variance with the laws of aesthetics), I can act in an un-economical, un-loving or un-righteous way. I can also be un-believing, namely possess a faith that is not in harmony with God's laws for faith. Trespassing these norms is, of course, sin.

3 How is reality constructed?

What about the things we see around us? Is it not the case that they do not function just logically or ethically but that the logical and ethical are only aspects of them which together constitute reality?

Indeed, we ought not close off anything in one or more aspects of reality, in one or more functions, for then we would no longer have real things but only abstractions. All things function in all law spheres and exhibit a certain structure, whereby the law spheres are uniquely suited to that structure. In other words, in every law sphere, every structure has its structural function, which differs structurally from the structural function of another thing-structure. Here too, we should differentiate between a law side and a subject side. How is it possible, for example, for the state to exist? Is it a 'creation' of humankind? No, the state only exists because, in his world order, God has in principle given the structure of the state, while it is the task of humankind to give shape and form to this structure. How do things stand with, say, an animal or a plant? We say they function in every aspect, but animals or plants do not speak, believe or think. Indeed, even though they don't believe, speak or think, they do function objectively in those law spheres. What is an object in one sphere may be a subject in an earlier, lower sphere that returns in a higher one. The subjects in those law spheres stand in a subject-object relationship. Thus we ought to believe that a plant is a creature of God. We can praise God, for he wanted to create it (faith object). We can admire the plant for its beauty (aesthetic object). We give the plant a name (linguistic object). We can make logical distinctions between it and other plants and kinds of plants (thought object), and so on.

In every structure there is a function that guides and directs everything. For example, in a work of art everything is directed and guided by the aesthetic function. For that reason we call this the leading or qualifying function. And because in a work of art the aesthetic function is the objective one, we call that an objective thing-structure. But there are also subjectively qualified structures, such as marriage, which is qualified by the love function; the state, qualified by the juridical function; the church, by the faith function; and business, by the economic function. These are all normative structures, because the leading function is normative. Besides them, natural things (stones, plants, animals) are qualified by one of the subjective natural functions (in order: the physical, the biotic and the psychic sphere).

The structures also have sphere sovereignty. That means, that the one (normative) structure may not interfere in the internal structural matters of the other. Thus a church may not meddle in the specific task of the state: the making of laws. Nor is the state allowed to force a church to adopt a certain article of faith. And the same applies to the structures of the economy (the business enterprise), marriage, the association, the school, etc. If one of the structures exceeds the God-given boundaries and interferes with the internal affairs of another one, then it is inevitable that one of them will be harmed.

Imagine, for example, that a church as church were to meddle with artistic life. The church could never apply the norms as they exist for art, but would always have to pay heed to the specific norms of the denomination. If the church did not do that, it would be acting as a 'Society for the Promotion of Christian Art' or something similar, but no longer as church. If it really acted as church it would mean the death of art.

Of course, the various structures are not independent of each other. They stand in all sorts of external relationships alongside each other. For example, the state ought to ensure that on a Sunday people can go to church in peace and freedom. Parents ought to ensure that the children born to them receive a good education and therefore should send them to school. The hotel businesses will be interested in getting many people to visit their cities and (through their societies for the promotion of tourism, for example) will draw the attention of foreigners to all the art treasures in their city, and so on.

4 What is the use of philosophy?

The 'invisible church', the *ecclesia invisibilis*, contains all born-again and true Christians, all of whom want to do God's will in this temporal life. Not only in every aspect of reality but also in every structure they will try to see to it that the law spheres and structural laws of the Lord are obeyed. The revelation of the invisible church in the temporal sphere is the visible church. The visible church contains the subjective Christian life in all law spheres and in all structures, one of which is the church. We may call the church the most important structure, as long as we understand that the church may never exceed her own sphere sovereignty in order to rule in other (non-ecclesiastical) contexts. If she were to do so, then the whole Christian life would be torn to shreds, as we illustrated with an example. We call the struggle for obedience to God in all areas of life the struggle of the antithesis. In the first article we saw how everyone who does not, or does not want to, know God has to make his or her god out of something immanent. And this is the reason for the great antithesis (opposition) between those who know and love the transcendent God and those who worship a creature of their own making (in principle there is little difference whether one worships one image or another, one abstraction or another). For from the heart come all our behaviours, either with the desire to serve God or in apostasy from the Lord.

This also applies to the scholarly arena. That does not mean that all Christians have to become philosophers and scholars. No, everyone may fight for the Lord in her or his own place and with his or her own capacities. And we can do that when we humbly bend the knee to receive his word and witness, praying that he will give us strength. The saying, 'Let not the wise man boast of his wisdom . . . but let him who boasts, boast about this: that he understands and knows me' (Jeremiah 9:23-24) should prevent us from thinking that only those who have studied a lot and know much about philosophy can be wise and profound, not 'ordinary people'. Know this: to the Lord there are no 'ordinary people'; all who know and worship him are wise and profound.

We do not need philosophy to be a good Christian (1 Cor. 2:2; 2 Timothy 3:16–17). If we live close to the word of God we are fully equipped to discern the spirits of this age and to stand strong when we are tempted to err (Ephesians 6:10–20). But it is true that Christian scholarship, which should be based on a Christian philosophy, could be of immense use and support in fighting for God's kingdom. But this will not be so if we persistently and proudly believe that we can build the kingdom of God because we know the principles and are so good at handling Christian philosophy, so competent to argue that which is correct and incorrect. Then even the Philosophy of the Cosmonomic Idea can become a curse, and we shall be like the Pharisees who, though they lived by the letter of the Scriptures and the laws that they had derived from them, forgot the Lord. God's judgment over us will be as in Isaiah 29:13: 'These people come near to me with principles and honour me with philosophy, but their hearts are far from me, and their devotion is but a human science learned off by heart'(paraphrased). And Christ will say to us (cf. John 12:48): 'You brood of vipers'.

We know that we continually fall short; we sin. Therefore, we should humbly bow before him, who is, who was and who is to come. In obedience to the Scriptures we should become obedient slaves (to whom the Lord owes no thanks), who fight for his kingdom. Then this philosophy can be a weapon for which we cannot thank God enough as we pray for the answer to our prayer: 'Your name be hallowed, your kingdom come and your will be done.'

What the Philosophy of the Cosmonomic Idea has Meant to Me[2]

After so many have already written in this magazine on this subject, I would very much like to tell of my experience, because I am of the opinion that it is somewhat different from that of the others.

I come from a family that can in no way be described as religious. There was no profound opposition to religion. My father did believe that God existed and that the Bible was a worthwhile book – perhaps his grandparents had been Protestants – but that was all. They even forgot to have me baptized. As a boy I did go to a Christian secondary school – because it was such a good one – but I was not in any way reached by the gospel there. It is really remarkable, by the way, how little mission-minded Dutch Christians often are. Apart from one conversation with one of my teachers no one ever tried to tell me anything more of the gospel.

In 1939, after sitting my final examination, I commenced naval training as a midshipman. That came to an end after the German invasion of the Netherlands in May 1940. I then went to study in Delft, to await the end of the war. In those days I began to think more seriously about matters, and sometimes I had the feeling that God could play an important role in our lives. But only when I, along with other professional officers, was made a prisoner of war and landed in a camp near Nuremberg did I begin to think about seriously reading the Bible. There were no other books available and, as a civilized man with cultural interests, I thought it would be good to know something about it. As I was reading, I gradually came to the conviction that the Bible reveals the truth to us.

I spent a lot of time thinking about the Christian faith, but read very little about it. Apart from this I made good use of the time. Gradually, especially after our POW camp was moved to Stanislau, more books became available. One man had this book and the next, another. I read philosophy, psychology, literature and especially the history of literature; in short, from all sorts of fields in the humanities. I also continued to work clandestinely to finish my training as naval officer while we officially had the opportunity to continue our studies for Delft University; I even sat exams. I did all the mathematical subjects.

Slowly, while continuing to think and study, a consciousness of a fundamental conflict grew in me, which I formulated in this way: Can I become a Christian and be active as a scholar at the same time, especially in philosophy? Or, to put it more precisely: Is it possible to be a Christian and to believe the Bible to be God's word, and at the same time to be a Kantian in philosophy?

One remark before we continue: I do not think it is possible that someone can come to know God and his Son through the Bible and then end up as a liberal. If one is confronted with the biblical truth, as I was in those days, then it is a question of accepting or rejecting it. The Bible is either true or not true: there is no alternative. Of course, nobody who is going to read the Bible in this way, even if he or she does not accept it, will deny that there are beautiful words in it, wisdom and insight, but such a person will also see that in the end this is not the issue. The Bible comes to us, and came to me, with the demand to accept the gospel as a joyful message, God as Father and hence also his Son as Saviour. That is not to say that a person, such as I was at that time, pondering everything the Bible was telling me and trying to understand the biblical world picture (in an all-encompassing sense, not limited to the physical structure of our cosmos) did not see any problems. On the contrary, I still find it rather striking that at that time I personally experienced the entire dogmatic struggle of the early church, and finally came to an insight that later turned out to be called 'orthodox biblical Protestant'. But I only realized this later, when I studied church history.

To return to my subject, when I came to the point of making a definitive choice, I struggled with the question whether there would still be a place for philosophy. I had not made a choice as to a specific school of philosophy, but I formulated it as, for example, Kantianism. This struggle for insight was very foundational. For me everything depended on it at that time. If as a Christian I had to stop thinking and was not allowed to look for insight into the given reality, then being a Christian was difficult to accept. For it is inhuman not to be allowed to think about this reality. At the same time I realized that it was difficult to make Kantianism compatible with biblical truth.

During that decisive time I was introduced to Captain (later Professor) Mekkes. It was just at the time that we were being evacuated to Neu-Brandenburg. I heard about Dooyeweerd from Captain Mekkes and started to read Dooyeweerd's book. Rather, I devoured it. For I discovered, right from page 1, that someone was speaking who started with precisely this question, and offered a clear solution, namely that being a Kantian and being a Christian were irreconcilable but that, nevertheless, the Christian has a clear task, also as a philosopher. He stated that the Christian's thinking is not closed off, but is actually opened up.

This is how Dooyeweerd's work became decisive for me. It removed the last obstacles that were still obstructing the way to the biblical Christ. At the same time it was for me a wonderful kind of catechism.

Having once taken this step, I learned a lot from Captain Mekkes, and through him I was further inducted into the Philosophy of the Cosmonomic Idea. We had very many discussions, and in this way I was shaped as a scholar.

After the capitulation of Germany I returned to the Netherlands and was almost immediately, after an interview, baptized and admitted to the Reformed Church. During that interview the people came to hear of my exclusive Dooyeweerdian catechism. And they also heard about the preceding, intensive reading of the Bible that resulted, amongst other things, in my first lecture (while I was still in Stanislau), on God's way with Israel and the prophecies regarding the future.

After the Japanese surrender I asked for and received my discharge from the Navy and started to study art history. A study of aesthetics, which I had completed under Mekkes' guidance in Neu-Brandenburg, was soon after published in *Philosophia Reformata*.

A final remark: I have personally experienced how the Philosophy of Cosmonomic Idea can have an evangelistic significance. Are we in general sufficiently aware of this? And do we make enough use of it? Do we realize, for instance, how important the work of the special, endowed chairs at the State Universities is, and also of those at the Free University?

The Philosophy of Unbelievers[3]

1 Philosophy and the human heart

What is philosophy? It is the human desire to be wise, namely to have a true and meaningful insight into reality, to understand 'what is happening under the sun' and thus to know what we ought to do in order to take our proper place among all the other creatures and things, and to determine our attitude towards them all. Philosophy is the attempt of people to orientate themselves in this creation.

For the unbeliever, whether a heathen who has never heard the word of God or a modern who no longer knows this word because he or she is apostate and therefore does not want to listen to it anymore, there are thousands of questions to be answered, with answers that can never be found if God's word is not recognized as such. It is not the case that the true state of affairs cannot be discovered from 'creation'. Paul writes that this is precisely what is possible, and that is why unbelievers will not be considered innocent. Human beings, in their 'natural' heart, simply do not want to admit that there is a Creator who is completely sovereign because 'by nature' they hate the Lord. In this way people are looking for an answer to the very many questions that fill their hearts simply because, even after the Fall into sin and in all of their lack of repentance, they remain unchanged as to their humanity. They are still equipped with all human characteristics, whereby they are apt to recognize God and to understand matters. They continue to be prophet, priest and king, also in their apostasy. But as such they progress no further than false prophecy, false religion and, related to this, bad kingship. Having cut themselves off from the true knowledge of God, people will attempt to gain an insight into the surrounding reality according to their own wisdom, with their own intelligence, and in their own strength. In this they will suppress God's word and the truth it contains in unrighteousness. We will limit our discussion to moderns who are living in a world where the gospel was once preached and is still being preached.

By means of science and philosophy people continue to attempt to answer thousands of pressing questions. These include: How did this reality come into existence? What is its meaning? How is it structured? And so forth. Philosophy consists in the first place of a systematized wisdom of life, a thought-out world view. This is where we find the false prophecy, the false doctrine, the confession of the unbeliever.

What is a world view? It results from the attempt of human persons to orientate themselves in the reality in which they are placed. Hence, world view is shaped, on the one side, by human subjectivity and, on the other side, by the reality in which people orientate themselves.

First, a word about the people who wish to orientate themselves in the creation in which they are placed. If they do not love God from the heart, and do not recognize him as Creator – not even mentioning his Fatherhood – then it is ultimately self they are looking for. They want to maintain and realize their own freedom, serve self and all the tendencies that live in their hearts.

Indeed, structurally persons are not changed; they are always 'designed for' God. The recognition of God is 'normal' and every denial of him violates the state of affairs. This is why humans will start to conceive a god for themselves. They choose something from the creation, since they no longer know anything other than what their creaturely eyes see. They declare as god whatever they consider to be more important, or greater, than everything else. For the heathen these are the natural things such as the sun, the moon and so on. After more thought, it is the powers of nature that are regarded as being ultimate. But for moderns, who have learned from the gospel that 'nature' is not God, this is not a possibility. Besides, modern people have come to know themselves better precisely because of the Bible. Thus we see that the apostate person now looks further and chooses a principle that is ultimately typically human: Reason (with a capital letter), i.e. human understanding, or History or Beauty or . . . whatever. Anything can be elevated to the status of being 'divine' by wisdom that has become foolishness. The more deeply humans think, and the further they continue on this road, the more they shall see and recognize that it is they themselves who are choosing and making their own gods. And then the realization will come that ultimately they themselves have to stand in the centre. In the end, all apostate philosophy is humanistic. Everything focuses on human being as the centre and starting point of all thought and action.

Two attitudes to life are ultimately possible. In the first place, apostate humans will emphasize their own freedom more and more consistently. They declare themselves to be independent of all that is outside of self; they want to be their own lawgiver and creator. But when they do this they come into conflict with created reality, with the world order in which they are placed. Reality does not allow itself to be used like that, to be 'forced' by the whims of the supposedly 'free individual'. Thus creation, in the first instance a person's own body, becomes the adversary, the counter-instance that restricts and limits human freedom. For precisely on the nature-side of reality laws are compelling, inescapable.

Then we see humankind take up a second attitude: they abandon themselves to their 'nature', arrange their life according to their own wishes and desires, in order to gain the possibility of living a free and untrammeled life. To this purpose they try to put nature, with all its laws, in their own service, in order to rule over it like a [proverbial] Oriental despot. There is no longer any talk of freedom but rather a submissive following of their 'nature'. We have to remember that what we here call 'nature' comprises not just the human body with its 'natural' demands but also what Paul in his epistles calls 'the natural man', the flesh, in which are seated all sinful tendencies and desires.

In this way, humans become slaves to sin in a very conscious way, for they want to walk in the way of the flesh. The natural functions will gradually come to be the centrepoint – eating, drinking, sex – and all their strivings may be summarized in the word 'eudemonism', that is, the search for happiness in the possibility of satisfying all one's desires without compulsion or trouble, and avoiding all affliction. It is especially for this purpose that humans want to rule over non-human nature. They try to make it serviceable to themselves by way of technical development. But ultimately it is all subjected to the sensual desires, to the needs of the human body. All decisions that have to be made – in the ethical and economic areas, and so on – are made to this purpose. All cultural activity is made to serve such 'natural needs' and is directed 'eudemonically'. The 'lower' human functions will come to stand so much at the centre that, with a continuing consistency, humankind would ultimately lose their humanity; they become merely a 'piece of nature'. However, this will only come to pass, and only to a certain degree, when apostasy has reached its lowest and final point, that is to say, with the so-called primitive peoples. The tendency to reach this low point occurs more often in our time than would be imagined. In the twentieth century there is a strong inclination towards the primitive, which is sometimes glorified as the 'original good state of nature'. This 'primitivism' stands in strong tension with the much-developed civilization in which we are placed. Science, art, politics and so forth have unfolded, as a result also of the centuries of influence of the gospel on our civilization, in a way that we simply cannot pass by and which cannot be reasoned away. Moreover, moderns are much too strongly aware of their humanity and, finally, do not want to abandon their own freedom altogether.

Humans become slaves to sin also in their proclamation of freedom. Their striving for freedom can never be consistently realized. All of life and every activity simply become impossible if people truly want to detach themselves from all norms and laws. If they do not want to conform to any law, nor submit to any norm, complete chaos will ensue. As soon as a person does anything, from satisfying natural needs such as eating to doing arithmetic, as in 3x4=12, he or she has already submitted to a law not made or designed in human freedom.

It is remarkable that those who want to proclaim their absolute freedom, independent from God or whatever, become the most tightly bound slaves. With everything they do, they first have to, according to their own notion at least, give up their freedom. Suicide is really the only possible consequence, but even in such extremity they use laws and possibilities not designed by them in freedom. Thus, in this too, humans are slaves to sin and anything but free. True freedom consists only in keeping the laws of God – as a fish can move around freely in the water but can only struggle and expire if it should seek 'freedom' on land.

In the twentieth century much progress has been made in thinking through these issues. People have begun to see that all principles, all 'gods' chosen by humans, have indeed been imagined by such persons themselves. Moreover, they have become conscious, certainly in a more consistent and radical way, of what it means to have a world without God. People want to maintain their own freedom at any cost; they have come to see this as being at the centre of all human activity, thus completely suppressing the truth in unrighteousness. For this reason, reality is completely meaningless in their eyes, since reality, the world order, seems to be something that forces itself on human beings from the outside, and something from which they cannot escape. People are 'thrown' into a completely strange and incomprehensible world, which oppresses them and restricts and opposes their freedom. These two basic tendencies in the human heart are in reality mutually exclusive. If there is complete freedom, 'nature' is not followed. If, however, 'nature' is followed, then freedom disappears. But apostate humans want to hold on to both elements. In their search for the absolute realization of their own freedom they do not want to lose their 'nature' with all its desires. They would like to see it assimilated into their freedom, but that is exactly what is impossible. Or else they want to follow nature and still gain their freedom, through the back door, as it were. But that way too they fall into slavery again. Thus freedom and nature become the two poles in the human heart between which it oscillates. If, for a while – as in Romanticism – they exercise freedom exclusively, then all the shortcomings of that attitude come to light in the practice of life. To which they react by bringing nature more to the fore – as in positivism. But in all cases the search is for a balance in which justice is done to both elements. This state of balance, however, cannot be anything other than unstable, since the two poles repel each other constantly and each of them, according to its character, strives for a more consistent realization. Time and again circumstances will disturb the balance and the world will be on the lookout for a new attitude, adjusting as much as possible in order to meet all the demands.

2 Philosophy and the world order

Thus far we have talked about the impulses arising in the apostate human heart. Now we wish to see how world view is also shaped by world order. By world order we mean created reality, with all its norms and laws and structures, as it is, now. The reality in which we live is not the same as the paradise in which Adam and Eve moved. The power of sin has come with its destructive effects. We live on a cursed earth and have to work for our daily bread by the sweat of our brow. But there are also many possibilities, which God had put into his creation and which people have disclosed, opened up, and realized in continued cultural activity. Humanity, apostate humanity included, has devoted itself very seriously to its cultural task. The people of today are concerned with many different matters that did not exist in earlier times: think of law, technology, economics, politics, traffic, art, and so forth. Many possibilities are disclosed; form has been given to norms that ask for this kind of formation. To give a few examples closer to home, just think of our traffic rules, the fashion of our clothes, and our notions of politeness.

Humans will have to orientate themselves in the world. It goes without saying that this world order will put a stamp on their world view. Modern people have a picture of the world that is completely different from that of people living 3000 years ago. Not only is our world map much larger and more precise but also our astronomical knowledge and our knowledge of plants and animals, for instance, have increased enormously. Those who are now forced to orientate themselves have to take much more into account than the people of 3000 years ago. To give another example: an artist today who is absorbed in art and its possibilities will make his or her acquaintance with art from the many periods and peoples gathered in our galleries and museums. He or she has to take account of all the possibilities discovered through the work of past generations. For that reason his or her insight into art and philosophy of art are irrevocably different from that of an ancient Egyptian living 3000 years ago.

Also included in world order – as we have already mentioned – are the norms put into the creation as they are given form in our time. These positive norms, the laws that regulate all our actions – think of decency, politeness, our rights and obligations in relation to the authorities – of course also shape our attitude to life. For example, a humanist will have all sorts of opinions about law and decency that may look very much like those of the gospel. That is simply the result of the fact that those laws have been brought to light by God's revelation and were formulated by an earlier, believing generation. Humanism, in as much as it is a secularized Christendom, maintains these laws. Only when there is a continuing, consistent cultural work in an apostate direction will people try to change their ways. I will not develop this point further.

In summary, world view is the result of humans, with their apostate inclinations, orientating themselves in the world order, the reality that presents itself to them at any given time. Their vision will be determined by the 'gods' they have chosen for themselves, or whatever principles they have declared to be 'absolute', and most profoundly by the sinful tendencies of the human heart, unwilling to recognize God as Creator or Redeemer and therefore also rejecting God's word. Personal freedom and 'nature' are the poles between which people are repelled and attracted – neither the one nor the other can be carried through consistently. Both keep on being decisive factors shaping the human world view. The emphasis will sometimes be near the one pole and at other times nearer to the other.

This is how nature and freedom determine the direction of people's attitude in today's world when they attempt to find their way in their own strength.

Even when people no longer choose 'gods', they will often absolutize a certain aspect of reality. The essence of reality and of human selfhood will be sought in that which is considered to be most important. In close connection with their directedness towards 'freedom' or 'nature', people will choose one aspect from the world order as being fundamental to all else, one aspect from which all others are seen to be derived. This choice will, of course, be influenced by the contemporaneous state of scientific knowledge or by special circumstances or events. When the emphasis lies on the control of nature, people will tend to absolutize the psychical, or the biotic, namely 'life' in the more restricted sense, or the physical. In the latter case, for example, people will say that everything, also life, also the psychical, as well as history and so forth, are determined by the physical laws of nature. When the emphasis lies on freedom, people are more inclined to look for an area where human freedom of choice is indeed present, for example the historical – as in historicism – or the economical, or the aesthetic – as in aestheticism – and so forth. The actual structure of human knowledge demands and seeks for an original principle, a 'starting point' from which all else flows forth. If people do not want to recognize God as Creator, then there is no other way than to derive all facets of reality from one of these principles, or sometimes from a combination of two or more. This is then declared to be primordial and to be the essence of human being and the world. If people refuse to honour the transcendent God and Creator of all things, they inevitably come to have a false insight into reality and can no longer see reality in its structure and order as given by God.

Philosophers are the prophets of this world. They formulate the confession in which their own attitude to life in the midst of the surrounding world is worked out. That is why philosophy plays such a large part in the lives of unbelievers. Philosophy indicates the place and task of a person; it says what the meaning of this world is and how things cohere 'in principle'. Every apostate philosophy, whether explicitly formulated or not, starts with such a confession, in which its world view is preached in a systematic form.

However, this confession is only a part, albeit the core, of philosophy. For philosophy is also a science. Sometimes, and that is where the connection with this apostate view of life is very close, an alleged science.

For it is insight into and knowledge of those matters of which people, who suppress the truth in unrighteousness and refuse to recognize God's revelation – in the first place in the order of creation, not to mention the revelation in God's word – will never be able to gain true knowledge, namely knowledge of the Creator and his creative deeds, including the place of humankind, the meaning of this world and the meaning of history. However, philosophy is also an authentic science, investigating and gaining knowledge of that which is knowable and visible. Science, as the attempt to gain insight into the state of affairs within reality, is a task given to humans and part of the cultural mandate. For unbelievers this gains a strong emphasis and a certain character, because they hope to prove by science that they are indeed correct in what they in an as such unprovable prophecy confess regarding reality. This is how the scientific ideal has originated, an ideal that gives a prominent, central place to science in all human activity. But this should not blind us to the fact that unbelievers also engage in authentic science. By its very nature, science is strongly bound to reality itself, to the 'phenomena', while it also serves the fullness of life, which continually presents questions and problems for solution that require scientific endeavour. Technology, economy, jurisprudence, politics, and so on, demand a solution from science for their specific difficulties and problems. Since, as we said, these are problems of the fullness of the reality of life, science is inevitably directed and bound to this reality.

We have talked about science as if it were a unity and, indeed, it is a unity. Originally this unity were actually present as a single science, namely philosophy. However, because the fields of investigation expanded so much and extensive specialization developed, the various special sciences necessarily became differentiated. Philosophy acquired the task of trying to preserve the connection between these diverse areas, and then to coordinate the findings and to assimilate them into a single system, and to investigate the epistemological presuppositions on which they were based. In this way the unity of the sciences was supposed to have been preserved. However, because the practitioners in all of these diverse fields of endeavour began to consider their own discipline as the most important, indeed even to absolutize it and to argue that all the rest was not only connected to that discipline but also dependent on it, that unity has to a considerable degree been lost. In addition, philosophy has given so little direction (except to those sciences that investigate areas similar to what philosophy absolutizes) and has been so easily refuted by the facts that people, as a result, have left philosophy to itself. They have given it the cold shoulder, at least in so far as it has been concerned with science in the narrow sense. However, as prophecy philosophy blossomed, increasingly so as its task in relation to the sciences was considered less important.

In summary, philosophy is a view of the whole of reality that gives each of the special sciences its place and in which their findings are assimilated into a system. The attempt is made to coordinate the abundance of true knowledge, based on reality itself, and to make it serviceable to a confession that systematizes the world view and on which both the world order and the direction of the apostate heart inevitably make their impact. It goes without saying that such a composite whole has to be full of contradictions, since the diverse elements can hardly be harmonized with each other. These contradictions cause philosophers to become entangled in many odd problems.

Book Review: Dr J. Stellingwerff, Origin and Future of Creative Man[4]

It is not easy for this reviewer to discuss Stellingwerff's book, as I am in agreement with the general thoughts expressed. This could result in the review becoming a wish-list. For example, why did he not say more on this subject? Why did he not touch on that? Why did he not make this or that connection? We do not wish to give a list of the few typographical errors. Any reader will discover them and read past them. The book is a philosophical study that deals with our humanity. It is not philosophical in the strictly technical sense, but rather as an indication of the direction of interest. The study is very readable, also for those who are not at home in the jargon of professional philosophers. Incidentally, the section on Hegel is not easy, but it is written so clearly and lucidly that anyone with a university education should be able to follow the argument. In brief, it seems to me that the author had a readership of educated people in mind, though not specifically philosophically trained people.

We can indicate the starting point with the help of two quotations from the beginning of the book. I think that these in themselves can arouse our attention and, in general, have our assent. Stellingwerff writes: 'We wish to maintain that also in our time the Christian faith is and remains the universal and undoubted faith. We are also of the opinion that this faith ought to acquire a new articulation in philosophy and world view' (p.18) and '[It] is possible to be radically Christian as modern people who participate in the life of this century.'

Stellingwerff sees the uniqueness of this century in our new situation in history, in which humans have become mobile and can make worldwide contact through new communication systems. However, the orientation of people in this situation is being affected by the crisis in which Western society has landed itself. To gain insight Stellingwerff discusses the dialectical person, the inwardly torn person, for whom yes and no, this world and the next world, positive and negative, always go together. We would especially like to refer to his lucid discussion of Hegel, who via Marx and Kierkegaard, amongst others, had such a tremendous influence and who determines the spirit of our time. This is especially important since Hegel is, unfortunately, a great unknown in our circles. But this dialectic itself is being undermined in our time by relativization which, as a result of intensive worldwide contacts, gives birth to the functional person (as analysed by phenomenology and such), in essence, the uprooted person. One highly elucidatory paragraph explains how this functional person could come into being because 'God is dead', as already proclaimed by Nietzsche. But, in reality, this god who is declared to be dead, murdered by Western humanity, is the god of

Greek philosophy, the theo-ontological god. Unfortunately, many have confused this god with the God of revelation. As a result they have not come to a new understanding of the living God. To the contrary. The crisis of today's Christendom is partly the result of this.

Stellingwerff's own vision is strongly influenced by the Philosophy of the Cosmonomic Idea. In a beautiful and original way he starts his exposé with God's revelation in creation: God is powerfully active. Then Stellingwerf deals with revelation as it takes place in history, to historical people. The extensive discussion of the problem of Adam is interesting. Was Adam the first man? Or is he, as a historical figure, no more than the first head of the covenant? The arguments for and against are weighed and offered for our consideration in a manner that is almost too dispassionate. He opts for the latter, although not without certain reservations. It is true that this point still requires a lot of study. For the time being we would emphasize his reservations.

In the following chapters, on human being, Stellingwerff deals extensively with the theory of evolution, lucidly summarizing what has been thought about these things in our circles during the last years. He does, finally, turn against this evolution-faith, since 'the scientifically reliable facts are insufficient to prove the doctrine of evolution. The philosophical objection is against this postulated Hegelian 'discontinued continuity' that has sneaked in. It is this that seems to mask what lies at the core of the evolution theory' (p.197).

In a chapter at the end of his expositions concerning the structure of human being, Stellingwerff speaks about judgment. I think he pays too little attention in this chapter to sin as a corrupting power, which endangers humanity as such, and hence also too little attention is paid to Christ's renewing work in human life. He presents an original vision here, namely that after the Last Judgment, in the second death, those who are not in the book of Life will disappear completely. Hence, they will not suffer eternal punishments; no eternal immortality for the evil ones. This vision certainly requires further structural elaboration and additional consideration. For the present, we wonder whether all of the scriptural givens have been taken into consideration.

A final chapter discusses the difficult situation into which humans have landed, now that they have made such tremendous discoveries, which certainly can be put to good use but which also can destroy all of human life. In this way, functional human being has landed itself in a dialectic of progress and war, of paradise and apocalypse, according to Stellingwerff. He is correct to reject this dialectic but, in our opinion, he deals too little with the problem itself and with the road that should be taken to overcome it.

Here lies our point of criticism: the Christian vision has been placed too much *alongside* of the non-Christian vision. Stellingwerff has not observed sufficiently that we Christians also have been brought into difficulties, through the influence of the dialectic and functional attitudes in the cultural reality in which we have to live and work. How can we, with our insights, taught by the Scriptures and in principle so beautiful, cooperate positively in the finding of real solutions for the real problems of the present crisis? For in this way it is possible not only to be a radical Christian in our time but also to practise our Christianity by offering a meaningful contribution. But perhaps we have here exceeded the goals of Stellingwerff's book and are now asking for answers to questions that preoccupy ourselves. And yet, this lack is perhaps connected to another criticism: Stellingwerff speaks about the difficulties caused by the present situation, the origin of a new phase in world history in which human beings become mobile through their communication systems, and alongside of this he speaks of the crisis caused by the new dialectic and by functionalism. But how these two issues are connected, how they intersect with one another and make the picture of our world so complex, is barely elaborated, even though more than once he indicates the connection, especially when discussing the functional person. This is why his own Christian consideration stands somewhat 'timeless' alongside the other influential visions discussed. The Christian vision should, after all, not just critically confront other visions but also offer solutions, even redemption, to them. The building blocks for this are implicitly present in this book.

In short, this is an interesting, instructive and very lucid book. It is clarifying with respect to the ruling insights that determine our world. It presents concisely and originally the main lines of Christian thinking regarding our view of human being. We do have a criticism regarding the title: it speaks about 'creative man', while in the book itself, unfortunately, very little is said about creativity and its meaning for human life.

Finally, the book is illustrated very attractively with woodcuts by Flip Vanderburgt. They are valuable in themselves and provide a visual commentary on the text.

Sketch for an Aesthetic Theory based on the Philosophy of the Cosmonomic Idea[5]

General introduction

Before we begin with the actual aesthetic theory, we will consider its task and goal. An aesthetic theory will have to give account of what (naïve) experience apprehends as beauty in the given meaning-systasis. For that purpose it will have to subject the aesthetic law sphere itself to a closer investigation and explore especially the different types of individuality (meaning-individualities) within this law sphere. Since experience never apprehends a function explicitly, but always in the meaning-systasis, always as a function of a structure of temporal reality, we will also have to include these structures in our field of research. It is mainly aesthetically qualified structures that come into consideration for this, because in these in the nature of the case the aesthetic aspect plays an important role. Precisely because works of art, which are of course aesthetically qualified structures, can not only be functionally-aesthetically investigated but must also be examined in terms of their founding function, their founding structure, and so forth, we will have to venture outside of the domain of aesthetics in the narrower sense. We can perhaps best refer to this part of aesthetics as the science of art. The science of art is the science that investigates the construction of aesthetically qualified structures and their interlacement with other structures.

In summary we can thus say that aesthetics consists of two very closely connected parts:

a) aesthetics in the narrower sense, which has the aesthetic law sphere as object and for which the initial definition is valid;

b) the science of art, which primarily has aesthetically qualified structures as the object of its act of knowing and for which the above mentioned definition is valid.

Given this division we will discuss our subject matter in two parts, respectively titled 'Aesthetic theory' and 'The science of art'.

An aesthetic theory cannot of course begin 'just like that', but will have to be based on a philosophy. The idea of law of such an underlying philosophy will exert a profound influence on the theoretical definition, demarcation and elaboration of the aesthetic theory.

An aesthetic theory actually provides the 'encyclopedia' for the various sciences that study art and beauty, such as art history and the special sciences for the various arts such as music theory, and so forth.

An aesthetic theory can never replace living art or beauty itself, but must give a theoretical explanation for the naïve experience of beauty. The theoretical character of science (i.e. that it works by abstracting from the systasis) means that, although it is founded in naïve experience, it cannot and may never step into the place of naïve experience.

I Aesthetic theory

#1 The aesthetic law sphere

First we need to form a concept and an idea of the aesthetic law sphere for ourselves. To do this we need to analyse *the functional structure of this meaning-aspect* of the cosmic order of the world.

The meaning nucleus of the aesthetic law sphere is beautiful harmony. All moments of meaning are determined and qualified by beautiful harmony, since that is what guarantees the sphere sovereignty of this meaning-function; for it is the meaning nucleus (or the essential moment) that maintains the original and irreducible character of this aspect of temporal reality in opposition to every other aspect.

Cosmic time too must express itself, just as it does in every meaning-aspect, in this law sphere. We find it in aesthetic time: the aesthetically correct moment. We discern it, for example, in the actualization of music: each voice must enter at the aesthetically correct moment, lest it seem definitely unaesthetic, or ugly. The correct moment is naturally very important in works of art, but also in non-aesthetically qualified structures such as social structures. Let us give an example to illustrate the latter: it is definitely not aesthetically responsible to start playing a Beethoven symphony at the market or in a similar area, because it is not the right moment for it. For the same reason it would not be fitting to play a cheerful tune at a funeral.

We will proceed to investigate *the concept of beauty, the aesthetic*. This concept forms the logical scope of the general basic meaning of the aesthetic in its still 'restrictive', 'rigid', 'not-disclosed', 'not-deepened' function.[6] For this purpose we will have to undertake an investigation of the relationship between this law sphere and its founding law sphere. In other words, we will investigate the retrocipations or analogies. This investigation will be very brief.

Retrocipation to the economic sphere. This retrocipation we find in the barring of excess,[7] the *meden-agan*. Everything that is aesthetically excessive will be aesthetically experienced as superfluous. That is why when we read a truly beautiful literary work of art we say: 'There is not one word too many or too few written here,' just as we may say of music that each note is in its place, that there is not one note too many or too few. The addition or removal of one word or note can in such circumstances destroy the beauty. In general we have to say: every surfeit has to be avoided, but also every deficit.

At different times and in different ways a positive form has been given to this analogy. One only has to think about the difference between Baroque art and modern art (especially noticeable in architecture). In the Baroque style there is an exuberant amount of decoration, detail, ornamentation and so on, while modern art features an extreme austerity and frugality.

Retrocipation to the social aspect. This retrocipation we find in the 'not jarring or clashing with its surroundings' of the truly beautiful. Subjectively (i.e. with regard to the subject, which as aesthetic subject discloses the aesthetic object function) 'taste' corresponds to it. In this meaning-moment the aesthetic aspect appeals to the meaning of the social group. Only if the beauty of a work of art is not incongruous, if it corresponds with the taste of the members of a specific 'culture',[8] can that beauty really be experienced as beautiful (this experience will turn out further on to be a symbolic analogy). Thus the contemporary artist can create a work of art in the Baroque style, but it will then be out of place and will not appeal to the taste of the present-day person; one may view it as a more or less successful anachronic experiment but never as living modern art, which we enjoy for the sake of beauty itself. This analogy also appears clearly in the following example: if a poet presents an impression, an emotion, a thought of his or her own in a poem, one can 'empathize' with it and understand it, even though one has never experienced anything like it oneself. If there were no connection between the aesthetic and the social, this would not be possible. In this way the portrait of an unknown person can say something to me, so that I can read the person's character and personality from the portrait. On the other hand it is sometimes difficult for us to understand works of art from the past or from a different cultural circle. Only insofar as something 'generally human' is rendered would one be able to grasp it without more ado.

It was already clear from the above, when almost unnoticed we stumbled upon the symbolic analogy, that this retrocipation is founded in the other retrocipations and only has meaning in correlation with them. We may not eliminate any of the founding meaning-aspects in our theoretical consideration, since without all of its founding functions the aesthetic aspect is not viable at all. Thus the sphere sovereignty of this law sphere can maintain itself only through the connection with the other meaning-aspects, through sphere universality.

It is clear from the chosen example that this retrocipation directly refers even further back, to the historical aspect.

Retrocipation to the symbolic law sphere. The truly beautiful will as such appeal to us, it will have something to 'say' to us. If it did not appeal to us, speak to us, then we would not be able to experience its beauty. 'Experience' is thus what corresponds subjectively with the appeal. It needs no further argument that art which we cannot experience as such is meaningless.

Furthermore, we see this retrocipation in aesthetic symbolism, as we find it for instance in the 'plasticity' of a poetical work. As an example here we would like to cite a line from Coleridge's 'Rime of the Ancient Mariner': 'Down dropt the breeze, the sails dropt down,' in which the first 'dropt' indeed aesthetically symbolizes the sudden falling away of the wind. Also in Homer's *Odyssey* we can find a lovely example in the first book: 'And down she darted from the topmost summits of Olympus', where the descent is clearly depicted. (That this 'dropping' and 'descent' can only be understood if we also take cognizance of the kinematic and spatial analogies clearly manifests the founding relationship as it reveals itself in the mutual relationships of the different retrocipations.)[9]

Retrocipation to the historical law sphere. This we see in the aesthetic moment of 'style'. Style is the manner in which the (aesthetic) norms based in the divine world order are positivized. Style is therefore the answer to the question of how the aesthetic norms are given form (originally a historical moment). Later we will submit style to a more extensive investigation.[10] The aesthetic also retrocipates to historical time, which we see in the different style periods, in which we find an analogy to cultural periods.

This retrocipation is also manifest in the 'aesthetic development' of a work of art. Thus in music or literature a work of art will rise to a climax and then that climax, with its aesthetic suspense and tension, will 'resolve'. Thus the climax of the sonnet (its aesthetic climax) often follows the two quatrains and finds its resolution in the ensuing terzas. It needs no further proof that here not only the other aesthetic retrocipations but also the historical analogies play a role. (Such a historical analogy we see immediately in, for instance, the moment of 'development'.)

Retrocipation to the logical aspect. This meaning-aspect expresses itself within the aesthetical aspect by maintaining even there its *principia identitatis* and *contradictionis*. If the parts of a work of art do not stand in aesthetical logical connection to each other, the Dutch say that the work 'hangs together like loose sand'; the aesthetically logical unity is missing. In this last-mentioned moment the aesthetical refers back to the logical moment of logical unity, which is in itself a logical numerical analogy.

The aesthetic aspect also refers back to logical time: something is only aesthetically justified – we will only then be able to understand it, it will only then speak to us (here we meet the founding relationship again) – if it aesthetically logically follows from that which precedes it. In music we see this clearly when we consider that the 'development' can only take place once the exposition is completed.

Further we see that the meaning-aspect of beautiful harmony points back to the movement of thought, a moment that is a logical kinetic analogy. This aesthetic movement of thought appears to be very important when we think of the rhythm of a motif such as the meander. Only if in the aesthetic movement of thought we 'go along' the 'repeating' motif do we experience its rhythm.[11] For simultaneity by itself is not automatically rhythmic. In paintings too this rhythm is of great importance.

Retrocipation to the psychical meaning-aspect of temporal reality. This retrocipation we see in the first place in aesthetic emotionality, wherein the artist expresses her or his feeling for beauty. This emotionality can be passionate, sober, and so on.

Furthermore we see this analogy in the moment of aesthetic intensity. In all spirited[12] art we will encounter this intensity, which we will need to distinguish sharply from the aesthetic tension dealt with below. If this intensity is not present, the beauty will not appeal to us; no, the beauty is not even (completely) there any more. In such a case we refer to the work as weak or feeble. Subjectively speaking this intensity corresponds to one's being moved by the beauty.

In another way this analogy can be seen in the aesthetic moment of the mood (for mood, like emotionality, is an original psychical moment). We find this moment in the 'colour', the 'tone', the atmosphere of the work of art. Especially in music this is very important. One only has to think of the key (major, minor), or in general of the lightness of tone, the seriousness, the sorrowfulness of a piece, such as for instance the cheerfulness of mood in Beethoven's *Eighth Symphony* (which we certainly may not call programme music); the sinister mood in F.W. van Eeden's *The sun, dying, sank into the sea*; the intimacy in Tennyson's song from *The Princess*: 'Sweet and low, sweet and low'; the dreaminess in the narratives of Aart van der Leeuw, as in his collection of short stories *De Gezegenden*, and so on. In music we distinguish between the masculinity and femininity of motifs (e.g. in the overtures of Beethoven), which we should also perceive as falling under this analogy, similar to the differentiations made in painting, such as a delicate or solid or bright or warm or cold colour.

Psychical time also turns up as an analogy in the aesthetic function, as for example in the fact that a moment of silence in a musical composition or in the reciting of a poem can be experienced (aesthetically) as very long.

Retrocipation to the biotic law sphere. This retrocipation we see in the 'soulfulness'; the work of art must 'live'. Only soulful, spirited art may carry the name art, since, if the soul is not there, the work of art – aesthetically – is dead. Then it cannot show any emotion, will lack intensity, will not grip us and impress us as beautiful art. From this the founding relationship is again evident.

Retrocipation to the kinematic sphere. This we see in the first place in the aesthetic movement, the kinematic analogy of what happens in the aesthetic movement period. In connection with a musical composition, do we not speak of a background full of movement, of fast allegro and slow andante, the fast and slow of which can indeed only be explained as the analogical return of the meaning of movement within the aesthetic meaning?

We also find aesthetic causality here. A certain phrase, line, movement, follows causally from the previous one. (If one begins to sing a melody there are many ways in which to complete it, but it has to move on in such a way that the following part follows aesthetically-causally from the previous part; if not, it will also be in conflict with aesthetic logic.) How often do we not notice while examining true works of art that one detail necessarily, that is aesthetically-causally, follows from the other. With respect to music especially this is even more conspicuous if we consider, for example, that dissonant chords constantly ask to be resolved; that which follows is aesthetically-causally demanded by that which comes before.

Aesthetic tension too falls under this movement analogy. Such tension can arise from shifts of rhythm (think, for example, of syncopation), accelerations and reductions of speed in the movement, while such tension can be alternated with or followed by a release of tension. We often find this tension very strong in many of Wagner's works, for example the 'fierce' unison violin part in the beginning of the overture *Die Meistersinger von Nürnberg*. In modern American dance music, the so-called 'swing', this tension is brought to such great heights that we can say it is misused.

In the visual arts (especially in the case of decorative ornamentation) the moments of movement, tension and causality appear in the movement of thought already discussed above.

Furthermore, the movement aspect surfaces in the aesthetic sphere in the moment of the aesthetic equilibrium. Balance is very important for all works of art, but it is especially noticeable in sculptural art. If, for example, an artist depicts a walking person without taking this equilibrium into account, which will be apparent in an incorrect choice of the movement-moment for the walking person, then we may say that it looks as if the person is falling over. Only aesthetic subjects will experience this: the person depicted does not really, physically, fall over of course; and a dog would not notice this about the sculpture; from all of which it is clear that we are dealing with an aesthetic moment.

Retrocipation to the sense of space. In the first place this appears in the aesthetic space for the aesthetic movement. This we see, for example, in the aesthetic interplay of lines, as is so evident in the polyphonic music of Bach. But also in connection with decorative drawings we will experience this interplay of lines in the aesthetic thought movement.[13]

Further, we apprehend the spatial configuration of figures as a spatial analogy: the compilation, their arrangement, in other words, the composition. Thus we see, for example, that in the composition of a painting the 'geometrical lines', for instance the diagonal, the horizontal and the vertical that divide the surface in two, are very important. Indeed, we can check this with a ruler . . . yet it can never be spatially, geometrically understood. After all, spatially, what sense does it make that in a painting the diagonal, for instance, is strongly accentuated? It only acquires meaning aesthetically, even though that would be impossible if the aesthetic did not refer back to the spatial, if the aesthetic, in the cosmic-temporal context, did not show a connection with the spatial meaning. And this is possible only if both possess sovereignty in their own sphere.

In addition we also need to mention the aesthetic measurements and relationships. One thinks for example of the application of the principle of the golden section. In these measurements and relationships the meaning of space reasserts itself analogically within the aesthetical. We can explain this as follows: if we put a mount around a picture that we are framing, we can – aesthetically – make it too big or too small. The relationships and measurements are then not aesthetically responsible, not in agreement with the norms of beautiful harmony.

Retrocipation to the arithmetic meaning. This analogy we see firstly in the aesthetic unity in multiplicity. A work of art must involve all its parts[14] in an aesthetic unity. For example, one thinks of the classical demand for the drama: 'unity of the plot'.

Furthermore we see the discrete quantity express its own irreducible meaning within the aesthetic sphere: one thinks especially of rhythm, which consists after all of discrete 'rhythmic pulses'. We could never explain these discrete, distinct pulses without referring to the mutual relational-meaning between the meaning of the harmony and that of discrete quantity. (Recall in this regard the logical retrocipation in the movement of thought.) With this, however, account has only been given of rhythm in the visual arts and in architecture, and so on. The rhythm of music and of poetry is more than 'just' a retrocipation, as we will demonstrate later on, see 2B below.

Up till now we have analysed the concept of beauty. Now we would like to focus on the idea of the aesthetic. This idea takes the general basic meaning of the aesthetic law sphere in its deepened, anticipatory, disclosing function, in its ultimate reference to the supratemporal significance of the beautiful in Christ as root of the new human race.[15] It is beauty in its deepened sense, being directed to the consummation of meaning. The investigation of this idea leads us in the first place to the mutual coherence of meaning between the aesthetic aspect and the law spheres that follow it. The deepening, or disclosure of the general basic meaning of harmony that we understand in the idea of beauty, is the dynamic factor in the formation of beauty, since if the functional structure is deepened, the retrocipating moments are implicitly deepened in their meaning.

In this way we find in the aesthetic norm aspect the following anticipations (which anticipations themselves reach ahead directly to the supratemporal fullness of meaning).

Anticipation to the meaning of retribution .[16] We see this anticipation in the weighing of the different moments against each other. That this anticipation deepens the retrocipations in their meaning will, with any consideration, be clear. We would especially like to point to the deepening of the economic retrocipation (which we previously defined as the barring of excess): the 'barring of excess' will, through this deepening of meaning, have to 'save', through a process of equalizing[17], elements that are no longer judged equal, since these elements, when weighed in a way which anticipates the meaning of retribution, are no longer judged equal. Thus, through this consideration it can appear that the one part of a work of art is much more important – that is, aesthetically more important – than the other.[18] In painting for example, one figure, one component, will be given much more attention than another. The accepted distinction in art history between analytical and synthetical[19] is a state of affairs of which we can give a more exact account as a result of this disclosure. Someone like van Eyck, for example, paints analytically; every part is worked out with about the same amount of care, as not one detail was more or less important for him than another. By contrast, someone like Rembrandt paints synthetically. For him one detail – aesthetically speaking – is much more important than another, and therefore he gives more attention to the important detail; he makes it aesthetically prominent. One only has to visualize his renowned *Nightwatch* to see this clearly illustrated. It appears from this that the disclosure of the aesthetic meaning had progressed further in the time of Rembrandt than in the time of van Eyck. This does not mean that art in the time of Rembrandt was better than the earlier art![20] We may not interpret the idea of disclosure evolutionistically!

Furthermore, in speaking about anticipation it will obviously not be right to overemphasize one of the aesthetic retrocipations. In subsection #8 below, we will show that this will be the situation if the activity of the artist stems from an apostate attitude of the heart, in which the latter is directed to an absolutized meaning-aspect of this temporal reality.

Anticipation to the meaning of love.[21] In the first place we see this appear in what is noble. Art must be aimed at the refinement, the uplifting of humankind. The disclosure of beauty is revealed here in the direction of love for one's neighbour. If a 'work of art' degrades human being, if it makes an appeal to the sinful instincts of humankind and attempts to stimulate them, then this anticipation has assumed an anti-normative direction.[22] With the disclosure of the aesthetic law sphere through love for one's neighbour, honesty and sincerity also become apparent. When, for instance, in a work of art a lack of ideas is 'camouflaged' by a 'lot of humbug' or by outer appearance, then someone is trying to pull the wool over our eyes; the aesthetic aspect then has a negative relation to the meaning of love. The beauty of the work will undoubtedly suffer or be destroyed by this. It would be the same if artists did not stick up for their opinions, for their world views, but attempted to suggest that they adhered to certain ideas while actually they believed something else. Justice is also not done to aesthetic honesty if an 'ugly' (that is ethically bad) content is flattered by a beautiful form, and the beauty as a whole is marred.

Anticipation to the pistical. The whole process of disclosure, thus also the deepening of meaning of the aesthetical aspect of meaning, is led and directed by faith. Music or other art which is conceived under the leadership of the scientific ideal or the Enlightenment ideal is necessarily different from either Christian art or an art which is guided and disclosed by a Romantic faith in genius. With regard to this, note that Dooyeweerd calls attention to the rigidity which appeared under the guidance of the scientific ideal because people wanted to mathematize art too.[23] The influence of faith on the process of diclosure is clearly apparent here. We will return to this subject when dealing with style.

#2 Meaning-individualities within the aesthetic meaning

We have just discussed the general basic meaning of the aesthetic law sphere. However, this must work itself out in the individuality structures of temporal reality, it must individualize itself into the meaning-individualities that have to form the modal structure functions in the various individuality structures. Thus we will encounter within the aesthetic sovereign sphere the meaning-individualities that form the modal structure functions of the individuality structures, which belong to the radical types of animals and plants, and so on. These individuality structures taken together, in interlacement with the *Umwelt*, form within the aesthetic meaning the meaning-individuality of beauty. The individuality structures qualified in the normative aspects also have their modal structure functions here. Thus we see here the meaning-individualities of the structures of family, state, and so on, as much as of those of the synthetic societal interlinkages. The thing-structures that are objectively qualified in one of the normative aspects also have modal structure functions within this aesthetic aspect, as do, for example, implements, symbols, pistically qualified things, etc.

However, in the first place we are interested in art, the work of art. Works of art are all objectively-aesthetically-qualified structures that have a historical founding function. They belong to the radical type: work of art. (A radical type is that structural principle that governs, though only modally, the structures it encompasses, according to the radical functions.)

The general basic meaning individualizes itself first into the meaning-individualities of the different arts. These meaning-individualities form the leading functions of the structural principles of the different genotypes. These individualize themselves again to those that form the leading functions of the subgenotypes.

Since the structures belonging to this genotype are all historically founded, all the mentioned meaning-individualities and thus also all the leading functions in question will be of a founded, retrocipating character.

Here below we would like to present the different genotypes and subgenotypes schematically:

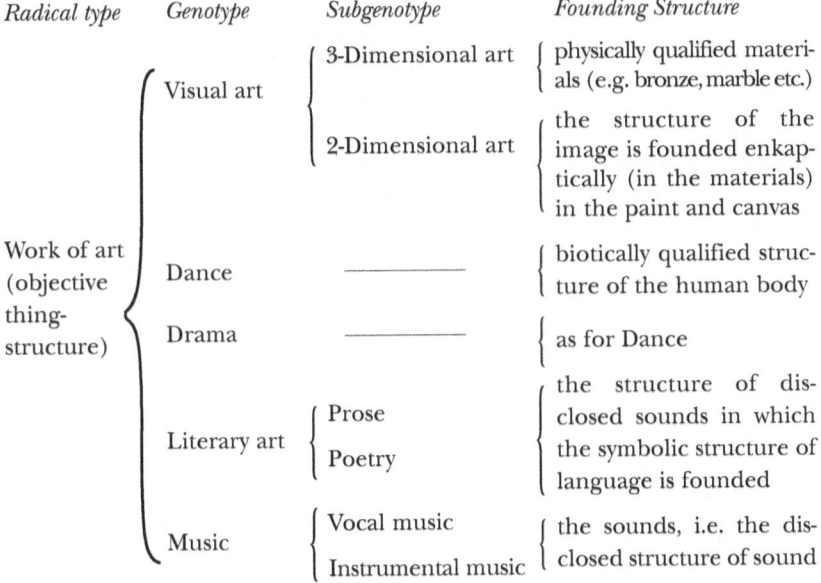

The sequence of the arts in this diagram is totally arbitrary; no preference is given to any of the arts.

In 2A, #3 below, we will take a closer look at the different genotypes, while in 2B we will look more extensively at the structure of music. There we will discuss the founding structures as presented summarily in the last column as well.

#3 Style

Style is one of the most prominent qualities of any work of art. We referred to style earlier as the retrocipation of an aesthetic sphere to the historical. Style is founded (within the general basic meaning of the aesthetic sphere) in all retrocipations to the cosmically earlier spheres, while those to the post-historic spheres are again founded in style. In this way we see that Baroque art now often strikes us as excessively boisterous;[24] however, for the people of that period it corresponded with their taste,[25] while they might have referred to modern art as bare and too frugal.

That style is indeed a historical analogy is manifest from the fact that style is the manner in which the aesthetic norm principles that are anchored in the divine order of the world are positivized in a certain period. Style therefore gives an answer to the question of how the aesthetic norms are given form in a certain period (originally a historical moment).

When the general basic meaning of a law sphere is deepened in its meaning, the moments that are to be positivized are also implicitly deepened, and thus the disclosure process will have a profound influence on the positivization.

We already saw this in the discussion of the juridical anticipation in the previous section. Now, guided by the aesthetical function in its disclosure, the pre-aesthetical functions are also disclosed. The meaning-individualities in the law spheres 'between' the aesthetical and the historical are positivized on a historical basis, which positivization is guided, however, by the aesthetic sphere (since this is the leading function of a work of art). The positivization of the norms in the different law spheres will thus be in 'correlation' with those of the aesthetic meaning.[26] Hence, when we investigate a particular style we are not finished when we have studied the aesthetic sphere in its positive form, since how the norms are positivized in the other functions also needs to be investigated. A work of art is more than the aesthetic function alone. (One also has to think in this regard about the intermodal coherence of meaning within the structure.)[27]

The investigation of the non-aesthetic structure functions of the work of art is obviously the task of the science of art. Thus this investigation will have to include a study of the 'form',[28] among other things. Although we may not ascribe to style the manner in which the non-aesthetic structure functions are positivized, since style appears in the proper sense only within the aesthetic law sphere, nevertheless we could, given the direct relationship between the positivization in the aesthetic and non-aesthetic law spheres, roughly expand on the above-given definition as follows: style is a normative requirement demanded of a work of art in a particular period.

Since positivization, as has been argued in the above, is dependent on the disclosure process, we will have to investigate the influence of disclosure on style. Disclosure and positivization are founded on the historical development led by the direction and with the social cooperation of successive artists as leading shapers of history. The disclosure process is guided by the pistical meaning-function. We will illustrate some of this in more depth with the following examples.

In the Middle Ages the whole of Europe was permeated by the ideal of a church that encompassed all the spheres of life and of a life that was focused on God. This finds its expression in style. Think, for example, of the Gothic churches with their verticalism, in which virtually the whole church building is a symbol of the central position the church, and Christ, held in the hearts of the people in a God-centred life and world view. The glory of the church is expressed in the Baroque church buildings of the Counter-Reformation. In contrast, the Protestant churches clearly express the centrality of the word of God, fulfilled in Christ.

In Renaissance art we find two moments or ideals at work. Firstly there is freedom, as in the Faustian unbridled desire for unlimited freedom and potential; secondly, rationalization of style as in strictly maintained, rationally determined classicism.[29] As time passes, these ideals, which still held each other in balance in the Renaissance, grow further and further apart until in the Baroque period they appear as two entities, next to each other, which cannot be connected. Compare, for example, the style of Bernini with Palladian classicism. These two poles naturally do not stand totally loose from each other, and thus Baroque elements occur also in Palladio. In these two ideals one immediately recognizes the two counterpoles within the humanistic life and world view, namely the ideals of personality and of (mathematical) science. However, we will not investigate their development further.

Precisely here, however, it is apparent that people cannot permanently ignore the norms imposed by the divine order of the world. Despite themselves, all great artists have gone beyond the limitations of the norms[30] positivized partially by their own doing, since 'life' does not allow itself to be forced into a straitjacket of false views of reality. If they really wanted to create works of art, they had to adhere to the laws of the structure of temporal reality, whether they wanted to or not. We will discuss this further in the following section.

Modern art's most conspicuous characteristic is its great 'frugality'. We see this frugality, this shying away from everything excessive, in the strong stylization of modern art. We can trace this frugality and stylization to a striving for functionalism, which is the consequence of disclosure in a pragmatical sense, whereby everything comes to fall under the guidance of an (economistic) idea of 'functionalism'. As 'counterpole' we see the more purely irrationalistic tendency, which occasions the many isms in contemporary art that do not recognize any permanent norm, while each artist claims to be able to create a style on his or her own, apart from any historical development, and to be able to determine the norm for art and beauty by him or herself. Both the irrationalistic and the pragmatic poles are rooted in the vitalistic life and world view.[31]

While we said that style was the normative requirement for the 'how' of a work of art in a particular period, and while we emphasized that this indeed means that laws are positivized, we may never forget that the artist, as subject, assumes a position of her or his own with regard to the law. Wagner, for example, has positivized a style as a leading shaper of history, and many composers have worked in that style; and yet Richard Strauss, Bruckner, Sibelius and others each have their 'own' style, their own subjective behaviour within the positivized norm.

The forming of a style occurs via successive artists, leading figures and their respective 'schools', in social collaboration. Continuity of style is accomplished by two historic phenomena: tradition and progression.

We said that style is the manner in which norms are positivized. We must now direct our attention to the factors that have an influence on the positivization of the norms for art. We have already, above, discussed the influence of faith, of the transcendental terminal sphere of the order of the world, on the process of disclosure and thereby on the positivization. (We do not have to go any further into the fact that faith, as a temporal function of human existence, receives its orientation from the choice of religious attitude in the heart of the total human personality.)

The question that we now ask ourselves is whether we can indeed speak of Italian or Dutch, German, Indian, Chinese art.[32] In answering this question we have to focus especially on the political and biotic factors. The influence of these external factors is so great precisely because the positivization by the artists takes place in social collaboration. This social collaboration takes place in all kinds of different interindividual relationships, upon which intercommunal relationships and other interindividual relationships will have great influence. We will illustrate this too with some examples.

We already mentioned the influence of the organized community of the state as being very encompassing. That we can (usually) see a unity of style within the territory of a country (*staat*), that we can speak of a specific national style, is made possible by the strongly integrating influence of the state. In the first place we would like to refer to the influence on the biotic. The biotic cohesion of the generations within the territory of a country gives rise to a national-political type. For human being consists of a number of structures that form foundations for each other. Here we focus on the biotic structure. The above-mentioned national-political type is a biotic variability type occurring through the influence of the political. This biotic structure is in the nature of the case a disclosed structure, which is immediately evident if we realize that we are talking about a 'national-political' type, which indicates disclosure led by the different functions of the structure of the organized community of the state. After all, a (subjective) national structure (*staatstructuur*) has come into being on the basis of historically developed or acquired power, which has bound this nation (*volk*) together.[33]

Directly founded on the biotic is the psychic, in its meaning-individuality of the national feeling of solidarity.[34] It is exactly this feeling of solidarity that has a great influence on the inter-individual relationships within the organized community of the state. The unity of language, which originates under the integrating influence of the institution of the state, is also very important with regard to this feeling of solidarity.

But the state will also 'directly' intervene in an integrating way. Just think of projects commissioned by the state, the establishment of art academies and museums by the state, and so on. Conquests can also have a great influence, as elements of the style of the conquered territory will exert their influence on a country's own style. A striking example of this is the art of the Romans which was strongly influenced by that of the Greeks, whom they had conquered.

We see a clear illustration of this also in the Italian art of the Renaissance. In relation to that time, we can rightfully speak of the typical styles (especially in the art of painting) of Siena, Florence, Venice, Rome, Ferrara and other cities. And yet we see in these styles a certain unity. We are dealing here with two contradictory influences: political fragmentation, as opposed to unity of 'race', and a feeling of solidarity, based on it. We can most probably attribute the latter to the after-effects of the integrating influence of the Roman state in the time when Italy was still a unit. The feeling of solidarity here occurs especially in those who know that they are bearers of the same 'culture'. That the Italians felt this unity despite the fragmentation is proven clearly by the fact that, especially in the sixteenth century, they searched for and found a language that was the same throughout Italy.35

We may also mention the church as a factor that 'stimulated unity' in Italy at that time. This illustrates the integrating influence of the pistically qualified institutionalized community of the church, an influence which is also apparent in the unity of faith, united in one denomination, which is a very important influence that made it possible for the ideas and art of the Renaissance to spread over Europe so quickly. For in Europe the church had really 'integrated' a certain unity which, even when the church and the Christian monoculture of the Middle Ages were deteriorating, made rapid diffusion possible. (The Balkans, which are Greek Orthodox, fall outside of the European unity of (Renaissance) style.) The ancient unity under the Roman Empire will probably also have contributed to the feeling of solidarity of the West.

When Italy later becomes a political entity, it no longer makes sense to distinguish between the different city-styles; one can then rightfully speak of an Italian style.

With regard to this, we would also like to refer to the important differences between the art of the Northern and the Southern Netherlands. Compare, for example, Rembrandt with Rubens.

In the same manner we could explain the reasons for the existence of different styles in other countries such as Germany, France, England, Russia, India, China, Japan and so forth.

Only seldom will we come across the situation in which within a single state context we see two (or more) different ways of positivizing of norms. Such differences will usually be traceable to differences in biotic typicality. A very typical example is the United States of America, where we find a specifically idiosyncratic African-American music and Caucasian (European) music existing next to each other. We wonder whether we can indeed speak of the African-American as a national-political type. Yes, the biotic aspect is also disclosed here; it points ahead in a transcendental direction towards the historical aspect, since the

African-Americans who have been united on American soil by the power of the sword of the economically-qualified slave trade have intermingled intensely and have indeed formed a typical national African-American type. We will discuss the integrating factors for the formation of their own musical art and of other important matters having a bearing on this situation in greater depth in #11 below. That African-Americans in the United States are really a national-political type follows also from the fact that they distinguish themselves not only from the black people in Africa but also from the black people in other parts of America. Their feeling of solidarity is based to a very great extent on this foundation: African-Americans feel themselves to be citizens of the United States, but at the same time, definitely black. This is an important factor in the origin of an idiosyncratic black North American art, and it is further strengthened by the so-called colour-line: the typical position of the African-American community originates on the substratum sphere of the psychic emotional judgment,[36] which arises through the objectivization of the biotic structure in the psychic aspect. They have their own churches, associations, neighbourhoods, yes even their own regiments. And in their own 'context' they have positivized their own norms for music, which guide their own music. In the United States we see, as it were, two integrations, side by side: one amongst the white Americans and one amongst the black Americans.

Besides the factors discussed thus far there may be many others that have an influence on the positivization and development of norms for art and style. We will not discuss these more extensively here. But, to mention a few, there are economic factors (think of the Dutch 'golden age', which was also 'golden' in the realm of art); climate (especially its influence on the positivization of the norms for architecture); available material (the use of other materials brings about variability types: compare, for example, brick buildings in the Netherlands with marble buildings in Italy); the previously mentioned influence of language, etc. Nowadays we witness the tremendous integrating influence of easier methods of communication. One only has to think of the radio, gramophone, film, aeroplane and such, to realize that the different styles will have more and more influence on each other through this intensified communication,[37] since inter-individual relationships will come into existence which were more difficult or totally impossible in the past, for instance in radio concerts.

We hardly need to mention that, along with a progression of integration, a continuing differentiation will take place. We will not go into this any further.

#4 The artist

We have been confronted in the previous section with the influence of faith and world view on norm positivization. The act of positivization is always directed towards the positivization of norms and laws. The question now is whether, through this positivization, a positive form is given to the norms laid down in principle in the divine world order or whether laws are positivized in conflict with these norms. The subjects in the normative spheres can subjectively violate the norms given by God, but cannot break free from them; it would not be possible for them to 'create' something that is not determined and limited by the divine world order, since in that case something would be made that is independent of the law, autonomous, self-sufficient. This is not possible for the simple reason that if something is self-sufficient it no longer exists within the sphere of meaning; it becomes meaningless, that is, not in the sphere of meaning; it falls away into nothingness, a 'pure fantasy'. Only the 'Lord of Hosts', who is the giver of meaning, does not exist within the sphere of meaning.

As has already been said, laws will be given a positive form through positivization. If a law that is given a positive form does not comply with the divine law, with the norm laid down in the world order, then this positivized law becomes a 'law of sin and death'. Let us be thankful that in his preserving grace God made things so that, in spite of the fact that many leading norm-positivizers belong to the world-in-the-antithesis really beautiful things may still be made, real art still exists and that, in spite of the predominance of an apostate faith, norms still can be positivized that are in harmony with the norms laid down in the cosmic world order.

The individual artist is subject to the, perhaps also by his own doing, positivized norms. Thus the personal direction of faith, or rather the personal religious choice that exists in the heart of a specific subjective artist will also have an influence on her or his creative labour; for the subject is free under the law, is truly subject (not a special case of the law, or something of that sort).

Thus we come across various possibilities. Consider first the case of artists who want to base their whole creative activity on a theory of art or an aesthetic theory. Since this is a theoretical science that therefore proceeds by abstraction from the systasis of temporal reality, the artists can never use the method but, at most, only the results. Yet, if the theory is based on a false view of reality, its influence can be disastrous. This is also the danger of many modern art institutions that are 'concocted behind a desk'.[38] One finds good examples of this discussed in J.J. Vriend's *Nieuwere architectuur.*[39] Cubism desired to apply the method of science. It sought to portray the 'concept' of things instead of the 'natural random appearance'. It was strongly mathematically orientated in its search for 'eternal, lasting values' in contrast to the transient forms of nature.[40] It wanted to present the general and not the particular, partly in reaction to what Romanticism and, especially, Impressionism had produced. The fact that the artists who worked in this direction often managed to create true beauty must be attributed to the fact that, in spite of themselves, they never managed to be totally consistent with their theory. In the end the only result is that they have become an important factor in the many influences that lead to, and have led to, a new norm-positivization, thus to the formation of a new style. In this regard we would also like to refer to what was said in the previous section about modern art.

Fortunately, when artists create, they create 'naïvely', even though they are likely to have an especially strong aesthetically disclosed naïve experience. Therefore, on the basis of their naïve intuition they will often 'do correctly what their theory taught them to do incorrectly'. The greater the artist, the better his or her developed intuition will sense the norms, and the less influence false world views and theories will have on him or her. Therefore we read in Bernet Kempers's *Muziekgeschiedenis* [41] 'One should never forget that there is a considerable difference between Wagner's theories and his practice. His music is much richer, more interesting and more spontaneous than his often cool and intellectual theories. The artist Wagner was fortunately much stronger than the aesthete and one often finds his most sublime moments there, where he most strongly contradicts his theory.'

This is also why, if one wants to study a certain style period, one has to look for the clearest examples in the lesser artists. For they will follow the positivized norms more slavishly, precisely because they will have a weaker 'aesthetic personality' and will add less of their own personality to it; they will not be leading shapers of history.

It is however not imperative and also not always the case that artists base themselves on an art theory. On the contrary, in general they will be 'naïve' as creative artists and will not even want to base their work on a theory. They will recognize intuitively that beauty and the activity of creating beauty cannot be replaced by a theory. The fact that in the twentieth century philosophy and aesthetics worked with all sorts of nominalistic thought constructions that ignored the given reality contributed, of course, to the fact that these sciences have become discredited. As long as theories of art do not really attempt to account for what is given in naïve experience, naïve experience will constantly resist efforts to impose all sorts of intellectual constructions on reality. In the case of artists who do not base themselves on any theory, their life and world view will naturally have an influence on their art and, in general, on the norm positivization, just as in the case of those who do attempt to apply theories. For the religious choice in the heart of our temporal existence, which determines our life and world view, determines the direction of everything we do subjectively, including the direction of our faith. And this faith guides the whole disclosure and positivization process, as we have already shown in the preceding section. The individual life and world view of artists will naturally, except in the above-mentioned manner, have a great influence on their choice of subject.

One should think in this connection of Marsman, whose vitalistic outlook on life is strongly revealed in his poems.

#5 The intentional fantasy image and inspiration

Only further on will we look at structures in depth. However, we have already stipulated that works of art are objective aesthetically qualified thing-structures; the leading function is therefore an aesthetic object function. We now ask ourselves whether the aesthetic subjectivity of the artist is objectivized in this object function. We have to answer this question negatively, because it is impossible that a subject would function as the object within one and the same sphere. How then does the object function come about, since it is after all the result of subjective forming by the artist? The situation is as follows:[42] artists subjectively design their concepts. These concepts are objectivized on the basis of the (psychical) fantasy image. We now have intentional (i.e. only in the 'minds' of the artists, thus still not actually existing) aesthetically qualified objective structures. These objective fantasy images must now be actualized, objectivized by the artists, in a historically controlled forming activity. Works of art of the genotypes, which cannot be permanently objectivized, are rendered by the artists in a symbolic structure; we will return to this in more detail, see 2A below.

The above-mentioned subjective concepts, which are thus objectivized in intentional fantasy images, are devised by the artists when they are inspired. So, what is inspiration?[43] Would it be nothing other than intuition? Indeed, through intuition[44] we become cosmologically conscious that the different meaning-aspects of temporal reality are part of us, thus also the aesthetic aspect. In the pre-theoretical intuition we also knowingly experience the modal diversity of meaning, albeit without articulated distinguishing knowledge, without distinct conceptualization of the meaning-modalities. Thus artists become conscious through intuition of possessing an aesthetic function, through which it becomes possible for them to see the beauty of various (theoretically all) objective structures in the created cosmos and of things formed by us on a historical basis through human activity in submission to the God-given norms. From all of this it is clear that inspiration is based on intuition, since without a cosmological consciousness of the temporal coherence of meaning and diversity of meaning, inspiration would have no 'grasp' of reality. We have clearly shown in the previous section that the intuition of an artist will be a disclosed and deepened intuition. For even if inspiration is founded in the psychical aspect, it presupposes 'the will to form'.

What is essentially self-given (in the pre-theoretical intuition) is never that which is aesthetically rendered (or that which is incorporated in the intentional fantasy image). An aesthetically responsible concept is only possible in disclosure, opening and aesthetic deepening of what has been given in pre-theoretical intuition.[45] So, *inspiration is to have knowledge in a particular way of the aesthetic state of affairs, of the norms in the aesthetic meaning-modality.*

We are certainly aware that with this we have not exhaustively discussed the important problem of what inspiration is. However, it is not possible to explain theoretically why the inspiration of a particular artist expresses itself thus, in such a manner, in such and such a genre, since in order to determine this we would have to delve into the subject. Yet inspiration, if it were not structurally built into the world order, would also have no subjective existence. And the task of theoretical thought is precisely to address the structure (in the broadest sense of the word) of all that is temporal in its systematic, normative form.

Artists are aesthetic geniuses in the sense that, as aesthetic subjects, they are gifted according to the norms of this law sphere with a particular instrumental subjectivity. They have an exceptional gift of objectivizing their intention. Naturally artists have to have command of a highly developed technique[46] in order to objectivize, to realize their intentional fantasy image.

The motive for devising a fantasy image can be:

1. The artist has a psychic perception of a psychic object (e.g. a landscape, an animal, a beautiful human body), which he or she objectivizes aesthetically and it then becomes the occasion for devising a fantasy image; it namely inspires him or her to do it. This will most often be the case in the visual arts.

2. A structure qualified by one of the normative meaning-aspects can also be the occasion, such as love, a painting, one's native country, a city, and so on. This will often be the case in literature, as well as in dramatic art and in programmatic music.

3. An original (subjective) psychic moment can be the occasion. In this way the artist's own mood, or that of another person, can be aesthetically objectivized. We often encounter this in literary art (especially lyrical poetry) and in music. 'Pure' fantasy can also be a cause. Think of fairy tales, 'fantasy' books like Rider Haggard's *She*, etc.

The subjective-psychic moment is logically objectivized for this purpose (one must after all distinguish it from other 'moods'), whereby the logical anticipatory spheres of that moment are opened under logical functional guidance. Next it is historically objectivized in the same manner, then symbolically, socially and economically, all directed and guided by the aesthetic function of the artist. Finally it is aesthetically objectivized, and when this moment has in this way become an aesthetic object, then the artist can devise her or his subjective concept and objectivize it again in the intentional fantasy image. In fact, the instances in question will often occur simultaneously and be mutually interwoven.

4. As fourth possibility we see that the artist can also 'directly' design his or her fantasy image, without any external-aesthetic reason. We find this, for instance, in abstract decoration and absolute music. It makes no difference whether the artist working in the arts which cannot be objectivized permanently renders this symbolically or actualizes it immediately (improvisation).

#6 The viewer of art

The viewers of art have the position of subject in all normative law spheres in relation to the object functions of the work of art, which they will disclose (or open, in the sense of actualize). If the work of art asks for a subjective actualization (e.g. music), an aesthetically qualified inter-individual relationship will exist between performer(s) and listeners. In this, a feeling of solidarity will occur, namely that they will know themselves to be bearers of the same culture.[47]

The normative requirement placed on the viewer of art is to have opened him or herself to the art to be viewed. This 'opening', which takes place on a historical basis, must be guided by the (disclosed) aesthetic subject function.

Here we encounter a very important state of affairs. Since in any particular period in a particular nation the positivization of norms in the different law spheres is guided by the same belief for everybody, emanating from a similar religious attitude of the heart[48] and based on the shared development of that civilization, while naturally the intermodal meaning-relationship of the different law spheres is also very important, the norm positivization in the different law spheres and for the different structures will be very closely related. If we are 'members' of a certain culture it is not difficult to open ourselves to art belonging to that culture. The art is after all not separated from the other meaning aspects and structures of temporal reality but forms a systasis with them.[49] If we know the norms of the different areas of life in a culture we will not be surprised by the norms of its art. It is not so, however, if we [as Europeans] try to become acquainted with the art of a culture that is unfamiliar to us (e.g. Indonesian, Chinese, etc.). In that case we must first take note of the whole of the culture, all sorts of moments in that culture, before we can open ourselves to its art and understand it comprehensively. We need to know how norms are positivized in the other culture. We need to reckon with this different norm positivization in the assessment of its art. We may never apply our own norms to it, the norms as they are positivized in our 'own' culture! Only when we know how norms are positivized in the other culture can we judge the aesthetic calibre of its works of art; only then can we judge to what extent this art satifies the normative demands embedded in the divine world order (since positivization is, after all, the giving of a positive form to the said norms).

We need especially to take note of the above in judging the art of a primitive culture. We will devote a separate section to this.

With regard to what was said at the beginning of this section we want to quote Dooyeweerd: 'To comprehend the objective reality of this work of art, the observer must contemplate it as the structural objective realization of the subjective aesthetic conception of the artist. He must indeed possess a reproductive aesthetic fantasy, to which end his natural aesthetic vision must be disclosed and deepened.'[50] We will see in the following section that a constructive critique, indirectly an aesthetic theory, can lead to a good disclosure. It is of course clear that the same norms apply to critics as to viewers of art. Moreover, as critics have a very responsible task because they have to test art work according to norms and their judgment can have great influence, they will need to comply very closely with the norms; the normative demands placed upon them will be much heavier.

#7 Art criticism

Aesthetics is very important for art criticism. Without a theoretical determination of the moments we need to search for in art – an aesthetic theory – we cannot get any further in our critique than postulating clichés. It becomes very clear that the cosmonomic idea is of importance for aesthetics, and thus also for art criticism, when we consider irrationalism. Irrationalists can, after all, never say: 'This is beautiful or ugly'; they can only say, 'I find this beautiful or ugly'.[51] By their basic premise they have given up the possibility of a universally valid critique. Only those who acknowledge that art is bound by norms can offer a critique. To that purpose they must know what the norms are (which in aesthetics, at least in principle, will have to be read from the divine world order). They can then 'confront' an individual piece of art with these norms and so arrive at a generally valid judgment. Personal taste does not have to have any influence here; the greater or lesser degree of disclosure will obviously have an influence.

As we already noticed, critics who want to confront an individual 'piece' with the norms must have opened themselves comprehensively to the work of art that is to be criticized. An extensive knowledge of style is necessary, and they should also have studied the other arts and the whole culture from which the artwork stems that is to be criticized.

Anyone who adopts the standpoint of the Philosophy of the Cosmonomic Idea has to acknowledge the existence of norms. A critique that consists of clichés or undefined remarks serves no purpose, since it lacks general validity. Obviously a critique based on a different idea of law from that of the Philosophy of the Cosmonomic Idea may contain many elements of truth.

A good critique, namely one based on good aesthetics, can have a great influence on the creator(s) as well as on the performer(s), since it points out the moments that can be improved upon. A good critique is especially important for art lovers. Through such a critique they can receive guidance and direction in their opinions about art, their enjoyment of art and their critical viewing of art.

It is also clear from what has been discussed here that a purely destructive critique has no value.

#8 Christian art

By Christian art we do not primarily mean ecclesiastical art.[52] Christian art is art that is conceived, and of which the norms are positivized, under the guidance of a Christian faith stemming from a religious attitude directed towards God and Christ. Therefore only if hearts are truly in Christ may we expect Christian art. We discussed Christian art in considering the art of the Middle Ages in #3 of this chapter not because that is mainly ecclesiastical art but because of the Christian attitude focused on God. No art can be truly Christian art, even if it is employed to build churches or to paint Christ on the cross, unless the above-mentioned requirement is met. We therefore cannot refer to the bulk of the art of the Renaissance as Christian art, even though many 'Christian subjects' are represented, because these works were made under the influence of the humanistic ideal of personality (or the scientific ideal based on it).[53]

Thus Christian art has to meet two requirements: norms must be positivized under the guidance of Christian belief, in submission to the God-given law, and the artists must let themselves be led in the conception of their art through this faith, their creative activity must find its roots in this choice of religious position in which the heart is directed towards God, who is revealed to us through Christ. Now if an artist or a group of artists make works of art according to the norms which are positivized in their time – for they can and may neither break through the historical continuity in style-development nor ignore the norms in their positivized form – while living and working from a Christian life and world view, then that which is hybrid, which gives too much evidence of the rebellion against God, will undoubtedly be softened and will find little or no expression in their art. If a similar attitude were to be pursued over several generations and if it were to have the opportunity to form its own tradition, then we could expect a Christian art, since in the continuous historical development the positivization would have come about under the guidance of Christian belief. We see something of this in the Dutch art of the seventeenth century, which is why it is hard for us to speak of 'Baroque' in connection with the art of the Northern Netherlands in that period as we would with regard to art in the countries lying further to the south.

Christians should not make themselves guilty of absolutizing one of the meaning aspects of temporal reality. In practice such an absolutization always becomes manifest in the over-accentuation of the absolutized law sphere, which causes its anticipations and retrocipations in the other law spheres also to be overly accentuated.[54] A work of art will become somewhat unbalanced as a result. Thus Romanticism wanted to turn beauty into something psychical (which in our terminology would say that they looked for beauty exclusively in the aesthetic anticipation in the psychic aspect). However, in Romantic works of art we see – and in this they had actually surrendered to the cosmic world order – that they over-emphasized the psychic retrocipation within the aesthetic aspect. And here one should look for the explanation of why non-Christian art will not completely satisfy the serious art lover in the long run. We also see then that those generally acknowledged as greatest among artists, such as Bach, Rembrandt, van Eyck, etc. were Christian artists, who in their artworks did justice to all aspects of the aesthetical. Is it not so that, without denying its superb qualities, many find the art of the Italian Renaissance a bit 'cold'? On the other hand they are full of admiration for Gothic architecture and sculpture which, even though a lot of ornament and decoration is used, is rarely referred to as 'boisterous', as regularly happens with regard to the Baroque. This evaluation comes not only from the Christian side but also from many non-Christian art lovers who, without wanting to acknowledge that the cause may be found in its Christian character, acknowledge this 'balance' of Christian art as a fact.

Now, if a Christian artist works according to norms positivized under the guidance of an apostate faith, then we can expect 'partial-Christian' art. Likewise partial-Christian art will originate if the creative activity emanates from the unfaithful heart of an artist who may otherwise be working according to norms positivized under the guidance of the Christian faith. Since nowadays there simply is no Christian norm positivization we can only expect partial-Christian art, emanating from an attitude of faith that is conscious of the fact that art too belongs to the realm over which Christ must be king. After all, art is not a neutral area, or an area that belongs in essence to the *civitas terrena*. It is true that common grace stops the penetration of sin also in the area of beauty and that consequently much beauty is brought forth by the world, but this area too, according to the norm, belongs to the *civitas Dei*, to the visible church, in which the invisible church expresses itself in the temporal realm. It goes without saying that this does not mean that art is supposed to be under the leadership of the church. If the church were to meddle actively with art, then it would exceed its sphere sovereignty. And this would surely mean the death of art, for the church, if it truly acts as church, will apply the norms as they apply to the church as institution and not as aesthetic criteria. If it were to apply aesthetic criteria, then the church would no longer be functioning as a church but as an 'Association for the Promotion of Christian art', or something like that. The church is the institutional manifestation of the invisible church in the temporal sphere, to be sure, but it remains bound to its own sphere sovereignty. If it wants to 'swallow up' the entire visible church, then this must inevitably lead to the destruction of the Christian life as a whole in all its interlacements. After all, the visible church is not limited to a temporal church institution but, in principle, includes all the social structures of this temporal reality. The religious root community in Christ, the invisible church, in which all who are truly born again are incorporated, must be temporally expressed in every social relationship.[55]

It goes without saying that Christian art is possible only when people really bow before God and his word rather than claim in a proud, pharisaic manner to be able to do something for God, for which God would then be indebted to them.

#9 Primitive art[56]

We will not discuss this in depth. Suffice it to remark that primitive society is characterized by rigidity; its law, art, religion, morals and so on are totally determined by tradition and this tradition is enforced by the tribal chief. The tribal chief is the 'curator' of the tradition and as such functions both as judge, priest and military commander.[57] We also note that in primitive culture there is not yet any differentiation; the different structures do not yet appear 'separately'.[58] Therefore one notes that primitive art does not function autonomously, independently, but rather functions in relation to other structures such as religion, dance (as such also still undifferentiated) and so on.

If through any influence the narrow walls of tribal relationship and tradition are broken and integration occurs, the possibility for further specific differentiation is created. If that has 'only just' taken place in a 'young' culture we may not expect that the different differentiated forms, as positive manifestations of the structures, will occur as independently as in a more fully disclosed culture.[59] The disclosure, integration and differentiation will continue to progress until finally such a far-reaching differentiation has taken place that we see the different structures next to each other, totally independent with each having its own sphere sovereignty. Only then may we expect 'autonomous art'.[60]

This means that in judging primitive art as well as in studying it we need to be careful not to seek art-for-beauty's-sake, but to be constantly mindful that little or no differentiation has taken place here.

We cannot determine the primitiveness of an art or culture from a single work of art. In order to do this we need to know what place the work of art has in that culture.[61]

#10 Style and beauty of non-aesthetically qualified structures

The beauty of natural things is a styleless beauty,[62] since this beauty is based on the leading function of the thing (which is qualified in one of the nature aspects) and thus not in the (historically) controlling formation. We can nevertheless recognize style in all objective thing-structures that are structurally based in the historical function; for the thing has come about as a result of formative human labour. Style is thus no 'privilege' for works of art or aesthetically qualified things. Therefore we notice beauty and style in socially qualified structures such as chairs, glasswork, washbasins, etc. In general one refers to glassware, wrought iron[63] and other socially qualified, historically based structures, as applied art. As appears from what we discussed here, we do not have to make any objection to the term as such, as long as we remember that these are not works of art. One sometimes refers to beautiful pottery (say, vases), jewellery and such like as decorative art, but we must object to that since decorative art, as will appear in the following chapter, is a case of enkapsis whereby visual art is bound (to another thing-structure).

Since in a certain culture all structures are based on the same historical development of civilization and they all possess 'the same' aesthetic function, we will notice, also in everyday objects, a certain unity of style. Therefore in #3 of this chapter we could take the church building as an example of the style of the Middle Ages since, although not an aesthetically qualified structure, it is representative of the art of that time with regard to style. We also come across this specific unity of style in our contemporary world – think, for example of the style of cars,[64] trains, radios, furniture, cutlery, advertisements and so on. Strangely enough, art proper can fall more or less outside this scope. If this is the case, as it often is in, for instance, modern irrationalistic art, it appears as if the artists, anti-normatively, do not want to submit themselves to the course of continuous historical development; their art will then also not satisfy the taste (social analogy) of their contemporaries.

The above-mentioned unity of style of artworks (paintings, etc.), applied art (vases, lamps, etc.) and other appliances (radios, telephones, etc.) is the necessary condition for achieving an aesthetic unity in furnishing, for instance, a house. This unity is an aesthetic requirement – remember, what was said earlier in the discussion of logical and numerical analogies.

In conflict with this logical analogy is the fact that not so long ago the interiors of mail-ships and the like were decorated eclectically by mixing all sorts of styles (which in itself is already in conflict with the norm in question) in contrast to the 'exterior' view of the ship, which was modern. With ships built in recent years (*Queen Mary, Oranje*, etc.) this mistake has not been repeated.

That style, beauty, is not the privilege of works of art is clearly apparent in architecture. After all, architecture belongs to the socially qualified structures and yet it is especially in architecture that one can study the different periods of style; various new directions in style were first expressed in architecture. Think, for example, of the renewal brought about by Berlage that heralded a new period not only in architecture but also in the visual arts. Since architecture is not an aesthetically qualified structure, one may object to the Dutch term for architecture, namely *bouwkunst* (literally, the 'art' of designing and constructing buildings). However, since this term is well established it is better for practical reasons to maintain it, and it is not a bad term if one only keeps in mind that one is dealing here with structures of a different radical type from works of art.

#11 An example . . .

In this section we would like to expand further upon an example in order to elucidate various situations mentioned in the previous section. For this we have chosen the music of the African-Americans.

First we should say something about the people in Africa and their music. The Africans lived, and sometimes still live, in a 'primitive' society. Therefore we cannot speak of state, family, economic enterprise and so forth, since these structures are very closely interwoven with each other and have not yet, as is the case in a disclosed culture, differentiated and manifested a distinctive form with a distinctive sphere sovereignty. As to tribal relationships we can speak of culture, but cultural development has 'stranded', so that we cannot speak of history in connection with them.[65] Everything that once was formed and positivized by previous generations remains statically the same, since it is strictly guarded by tradition. This tradition, which is maintained by the tribal chief, who is at the same time supreme judge, high priest, tribal chieftain and military commander, narrowly confines the acquired culture. Such cultures are totally rigid, since here tradition does not, together with the (equally historical) moment of progression, produce a continuous historical development as it does in a disclosed culture. What causes this rigidity, this confinement within the walls of tradition, this absence of every manifestation of progess, this 'historylessness', is the belief in nature gods, the deified powers and phenomena of nature. Because of this belief African culture misses a sense of personal identity . . . the people are, or feel themselves to be, part of the surrounding nature and they worship its powers. Precisely by directing the pistical to the powers of nature, they shut down the whole process of disclosure.[66]

African culture obviously has its own music. This is not the place to discuss the typical characteristics of this music. However, it does need to be pointed out that we can not speak here of art music, entertainment music, dance music and sacred music. The music reveals its primitive character specifically in its being totally undifferentiated. All music is simultaneously cultic and social and art. Thus, although we can distinguish between battle songs, religious songs, community songs and so forth, these all manifest the same lack of differentiation. Differences exist only as a difference in text.

It is fundamentally impossible to write a history of this African music. It has no history and one cannot speak of a development of style. Therefore it makes perfect sense that in order to learn about African music in the seventeenth century, one could study the music of the primitive tribes in the interior of Africa as it is today.

In the course of the seventeenth and following centuries, many black Africans were transported to America as slaves. In the process their old tribal relationships were torn apart and the possibility was created for differentiation; the walls of tradition had been violently torn down. The danger existed that they would form new primitive 'tribal' relationships. However, something remarkable occurred. The Africans in North America who became christianized, in whom Christianity became deeply rooted, no longer formed primitive relationships, not even after the Civil War when they became free men and women. That direction was cut off because their hearts were no longer directed towards the old nature gods; they had become free in Christ. And nowadays there may be a lot of apostasy amongst African-Americans, just as there is in the surrounding white American culture, but they will not revert to a primitive form of society because their sense of personal identity, under the influence of Christianity, has become too developed for this. They may bow down to humanism or pragmatism or any other non-Christian life and world view, but not to a natural religion such as sun worship, beliefs in mana, taboo and so on.

To the contrary we note among the Africans of the Antilles and some regions of the South American continent that as soon as they had the opportunity, which could only take place on a large scale after they were emancipated, they started to form primitive tribal relationships again. And if one listens to their music it sounds exactly like that of the tribes of their forefathers in Africa. The reason for this is that they were not christianized, or if they were christianized it remained very superficial, and they fell back into natural religion.

We now want to deal only with the music of the African-Americans in the USA. They were rather quickly christianized, as noted above. This brought them into contact with Western (church) music. Over a short period of time they adopted Western tonality, although certain characteristics are still reminiscent of and can be traced back to their old tonal systems. We will not explore in detail how easily this process of adaptation took place and what all its characteristics are. Suffice it to say that the African-Americans quickly started to form their own spiritual songs, the so-called Negro spirituals. These are very clearly black songs. They possess the typical characteristics of all black music. The lyrics have mostly been inspired by biblical texts. Since black Americans were not taught reading, they were totally dependent on hearing Scripture through public reading. They memorized the key verses from the Scripture passage that was read aloud and reworked it into a song. The following is an example:

> There's a handwriting on the wall
> Oh, won't you come and read it, see what it say.
> There's a handwriting on the wall.
> Oh, Daniel, there's a handwriting on the wall
> Who writes the letter, there's a handwriting on the wall

> God writes the letter, there's a handwriting on the wall
> Tell old Nebucadnezar that he is weighted in the balance and found wanting
> There's a handwriting on the wall.

The text is sung by a cantor, while the choir sings the 'core' of the song after each line of the cantor, creating the repetition of the key sentence as in the example above. There are also texts that arose directly from their Christian experience. It is striking how well these people knew their Bible and how their thoughts were filled with Scripture. We give the following song as an example of a Negro spiritual that is not based directly on a biblical text:

> Rise, mourner (seeker, sinner) rise
> Oh, can't you rise and tell
> What the Lord has done for you?
> Yes, He has taken my feet out of the miry clay
> and He placed them on the right side of my Father.

Alongside these spiritual songs,[67] for which the norms were positivized around 1800, the African-Americans had also community songs (coon songs), work songs, plantation songs and others, for which the musical form differed little from that of the Negro spirituals.

In the American countryside there were brass bands, just as in the Netherlands. African-Americans also wanted their own orchestras, for which the opportunity came only after their emancipation. Such orchestras were naturally very modest, rarely consisting of more than a clarinet, trumpet, trombone and percussion instruments. They played marches and other music, but the music they played was typically black music. They did not just adopt Western music. Later, African-American jazz would arise from this.

After the emancipation of the African-American slaves, their secular songs acquired a more fixed and typical form. Of the many different forms that had developed, blues became established as the foremost form, the most used and loved. The blues as a song form is based on a chord progression of twelve bars sung by one person – the Negro spirituals and the older non-sacred songs were always sung by a choir – to the accompaniment of a guitar, and later also a piano and sometimes a melody instrument. The blues is sung by both men and women; as in the other forms of black music, women have 'equal rights' without it resulting in a levelling, as for instance in Western women's liberation.

The Negro spirituals, the vocal blues, and instrumental African-American music are all authentic forms of folk music. The first two retained their 'folk' character, while the latter would develop further. What is folk art? Folk art is art that has not been further differentiated and in connection with which one cannot speak of style-forming leading personalities. Everyone can practise folk art and everyone does it in the same style. It is not yet a free art but still strongly interwoven with the social aspect. Although an important development would take place in instrumental music – which we will discuss later on – also the instrumental folk music continued to be played 'at home' by many African-Americans, just as around 1920, in a style that has not appreciably changed since then, alongside the more evolved jazz. We can therefore conclude that African-Americans made use of the possibilities for differentiation that were offered to them to such an extent that up till now they have formed what is essentially a spiritual song, a secular song and an instrumental music. With reference to the last two, however, we cannot yet speak of free art,[68] but neither can we speak of pure social music (comparable to our own entertainment and dance music) since the structures are still interwoven in a primitive manner. Yet, it is remarkable how fast the differentiation and further disclosure have taken place, especially in the years following emancipation – in spite of the fact that their circumstances have never been particularly favourable (think of the social and economic position of African-Americans, while also life amidst white Caucasian culture must have inhibited the formation of an own art).

Around 1900 the instrumental music of the African-Americans, then already known as jazz, obtained a fixed form. It also attracted the interest of the whites. But more about that shortly. This instrumental black music was then still pure folk music. However, over the years a number of black musicians appeared who served as leading formers of history, formers of style and this music developed very quickly, especially after 1920. In the beginning there was practically no difference between their instrumental folk music and the developing African-American jazz. As the years passed, however, the distance between these two grew steadily and by today has become considerable. Still, even in the case of the development of jazz the differentiation between art music and entertainment music and/or dance music has only just begun. At this moment we can no longer call jazz music pure 'folk art', but it has not yet lost its primitive character. The narrower genotypes of vocal and instrumental music have already become differentiated, but (here too) the distance between them is still relatively small. Practically every instrumental African-American melody is still easily 'singable' (and can be provided with a text).

To shed more light on these matters we would obviously have to go into much greater depth than would be useful here. Yet it must be strongly emphasized that this African-American jazz is *not* considered primitive because practically only one musical form – namely theme with variations – is used, because improvisation still plays such a big role; rather, it is considered primitive because the different structures that belong to the world order are not yet differentiated, inasmuch as these structures are still interwoven with each other without being able to manifest their own sphere sovereignty. For the African-American this music continues to be simultaneously art music, entertainment and dance music.[69] Only the cultic element has disappeared completely, so in that regard differentiation has made important progress. Our conclusion must be that we are dealing here with a type of music that is still primitive but in which we no longer find the element of rigidity. As shown, black American culture has not only left the stage of extreme rigidity and closeness but also can no longer revert to it. We see before us, we experience as it were how the differentiation and, more specifically, disclosure takes place. That is precisely what makes this music and its development so extremely interesting.

Can we expect, after some time, perhaps after a few centuries, to have African-American art music and next to it African-American entertainment music, and so on? If black Americans had the chance to develop their own culture in peace, yes. But the possibility of this is extremely small. The black American dilemma here [in 1947] is: either emancipate oneself and become totally 'white', as it were – in other words totally abandon one's own black culture – or remain oneself but then – partially because of the 'colour-line' – remain mired in one's present social position. Exactly this dilemma forms part of the tragedy of the development of this music. Another factor, perhaps even more intrusive and far-reaching, that prevents a 'normal' development is the fact that the white Americans have actively interfered with this music, with extensive 'commercialization' as the result.

In the years after 1900, instrumental black American music entered the white American sphere of interest. It is a singular fact that we observe here contact between whites living in a well-differentiated civilization and a type of music that manifests hardly any differentiation at all. Understandably, those whites did not grasp what they were dealing with. The mistake made by a number of them – and where that would lead we shall see shortly – namely, to think they were dealing with a form of social music here (thus with a case of enkapsis), with pure dance music, was therefore virtually unavoidable. These whites, who lived within a pragmatic life and world view that regards everything from the standpoint of whether there is money to be made from it, saw all sorts of commercial possibilities in this music. Black music is, after all, very dynamic ('dynamic' here not in the specifically music-technical sense), works with strong tensions, has a strongly pronounced rhythm, in a word, works 'on the legs'. They did not see that this music, the external sound of which was indeed still raw and rough, also had something to 'say' in a musically aesthetic sense. Whites began to imitate this music, at least its external form. The war of 1914–1918 gave them a particularly good chance. After all, more or less 'running wild' because of the war, the American (as well as the European) public was asking for something wild, rough, uncivilized. These white musicians gave this to them in the form of a dismal caricature of the authentic African-American music.

Precisely those elements that had commercial possibilities – such as the pronounced rhythm and the strong 'dynamics', that were used in an aesthetically fully responsible way – were overaccentuated and exploited, and these elements were, given the taste and attitude of the (American) public, never the purely aesthetic characteristics. During the postwar years a lot was 'brushed up' and 'civilized' in this 'pots-and-pans-music', since the public began to long again for something more melodious. The drums were pushed into the background, the orchestras somewhat expanded, sometimes violins were added and sentimental tunes introduced, sung in a soft and crooning way. Whites also introduced the saxophone. Slowly but surely modern dance music developed. In the years after 1928, when the black Americans had finally come out with their own music, (external) African-American elements were once again injected into this dance music. For, the white public that listened to distinctively black American jazz were not touched by its beauty – since they did not understand it – but were touched by the strong dynamics, which in the course of the years had vanished from commercial dance music as it was polished up. Producers of dance music now looked for ways to put more tension and dynamics into their music, and were reasonably successful. And now we cannot but observe that this dance music in the form of American 'swing' music is very popular. That it is anything but Christian art goes without saying.

Where will this lead? We obviously cannot identify with this music, its origin and intention. However, it cannot be removed from our society – revolutionarily – with a single stroke of the pen. It will drift further and further away from African-American music and become increasingly 'Europeanized'. There are discernable tendencies in this direction (the augmentation of orchestras, increasing use of 'symphonic arrangements', etc.). There are, however, also many tendencies in the opposite direction as white managers have used enticing contracts to bring African-Americans into the commercial camp. This has naturally brought with it an intensification of the black elements in this music. And it is precisely there that great danger lies for the black Americans themselves and the development of their music. Young black musicians often no longer play and develop their own music but immediately become dance musicians. Thus, from a black American perspective a differentiation has perhaps indeed taken place, but then only of social music, while the chance of developing an art music has been virtually lost. And we may not even call that dance music an expression of black culture. It has become too saturated with white influences for that. The (pragmatic) intervention of the whites has made a distinctive, peaceful development – a further disclosure and differentiation – of black culture in its musical expression practically impossible and has put it onto the wrong track.

Besides the whites to whom we have devoted some words above who did not understand African-American music in its dinstinctive character, there were also a number of whites who intuitively understood this music. They attempted to play jazz music in the way of the black Americans. And since this time – the first of them began around 1910 – many whites have shared the ideal of approaching the musical idiom of the African-American as purely as possible. However, it has become obvious that a white person can never produce the pure black music. It always remains white music. These whites, who in principle considered black Americans to be their teachers in the realm of music and allowed themselves to be inspired by their music, are nevertheless much less dangerous to the undisturbed development of black music. On the other hand, they contribute to the softening of the differences between white and black Americans. Although we cannot share or justify their ideal of playing music just as the African-Americans do and thus of abandoning their own culture at this point, the objections against them are much less serious than those against the group of commercially-oriented white musicians.

We discuss these matters so extensively because it would be wrong to ignore these problems. We can 'bury our heads in the sand' and ignore jazz (in its commercial form) – we can leave the study of black American music with a serene heart to those who take an 'ethnological, folkloristic' interest in it – but it is a fact that the radio uses more than fifty per cent of its time to broadcast this music and that many people never listen to anything else on the radio, that 'classical' music is now regarded by many as taboo and out-dated. There are also other reasons why we need to acknowledge the popularity of this music as a fact. These problems are highly relevant and cast their own light, the importance of which we may neither ignore nor underestimate, on the spiritual condition and structure of our twentieth-century culture.

Now we return to the discussion of black American music. When we listen to it, the question immediately arises of how one should judge this music. If we intend to judge this music according to the norms that we as Europeans have positivized for music, which hold for 'classical' music – this last taken in the very broad sense of general usage – then not much good can be said about it. For not only do African-Americans use the tonal system that they took over from Europeans in their very own manner, but they also make an entirely different use of the various instruments, while in addition they give rhythm a much greater emphasis than Europeans probably ever have done, and their melodies also deviate from those of European classical music. With regard to the tonal system, the black Americans use chord progressions that are very unusual for whites, while they sometimes play notes that strike the Western 'classical' ear as particularly out of tune. On the other hand, we almost never come across the complicated dissonant chords of which modern Western music so gladly makes use. Black Americans play the instruments in their very own manner. They have positivized their own norms for this. Thus a clarinet, for example, is played with vibrato (imitated by all white jazz musicians, commercially inclined or not). One can also attribute the invention of the use of mutes and such with brass instruments to them. But all this does not mean that this music would not satisfy the norm given in the divine world order.

If we want to judge this music, to give an answer to the question of whether it is aesthetically justifiable or not, then we need to acquaint ourselves with black culture (to what degree can it still be called primitive, what belief guides it, how much differentiation has already occurred) and study this music extensively. Only then will we be able to judge whether, and to what extent, African-Americans have given positive form to the aesthetic norms in their norm positivization, or whether, and to what extent, instead, they have formed laws of an anti-normative character. If we set to work in this manner we will have to come to the conclusion that this music obeys laws that are indeed in accordance with aesthetic normative principles. This music is thus truly aesthetically justifiable, insofar at least as non-Christian art can be aesthetically justified.[70] Unfortunately, among the black Americans too apostasy has assumed large proportions since their emancipation (especially in the big cities). Yet music is still being played that we, albeit only partially,[71] can call Christian. Particularly in the Negro spiritual we see a truly Christian art expression.

2A The science of art, general

#1 Aesthetically qualified structures

The radical type, as we observed earlier, groups together the definitions of both of the radical functions; in the radical type work of art we found the aesthetic function to be the leading function, and we must look for the foundational function within the historical law sphere in its original meaning-individuality (even if it is one of a disclosed, anticipatory character), which is the technical form. The leading function is thus of a founding, retrocipatory character.

All structures that are determined by this radical type are objective thing-structures. Therefore they will only be actual in a patent subject-object-relationship, in which the different object functions are disclosed by the subjects functioning in the different spheres. As is known, each structure functions in all aspects of reality; thing-structures cannot be closed off in any aspect, since that would leave us with some sort of metaphysical *Ding an sich*, 'a thing in itself'.

None of these structures can function outside of a foundational enkapsis with its own foundational structure. Therefore they will always be structurally founded structures such that one will always find one structural function in each law sphere. Changes in foundational structure will give rise to variability types. For variability types always originate as a result of external factors, namely factors that as such do not affect the internal structural principle itself. All variability types are thus subjective individual totalities that are determined and enclosed by the same structural principle.

Within a radical type we find structures that are and structures that are not objectifiable as enduring entities. The latter rely on subjective actualization to ensure their actual objective existence. To these structures, which can be newly actualized again and again, belong all the genotypes: the art of dance, literary art, drama, and music. To be sure, these structures can be objectified enduringly in a symbolic structure (e.g. a book, a volume, a music score). Structures that are enduringly objectifiable only need to be objectified once, however, by the creating artist or under the artist's guidance. They do not require repeated subjective actualization, only opening, which is to say disclosure of the in themselves latent object functions in a patent subject-object relation.

Here we would still like to refer to the difference between the disclosure-relationship and the actualization-relationship of the functions of an objective structure in the different aspects of cosmic reality. In the disclosure-relationship we open (reveal) the latent object functions in the actual subject-object relationship. This relates to the experience of the objective reality of the thing, a reality which never changes as long as the thing maintains its identity. Moreover in a law sphere one also finds the actualization of the thing according to its objective destination, the so-called actualization-relationship.[72] We hereby use and handle it. In the nature of the case this actualization-relationship is also bound to norms. Thus we can play a schmalzy popular song in church, but such an actualization, as needs no further elaboration, is a-normative. In the actualization-relationship changes can take place. Thus inactualization is discussed by Dooyeweerd, taking the ancient knight's attire as an example.[73] We can no longer use it as clothing; in the subjective actualization-relationship this structure has been inactualized in its function of destination; yet the experience of the objective reality of the thing, thus of the thing in the disclosure-relationship, naturally has not changed. Even we will always have to experience it as a socially qualified structure, as a piece of clothing, even though we do not use it as such anymore.

For the sake of completeness, let's summarize as follows. All structures of the radical type work of art consist of an enkapsis of a founding and a founded structure, which together form a single structure with one structural function in each law sphere. In the first three (or as the case may be four) law spheres this structural whole thus has a subject function. All its functions in the cosmically later spheres are object functions. The founding function is the historical, which is initiating, albeit of anticipatory character. All functions in the pre-historical law spheres are pre-anticipatory; all functions in the post-historical spheres are of a founded, retrocipating structure. The aesthetical is the leading function.

#2 Structural interlacements

In #2 of the first section of this article we gave a summary of the different genotypes and narrower genotypes.[74] These obviously do not stand isolated and apart, outside the cosmic systasis, the structural coherence in the cosmic world order. They always exist in interlacement, in enkapsis with all sorts of other structures. Insofar as the foundational type of enkapsis is concerned we would like to limit ourselves to the few remarks that we made in the previous section. Here we want to take a somewhat deeper look at the correlative type of enkapsis. In the case of correlative enkapsis, in contrast to that of foundational enkapsis, the enkaptically bound structures each have their structural functions in each law sphere. Thus these structures do not form a single structure with just one structural function in each law sphere, as is the case with foundational interlacement.

An enkapsis is a type of structural interlacement wherein the bound structures maintain their sphere sovereignty.[75] However, it will call variability types into being. The interlacement will express itself, will have to express itself in the enkaptically bound structures. The node of the enkapsis is the (historical) form. Thus we see that a literary work of art cannot be put on the stage, just like that. It must first be totally rewritten for this purpose. Once that has happened, the enkapsis with the drama will express itself clearly in the form of the literary work of art. *It is a normative requirement that the interlacement expresses itself in the bound structures*, otherwise no real enkaptic structural interlacement will be obtained. If the bound structures in the conception of the artist are 'acuminated' to each other, then they are intended for the enkapsis and it will naturally leave its mark on each of them. However, an enkapsis involving a structure that is not especially intended for it will only succeed if it lends itself especially to this, that is, if the enkapsis *allows* itself to be expressed in the structure. We see this, for example in song, in which a poem, which is usually not specifically intended for music, is set to music. We see in such a case that if the enkapsis allows itself to be expressed in the structure not-especially-meant-for-enkapsis, a real enkaptic structural interlacement is obtained. If it is not, then there is no true structural interlacement and therefore certainly no harmonious work of art.

It needs to be emphasized that *structural interlacements cannot be determined a-priori*. In accounting for cosmic states of affairs, we need to *refer continuously to naïve experience*. We need to 'read' the norms and states of affairs 'from' the meaning-systasis in which the world order presents itself to us. Thereby, in order to arrive at the meaning-synthesis, we will naturally have to analyse the constellation (εποχη) of this coherence of meaning, thereby achieving a *Gegenstands*-forming, in which we will direct the logical function in the meaning-synthesis towards the *Gegenstand*.

We would like to discuss some examples of enkapsis here. First we will look at drama. In reality we seldom if ever come across works of art which belong to this genotype outside of an enkaptic relationship. A pantomime without backdrops could perhaps be referred to as free drama. Drama always exists in enkapsis with literary art – the classical drama usually with poetry, today's drama mostly with prose. Further, we almost always see enkapsis with the visual arts: in the backdrops, etc. Drama is sometimes also combined with music, as in opera. Dance too, usually in the form of ballet, may be interwoven.

Up till now we have directed our attention to the enkaptic relationship of drama with other genotypes of the radical type work of art. But enkapsis can also occur with structures of another radical type, as in the social interlinkages in the cabaret and the revue or the drama aiming at entertainment in general. The same is true with pistically qualified structures: think of church drama in the Middle Ages and of propaganda pieces for a political party (a political party is after all a pistically qualified societal relationship).[76] Consider further, for example, the advertisements (for an economically qualified business relationship) that we see currently in the cinema.[77]

We now notice that with interlacement *one of the enkaptically bound structures can be the leading one.* Thus in opera, music is without a doubt the leading one; in so-called *bel canto* opera, in particular, everything centres on the music. In the case of a play that is not bound to music the structure of the play will usually be the leading one, and all the other enkaptically bound structures will then be the guided structures. Occasionally it will happen that the literary art is the leading one, as with so many pieces by Vondel and other playwrights.

In the case of enkapsis in which a non-aesthetically qualified structure is the leading one, we will call this qualifying function of the structure the *function of destination of the interlacement coherence*; the leading function of the work of art remains in the nature of the case the aesthetical function. Thus the above-mentioned piece of propaganda has a pistical destination, the advertisement has an economic destination. However, one notices that the function of destination does not necessarily have to lie in another, higher or lower, law sphere; this is already apparent from the examples mentioned above – with the *bel canto* opera, the function of destination of the dramatic work of art is clearly an aesthetical one. It will be the leading function of the leading structure in its positivized form, dependent therefore on the disclosing process and the positivizing process, which will guide the whole structural coherence. We can expand the definition of the function of destination given above as follows: *In cases of enkapsis the leading or qualifying function of the leading structure will always be the function of destination of all the other enkaptically bound structures.*[78]

As our next example we will discuss the enkapsis architecture-visual art. Abstracting from the enkapsis with the societal relationships or with the interlinkages, as the case may be, we see that visual art (sculpture: think of Gothic cathedrals, etc.; paintings: think of frescos, etc.) can be bound to architecture.[79] Architecture is in that case still the leading structure, so that the visual art is totally guided and directed by the social meaning-individuality of the architecture, which will be the function of destination.[80]

This interlacement coherence, however, will be bound in its own turn to a societal relationship or interlinkage, the leading function of which will be the function of destination of the enkaptic whole. Thus a church building may be bound to an ecclesiastical community, a house to a family community, a ministry to the state community, a warehouse to an economic corporate community, and so forth.

That enkapsis, several examples of which we presented above, expresses itself in the form, speaks for itself. Think, for example, of the difference between a Protestant and a Roman Catholic church building, which is the result of a difference in the function of destination. That these destinational functions are different occurs because the Protestants and the Catholics have given a positive form to the norms of the leading function of the church community, each in a different way.

We now need to look at the phenomenon of inactualization. For an enkapsis can also be inactualized. We notice this, for example, in a minuet by Mozart. Here the enkapsis with a socially qualified interlinkage is inactualized. This music, which was dance music in the time of Mozart, is no longer used as such today. The aesthetically qualified work of music, which originally functioned in interlacement, is actualized by us as a free work of art, separated from its enkaptic bond. But we are still supposed to experience the above-mentioned minuet as having been conceived as dance music; after all, the way that we experience the thing objectively has remained the same. It is only the subjective actualization of the destinational function that has 'changed'. One can see from this example that this music was not only aesthetically qualified, but also aesthetically justifiable. If we see that a lot of modern dance music is no longer valued as truly beautiful as soon as it is 'out of fashion', then we may draw the conclusion from this that here the norm has clearly not been satisfied.

It needs to be said that inactualization too cannot be determined a priori, but only in reference to naïve experience. Thus, we will for example never see that the enkapsis between drama and literature becomes inactualized in the sense that the drama is actualized free of its enkaptic bond; however, the literary work of art can be actualized separated from the enkapsis. We can only say this because this is what naïve experience teaches us; this can never be determined a priori through some rational construction.[81]

We would still like to give some other examples of inactualization of enkapsis here. Consider the ancient Greek statues of the gods. We actualize these as free works of art separated from the bond to the pistical. For us they no longer have a pistical destination. In the same way, the statues of saints in the Catholic Church have also 'lost' their pistical destination for Protestant Christians. When Protestants see such statues, they will have to experience it as conceived with a pistical destination, but they will no longer be able to actualize it as such themselves, since for them the enkapsis with the church will be inactualized.

#3 Some comments on the genotypes within the radical type work of art

In chapter 1, #2 we summarized the different genotypes within the radical type work of art. We need to mention here that these too cannot be determined a priori. Thus the division presented is also open to criticism and can be replaced by any other division, if it can give a better account of reality. We would like to make some brief remarks about the different genotypes here in order that we may discuss music in greater depth in section B of this chapter.

a. *Visual art.* We have to keep the state of affairs as set forth in #5 of chapter 1 well in view here. A work of visual art can and will very often be inspired by a psychical object. It can also be the case that no extra-aesthetic consideration has occasioned the forming of the work of art. We will come across this often in decorative art. We would like to define this as follows: *decorative art is visual art bound to another objective thing-structure.* Thus the sculptures in a Gothic church have no independent 'function' but fulfil a decorative task in the whole; the sculptural art in this case is bound to the architecture. It is obvious from the following examples that with such decorative art we will often encounter a situation where the work of art is not inspired by an extra-aesthetic consideration: decorative surface ornamentation, which usually consists of a number of 'motifs'; modern (Cubist) stained-glass windows; the decoration in Jugendstil (a style which attempts to level out the structural difference between architecture and decorative (visual) art); the decoration of plates and cups or the decoration on the spine of a book, and so on.

We seldom come across visual art that is not bound, art that does not portray any extra-aesthetic givens (so-called 'abstract' art).[82] Some modern sculptors occasionally venture to undertake more or less successful experiments in this direction, for example Belling's succcessful sculpture *Dreiklang*.[83] There is no need to say a priori that abstract sculpture (like abstract painting) is ugly. It is just a question whether it can have anything to say to us as a free, unbound artistic expression. Used decoratively, in enkapsis with architecture for example, such works of art can come fully into their own. For the time being we see in them an expression of human hubris, where people, irrationally, just want to be different.

That is why people want to make visual art that for once does not portray anything. In practice they demand from us that we view what is essentially bound art, decorative work, on its own as a free artistic expression.[84]

Appealing to naïve experience, we need to say that free visual art consists of the portrayal of something (non-aesthetically qualified), and that it has produced its greatest works in this way (in contrast to music, where free art is usually 'absolute' music).[85]

Within the genotype visual art we see the narrower genotypes of three-dimensional and two-dimensional visual art. We would like to begin by taking a closer look at the first of these. As the founding structure we see a physically-qualified material (sometimes in intimate enkapsis with another physical structure such as paint, in which the structure of an objective psychical observation is founded, for instance in polychrome majolica and in painted sculptures).

If the sculptural work of art portrays a structure that the artist observed in an objective psychical observation, then we need to realize that the artist has not copied what he or she observed. The image presents the artist's aesthetic vision of the object. The beauty of the work of art is also never the beauty of the aesthetically depicted object.[86]

We encounter a similar state of affairs with two-dimensional or pictorial visual art. Here we see an intimate enkapsis between 'canvas' and 'paint', in which the structure of the beautiful, disclosed, observed image is founded, in which, in its own turn, we find the aesthetically qualified structure. It is obvious that this founding enkapsis expresses itself in the 'form' if we think of the difference between: oil paintings, watercolours, frescos, pastel drawings, lithographs, and so on. Variability types also arise through a different choice of subject. Just think of the difference between seascapes, interiors, nudes, landscapes and still lifes. Each of these variability types has its own characteristics that place different demands on the artist for painting each type.

This genotype clearly asks for a *disclosed reproductive imagination.* Consider, for example, a drawing in which with a few lines a face is represented. It would not be possible to recognize the face without reproductive imagination; yes, even to see that a face had been portrayed. Think also in this regard of a caricature. In sculptural art this is very evident if we think of spatial figures consisting of wire windings as Archipenko makes them, for example.

b. *Dance.* As the founding structure here we see the human body. We then also notice a clear difference in characteristics between 'masculine' and 'feminine' dance. In the nature of things the body is a strongly disclosed structure: e.g. do we not speak of controlled movements,[87] etc.?

c. *Literary art.* Founded in each other here are the structure of the disclosed sounds, the symbolically qualified structure of language, and the structure of the work of art. Differences in language also summon variability types to life; just think of difficulties of translation. The 'musicality' of a poem is founded on the disclosure of the sounds (alliteration, assonance). Variability types also originate from handling different subjects (epic, lyrical, didactic, historical novel, psychological novel, etc.).

We encounter correlative enkapsis in propaganda-literature, satire, St Nicholas rhymes, etc.

d. *Drama*. In the previous section we already discussed the different cases of enkapsis. We also need to see the human body as the founding structure here. This structure is also strongly disclosed here: think for instance of mime, through which joy, sorrow and the like are depicted.

2B The science of art, applied to music

Of all of the different art forms, we will discuss only music in greater depth here. An aesthetics (science of art) that aspires to be complete must in the nature of the case account for all art forms. Since it is our intention to present only in broad lines the framework, method and direction of such an aesthetics, we will limit ourselves to music.

#1 The leading or qualifying function

Earlier we said that the general basic meaning of the aesthetic aspect individualizes itself to meaning-individualities. We also spoke then of the meaning-individualities which form the leading functions of the genotypes within the radical type work of art. One of these meaning-individualities is that of music. It encompasses the meaning-individualities of vocal and instrumental music. This is evident when, among other things, we consider that a musical phrase, a melodic sentence that is meant to be played on an instrument, cannot (or usually cannot) be used directly for song. By the same token, a 'vocal' phrase cannot serve for an instrument. This is especially clear if one considers that a score for a choir can not be used for an orchestra. What will be beautiful for a choir will sound boring and long-winded when played by an orchestra. This is also true the other way round. In the seventeenth century when instrumental music started to differentiate itself, people began to use melodies for it that were meant for song, for which they then had to provide 'decorations'. This example makes it also evident that vocal and instrumental music are not variability types but definitely different genotypes. In the following we will speak of music and its functions in the different meaning-aspects, thereby combining instrumental and vocal music.

Upon closer inspection, the meaning-individuality of music appears to consist of three parts: *the meaning-individualities of melody, harmony*[88] *and rhythm*. Each of these meaning-individualities is an 'individualization' of all retrocipations within the aesthetical basic meaning. They are the leading structural functions of the structures of melody, harmony and rhythm, respectively.[89]

Since neither melody nor harmony or rhythm has an independent leading function, each stands in relation to the total work of art as a part of a whole. For a part has a relatively autonomous part destination within the whole, but it can reveal this only in the structure of the whole, which continues to express itself also in this part.[90] To avoid needless repetition, we will not investigate these part-structures any further in their different functions; however, it should be mentioned that in each law sphere the relationship between the general basic meaning, the meaning-individuality of music, and the meaning-individualities of the part structures corresponds with that in the aesthetic meaning.

The whole-part relationship discussed above is situated in the law-side [of the created cosmos] and will thus reveal itself in the subject-side in submission to this norm. However, with the conception of a piece of music the artist will also call whole-part relationships to life which, although they naturally do not stand separate from the law aspect, can not as such be found there. We mean the whole-part relationship that reveals itself for instance in the relationship of the whole of a symphony to its parts (movements). This applies also to the relationship of the sections within a movement, such as the exposition, development, coda and so on. So this is a whole-part relationship that reveals itself on the subject-side of the world order as an individual totality. We mention for clarity's sake that we also find a similar state of affairs in the visual arts, for instance in the relationship of a finger, a hand or a leg to the whole of a depicted human figure.

It is a demand, which has already been formulated by the meaning nucleus of the aesthetical aspect, that the different parts (in the first as well as in the second sense) are joined in truly beautiful harmony, that together they really form a beautiful whole.

#2 The founding enkaptic interlacement

A work of art can, as we already noticed, only exist in a founding enkapsis, in which an irreversible founding relationship exists between the enkaptically bound structures. In music *the founding structure is that sound that has been formed into beautiful tones*. This structure has, as is already apparent in the formulation, a disclosed, anticipatory character.

In the form, which is the node of the enkapsis, the interlacement naturally expresses itself. The different variability types are thus also based on the differences in the founding enkapsis.

We will first analyse the structure of *sound*. We find the leading structure function in the psychical meaning-aspect. It is the initiating objective meaning-individuality of the 'objective sensual perceptibility of sound'. The biotic function, which like all other pre-psychical functions is anticipatory in character, is also an object-function: sound must have access within our 'living-space' to our auditory organs if we are to hear it. In the kinematic aspect we find an anticipatory subject-function:

sound consists of physical vibrations, vibrations that need room to vibrate (spatial function) and that have a number of vibrations (arithmetic function).[91]

Sounds that have been formed into music have a disclosed, anticipatory structure, as we already mentioned. The psychical function, which was initiating for the disclosed structure, is also anticipatory. We clearly see that sounds are really disclosed, formed sound when we consider the fact that of all the sounds within the reach of our hearing we have selected only some, namely those that have a particular mutual relationship of vibration. We see it further from the use of sound with a particular number of vibrations and with overtones, on which the 'timbre' of the different instruments is based. In order to obtain a large variety of timbres people have created a great diversity of instruments.

It is not necessary to actualize the sounds in order to actualize the beauty of a work. A well-trained musician can, in reading a score, 'hear' the sounds in an aesthetically qualified imaginative image and thereby enjoy the music and its beauty. One can also 'repeat' a piece that one knows well in one's 'thoughts', namely in a fantasy image.[92] The structure of the sounds is in that case replaced by the imagined sounds, which are incorporated in the fantasy image. (Something similar will often take place in poetry. We know all the symbolic representations – including printed letters – so well, that we enjoy the beauty of the poem without actually hearing the sounds. This will practically always be the case with prose.)

#3 The structural functions in the relationship of disclosure

In chapter 2A we discussed what we understand by the relationship of disclosure. Since in a founding enkapsis, as we know, two enkaptically bound structures together form a single structure with one structural function in each law sphere, we no longer need to discuss the pre-logical functions, because these will coincide with the functions of the sounds that we already investigated in the previous section. We analysed the aesthetic function in #1 of this chapter. We will now begin with the pre-aesthetic functions.

The economic structural function. We find this in the 'economy' of a work of art, the way in which the 'value balancing frugality'[93] is positivized under the guidance of the aesthetic aspect. This function is therefore, like all the subsequent functions, of a retrocipatory character.

The aesthetic function is in the first instance founded in the economic function; it in turn refers directly back to the social function, which in turn is founded in the symbolic function, which retrocipates to the historical function. We find in the latter, in the founding direction of time, a resting point, since the historical function is of an initiating character.[94]

This structural function is expressed, amongst others, in the length of the work; the length needs to be economically measured in 'value balancing frugality', under the guidance of the aesthetical function. The number of movements also falls within this law sovereignty, as do the number of motifs[95] and the number of instruments. Compare, for example, a symphony with a quartet: the economic function is different, although the economic retrocipation within the aesthetic meaning can have an equally positive form.

The social function. This is retrocipatory, as stated above. Art must appeal to the musical taste[96] of the 'community'; art is after all *community art.* If, as is already the case with a great deal of modern art, art is 'detached' from the community, from the culture from which it stems, then that will be indicative of a disharmony in the development of that culture. We can be sure that in that case various norms will have been seriously violated, and that in the first place the norms of the social function will have been handled anti-normatively.

Perhaps we could, with an eye to these structural functions, albeit with some caution, speak of 'art fashion'. A style can only acquire historical cultural power if it is able to captivate humanity, if people take an interest in it and it becomes indeed a generally acknowledged cultural expression.

The symbolic function. In a work of music various symbols can be used. We need to clearly distinguish this from the aesthetic symbolism referred to in chapter 1, #8. Here we are talking about real symbolism, which we may not try to locate in the aesthetic meaning-aspect, although it obviously cannot be detached from it. Think, for example, of the leitmotiv, as Wagner frequently used it. The playing of the same melody or motif announces or symbolizes the reappearance of a person who is 'associated' with that motif. This structural function is therefore extremely important for programme music. It goes without saying that the norms for symbolism also require positivization. This is clearly revealed in the following: 'Oddly enough, we no longer connect with the programmatic references and illustrations in programmatic eighteenth-century works.' [97] We no longer know the positive symbolism of those days!

But this structural function is also important in absolute music. We will often see that a few notes or a single motif symbolizes the whole spirit and style of a piece (think for instance of the first measures of Beethoven's *Eighth Symphony*). Think also of the so-called cyclical form, in which the cyclical motif symbolically represents the belonging together of the different parts. We see another typical example in Beethoven's *Quartet Opus 59, nr. 2* in E minor. The rondo motif from the last movement is set in A major, in conflict with the norm positivized for it. Symbolically Beethoven reminds us that the whole piece is in E minor by continuously returning to the key of E minor at the end of the motif. Within this 'framework' we need also to recognize the norm, which is positivized by classical and Romantic music, that a work must always end in the key in which it is written.

The historical structural function.[98] As we mentioned above, in this function our thinking finds its resting point in the foundational direction of time. This function is, namely, the founding function of all structures that result from a human formative activity. Therefore it is also the founding function for the structure of the musical work of art. The meaning-individuality in this law sphere is of an initiating character, albeit also of a disclosed, anticipatory structure.[99] It is the *technical musical form*. From the apposition 'musical' the aesthetically-disclosed character of this function is already obvious, since one can only speak of musical within the sphere of aesthetic sovereignty. This technical musical form is the result of subjectively controlled forming. At different times the following positive musical forms have been called to life: sonata, passacaglia, song form, and others as well as the symphony form, the concerto form, and so on. Each style will look for that form in which it can best express itself.

The norms regarding the manner of use for the different instruments are also located in this law sphere; for this function exists, just as the other functions do, in objectivization of all of the preceding functions, thus also in objectivization of the sounds.

Logical structural function. This function has, just as all the following ones, an anticipatory structure. It points, namely, towards the historical aspect; for these aspects are disclosed by historically controlled forming; in our case this occurs, of course, under functional aesthetic guidance.

Logical multiplicity must be connected to logical unity,[100] whereby the pre-logical aspects of a work of art are objectified. Here we are dealing with the logical-functional synthesis, which appears in naïve experience. Here we would also like to point out the following, although it does not concern music directly. We speak of an illogical reproduction or portrayal of something that is also (even specifically) rejected in naïve experience. It does not appeal to us and can therefore also not be really beautiful. That would be the case if someone put three legs into an illustration or depicted a person holding an object in a definitely impossible manner. We must remember here that in the logical aspect all the pre-logical functions are objectified. Illustrations such as those just described will eventually start to irritate us. Even in the representation of situations from fairy tales or unreal events in which an appeal is made to our imagination (think of the paintings of Hieronymus Bosch), this still applies. That is also true of the 'absurdities' that cartoons sometimes show.

The psychical structural function[101] and all the other structural functions in the spheres of nature coincide, as mentioned above, with those of sounds, which we have already discussed in the previous section.

We have not yet discussed the object functions of the musical work founded in the aesthetic function. Thus these all have a retrocipatory structure in the objectivization of all earlier functions.

The juridical function. All moments that ought to appear normatively in a work of art must be done justice. In the first place, justice must be done to the conception in a work of art. A large number of aesthetic 'ideas' should not be 'disposed of' in a few bars, since we otherwise would have to say that what needed to be 'said' has not been given a just treatment. By the same token, one little idea should not be presented in a very extensive form. Furthermore, one of the instruments or groups of instruments used may not push itself forward at the expense of the others. That last point is also very important in the actualization. The same applies to the movements or the part-structures of melody, harmony and rhythm. When one pushes itself forward, justice is not done to the other parts.

Furthermore, juridically speaking, in the sense of retribution, it will not be right if any one of the functions is overemphasized. This would be the case if, for example, a creating artist were to be led totally in his or her composition by the taste of the public, by 'fashion'.[102] In the conception we may especially not devote all our attention to the technique or the technical form, at the expense of the aesthetic quality. Professor Dooyeweerd writes, 'Technical form and the leading aesthetic expression of the artist's conception are the two aspects characterizing our experience of every work of art. Their inner structural unity is a requirement of every good and mature artwork.' [103]

Ethical structural function. In general we can define whether a work of art expresses *love or hate* towards society. A work of art ought not, however, to be deliberately meant to offend a person or a group of people, unless by doing so one wishes, precisely out of love for one's neighbours, to bring them to better insights; it must truly, objectively satisfy the requirement to love one's neighbours. If a musical work consists only of shrill sounds it is not only not aesthetically justified but also in conflict with this requirement.

In chapter 1, #1, in connection with the aesthetic anticipation of the meaning of love, we discussed the honesty and sincerity of a work of art. We said that in a work of art what the artist wants to say should be expressed 'honestly', without 'ugly' content in a 'beautiful' form, and that 'emptiness' should not be disguised by outer appearance. If the beautiful is not disclosed in this respect in the correct manner, it is obvious that this structural function will not satisfy the norms either. For the aesthetic function is also objectified here. We could have made a similar comment already when discussing the juridical function.

The pistical structural function. In the first place we need to point out that a work of art can express a particular faith. The *St Matthew Passion* is a true confession of faith in Jesus Christ; but man's faith in himself can also be expressed, as in the words of Kloos: 'I am a god in my deepest thoughts.'[104] We see another example in a painting by Jan Steen, *Christ drives the money-changers out of the Temple*. One cannot detect anything of the holy indignation, of the greatness of this fact, so that someone who has looked at the painting for a long time without knowing what was being portrayed might finally say that he or she cannot work out what it represents. It might just as well have been a scene at any inn. Compare this with the painting by El Greco on the same topic.

In the case of a particular work, we will often find it difficult or impossible to determine what type of faith is expressed or under the guidance of which faith it has been conceived. It is especially difficult in the arts where no words are used to express thoughts, for instance in the visual arts and in instrumental music. I believe we can attribute this to the fact that, although we are in antithesis with this world, we are still *zeitgebunden*, children of our time and members of the culture in which we have been raised. Now, this culture has for many centuries been guided by a science ideal, which though it found its roots in the personality ideal, yet kept its eyes fixed on the functions in the founding direction of time. This has taught us to distinguish more or less clearly the state of affairs in the spheres of nature (mathematics, physics[105]). We have also learned to see logical and symbolic states of affairs. The personality ideal which was just mentioned has often been strongly 'aestheticistically' tinted – in the Renaissance, for instance, by the ideal of the harmonious person, the so-called *uomo universale*, and also in the Romantic period – think of *Sturm und Drang* with its 'aesthetic genius'. Through this we have learned to see the aesthetic function as well; but the functions that lie higher in the transcendental direction have, in contrast to those lying lower, been more or less neglected, so that we have to be endowed with a particular intuition if we want to recognize faith in a work of art except when it is explicitly expressed. We need to exercise our intuition, open ourselves and increasingly improve in opening ourselves to the meaning-fullness in Christ, in order to be able to apprehend how non-Christian art and norms that are positivized under the guidance of faith in an idol – whether the idol is a humanistic or a modern vitalistic 'conception' – belong to the world-in-antithesis.[106]

All the mentioned object functions need to be disclosed by the subjects in a patent subject-object relationship. If people hear a piece of music but call it just sound, they evidently have a *false experience* of reality. Subjectively, however, we can 'unveil' its functions either more or less perfectly. To do this really well, we first need to open ourselves to art in general, but then also to the individual work. That is why so often we only start to understand a work well after we have heard it a number of times, that is, if we have opened ourselves to that work.

It can be that in this subjective disclosure we do not unveil all functions equally 'intensively'. Thus it is possible to judge the aesthetic quality of a musical work even though we do not precisely know how the work is 'put together' technically and even though we do not know in detail which instruments are involved. The same applies with regard to the symbolic function. If in a programmatic work we do not precisely know the programme, and thus cannot follow the symbolic representation in detail, we may still enjoy it greatly, namely disclose the aesthetic function. The pistical function will, as we already discussed above, often remain closed. Only when we disclose all functions subjectively, in their true form and in their true relationships, do we satisfy the norm expected of the lover of art. Only then will we know the work fully and achieve an experience of maximum musical enjoyment.

#4 The musical work in the relationship of actualization

As subject in all normative spheres, people should actualize a work of art according to its objective destination.[107] Performers and listeners usually actualize the work in an *organized, aesthetically qualified, social interlinkage*, such as a formal concert. The work can also be actualized in a (synthetic or institutional) community. We will return to this in what follows. We will discuss the orchestra or choir as a community of performers in a separate section.

Both the performers and listeners have to be *present according to their biotic structure* for actualization to take place.[108] The performers in the actualization are bound to their biotic possibilities. The composer needs to take this into account while composing. A pianist can never strike more than ten notes at once, while also the speed of his or her fingers has limitations. Similarly, the 'length' of breath of the players of wind instruments needs to be taken into account.

The actualization of the work of art in the aesthetically qualified interlinkage is also revealed in this, namely that when building concert halls one needs to take account of the acoustics in connection with the subjective spatial function of sounds.

The relationship of actualization in the psychic meaning-aspect. This relationship is manifest in the fact that we can start to fantasize as a result of a work.[109] This is especially important in programmatic music. In this case a fantasy image *must* arise in us that represents what is reproduced in the work of music by symbols. Thus we encounter here again the reproductive aesthetic imagination that we have already discussed.[110]

Furthermore, it is possible that a piece can bring us into one or another mood. We make use of this when we feel low by listening to music that will cheer us up.

A work of art can arouse a feeling of community[111] that 'speaks' to the performers and listeners who know themselves to be bearers of the same culture.

In the logical sphere we actualize the piece by distinguishing it logically from others. We then distinguish it by all its characteristics, so that we can 'confront' it with other works.

The relationship of actualization in the historical law sphere. As we noticed at the end of the previous section, we need to open ourselves to art and works of art. This disclosure takes place on a historical basis. As historical subjects we determine which piece we want to hear or play, and where and when. This historical actualization is also obvious from the fact that some works have become 'repertoire-pieces', while others are seldom or no longer played.

Technical ability is required of the performers in order to actualize the work of music in a controlled forming.

In general we can say that the work of music is an object in relation to the act of actualization, for both the listener and the performer, for whom actualization can only be done justice to on the basis of a historical development under guidance of the disclosed aesthetic function.

The relationship of actualization in the symbolic meaning-aspect. To start, we notice that a work of music can be reproduced symbolically in a score. We will devote a separate section to this.

Further, we notice that the symbolic subjects can use a particular work as an example of the style of a particular period or of a particular composer. The work can be representative of such a style. Since the aesthetic meaning (and thus also the meaning-moments) cannot be symbolically objectivized, it is not possible to express precisely in words the how and what of a certain style, to comprehensively express what the concrete beauty of a specific work of art is. We can only approximate it, hint at it. However, we can easily speak about its form, and so forth.

A work of art can be actualized by a community, since it can symbolically represent that community. For the institutional community of the state it may be the national anthem, like the Dutch *Wilhelmus;* for a synthetic community, for instance, that may be the club song.

The relationship of actualization in the social aspect of temporal reality. It goes without saying that in the actualization of a work of art by performers and listeners, the social function is of eminent importance. In the already mentioned aesthetic interlinkage the social norms need to be taken into account. For instance, evening dress needs to be worn to formal concerts and the musicians will not be allowed to appear on the stage in their shirtsleeves.

Music naturally can also be used to heighten a pleasant atmosphere. Think especially of light entertainment music,[112] which has a social destination.

The relationship of actualization in the economic law sphere. This actualization is manifest in the first instance in the fact that the artists (and publishers) can earn money from the actualization of a work of music. Consider in this connection the commercial gramophone companies. Nowadays people even speak of commercial music, that is, music for entertainment, which is made solely for commercial purposes and in which the composer aims singularly to humour the popular taste.

The relationship of actualization in the aesthetic law sphere. The act of actualization for both the listener and the performer must be under the guidance of the (disclosed) aesthetic subject function. It is required, especially of musicians, that they indeed be able to justify their subjective actualization (including all retrocipations and anticipations). This is a normative requirement. Violation of the norm or anti-normative behaviour we indeed have to call *sin*, in the full sense of that word.

Both the artist and the recipient need to be fully aware of their being in the 'mode-of-being of meaning' and of the inescapable requirement of this 'mode-of-being of meaning': submission to God's law with their whole heart and their full personality.

However, no one can ever say that the enjoyment of beauty is sin, that it is 'from the devil', for 'everything God created is good, and nothing is to be rejected if it is received with thanksgiving' (1 Timothy 4:4). Did God not in his world order give us beauty for enjoyment and impose the *duty* upon us to give the norms, thus also the aesthetic norms, a positive form? And is it not our duty to actualize the beauty, with our heart directed towards the meaningfulness in Christ? We also may, and in fact must, subjectively disclose the beauty of the things of nature in the patent subject-object relationship, 'with thanksgiving'.

The actualization in the juridical meaning-aspect. We will, when we actualize works of art, weigh these against each other according to their aesthetic quality. The performing artists too will be weighed against each other according to their capacity to actualize; we will pay the superior better than the inferior.

With the actualization, justice needs to be done to all moments, just as we already mentioned with the juridical disclosure relationship and the juridical anticipation in the aesthetic meaning. Therefore, in their performance, musicians will not be allowed to pay all of their attention to technique. In general we can say that they need to do full justice to the composition. Therefore they may not subjectively introduce any changes or actualize it in any other way than the composer meant it to be.

It goes without saying that a work of art can also be actualized as juridical object, as in a struggle for copyrights.

Actualization in the meaning of love for one's neighbour. We can express our love in music (think, for instance, of the 'dedicated to . . .') or we can put a piece of music to such use (as, in earlier times, with the serenade).

We, the listeners, have to love music, while the musician, in the actualization of a musical work of art, has to do it in love towards that work. Such a piece truly becomes an object of love, for the performer as well as for the recipient!

The relationship of actualization in the pistical sphere. We can believe in the primacy of a particular style; or we can believe that with a particular style, such as that of the Renaissance, the sovereignty of the aesthetic personality is proven.[113] In connection with this 'aesthetic personality' we also think of Romanticism. Thus, in many ways, we can actualize art in general or a work of art in particular as an object of faith. However, the norm is that we need to thank God for allowing this beauty to exist within his creation order. Art, the work of art, must in the first place be to his honour, '*ad maiorem gloriam Dei*'.

#5 The orchestra and/or choir

(We also include the smaller 'units' here, such as the quartet.) In the previous section we discussed the actualization of the musical work of art and the norms imposed by it on the performing artist. These norms are in the nature of things also the norms that apply to orchestra and choir.

The orchestra (choir) is an aesthetically qualified, synthetic social community,[114] which is founded in the historical law sphere. We see this also in its organization.

It is directly apparent from experience that an orchestra (choir) in the 'musical meaning' is indeed a community with its own identity. After all, we can rightfully speak of the 'typical sound of the strings' in one or another orchestra. That a choir is a community is also apparent from the fact that here a single person does not 'descend' in pitch while singing, but that everybody does it simultaneously and by the same amount. We can also offer the argument that we often hear all the members of a 'section' of an orchestra (or choir) place a particular accent at a specific moment, that they all make the same mistake, and so forth. The whole orchestra (or choir) is also in better form at one time than another, which cannot be inferred from the better or worse disposition of the different members at different performances (for it would be rather coincidental for all members simultaneously to be in especially good form on the same day). Every individualistic approach proves deficient here.

When new members join such a community they will first have to be 'worked in', that is, they will have to allow themselves to be incorporated into the community and become a true 'member of the identity' before the community can perform as a completely 'homogeneous' entity again.

We also discern a norm in the manner of arrangement of an orchestra (or choir). This is traditionally determined, which is indicative of the positivization of the norm over time.

#6 Music and its enkaptic bond

We will begin with discussing the *structural interlacement between the narrower genotypes*. Earlier we found these to be vocal music and instrumental music. Both can occur freely (vocal, as in a capella singing, for instance Gregorian chant; instrumental, practically all concert music). However, vocal music is usually found in enkapsis with instrumental music. It is then often the leading structure, with instrumental music having an accompanying function. That is for example the case with most songs in the Italian *bel canto* opera. Sometimes, however, the instrumental music has the leading structure, as in Beethoven's *Ninth Symphony*.

Now we will discuss the *enkapsis with other aesthetically qualified structures*. In the first place we see enkapsis with the already often mentioned *aesthetically qualified interlinkages*. An interlinkage will also express itself in the form of the work. Consider, for instance, the difference between a symphony and a quartet. The latter can rightfully be called chamber music, since it is intended to be played in a small, limited circle. The difference between 'concert hall music' (such as the symphony) and chamber music can now be traced back to a difference in enkapsis; they are bound to different interlinkages. And exactly because of this it is not good to present a chamber music concert (such as a piano recital) in a large concert hall.

Enkapsis with the aesthetically qualified community also occurs. Usually composers prescribe the strength of a symphony orchestra, departing rarely from the normal strength (this obviously only applies if the composer makes 'concert music'). Thus we see enkapsis with the aesthetically qualified community of the orchestra. However, this interlacement is still more apparent if the composer writes music for special orchestras. Haydn, for example, wrote pieces specially for the strength of the orchestra of the Esterházy family. Mozart wrote arias for particular soloists. Think of Beethoven's 'Wellington's Victory', where he inserts a fanfare for an automatic trumpet.

We come across very clear cases of enkapsis in jazz music, as discussed in the last section of chapter 1. Since improvisation takes on a large role in this music, we see that arrangements are written especially for this or that orchestra. Moreover, the style of the different soloists is taken into consideration. Thus an arrangement for one orchestra cannot be used for another. It is unnecessary to say that if one does not take the style of the different soloists into consideration with the arrangement, one will never be able to arrive at a musical unity. And such unity is an aesthetic norm.

Up till now we have discussed the enkapsis of music with subjectively qualified structures. We will now focus on the interlacement with *objectively aesthetically qualified structures*.

First we will discuss the interlacement with the literary work of art. We usually see interlacement of the narrower genotype poetry with vocal music, while the narrower genotype instrumental music can obviously also be interwoven in the interlacement coherence. We seldom come across vocal music that does not function in enkapsis with literary art. As example of such an exception we mention Debussy's *Les sérènes*.

If the interlacement in question centres on the 'music', and the words are only an 'aid', then the musical (vocal) structure is clearly the leading one. In *bel canto* opera the singers could just as well be singing something else, without causing any harm to the aesthetic quality. The music can also have only a serving function; in this case the music must be totally 'adapted' to the text, since the leading function of the structure of literary art will be the destinational function of the music. As example of the latter we can point to the melodrama and to madrigalisms [word-painting], and this will also be the case in most songs.

For many, in different times, the ideal was that the enkaptically bound structures would stand next to each other as 'equal partners', such as Wagner's ideal of the *Gesamtkunstwerk*. However, this ideal was seldom or never realized.

Furthermore, musical art can be bound to drama (which in its own turn, as we already noticed earlier, nearly always functions in enkapsis with literary art). If drama is the leading structure, music has an accompanying, complementary, sometimes mood-suggesting task. We see this in Grieg's *Peer Gynt* music to the drama of Ibsen, in the *Egmond* music of Beethoven, in Badings' music to the *Gijsbrecht* of Vondel, in Pijper's music to *The Tempest*, for which Shakespeare himself even prescribed the use of music.[115] In contrast to this we notice that in the Italian *bel canto* opera the music is clearly the leading structure. Also in this context we can point again to the indeed unrealized ideal of Wagner to arrive at a *Gesamtkunstwerk*.

Music can also be enkaptically bound to the art of dance. Just think of ballet music. Dance will usually be the leading structure here. We find examples in *La valse* of Ravel, *La création du monde* of Milhaud, and furthermore all music written by different composers for the Russian Daghilew ballet in Paris around 1920. The music could also be the leading structure in this enkapsis; however, examples are difficult to find. Moreover, experience teaches us that dancing to music that is not especially structured for it, does not satisfy. In such cases the enkapsis apparently does not allow itself to be expressed in works of music.[116]

We now want to proceed to discuss the interlacement of music with non-aesthetically qualified structures.

Thus we see that music can be bound to a (subjectively) *socially qualified structure*. Consider entertainment music. From the requirements that we place on it, it is obvious that this music has a social destination. It may not be 'heavy'; it may not pose any 'musical problems'; it must on the other hand be 'light', have an easy appeal, at first hearing be directly congenial and strike us as pleasant. It must also not be too 'imposing' – think of café music. The socially qualified structure, to which music is bound, is an interlinkage. Music can also be bound to dance, while the [internal] interlacement coherence of music and dance can be bound in turn to the above-mentioned [external] interlinkage. We see this for example in modern dance music, and in the waltzes of Strauss. In general we can say that the already mentioned enkapsis (the interlacement with literature, with drama and with dance) can have a social destination. So we may point to the operetta, the popular song, the songs of Lou Bandy and others.

Music can be bound to a *pistical structure* such as a church community or denomination. We call this sacred or church music, and examples include Gregorian chant, the 'composed' masses, the Protestant chorale and so on. We already gave the reasons for the typical differences between art bound to the Roman Catholic and the Protestant denominations in chapter 2A, #2.

Music can also be enkaptically bound to all sorts of other structures. In this regard, think of marching songs, folk songs, lullabies, camping songs, war songs. We will not discuss all these cases of enkapsis any further.

We would also like to emphasize that we are not dealing with a case of enkapsis with the *Wilhelmus*, the Dutch national anthem.[117] This is a case of subjective actualization of the work of music according to its objective destination by the community (of the state). This music is used by the community as a symbol for its unity. This does not express itself in the form or in the text.

In summary we notice that variability types can originate: i) as a result of differences in the founding enkapsis (think of the difference between a brass band[118] and concert music); ii) as a result of (correlative) enkapsis; iii) as a result of a difference in style (historical variability); iv) as a result of a different positivization of the norms because of external factors (actually also a difference in style, likewise a difference in historical variability).

#7 The score and the instrument

In music we meet the peculiar state of affairs that it cannot be permanently objectivized. We already noticed this. It explains why one uses a score, in which all the lower-symbolic functions (i.e. the sounds and the form) are symbolized, objectivized.

The score is a symbolically qualified structure with a historical founding function, but this structure only exists as founded in another structure that is qualified in one of the natural aspects.[119] Further, we see correlative enkapsis of the score with the musical work which is symbolized by it. The latter is naturally expressed in the 'form' of the score and also in that of the musical work. Consider that a composer can never write music that cannot be notated in a score. Musical notation poses limitations; one cannot notate every arbitrary nuance (not even considering that otherwise it would be 'unreadable' for the musician). The score therefore symbolizes a non-symbolically qualified structure, namely the intentional conception of the artist in his or her pre-symbolic object functions, without that structure really being portrayed or represented.[120] In this way the rhythm is symbolized by bars [and whole-notes, half-notes, dotted notes, etc.], the sounds by notes. A work of art can be symbolically notated only if the symbolic meaning-aspect is disclosed by the aesthetic meaning-aspect.

The structure of the score obviously expresses itself in all the meaning-aspects of temporal reality. We will only look at a few functions that are important in this connection. We see a biotic object function: we need to turn pages; we can take it into our hands. The psychical observation of the notes is founded directly in this biotic objectivity. In the historical and symbolic meaning-aspect, we mention the relationship of actualization. The performing artist has to actualize the work in an act of controlled forming based on his or her understanding of the symbols. The disclosure of the objective language function which still lies closed in the thing-structure is done by the musician who, because of his of her subjective 'community function', based on historical development, understands which sounds must be played.121 On the basis of the sounds and form that are symbolically incorporated in the score, the post-symbolical functions can also be actualized in the actualization of a musical work.

A second important 'aid' in the actualization of a piece of music is the *instrument*. This structure belongs to the radical type 'utensils', which is a *socially qualified structural principle*. Within this radical type we find the genotype 'instrument', while the different structures within this type can be interlaced in an enkapsis with other structures. In this way we see that the musical instrument has a socially qualified structure that is historically founded and that exists in a foundational enkapsis with a physically qualified structure (wood, copper, etc.). The total structure of the instrument as object exists in an enkaptic interlacement with the aesthetically qualified structure of the music. Thus it goes without saying that the instrument has an aesthetic destinational function, for it has to produce musically aesthetic sounds. A musical instrument is thus well formed only if it fully satisfies the normative requirement that it must produce beautiful sounds.

The musical instrument presents different variability types: wind (wood and copper), string (bowed and plucked) and percussion instruments. The difference between these types stems from a difference in historical subject-object relationship in the technically controlled playing of the instrument.122

Epilogue

In this article I have attempted to discuss, albeit very briefly, the direction and broad outlines of a yet-to-be-built Christian aesthetics. Such an aesthetics must unavoidably be based on a Christian philosophy. Such a philosophy may be found in the Philosophy of the Cosmonomic Idea. I have, as is evident, presupposed the knowledge of the main lines of this philosophy as it is discussed in Professor Dooyeweerd's tripartite work *De Wijsbegeerte der Wetsidee*, translated into English as *A New Critique of Theoretical Thought*. I am well aware that my work is not nearly finished; on the contrary, many problems have been briefly pointed out without further elaboration, while at the same time there are many moments which an aesthetic theory should take into account that have escaped my attention. There is of course also the possibility that I may have seen or interpreted some states of affairs incorrectly.

We may not rest in our scientific work until the states of affairs that we have elaborated account fully for cosmic reality as given to us in naïve experience. In other words, our work must comply totally with the demands of truth.123 Moreover, we need to be continually aware that we can never fully, exhaustively, grasp the *Gegenstand* in our concept or idea, but can only approximate and approach it.[124] Thus we may never ask of aesthetics to give us a completely adequate, clear view of the 'essence' or 'identity' of beauty. For the true identity of beauty, as of each other meaning-particularity within this meaning-diversity, lies in its meaning-fullness; one can therefore only approximate it in the idea but never fully grasp it (in a concept).

We need to be especially imbued by being in the 'mode-of-being as meaning'. As soon as we no longer see the *Gegenstand* as meaning, as soon as we lose sight of our relationship of dependence on the Creator of all meaning, we lose that 'grasp of truth' that points towards the meaning-fullness of truth, or the *Gegenstand*. Yet, this should be the leading principle: to look for the truth, to read the true state of affairs, with the help of a disclosed intuition, from the divine world order while pointing towards the Truth, the meaning-fullness, that Truth which lies in Jesus Christ as the Perfecter of meaning, the new Root of the human race.

Yes, truth must be the leading principle. We must not try to impose our thoughts and opinions in a nominalistic manner on the world order, nor attempt to impose our theories on reality. Instead, and this is perhaps much harder, we need to attempt to read the real states of affairs from reality. In this way we will never fall into a rigid art and art theory, for pointing towards the Truth and acknowledging our being in the 'mode-of-being a meaning' is the dynamic factor for development, for disclosure, for intensification of meaning.

It must be directly evident that for a Christian science, truth in the above-mentioned sense is the only possible truth. Anyone who says that science in this way is no longer science but theology, that working on this basis is not scientific work but preaching, proves to have no insight into the totally religious character of each act of the temporal human personality, proves to be still caught in the dogma of the *Voraussetzungslosigkeit* ('presuppositionlessness'). Yet, are treatises such as Kant's glorification of duty or the 'slanging matches' and the glorification of 'life' in Nietzsche's *Der Antichrist* not also 'preaching', albeit directed to another 'god', or are they perhaps 'neutral', 'purely scientific' and in no way religiously determined?

In a Christian science it has to be clear that lying, i.e. everything that is not directed towards the true meaning-fullness of truth, is sin, in the same way that ugly art or an act of hatred or, in general, any anti-normative behaviour is sin.

Obviously we may not, in a proud hard-hearted attitude, think that we, by ourselves and in our own strength, can fight for God and his kingdom because we have such pure principles and on the basis of such a pure Christian philosophy can argue so well how everything ought to be. We would then be no better than the Pharisees, who lived by the laws that they derived from Scripture but forgot the Lord. God's judgment would then be on us as it was in Isaiah 29:13 when he declared: 'These people come near to me with their principles and honour me with their philosophy, but their hearts are far from me. Their piety is only a human science, learned by rote.' But if we bow ourselves before him in humility, in submission to his word, praying that he will be with us by his Holy Spirit, as obedient and yet unworthy servants doing our duty, then we may expect God's blessing (1 Corinthians 15:58).

May science and also art continuously be, not to the glory of man, not to the greater honour of the scientists or artists thimselves, but *ad maiorem gloriam Dei.*

Style and World View[125]

1 What is style?

Before we look at our topic closely we must ask what style really is. Although the word style is also used metaphorically, in expressions such as lifestyle, thinking style, and so on, we can be sure that it commonly refers to an aesthetic condition. Is style then a characteristic of everything that is aesthetically beautiful? Certainly not. You only have to think of the beauty of nature. The beauty of nature is a beauty without style. Before we can deal with the problems that arise here we first ought to say what, in fact, beauty is. The aesthetic aspect is one of the aspects of the world order that is sovereign within its own sphere. Each thing functions within this aspect. Does that imply that all things are beautiful? Certainly not, but also the ugly can exist only because there is an aesthetic aspect to reality. That something is ugly means that it is not-beautiful, un-aesthetic, that it goes against the norms for beauty, but not that it could exist without taking part in the aesthetic aspect.

The aesthetic aspect is normative. That means that God has given this aspect in his world order, in which norms are given, in principle. Nothing can be beautiful if it does not satisfy these norms. People have been given the task to give a positive form to these norms; these norms are such that it is human beings who give them a concrete form. In the course of historical development, and under the leadership of great artists, who in this area are the leading culture-formers, a different positive expression is given to the aesthetic norms in each era; these norms are positivized in different ways over time. And style describes the manner in which these norms are positivized at any particular moment during a particular historical period.[126] Works of art originating from different periods show differences in style. It means that the beauty in these works of art has been realized in different positive forms. In order to be truly beautiful, these works must always satisfy the norms as they have been laid down in principle in the world order, otherwise they certainly could not be beautiful.

As we said, all things function in the aesthetic aspect. Therefore, all things made by human beings show style. For example, a modern home interior will display a modern style not only in the modern paintings hanging on the wall but also in the chairs, the telephone, how the paintings are hung, how the furniture is arranged, also in the vases, the floor coverings, the cutlery and crockery, and so on. And is it not true that when you go out the cars, the advertising billboards, the modern buildings too will display a certain unity of style, for they all obey the laws as they are aesthetically positivized at that moment? Therefore, style is clearly not just the privilege of the fine arts.

By contrast, things in the created world, such as flowers and mountains, do not have their origin in human formation. It goes without saying that we therefore cannot speak of style in relation to the beauty of nature.

2 Who influences style?

We will now discuss the influence that the world view of those who positivize the aesthetic norms, i.e. the formers of style, has on the style being produced. Every human action, and therefore also the creative work of artists, their activity as leading positivizers, as well as their faith, finds its deepest root in a religious choice of position, which is concretized in a world view. Of course, a person is not necessarily always aware of his of her world view, although it will come to the fore in the opinions he or she holds on various matters. Neutrality is impossible when trying to solve the smaller or greater problems being presented to humanity for solution. The positing of the demand for neutrality and the belief in its existence also find their root in a world view which is strongly influenced by the (positivistic) philosophy that came into being in the nineteenth century. It is important to remember that when problems are being solved, of whatever nature, it is never a matter of facts as such, but always a matter of the interpretation of those facts.

In this religious choice of position by people, mentioned above, there is really in principle only one choice: for or against God; for Christ or against him. The antithesis finds its deepest root and ground in this possibility of choosing for or against God. But if a person has chosen against God there are still numerous possibilities. For people have to choose their god; they are made that way, structurally, and as they close off the view of the transcendental (since God is the transcendent God, exalted above his creation), they will always create their own god, by 'proclaiming' something temporal within the creation as god. It could be one of their own functions, such as intelligence or reason.

Faith also finds its root, its orientation, in the religious choice of position. Don't think that faith is a privilege of the Christian only. Everyone, whoever she or he may be, has a faith function and an actual faith, but that of the Christian has taken a different direction (and content) than that of the non-Christian.

All this is of such importance because the whole process of positivizing is led by faith. The direction of faith shows the direction of the positivization process. This is true in every field, in the positivization of legal, economic and social norms, and also of aesthetic norms. I want to emphasize the latter especially, because too often the opinion is expressed that the field of art is either a neutral field or a field that has nothing to do with the Christian faith, that at most art can be assigned to the of 'common grace', or, inevitably belongs to the 'world', the *civitas terrena*. We will return to this topic later. First we will deal with a few examples from the history of art.

During the Middle Ages all of Europe was pervaded by the ideal of a church that embraced all spheres of life, and an attitude of life directed to God. You can find expression of this ideal in style. Think, for example, of the Gothic churches with their vertical lines, in which the church building represented the central place that Christ and his church took in the hearts of the people. We find the glorification of the church in the Baroque churches of the Counter-Reformation. In the Protestant Christian churches dating from the same period, the central place given to the word of God as fulfilled in Christ is clearly expressed.

Also in the paintings of the Middle Ages the above-mentioned world view comes to expression. I refer you to an article that appeared in a previous issue of this journal – 'The Christmas Story in the Visual Arts'. Allow me to cite a few lines from that article. In a discussion of the painting by Geertgen tot Sint Jans of the Bethlehem story, it speaks of

> the pious and intensely individual emotional life ... What a serene simplicity shines forth from this work, what a timid approach as if on bare feet, because the place on which we stand is holy ground ... The Light that has come into the world shines from the little baby. Here we are more concerned with the rendering of the Light, that Mystery, than with the rendering of that tiny being lying in the manger ... The work of this painter, who still has to be included with the Flemish Primitives, is penetrated by such a pure feeling, that it has become one of the most beautiful expressions of the Christmas mystery. When we compare this with the paintings on this subject of the great Italian masters, the Spanish, the Flemish, Rubens and other masters of the Baroque, then you see the difference. With Geertgen we find serene simplicity, the expression of what is important here at the deepest level: the Mystery of the incarnation of God. With the others we find the pomp and splendour of the Wise Men, the kings: elegant garments, beautiful madonnas, lovely children, magnificent ruins or grottos, glorious landscapes as background, but devotion is lost. A feeling of admiration for the work of art as such remains, but the adoration of the Christchild, which is what it is all about, is left out.

We ask ourselves how it came about that in the works of the later masters, the painters of the Renaissance and the Baroque, this devotion was lost.

3 The influences of style on art

During the Renaissance we find two moments in art: firstly the Faustian, with unbridled striving for unbounded freedom and possibilities; and secondly the rationalization of style in a strictly maintained and rationally determined classicism. Also this phenomenon can be traced back to the world view of those times. After the decline and undermining of the ecclesiastical monoculture of the Middle Ages we see the rise of a new religious attitude in the hearts of the people: the personality ideal. It proclaimed humankind itself, 'universal man', the rational, moral personality as the lawgiver and creator of the world order. And humans immediately started to exercise their self-sufficient kingship over nature. Science became the vehicle for that kingship: not satisfied until everything was reduced to simple basic formulas, they could, with these formulas as starting point, build up the cosmos rationally. This has become known as the scientific ideal, which, although it was itself rooted in the personality. ideal, came finally to stand in sharp contrast to it, since it also wanted to build up human being itself from a few basic laws, and thereby came to threaten the freedom of the sovereign personality.

This polar contraposition within the humanistic (or Renaissance) world view comes clearly to expression in the artworks of this period, as we already indicated. During the Renaissance, both moments – the struggle for freedom and rational classicism – are still more or less in balance, but increasingly they find themselves in opposition to each other, until we see the two moments stand side by side as incompatible forces during the Baroque period. Thus we see the indomitable struggle for freedom expressed in one style, and next to it, or opposite it, another style that arises out of the scientific ideal, which has pledged its heart to mathematics.

After this period we come to the time of the Enlightenment, when the scientific ideal had seemingly won the day. Under the influence of this faith in human reason all of art threatened to fossilize, until the personality ideal once again comes to demand its due, and Romanticism comes to the fore with the *Sturm und Drang* movement. Don't think that the old polar contraposition is immediately done away with. Romanticism arises out of the same religious basic attitude as the Renaissance and Baroque. On the one hand we see in the visual arts a style that is very strongly classicist, where one is more or less subject to rationalistic norms borrowed from Greek and Latin antiquity. On the other hand we see a blossoming of personality, especially in literature but also in music.

Tensions necessarily arose out of the basic humanistic ideas. On the one hand the scientific ideal set its sights on nature and, as a result, regarded everything as subject to the laws of nature, to causality and to determination. On the other hand the personality ideal taught the absolute freedom of human being. Romanticists attempted to solve these tensions in adoration of the feeling of beauty, as they thought that the contrasting attitudes had thus been reconciled. That is why early Romanticism assigned such a prominent place to art and why artistic genius enjoyed such veneration. In contrast to the Renaissance, people were less set on dominating nature through their intelligence than on finding unrestrained ways and means of expressing their emotions. People had to bring to expression the stirrings of the soul in art, but the 'soul' was really no more than their psychic, emotional function. Because while it is true that in Romanticism the aesthetic was valued highly, it is also true that the aesthetic was in their eyes not much more than a 'kind of feeling'. Hence Romanticism is focused strongly on the psychological – everything is centred on feeling. The irrational, that is to say the elevation of the person above any norm or law, uniqueness, limitlessness, dominion of feeling, this is what the Romantic person worshipped and aimed for: this was his [or her] faith. For this reason we see that when Wagner appears – in music history we speak of High Romanticism by then – aesthetics had been influenced for so many years by faith in the psychologically-tinted personality ideal, the ideal of emotional expression of the 'soul', that many call this music almost sensual, for it affects us psychologically more than aesthetically.

The visual arts have also gradually yielded themselves to the Romantic personality ideal: in painting, see Delacroix and Géricault; in sculpture, Rodin.

4 Style and world view in the twentieth century

Around 1900 we see great stylistic changes taking place, first in architecture, but soon also in the visual arts and music. We shall now investigate the origins of these changes.

During the first half of the nineteenth century the Romantic ideals were breached because the personality ideal was dethroned. Influential in this was the revival of the scientific ideal, this time more in the form of the natural sciences, as a result of the blossoming of technology. This scientific ideal no longer found its root and impulse in the personality ideal, as it had in the time of the Enlightenment. The admiration of history and science as a revelation of the (rational-moral) human spirit (this is something that originated in the personality ideal) made place for a simple acceptance of what happens, of what had been accomplished. The result of all this was a barren (positivistic) attitude towards life, which thought to restrict itself to the facts, but only to those which could be scientifically explained. Only rudiments of the formerly proud personality ideal remain, as in the historicism of Dilthey, for example, who described the glory of humanity in the awareness of its transience. The ancient humanistic streams combined in the philosophies of death, in which humans rise above nature only in their awareness of having to die one day.

Yet all these are but the convulsions of an attitude to life that is actually already dead. Nietzsche had shot this humanism in the heart, and with it all of Western culture as it had developed over the course of a few centuries, when he relinquished the old faith in rational human nature and scoffed at the idea of the equality of the human race. The ideal of the superman (*Übermensch*) and the doctrine of the *Herrenmoral* made their entry.

And so we find, confining ourselves to the main issues, two sources out of which the new world view arises: firstly the natural scientific attitude of the nineteenth century, which led to biological speculations – just think of Darwin; and secondly Nietzsche, for his ideal was the superman, the man of power, but an ideal man almost exclusively in a biological sense only. This new world view, which found its sources here and seized the spirits from the end of the nineteenth century, was vitalism. Instead of finding the foundations of human existence in morality, beauty and so on, people are now looking at the natural instincts of life. Instead of seeking a starting point *in cogito*, 'I think', people find it *in vivo*, 'I live.'

Around 1900 we see, amongst others, three new world views being preached by Bergson, William James and Dilthey. They are vitalism (in its narrower sense), pragmatism, and historicism, respectively. These are various faith-directions that are all based on the same religious choice. That one religious root is, as we said, vitalism whereby 'Life' is explained as the origin and root of everything. But biotic life alone does not get us very far in explaining the many problems of human existence. That is why people say that this Life creates its own values, and creates more and more different values. Art, religion, the state, are nothing but 'manifestations', forms of expression, of this Life. And they are not subjected to any norms (this is what is irrational in these views). You only have to concern yourself with the forms of the various areas of life, as these are formed by Life, for tomorrow Life may present you with entirely different norms . . . and then that is fine as well. That is how, by starting from vitalism, people end up with historicism, of which Dilthey is the most important representative, as we have already mentioned. We may also mention his pupil Spengler in this context. But pragmatism also grows out of this religious root. People should not wonder about what is good, beautiful and true, but only about what is directly profitable. Only the things that human beings want to assign value to are valuable, and these are always things that are useful and conducive for Life. We have been able to see, and can still see, the horrible results of this world view in the National-Socialist revolution and in Bolshevism, where the 'élite' ask the question only of what is good for themselves, for their power, and design their slogans to blind the masses.

We are dealing with this in such an extended way because, once we have seen the religious root of all that is 'modern', we will gain further insight in the various modern cultural expressions, to which also belong the new stylistic directions in art. But let's see what these modern expressions of art look like.

On the one hand we see a pragmatic direction in art, usually called functionalism. Here art is under the guidance of an economic idea of what is functional and useful. Pragmatists have, under various influences, taken an economic turn and now pay special attention to technology. When dealing with technology people have to be concerned with the laws of nature, and therefore this world view seems to lose its irrational character: when producing technology people cannot say, without expressing clearly discernable foolishness, that they themselves (each individually) are the ones who make those laws of nature – and that tomorrow they could invent different laws of nature. The artistic direction that flows from such pragmatism, namely functionalism, is not half as irrational in its forms of expression as the other modern stream of art, which we will examine shortly. In functionalism one still looks for laws or norms to which beauty is subjected. Functionalism we find first of all in architecture (Berlage), but it also finds expression in the visual arts. It produced the stylistic direction that usually puts emphasis on technical proficiency and that works with stylized representations. As examples we can mention the painters Toorop, C. Lebeau, R. Hyckes and K. van Veen, and the sculptors Maillol, Dobson and (sometimes) Hildo Krop. In general one can say that this style is liked by modern people (that is why advertising posters are also produced in this style). This is something that cannot be said of the other stylistic direction, which we are going to discuss next.

Alongside functionalism we notice what we would call an irrational style. Although, especially after the First World War, architects tried to design buildings where these ideas came to expression (especially in Germany), the faith that was founded on historistic vitalism obtained the most far-reaching impact on the style formation of the visual arts. It has led to more or less abstract, whether or not cubistic, style directions. These are generally referred to in the language of the common people as 'crazy' paintings and sculptures. For these artists do not want to subject themselves to any norm but claim to have the norm within themselves. They call it beautiful if they find it beautiful. Many second-rate artists have abused this situation and have taken the opportunity to declare everything 'crazy' to be great art. Generally the public rejects this, but many who are inclined to be somewhat snobbish allow themselves to be fooled. More or less gifted artists who have worked in this style include the painters Picasso, Braque, Mondrian and Permeke, and the sculptor Boerderelle.

These stylistic changes, which occurred in a relatively short period of time, have been very noticeable at the exhibition of French art that (recently) took place in The Hague. At the exhibition the well-known sculpture by Rodin, *L'Age d'airain,* and a large female nude by Maillol called *L'Isle de France* were on show. A great tension was noticeable with both sculptures, but how totally different! With *L'Age d'airain* there was a great psychological tension, such as occurs in an adolescent (which is partly expressed by the hand, which the male person has placed on his head), while the tensions that came to expression in the female figure were rather of a different kind. They were more physical tensions. But we should also point out the tremendous aesthetic tension, the dynamics that give such an aesthetic power to the work of Maillol. And indeed, there is a strong aesthetic tension, a dynamic that often borders on the demonic, which is a remarkable characteristic of modern art, especially of the more functionalistic art.

We could say a lot more here but intended only to show by way of a bird's eye view of stylistic developments since the Renaissance the radical influence of world view and the faith that is rooted in it on the resulting stylistic directions.

5 Style and Christian art

If we think about this stylistic development as I have sketched it, then it is striking that since the Renaissance stylistic development has never been influenced by the Christian faith, and therefore we cannot speak of Christian art. For Christian art must be an art of which the norms are positivized under the guidance of faith in God and Christ. At the same time the individual artist's creative activity must be rooted in a religious choice of position, whereby the heart is focused on, directed to, God, as revealed to us in Christ.

If artists as individuals or as a group make works of art under the norms as they are positivized in their time – they can and may not break through the historical continuity in the development of style, nor can or may they abandon the norms in their positivized form – while they live and work from a Christian world view, then undoubtedly all that is too much of a hybrid or that witnesses too much to the rebellion against God will be softened and will find little or no expression in their art. If such an attitude were to continue during several generations and have the opportunity to form its own tradition, then we could expect Christian art to come into being, because the continuing historical development would then have come under the influence of the Christian faith. An example of this we see in seventeenth-century Dutch art, which is why it is difficult to speak of 'Baroque' art in the Northern Netherlands in the sense that we speak of it in the countries further to the south. From this we can see how great the influence of Calvinism was at that time in the Netherlands.

But already soon after the seventeenth century this tradition was broken. Nowadays we can hardly speak of Christian art. We are not talking here about ecclesiastical art, art that deals with and pictures biblical subjects. Even the Renaissance dealt almost exclusively with this kind of subject because of the continuing influence of the medieval tradition, but we dare not call that Christian art. No, Christian art is not in the first place art that seeks its inspiration in biblical subjects and scenes. Nor does Christian art mean art that is under the control of the church. For if the church would really want to control artistic life, then it would break through its sphere sovereignty. It is always the case that when two sovereign spheres encroach on each other's domain by obliterating the boundaries between them, it will mean the end of one of those spheres. For example, if the church, truly as church, would meddle in politics, then it would be the end of the church as such and she would become a political party. If the church were to meddle in art, it would certainly kill art because the church, acting as a real church, will always apply the norms that are valid for the ecclesiastical institution, and not aesthetic criteria. If the church would apply aesthetic criteria, then it would no longer be acting as church but as an 'Association for the Promotion of Christian Art', or something similar. What we have to aim for is that the Christian artist becomes aware that the struggle between the *civitas Dei* and the *civitas terrena* must also be fought in the field of art. Calvinism, perhaps most of all the Christian persuasions, has always been very conscious of the need to bring all areas of life under Christ's sovereignty, and has known that the antithesis is a reality that is valid in all of life, and that we must fight for the kingdom of God in all of life's domains. This implies that we may not just leave art to the 'world'. The field of the fine arts is not a neutral field, or a realm that belongs in principle to the *civitas terrena*, to the world in the antithesis. For, even if artists are Christians and confess their Christianity not only in the church but also politically etc., as long as they do not recognize that art should also stand under the lordship of the Christian faith we will never attain a Christian art; then art will always remain 'of the world'.

I pray that these considerations may contribute to the recognition of the truth of the following lines, written by one of our young poets:

> All beauty that does not carry
> God's stamp and mark in itself,
> Is a temple for sin,
> Is a lie in its character.

The Aesthetic Sphere and Disclosure[127]

The aesthetic is intensified and disclosed in its meaning in a disclosed culture on the foundation of historical development guided by faith. In a primitive, undisclosed culture, we see that only the primary structure of a law sphere, namely the meaning nucleus with the retrocipations, has come to a positive development. Certainly things are then made in a specific style, with a specific beauty, but this beauty and style manifest a rigid, restrictive character. Only when the opening process of disclosure begins will beauty start to reveal its restless, temporal meaning-character, as a result of the fact that the moments which anticipate the law spheres founded in beauty and which point ultimately towards the completion or fullness of meaning, develop and start to manifest a positive form. This deepening or disclosure of meaning is the dynamic factor in the formation of beauty, since if the aesthetic function is deepened in its meaning, then not only the meaning nucleus but also all its retrocipations share in the disclosure and expansion of meaning. Only now does the law sphere actually develop, only now does it start showing its own, inexhaustible richness and possibilities.

In the investigation of the process of disclosure we are immediately struck by the inter-modal relationship between the aesthetic and the juridical function. In anticipation of the meaning of justice all elements within the meaning of beauty need to be weighed against each other. That the economic retrocipation is thereby also deepened, I discussed more extensively in a previous article, 'Sketch for an Aesthetic Theory based on the Philosophy of the Cosmonomic Idea'. That this anticipation is never complete in itself but points directly towards the pistical meaning and the religious fullness of meaning becomes evident the moment we realize that it is exactly in this respect that non-Christian art (and that is almost all art) clearly falls short. Constantly, too much emphasis is placed on one moment in art at the expense of other moments. Thus in classicism, for example, since this is led by faith in human reason (often in the sense of the mathematical science ideal), the aesthetic-logical is overemphasized. As a result this art is often very cold and uninspiring. In the heyday of Romanticism, on the other hand, when the pistical was more psychologically tinted, people endeavoured to express the 'stirrings of the soul', the psychological movements of feeling. This was then often accompanied by a depreciation of the aesthetic-logical (the composition becomes 'more loose'). As a consequence the art of Wagner, for example, may move us, grip us, overwhelm us, yet often leave us with an unsatisfied feeling after the performance; we have been moved psychologically, but not necessarily aesthetically. In such a case one feels deceived, as if one has been cheated. From this it is clear that the juridical function does not rest in itself but points immediately towards the ethical.

The different objects that are represented in a painting, the different characters in a literary work, and so on, also need to be weighed against each other according to their importance. In more primitive art each detail is equally elaborated upon. Everything is equally important. But given advanced disclosure, all attention will be focused on one point, aesthetically the most important one. Think, for example, of Gustav van der Woestijne's *Crucifixion*. In this painting the attention is not focused on the suffering of Christ, although that is represented, but on his eyes. These eyes demand our attention, our focus is constantly drawn to them, to eyes that say: 'What are you doing? Are you walking past me, who is suffering here, also for you?' These telling, accusing, questioning eyes are aesthetically the focal point of the canvas, and in this way the work obtains its meaning from its content. For 'content' and aesthetic value cannot be separated. Art is always about an 'adequate aesthetic representation' of something. A work of art therefore can never be good only because the content is 'good'. Thus the main character in a story can never be the central point of focus in the story without attention being focused on that character aesthetically as well. Hence it is said that form and content have to be in agreement with each other.

Now we will move on to the ethical anticipation. Here we are immediately confronted with the controversial matter of the relationship between the ethical aspect and the aesthetic aspect. All the arguments that people have advanced to prove that art has nothing to do with ethics show us that beauty and ethics can indeed not be reduced one to the other, that the good and the beautiful are totally different in meaning, that they pertain to different law spheres. Beauty as such can never be ethically good or bad. Yet – and here we find the solution to the problem – this does not mean that a work of art has therefore nothing to do with ethics. As a result of the fact that people regard a work of art as something purely aesthetic and have no eye for its full structural reality, they inevitably end up with such a falsifying conception. Precisely because a work of art functions as a real thing in all law spheres, one may find that it conforms to the norm aesthetically to a certain extent but that one still has to condemn it as a concrete work of art because it is ethically anti-normative.

Till now we have focused on the fact that a work of art has an ethical as well as an aesthetic structure function. The ethical anticipation in the aesthetic sphere is expressed in honesty and sincerity. Thus artists should not act as if they have something to say if that is only so in appearance. It is a lack of (aesthetic) honesty when an artist pretends to be tremendously inspired while actually only playing with empty forms. An artist's work may be clever and, when measured according to the primary norm-structure of the aesthetic sphere, good; nevertheless, that work may also lack the aesthetic sincerity and honesty to make it a truly beautiful, enduringly beautiful thing capable of charming us for more than just a brief first encounter. We sense in such a case that the work has originated from routine and technical skill and not from inspiration. Then it often lacks soul and the work is cold (psychological retrocipation). This is often the cause for the loss in value of the work of artists who take on too many assignments.

Lastly, via justice and love, the aesthetic anticipates faith. We see that in different periods art is led by different 'leitmotivs'. Art needs to find ways to reflect the ideas and ideals of its age. Each era confronts art with the problem of looking for ways to adequately 'conform to its leitmotiv'. Once that problem has been solved, the art of that time is in its mature phase. It is then an adequate medium to express the ideals and beliefs of that period. It can then say with certainty and conviction what people want to express with it. Somewhat later, art often lapses into 'mannerism'; the means of expression become devices and people start to play with the found motifs. After all, the stated problems have been solved and no one has to search and strive any longer. Therefore these mannerist late works of a particular period often lack aesthetic persuasiveness (the 'it is good only in this way and in no other') and often reveal a certain emptiness and hollow gesturing.

When studying the art of a particular period we should always ask ourselves what problem was posed for it, which 'leitmotiv' led its searching and striving. Do people want to copy reality precisely (following the teaching of the classics) as was done at the end of the eighteenth century or are they trying to represent an emotion, the *Sehnsucht*, the mood as in the Romantic period? Or are they trying to express the truths of faith, the dogmas and facts of salvation as in the Middle Ages? Or do they want to present each thing as it is in itself, in all its richness and detail, perhaps embedded in a supernatural world of faith and grace as in the fifteenth-century late Gothic style north of the Alps? Or do they want to express the vital, the normless but also the hopeless, the uncertainty and the anxiety, as well as a 'let yourself go' attitude as in modern art? (Do not forget that Picasso and the Surrealists are real twentieth-century people who are far more authentic symptoms of the times than many neo-schools.)

Mature art has aesthetic strength because it is aesthetically convincing. It can say with great certainty what it wants to say, with honesty, soulfulness and enthusiasm. We must not forget this. As long as artists convincingly reproduce reality as they see it, with great beauty and honesty, with full conviction – since they also express their faith – we can enjoy their work truly aesthetically; of course we may and must not forget that such artists see reality from a specific perspective and that in their art, beauty is guided by a leitmotiv in which belief is expressed in an anticipation of a faith rooted in the contemporary religious community motif. Just as we can admire the depth and breadth of non-Christian philosophers without forgetting that their insight has its roots in an apostate belief and that therefore their view of humanity and reality is unavoidably falsified, so too we can admire non-Christian art, even though we know that this art is necessarily one-sided and does not disclose all the facets that beauty can offer us. On the other hand, a non-Christian aesthetic genius can create art that better complies with the norm than does the work of an incompetent Christian artist.

Science, Aesthetics and Art[128]

Science

Many people today maintain that there really is no such thing as naïve everyday experience but that a theoretical attitude towards reality is the only true one. They claim too that there is no such thing as a non-theoretical attitude to reality, but that in daily life human beings have a certain theory, a so-called naïve realism, that science must thoroughly reject. What happens here is that the matter is turned upside down. Instead of starting with non-theoretical experience of reality as a given and telling us subsequently what science is, i.e. the theoretical mentality, they start from the scientific attitude and try to look for an explanation of the everyday non-theoretical. And in this way they are obliged to ascribe a kind of theory to the latter. The result is that they produce of a theorization of the humanistic world view that humanistic philosophy then penetrates in its popular form. This is also a result of their limitless overestimation of science as the only instrument by which human beings can grasp truth. People came to believe that theoretical thinking was unprejudiced and sovereignly infallible. In this way they deprived humanistic philosophy of the counter-authority which had always obtained for ancient and medieval philosophy in the religious world view of the people or the church. Humanistic philosophy lost the urge towards religious self-criticism and as a result the dogma of *Voraussetzungslosigkeit* ('presuppositionlessness'), the absolute neutrality of theoretical thought as an infallible means to get to know reality, obtained a firm footing.

Some time ago I heard someone say in all seriousness: 'Look, if a number of people are looking at a rainbow and say, "How beautiful," then that is in fact not tenable. It is in fact nonsense what those people are saying, because the rainbow does not really exist.' Now, how did this person arrive at the pronouncement that 'the rainbow does not really exist'? He simply identified reality with its physical aspect. Indeed, physically speaking the rainbow does not exist – it cannot be weighed or measured accurately; according to its physical aspect, the aspect investigated by science, a rainbow is only explicable by the effect of refraction. It was strange that none of the listeners brought any objection to that statement. For the rainbow does really exist. We can see it, and really, it is beautiful. Moreover, in the Old Testament it is a sign of the covenant between God and humankind. This is how a world view allows itself to be deprived of its vitality, without offering the slightest opposition. It loses the awareness of the irreplaceable significance of the naïve attitude towards reality over against the theoretical attitude. It becomes abstract and rigid, loses its down-to-earth character, its proximity to life, and starts to make pronouncements about questions of life and the world from a theoretical distance.[129]

Before we continue, I would like to tell you a story, to which I will refer later in my argument. On the Leidseplein [a public square in Amsterdam] you can buy a cocktail in which a fig is placed. One day a horse arrived on the scene, sat down and ordered that cocktail, saying very particularly that it did not want the fig in it. They brought him the cocktail and the horse downed it in one draught. Now everyone was watching this peculiar sight. The horse looked around for a bit, neighed in a smiling sort of way and suddenly said: 'What's the matter, do you find it so odd that I don't like figs?'

If we apply the above-mentioned ideas to this very modern joke, a few things become clearer, I hope. If I were to tell you that the joke is not real because it only consists of some physical vibrations, you could rightly call me crazy. Some of you will say that the joke obeys a totally different reality. Perhaps a historical reality? Fine, but then I would have to be a historian before I could understand this joke. It is true: 150 years ago this joke would not have been told. There is definitely a historical facet to this joke. But even if you could tell me in great detail the course of development of the history that led to this joke being told, then I still do not know, on account of its history, whether it is a funny one or not. Another person could perhaps ascribe the origin of this kind of joke to a certain economic structure of society. And yet another would have drawn attention to the logical aspect, whether or not it came to expression in this joke. Yes, it is true, the joke as it is being told consists of physical vibrations but, in addition, those vibrations can be received and heard by my ears, and the sounds that I hear do have a linguistic meaning, and those words reproduce a certain logical or illogical thought process. Is it then the case that the joke consists of the sum total of all the facts as mentioned? Woe unto us if that were true, because the awareness that we have of the unity of such a phenomenon would be a mirage, a chimera. And then we would have to be practitioners, even experts in all those various sciences. We would have to unite the results of our various studies, if that were still possible. And only then would we be able to laugh at the joke.

I have gone into such detail because we must break with the overestimation of science as the only instrument with which we can truly get to know reality. It is not true that only science has any right to speak and that the everyday attitude is a theoretical one, and one originating from a false theory that has to be refuted. The problem is rather: How is science possible? We know that in science we work with abstractions. Out of what do we abstract? And what does it mean that we make abstractions? In brief, the answer is this: In science we separate one aspect of reality and abstract it, we look at it individually and investigate it, separated from the concrete coherence in which that aspect was found.

Therefore researchers continually deal with so-called naïve experience. Without that they would not even be able to carry on their work. Imagine naturalists doing a test. They have to base their work on their complete experience of life. For example, if they do a test with crystals, are they not observing real things rather than abstract matters? It is true that the crystals are not visible to the naked eye and that the scientists experience them as strongly disclosed. When they finally express the results of their test in formulas and draw their conclusions, it seems that they have abstracted the physical side from the concrete things. But aestheticians could also have been present at the test. For them it is also very interesting to investigate the beauty of these crystals. They will direct their eyes especially toward the aesthetic aspect of those crystals. I stress this because the task of aestheticians is not limited to researching the beauty of products of human formation or, even more narrowly, to works of art. The beauty of natural objects is also to be included in the aestheticians' field of study.

What then is the real task of science? We already claimed that science cannot be a substitute for everyday experience and that science is by no means the only source of knowledge. The task of science is precisely the disclosure and deepening of naïve experience. However, I do not want to claim that disclosure and deepening can only occur through science. Pre-theoretical experience is focused on the whole of reality and implicitly apprehends all meaning-moments and aspects of it. Science has the task of deepening this experience, of enriching it, of showing it all sorts of things that can be known. Just imagine you are wearing a coat. Someone points out a stain on it that you yourself had not previously noticed. But from that moment you will always see it. The everyday experience of modern people is not the same as that of a Kalahari bushman. Telephones, telegraphs, aeroplanes, gas and electricity are things that belong to the disclosed temporal reality of modern people. These are not theoretical abstractions, but I do not need to go into that again. As long as we perceive these things in their complete structural reality, without deliberately making ourselves theoretically accountable, we have an attitude of naïve experience, even if our experience had to undergo a certain formation in order to be able to live in the modern culturally-disclosed reality. If Kalahari bushmen who have never before seen an aeroplane see one for the first time, they do not grasp the concrete reality of this modern cultural item because they lack the formation and the disclosure of their experiential horizon to do so.

So what is the task of aesthetics, or perhaps more widely, of all science that is concerned with art and beauty? It is obviously the task of disclosing experience, of opening it up to beauty. Thus we speak about the composition of a painting, about consonants and discords, about a seventh and about a tonic chord in music, about economy of means and, in poetry, about alliteration, enjambement (carrying the sense of a poetic line over to the next line), and so on. These are all means the artist uses in the creation of a work of art. The concepts we mentioned are the result of the disclosure of our experience, of which both the artist and the art lover have gained knowledge, but not the Kalahari bushman. And yet, these are not theoretical concepts. An artist is unable to put together a work of art out of purely theoretical concepts. And, given a headful of concepts, we may still not be able to understand the beauty of a concrete work of art. The concepts, discovered by aestheticians over the course of the centuries, have entered into the experience of reality of modern people, although it is true that all people must first, when making their acquaintance with art, learn to see and distinguish these things. I do not mean that they should study aesthetics, but they have to open themselves to art and make use of the treasure of experience that has been collected over the ages. Alongside aesthetics is the science that should investigate the foundations and methods of art history.

So what is the meaning of art history? As the name suggests, it ought to investigate the course of artistic development; it focuses on the historical side of artistic life and works of art. It will also disclose naïve experience. If you are in a museum and see a number of paintings that are properly arranged, each with a name and a date and, moreover, ordered according to their school, time and location, then all that is the result of such disclosure. Anyone who is somewhat interested in art will also know distinctions such as Romanesque, Gothic, Renaissance, Baroque and others, which would not exist without art history. However, it does not require a scientific view and attitude as such in order to see and confirm that a concrete work of art is Gothic.

It is clear that also researchers have to base their work on strongly disclosed, non-theoretical experience. How can one discover something of art-historical importance if one has no solid knowledge of the works of art that have been created over the centuries? One must be a connoisseur. It is also absolutely necessary for aestheticians to be knowledgeable about art; in a certain sense they need an even more comprehensive knowledge than art historians need. The latter can, to some extent, make do with a knowledge of the products of the visual arts, just as music historians first and foremost need to know musical pieces. The aesthetician, by contrast, should be at home in all those fields, and the more thoroughly, the better. I do not care for an aesthetician who is not an art connoisseur.

To return to the task of science, I would like to say that we should not ask for practical usefulness. It is true that people do ask for that in these modern times, now that they are starting to break with humanistic considerations and going to the opposite extreme, which is a complete depreciation of science. The question of usefulness arises most often out of a pragmatic vision. Everything is measured according to usefulness. But what is usefulness? Useful for what? For the pragmatist something is only useful if it is economically useful, and thus indirectly useful for life, life in a biological sense. But others will look at the question of usefulness from a different angle. For example, something is only meaningful if it is socially useful, or historically, or theologically – yes, even the latter can occur. We should not start with the question of usefulness, but with that of calling. Human beings have the calling to investigate all things. And that will definitely have meaning and bear fruit for 'practical' life. We have already illustrated that with respect to art history and aesthetics. I would like to give another example to clarify this. Scientists, who more than a century ago started to investigate the structure of atoms and molecules, could not suspect in any way what meaning this would have for the world later on. I am thinking of the atom bomb. They were not motivated by the question of usefulness in their research, but rather by innate human curiosity that demands an answer to every question.

For us, only our calling can be the justification for our work. The calling comes from God. We get to work as living members of Christ in obedience to God. As a direct result of this, there is a requirement. This requirement is not at all an annoying constraint or a self-imposed restriction. It asks that we take God and his word into account when we do our scientific work.

If we live close to the Scriptures in a healthy way, and are continually aware of the reality of God's work and his intervention in human affairs and history, then we cannot do otherwise but take that into account in our scientific work. If not, we would be keeping a large piece of reality, as we know it by God's grace, outside of consideration. We are not here concerned with lacing our scientific work with Bible texts, and even less with the application of theology. Because theology too is one of the sciences and in no way can teach us the whole truth. Just like all other sciences, theology must have real knowledge of Scripture as its starting point. We are not concerned with the application of theological theories to other disciplines, but with living in obedience to our God in Christ, also in our scientific activity. In science too, there is no neutrality. Even naïve experience is already determined through and through by our particular religious vision of the world, by our world view. Our whole life is saturated by that vision. For example, a Christian may be very sad because of a certain course of events in the church – not as a result of some theoretical topic, but because of something real and concrete. The Christian may also be psychologically very moved by this, while for a non-Christian the same events would appear to be completely incomprehensible and unimportant. All facts are viewed by people from a certain angle and tested by certain norms. Facts 'in themselves' do not exist; they are abstractions. We cannot even observe events in and of themselves. It is true that when we see and learn a list of dates, they remain unrelated facts. But even the selection of dates is already indicative of a certain insight as to what is important for the course of historical development. But by noting down the dates we have only determined what has happened. We are not yet doing history, and we have not yet understood the events in their mutual coherence. For example, what happened during the Renaissance? Did the people take a step towards freedom, and did they gain this freedom by denying all authority above themselves? Or did they free themselves from domination unjustly usurped by the Roman Catholic Church, while departing further from the faith and coming into true freedom only during the Reformation? What about the events in Czechoslovakia in 1948? Was that the victorious march of Communism whereby people were finally liberated, and whereby true society was allowed to break through? Or was it a threatening step in the direction of the West and the end of all human freedom there? And is it a historically necessary event, one bound to come because of a historical constellation being a certain way, so that the future belongs to Communism, which must come? Is it all explicable in terms of economic circumstances and relationships? Or does God have something to do with this, and his judgments on the world? And why does it happen this way? Or does God just allow these things?

All of these questions show how a concrete event is inseparable from the light and the norms by which we see things. Here too we see the validity of Calvin's opening statement in his *Institutes*: 'Man knows the cosmos only insofar as he knows God.' For example, if people see the origin of everything, that out of which everything arises and by which everything is directed, as the stream of life, then this determines their whole vision of the world and of others, their whole awareness of what is and is not allowed, of what is or is not good. Then all of reality is directed to and becomes meaningful only through the purely vital. Or perhaps it is the case that emotions are the source and origin of everything, and we should say with Freud that all religion is nothing but sublimated libido. Or perhaps we should say with historicism that human beings with all their ideas are absorbed in, and are the product of, the course of history. Should we say that laws and norms are only meaningful in a certain period of time, and therefore that what is good today may be wrong tomorrow? Ultimately, on the view of historicism, human being distinguishes itself from animal life in nothing more than the awareness of the inevitability of death. One step further and being human is nothing more than a *Dasein zum Tode* ('existence unto death'), a coming to self-knowledge through fear. We need not go on to show that all this cannot be separated from people's religion and their attitude towards God. When we investigate and confront their systems with concrete reality, we become acquainted with their value, depth and meaning. Systems that are good should be able to really give an account of reality and not contain any absurdities or contradictions.

Finally, and this is really inherent in what we just discussed, we ought to use the word of God to test both the results and the core of the faith and religion out of which these systems arise, in order that we may know what the Spirit has to say about them. For we know that we are better informed by the truth not because we are so clever but because we have come to know the truth by grace. And we know that there is a lot of brokenness and half-heartedness and imperfection in us, for sin is still part of the picture.

Aesthetics

We have determined the place and task of aesthetics as a science that investigates the aesthetic aspect, or beauty, and which gives us the basis for art history. Now we want to turn to the treatment of a specific area of aesthetics.

You are probably all familiar with the fact that in Dooyeweerd's Philosophy of the Cosmonomic Idea there are fourteen so-called 'law spheres'.[130] These law spheres or functions are not mental categories or working hypotheses; they are present as such in a very real manner in the cosmos. They are also known in naïve experience. People have got to know them just by appealing to everyday experience. However, in pre-theoretical experience we do not distinguish them sharply. Naïve experience knows about them but does not work with the methods of abstraction whereby one learns to articulate them sharply. These law spheres are the functions that all things have in common. All things function in all law spheres. In other words, they possess all fourteen functions. You could say that the law spheres constitute the universal in the cosmos, the structures; but things constitute that which is individual. A work of art therefore also operates in all functions. A work of art is not an abstract aesthetic law sphere but a strictly individual thing, which has the distinction of having the aesthetic as its leading or qualifying function. I emphasize this, because insight into this state of affairs can make all sorts of problems transparent. We hope to return to this later.

Let us now have a look at the aesthetic law sphere. As we already noted, all individual things, all structures, function within this law sphere. In other words, all things have beauty. Therefore, after investigating the typical laws of that which is beautiful, it is the task of the aestheticians to account for the manner in which beauty comes to expression in the various structures. For centuries this task has been neglected with respect to societal relations.[131] Our experience in this is as yet very little disclosed and this task is far from easy. Several researchers have been occupied with beauty in the objective structures, somewhat less with the typical beauty of nature but especially with the beauty of human cultural products.

I said just now that all things possess beauty. Perhaps you protested inwardly and said: 'What about all the ugly things?' When I say that all things function in the aesthetic function, then that does not mean that all things are beautiful. There are also ugly things, things whose aesthetic side does not satisfy the norms of beauty. The aesthetic function is a normative function and the rules of beauty are rules of what ought to be. When a thing is ugly it means that its beauty cannot pass the test of the norms of beauty. We need to realize that we can only say that something is ugly, or un-beautiful, if we test it against the norms that are valid for it. If a thing did not function in the aesthetic mode, it would be neither beautiful nor ugly, because it would simply not be confronted by the aesthetic norms. But such a fantasy-thing would fall outside of the coherence of the created world, and can therefore not really exist.

The aesthetic function is therefore a normative function and this means that its norms are applied to human formative activity. On the foundations of civilization's development these norms are given various positive forms in various times, they are positivized in different ways. Here we are dealing with what we call style. Style is the manner in which the aesthetic norms are positivized at a certain time. We hope to return to this subject shortly.

What is the relationship between the various law spheres? We usually express that in two terms: sphere sovereignty and sphere universality. Let us discuss the first. I do not want to engage in a discussion about various objections that have been made, possibly correctly, against the terminology as such. Sphere sovereignty says nothing more than this: the laws that hold in one area (sphere), do not hold as such in another. Therefore, economic laws should not be applied to aesthetic states of affairs, nor should aesthetic laws be applied to the juridical area. It is not right to confuse the symbolic with beauty, historical development or ethical norms with aesthetics, or to apply the norms of one sphere to another. It seems to me that no further elucidation is needed. Although at first sight this seems quite self-evident, sphere sovereignty is often violated. We would like to elucidate this with an example. For about two centuries the leading trend, and especially the one concerned with beauty, was more or less focused psychologically. This is why aesthetics, and especially the experience of beauty, slowly but surely came to be equated with the psychical, with feelings. Due to this certain problems arose. For example, there was the problem of how a painting that illustrates something quite unpleasant, something which people considered repulsive that aroused feelings of disturbance, could yet be beautiful. How is the beauty of a discordant note to be explained? Once we free ourselves from this confusion, the answer is simply this: if such a work of art is beautiful it thus satisfies the aesthetic norms, and the artist by his or her choice of subject, say death or an ugly woman, has created something that just does not please us psychically. He or she can even use this as a means of constituting beauty. In music, for instance, a well-placed dissonance ('well-placed' means it obeys an aesthetic law) can create for us a very special beauty and can also convey something horrible in a moving manner. We need to be especially careful in connection with being repulsed psychically when judging art forms that are foreign to us. For example, to our Western ears, which have been subjected to a totally different education, Chinese music consists of ghastly sounds. For that reason it is impossible for us to give an honest judgment about this music. Only after our hearing has been disclosed for these sounds can we penetrate their aesthetic value and form an accurate judgment.

In this connection I would like to say something about aesthetic judgment. Is it possible for us to give a judgment about something that is absolute and universally valid? Or does such a judgment necessarily remain subjective? What is a true judgment? A true judgment is one that tests the given reality by the norms as they are actually operative, and whose content represents a real state of affairs. Such a universally valid judgment is indeed possible. Of course, what is required is that the person is normal, and hence has a healthy experience of reality, and that the person who judges is disclosed for that which she or he judges. Someone who has never become acquainted with medieval or Chinese art, which I mentioned before, will not be able to give a true judgment because his or her experience and knowledge of the material is too limited to confront it successfully with the norms. A judgment that is true is of necessity also universally valid. For it reflects a state of affairs as it really is. To give a trivial example: say you are crossing Times Square with someone. There is a statue, and your companion insists that he sees not a statue but a piece of bronze. That may be his personal insight, but his judgment is nevertheless wrong, nor even worth any consideration. It is true that people have different characters and inclinations, which means that you can indeed talk about differences in taste. But these do not invalidate a universal judgment. For example, it is possible that someone says: 'I would rather listen to Chopin than to Beethoven', without implying that his judgment has to be that Chopin as artist is the better one. It is remarkable that many people, when talking abstractly, emphasize the strict subjectivity of judgments, whereas in actual practice they do not act this way at all. Is it not true that when a person says that she or he does not like Bach, others quickly point out that she or he is not yet ready for Bach? Do they not revile the vulgar taste of the uneducated population? Do they take seriously the judgment of someone who totally denigrates something that is universally acclaimed as beautiful? If they are made aware of that, they usually appeal to the difference between theory and practice. I wonder what meaning theory has, if it gives so little consideration to reality. By the way, this discrepancy between theory and practice is connected to the foundational idea of humanism. However that may be, when one denies the existence of universally valid judgments, then such things as art history, art criticism and the so-called education of public taste no longer have any meaning at all. Those people we discussed, who do not recognize a universally valid judgment, say that in principle we can never claim anything other than: 'I think this is beautiful or ugly.' But we also say: 'I think', and mean to say that according to our interim judgment something is so, while we leave a place for discussion and revision of our judgment. For even those who recognize universally valid judgments do not have a monopoly on wisdom.

We just spoke a little about the theory of law spheres and expanded somewhat on sphere sovereignty. But sphere sovereignty has no meaning or purpose if we do not take into account its counterpart, namely sphere universality. The various law spheres are not independent of one another but form a coherence. Sphere universality means that the laws of one law sphere return in all others, but then with a totally new meaning, determined and directed by the typical, peculiar character of those other law spheres. We should distinguish two directions. On the one hand, in any particular law sphere all law spheres upon which it is founded return with a new meaning. In other words, this law sphere refers back to all spheres upon which it is founded. On the other hand, this law sphere refers forward to all spheres founded upon it. If we speak about a normative sphere, and we look in the founding direction, then it is clear that these referring elements, called retrocipations, always have to have a positive shape. For, how shall something exist without the foundation upon which it rests? The aesthetic will never exist without style. We already discussed how style was the historical retrocipation within the law sphere of beauty. Similarly aesthetic logic, namely the retrocipation of the beautiful to the logical, has to come to expression. If the various moments of beauty do not stand in an aesthetic-logical connection but relate as loose ends, the aesthetic unity is lost. Retrocipation of a social nature should also always be given a place. When a poet or a painter wants to show us something, to give us an emotion or an impression, we can sympathize with that and understand it, even though we ourselves have not experienced such a thing. If there were no connection between the aesthetic and social law sphere, then that would not be possible. On the other hand, if an artist presents us with such strictly individual visions or nightmares that they will not be understood, an anti-normative and sinful shape is given to this aesthetic moment. We quite often meet with this in modern art.

We now want to discuss 'anticipations'. They are the aesthetic moments that refer to the law spheres that are founded in the aesthetical. By giving form to these moments the aesthetic law sphere becomes disclosed and deepened in meaning. (Disclosure and deepening have a similar meaning here as above, when we discussed science. It always involves an opening, enriching, enlarging of the potencies of what is being disclosed. But here we are concerned with disclosure of the aesthetic function, first of all with disclosure of naïve experience. Some things will become clear from the context.) In a primitive, non-disclosed culture we see that only the primary structure of the law sphere, that is to say, the core of that law sphere with all its retrocipations, has come to positive unfolding. It is very true that in such cultures objects are made that possess beauty and style, but of a rigid, restrictive character. The development of culture has run aground here, and neither development nor disclosure plays any real role. Only when such a primitive culture for one reason or other is broken open and the rigid walls of tradition are demolished can the process of disclosure get going and the anticipatory moments start to unfold and take a positive shape. If the aesthetic function is deepened in its meaning, then all the retrocipations are also deepened in their meaning. We shall elucidate this shortly with some examples. This deepening of beauty, this disclosure and unfolding together form the dynamic factor in the formation of beauty. Beauty can only come to unfolding through this disclosure and deepening. Only because of this is it possible to show beauty's own inexhaustible riches and possibilities.

As the first anticipation we should have a close look at the juridical function, the law sphere of justice. In anticipation to justice all the elements within the aesthetic function must be balanced out against each other. In this way, the meaning of the economic retrocipation for example is deepened. This could be represented with the words: the barring of excess. We see that if art and beauty have not yet been disclosed, the barring of excess is faced with an equality of elements. Once this anticipation is unfolded, then the various moments are no longer simply equal. One will be aesthetically more important than the other. For example, in early medieval art every detail, every element was equally important. Each little part was executed and looked at with equal care and love. If we compare this with one of Rembrandt's works, we see that the various elements are no longer aesthetically equal – the one is much more important than the other, that is, more important aesthetically. And these unequal elements must now be joined together while barring excess. You only have to think of Rembrandt's *Nightwatch* to see this clearly illustrated.

Such an anticipation is never closed in itself, but points beyond itself directly to the following one, here namely the ethical and the pistical anticipation. That this is of such great importance becomes clear when we see that here a major deficiency of non-Christian art manifests itself. In this art, time and again too much emphasis is placed on one moment to the disadvantage of another. For example, in classicist art, because it is led by a faith in human reason, and then often in the sense of a mathematical scientific ideal, the aesthetic-logical is overemphasized.

This is what often makes this art so cold, devoid of apparent inspiration. By contrast, at the time of High Romanticism, when faith had a more psychological tinge, people were seeking to bring to expression, especially in art, the stirrings of the soul, the psychical movements of feeling. That usually went hand-in-hand with a depreciation of the aesthetic-logical. Composition became more free. Wagner's work, for example, overpowers us; it carries us along, it engages us, but often after the performance we have a dissatisfied feeling because we have been seized psychically, not aesthetically. We get the feeling of having been fooled, so that the connection with the ethical function clearly manifests itself. Over against this we see the art of Bach in which complete justice has been done to the various moments. That is what makes this form of art so rich and complete. It always has something to say to us, no matter what mood we are in. That is why the riches of this art are so inexhaustible and of such incomparable, lasting meaning and beauty.

The various objects that are to be rendered in a painting, the various characters in a literary work, must be balanced according to their aesthetic importance. In more primitive art every detail is dealt with equally minutely. Everything is equally important. But with a more disclosed art all attention will be drawn towards one point, the one that is aesthetically the most important. Here I am thinking of Gustav van der Woestijne's *Crucifixion*. Our attention is not concentrated on the suffering of Christ, although this does come to expression, but on his eyes. These eyes again and again draw our attention; our gaze is drawn to these eyes that say: What are you doing? Are you passing me by, the one who is suffering for you? These eloquent, questioning-accusing eyes are the aesthetic point of concentration of the canvas and this is how the painting gains its meaning. For we cannot separate content and aesthetic value. We are always concerned with an adequate aesthetic rendering of something. A work of art can never be good purely and merely because the content is good. In a narrative the main character can never stand centre-stage with respect to the story in and of itself without also having all attention concentrated on that character aesthetically. Content and form must be in agreement with each other.

We should not draw the conclusion from what has been said about this deepening through anticipation that we are dealing here with a kind of evolution theory. Beauty is something that satisfies aesthetic norms and is not dependent on the degree of disclosure of these anticipations. If at a certain time this disclosure is further advanced, it does not mean that solely for this reason all works of art are of a greater quality. That depends on the presence or absence of great artists. Furthermore, it is possible that disclosure during a certain period of time can take on an anti-normative direction. We will return to this shortly.

Now we shall look at the ethical anticipation where we touch on the much-disputed point of the connection between the ethical and the aesthetical. It is true that the many proofs that people have brought to show that art and ethics have nothing to do with each other show that the beautiful and the morally good are not mutually reducible, and that the good and the beautiful are indeed totally different in meaning. In other words, we are dealing with totally different law spheres. It is true, beauty as such can never be ethically good or bad. But, and here we find the solution to the problem, that does not mean that the work of art has nothing to do with ethics. The work of art does not consist of an abstract aesthetic function but functions as a real thing in all law spheres, therefore also in the ethical. A work of art can certainly be good from the abstract-aesthetic point of view, while it has to be rejected on ethical grounds. By the way, this opinion that art and morals have nothing to do with each other is often expressed by those who wish to display all sorts of indecencies under the guise of art. On the other hand, we sometimes read in the critiques of Christians the remark: 'Look, it is a beautiful work, but it cannot be accepted by us.' Then it seems as if the world has something – culture – that we do not possess and that we are not supposed to enjoy. First of all, the critics should make it clear to us – if this is possible and if they see it – that beauty also has suffered under the misguided attitude of the maker. And then, if the work does not stand up ethically or in any other way to the test of critical insight enlightened by Scripture, then not only may we not accept it, but the work itself is not good, and truly not merely because it does not suit our purposes.

Now we get to the real ethical anticipation that comes to expression in aesthetic honesty. An artist should not act as if tremendously inspired if that is only a pretence. He or she should not act as if having much to tell us while just playing with empty forms. In that case the artist's work may be clever. It may even be good when measured by the norms of the aesthetic law sphere in connection with its retrocipating moments only. But it lacks the aesthetic sincerity and honesty which make it a truly, lastingly beautiful thing that will delight us more than just at first acquaintance. We then learn that the work of art originated from technical routine and proficiency, and not from true inspiration. Such works often strike us as cold. This is often the case with the work of artists who have too many commissions. The works of art lose in value and regress.

Finally, the aesthetic points us via the juridical (law) and ethical (love) towards faith. But before we deal with that, we want to make a few remarks.

All our acting, thinking and striving is determined, in the final analysis, by our religion, by our religious attitude towards God. People are religious beings whose total humanity is determined and directed by their religious choice. This choice is made with one's complete personality, in the heart of one's existence, as the Scriptures teach us. This choice can be for God or against God, in obedient submission to or in rebellious apostasy from the Creator and Lord. This religious choice comes to expression in each person's world view and determines if not the what at least the how of his or her actions and behaviour. Religion is not the same as faith. Faith, the pistical, is one of the human functions based, for example, on history. So then we could point out that Abraham, Jeremiah and Paul all had the same religion, the same basic attitude towards God. But their faith was different. Think, for example, of their different attitudes towards the Law, their different knowledge regarding the life, death and resurrection of the Messiah. In this world, which has alienated itself from God, we do not know any such attitude towards life that remains the same through all centuries. We see that in the various time spans of history new and different positive content is given to the apostate direction of human hearts. In other words, we see different religious ground motives operating in the various periods of world history. These religious ground motives always consist of two opposite poles, such as form and matter, nature and grace, nature and freedom. Sometimes the one is dominant, at other times the other. But we will not elaborate on that now. Within one religious attitude there is the possibility of many different faiths. For example, within humanism, which is first and foremost a religion, people can be rationalists or irrationalists, historicists or 'psychologists', individualists or universalists. These terms indicate different contents of faith. However different the humanists are in attitude, and however much they may quarrel among themselves, they know themselves in their heart of hearts to be united because their basic religion is the same.

So we see that in the various periods of history, artists in their artistic activities are driven by their religion, but when looked at functionally their aesthetic activity is governed by their faith. In summary we can formulate that as follows. In the various periods of history, art is guided by different leitmotivs, different ideals. Art has to find ways of expressing what is alive in each period. In each period art has the problem of conforming adequately to its leitmotiv. Especially in transitional times, when one religious ground motive is making way for another, this leads to a difficult struggle for art, to seek new forms. Slowly but surely it has to do away with the old forms and positive norms, which often maintain themselves for quite a long time through strength of tradition. When the problem has been solved, that is, when it has gained an adequate means of expression of the ideals, art is in its mature, classical period. Art can then with certainty and conviction – aesthetic certainty and conviction – express what people want it to say. After that art usually degenerates into mannerism, the means of expression become a manner and people start to play with the motifs that have been found. The problems posed, after all, have been solved. The technique has been mastered for the purpose intended and the materials offer no resistance anymore. There is no need to seek and strive anymore and a kind of fossilization takes place. These manneristic late works from a particular period therefore often lack the aesthetic power of persuasion – the 'this only is the right way and no other' – and they often reveal a certain emptiness and hollow gesture.

We always should ask when we study art of a particular period: What was the problem posed? Which leitmotiv guided its seeking and striving? Did they want to represent reality precisely, whereby they became disciples of the classics, as in the time around 1800? Or, were they seeking to represent emotion and mood, such as *Sehnsucht*, as in Romanticism? Or were they seeking to express the truths of faith in art, to depict the dogmas and facts of salvation, did they try to put something of faith in God and his angelic hosts into art, as in the Middle Ages? Or did they want to represent everything as it is in and of itself in all its riches of detail, inserted perhaps in a supernatural world of faith and grace, as in the fifteenth-century Northern European art? Or did they want to give artistic expression to the vital, the normless, as well as the hopeless, the feeling of 'Let the mountains fall on us,' the insecurity and the fear but also the idea of 'letting yourself go', as in modern art? We will return to this later.

Art

We now come to our final point. Here we pose the question: What, as confessing Christians, should our attitude be towards art? This is not at all an academic question. It is a question that arises in and through the way we live. It is a question that arises out of our proximity to life, not from the seclusion of the study. It is actually part of the more general question, What stake do we have in worldly culture? The direct sub-question is: Is there a Christian culture?

We just said that during any given period all human striving and acting, art, science, social relationships and so on find their ultimate driving force and basis in the religious ground motive. That is where the apostate human heart has formed its own gods – idols which no longer consist of wooden and stone images as in the primitive heathen cultures but which are, in principle, no different from them. The idols of today are ideals and fantasized ideas about the origin of everything. People project something out of which everything arises, a goal or an idea, to which everything has to be directed, through which things receive their meaning, and therefore also through which norms are determined and to which they are bound. It is often difficult to determine how people come to this basic orientation. Most of the time it will be the case that, in order to justify their own deeds and strivings – after all the human heart is crafty – they will engineer their basic ideas in their faith fantasy. In this sense all apostate faith is mythology. But the law and norms they design will often quickly turn against them. Then they become slaves to their own thought objects. That can be the occasion for designing new gods. That is why, behind all religious ground motives in the human heart, these people themselves grimace at us, people who do not want to recognize God and do not want to bend the knee before him or serve him in obedience. Because people no longer know God, they have lost their view of the transcendent. The origin for their thoughts will then always be a deified part of creation. This is why we call these philosophies and systems immanence-philosophy, for its origin, that which gives everything its meaning and existence, is a deified creature. Of course that creature does exist concretely, truly, really, but it is being torn out of its connection with other creatures by the process of deification, and through this all relationships go awry. People subjectively distort the relationships in the cosmos – but God maintains his laws and norms. This results in great tensions, difficulties and contradictions. People are often forced to capitulate to the divine world order, even when they do not want to admit this in their theories. For example, the Leninists after the Revolution in Russia thought that marriage was an unnecessary evil. A few years later they were forced to reinstate it quickly, in order to prevent further disaster and disruptions of life. Of course they did not want to admit it, but they did capitulate to God's will, his ordinances and concrete reality. In theoretical speculations it is possible to defend and maintain just about anything, but here we are concerned with action and with how these theoretical speculations work out in practice. In the historical development of the world we see that humanity falls from one extreme into another in matters of faith, religion and ideas. No extreme can be maintained, so people veer to the opposite extreme. So we see actions and reactions in the history of the world. These themselves call up new consequences of historical causality, whereby new situations are created where people have to adjust their ideas. In this way the generation that follows always bears the consequences of what the previous generation thought and did, or it acts in opposition to it by choosing exactly the opposite standpoint.

What is our place and position in all of this? I do not now want to speak about our task of witnessing and evangelizing but about what our attitude should be regarding this course of development. It is clear that the struggle of the worldly person, a struggle that goes more and more downhill – as we know from the Scriptures and from history – is not our struggle, and we do not need to play too much of a role in it. And yet, we are not independent of other people; we cannot isolate ourselves, even if we wanted to. We would not even succeed by living as hermits in the desert. It is true that we should keep ourselves pure and take care that we do not get tainted by the apostate ideas of our time. But when the world comes to recognize a fault, we may see the good in that new striving and help with that. However, we must watch out that we will not along with the world fall into an opposite fault. We are allowed to rejoice and lend our energy when the world comes to see that science has been overestimated, but we should not start to depreciate science. We will discover to our horror that we have not been free of this overestimation of science either, we who should have discerned it from the start. We are not free from it either and this often manifests itself in a far too great respect for theology. But let us also not under-appreciate the science of theology and regard it of no value. The world has come to see that it has paid too little attention to the lot of the workers, and that makes us ashamed because we see that we have gone along with that much of the time, instead of witnessing against it. We can now go along with these social strivings, but let us not become socialists, who forget all else apart from the workers and the improvement of their lot, and who want to see the so-called ruling class bite the dust.

So, should we build our own Christian culture over against that of the world? Let us be careful here. If we want to build a Christian culture on principle because we think we are strong and have such good principles and such an insight into the status quo, and because we have such good scientific knowledge, then we will surely fail. Our work will crumble in our hands because it is merely man-made religion; we ourselves determine how we should serve God. A Christian culture can grow only when God blesses our work. We only have to do our task and duty obediently. We should start with being faithful in small things and not immediately focus on the so-called important matters of principle while neglecting the small ones. If we are simply faithful and leave the outcome to God, if we first seek his kingdom, then all other things will be added to us. This is our confession, but it has also been confirmed many times in the history of the Netherlands. In the sixteenth century the people returned to God and his word and in the seventeenth century we were blessed with welfare and success in all sorts of areas, and also with national freedom. We became one of the leading nations. Alas, while the warning example of Israel was not heeded, we also suffered decline and corruption. Again, in the nineteenth century the work of the Réveil and of Groen van Prinsterer was blessed in such a way that we soon had a large political party that gained control and has been able to be a great blessing to our people. And now again we see apostasy and the spreading of willfulness and self-righteousness. Therefore, our first task is conversion and reformation and not the building of a Christian culture.

So if we return to the subject of art, we see that a Christian form of art can never originate from considerations of principle. It is clearly not an art laced with Bible texts and the naming of God's name in and out of season. It should not be a matter of reasoned activity this way or that, but a holy compulsion, a feeling of 'We cannot help but do this.' It can grow and will take shape when we start to work very simply, faithful in the small things. But if we think that in this time of apostasy and desertion of God's word we can 'just' start to make Christian art – after all, we have such good principles now – then nothing will come of it. We must follow Christ in this too, and not determine our own way. We must wait and see if he gives us the times and opportunities. Christian art will have to grow: it cannot just be proclaimed. And I firmly believe that we would misunderstand our time if we were to speak seriously about the formation of Christian art, or even more generally, a Christian culture. Of course, theoretically a Christian culture is possible, but that does not answer the question whether it is possible today. On the contrary, the time will come when nothing but a simple witness will remain for us.

I now return to the question we posed at the beginning: What are we to do with art of the world? After all, when we become involved with art, we have to become acqainted with non-Christian art. Artists and works of art that are rightly called Christian are by far the minority. There has been little in the way of Christian art, and what there is has been strongly influenced in form and style by the world, which we therefore must not neglect if we are to have a good grasp of this art.

Let us be thankful that God has allowed beautiful works of art to be made in the history of the world, despite all apostasy and unbelief. And when I say beautiful that also means works that are in agreement with the norm to a large extent. By this I do not mean that apostate faith and religion have not left their mark on works of art from the past. That is generally recognized, not just by us. Art from each period is a pure expression of the spirit of that period, and as such it had great propaganda value for those new ideas, even if it was not at all deliberately conceived as such. We already mentioned that art strives to represent reality with certainty and in an aesthetically convincing way, as seen by people of that period with their particular attitude. As long as an artist succeeds in this and represents reality in a truly beautiful way, we may enjoy it. We may note also that it is the particular attitude that gives it its partiality, as we discussed with the juridical anticipation. We do not need to close our eyes to the fact that in some works of art things are represented that are not in conformity with the law of God. Finally, we can and may not forget that the artist looks at reality in this way or that, has these or those ideals, in conformity with his or her world view. We admire works of art from the aesthetic genius who can sometimes express him or herself in a truly masterly way. Artists who want to make true works of art must subject themselves to the world order so that, no matter how they think about matters, they always still work aesthetically and the result becomes a matter of emphasis, of too much emphasis on certain moments. Indeed, great artists honestly give us their vision with the power of persuasion. A beautiful poem or a splendid piece of prose is more likely to convince us than a deadly dry argument. No, they do not convince us by their inner truth, but by the aesthetic power of what is aesthetically convincing. And precisely for that reason its propaganda power can be so great. Old art, indeed, also the art of the Greeks, of the Middle Ages, of the Renaissance, of the eighteenth century and of Romanticism all have the convincing effect of their aesthetic power governed by the faith that inspired them. We all know and experience that. The way in which a piece of art can reflect the spirit of its time will be clear to you if you conjure up in your mind a Dutch family piece from the eighteenth century, one of those pieces that are sometimes called *babbelstukken* ('chatter pieces'). With one look you see everything, the complete character of that time as you are familiar with it, probably from the book *Sara Burgerhart*. For the people of that time it was perhaps not so clear, they only knew that it agreed with their taste and that they thought it was beautiful. But for us it becomes a symbol of that time, in it we see the people of that time with their view of life. Every object, even the simplest utensil, communicates to us something of the atmosphere and of the surroundings that produced it. Art, especially if somewhat progressive, can effect a tremendously propagandistic power on the contemporary person, even though this power may be impossible to calculate. For us today this art [of bygone times] has lost this power because, although they also see and recognize these things, non-Christians will not automatically be tempted to adhere to the ideas that are advanced. If on occasions they allow themselves to be inspired and guided by them, it is because they have to a certain degree similarly directed goals already. In short, we shall certainly note the attitude towards life of bygone ages through their works of art, but we can and may enjoy them if the art is truly beautiful and enjoyable. It will not harm us; on the contrary, it will enrich us.

I just said that we can enjoy art if it is truly beautiful and enjoyable. Above all, we should stay alert and level-headed. An artist is a human being like all of us, with the difference that he or she has a particular profession. An artist is not a special kind of person, a person who is allowed to do everything and whose every opinion is very important. Not every sketch or scrawl, not every sentence is important just because an artist made it. We must do away with the typical Romantic notion of the artist as a very special, brilliant person who, partly for that reason, is not bound to any law or norm. The artists themselves have often been keen to adopt this idea and have lost their humility. This is also the basis for the status quo of modern art. Aspiring artists are all of the opinion that, just because they are artists, they have the right to receive support and protection, while at the same time asking the highest prices. And they also think they should immediately give a very personal style and mark to their work. Artists should again learn to start very modestly by being a good craftspeople who, if they possess talent or genius, will rise above their colleagues quite naturally to obtain the appreciation through which their work will soon be in demand. And then it will automatically rise in value. Let us not admire artists and put them on a pedestal just because they are artists. But if there is one who deserves to be honoured, then we should honour him or her as a person of talent, a good craftsperson. Yes, and let us also be very sober in this matter.

To return to our subject after this digression, I said that art of a certain time gives expression to the spirit of that time and as such can possess a great propagandistic value. This is also valid for modern art. But contrary to the art of past times we are not so immediately conscious of it and that makes modern art so dangerous. True, there are positive points to be noted. Modern art has taught us to do away with the dogma of naturalism, the concept that the only task of art is to reflect reality as precisely as possible according to outward appearance. Furthermore, the work of style formation has led to a big improvement in industrial design. One only has to think of modern utensils. Stripped of all redundant ornamentation in form and design, they are aesthetically responsible and so help to make our lives pleasant. This comes to expression in the most ordinary objects such as cutlery, glasses, telephones and irons. But the modern world comes to expression far more explicitly in art proper. Most modern artists are very progressive, seen from the development of ideas of the world. Many are very much on the Left, politically, and some are unashamedly communist. A modern collectivism manifests itself here, a universalistic vision of reality. Primitivism – that is, acting as if one were primitive – is also connected with this. They seek their ideal in spontaneous expressions, where all restricting influences of the intellect, culture – the so-called conventional forms – are set aside in order to come to a pure, honest and free creation. They sometimes even learn from children and insane people, as those are free of the restrictions of our customs, conventions and prejudices. They are searching for an immediate expression of human being, passion for life and subconscious life, whereby every norm, law or tradition is perceived to be an annoyance that should be permanently discarded. We do not need to explain further what comes about when people allow uninhibited expression of their deepest instincts and give free rein to their sensual passions. It is not so pretty. In an irrational way every norm that could restrain them is set aside. 'The coming of the lawless one will be in accordance with the work of Satan displayed in all kinds of counterfeit miracles, signs and wonders' (2 Thessalonians 2:9). In the Scriptures this person, the lawless one of the last days, is called the unrighteous one, without restraint or discipline, loveless, more attached to pleasure than to God, foolish. It is thoroughly revolutionary living; no single value or truth has any meaning for them. Whatever stimulates the sensual passions of life is good. For them that is often the only touchstone. And therefore in art also free expression has to be allowed. We limit ourselves here to what we consider to be the most important, vitalistic, pragmatic-surrealistic branch of modern art. The Cubist and abstract directions may differ a great deal from that in theory, but in their inmost being they are very similar.

However it may be, all this modern stuff has one thing in common: nihilistic despair! The norms that people set themselves are seen as completely relative; no one really believes in them. People no longer believe in norms: they have stranded in nihilism, the most extreme consequence of a world without God. Everything has become absurd and meaningless. We come across this again and again: the absurdity and the meaninglessness, the complete despair with nothing to hold on to. Just think of Kafka, Camus, Sartre and many others, also visual artists. Such people who can no longer believe in anything, who consider everything meaningless, are left only with despair and fear, fear for the unknown, for the nothingness that they have wrapped around themselves. This is what we have referred to as the feeling of 'Mountains, fall on us' (with Isaiah 2:21) that grimaces at us in modern art. On the other hand, we must not forget that great modern artists honestly express what lives in them. We should not ask them to give us more conventional art or art that is more to our taste. That would mean asking them to be hypocrites, apart from the question whether they could indeed sound out a different spirit in their work, whatever themes they were to choose. We can only appeal to them to be converted and pray to God to be gracious to them. Of course, a lot more could be said about all of this. I was primarily interested in a general characterization, to give you a feeling of what is going on. Everywhere and always we are surrounded by modernity and we also understand the language of our time very well. Therefore, we do not always notice so quickly what spirit is speaking. Picasso and his disciples, Sartre and his, may perhaps inspire us with fear. Much of modern art is so peculiar that we have to study it for a long time before we can even understand its outward form. The very fact that in Picasso's work every tradition has been crudely broken may mean that it is not so dangerous after all. But the danger is in the more measured expressions such as film, literature, poetry, jokes, in the more accessible forms of our culture. Again, exactly because modernism does not come to such a pronounced expression here, and we as children of our time can easily understand it and therefore fail to perceive the spirit that it expresses, we must take care and not come too quickly to the conclusion that all this will not have any influence on us, and that some of it may be fairly innocent. You have every Christian liberty to become informed about modern expressions of art, but keep your eyes open and do not forget to study the Scriptures well, so that you may know from its light what the Spirit says about it. In this way, you will understand your time and the signs of the times and will not be deceived, for the time will come and now is that, if it were possible, even the elect would be deceived (Mark 13:22).

The Iconic Function[132]

In what follows I shall attempt to summarize in a schematic way the results of my studies in this area. I also hope to use what follows as a working hypothesis for further research. For this reason I will be pleased to receive any edifying critiques, references to further literature or other help.

Already in previous reports and lectures for our circle I have defended my position that the element of 'representation' in a painting or sculpture could be localized in the symbolic function. It has become clear to me that the term 'symbolic function' causes more confusion than clarification. That is the reason why I now propose the term 'iconic'. In this we will be using a term that is current in art-historical circles, but is not so heavily weighted historically.

Thus we can conclude as follows:

In the modality referred to by Professor Dooyeweerd as the 'symbolic' law sphere – whether or not we can maintain this nomenclature is outside the scope of this article, but I think we can – we can distinguish at least two meaning-individulalities, namely, the linguistic – relating to the written and spoken language – and the iconic – relating to pictorial language.

There are iconically qualified structures – namely, those in which this iconic function does not form a modality of a work of art – in the same way that language can be used without being part of a literary work of art. Think of pictorial statistics or of some traffic signs: Caution! Pedestrians. School. High Bridge – indicators, such as a stop sign with a raised hand, as well as warning signs, for example a skull to indicate danger. For the latter, these icons are interchangeable with written signs. Indeed, writing often accompanies them. With the skull there is nearly always a notice saying 'Danger!' But a pictorial statistic can hardly ever be changed into just numbers or words without losing clarity or expressiveness. With instruction-drawings used for the construction of machines, ships or buildings this is totally impossible as it would cause ambiguity and lack of clarity. Iconically qualified structures convey schemas, constructions, designs, warnings in their own iconic way, just as language does it in its own way. The norm of clarity is of primary importance. Here also, we can speak of positivizing.

Thus we can conclude to a similarity between the visual arts and literature, as I have explained,[133] namely, that we should distinguish three structures that are founded in each other: (1) an objective psychological structure, (2) an equally objective iconical structure, and (3) an aesthetically qualified structure.

For example, what is depicted in a painting does not stand primarily in a relationship of exact representation to reality. Only naturalism, which reigned supreme in the visual arts from the Renaissance until the twentieth century had this starting point. If you were to analyse works of art from the time prior to the second half of the nineteenth century, you would, however, often come across elements that are not accurate in a naturalistic sense, that is to say, they are strictly speaking not found like that in real life. It is only in the second half of the nineteenth century that naturalism existed in a consistent manner, resulting in an extreme lowering of quality. It is partly because of this low ebb in the development of art that modern anti-naturalism could arise and gain such a strong foothold. Photography was developed under the influence of this artistic naturalism. In photography we indeed find a mechanically achieved relationship of exact representation that is determined by the objective-psychical aspect.

In each good work of art, however, there are 'misrepresentations' in relation to the given reality which have an iconic meaning. In this way the artist intends to say something, to express something, to reflect on something using pictorial language. This is very clear if you look at art outside of the period of naturalism. It is very enlightening, for example, to read the criticisms of Chinese courtiers on the portrait by a Western painter in the nineteenth century of the empress: in their eyes the portrait is not correct because the cheeks of the empress should have been the same on both sides, that is to say, they rejected the depiction of shadow. The Japanese found the perspective in Western portrayals ridiculous and a disfiguration of reality. Another example would be a really 'apt' caricature, which can never be explained by a naturalistic theory of representation.

The laws that determine the iconic visualization do not have the nature of a relationship of exact representation, which occurs perhaps as rarely as imitations of sounds in the spoken language, such as cuckoo, or other onomatopoeic sounds. The structure of the icon should do no violence to the structure of that which is given in reality. Think of the two drawings out of little Johnny's drawing book. The one is a man with two legs underneath his body, which is correct, clear, and does justice to what is given in reality, even though it is no work of art. The other one, by contrast, has the legs sticking out from the top of the body and is incorrect, even anti-normative, falsifying reality, as it does not honour the given structure.

Keeping these matters in mind, one can do justice much more easily to all kinds of artistic phenomena, such as Expressionism and the like. In this connection, you are invited to compare the works of art dealt with in my article on Altdorfer.[134]

I hope I have not been unclear on account of the concise nature of this article.

Norms for Art and Art Education?[135]

Some time ago a number of people involved in the art education of young people put the following question to me: How can we point our students in the right direction and teach them a view of, say, modern art without imposing our own opinions on them and talking them into accepting a number of norms which they do not really believe? One of the difficulties in bringing art to students lies in the fact that they expect a very definite guidance from the teacher, a positive choice of position, which leads to definite pronouncements: this is ugly and that is beautiful; this is bad and that is good. This problem is the more acute as today's art is often very problematic and does not seem to be beautiful, neither from traditional nor from contemporary points of view. Sometimes the ugly is even a conscious goal. The famous statement by Schierbeek that in our time beauty has burnt her face is true not only from the point of view of the observer but also from that of the artist. In former times, roughly before 1910, art that was not beautiful was considered as unimportant. Today the problem is rather that art which tries to be beautiful hardly receives serious attention, whereas the horrible things of the old and new Dadaists are considered of great importance by most art critics. In short, we live in a time when art is extremely manneristic and in many ways expresses a sense of crisis, of the end of all norms, of decline, a shaking of the pillars on which civilization in former times depended. Over the period of a hundred years the situation has completely altered: a hundred years ago the academicians were 'in' while the young revolutionaries received no attention; today the revolutionaries are 'in' and those who are faithful to tradition or in some way try to make 'normal' art are neglected . So much so that when we visit large exhibitions we sometimes wonder whether we are actually looking at the 'salon' of today, just as dismal, and unimportant as the Salon of the academicians a hundred years ago.

The problem of our time

What we have said so far raises more questions than it answers. But that is precisely the difficulty of our time. It is a problem for everyone who has to talk to people who are not yet 'in', who have not yet 'accepted' the extensive brainwashing of contemporary art propaganda, which aims at undermining any notion of normativity and the certainty that in some way there should be beauty in art. Modern art has an esoteric quality, apparently only understood and appreciated by a relatively small group of initiated. The majority of people, whether they are unartistic folk, students, intellectuals, or simply 'not modern' artists, have questions and are tempted to discard the whole of modern art as a misunderstanding or a kind of spiritual charlatanry or even a conscious deceit. If the number of those who appreciate modern art – the avant-garde art, that is – should increase, we may ask ourselves whether we have not lost something and whether a positive resistance has not been broken down by continual propaganda. The trouble is that this again is a too simple and one-sided a way of posing the problem because the leading modern artists are undeniably serious and honest people with talent – in the sense that in their art they seek to express the truth. The question therefore becomes: Are talent, seriousness and honesty enough? An anarchist can have talent, seriousness and honesty in his endeavours, yet we do not follow him. Perhaps this is an indication, for who still dares to condemn a work by De Sade or dares to interfere with gangs of young people who consciously want to disturb order? Who dares to denounce these people as 'wrong' and not to be taken seriously? Questions like this lead us into the heart of the problems that this article wants to address. Why do we no longer dare to judge? Is it perhaps because we no longer have any norms, or maybe no longer dare to apply them? Or, as educators, no longer dare place them before our children as certainties? Is it because we are afraid that in teaching them thus they may become bourgeois? Are we afraid to give them firm certainties? We realize that these problems are not easy. And if we want to speak meaningfully, we should not avoid the real questions. That is why we want to begin to look deeper into the situation. There must be an answer to the question of why it is so difficult to establish fixed norms. In first instance we will only try to describe.

To avoid misunderstanding we should point out that in some places in this article we have treated modern art rather negatively. It should be clear that we do not want to generalize and denounce all twentieth-century art. The works of Rouault, Feininger, the young Matisse, some works of Picasso, Maillol, Mascherini, Moore and others we will mention later, can be appreciated and sometimes even admired. But in writing this article we concentrate on and have in mind the most extreme modern art, because this is the kind of modern art that calls up the questions and brings our students to sometimes very passionate rejection. So we think of Schwitters, Magritte, Guston, Tobey, Rauschenberg, Fontana, Saura, Bacon, Dubuffet and the like. It is by no means our intention to denounce them as charlatans or dishonest people. On the contrary, with all those who are deeply engaged in this study of modern art, we recognize their talents and their individual greatness. But we do not want to close our eyes to the problems their works raise, especially for those who are teachers and who cannot escape dealing with them.

Norms for art

Why is it so difficult to point out which norms are valid for art? Most likely the eighteenth-century movement which rather conceitedly called itself the Enlightenment is to be blamed. Now light would be brought to the world by human beings, humans with their rational-moral souls.[136] All laws, norms and insights spring from humanity, and all humans are equal. No persons have the right to impose their insights and norms on others. All opinions are equal.[137] This starting point robs every norm of its power. After all, a norm is fixed and valid, even if some people do not want it. But in this system a norm can be at most an agreement to which all voluntarily subject themselves; or a norm could be a rule that immediattely and undoubtedly follows from our humanity itself, thus finding its root in human being, in the subject. Philosophers like Kant have made attempts to formulate the general validity of certain rules in this way, but basically their efforts have been in vain. After all, even if there are only a couple of people who think differently, the validity of the rule is affected and essentially ought to be discarded as worthless.

At the time the results of such thinking were not yet fully felt. Much was still considered as self-evident, many traditions were not yet questioned or were doubted only by the intellectual avant-garde, if at all. But in the twentieth century the results of these ideas have become fully visible, although even today such thinking is still opposed by many. It turned out not to be so easy to overthrow the whole world order and introduce a new subjective order based on human reason. By the way, later on, reason itself was questioned too.

People search for solid ground. They want certainty, and truth. Hence all that is considered to be merely subjective, all that has no general validity, loses its power. Therefore people started to look for certainty in something higher than subjectivity, something that would be inescapably true. This was found in nature, in what is simply given and not open to discussion. Of course there is such a thing as optic delusion and therefore things must be investigated to establish them as indisputable. Thus this certainty came to be based on the natural sciences, and in the course of the years also on those fields of the humanities that operate on the basis of the scientific method established in the natural sciences (economics, sociology, etc.) This positivism, with its one-sided interest in natural laws – of vital interest for people who looked to these for solid ground – was very succesful because it propagated itself with the 'wonders of technology'. Its success was so great that today it makes sense to talk of technocracy. With peculiar side-effects.

We have already mentioned that natural science did not restrict itself to physical or biological nature. It also examined the phenomenon humankind, and found many rules governing it. So many, in fact, that more and more the basic assumption (that all things are equal) seemed to be true. After all, everything is governed by natural law, and on this level humans are essentially the same as stones or animals.[138] One tried to prove this by means of the evolution theory. Human being is only a very complicated mechanism that has developed from matter by a long process of evolution. It is nothing more than other things to be found in nature and as such determined by laws of nature. Inevitably people revolted against this statement as they did not want to lose their freedom (for, curiously enough, the right to freedom was also a slogan of the Enlightenment). Gauguin puts it rather poetically when he speaks of the effect of this positivism on art, namely increased naturalism:

> Primitive art proceeds from the spirit and uses nature. So-called refined art proceeds from the senses and serves nature. Nature is the housemaid of the former and the mistress of the latter, but the housemaid cannot forget her origin and degrades the spirit by allowing him to adore her. This now is how we have fallen into the abominable error of naturalism.[139]

Where would humankind now be able to find their humanity? And their freedom? For people know, and their experience tells them so, that they are free, not determined by the laws of nature, and they are more than what the natural sciences can record about them.

One thing is certain: what is essential and 'higher' to being human should not be scientifically approachable. For science would inevitably rationalize it, dehumanize and kill it by scientific statistics. That is why people in the twentieth century have attempted to find the essence of human being, our humanity, in an existential experience, in 'something higher', something that cannot be explained rationalistically. It is a kind of mysticism that remains strictly subjective, strictly individual, not to be captured in words, for as soon as that were the case, psychology or some other science would again incorporate it in the scientifically known rational reality. Thus alongside technocracy an irrational mysticism (which is dialectically related to it) arises, in which humankind find a deeper experience of their humanity.

The expression of this, the revelation of what is higher, deeper and more essential, becomes pre-eminently the task of art. It must be human, which means opposed to technocracy, positivism, and rationalism. That is why much modern art is technically bad on purpose, because thus it is clear that it is not of the same order as products like cars and washing machines. It also should not be understandable. For then it would fall within the province of reason again, in which case the danger would be immense. It must give a free 'polyinterpretable' (that is, for all to be interpreted in their own way) meaning to the human or the natural.

In any case, norms should not be mentioned. For that would bring us right back into rationalism. Art is purely subjective and it reveals the truth of human being, which lies deeper and is therefore irrational. It is not in any way related to normal reality. It goes beyond that. It is that which is higher. Or, to put it differently, its relation to reality is dialectical, that is, it interprets reality by denying it, or by refusing to attribute any meaning to it, by unmasking it as being inhuman and degrading. Therefore, why still talk about norms? Why talk about art? Art and beauty . . . no! . . . don't talk about that. Beautiful things? Why? Art is religion, mysticism; and the artist is a prophet.[140] Art reveals the real reality, human reality. Reality is not the meaningless world the natural sciences deal with. To be sure, science has discovered the truth about a part of reality, yet in doing so it has robbed humankind of their humanity and thus evoked meaninglessness. So modern art is at one and the same time a denial of positivism – there is no essential truth and certainty to be found in it – and an affirmation of it – that which is human can only be found elsewhere, for what science teaches us is correct and inescapable.

This dialectic is an essential feature of our culture. The effect of it is, and therein lies our difficulty, not only that art cannot be judged according to norms but also that art cannot be regarded as art anymore. Art has become something different: it is religion, expression, art that reveals and philosophizes. Therefore, do not talk about beautiful things. An automobile can be beautiful. Art? Art must be authentic, honest, and based on deep existential experience, which at the same time exposes the meaninglessness of the technocratic reality.

Have we overstated our case? It is possible that not all avant-garde art is like this, at least not completely. But read such journals as *Quadrum* and *Le Vingtième Siècle*, written by those involved in modern art who know it closely and translate the ideas into words.

Beyond words and proof

We would like to mention another difficulty that we face when speaking about norms, particularly for those of us who have to teach. The difficulty lies in the fact that aesthetic norms are valid and are known, but essentially cannot be put into words. They cannot be proved either, if by proved one means asserting them to be scientific and mathematical certainties. For what is typical of norms is that they do apply but that the subject, who stands under the norm and for whom it is valid, can nevertheless neglect it. A norm for example states that one should not steal, yet thousands steal in a brutal or somewhat more refined fashion and this does not immediately threaten their existence. With natural laws, for instance technologically applied, this is not the case. One can prove that a car engine needs gasoline and not water. Try it with water and the thing will not work. But if you make a painting that sets at naught all aesthetic norms the result is nevertheless a painting, though not a beautiful one. And if some want to think it beautiful, important, interesting or in some other way have a positive reaction to it, no one can stop them or forbid them to do so. Discussion about taste is certainly possible, but individuals can deliberately go against the grain.

One can talk about aesthetic and artistic matters in words. For this purpose a great number of words have been developed in the course of years, terms like pictorial and linear, concepts such as tension, rhythm, classical, expressive, and so on. These words express particular aesthetic and artistic qualities and characteristics: a functioning under the norm in a particular manner. However, while analysing one will hit certain boundaries. Sometimes one can only point out that a certain passage is beautiful or another part inferior. If the persons addressed are open to look and understand, they will experience the same thing – or perhaps contradict it if the speaker is wrong – but to put it into words is not possible, let alone to prove it. One has reached the boundary of the sense of beauty, which cannot be further related to something else. Art does refer to the outside world and these references can be put into words: boisterous or frugal refer to aesthetic economy, fierce and intense or restrained and quiet refer to emotional qualities. But beauty is in essence a norm and a possibility which is given us, beyond which no questions can be raised and no words used; one is dealing with the very core of the aesthetic aspect itself. At most one can attempt to say something by other aesthetic means, for instance by poetical comparisons.

But this does not contradict the existence of the norm, even if it reaches beyond our proof and words. It is also not irrational or arbitrary – a matter of taste – even though it is not rational. Beauty is a province of human possibilities and experiences that is peculiar to itself. It is not determined intellectually, nor emotionally or symbolically: it exists in its own way. Not only that which we can grasp with our reason is real. Also what we can experience consciously is real. It is a fallacy that all that cannot be put into words is therefore by necessity unconscious.

We all use norms

If there were no norms, it would be meaningless to talk of art or beauty. Consequently, it is only human that young people ask for certainty and for positive statements, because the knowledge and use of norms is an essential element of our humanity. Students want no vague talk about art: look, it is very important, but you don't have to think it beautiful. Time and again we found that they are dissatisfied with the assertion that modern art is really art but that one should not enquire after beauty or ugliness. What they see, they find ugly and they want to know whether they are right or not. They are open and want to learn. And if they are wrong they want to know the reason why, or at least a way to transcend the situation in which all they can say is strictly subjective. They ask for certainties. And perhaps there are many young people who, as a result of their 'aesthetic education', have turned their backs on all art: it is only a lot of talk anyway and no one can say anything sensible about it. They are right if art criticism is nothing more than a strictly individual reaction to a work of art; then it is poor and not worthwhile to engage oneself in it. And if all talk about art were a strictly individual expression of a strictly individual emotion, why should we trouble someone else with our emotions?

In whichever way we look at it, there will be only a few people, if they exist at all, who really accept the consequences of such a normless point of view. We must not forget that every exhibition is the result of choices and judgments and that each museum presents a selection out of thousands and thousands of high quality works. The choice was made by the museum director and his or her staff. If they choose to show us clumsy works, paintings of no talent or taste, then we critisize them violently. Rightly so. And they cannot afford to keep on doing that, because if they do they will be sent away on the grounds that they are not up to the task. In short, when we talk about art we all use norms, otherwise we would not even know what art was and the distinction between a work of art and any other human or natural thing would fall away.

Why then is it so difficult to make clear what these norms are, apart from the difficulty we already mentioned? We want to point out a number of aspects of this problem.

Historicism

In the course of the nineteenth century historicism came into existence. Historicism is one of the most influential and generally accepted philosophical trends of the twentieth century. It has influenced existentialism and other philosophical schools.[141] In the Anglo-Saxon world historicism has been much less prominent than on the European continent. However, that does not mean that its basic ideas were not active there as well. Historicism teaches that all human ideas, insights, norms and values are historically conditioned and are valid only in a particular period of history. Each period has its own system of norms. In art we call that style.

In fact, one wonders whether anything meaningful can still be said about the past. This is especially important for the art critic, who has to pass judgment on the art of earlier times.

It is clear that historicism can easily lead to an extreme relativism, for from a historical point of view our judgment is necessarily relative and determined by the time in which we live. From this point of view we can say nothing meaningful about art that was made during an earlier period. Unless we take the point of view of Malraux who argues that we must accept this position positively, so that the work of art, regardless of what it meant in the time it was created, means what it means to us now.[142] Moreover, we all know that in any given period a variety of trends often exist side by side, each reflecting its own values and system of norms. Who will say who is right? Historicism leads inevitably to relativism because it recognizes no fixed norms but regards each norm as historically determined and belonging to a specific group. Stated like this, there is indeed little sense in talking about norms. Every time and every group has its own truth. And though one can speak about norms within one's own circle, one has forfeited the right to talk others into accepting them, let alone to impose them on others.

Historicism does try to take into account the situation as it really exists, but it draws the wrong conclusions. First of all, it is clear that we must be careful in our evaluation of art from the past. People of that time often understood these artworks in a different and more direct and refined way, simply because they knew the situation out of which the works stemmed far better than we do. Moreover, the artist of a former period uses a different artistic 'language' that we must learn to understand. We all know how difficult it can be to make students approach a painting of the seventeenth century in a correct way and to teach them how to 'read' the visual elements. Just as we, when we want to read Chaucer, have to acquire some knowledge about Middle English, otherwise we will for instance take a word to be vulgar which at that time was not vulgar at all. The same is true when we look at a miniature from that period.

Here we run into the reality of the norm positivization. Each period has realized the norm in its own way by giving it a positive form or content. But that does not mean that the norm itself is determined by time. For example, in all times it has been wrong to steal. But the punishment will be different in each period and the seriousness of the crime can only be understood within the context of the whole culture of that time. But stealing remains stealing, even if contempories would find no fault with it. In this way we can also form an opinion about the art of an earlier time. We have to be careful that we 'read' a work correctly and take into account the stylistic features peculiar to that time, but if we do, we can come to a right pronouncement about it. If this were not true we might as well stop all art history. We would not even know what were the relevant works of art during a given period in the past. Or, to put it less extremely, we would not be able to understand why a particular work of art met with great admiration and why such a highly esteemed work exerted such a great influence. But whoever stands in front of a Michelangelo understands, even today, why he is so great. Michelangelo's work is artistically excellent and he is considered great, even today. Similar statements can be made about art that is further removed from us in time and geography. We can find beauty in Chinese landscapes of the twelfth century, though we have to add that many details probably escape our attention, as our knowledge of the world from which they stem is very limited and we consequently cannot estimate all their stylistic peculiarities to their full value. All this is not contradicted by the fact that we can make mistakes. We always have to guard against pronouncing an anachronistic judgment. Whoever judges Romanesque art from the point of view of the Renaissance will find nothing but stiff and clumsily formed puppets instead of masterworks which are still famous. The fact that we often go wrong in our judgment of works of art of the past should not discourage us. Besides, the fact that the use of norms with regard to modern art calls up many difficulties, makes clear that the problems lie much deeper. In short, we can say that the people of former times were just like us in that they lived in the same world we live in, even though they spoke a different language and had a different style. In other words, they positivized the norms in another way or gave another positive form to the same norms.

Subjectivism

People often say, on the basis of a typical Expressionist art theory, that art is purely subjective expression. Then it is very difficult to judge a work, because in fact we then are not judging a work of art but a person – one (according to this view) who has, as artist, in her or his own peculiar manner, given expression to her or his feelings or thoughts, a person who actually withdraws from our judgment as non-artists. By the way, if this were true all discourse about art would indeed be senseless unless the critic were as great an artist as the one being judged. Especially those who hold the thesis that art is prophecy have in fact silenced themselves. We cannot judge anymore because we may only listen respectfully. But we know that different artists contradict each other: only if one maintains an extreme relativism can one hold the thesis that artists reveal the truth.

It is obvious that in this way any mention of norms with regard to art becomes difficult. We certainly do not want to deny the personal element in each work of art – or at least in many great works of art. But a work of art is more than a purely individual expression of a purely individual emotion. Artists speak as human beings about human affairs, in an artistic manner, within a normative realm that transcends their individuality, regulates their work and makes it possible at all. Only those who conform themselves to the laws of language can communicate verbally with others. In the same way artists can only create art that others can experience as art if they create art, that is, if they conform themselves to the rules for artistic structures and to aesthetic norms. How could we otherwise distinguish artistic expressions from other personality expressions? People who get red in the face because they are angry also give expression to their feelings, but that does not make them artists, and the possible result, a slanging match, is not a work of art.

Aestheticism

Art is sometimes referred to as autonomous, as being a law unto itself – art for art's sake. If that were true, and actually were realized, then art would only make sense to professionals. The general public would walk past it and perceive themselves as uninitiated and redundant. Indeed, if a work of art might only be judged by its own norms, then it would in fact be a phenomenon standing outside of reality. By the way, it is remarkable that historically 'l'art pour l'art' was not proclaimed in order to make art that would have artistic characteristics only – namely non-figurative art – but to create art that did not conform to ethically and morally accepted norms.

However, almost paradoxically, people have often felt the need to appoint a high function and task to art, starting precisely from the premise that art is autonomous.[143] It should be prophetic, an eye-opener, an expression of personality, the highest spiritual achievement of human being, and so on. It appears as if the further art is removed from, or is in fact separated from, daily life, the more its meaning is exalted. Because of this it becomes even harder for the public to judge art. What is remarkable is that in order to defend art, one appoints a place and task for it which is in actual fact not artistic. Which criteria are then valid? If a work of art is prophetic, how must it be judged? By the prophetic calibre or by the artistic qualities? Can only works of aesthetically high quality be prophetic? Do I not then actually judge a work by other norms than the supposedly autonomous aesthetic criteria?

We could briefly formulate our solution for this problem as follows:[144] the aesthetic or artistic has its own place and meaning that cannot be fulfilled in any other way than through art. Music, sculpture, literature, do not require any other justification than that they are art; they are meaningful as such, and as such have their own task and place in human life. A painting or a novel serves no other end than to be a painting or a novel. They are definitely not required to be prophetic, didactic, moralistic, or whatever, in order to be meaningful. They have their own meaning, and they may also hold or reveal morals or other values, but the real task of art in general is not described by this. One does not solve the problem by claiming the work of art to be autonomous, since one then severs the diverse connections that link a work of art to reality. In the same way, for instance, the state has, as a given structure, its own meaning within the existing social order. But if one absolutizes the state and attempts to declare it autonomous, one either makes the state a meaningless entity without contact with and meaning for social life or one is compelled to make everything state-centred and to let everything within the state that has its own structure fall by the wayside – which is indeed attempted in totalitarian states to the detriment of much human activity – think, for example, of the position of art. Art has its own meaning, but only when it is willing to take its own position within human life and does not sever the thousands of connections that link it to reality. Otherwise it becomes sterile and meaningless.

There is art that is exalted, that fits in the church; there is also art that wants to portray obnoxious things. How do we react towards pederastic art, or cursing art? If we say that its interplay of lines is so very beautiful, it can be true, but then we have probably missed the true meaning, because the artist wanted to say something by those means. It could even be hurtful to the artist to ignore the contents of the work. If you should object that we are now expressing moral or religious judgments, we will not deny this, but one has to realize that the work of art was approached in its aesthetic-artistic nature, and not separately from it. These are difficult problems, we are certainly aware of that.

The fear of the future generations

We want to briefly mention a peculiar phenomenon. How often do we not hear at an exhibition of modern art: 'Watch out that you do not condemn too quickly. Our forefathers didn't honour van Gogh, and look at how foolish they were!' The moral of the story is that if you judge negatively you are just as foolish as your forefathers were, and your descendants will laugh at you. This inferiority complex with respect to our descendants is a poor counsellor. It can only make snobs of those who believe in it. In the first place it is debatable whether the example of van Gogh is properly dealt with. But the moral is certainly destructive. It means that we must accept the most contemporary/avant-garde art, or that which is presented as such, regardless of what the content, meaning or quality of it is. If art is a facet of cultural life, then by its nature it is embedded in today's cultural struggle. Then we cannot accept it just as it is. To state this with a wordplay: they who accept Karel Appel are co-responsible for the future generations. If they are 'appelized' (spiritually speaking), and we evaluate this negatively, we have lost the right to speak. If we hold to the values that Appel represents in an artistic manner, we must be in favour of these ideas and consequently accept our responsibilities as living and cooperating individuals; if the opposite is true, we also need to say so. It could be that the accelerated revolution we are experiencing in life is also caused by people neglecting to think along critically, or to fight at the cultural level, while they relativistically accept everything that is new as valuable simply because it is new. Let us not forget that art belongs to cultural life and is sometimes a powerful factor in the cultural struggle for values and truths.

Art is difficult

A remarkable facet of present-day art life is that people want to apply norms and that they demand that works of art be beautiful. They go to the museum trusting that 'of course beautiful things will be hanging there.' They enter the first room and do not discover anything beautiful. Perhaps unjustly, because they have not learned to understand the new norm-positivization. Perhaps justifiably, because they see works in which 'beauty has burnt her face'. In any case, because they do not experience any beauty they conclude: I do not understand it; modern art is too difficult for me; come on, let's leave. The occasional cynic could then reply that we should let them go; life's revolution will take place anyway, without them, a crowd that doesn't know the law. Others may reply, just as cynically, that it is fine that they leave this art; at least it does not have any influence. In this manner some people think they can make modern art ineffective. But it is exactly this unrecognized danger that is pernicious. If modern art remains uncomprehended it can, in subtle forms and along devious paths, have an even deeper influence. In short, those who take today's culture seriously must attempt to speak normatively about modern art, in order to take a responsible position in the face of the many phenomena. The position that they choose depends on their own spiritual attitude, and on their own cultural ideals. Nevertheless, they have to adhere to norms, with wisdom and insight and knowledge.

It doesn't seem necessary to us to denounce the opinion here that modern art is actually just charlatanry, that is, not art at all and therefore not worth talking about. However, that is the most dangerous opinion that one can have about modern art. And also the most uncompassionate.

The structure of a work of art

We will limit ourselves here, just as we did in the above, mainly to paintings. Not because other arts would in principle be any different, but to exclude all sorts of secondary problems.

Art has structure, or rather, art is determined by a structural law. Without this structure we would not know what art is. This structural law is a norm and, to a certain extent, simultaneously a fact. A norm, in the sense that its being a work of art is recognized and identified by us, even though we think – rightfully or not – that the specific piece is horrible, ugly, imperfect, clumsy, or whatever. It is therefore not only successful works of art that may be called works of art. This would lead to total subjectivism, and lead us into many irrelevant problems. Imagine that an artist who usually creates good works also, for whatever reason, displays a horrible piece under his or her name. Would he or she then suddenly have stopped being an artist? And is it not true that the statement 'it is a horrible piece' is possible only through testing by a norm that is valid for the work of art? How could I otherwise state meaningfully that it is horrible? If it could not be called a work of art anymore, at that same moment I would no longer understand why it would be horrible. What would it then be? A canvas with paint on it? Obviously, because a good piece of art is also that. But we perceive painted canvases differently if they are not works of art. For instance, we have, and rightly so, different requirements for wallpaper, and therefore we have other norms for judging it. Yes, also that it should be beautiful, but then still in a different manner from a painting.

Analysing the structure of a painting falls outside our scope here. It is sufficient that we observe that there must be a physical carrier – say, oilpaint on canvas – that makes the colours and lines visible to us in a specific configuration. These colours and lines have an iconic character and reveal a harmoniously beautiful cohesion. The iconic is just as the aesthetic not reducible to the psychical, just as we already mentioned with regard to the latter. With the iconic we mean the remarkable characteristic of lines and colours to present, represent and mean something. Draw a line on a piece of paper and someone will say: hey, that is the face of so and so. The relationship between that line and that face is iconic – it is meaningless to speak of imitation or copy, for what is the correlation between the face of the person and the line on this piece of paper? In the same way, colour indicates something, makes something clear. We can require a painting to be iconically clear, to express what it wants to say, to speak to us. We will not have to explain any further that the iconic, just as the aesthetic, is a possibility that needs to be positivized, so that different visual languages are possible, all of which can be clear in their own way. The state of affairs in this is similar to that of the aesthetic norm, of which we spoke previously.

The mutual relationship of the things represented in colour and line should be a beautiful, harmonious one. It is questionable whether it makes sense to speak of colour harmony and the beautiful interplay of lines apart from, or while ignoring the matter that is iconically represented. We think that such is possible as a thought experiment, but is hardly realizable in practice. If we see a piece in front of us, we immediately notice a head, a character, a tree, and we recognize their mutual relationship. It is very difficult to abstract from the representation, and we also seldom do it; by which we do not want to say that colour and line configuration as such should not be beautiful together. Obviously, the work of art forms an entity. It is certainly true that in one work the subject matter, or rather the representation, plays a larger role than in the other, and is more serious in content and meaning. But also in the light-hearted sketch of, say, a tree, the fact that the drawing is a tree plays a role in our judgment. We know of course that there is an a-iconic art, i.e. an art in which no recognizable representation is given. In such a case the expression is brought about in an aesthetic manner only, although we need to ask ourselves whether the interplay between colour and line does not iconically express something, even in an abstract manner, though it does not designate or show any object in reality? Does a 'wild' line on an Appel or a Pollock not also speak and express something, say something?[145]

We spoke very candidly about beauty and harmony. We believe that even in our time it still makes sense to talk about these things. We will go even further: if it is said that in our time beauty has burnt her face, then we can only understand this by acknowledging that we are in fact dealing here with a remarkably negative relationship with beauty. Otherwise it would be incomprehensible. If the message of the work of art is that beauty is depraved, destroyed, or ought to be destroyed, that can – almost paradoxically – only happen in the manner of the work of art itself, through a strong expression in the iconic sense and through a direct relationship to the norms of beauty. Furthermore, it is remarkable that even in the work of those who claim not to care for beauty, one can often discover much beauty in the colour, lines, composition, or whatever, nearly against the will of the maker. However it may be, the dilemma that is mentioned here forms a complication, but does not contradict the above.

Art and world view

That people have a world view is inescapable. People have a certain way of understanding and seeing reality. Seeing spiritually obviously has everything to do with seeing visually, for depending on what they consider essential, people will notice certain facets and disregard other elements as unimportant. This will also leave its mark on their art. And if 'their' movement, the group of which they are members, which perhaps even determines the Zeitgeist, has the opportunity to be creative in the formation of a style, then their way of seeing will also influence the visual language and style.

As much as we are inclined to attribute great importance to world view, nevertheless we have to state clearly that its influence will always be relative. After all, it remains a view of reality, the same reality that is viewed by all artists. This is most clear in landscapes. That is precisely why landscape art reveals so well what a specific movement found important and how it viewed reality, sometimes to such an extent that the landscape is practically absent, when the natural environment was judged as not having much consequence. We should never forget that art will always aim to represent what is considered relevant, significant and worth portraying. Especially in the case of landscapes it is clear that the manner of portrayal is very important and can speak volumes. It can make the time-bound human understanding of reality visible.

Reality itself always plays a great role. Styles may come and go, manners of expression can change, accents can be shifted, and yet it will be reality itself in which people live, about which they think, which they experience, and which they portray visually in their art. After all, no one is able to withdraw from existence itself within our human reality. And with 'reality' we are referring not only to trees and people and love and hate but also to God, angels and devils, as well as dogmas, ideas and values – therefore to much more than what can be seen by the eye. And to our fantasy as well. Only in exceptional cases, as in the art of the third quarter of the nineteenth century, do artists as human beings know only the reality that they can see and experience physically – with which we note that this was also a world view.

Reality plays as it were a role in a plurality of ways. As living space, a natural given; as human-spiritual world in which ideals, faith and experiences play a role; and as norm, in particular in art as norm for art, the norm that as tradition (positive norm) is known and understood – and that one sometimes, gradually, under the influence of new concepts, will start to change or renew. In short, reality will be present in the work of art as a given, a point of departure, and as norm on the one hand, and as vision, ideal, faith and insight on the other. Or to put it in yet another way, reality comes to us in a work of art as norm and fact, and as vision and insight. In short, as seeing, understood in two ways.

Reality is not static

In the previous section we spoke about the relationship between the work of art and reality, a very important relationship for our understanding of the work and for the possibility to judge it.

Therefore we would like to think further about reality. We just considered the landscape as an example. That is only relatively static, in terms of being the same at all times. Our landscape, or our 'countryside', is different from that of our distant forefathers. Homes, bridges, afforestation and deforestation, roads and paths belong to the phenotypic landscape, which is altered in history – it is only the jungle and the inaccessible, high mountains that are in a certain sense free from this. And our city environment changes even more distinctly and markedly. The social and 'spiritual' reality changes more deeply still. Also here we have to do with human design and norm positivization in history, with vision and insights, which are realized, at least to a certain extent, in human cultural labour.

How then can we ever understand old art, if its language and style change and the reality with which it was concerned changes and can be even radically different? What if reality itself is no invariable?

Here it applies again that people can do nothing but work and act within the given cosmos. We cannot do as we like. We can only act within the given possibilities, structures and norms, so that we do not have to be afraid of the historical unintelligibility of the past. Style, form, vision, accent, power, insight, positive law, all can change but reality as such remains the same; it changes its appearance only, no matter how far-reaching this may seem to us.

By way of illustration, people are people at all times. Naturally medieval persons expressed their anger in a different manner from sixteenth-century people or moderns, just as Japanese will do it differently from Dutch, and they again differently from Italians. It can also be that anger is aroused by totally different matters. But anger remains anger, and if we are people we can understand anger as anger. Even if we may need to learn to understand its language and manner of expression and the cause of the anger, in all its nuances: anger can mean regretting a lost chance, dissatisfaction with the work of another, irritability out of an exaggerated sense of self-worth, distress because of an assault on those things which were esteemed holy and high, and so on. Love, fear, greed, joy, sorrow, and all else that is typically human with regard to feelings, are timeless, no matter how different the manner of expression may be. The same applies if we start talking about law, state, trade, traffic, celebration and mourning, and so forth. Reality is not static; its appearance changes but reality itself remains the human living space for all times and all people, as given, as possibility, as inescapable reality.

Judging art

Our judgment of art is in direct correlation with our understanding of that art. If we do not understand it, then it is better not to judge it. We are in a position to distinguish clearly what is pornography in our own Western world, since we know the positivized norms with regard to morality and sexuality, but whether a specific work from a distant culture was or is such we can only determine if we 'know more about it' and therefore have learned to understand what was the positivized norm there. Not that it is always easy. Even in our time norm positivization, values and morals shift so quickly that it often proves difficult. The situation is seldom without ambiguities.

Obviously somewhat schematically, and certainly not exhaustively, we would now like to indicate the factors that determine our judgment of a work of art.

To take the most complex situation, if we read a review by someone else of a specific work of art, then, in order to judge both the work of art as well as the review, we will have to take at least six factors into consideration: the reality, the world view and the personality of the artist, the situation in which the work came into being, the work of art itself, and finally the viewer. Six unknowns! How will we ever be able to make a sensible judgment?

Now there is a rule in mathematics that one must have just as many equations as unknowns if one wants to solve the unknowns. A problem such as 'a cyclist drives from A to B, a motorist from B to A – how long will it take for them to meet each other?' is unsolvable. If I specify how fast the cyclist is riding, how fast the car is driving and how far the distance is between A and B, then I can solve the problem. Three givens along with three unknowns make it possible to solve the problem. Algebraically, if there are two unknowns, x and y, one must make two equations, e.g. $x + y = 4$; $x - y = 2$. Then one can solve x and y.

And in a similar way one can judge a work of art, since we have six factors, which are each unknown, but along with it also six 'equations', six relationships.

There is the reality to which the work of art is related; there is also the relationship between the world view and the work of art (and reality). If we know nothing about the artist in question – if he is, for example, a medieval anonymous – then he still expresses himself in the work of art and thereby is in a relationship with the Zeitgeist or the world view of a group. Sometimes we have even more than six 'equations', through which we have possibilities to verify. The most difficult will sometimes be the setting. Was this work an altarpiece, or a cabinet piece, was it made for political propaganda or as a satire? Such questions can sometimes only be answered through a thorough historical knowledge. Fortunately the number of possible settings are in general limited, so that in many cases a subtler judgment with knowledge of the setting will bring very little change.

We will now briefly investigate each of our 'unknowns' individually. We know reality from our human experience, enlarged by our being culture bearers in a specific world. If it concerns a work from the past, then our knowledge and historical experience will also play a role. As example we will take van Eyck's *Eve* from the Altar of the Lamb of God in Ghent. The question that is often asked is: Is this Eve pregnant? Where does the remarkable bodily shape come from? Is it a pure life study, or an idealized image, for example van Eyck's representation of the ideal woman, and/or that of his contemporaries? We understand that the figure is painted very precisely – perhaps it is exactly this that raises these questions. Here our knowledge about reality, our insight into the fashion ideals of the time around 1430 (think of the woman in the double portrait of Portinari and his wife by van Eyck, in which the woman also has a stout abdomen and yet we sense that she presents a very fashionable appearance) and our understanding of the style of van Eyck plays a role (i.e. in the relationship between the work of art and reality). It is true that it remains a difficult problem to give a clear judgment here, but our own being human, added to our experience and historical knowledge, makes a solution possible, at least not necessarily impossible.

The second point concerns the world view. In the first place we must again start from our own humanity and our experience (possibly increased by historical knowledge). It is only a very shallow and ignorant viewer who would say that the *Venus* of Giorgione, the *Danae* of Rembrandt and the *Olympia* of Manet are the same. That the artists' views of reality are totally different becomes clear to us through observation. The reality as seen by the first, who in fact is painting an allegory of love and beauty, is different from that of Manet, who no longer knows such general human ideals. Our judgment of the content of works of art is coloured by our experience – we understand, as human beings and as art viewers, that these works of art have something different to say. And so one could lay a Jan van Goyen next to a Both, from the same period, but so totally different in perception and content. One could then place a Monet next to them. Three worlds, which we do not distinguish only by tracing sources and reading further about what moved these people – in this case, not that easy – but which we experience from the works of art themselves.

Thirdly we consider the artist's personality and talent. Also here our own humanity plays a role, our experience, our knowledge of human nature, and also our reflections about these things. How do we know something about Jan van Eyck? We know that he possessed amazing talent, had a tremendous intellect, could make sharp observations, was obsessed by reality as natural reality, and so forth. We know this only from the works themselves. The sources are silent at these points; his contemporaries tell us little or nothing. Does one really need to know Karel Appel and Corneille personally to be able to say something about the difference in their characters and talents? What if we are dealing with artists from an earlier period? Take Picasso and Braque during their collaboration between 1907 and 1911 – their works speak a language that can be experienced by everyone who wants to look. Because we too are human beings who know people and can understand their actions.

Next there is the work of art itself as it is built up with lines and colours on a surface through a specific composition; it speaks iconically and has aesthetic qualities. We can analyse and understand this in relation to the aspects mentioned, but also in relation to the structural norm of the work of art, which makes judgment possible. That Kirchner did not paint a blue woman but a woman, blue, we 'see' and understand by observation. Kirchner does not need to have written about that himself. Ultimately this understanding rests in our humanity, our existence in this world, undoubtedly coloured by and more fully formed by our being a culture bearer in this Western world. If we abstract from these givens, yes, then it becomes difficult. But also unreal.

Finally we consider the viewer. We get to know the viewer from her or his observations in relation to the work of art, which has a specific relation to the mentioned givens. Winckelmann, Berenson, Wölfflin, Gombrich, and the art critic whose review we read in the newspaper last night, we understand their judgment, we judge along with it, learn from it or feel we have to contradict it because we know what they are talking about and because we recognize and understand their basic assumptions and relationship to the work of art. This is possible because we ourselves know what it is to judge, what it means to think about a work of art, because we ourselves are human and have experience.

It can be that persons judge incorrectly because they did not know or did not judge the setting in which the work originated, the commission, correctly. If one happens to know better, one can understand where and why they made mistakes. The setting is sometimes the hardest to understand and always takes the most study. Why do the Expressionists paint with such bright colours and such 'crude' forms? Without doubt in hefty reaction to nineteenth-century naturalism! They are against a hollow tradition, against shallow, expressionless art that expresses a knowledge only of the 'surface'.

In conclusion we can say that a work of art can be judged, because we as people and as art viewers are truly human and are involved in life as culture bearers. A review of a painting by Raphael, Giotto, van Goyen or an unknown artist is not a wild guess, even though there are no written sources to refer to. We can see the things. Here too we can see in two ways. If there are sources, then that would only mean that we were dealing with the judgments of an art viewer that was contemporary with the artist whose judgment we also have to weigh. Not an impossible task. Indeed, such a viewer can initiate us further into the setting. And that is of great importance. To know whether something is a sketch or a complete work of art can alter our judgment. Think in this respect of deep and lengthy discussion about the 'unfinished' work of Michelangelo. Whether it was one or the other changes our insight into his accomplishment and our view of the works. And they who say that that makes no difference because they find it beautiful either way, are shallow and satisfied with too general a judgment. They make it too easy for themselves, and therefore they will fail to notice many subtle facets of the works of art.

Conclusions

In short, our conclusion from the preceding discussions is that we must judge as human beings, not as an abstract *homo aestheticus*, or as art historians, or as artists, but with our full human being. Just as art can only be meaningful when it is integrated fully into life and, no matter how 'beautiful', loses its significance when it attempts to lead its own life in higher spheres. We also said 'or as artists', because art really should not be made just for artists. If only artists were capable of judging, art would have little meaning, certainly no fraction beyond the borders of the art world. But everyone may and can judge art. The difference comes between a practiced judgment, based on experience, and the judgment of someone who is just beginning to look. The latter must still learn a lot – in the first place, to see. And that is exactly the situation of our students. We also need to teach them to look as human beings. All of education is concerned with the humanity of young people. The point of departure is their humanity, their young and inexperienced humanity. They need to develop competence in judging, they need to gain experience and insight. They will have to do that themselves. It is all too subtle and too richly multi-coloured for us to be able to teach it to them as one teaches a maths sum. But we will have to show them the way. Help them. Pass on something of our experience and our knowledge by which they at least can be guarded from the most obvious misconceptions and dead ends.

That means, taking a stance. The person who does not know how to say more about a painting than 'it is of good quality', or 'the composition is quite beautiful', has in fact revealed his or her lack of real interest. And she or he who finds art so interesting and so cultural, says in fact that art is not important and is removed from life. If art is important and holds real value in society and in human life, then, in the first place, it may demand our personal commitment. After all, the artist did not create the work to be coldly judged by us as to its fashionable requirements, competence and 'cultural' interest. Some works were born staking someone's whole life on it, painted from the depth of the heart, with all fortitude and from deep inner conviction. If artworks are not that, they are routine works, competent and interesting maybe, but in actual fact not worthy of our continuous attention and energy.

The student expects that you will judge as a human being. He or she does not expect you to be a nobody but to be a person with conviction, a point of view, a person with a warm heart who can get angry and can also say why you were so moved or became so enthusiastic, can explain why something had such an impact on you. We may talk about works of art, preferably close to the works of art themselves. As long as it is not an argument for argument's sake – so interesting and so cultural – as long as the real commitment is to find the truth, to say the right thing, in order to do justice to the artist, the work in question, and to the students and ourselves as well.

Besides, we can be sure that our work is never perfect. But it certainly can be meaningful. It is possible to work and deal with art and with students in this way. If it were impossible, it would be better never to speak about art again, no, even stronger, to never look at it again.

After all, the work proves to be humanly impossible to approach and does not really require our reaction, the input of our personality. Basically these things are about love for our neighbour and for the truth, because only these can make us free and make our work meaningful.

Our mathematical example above, of the multiple equations, as many as there were unknowns, would that also apply to modern art? Or is the problem different there? To begin with, if modern art is art, we may treat it as art. If it is not art, then it is interesting but we can leave it to the sociologist, the philosopher of religion or the politician.

But is the element of 'reality' not very small in modern art? Sometimes, indeed, it is very small because the world view relates itself in such a negative manner to reality that it becomes almost totally distorted. But the reference to reality is still always there, in spite of this; it has to be there, because it was made by living human beings. It may be that modern art wants to show up the problems too much, wants to be too intellectual, too 'prophetical' as a result of which its art-ness is affected. People say that beauty's face has been burnt. This is not true. Our concept of beauty, our experience of beauty, our perception of beauty, is mutilated. Ours? Or only that of a specific group, those people whom we as to their philosophy ought to call gnostics; namely those who claim that reality as such is bad and wrong and therefore meaningless, in the same way as some contemporary philosophers claim that death, in essence meaningless, is yet the only meaning-giver in life.

But even then we cannot remain indifferent. We must know 'what lies behind it', why it was done like this, to what extent the work of art is indeed worth looking at and worth discussing, to what extent it betrays talent, intelligence and insight, artistry and content. We can on occasion, maybe more than once, be forced to arrive at a paradoxical judgment: this work has tremendous weight and is made with great talent and insight – and for this reason is so appalling. In such cases it is still so that the better we understand it, and the deeper we can empathize with it, the stronger our experience, the deeper will be our disgust, simultaneously with our admiration that someone knows how to express all of this.

This peculiar situation is in the deepest sense the result of the brokenness of this world. And where in our time everything is turned upside down, all values are questioned, everything is thoroughly thought through and the utmost consequences are drawn, everything is expressed more intensely. If our fellow human beings, intensely passionate and with much intelligence, attempt to speak the truth or to find it, even though this would mean that the senselessness itself must be admitted and the beauty must be burnt, then we may not stand next to it and say 'how interesting'. They are deeply involved. And that requires our response, our reaction.

Therefore our answer to the problem that was the departure point of this article – what are the norms and what will we tell our students – can, basically be very simply this: you, as lecturer, must involve your full personality. If you find that essential values are being attacked, a world view is being unjustly demolished, a false and unworthy 'gospel' is being preached, art is being created that is essentially not art, then say so. Prove it. Let it be seen. Let them think along with you, look with you, understand with you, experience what you see and experience. If along with the ultramodern artist you find that present and former values no longer count, and need to be abandoned, that reality is really meaningless, that it is a good thing that the last leftovers of Christianity are being blown up, then go for it, fight for it, preach it, honour your predecessors. Be accountable for it. Maybe you will discover in the process that there is meaning in your work again, no matter how paradoxical this may seem. In short, be yourself, be human, and fight for the truth.

Art, Aesthetics, and Beauty[146]

Art

The modern schematization of the arts found its form in the eighteenth century. It distinguishes the fine arts from the applied arts or crafts, which without any well-defined boundaries are further differentiated from utensils, artifacts, etc., some of which in our days have once again gained some aesthetic significance under the heading of industrial design. Within the fine arts are distinguished the literary arts (prose and poetry), music, drama, dance, and the visual arts – architecture (which can be called 'fine building', since building as such is often not considered architecture), sculpture, and painting, together with the minor arts, graphics (woodcuts, engravings), and drawing. Under the applied arts are considered (fine) ceramics, tapestry, textiles, gold- and silverware, etc. These distinctions have been created mainly by the collectors of artistic objects, or with them in view, and by the art lover in general. The great tradition in European art, beginning with the Renaissance, looks to the work of art as the individual creation of an artist considered to be in line with poets, philosophers, and in general with men of letters. In other cultures and in the Middle Ages this system was unknown. The arts were considered under the *artes technicae,* distinguished from the seven *artes liberales;* in this system music was placed under mathematics, as a science of tones, and not as the actual music which was played or sung.

What is art? Is it to be defined by quality, or by structure? In the first sense a bad sculpture and a qualitatively poor novel are not art, while in the second they are, even if bad, art. The latter offers advantages, as the normative approach is clearer, and an analysis of the structure of art can be accomplished; so we may treat a painting simply as a painting and not as a work of 'fine art' nor as a nonentity, which would conflict with experienced reality.

Art can be defined as human-made beauty, and as such has much in common with natural beauty (cf. 'Beauty' below). The beauty of a human-made thing is directly related to its meaningfulness, which as such includes its function, but is never identical with it. An ornament is beautiful if it is meaningful, just giving the accent needed at that spot, making the structure and use of the thing it adorns clearer, and adding to life and beauty in the human environment. An abstract (non-figurative) playfulness with forms and colours can be beautiful and as such fascinating if it meaningfully makes the surroundings more agreeable, more humanely liveable, and at the same time serves the purpose of the environment.

But human art can also express something, often by depicting human or natural forms, telling a story, singing about a situation, and so on. This can be very meaningful: in this way we can honour the head of government or hint at a great tradition, as on coins or stamps, or focus attention on that which gives meaning to a certain building, as a picture of the judgment of Solomon in a courtroom (not uncommon in previous centuries). Good quality in the work chosen for such use is a prerequisite; a bad and cheap painting is detrimental to the function just described, and impairs its meaning.

Before our own times works were never made just for the sake of art; art for art's sake is a very recent invention. A work of art was always given a meaningful place in a larger context. Think of the fountains by Bernini on the Piazza Navona in Rome, or the obelisk in the centre of Washington, D.C. Altarpieces, frescos with biblical stories, capitals on the columns of a building, mosaics on the floor, garden sculptures, all were chosen to play a meaningful part in a total human-made structure, in which they fulfil a function – although the fact that they can be taken out of context and still remain beautiful shows that one cannot equate beauty and function. On the other hand, one can only understand the full beauty, for example of a Roman Catholic devotional image if one understands its intended use and considers the way it answers a specific religious need. The function the work of art has to fulfil specifies its form and therefore its beauty. Even cabinet paintings and the little decorative sculptures one has in one's room, which simply add to the humanity and quality of life of our surroundings, have a function that as such can never be equated with utility. In this we see a norm for art: it has to be in place. Marching music and chamber music can both be beautiful, but must be used according to their intended function.

The history of art shows that people have a need for depicting things dear or important to them – the human image itself, the portrait of the beloved, the animals around us, the scenery that is important to us. People depict the things directly around them, sing about things they know, tell tales of the social world in which they live. Or must we rather say that these things, to some extent, become dear to us through depiction? The picture of the window view, the tale about the garden well, along with the objects with which we surround ourselves, such as old cartwheels and old weapons, help build emotional contact with, as well as an intellectual understanding of, those people or natural things around us, our environment. In this way art is related to life. It 'works' in conquering realities for us, opening up their meaning, deepening our love for them, focusing our attention and discovering hitherto unknown aspects. Humanity with little or no (figurative) art is poor in its relation to reality (therefore one finds clean and empty unadorned spaces where mystical people meditate, just because they want to break their contact with reality).

Art in this sense is constituted by reality as such, and, on the other hand, by our vision and understanding of that reality. In the tension between these two lie our appraisal and appreciation of the work of art: we like to see our vision affirmed, but we look for the true, the natural and real. Contrary to most critics today, we do not believe that quality is the ultimate, and maybe even only, criterion for art. Quality is a prerequisite. When this fails, we never come to assess the really important questions. The what, not the how, is the final test; quality is the first norm for art, but its final norm is love and truth, the enriching of human life, the deepening of our vision.

Of course, this content can only become true, real, and expressive in the technical and artistic achievement. One can never sever content from form. The content can only be experienced through the form and the form is created in order to express the content. In a good work of art one can almost say that form and content are an inseparable unity. Content here is more than only subject matter. Subject matter concerns that which the work of art talks about, while content means what it says about it. So a work of art – a song, a poem, a play, a picture – is not Christian by having a biblical theme, but is so only if the understanding of that theme shows a Christian mentality and inspiration. Many biblical stories are depicted in a humanistic or unblibical sense, while a landscape or daily occurrence may be depicted in a Christian way with biblical insight. Only on this level can any discussion of Christian art be fruitful.[147]

Aesthetics

Aesthetics is the philosophical theory of beauty. Since the eighteenth century it was pursued in an almost rigid intellectual way aside from the realities of art, though today it often comes much closer to the practical issues of art theory. Both are thus considered to be very close to art criticism. Of course, the development of these theoretical activities has always been related to the arts as such.

In ancient times two philosophers stand conspicuously at the beginning of aesthetics, defining its problems and offering two different ways of approaching the arts that have had a long and deep influence. Plato defined the artist (speaking of the poet, and not at this stage the artist working in the visual arts) as a seer, someone who through inspiration could see the Ideas and express them. Aristotle, however, defined art as mimesis, in a direct relation to experienced reality; for him the artist must concern himself with matters of probability, necessity, coherence, and completeness. Xenocrates followed Aristotle's art criticism, while the Romans adopted his main ideas in a classicistic art theory. The Neoplatonism of Plotinus, in which 'beauty' (and not in the first place 'art') was a key word, defined the basic ideas for aesthetics and art theory that have been decisive up to the twentieth century, often in the Christianized form of the work of Pseudo-Dionysius the Areopagite.

In the Middle Ages, particularly through the work of Thomas Aquinas, Aristotelianism again became influential. The arts as we conceive them today, however, were considered under the heading of *artes technicae* (technology). The function of the work of art was the first consideration, in which the following notions were considered: the narrative or literal, the moral, the allegorical and the analogical. By the latter was meant the influence of the work on the beholder, its total impact, its motivation and direction, and it is the highest and deepest effect a work of art can accomplish. The universal was experienced in the perception of the work of art, and it was the universal that imparted beauty to it.

At the time of the Renaissance, art theory again reverted to Platonic or Plotinian concepts, in the work of Ficino, Pico della Mirandola, Bembo, Michelangelo and many others. The sixteenth century is rich in art-theoretical treatises, either in the Platonic or, particularly in Venice, a more Aristotelian vein. The latter type became once again the leading factor in the art theories of the seventeenth century, when Agucchi and Bellori very strongly influenced the ideas of Poussin and the French academy. The main trend of these theories, stressing the imitative and the ideal combined with a high regard for the arts of Graeco-Roman antiquity, exerted a deep influence on the following centuries: on Winckelmann, neoclassicism and on nineteenth-century academicism.

Meanwhile, a more subjectivistic stream had gained priority. Its roots lie in the beginnings of the Renaissance, which stressed *disegno* or conceptual form, the creative act of the artist. This moved the emphasis from the work of art to the artist. With Leonardo, the scientific, the intellectual and experimental were introduced. But with the Cartesian influence the aesthetic experience was more and more internalized and made resident in the subject. Taste and rationality, and now also feeling, were determining thought on art. In this time too the first philosophical aesthetics in the modern sense was written by Baumgarten, leading up to Kant who determined later aesthetics through his *Critique of Judgment*, surpassed in influence only by Hegel's aesthetics.

The Romantic movement reacted against the rationalistic ideas, often reverting to Platonic or Plotinian ideas, with great stress, however, on the idea of the artist as a genius, as for instance evidenced by Schlegel, Schopenhauer, and Baudelaire, for whom the main motives were immediacy, intuition, idealization, inspiration and genius, while the symbolic replaced the older concept of allegory. Another line of thought in the nineteenth century is that of positivistic naturalism, particularly in Taine.

In the twentieth century, with Croce, Cassirer, Wittgenstein, and Susanne Langer, the stress is on language and symbolic expression. In addition much aesthetics is influenced by new psychological trends, or by phenomenology.[148]

Beauty

As a concept, beauty stands in a line with truth, love, reality, life, righteousness. Like these concepts it has a wide and all-pervading scope and importance and a tight definition is difficult. These universals however always manifest themselves in the particular, the individual, and the personal.

These concepts, moreover, are closely tied together, so that one cannot speak about one without also touching on the other. Beauty will always exist where there is truth, love, life and reality, while sin, lies, hatred and death (in its deepest sense), being negative realities, are ugly and lead to ugliness. In this sense a marriage, a group of people in their communal relationship, an action or an attitude can be called beautiful when they show love, unity, freedom, and so forth. In a certain respect one can call this 'inner beauty' (cf. 1 Peter 3:3), but it will also express itself in 'outward beauty', visible, perceivable beauty. At this point one can begin to speak about human-made beauty and art.

Beauty is always related to meaning and sense. In this it shows similarity to the beauty of nature, the distinctives of which also apply to beauty in human artifacts and in humanity itself.

Beauty in nature is related to meanings; for example, the tree is beautiful as a tree. Trees are meaningful as such, being created by God. They have a meaningful place in the total structure of nature, together with mountains, rivers, moon, sun and light, weather conditions, other plants and animals, the total ecological structure – humans not excluded. Trees have a definite function in this whole, yet we should not define their meaning in a functional way, for their meaning is more than the sum of their functions. The concrete meaningful reality of the tree in itself, not referring to anything outside the tree – except God – even if always open to all kinds of relationships with other creatures, constitutes its beauty.

The beauty in nature as God's creation shows God's 'style': endless variety and great unity. The unity is the result of the inherent simplicity of nature: for example, all animals have a few particular qualities in common, such as movement, perception (with a limited number of senses), feeding, breeding; some of these they have in common with plants too. Yet, within these basic simple structural patterns an almost endless variety of species, each having a specific place in the total ecological structure, is realized in creation. But the variety does not end here: even within one species each specific individual example is different from the others, not in a random way but in relation to its place and environment, to its own history, its relation to other representatives of the same or other species.

In this way the beauty of nature becomes manifest in its meaningful totality, in which nothing is autonomous or stands by itself, yet everything has its own peculiarity and a meaning transcending the functional aspect.

It is a superabundant beauty, and as such is also open to people; in this God's creative love is discernable (cf. Rom. 1:20), for human beings have been placed in this abundance to use it and to guard it (cf. Gen. 2:15). People discover its possibilities, giving it names and putting it to use. They have to do so in love and in reverence for God's purposes and the meaning of things. Human creativity (as humans in the image of God) lies in the opening up of the natural possibilities by adding to life and, in love, creating new beauties; whereas sin is always detrimental to life, 'wounds' nature, brings death and results in ugliness. Here we can point to the ecological problems of our time. In the same sense people in their relation to others and to God can be creative in realizing harmony, mutual love, care, adding to life and enlarging its freedom, while sin leads to confusion, hatred, takes away freedom, leads to death and ends in ugliness. To act in truth, to do the truth (John 3:20f.), fulfils both life and freedom and inevitably also beauty.

Art, Philosophy and our View of Reality[149]

From the beginning of our history, we human beings have been placed at the centre of the world, God's creation. It was left up to us to orientate ourselves in this world. As such, much is uncertain, since our knowledge and insights are human, relative, disputable, more in the order of hypotheses than certainty. God, in his revelation, has given us the key to understand reality; but much has been left up to us to discover, to study, to try to understand. In this sense, all of our knowledge is *a posteriori*, a reflection on that which is given.

We look, we think and we talk about reality. In a certain sense, talking about reality, or better, discussions of what we humans claim to have seen and understood of reality, are essential to what it is to be human. We offer arguments and consider the correctness of interpretations. The history of thought, in philosophy and literature, and the history of looking, in the fine arts, is in a certain sense the history of humankind. Of course, there is more to it than just talking. We also act: we use the knowledge we have gained, apply it and, if things go well, a contribution is made to an ongoing discussion. In and with all of this, we reshape the contexts, the ways of life and the views we have of reality.

The philosopher and the artist are both engaged with reality. The philosopher speaks through concepts, trying to represent and express his or her thought in order to communicate and contribute to the discussion. The artist gives concrete form to what she or he has een and, hence, contributes to the discussion by means of visual communication that which she or he believes to have seen. Discussion of art is an intrinsic part of art, both verbal and visual discussion – insofar as one artist reacts in image making to what another artist has put forth.

Before proceeding any further, two remarks need to be made. We are limiting ourselves in this article to one facet of the fine arts, namely, to visual communication. All of the other things which could be said about art – and there are many – will not be discussed here. Secondly, it is of course interesting to consider what philosophers have said about art, but that also will not be discussed here.

We see what we know

What interests us right now is the idea that philosophers, regardless of their insight into art, simply cannot think without it. (The connection between philosophy and literature is also much stronger than people usually realize, but neither will we discuss that here.)

For the fact is that philosophers think about reality, that is, about reality as they know and have seen it. But what they and their audience often do not realize is that what they see is not simply something neutrally presented as a given, but the very way they see things is determined in part by the arts. The arts have represented what we can and want to see of reality, in an equally human and fallible way. Artists 'philosophize' about reality in their own manner, namely with eyes and hands; they express themselves not in language and concepts but through visual communication, using images, which in their own way are just as clear and definite as verbal communication in language; both ways of communicating have their own possibilities and limitations.

What we need to realize is that seeing or looking is a complicated activity. Neither is it true that everything we know is solely dependent upon what the senses offer us – as though they were the only contact we have with reality. It is not so that we know what we see, as is often implied in theories of knowledge such as those of Locke and ultimately also of positivism. Sight is not our only source of knowledge. If this were true, the philosopher would in fact be totally dependent on the artist. It is actually quite the reverse: we see what we know.

We see what we know. This also implies that we do not see what we do not know. Take a walk through an orchard with a tree specialist. You see trees, he or she however, sees this kind and that kind and is surprised by a certain tree which differs from the others of its kind; he or she notices the insects at work in the trees. He or she can show and teach us to see, although this is not always easy and it will take time before we are really able to see the things that are obvious to the initiated. All education consists of opening our eyes and learning to see. And this is anything but simple. Our problem is impatience; we want to see too quickly. We are careless about seeing, we constantly overlook things; we are even worse about seeing than we are about listening or reading.

We see what we know. This kind of knowing is determined by tradition – in particular by traditions of seeing – and by our knowledge. Philosophy and science have certainly contributed to the latter. We can put it like this: as long as we know less than the painter and are still learning from her or him, we see what she or he wants us to see, at least if we are patient about looking and trying to see. But if we know more about something than the painter, we can have a discussion with her or him and notice errors. Someone who knows a lot about anatomy sees mistakes in that area. Someone who is knowledgable about the way a sailing boat is rigged, sees where the one who draws a picture of a boat 'didn't see well', probably because she or he does not understand how it works. Hence, seeing and knowing, understanding and seeing, are very closely related.

We see what we know; if this is true, one might then claim we are captives to our limited knowledge and that we can never really see. Neither could we then appeal to philosophy or science, because they too could only deal with reality as they have seen it. As such, all of us would be captives. But the situation is not really like this. For we are capable of seeing creatively. Locke, and many others with him, thought too naïvely about perception and the senses in general. They acted as if seeing were a simple or obvious process; we see what we see, don't we?

Human seeing is anything but mechanical, passive registration. We can see actively. What takes place is not merely 'from outside to inside'; it is just as much 'from inside to outside'. When we see, we use our imagination (*imaginatio*), as the twelfth-century Hugo of St Victor claimed, and so we can discover while we see, creatively grasp that which we missed before. By means of the power of imagination we can discover the structure and context of that which is offered to the senses. Indeed, they who see creatively must exert all their powers of imagination. If, for example, biologists look at a membrane through a microscope, they must use their scientific power of imagination to see something, to discover and to understand what they see. Art historians have to see creatively in order to discover new things in the artworks they have looked at many times already. It is amazing how we sometimes suddenly begin to see something that before has always eluded our notice. In short, when looking, we need the help of a creative imagination in order to discover what there is to be seen. Of course, it is possible for our imagination to run wild and for us to start seeing ghosts. But even this can become the subject of discussion.

This is how we human beings stand in the world, our cosmos – with our eyes and our understanding, our imagination and our creativity. This is how we pursue our quest for discovery. Dead ends are not excluded. Nothing human is certain. But in discussion with others, and with renewed seeing, we move forward and sometimes make progress. To this we can add that at every new point we reach with any degree of certainty or presumed certainty, new perspectives, new facets for seeing, open up. Reality is inexhaustible, infinite in depth, diversity and richness. It will never cease to fascinate us – the Lord be honoured and praised, we should add to this.

Against subjectivism

Now I want to turn to the second main point of this article, namely that there is a great deal that is definite and certain. If this were not so the preceding could give the impression that we are captives to total relativism, that everything is uncertain and endlessly disputable. No. The reality that we think about, which forms the basis for our observation, is a given which as such is definite and certain. Our humanity too, and the structure of our orientation in reality, our ability to think and see, is definite and certain, something given to us by God in our creatureliness.

It is certain that you who read these words at this moment, exist, can read and, moreover, can read (understand) English. Otherwise you could not be reading this, and you would not be reading it. Our reality is full of certainties, which, as such, are the starting point of all our work. Put differently, the world is not in chaos but in order, an order that is not dependent upon us. Even if our thinking is chaotic and confused, this definite reality, which at every moment offers correction to our thinking and seeing, remains there. In it we have a guardian. And this is what the discussion is about, whether or not our thought and our seeing are in agreement with that which is given in reality itself.

Anyone who has understood the above will understand that all of our seeing is coloured. Our own starting point is subjectively determined by our own personal history – where do I come from? What are my life experiences? Our faith, our own personalities too, colour our way of seeing and understanding. But we must not therefore fall into subjectivism. Consider this comparison: coffee, tea, wine and Coca Cola are all drinks, but they differ in appearance and taste. The latter is the essential point. Still, they have a lot in common. Each consists, namely, of more than 90% water. Similarly with people, our insights and our ways of looking at things are coloured differently but there is so much we have in common – our humanity, our being placed in the same cosmos. And therefore we are able to communicate with each other and we don't have to be afraid of getting stuck in a chaos of unintelligible misunderstanding.

No, this is the greatest miracle, a discovery that surprises us anew, time and again, and which we cannot, or can hardly, explain, namely, that there is communication in spite of the fact that our subjectivity has such a profound influence on our understanding and our seeing, on our reality itself: we are able to see and hear what another person wants us to see and hear. In this we can distinguish between what belongs to the 'colour' of another person and what is the real reality that is incorporated in it. Our perception is coloured, also our observation of that which others communicate (which in itself is again determined by its own colour) and still we can discern and acknowledge what is real and what is certain in it. This amazing fact alone, namely that we are able to enjoy substantial communication and are not captive to subjective relativism, means that we can really discuss things and make progress. Therefore it is worthwhile to read the writings of philosophers and listen to them. Looking at a painting is meaningful and so is discovering what it makes visible and, thereby, what becomes evident about reality – perhaps even new things, things we never imagined before.

The question then is which comes first, thinking or seeing, philosophy or the fine arts? It is certainly not the case that it will always be philosophy. Thinking is, indeed, important, but it is thinking about a reality which is seen and which as such is partly determined by the artist who influences our seeing. In this way philosophers and artists need one another. The former can make progress only if the latter has kept up with them. Hence, the question of who is first will frequently be like the problem of the chicken and the egg.

Three examples

Think of the German art of the tenth century, the so-called Ottonian period (named after various Emperors of that name). There never was a more spiritualized art. It contains practically no reality in the sense of anything tangible or visible and insofar as it contains any reality, that is completely spiritual: bodies cast no shadows but are themselves light. This art, in all its expressiveness, is totally inspired by the mysticism of Duns Scotus. This eighth-century theologian-philosopher spiritualized the image of God in man completely: the body itself is perceived as the image of the divine image in the soul. As such, the body is a transparency of a spiritual reality, and this art is the art of those transparencies. There never was an art which could represent the deepest Christian truths so clearly but which at the same time had so little eye for the 'ordinary' beauty of 'ordinary' things, thereby failing to do justice to God's work of creation. Nevertheless, these people were good observers, as we can see from certain details, for instance the representation of flapping sails, the folds of robes, and so on.

In a depiction of Christ of this time we see something we could never see with our everyday eyes, but which is still true; something which is a given in the Bible. We say yes to this view; it is one that is not merely a vision but a glimpse into the essence of things. We see Christ with the book of life on his lap, enthroned in majesty. He is also the source of life and below Christ two deer, panting after water by the stream, are depicted. In his uplifted hands he holds (it could not be taken more literally) the Gospel of Luke, symbolized in the manner of this time by a winged bull. Above it we see Luke, the Gospel writer himself. All around the scene are the Old Testament prophets who have been quoted and who have contributed to the Gospel – their names are written alongside them. Out of all of this, like illumination from a candlestick, comes light – light represented by the hands, which we see coming out of a cloud of witnesses. All around is a decorative bow and many playful birds. A grand, but true, vision; a creation which almost makes us forget the one-sidedness of this way of thinking about reality, in which corporeality and materiality are swallowed up by the spiritual.

A second example dates from the time of the Renaissance, when a new representation of space came into being – by means of perspective. Panofsky has made clear how antiquity had not been acquainted with this because it did not yet see space as being homogenous. Things were, indeed, seen in a kind of perspective, but one represented as discontinuous, and they were not clearly related to each other. Only after the development of art in the high and late Middle Ages, did a new way of portraying space come into being, one which assumed a continuity in which things were related to each other in their 'object' appearance. But at the same time, just because it was now objective, space was de-theologized and came to stand alone in itself. Later, according to Panofsky, and I agree with him, space became rationalized by Descartes and still later, formalized by Kant.[150]

Furthermore, this meant that the space that Kant talked about, and which he elevated to a category, was no longer simply the given one but rather one subdued by humankind in its art. The space Kant talks about can be seen even earlier in a Massaccio or Piero della Francesca. Kant believed that he had seen something, but he was probably not aware that what he had seen was an interpretation – a human accomplishment and as such also disputable.

A third example can be found in the art of our time. The absurd, the chaotic and discontinuous, the breaking down of the old world view is nowhere better seen than in modern art, particularly at the beginning of the twentieth century. It was only later that the philosophers began reflecting on this development. In some cases we can directly point out the influence of this art on philosophy, or at least easily assume the possibility. Sartre was part of a group of people interested in Picasso and intensely engaged with his art. His own early philosophy may have been an attempt to understand the images which brought to expression a new vision of reality. He saw the world like this and then tried to articulate it in his thought.

Modernism is, moreover, the end point in the de-Christianization of Western art and philosopy, a process that began in the Enlightenment. The extent to which Christianity was taken to be dead – to say nothing of the death of God – can be seen in Picasso's drawing of a crucifixion in which everything consists of dead bones. In earlier times, the crucifixion was depicted not so much as a reconstruction of what one would have seen at Golgotha, but as a confession of Christ who suffered for us. This confession itself is presented here as dead.

It is up to us to discover reality once again, to learn to see and understand reality in its createdness and hence also in its openness to heaven. This is the purpose of Christian philosophy. This is also the purpose of a new art, of which we can see the first delicate beginnings here and there. In any case, if we ever hope to experience the reformation for which we pray and work, a revolution which is so deep and which we can never bring about ourselves, but which must be given by God – then it will be necesssary for both our thought and our seeing to be renewed, both philosopy as well as art. The body of Christ cannot be heart only – faith; nor head only – philosophy, science and theology; nor mouth only – preaching; nor arms and legs only – activity. No, it must also have eyes, and for this purpose it needs art. The one simply cannot do without the other. Through all the ages, the Lord has given his church both the one and the other. It is up to us to thankfully receive these gifts and to develop our talents. We need a kind of thinking that never stands still and an artistic activity that can open our eyes to the openness and depth of a reality that is more than an autonomous collection of atoms or living cells, one that contains not only what is human but, beyond this, also so many spiritual principalities and powers.

Book Review: Calvin G. Seerveld, A Turnabout in Aesthetics to Understanding[151]

This review is long overdue. As a friend and colleague, having discussed the problems that are touched upon, densely but succinctly, in this inaugural address, I find it hard to go into Seerveld's argument, as I know how many subtleties, slight differences in matters of terminolgy, background and situation go into assessing it. Yet, we owe him a hearty and friendly welcome, as he is a pupil of Vollenhoven, a friend of our group, and a distinguished member of the staff of that small but versatile Institute of Christian Studies in Toronto. So I had to overcome my reluctance to write about this paper, a reluctance not because I find it wanting but because I'm afraid not to do justice to the riches of its content and its depth of insight. Many things are touched upon – art, aesthetics, Christian life, our position as Christians in the world today, as scholars and as a community, faith, science and scholarship, not as seperate fields but in their relationship, their interdependence and their meaning.

Very rightly Seerveld begins to discuss the problem of aesthetics as such. As a modern philosophical discipline it is rather new – a product of the Age of Reason – dealing with the things that were left over after the rationalization of the sciences and many fields of life, namely art. But thinking about art is much older, and we have to go back to Plato and Aristotle to see how they determined in many ways what people thought about the arts for many centuries, up to the present. Much confusion resulted out of all this: the arts were asked to perform very high tasks but, on the other hand, much of what Seerveld calls 'aesthetic life', the artistic element in everyday existence, was neglected and bypassed and not reconized as of importance. The visual arts only gained a place among the fine arts after the Renaissance, having been considered a craft before that time. Happily, life is stronger than theories and much has been accomplished by artists over the course of time, even if the thinking about it was confused. Yet when art became autonomous and almost religiously high during the Romantic period and afterwards, aesthetic life, in some ways enriched, was also found wanting in many ways – note in particular the low tide of the popular arts, the emergence of kitsch, the loss of taste. Also aesthetics suffered very much and became sometimes really quite academic in the bad sense of the word, as it was often nothing more than an obligatory chapter for philosophers to deal with, even if their knowledge and understanding of it was very poor and they had not followed in any way the development of art history and art criticism.

This is Seerveld's argument told in my own words, and I do agree with his views almost entirely. It is therefore a bit surprising that Seerveld contends that aesthetics is not such a dangerous activity (p.13), and that church councils and, today, the mass media are much more dangerous threats to the arts. I think this is optimism, especially in the light of his own argument. The ideas that motivate the decisions in these powerful bodies are, after all, the result of the thoughts of philosophical aestheticians from Plato and Aristotle to Thomas, Ficino, Baumgarten, Kant, Hegel, Schelling and so on, even if their achievements only reached the world of art, of artists and patrons, in a very diffused and watered-down form. This has often lead to the anti-intellectualism of the artistic world, as Seerveld also rightly notes; any infringement on the freedom of the artist, whose genius should not be hampered, must be shunned. This anti-theory has itself become a theory that is taught, even if not in a formal way, in many art schools.

Seerveld asks for a turnabout in aesthetics, a new approach that tries to do better than this age-old tradition. He wants aesthetics to take into account the aesthetic aspects of all of life, not to bypass the arts but to focus our attention on so many more aesthetic elements in reality. He therefore searches for a new formulation of the modal nuclear meaning in 'suggestion' – or explicitly in a recent lecture held in the United States, in 'allusiveness' – as he is afraid of the term 'beauty', which he feels is too loaded with Platonic or Plotinic content. He hopes to gain an understanding in this way that will open up many new possibilities: 'A low-profile theory which by analytic deeds invites the aesthetic lost in to serve with joy on what is fruitful aesthetically, artistically, and can be blessed.'(p.20.) Even if he is very much aware of the age-old tension between the intellectual and the non-intellectual in our Western tradition, yet he optimistically asks for a leadership of the aesthetician (note, the doxological aesthetician) to lead towards a more rich, imaginative way of life. I do agree with the dream; it is what I have called somewhere the 'liturgy of life', the imaginative form of the free and open content of life. But I deem it utopian.

I see in it a cultural and intellectual optimism that characterizes much of the thinking of our brothers [and sisters] abroad. Seerveld asks for aesthetic theory 'to join its hand in leading God's weak little people in developing a biblically reformed, wide-open christian culture, a minority culture in our post-christian age'.

The question is whether this is feasible. It is the dream of the new earth now. Indeed, something of this creative dream ought to be part of our thrust, but yet I feel that our energies are already completely exhausted if we try not to fall for the idols of our time, to keep ourselves pure and clean, to withstand the indoctrinations, to unmask the heretical or anti-Christian theories, to hunger and thirst for righteousness, humanity and life. Indeed our Lord himself has asked us to be salting salt, i.e. to preserve, to fight the evil and the destructive. Maybe we will have some kind of sub-culture, but I cannot see this as an ideal. And certainly it will be only partially Christian, as we cannot avoid being children of our age.

We are not looking for a utopia in this time. But we can pray, think and work towards a reformation, and if the Lord comes with his Spirit and blesses our work, maybe a renewal can take place. The battle against evil – against the evil spirits in the air – can be turned by the Lord into positive renewal, even if there is no definite promise in that direction. Rather, we are promised persecution and hardship. One thing is certain: if that reformation will ever come, the arts will be part of the total activity. A reformation cannot be the work of theologians, or scholars and scientists, even if they too are needed, but it will encompass all aspects of life. And without the arts it cannot work: the arts will give the form to the new content, and bring it home to the minds of the people. As it was in the time of the Reformation, with its renewal of psalm and hymn singing, and the participation of artists in the illustration of books, in poetry, literature, the visual arts and so forth. Indeed, we do not read much about these things in our history books, not even in the specialized ones, as since the Enlightenment – with its ideal of a neutral science – history has been falsified and the role of faith has been, at least, underrated. Just as Groen van Prinsterer had to rewrite Holland's history, so we have to do something similar in the artistic fields today. Rather than develop a kind of sub-culture view of history, Christians have in this completely followed the views of the world around them, even reinforcing them by focusing all attention on politics and economics or on abstract philosophical thought.

Yet I feel also a little bit optimistic. Seerveld's optimism is at least a strong incentive to work, and so we can hope for much more from his hand and from the people he has influenced.

The booklet itself is produced in line with the ideals he preaches in quite a special way. It gives a good introduction to the thought of an important man and of a positive movement. As such we can recommend it, even if it is not easy reading.

Part II

JAZZ, BLUES AND SPIRITUALS

Preface by Hans Rookmaaker to the First Edition[152]

This book is an attempt to give as complete a picture as possible of developments in black music, past and present, in the USA. I have tried to explain the origin of new genres, the circumstances and reasons behind such developments, and also the comparative development of the different types of music, how they affected each other, degenerated or flourished. Besides the history of jazz music I have also focused on Negro spirituals and gospel music. Considering recent developments in this area it seems strange that relatively little has been written on this subject so far.

I hope that this book will provide more insight into the spiritual background and qualitative differences of the various genres. Perhaps it will contribute to answering the many questions raised by pseudo-jazz, a poor-quality entertainment music, but also by modern jazz, which often boasts high quality but an existential spirit.

One significant drawback of any writing on the subject of music is that the audience cannot listen to the pieces in question. I have endeavoured to overcome that problem by referring as much as possible to records (cassettes, etc.) that are still available [moreover, an updated discography has been included on p. 312]. Musical notation would be of little use since it would not do justice to the style of rendition, to the typical accents and timbres. In many cases the notes would be counterfeit anyway, since they would inevitably be the victims of westernization.

H.R.R.
Leiden, 1960

Acknowledgments to the First Edition

Here I would like to thank the many friends and acquaintances who have helped me in so many different ways. I will not mention them by all name for fear of forgetting someone, but I have to make an exception for Mrs M.H.L. Boom-Sybrandi, who made available her late son's study of the blues which was unfortunately never published.

I must also thank the following people and organizations for helping with photographic material and copyrighting: Mr R. Blesh (from whose book *Shining Trumpets* the photographs of the Superior Band, Ma Rainey, Bunk Johnson's Band and Jelly Roll Morton were taken); H. Courlander (photograph of Doc Reed and copyright of songs by Doc Reed, Richard Amerson and one of the children's verses); W.L. Grossman; Alan Lomax (copyright for extracts from Mr Jelly Roll [Cassel & Co., 1952, pages 64–109], copyright for 'Whoa black', 'Jumpin' Judy', 'No more, my Lord', 'John Henry', which were collected, edited and published, and who holds exclusive copyright; the songs 'Ain't no more cane', 'Here, Rattler, here', 'Do Lord, remember me' were published by the Library of Congress and taken from *American Ballads and Folk Songs* (MacMillan, 1934, copyright John A. and Alan Lomax); the copyright for 'Roll 'im on down' was from David Pryor and Alan Lomax; F. Ramsey Jr. (photographs Of Jack Wimes, Scott and Celeste Dunbar, the Starlight Gospel Singers and the Alabama Skiffle Band, and also songs taken from the Folkways *Music from the South* series); Vogue record company (for copyright of Big Bill Broonzy's 'Black, brown and white'); Philips Phonographische Industrie, Baarn (for the photographs of Mahalia Jackson and Bunk Johnson, and for helping deal with the question of copyrights, especially Mr. H. van Baaren who has assisted me in all sorts of ways); United States Information Service (photographs of the Kid Ory Band and from the blacks church); WDIA Radio Station, Memphis, Tennessee (photograph of the Spirit of Memphis Quartet); Peacock Records Inc. (photo of the Dixie Hummingbirds); Decca Record Co., London (photo of Rosetta Tharpe and permission to quote two of her songs); Rinehart & Co. Inc. (for permission to quote from N. Shapiro & N. Hentof's *Heah Me Talkin' To Ya*); Cassell & Co., London (for mediating on the issue of copyright) and A.A. Knopf's Publishing Co. Inc. (for the same). Finally, rights were obtained from *Life* (photograph of Gillespie) and Ed Basart (rights for publication of texts from 'Out of the depth' and 'I'm going to move up a little higher').

The photographs of the chain gang by Doris Ullman and several other photographs were taken from Richard Wright's *Twelve Million Black Voices* (New York, 1941).

H.R.R., 1960

1
Origins

African music

'Orin Muritali Alhaji'

Africa, the land of rhythm, the land where 'the gods speak through the drums' is the creed. You would be hard pressed to find such a diversity and sophistication of rhythm elsewhere. To the uninitiated, African music is an almost indecipherable pattern of rhythmic sound, frequently evolving from a large number of rhythms of different character and nature, played simultaneously on heavier and lighter drums and other percussion and plucked instruments.

Is this music primitive? That depends on the definition of primitive. Performing this music is certainly no mean feat. It requires knowledge and skill. Some would describe it as the voice of primitive humanity – an unrestrained human spirit, unspoilt by civilization. But even without the testimony of the Bible, it would still have to be proved that this art is more direct, more spontaneous, more authentic and purer than that of Western Europe. The Africans have their own culture, which may in a sense be regarded as primitive. However, 'primitive' in this case refers not to origin or virginity but more to paralysis, a deadlock, a closing of the route to development and progress. Here 'primitive' also refers to little people in an awesome world – frightened mortals amidst the incomprehensible forces of nature, threatened by demons, spirits and mysterious powers, sometimes products of the religious imagination, sometimes real, and certainly evil.

The multifarious and complex rhythmic patterns cannot be said to express joy. Like magic it often evokes hostile gods and demonic forces. It incites a trance to allay fear or to overpower the hostile forces. African rhythms can often be compared with the masks used by the indigenous peoples to disguise themselves during religious ceremonies, to repel, summon or tame powers. They show us how pagans have lost positive touch with creation, paving the way for fear and alienation.

The rhythms are undeniably characteristic of Africa, and also of the Dahomeys and Yorubas who live on the Gold Coast of West Africa, but that does not mean that we have exhausted the subject of their music: indeed, it is more closely related to ours than we may realize. They have developed their rhythms further than Western Europeans have, who since the Middle Ages have paid more attention to harmony, to the sounding together of different notes. Still, African and Western music are undeniably similar in many ways: in the scales used, in the musical approach, in the nature of the melody. We do not know whether this can be attributed to the influence of those blacks who occupied an important place in the court chapel of the Egyptian pharaoh (and which we see portrayed in many murals) or whether there are other factors involved. But those who listen will certainly discover that African music is more closely related to Western European than to Indian, Chinese or Arabian music, for example. Listen to 'Orin Muritali Alhaji',[153] a solemn song of the Yorubas of Nigeria, one of the highest black cultures before the arrival of the Europeans. We hear the polyrhythmic sound of the drums as the foundation, the melody sung by a male-voice choir. If we listen to the royal drums of the Abatusi – possibly the most impressive of pure rhythms – let us not forget that the girls of this tribe from the Congo can sing very melodically whilst clapping their hands in accompaniment.[154]

White folk music

'Blow the man down'

Since the Europeans settled in America, they have regarded it as their own, to do with as they please. When its indigenous population did not prove to be as subservient as required, slaves were quickly sought and imported. Murderous battles between African tribes supplied the slaves – prisoners of war – who were sold to the slave-traders, who in turn disposed of them in the New World while pocketing a tidy sum. The Spanish slave-owners preferred Yorubas, the French opted for Dahomeys, while the English were partial to Ashantis.

It goes without saying that the slave-traders were no gentlemen, and that the quality of their ware was of little concern to them. As long as enough were imported, alive, to secure a decent margin – that was all that mattered. Their victims, spoils of war from the neighbouring black tribes, had already been stripped of anything of value before they were sold, so we can be sure that they took nothing with them to their new destination – at least nothing tangible or portable. What lives in a person's mind is less easily displaced. These people took their music, their religion, their views with them – invisible but nonetheless present.

En route and on arrival the slaves were immediately confronted with Western culture. They were certainly subjected to the crudest and least pleasant side, but they were also introduced to its music, shanties and possibly even psalms. One of those shanties was 'Blow the man down'. Although it originated in England, it was often sung by American sailors. It is actually a work song, sung whilst reeling in the anchor chain. The song has eight beats to a bar and includes a chorus-like stanza:

> Oh, blow the man down, bullies, blow the man down,
> To me way, aye, blow the man down.
> Oh, blow the man down, bullies, blow him right down,
> Give me some time to blow the man down.[155]

This tune can be traced to the Bahamas where it is sung, in almost identical form, by the black fishermen as they haul their boats up onto the sand for the low season. The recorded version allows us to hear what fantastic singers they are:

> So pull 'im along,
> Well, we pull 'im along,
> Hey, aye, pull 'im along,
> Now we pull 'im along from this old shipyard,
> Give me some time to roll 'im along.[156]

African music in South America

'Jesha for Oshun

The blacks who were slaves to the Spanish or French in South or Central America or on the large islands in the Gulf of Mexico seldom saw their own bosses. They lived elsewhere, leaving the supervision to a few overseers. The slaves worked on the plantations, which were often large, and as long as they worked there was no need for their owners to bother about them. Their religion, their music, their lives was of no interest to their masters. If missionaries wanted to evangelize them, that was fine.

Since they had arrived in a Roman Catholic country the blacks became mainly Catholic, but nowhere has the principle of mission, of christianization by the simple renaming of pagan religious customs, been so avenged. These people did become Christians, but they were often unaware of the basic principles of the gospel. This led to a range of mergers. A Roman Catholic saint might be likened to an African god. The Dahomey god Legba, protector of crossroads, might be likened to St Antony, for example. Both were portrayed as old men with weathered faces. African religion sometimes existed unashamedly alongside the Roman beliefs.

We can hear pure African sounds in the former Spanish and French colonies; not only work songs, but also cult music, such as the song of the Brazilian, 'Jesha cult followers, which is a call to Oshun, the goddess of Pure Water.[157] This sort of song can also be heard on Haiti. There the god Legba is evoked in pure African style. The drums form a complicated, repetitively rhythmical pattern, whilst the solemn melody is sung by the priestess and all the believers alternately.[158] The alternating solo call and group response is typically African. We call it responsive song because it has the character of a game, of question and answer.

The blacks also became familiar with the music of their Spanish or French owners, depending on which country they ended up in. Some of the European folk songs were adopted in their original form, and some became hybrids. This is apparent on Haiti nowadays where the meringue,[159] French in character and related to the chanson, can be heard. On Cuba the habanera, which is almost purely Spanish, and the guaracha, which is influenced only slightly by African rhythms, are performed alongside the rumba, conga, son, etc. These dances, which are characterized by varying rhythms, have a stronger African definition. The more African the music, the more drums and percussion dominate; the more European the music, the more the percussion is replaced by instruments like the piano or guitar.

African-American work songs in the USA

'No more, my Lord'

Things progressed very differently in North America. The plantations were smaller there and slave-owners were less indifferent towards their slaves. Because fewer people worked on the plantations and the plantation owners lived there and were in charge, there was a much closer bond between slave-owner and slave. This was particularly evident in the case of domestic slaves – servants. The largely Protestant slave-owners were of English descent and, in order to defend their practises, they argued that the heathen slaves must be rescued from the dark realms of idolatry and brought to the true Light of the gospel. Indeed, it seems that efforts were made in that direction and that slavery in North America during the seventeenth and eighteenth centuries, without wishing to idealize it, was not necessarily an unbearable lot. Pagan religion has consequently all but died out in North America. It is still evident in superstition, which stubbornly manifests itself in voodoo, as a kind of degenerated remnant of paganism, just as folklore and superstition live on in old myths in our Western culture. The disappearance of the African religions meant that their rhythm, inextricably linked to the exorcism and invocation of gods and powers, also lost its meaning. Black American music was therefore always based on a simple rhythm, while a number of characteristics of African-style music only survived in a new form.

The nineteenth century saw the import of thousands of blacks and the slave trade assumed a much harder, less compassionate character. And even though slavery was abolished more than a century ago, there are still cases of black convicts carrying out forced labour in penal colonies [in the 1950s] in similar conditions to those of the days of slavery. It was only in the mid-1940s that things began to improve. These colonies have been home to songs of a similar character to the ones heard more than a century ago.

Besides blues and spirituals, which we will come to later, it is work songs that we most often hear in the colonies. The blacks worked there in shifts called chain gangs, supervised by a captain. While they were working they sang songs to help lighten the labour. The chopping of wood, hewing of rock, cutting of sugarcane, harvesting of cotton was accompanied by music strongly reminiscent of Africa. The rhythm was not provided by drums but was much simpler of character – the sound of the axe or the pickaxe. There is always a precentor, a convict like the others, but one who can sing well and has a wide repertoire, while the rest sing the 'response' together. This is another example of responsive song. The melodies are sometimes exuberant, frequently solemn, but always musical and interesting, each with its own unmistakable beauty. Here is one such song sung in the Mississippi State Penitentiary during work on the great cotton plantation in the Yazoo Delta:[160]

> *No more, my Lord, no more, my Lord,*
> *Lord, I'll never turn back no more.*

Precentor:
> I found in Him a restin' place
> And He has made me glad.
> *No more, my Lord, no more, my Lord,*
> *Lord, I'll never turn back no more.*

Precentor:
> Jesus, the Man I am looking for,
> Can you tell me where He is gone.
> *No more, my Lord, no more, my Lord,*
> *Lord, I'll never turn back no more.*

Another group would sing the next, more exuberant responsive song as a full ensemble, though the precentor's voice is still clearly audible above the rest:

> O well it's Jumpin' Judy
> O well it's Jumpin' Judy,
> Boys she was a mighty fine gal.
> You catch the Illinois Central,
> You catch the Illinois Central,
> Baby, go to Kankakee. [This expresses the desire to go north.]
>
> O well, and yonder comes old Rosie,
> O well, and yonder comes old Rosie,
> Baby, how in the world do you know.
> O well, I know her by her apron,O well, I know her by her apron,
> Baby, red's the dress that she wore.
> Etc.[161]

It is not easy to establish exactly who Jumpin' Judy is, in spite of her many appearances in this sort of song. Perhaps she is the personification of hard work, but that is admittedly a stab in the dark. The name Rosie – truly beloved – also appears regularly. The word 'old' is a reference to the faithful beloved. It does not mean that she is old, but refers to a well-established relationship, the name 'Rosie' having a familiar ring.

Children's songs/nursery rhymes

'Satisfied'

Children will play, irrespective of their situation. Slave children too, play. There was little in the way of toys, but an abundance of song. The repertoire consequently embraced both African children's songs and Western children's songs, and included all sorts of combinations of the two. This is still the case today, for there is after all nothing more traditional than children's songs.

The songs were sung whilst playing, mainly during so-called ring-games such as 'The farmer's in his den'.[162] The next example has both melodic and in its delivery strong Western (i.e. Anglo-Saxon) characteristics. It is striking how well these children sing. The child sitting in the middle is sung to by the others, and 'Sally Walker', for that is her name, has to make a hip movement at the end of the verse to indicate which child is to replace her:

> Li'l Sally Walker,
> Sittin' in the saucer,
> Cryin' for the old man,
> To come for the dollar,
> Rise Sally rise,
> Put your hands on your hips,
> Let your backbone slip,
> And shake it to the East,
> And shake it to the West,
> And shake it to the very one you love best.[163]

Once you have heard this song it should be obvious which source Armstrong used when he wrote 'Georgia grind' in 1926.

A song such as 'All around the maypole' is also clearly of Anglo-Saxon origin, but there are many others whose flavour is much more African. They have a typical responsive form whereby a game-leader-cum-precentor (usually an older girl) is answered each time by the children's choir singing the response. The lyrics also are in line with the artistic tradition characteristic of black Americans (which I will refer to in the coming chapters), and smack of self-mockery and irony – a sort of humour unfamiliar to Europeans. Here is a typical example:

> I'm going up North
> *Satisfied*
> An' I would tell
> *Satisfied*
> Lord I am
> *Satisfied*
> Some people up there
> *Satisfied*

Going to bring you back
Satisfied
Ain't nothing up there
Satisfied
What can you do
Satisfied
Mamma cooked a cow
Satisfied
Have to get all the girls
Satisfied
Their bellies full
Satisfied
I'm going up North
Satisfied
Etc.[164]

There are also adult versions of this type of song to be found away from the cities. A game called 'Liza Jane' often played at parties involves couples dancing in a circle while a solitary male performs the most amazing dance steps in the middle. He has to try to 'get' one of the dancing women, whose partner is then banished to the middle. There is also a jazz version of the folk song to accompany this dance.[165] The lyrics go like this:

Come my love and go with me
L'il Liza Jane
Come my love and go with me
L'il Liza Jane
O Miss Liza, *L'il Liza Jane*
O Miss Liza, *L'il Liza Jane*

I got a house in Baltimore
L'il Liza Jane
Streetcar runs right by my door
L'il Liza Jane
Chorus.

I got a house in Baltimore
L'il Liza Jane
Brussels carpet on the floor
L'il Liza Jane
Chorus etc.[166]

The connection between African-American music and the stories told by blacks to their children might not be immediately clear, but anybody who has witnessed a black storyteller in action (or a black preacher, as we will see later) will recognize that the intonation and rhythm used come close to music. It is a sort of rhythmic prose, like a recitative.

Many of these stories are related to African and, strangely enough, also to Indian tales such as those heard in South America. The latter creates a problem for us, which we will not discuss here.[167] An important series of stories has been preserved for us, thanks to Noel Chandler Harris who wrote them down them in 1880 from oral tradition. We are not confronted here with Western misrepresentations as Schulte Northolt contends[168] – the stereotypical image of a simple man, grateful for the privilege of being a slave, an idealized image fostered by the plantation holders of the Southern States. These are real black folk tales that can still be heard in remote parts of the South.[169]

The following is part of the 'Tar-Baby' story, the writer having tried to reflect the dialect characteristic of that period. If the words are pronounced out loud, the intention becomes clear. The fox has made a little figure of tar that he uses to bait the hare. This tar-baby is placed on the road and the fox lies in wait in the bushes:

> En he didn't hatter wait long, kaze bimeby here come Brer (Brother) Rabbit pacin' down the road – lippity-clippity, clippity-lippity – dez ez sassy ez a jay-bird. Brer fox, he lay low. Brer rabbit come prancin' 'long twel he spy de Tar-Baby, en den he fotch up on his behime legs like he wuz 'stonished. De Tar-Baby, she sot dar, she did, en Brer Fox, he lay low.
>
> 'Mawnin!' sez Brer Rabbit, sezee – 'nice wedder dis mawnin,' sezee.
>
> Tar-Baby ain't sayin' nothin', en Brer Fox, he lay low.
>
> 'How you come on, den? Is you deaf?' sez Brer Rabbit, sezee.
>
> 'Kaze if you is, I kin holler louder,' sezee.
>
> Tar-Baby stay still, en Brer Fox, he lay low.
>
> 'Youer stuck up, dat's w'at you is', says Brer Rabbit, sezee, 'en I's gwineter kyore you, dat's w'at I'm gwineter do,' sezee.
>
> Brer Fox, he sorter chuckle in his stummuck, he did, but Tar-Baby ain't sayin' nothin'.
>
> 'I'm gwineter larn you how-ter talk ter 'spectubble fokes,' sez Brer Rabbit, sezee. 'Ef you don't take off dat hat en tell me howdy, I'm gwineter bus' you wide open,' sezee. Tar-Baby stay still, en Brer Fox, he lay low. Brer Rabbit keep on axin' 'im, en de Tar-Baby, she keep on sayin' nothin', twel present'y Brer Rabbit draw back wid his fis', he did, en blip he tuck 'er side de head. His fis stuck, en he can't pull loose. De tar hilt 'im. But Tar-Baby, she stay still, en Brer Fox, he lay low.

'Ef you don't lemme loose, I'll knock you agin,' sez Brer Rabbit, sezee, en wid dat he fotch 'er a wipe wid de udder han', en dat stuck. Tar-Baby, she ain't sayin' nothin', en Brer Fox, he lay low.

'Tu'n me loose, fo' I kick de natal stuffin' outen you,' sez Brer Rabbit, sezee, but de Tar-Baby, she ain't sayin' nothin'. She des hilt on, en den Brer Rabbit lose de use er his feet in de same way. Den Brer Fox, he sa'ntered fort', lookin' des es innercent ez one er yo' mammy's mockin'-birds.

'Howdy, Brer Rabbit,' sez Brer Fox, sezee, 'you look sorter stuck up dis mawnin',' sezee, en den he rolled on de groun', en laughed en laughed twel he couldn't laugh no mo'.[170]

The story goes on to tell how the hare, in spite of being in a tight spot, manages to get free by bamboozling the fox. Almost all these stories have the same moral, of a hare who is too clever for the fox. Perhaps they reflect the hopes of the blacks who, in spite of their weaker position, were still able to outwit the 'stronger' whites.[171]

The first of the African-American Christian songs in North America

'Go preach my gospel'

When black slaves arrived in North America, still an English colony in the seventeenth and most of the eighteenth centuries, they were introduced to the Protestantism of their masters. There were various denominations, the majority of them dissenters or Nonconformists, i.e. Christians who did not wish to belong to the Anglican Church, the established church in England. These people sung psalms only.

Thanks to Calvin in Geneva, the psalms were translated and set to music, which in turn contributed greatly to the propagation of the Reformation. They were sung briskly and cheerfully. Even Queen Elizabeth I once made a reference to these 'Geneva jigs'. Since people at first were not familiar with English rhymed versions of the psalms it became customary to have a precentor recite a line, which was then sung by the congregation, and so on. The custom continued even when it was no longer necessary.

In the seventeenth century people began to sing the psalms slower – more solemnly and legato (this may still be heard in some old Calvinistic churches). It became so slow that it was impossible to hold a note for the required length of time. At that point 'grace notes' were introduced to replace the notes that were too long. These took the form of decorative melodies that swerved very closely around the tone. Since everybody had his or her own method of application, the result was curious. The original note became frayed and obscure. The beginning of the eighteenth century in England saw an attempt to improve the standard of singing in churches. Dr Isaac Watts, a clergyman from London, particularly devoted himself to the abolition of 'lining out', in which a precentor sings the line for the congregation to repeat. He was also responsible for revising the metrical psalms and writing a large number of hymns.

Let us return to the Africans in America, who at this time were learning psalms and hymns like those of Dr Watts, but performing them as described above. While Dr Watts had been successful with his hymns, his efforts to improve the standard of singing had rather failed. Having a precentor sing and the choir 'respond' sounded familiar to the black slaves. This was what they had been used to in their native countries – responsive singing of solemn melodies. The rhythm as basis was certainly lacking, but as we discussed earlier, for various reasons the intensive contact with biblical Christianity led to African rhythms being abandoned. These were considered pagan – after all, the gods spoke through the drums.

There is therefore much evidence that blacks, having arrived from Africa, were very fond of psalms and hymns. They simply could not stop singing them. That sort of song was in fact the most Western, European music to be found in America. Although it cannot be referred to as highly sophisticated, it was conceivable only in the context of Puritan, Christian Europe. At the same time, and without any modification, it was also African song in its purest form. There was no mutation necessary, no hybrids were involved – the music was purely African and purely Western at the same time.

It seems strange that it was the very hymns from Dr Watts that the blacks preferred to sing in this way. They still do for, as we shall see later, it was the 'songs of the old Dr Watts', alongside other sorts of sacred songs, that remained popular – a regular feature of the blacks' church service. The precentor 'lines out' a line, which is then sung very slowly, elaborately drawn out by the congregation. This sort of singing died out in other parts. It is only in the black American churches today that we can witness how the English congregations sung around 1700. Just how slowly and spun out the hymns were sung can be seen by the following hymn that took more than five minutes to sing.

This is one of Dr Watts' hymns, which is still sung today in the prescribed fashion.

> Go preach my Gospel, saith the Lord,
> Bid the whole earth my grace receive;
> He shall be safe that trusts my word,
> He shall be damned that won't believe.
>
> I'll make your great commission known,
> And ye shall prove my gospel true
> By all the works that I have done,
> By all the wonders ye shall do.[172]

The origin of the true Negro spiritual

'I want to be a Christian'

Dr Watts songs were sung by slaves (and free blacks) in the Northern states, and here and there in the South. In the South, however, there lived large groups of slaves who worked in remote plantations and who had hardly encountered Christianity. The eighteenth century in particular witnessed concern about the fate of the blacks, and a more conscious effort was made to preach the gospel to them. Baptists and Methodists were particularly committed to this work, but Presbyterians also made a contribution. Consequently, African-Americans were exposed to the sacred song of the whites – the hymn. It was not only the Dr Watts' hymns that were circulating; hymns by Wesley and his family were in circulation as well. The Wesley brothers were leaders of a spiritual revival movement in England in the middle of the eighteenth century. Methodism, as it was called, devoted much attention to improving and reforming the standard of hymns. They were more successful than Watts in breaking down the rusty traditions of 'lining out' and note-stretching. For their hymns they often used the tunes of folk songs.

It is evident that these hymns were also sung by blacks. The words were often too difficult for them, however, as they lacked the formal education of the average Westerner, and it was this that led to the simplification of the songs. Sometimes the hymns profited from it for, once it was stripped of its poetic frills, the essentials became more evident. Songs of this sort are still sung by black Christians. They often have an attractive melody which is sung slowly, either collectively or as a solo. It is possible that the following song stems from that period:

> Lord, I want to be a Christian in my heart, in my heart,
> Lord, I want to be a Christian in my heart, in my heart,
> Lord, I want to be a Christian in my heart, in my heart.[173]

The next few verses may read:

> Lord, I want to be more loving in my heart (x 3)
> Lord, I want to be more holy in my heart (x 3) Etc.

The following variations developed:

> When Jesus comes into my heart, into my heart (x 3)
> I'm filled with joy, Etc.

Wesley's lyrics are often constructed in four-line verses which, when set to music, require eight measures (four times two). This sort of Negro spiritual consequently consists of verses of eight bars.

At the end of the eighteenth century a great revival took place, also known as the Great Awakening, mainly in the Southern States of the United States of America. The influence of the Wesleys and others created a strong revival movement focused on a more personal, warm, authentic Christianity – biblical and primarily practical. Conversion was emphasized – a personal, direct relationship with Jesus, with a whiff of mysticism manifest in such expressions as 'Jesus comes into my heart.' There was also a certain moralism involved, and an emphasis on going to heaven to be with Jesus. Little attention was given to doctrine and a scriptural, solidly formulated confession. In practical terms the revival consisted primarily of camp meetings, social gatherings in large tents lasting several days. There was singing, prayer and preaching from the Bible. It was at these meetings in particular that the need was felt to make Wesley's new type of hymn accessible to everyone. That would promote the standard of combined singing. Simplicity was the key since these camp meetings were primarily attended by the lower classes.

An interesting feature of these meetings was that blacks and whites were on a par with each other, side by side and not separated. That was significant. It also made an impact on the singing, since the blacks were not only good singers with a sense of rhythm but their principle of responsive singing was a welcome addition. It worked by enabling the crowd to join in easily: the songs with tricky words and irregular word patterns were chanted by the precentor-preacher and the crowd responded with the chorus.

This is how the most well-known type of Negro spiritual probably came into being. Having said that, there are many unanswered questions in this area and there is little about the origin and the early development of the Negro spiritual of which we can be absolutely certain. In any case, the structure of this kind of Negro spiritual generally follows the pattern as described next.

Firstly, there is a verse consisting of eight bars, divided as four times two. Each set of two bars is allocated a single sentence, which is also a musical phrase. At the end of the line there is often a word or short sentence that is sung collectively which we might call a short refrain. After this verse comes the actual chorus, which we call the main chorus, also consisting of eight bars. This is sung collectively. Many variations are possible – the verse is sung twice and the chorus once, or a verse of sixteen bars is followed by a chorus of sixteen bars, for example. The main chorus is sometimes omitted. This type of song is still often sung in churches by blacks, briskly but not hurriedly. A rhythmic accompaniment such as the clapping of hands is regularly heard, but true African polyrhythms are never heard – they have barely survived in North America. The tune is always based on a simple, even metre and so is the rhythm, which is often varied, never monotonous. Rhythm, however, is never the feature of the spiritual. The following is an example:

>   When I am sick and by myself, (one bar)
>   *Do remember me.* (short refrain, also one bar) x3
>   *Do Lord, remember me.* (all together, two bars, last syllables on long notes)

Main chorus:
>   *Do Lord, do Lord, remember me.* (two bars)
>   *Do Lord, do Lord, remember me.*
>   *Do Lord, do Lord, remember me.*
>   *Do Lord, remember me.* (see the last line of the verse)

The first lines of the following verses are:

>   When I'm crossing Jordan. [which means, when I die and go to the 'promised land', namely heaven]
>   If I ain't got no friend at all.
>   When I'm going from door to door.
>   When I am bound in trouble, Etc.[174]

We can be reasonably certain that one of these spirituals, 'Roll, Jordan roll', came into being around this time:

>   Brother you ought to be there, (two bars)
>   *Yes my Lord.* (two bars)
>   A-sittin' in the Kingdom, (two bars)
>   *Just to hear old Jordan roll.* (two bars)
>
>   *Roll, Jordan roll, roll, Jordan roll,* (2x2 bars)
>   *I want to go to heaven when I die,* (two bars)
>   *To hear ol' Jordan roll.* (two bars)

Both the words and the music (which is a tune derived from an English folk song) are based on a song written by Charles Wesley, but it has undergone significant changes since the original.[175]

2
Nineteenth Century: Development

The development of the spirituals in the nineteenth century

'Go down, Moses'

In the eighteenth century the blacks formed their own church. There were many factors involved in this development but we will not discuss them at this point. What concerns us here is the songs that were sung in their services: first of all hymns, sung in the time-honoured style in which the hymns of Dr Watts were performed; moreover it is probable that many of the new hymns, those written from the late eighteenth century onwards in the spirit of Wesley, also penetrated the black churches. Here is an example of a white song of this sort, regularly sung in black churches and also popular among whites. The melody is American and dates back to the eighteenth century. The words were written by John Newton (1725-1807), who worked on a boat for fetching slaves until, under very adventurous circumstances, he became a Christian and subsequently a minister in England.

> Amazing grace! How sweet the sound,
> That saved a wretch like me,
> I once was lost, but now am found,
> I was blind, but now I can see.
>
> Thro' many dangers, toils and snares,
> I have already come,
> This grace has brought me safe thus far,
> And grace will lead me home.[176]

Many new hymns emerged from the black culture in North America, however. They essentially followed the pattern of the hymns of Wesley and others, but in contrast to the white hymns composed during the nineteenth century, which were seldom of a high standard,[177] many of these were particularly beautiful. This new type of black hymn, by blacks for the blacks, was called a Negro spiritual. The lyrics are often powerful, poetic though simple, and strongly biblical. Unlike white spirituals, the tunes were often far from sentimental with depth and beauty. These songs have been referred to as compositions because we believe that someone composed them – someone who functioned as a musical leader, who stimulated musical life and contributed his or her own work.[178] On the other hand we must not think of compositions as music written down once for all in musical notation and with a definite text. The composer and poet (we imagine it would have been one person in most cases) would have taught the congregation the song, i.e. the tune and the words. The song would have been performed in a traditional, very lively fashion, in responsive form. There would always have been room, however, to vary the number of voices and details in the melody, etc.

Believers have always sought comfort from events recorded in the Bible. These stories teach us, after all, how the Lord acted with his people, and they also show us how he will act today (see Romans 15:4). It is therefore no surprise to us that blacks, in their desperate circumstances in the bonds of slavery, also reached for the Bible; for all sorts of reasons the plight of slaves in the nineteenth century was harder, more inhumane and cruel than previously. In the face of that it is astonishing – and we may praise the Lord for it – that the blacks who were already Christians remained so. Not only that but, in view of the fact that those who were responsible for the sorry condition of the slaves professed to be Christians themselves, it is amazing that large numbers of the slaves also became Christians. They particularly sought solace in the stories with a message of hope and expectation, such as the history of the people of Israel in Egypt and their subsequent exodus. Would this not have taught them that the Lord does not let his people cry out in vain when they ask for deliverance? There are cases of slave insurrections, but it seems certain that these were led by slaves who were not yet familiar with the gospel or, at least, only superficially. Attempts to liberate themselves often led only to an aggravation of their circumstances.

The song 'Roll, Jordan roll' has already shown us that Christians were making associations with parts of the book of Exodus. An even clearer example of this is 'Go down, Moses', in which we are also struck by the poetic way in which blacks were able to present a situation in no uncertain terms, using a few strokes of the pen, a few well-turned phrases. The words are recorded here. Authentic renditions from church circles are very rare, a phenomenon which we shall be discussing in a later paragraph.

> *Go down, Moses, way down in Egypt land,*
> *Tell ol' Pharaoh to let my people go.*
>
> When Israel was in Egypt land,
> *Let my people go*
> Oppressed so hard they could not stand,
> *Let my people go.*
>
> When spoke the Lord, bold Moses said,
> *Let my people go.*
> If not I'll smite your first born dead,
> *Let my people go.*

> No more in bondage shall they toil,
> *Let my people go.*
> Let them come out to Israel's soil,
> *Let my people go.*[179]

The Civil War in the 1860s brought the long-awaited answer to prayer. A bloody war was fought between the Northern and Southern States to decide the future position of blacks. After the Northerners had won the war under the inspiring leadership of Abraham Lincoln, the slaves were declared free. Now they were free as people. But the faithful Christian knows that being free from oppression is only part of the battle; freedom is complete only in the spiritual freedom found in Jesus Christ. In him we are no more slaves to sin – no longer children of the devil. This gives us reason to think that the following song is a product of the post-Civil War period. It is a lovely example of words without a direct basis in Scripture, a black Negro spiritual which is able to express the heart of the matter directly, perceptively and deeply, in almost childlike, but far from childish, words.

> *Free at last, free at last,*
> *Thank God Almighty I'm free at last.*
> *Free at last, free at last,*
> *Thank God Almighty I'm free at last.*
>
> One day, one day I was walking along.
> *Thank God Almighty I'm free at last.*
> I met old Satan on my way,
> *Thank God Almighty I'm free at last.*
> What do you reckon old Satan said to me?
> *Thank God Almighty I'm free at last.*
> Young man, young man, you're too young to pray,
> *Thank God Almighty I'm free at last.*
>
> If I'm too young to pray, I ain't too young to die,
> *Thank God Almighty I'm free at last.*
> Oh free at last, free at last,
> *Thank God Almighty I'm free at last.*
> Old Satan mad and I am glad,
> *Thank God Almighty I'm free at last.*
> Well he missed the soul he thought he had,
> *Thank God Almighty I'm free at last.*[180]

Liberation meant new horizons for the slaves – new opportunities and wide perspectives. It also brought many new problems, worries which partly stemmed from the uncompromising attitude of the former slave-owners. Even without additional pressure from outside the liberated slaves had no easy time. Indeed, there were many for whom the temptation to stop working altogether became too strong. They sought refuge in the cities, far away from the rural areas where they had such a miserable existence, and gave themselves over to living a loose life that often culminated in crime. New opportunities had brought a new dilemma – freedom bred temptation, which bred crime, and evading crime became a tough test of faith. Many held on to the faith of their fathers, sung of in the spiritual 'Give me that old-time religion'. On the other hand we must not underestimate the troubles and sorrows of that time – pressure from outside and testing from within. That is what is expressed in the following song:

> I ain't gonna lay my religion down, (x 4)
>
> Ever since I've been free. (x 3)
> Nobody knows the troubles I've seen.
>
> Nobody knows but Jesus and me, (x 2)
> Ever since I've been free.
> Nobody knows the troubles I've seen.
> I ain't gonna lay my religion down. (x 4)[181]

The origin of the westernized spiritual

'Swing low, sweet chariot'

Emancipation of the blacks was marked by a declaration of their full dignity as citizens of the United States of America. At the same time it created a problem for their liberators, because there were thousands upon thousands of slaves in the Southern States who were suddenly granted rights and had to fulfil obligations with little understanding of the implications of either. It was a difficult matter to provide for these ex-slaves, the vast majority of whom were illiterate, had no financial resources and absolutely no property. The responsibility for the new task had fallen to the Northerners and, it must be said, they approached their task with much idealism and endeavour. An example of their achievements was the founding of schools and universities, one of which was of particular importance. It was the Fisk University, established in the Deep South in an area densely populated by blacks. At first it was probably simply a primary school for adults. It still exists and has become a very important institute for higher education.

A music teacher by the name of White became the principal of Fisk University. He heard the songs of the blacks, admired their beautiful lyrics and melodies, but decided that his pupils who were now full citizens of the USA should not sing 'so barbarically', so he began to transcribe and edit their songs. He met with all sorts of difficulties however because our tone system is *wohltemperiert* (of equal temperament). Since the eighteenth century there has been a definite (though somewhat artificial) division of the octave, which has made it possible to play in any key, and facilitated the playing together of various instruments. (Bach wrote his *Wohltemperierte Klavier* for clavichords and harpsichords tuned in this (new) fashion.) What the blacks sung however was partly determined by Western tone systems and partly founded on African systems, not in the least equally tempered, while it had its basis in natural intervals and the combined sounds resulting from them. In order to 'temper' these songs fully, White proceeded to refine them as he transcribed them. The style of their adaptation for male-voice choir was reminiscent of Schubert; these Schubertian adaptations became White's Negro spirituals.

Some years later the University ran out of funds and someone had the bright idea of letting the choir go on tour. By early in 1870 the 'Fisk Jubilee Singers' had already staged many concerts, the tours of the Northern States and Europe having been very successful. So much so that almost all spirituals known nowadays are the same as those first sung by the Fisk Jubilee Singers for white audiences: 'Deep river', 'Go down, Moses', 'Swing low, sweet chariot', 'Nobody knows the troubles I've seen', 'Little David play on your harp', and so on.[182]

The success can be accounted for by the fact that these songs were not difficult for white audiences to digest. The Schubertian style appealed greatly to them. In this way these often beautiful melodies and catchy or haunting lyrics were displayed in a way that was most agreeable to the Western palate.

Apart from the musical aspect there was another factor that undoubtedly contributed to the success of the choir: the words spoke of faith, oppression and liberation. Imagine for a moment that you were a member of the audience of that time. There on the stage a performance is being given by people who have been subjected to all sorts of wrongs, for generations – and then listen to the beautiful, haunting music. Would there have been a dry eye during 'Nobody knows the troubles I've seen'? Indeed, the success of these songs is definitely linked to a certain feeling of sympathy towards these oppressed and sorely-tested folk. The great popularity of the spirituals cannot be attributed to the real religious spiritual but to these songs, arranged for Western ears and concert stages and awakening all sorts of sentiments.

This is also why we know renditions of the spiritual 'Go down, Moses' from this setting, while it is hardly sung in church these days. This spiritual originates from the Fisk area and it is even possible that it was not known at all in other regions. But more importantly, in the living musical tradition of the blacks who keep producing new songs, a song like this will be forgotten because the content no longer has much bearing on the present circumstances. Only in the concert tradition of Fisk have these songs, while they are an enduring memorial to slavery in the past, been preserved artificially.

A few soloists have emerged from the universities where students strive for emancipation and complete equality with the whites. These soloists – Marian Anderson, Roland Hayes and Paul Robeson, for example – have in their own way contributed to the further westernization of the Negro spiritual. For them as blacks the Negro spiritual had become a kind of obligatory encore piece for every recital or concert. But even if they considered these songs as part of a tradition that still moved them deeply, things are different for a more recent generation of blacks. They often enjoy these songs less, and certainly do not appreciate that they more or less have to sing them: 'They remind us too much of the period of slavery.'

This leaves black people in a quandary. On the one hand they want to disown the things belonging to their own folklore, art or custom in order to be accepted by whites, while on the other hand whites keep on telling them that their spirituals are the only authentic contribution they have made to the world.

We called this type of spiritual 'Schubertian'. Indeed, people like Roland Hayes conveyed these songs with so much emotion, rallentandi and accelerandi, so much gesture and emotionalism of a romantic nature that the authentic character of this originally Christian church song is completely lost; pathos and romanticism are after all foreign to this kind of song, which has a steady beat – an expression of peace and certainty – and conveys an emotion of a very different kind. No, White's version, and those of his successors, did not only create technically perfect songs, they also translated them into a language with a completely different attitude to life, into a type of romanticism of which the roots are foreign to Christianity.

The words to the song 'Swing low, sweet chariot', made famous by the Fisk Jubilee Singers, mark the end of this chapter. This spiritual, written prior to 1860, is interesting and important enough to contemplate more deeply.

> *Swing low, sweet chariot,*
> *Coming for to carry me home,*
> *Swing low, sweet chariot,*
> *Coming for to carry me home.*
>
> I looked over Jordan and what did I see
> *Coming for to carry me home?*
> A band of angels coming after me,
> *Coming for to carry me home.*[183]

This imagery is most unusual. It is very probable that it is derived from the story of Elijah, who rode to heaven in a chariot. It is an image that apparently had a profound impact on the imagination of the blacks because we come across it often in various ways. Somewhere along the line the chariot was replaced by a train, and it is evident that the 'gospel train' evolved from this idea. There is a whole range of variations on the theme: 'If I have a ticket, Lord, can I ride',[184] 'The gospel train is leaving',[185] and it also makes its appearance in sermons.[186]

The background to the true spiritual

'Down on me'

The nineteenth-century Christianity which emerged from the evangelical churches in Anglo-Saxon countries has often been accused, and unfortunately not always wrongly, of speaking only of heaven and life in Christ without tackling concrete problems. People were ushered towards Christ as a way out of their problems, but no attempt was made to take action at root level. Of course, this is not the whole picture. These congregations were made up of the lowest social ranks. The simple and poor people had little say in matters outside the church and could do little else than accept their lot in faith and with hope for a new earth. The alternative would have been to take the revolutionary path alongside their socialist fellow-sufferers. If anyone is to blame, then not so much the evangelical Baptist and Methodist groups but rather the Anglican and Reformed churches, whose members were generally from well-to-do circles. But it is very well possible that much more was done by these people for social improvement than often assumed, perhaps due to socialist propaganda.

Be that as it may, there seems to be no justification for accusing the blacks of escapism, having their hearts set on heaven, far removed from earthly realities, in a sort of Christian stoicism. The Scriptures teach us to face up to difficulties and trust in God. That, in many respects, is what the blacks did. It is this aspect which emerges from their songs: joy, happiness, a love for others and hope for the future (including the future on earth). They did anything but deny their troubles, even in the face of the most awful circumstances imaginable.

The spiritual 'Down on me' is a classic example:

> *Down on me, down on me,*
> *Looks like everybody in this whole round world down on me.*
>
> Mary and Martha, Luke and John,
> All God's prophets dead and gone,
> *Looks like everybody in this whole round world down on me.*
>
> Ain't been to heaven, but I've been told,
> Gates is pearl and the streets is gold,
> *Looks like everybody in this whole round world down on me.*
>
> God is God, God is God, rain is rain,
> God's a man don't never change,['God is a man' here refers to the personal character of God]
> *Looks like everybody in this whole round world down on me.*[187]

This song shows a recurring feature of spirituals: they show us that focusing on the scriptural hope of salvation in Christ Jesus is anything but stoical. The joy that emanates from their songs, and particularly in the delivery, is a testimony to the depth of that joy and to how vital and real that faith and hope in the work of their Lord and Saviour was and is. In view of the circumstances of these people, in view of their songs and attitude, is it fair to accuse them of escapism? For those who are familiar with the arrangement and performance of these songs in the spirit of the Fisk Jubilee Singers only, this will not be easily recognized. It is sentimentality, escapism and sorrow which emanate from those versions; the vital, religious spirituals express strength, joy and a sense of reality.

Secular folk songs during the age of slavery

'Here, Rattler, here'

Although many black Christians sing exclusively spirituals, they also have a large repertoire of what we call folk songs. Some sing them, some do not, but it cannot be said that these songs do absolutely belong to a non-Christian culture. They are the property of all blacks whether they are members of a church or whether they are no longer Christians (in the strict sense of the word). It is necessary to make this distinction because the difference between being a member of a church and not being a member of a church is very marked in African-American culture, and mutual contact is virtually non-existent in some black villages. Church discipline is strictly adhered to, particularly with regard to conduct. One dance too many on a Saturday evening may provide sufficient cause for action.

Some of these secular – at least, non-religious – songs are work songs, some are solos – hollers – which we will come back to later, some are songs to be performed on social occasions (e.g. 'Saturday night hoe-down'[188]), some are dance songs (like 'Liza Jane'), while solid instrumental music, which played a significant role in the later developments, is also evident. The song 'Here, Rattler, here' dates back to the days of slavery. It deals with a subject that is reminiscent of the story of *Uncle Tom's Cabin*. It is about a black slave who escapes and is then tracked down and chased by bloodhounds, one of which is called Rattler. 'Here, Rattler, here' is the refrain which is sung by everyone together, while the verses are solos. It is another responsive song.

> Oh, b'lieve to my soul there's a nigger gone,
> *Here, Rattler, here,*
> Oh, b'lieve to my soul there's a nigger gone,
> *Here, Rattler, here.*
>
> *Here, Rattler,*
> *Here Rattler, here*
> *Here Rattler, here*
> *Here Rattler, here.*

The words of the song continue (somewhat shortened):

> Oh, he went right through the corn.
> I heard the old horn blow.
>
> Go and get the dog man,
> Go and get the dog man.
>
> Run that nigger to the riverside,
> Run that nigger to the riverside.
>
> Go and call old Rattler,
> Call old Rattler.
>
> Oh, he set so long with the sympathy,
> Oh, run that nigger right lost his mind.
>
> Oh, he run that nigger till he went stone blind,
> Oh, cross the river to the long leaf pine.
>
> Oh he run so far he didn't leave no sign,
> Oh, got a baby here, got a baby there.
>
> Oh, trip this time, I'll trip no more,
> Oh, going to the North where you can't go.[189]

The Arican-Americans also sang all sorts of ballads. A very popular one, is about a bad man called Stackolee. It is difficult to say how old it is, but it may have been written after 1870.

> Stackolee was a bad man, everybody knows,
> Spent about a hundred dollars, for just one suit of clothes,
> He was a bad man, that mean old Stackolee.
>
> Stackolee and Billy Lion, fighting on the floor,
> Stackolee pulled the trigger, of that smokeless forty-four, [a forty four is a revolver]
> He was a bad man, his name was Stackolee.
>
> Billy the Lion said: 'Stackolee, please don't take my life,
> I've got two little babes and a darling little wife,
> You're a bad man, your name is Stackolee.'
>
> 'Well, what I care for your two little babes, and your darling little wife,
> You done throw my Stetson hat, now I'm bound to take your life,
> I'm a bad man, my name is Stackolee.'
>
> 'Well', the judge said: 'Mister Stackolee, Mister Stackolee,
> I'm gonna hang your body up, and set your spirits free,
> Cause you're a bad man, your name is Stackolee.'[190]

Minstrel shows

Jim Crow

We can be certain that a considerable number of this sort of folk songs existed prior to 1860. Not only do we have the testimony of many that were resident in the South at that time, but the impact of the songs on Western popular music was also considerable. Minstrel music particularly owes its emergence to true black music, though they bore little resemblance to each other. It was popular music, composed by whites, and seldom profound.

As to the origin of minstrel music, it is set to date from 1828 when Daddy Rice put on a cabaret with his group in Baltimore, Pittsburgh or Louisville. Jim Crow owned the farm behind the concert 'hall' (which consisted of a number of tents) and his slave, who was named after his master as was customary, had a clubfoot. Rice saw this slave tending the cattle, stumbling around and singing:

> Wheelabout, turn about, do just so
> And every time I wheelabout, I jump Jim Crow.

Rice proposed that the slave appear in the show. The show was promptly threatened with a boycott, so Rice borrowed the slave's clothes and, having blackened his face, performed the slave's 'dance' and its accompanying song. It brought the house down. From this originated the cabaret routines in which whites impersonating blacks performed quasi-black songs and dances: the black-and white minstrel shows.

This is also the origin of the subsequent expression 'Jim Crow Regulations' for those rules that segregated black Americans from whites in public places in the Southern States.

Stephan Foster was responsible for the most popular and indeed often charming products of the minstrel show scene. He appeared in Christy's Minstrel Show and, prior to that, composed white American folk songs, some of which have become classics: 'My old Kentucky home', 'Swanee River', 'Old Black Joe', 'Camptown races' (mainly played as a cowboy song) and the well-known 'Oh Susanna'.

The minstrel shows, which toured the Northern States did not really produce any music that was directly related to authentic black music. Still, the existence of minstrel music is testimony to the fact that the influence of black music was present early on, and that black music was recognized as something remarkable.

Secular hollers

'Whoa black'

Blacks who worked as slaves or those who did manual work in poorly paid jobs after 1865 often sang while they worked. Some still do.

When they needed to convey a message to someone working further away, they would sing out the message. Those two functions produced the 'holler', a call, a song, a free melodic expression, sung exclusively as a solo. Although references to faith and the Bible may be heard, they are not typically religious in content but of a rather secular nature.

These hollers, often very beautiful, provide a distinct musical expression of great originality alongside the spirituals and, later, the blues. They are almost always sung very slowly and solemnly, thereby enabling the voice to be fully exploited, and falsetto is often heard. The melodic lines are very capricious, moving from phrases in spoken verse to drawn-out melodies, only to switch suddenly to a faster passage, a rest or something like a scream. There are pieces that resemble yodels albeit in slow tempo.

Where did the holler originate? This sort of music possibly has traces of African influence, but it seems more likely that it is connected with the church songs we discussed earlier, sung in the way of the psalms and hymns of Dr Watts. When these are sung solo, the result is very similar to the holler and we may suppose that churchgoers sang their favourite songs alone, whether working at home or on the land. We hear a succession of spoken and sung parts, the melodic structure of the latter being very capricious, strung out and free. If we listen to Suddie Griffiths, for example, who sings hymns that date back to the nineteenth century (and appear in nineteenth-century Baptist hymn-books),[191] the relationship becomes very evident. The holler may therefore amount to little more than the time-honoured hymn, but now fully secularized. The way in which it was sung would have been that of a hymn, the words freely composed, springing from the singer's circumstances, but as to content it was definitely not a church song.

This holler was sung by a farmer to his draught animal whilst ploughing the land. A recording of the music (by Lomax) is still available.[192]

> O ... a-whoooo ... whoo ... oo (etc.)
> Sometimes I plough the old grey mare,
> And then I plough the cuddy,
> When I make my fifty cents, Lord,
> I carry it home to Rosie.

Spoken:
> Come here Old Mule.

> Whoo ... Whoo ... Lordy Lord,
> Somebody stole my old coon dog,
> Boys I wish he'd bring him back,
> He run them big ones over the fence,
> Boys, and the little ones thru the crack.
> Hee, whoo ... whoo ... (etc.)

Spoken:
> Right Old Flat Tom, we're going to make some corn this year boy.

> I been rollin', rollin', rollin',
> Boys we gotta make that money,
> We're gonna take it home to Rosie.
> Whoo ... whoo ... whoo-a'whoo ...
> Black gal wear the brogan shoe,
> The yellow gal wear the slipper,
> I don't care what Old Flat says,
> We're gonna ride in a Lincoln Zephyr.

Here is another example. The farm-labourer in question would have been lying on his back in the shade during the very hot hours of the afternoon. Then he starts to sing – a holler, of course. He sings to himself, as it were, meditating aloud. It is not a story, neither a ballad, but an utterance that flows from his situation. On the other hand he may not be singing of his present circumstances at all but be making it up, though not just anything, as we will discuss later. Who is to say what the origin of the tune is? Unlike the previous example, which reminds us of a white folk song as sung by a cowboy, the tune is vaguely reminiscent of a spiritual. Rich Amerson of Livingston, Alabama sings:

> Well I said come back here black woman
> Ah-umm, don't you hear me crying, oh Lordy!
> Ah-hum, I say run here black woman,
> I want you to sit on black Daddy's knee, Lord.
> M-hmm, don't your house feel lonesome,
> When your biscuit-roller gone.
>
> I'm going to Texas mamma,
> Just to hear the wild ox moan,
> Lord help my crying time I'm going to Texas,
> Mamma to hear the wild ox moan!
> And if they moan to suit me,
> I'm going to bring a wild ox home.
> Ah-hum, I say I got to go to Texas mamma.
> Etc.[193]

It is evident that the singer lets his thoughts take over, alternating between fantasy and reality.

There are many more examples we could show here. The song of the assistant pilot, the man who is employed to take soundings by throwing a plumb line into the Mississippi[194] and who then sings the measurements to the captain on the bridge. Then there is the song of the foreman instructing his workers, who are unloading railway tracks. The holler is a type of song that is freely rhapsodic, with variable lyrics, springing from circumstance and the inspiration of the moment.

The origin of the blues

'Blues at sunrise'

After the spiritual came the blues, another pre-eminently African-American music style that originated in the nineteenth century, probably between 1880 and 1900. Its roots can be traced to the Mississippi basin, the land along the river where so many blacks live and work. The blues was not invented by city slickers or university students; rather, it is a pure form of folk music.

It would not however be true to say that the blues suddenly came into being, just like that. Nothing happens just like that, and something as well balanced as the blues certainly cannot simply be called forth. It was, we think, the brainchild of artists, a sort of compilation and refinement of all the existing black folk music. The primary constituent has to be the holler, but folk and work songs are also main ingredients, while instrumental music like that of the string bands (which we will be discussing later) may well have influenced the style of accompaniment. While it is certainly true that artists shaped the blues, we must realize that these were no sophisticated, trained composers in the Western sense. We suppose that the artists who forged the blues were real folk artists, wandering troubadours who accompanied their own songs on the guitar or mouth-organ whenever they were able to find an audience. We encounter the spirit and character of these people beautifully in Fenton Johnson's poem:

> There is music in me, the music of the peasant people.
> I wander through the levee, picking my banjo and singing my songs
>   of the cabin and the field. At the *Last Chance Saloon* I am as
>   welcome as the violets in March. There is always food and drink
>   for me there, and the dimes of those who love honest music.
> Behind the railroad tracks the little children clap their hands
>   and love me as they love Kris Kringle.
>
> But I fear I am a failure.
> Last night a woman called me a troubadour.
>
> What is a troubadour?[195]

A troubadour of this kind used many different sorts of folk music to make a new art form – the blues. This means that the blues cannot be referred to as the common property of all the blacks. The blues sung by ordinary people is almost always derived from the work of these troubadours, and this is plainly evident later, when the influence of gramophone recordings can almost always be demonstrated.[196] We may also see blacks from rural areas, who have not yet mastered the complex structure of the blues, translating the song back into a holler.

There is a nice example of this in 'Black snake blues'. This was first sung by Blind Lemon Jefferson, one of the best-known folk artists, and highly esteemed by blacks. The first few bars of his song (later recorded around 1925[197]) are a sort of drawn-out hum, reminiscent of the holler, but the song in its totality is very definitely a blues song:

> Oh ... ain't got no mamma now,
> Oh ... ain't got no mamma now,
> She told me late last night, You don't need no mamma nohow [The typically black expression 'mamma' means 'beloved', as does 'pappa'.]

Horace Sprott, a simple farmhand from rural Alabama, tells (in 1954) he had heard Blind Lemon Jefferson singing this blues song. He even recalls how it went and proceeds to demonstrate. It is the same song, the same lyrics, but the first line is not repeated; it lacks the twelve-bar structure and it is sung in exactly the same way as a holler.[198]

There was probably much experimentation at first and we may be able to detect remnants of this in divergent variations and in structurally simpler songs,[199] but the blues as a finished product has a highly original, fixed structure. It is constructed on a simple, gentle 4/4 time, harmonically based on a simple pattern where tonic, dominant and subdominant alternate. The 'blue note', a minor third or seventh within the otherwise major tonality, is often heard. These strange blue notes help to give the blues its own character; they also show that this music originates from a milieu in which our *wohltemperierte* musical system (or music system of equal temperament) was little known. (We will gladly leave the music-historical complications of this to the experts.)

Unlike the sixteen-bar scheme of white popular music and the eight-bar scheme of the spiritual, the blues uses a twelve-bar structure. This is then divided up into three parts of four bars. A phrase that is sung during the first four beats is repeated in the second four, while the third four bars close the verse with a line which, together with the first phrase, forms a sentence. The blues is thus based on an AAB pattern. The tune and lyrics form a close bond. Irrespective of the number of syllables, each line contains a number of strongly accented points that form the supports for the melody. These supports often occur on the first and third beats of the first bar, on the first and third beats of the second bar, and always at the end of a line. This last beat almost always coincides with the first beat of the third bar. The line for the vocalist therefore contains just two-and-a-quarter or two-and-a-half bars. The musicians then fill in the remainder of the line. There is almost always a caesura in the vocalist's line – a rest which coincides with the position of the comma. Here is an example, although it must be said that the accentuation rarely falls precisely on the beats. Furthermore, there will be all manner of small deviations from this pattern to ensure that the audience remains enthralled.

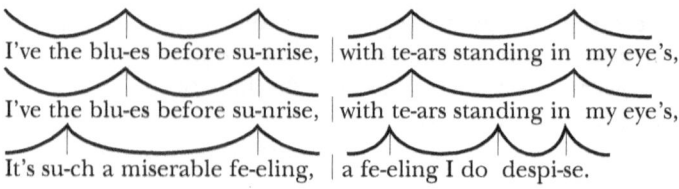

I've the blu-es before su-nrise, | with te-ars standing in my eye's,
I've the blu-es before su-nrise, | with te-ars standing in my eye's,
It's su-ch a miserable fe-eling, | a fe-eling I do despi-se.

The second strophe:

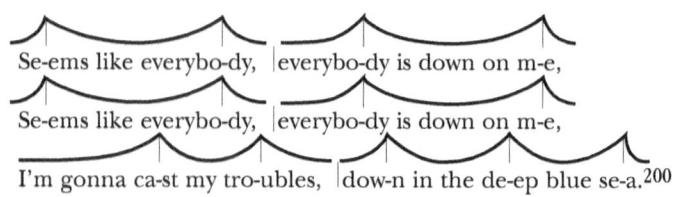

Se-ems like everybo-dy, | everybo-dy is down on m-e,
Se-ems like everybo-dy, | everybo-dy is down on m-e,
I'm gonna ca-st my tro-ubles, | dow-n in the de-ep blue se-a.[200]

The harmonic pattern is repeated in each strophe and the melody remains almost identical. The tension is built up during the first two lines, reaches its climax at the end of the second line and then disperses in the third line. The third line rounds off both the lyrics and the melody. Each strophe forms a complete unit. This example features all sorts of little tricks which are characteristic of one of the best blues singers available on record, Leroy Carr. He composed this blues music and wrote the lyrics. The repetition of the word 'everybody', strongly emphasized in the second strophe, is particularly beautiful. His language is very poetic. For instance, look at the following line:

> Sun rises in the East, and sets well in the West,
> Sun rises in the East, sets well in the West,
> It's hard to tell, hard to tell, which one will treat you the best.[201]

The singer is wondering here whether it is the beginning or the end of the day that is best for him in his troubles.

The blues song is meditative. Barely more than two bars are sung for every four played. The rest is given over to instrumental music by the guitar, perhaps, or other accompanying instruments. The guitar is, however, the most characteristic instrument of these blues singers-cum-troubadours and together with the Spaniards they may be called masters of this instrument. Big Bill Broonzy was such a master and his music has been recorded on a number of LPs.[202] The meditative aspect is strongly enhanced by the instrumental parts.

So the blues is the song of secular African-American culture. No black Christians would sing the blues; the content of the songs would be considered incompatible with their faith. The content is indeed curious. The songs tell of worries and troubles and presuppose a rather immoral lifestyle. It must be said, however, that this is partly due to the past, the slavery, when the owner was at liberty to sell his slaves irrespective of their family and to bring men and women together as he wished. The blues emerged from an impoverished world, a world of people who stand on the very bottom rung of the social ladder. It would hardly be fair to blame blacks for this, as the Jim Crow regulations made progress almost impossible.

It remains remarkable that while the main subject matter of the blues is love the songs are seldom or never coarse or vulgar. Sex is certainly referred to and taken for granted, but the blues is rarely 'dirty', and sexual relations, as such, rarely or never besmirched. That only happens with a certain type of blues, sung in nightclubs and intended for white ears. (We shall come to it later.) The blues is based on poetic fiction, as is the case in European songwriting. In the case of the latter, falling in love and flirting are central. It is widely recognized that the rather sturdy singer on the stage, declaring his love for the pretty miller's daughter as he sings Schubert's cycle of *Die schöne Müllerin* ('the pretty miller-girl'), has not actually fallen in love with this particular girl. In the same way the worries, troubles and strife which the blues singer laments, are not necessarily part of his personal experience. The subject of the poetic fiction of this black music is abandonment: the abandoned singer tells of how his beloved left him, and how he has got the blues, which proves how much he loved her. An appeal to return, a desire to contact her is often included and, at the same time, a desire to escape from the torment. Travelling as migrant workers was indeed characteristic of these poor people and the music speaks of a permanent state of migration. This is confirmed by the incidence of geographical knowledge of the Southern States in these songs. Finally, besides a healthy dose of characteristic humour, there is a certain amount of optimism, as in this traditional line, which is often heard: 'The sun's going to shine in my back door some day.'

Here are one or two examples of blues lyrics. Firstly, the 'Midnight hour blues' by Leroy Carr:

> In the wee midnight hour, long before the break of day, (x2)
> When the blues creep upon you and carry your mind away.
>
> While I lay in my bed, and cannot go to sleep, (x2)
> While my heart's in trouble and my mind is thinking deep.
>
> My mind was running back to the days of long ago, (x2)
> And the one I love, I don't see her anymore.
>
> Blues why do you worry me, why do you stay so long, (x2)
> You came to me yesterday, been with me all night long.
>
> I've been so worried, I didn't know what to do, (x2)
> So I guess that's why I've had these 'midnight hour blues'.[203]

There are few blues songs that deviate from the above in content. The following example is a particular exception. The background is that 'grades of skin colour' were prevalent in the USA – a sort of apartheid or segregation. School clubs were structured according to skin colour[204] and the males, in their search for a partner, strove for the 'bonus' female whose skin was lighter than their own. It is also useful to know that African-Americans were not particularly fond of South Americans, whom they referred to as 'monkey men'.

> So glad I'm brownskin, glad I'm brownskin, chocolate to the bone,
> So glad I'm brownskin, chocolate to the bone,
> And I got what it takes to make a monkey man leave his home.
>
> Black man is evil, yellow man so lowdown, ['yellow' here refers to light brown]
> Black man is evil, yellow man so lowdown, I walk into these houses, just to see these black men frown.
>
> I just like Miss Lillian, like Miss Lillian, I mean Miss Glynn you see,
> I like Miss Lillian, I mean Miss Lillian you see,
> She said: 'A brownskin man is just all right with me.'
>
> Yellow man won't quit, black man just won't behave,
> Yellow man won't quit, and a black man just won't behave,
> Got a pigmeat mamma crazy 'bout brownskin baby ways.
>
> I got a yellow mamma, got a yellow mamma, she always got a pleasant smile,
> I got a yellow mamma, she always got a pleasant smile,
> But that brownskin gal with her coalblack dreamy eyes.[205]

The background to the blues

Blues and trouble

There are other aspects of the blues worth mentioning before we bring the subject to a close, because it is evident that, in contrast to Western entertainment music, which abandons the concept of everyday reality, blues music is very realistic. This comparison is important because popular music, cabaret music, schmaltz intended for home listening, dancing to or otherwise, has replaced the folk music of the West. It has become the new folk music – the music of the 'folk', as it were. It is barely conceivable that entertainment music would sing of the sombre side of life. A reference to a valley of tears may occur in a sentimental song, but that same sentimentality removes it from everyday reality with little elaboration of the situation. I am convinced that the realism in African-

American music can be partly attributed to biblical preaching. Its influence is evident, even when the church has been abandoned by the songwriter. Christianity is not opposed in these lyrics; in fact there are many songs that show that writers were familiar with the Bible and, although they may not have lived up to it, considered it to be the truth. One well-known example is the traditional line, 'The Good Book (the Bible) says you got to reap just what you sowed.' The Bible does not teach us to escape from reality and neither does it teach us stoicism. It does not teach us to say 'all that misery does not bother me', but to face up to problems and hardships, to look to God for help and to expect it from him. The Scriptures teach us to break with superficial escapism, pretending there is nothing wrong. In the light of this we can understand the true-to-life realism of the songs, including the secular ones, of the blacks.

This spirit is anything but self-evident. Would it not seem more appropriate for the indigent blacks in their songs to seek escape from reality, to sing of their wishful dreams?

The blues and spirituals certainly share a similar realistic approach. We have already talked about 'Down on me'; this is another spiritual:

> Wait and see what your brother will do:
> Before your face have a love for you.
> Behind your back scandalize your name,
> Just the same you have to bear the blame.[206]

Can we imagine a European folk song like this?

> Death is awful, death is awful, death is awful,
> Spare me over another year.
> This is the way that death begins,
> You stretch your limbs and close your eyes,
> Death is awful, death is awful,
> Death, spare me over another year.[207]

That was a spiritual. The following line is characteristic of the blues:

> Blues and trouble, seem to be my best friends (x2)
> When my blues leaves me, then my trouble begins.[208]

Sometimes the blues cites a piece of proverbial wisdom like this. Another example is the recurring notion which Snitcher Roberts put into words like this:

> When I have money, I have friends from miles around, (x2)
> Ain't got no money, then my friends cannot be found.
>
> Some give me a nickel, some give me a lousy dime, (x2)
> Some people say: 'Baby, you was never an old friend of mine.'[209]

One of the most curious examples of this attitude can be heard in the 'Moppin' blues' by Big Bill Broonzy. It is a song which shows that in spite of their circumstances, the blacks did not display rampant revolutionary sentiments. It also shows that they had not yet learned to express the concept of human rights. They were not aware of society's obligation to provide for them. What they did express was great joy and openness – cheerfulness under the most testing circumstances. There was no escapism – they faced the difficulties positively; no bitterness, in spite of everything. A song like the following one shows the strong influence of scriptural preaching and its effect on a milieu which was anything but churchgoing. It also shows the secret of these people, how they were able to survive during all those years of oppression and poverty.

The joy that can be heard in the song is definitely real, and the chorus betrays no pretence – no superficial *que sera sera*. It is a typically Western thought, anyway, to assume that happiness and cheerfulness are superficial, and that melancholy, sadness and seriousness are the only deep emotions.

The singer tells how he is sweeping a building out, alone. He has nothing, no house, no money, nothing to lose apart from his 'moppin' broom' – his broom. Still, the chorus confirms, 'I'm the happiest man in town.' As always, the blues is played in a major key, apart from the blue notes (i.e. minor notes in an otherwise major key), although this example is played particularly briskly. Each strophe contains twelve bars, but the structure is unusual. In fact it is probably an early form of the blues, dating back to the time before a structure was established. Each line contains two bars.

> I've got the moppin' blues, (x5)
> But I'm the happiest man in town.
>
> You know I can't lose (x5)
> Nothin' but this moppin' broom I knew.
>
> I'm all alone, (x5)
> But I'm the happiest man in town.
>
> I ain't got no money, (x5)
> But I'm the happiest man in town.
>
> I ain't got no home, (x5)
> But I'm the happiest man in town.[210]

The blues as sung by Ma Rainey et al.

'Backwater blues'

Besides the mainly male, itinerant troubadour blues singers, there were also some women who played the blues. They were the core of the travelling shows – groups who toured from one place to another and held their gigs in tents. Bands of this type had already existed for some time in America – the minstrel shows, as we have seen, had been around a while – and it was understandable that black groups like this would also develop to perform for exclusively black audiences. Also blues were sung at these gigs where the climax of the evening was provided by the likes of Ma Rainey. She was regarded as a great artist by her own folk, and rightly so, for the many records we have of her music bear witness to this fact.

Usually accompanied by a small orchestra/band – she did not play the guitar, unlike most troubadours – she sang blues which she had composed herself, or drew on tradition. Her orchestra/band always comprised of a piano and a guitar, and was often joined by a trumpet, clarinet and trombone. The passages that were not sung – generally the last two bars of a four-bar line – were taken over by the instruments. Ma Rainey and other singers of her genre had no formal music education and their voices were not 'trained' according to Western standards. But that in itself does not make them natural voices. Here too we find a certain artistic, deliberate style of singing that builds on the tradition of the hollers and uses the voice in a very distinctive way. This style of singing is varied, not based on the violin like our Western singing tradition,[211] and the potential of the voice is fully tapped. The rendition is always based on the text, for the singer as well as for the musicians; madrigalisms, i.e. direct illustrations of the text, often occur: when she sings 'moan' for example, the trombone will make a moaning sound; when she says 'laugh' we hear the trumpet laughing; while other words like 'rain', 'whistlin'' (of a train), and so on are also depicted by the instruments. The tempo is usually gentle, never very slow, never sentimental, the rendition always powerful but at the same time never wild, rough or uncontrolled. The only way to recognize these characteristics is to listen to the music. This is no simple matter for us Westerners because the songs have their own style, which is anything but Western or Schubert-like, and equally little redolent of Africa. This art form is pure African-American; it is a new art form, completely the creation of North American blacks.

To give you an idea of the impression that 'Ma' (this was her nickname, and it testifies to her popularity) Gertrude Rainey made on her audiences, let me quote a poem by Sterling Brown, written prior to 1932. Ma Rainey's golden years as an artist were between 1900 and 1930; her stamping ground was almost exclusively the Southern States.

> When Ma Rainey
> Comes to town,
> Folks from any place,
> Miles aroun',
> From Cape Girardeau,
> Poplar Bluff,

Flocks in to hear
Ma do her stuff;
Comes flivverin' in,
Or ridin' mules,
Or packed in trains,
Picknickin' fools ...
That's what it's like,
For miles on down,
To New Orleans Delta
An' Mobile town,
When Ma hits
Anywheres aroun'.

Dey comes to hear Ma Rainey from the little river settlements,
From Blackbottom cornrows and from lumber camps;
Dey stumble in de hall, jes' a-laughin' an' a-cacklin',
Cheerin' lak roarin' water, lak wind in river swamps.

An' some jokers keeps deir laugh's a-goin' in de crowded aisles,
An' some folks sits dere waitin' wid deir aches an' miseries,
Till Ma comes out before dem, a-smilin' gold-toofed smiles,
An' Long Boy ripples minors on de black and yellow keys.

O Ma Rainey
Sing yo' song;
Now you's back
Whah you belong,
Git way inside us,
Keep us strong ...
O Ma Rainey,
Li'l and low;
Sing us 'bout de hard luck
Roun' our do';
Sing us bout de lonesome road
We mus' go ...

I talked to a fellow, an' the fellow say:
'She jes' catch hold of us, somekindaway.
She sang "Backwater blues" one day:
"It rained fo' days an' de skies was dark at night,
Trouble taken place in de lowlands at night.
Thundered an' lightened an' the storm begin to roll,
Thousan's of people ain't got no place to go.

"Den I went an' stood upon some high ol' lonesome hill,
An' looked down on de place where I used to live."

An' den de folks, dey natchally bowed dey heads an' cried,
Bowed dey heavy heads, shet dey moufs up tight an' cried,

An' Ma lef' de stage, an' followed some de folks outside.'

Dere wasn't much more de fellow say:
She jes' gits hold of us dataway.[212]

This is the well-known 'Backwater blues', inspired by a Mississippi flood and later made famous by one of Ma's pupils, Bessie Smith, who never bettered her teacher – just occasionally equalled her. 'Backwater' refers to the water which, having burst through a dike elsewhere, floods the area from the land side.[213]

The first brass band music

'I'm going up the country'

Socially, there was not much going on in the plantations; the odd party was held. But 4th July – Independence Day – was earmarked as a day of celebration. There were barbecues, and musical accompaniment was guaranteed. Slaves were often used as musicians in the brass bands. They played patriotic songs like 'Hail Columbia', 'President's march', 'Hail to the heroes whose triumph have brightened' and 'The star-spangled banner', but also less distinguished pieces like 'Yankee doodle' and 'Wait for the wagon'.

After the Northerners had won the Civil War, the slaves were freed and these blacks began to play their own music – spirituals, folk songs, early blues, etc. – on the instruments they had kept. They played mainly for dance parties, and the dances that were performed to this music were the real folk dances of the rural areas.

Such bands cropped up all over the South and, as we shall see, contributed to the emergence of jazz. In the 1950s they could only be heard in very remote areas such as rural Alabama, for example, where Ramsey made recordings of the Lapsey Band and the Laneville-Johnson Brass Band in 1954. These musicians are farmers who play at rural dance parties while they are waiting for the harvest. The Lapsey Band bears the name of the plantation where their ancestors, more than a century ago, were slaves. The Laneville-Johnson Brass Band was created through the amalgamation of the Laneville and the Johnson Bands.

The musicians play exclusively by ear on old brass instruments like the cornet, the horn, the valve-trombone, and on drums they inherited from their ancestors, instruments that would not be out of place in the nearest museum. They have a traditional repertoire that consists predominantly of spirituals and folk songs, such as 'Precious Lord, hold my hand', 'Take rocks and gravel to build a solid road', 'Preaching tonight on the Old Campground', 'Dixie' and 'Going up the country, don't you want to go'.

Their music is rough and little refined, but how would these amateurs have been able to refine their technique? Still, it seems to me that Ramsey's recordings, while they provide us with a valuable addition to our archives, are qualitatively misleading; the oompah of the horn, which sets the rhythm, has been recorded a bit too loudly in comparison with the other instruments.[214] This is not surprising since the recordings were made at night, in the open air and in poor weather conditions.

String bands

'Hootchie kootchie'

It is hard to say when the string band came into being. It possibly started on Saturday evenings, after the slaves had had a day off. They would dance and sing, make music and tell stories to each other. On the other hand, the custom to play like this may have arisen only after liberation. In any event, string bands seem to have been around as far back as we are able to trace. They are small, informal bands composed of amateur musicians. All manner of stringed instruments are played, guitar and banjo being the first to come to mind. One indication that this form of music has existed for a long time is the fact that the banjo – an instrument developed by the blacks – is now considered an old instrument, one that existed in the days of slavery and was used way back in the minstrel shows as an instrument to give the black parody its *couleur locale*.

There is little material to give us an exact picture of the string-band music of the nineteenth century. The few later recordings provide little insight as most of the musicians in question will have been exposed, remotely at least, to the development of jazz. We suspect that the character of the music played in the nineteenth century was not unlike the white folk-dance music that still exists today in the Appalachians – remote parts of Carolina and Virginia. These square dances were played on fiddles, five-stringed banjos, guitars, dulcimers (dating back to the seventeenth century) and accordions.[215] So the black string bands played a rendition of white folk music, which in turn was reproduced by whites in their minstrel shows – the cake-walk for example, which was an early form of ragtime.

The most important recording is once again to be found in the Folkways series,[216] recorded in Vicksburg, Mississippi. Old examples are very rare, because record companies seldom recorded music by amateur bands. We believe that the Dallas String Band, possibly a professional group who made famous the 'Dallas rag',[217] provides us with quite a good example of this sort of music.

Ragtime

'Maple leaf rag'

Although the 25 years after their liberation were in many ways not easy for the former slaves, they did have more opportunities and discrimination did not take on its really ugly forms until after 1900.[218] In any case, African-Americans began to feel their way in the world of music. It is quite understandable that the very first music they took hold of was minstrel music, particularly banjo music, which is distantly related to string-band music.[219] They tried to improve the music by arranging it more in line with the musical practice of their own background, and to develop it as a characteristic pianistic art.

This is a brief outline of the origins of ragtime. Shortly after its birth, between 1895 and 1900, it became the rage in the USA and, inevitably, its commercialviability destined it for a very wide audience looking only for rhythmic entertainment. We must not forget, however, that the musicians, mainly from St Louis and surrounding areas – such as Scott Joplin and Tom Turpin – were real artists with serious ideas and ambitions. Their music was far from straightforward and their use of the piano was particularly rich and versatile. Piano scrolls, published at the beginning of the twentieth century for mechanical pianos, give only a faint idea of the achievement of these musicians, also in an artistic sense, though it is sufficient to convince anyone who really wants to hear.[220]

Ragtime is composed music that is published as sheet music. The fact that all of the important ragtime composers were black (with the exception of Joseph Lamb) may be considered as further evidence that ragtime indeed had its origins in African-American music. We have already mentioned Scott Joplin, who even ventured a ragtime opera.[221] A striking characteristic of ragtime is the prolific use of the syncopation, but it was written of Joplin that,

> although syncopation remained an essential component of the musical resources he used, he pushed it aside to some extent. His phrasing is longer, his harmonies more complex. He uses more modulation and often more than one key within a sixteen-bar strophe. Three features of his art particularly stand out: greater freedom of the left hand, the attempt to make the beat more implicit than explicit, and a renewed or at least greater interest in matters of form.[222]

Joplin's ragtime, in contrast to popular ragtime, was not reduced to a formula, i.e. a particular type of melody with much syncopation, a definite rhythm produced by the left hand (referred to in the trade as 'pumping'), in pursuit of a stereotypical construction.

We would like to refer briefly to musical structure here, because it helps to explain some of the typical features of later New Orleans jazz. Firstly, the sixteen-bar form is central, constructed of a four-bar phrase, which is repeated, and repeated again (note that the basic chords of the repeated phrases may vary), plus a counter melody of four bars. The following structure however, occurs more often: a four-bar phrase, which is repeated followed by the counter melody, plus a repeat of the first phrase. These sixteen bars are then usually repeated and are followed by a new sixteen-bar section, which also is repeated, and so on, leading to the common pattern of AABBAACCAADD, or more frequently AABBC-CDD (each capital letter represents a sixteen-bar section). The various themes are not in contrast to each other; there is no mood change in the piece as a whole, neither does the tempo change (no accelerandi, just as in other African-American music). The metre is always even, mostly 4/4.

Little research has been carried out in this field so far. There must be much of aesthetic value among the large amount of sheet music published in the course of the first decade of the twentieth century waiting to be discovered. The following poem, published by Stark, has been reproduced with permission. Stark published a lot of work in this area (including all Joplin's work), continually emphasizing aesthetic significance as opposed to commercial imitations. He said, for example:

> Publishers are known to hold that the best songs never become hits. The pieces which are all the rage in the cinemas and bars are songs with a twist to draw attention or a dog barking, a cat mewing, hooters or ships' whistles [this was pre-1920, these things were still a novelty], and by the second hearing they sound as flat as a pancake. Sales techniques are also far removed from our idea of how the 'art divine' should be propagated.

He then continues by quoting this poem:

> Full many a gem of purest ray serene
> The deep unfathomed caves of ocean bear,
> Full many a flower was born to blush unseen,
> And wash its fragrance in the desert air.
>
> Full many a mushy, gushy song – and vile
> Is sold by methods – sure the devil's own,
> Full many a gem of art and love – the while
> Lies silent, sadly waiting to be known.[223]

This poem is entitled 'Maple leaf rag', taken from the title of Joplin's debut piece from 1897, which is also his best-known work.

3
Twentieth Century: pre-World War I

New Orleans around 1900

'Eh La-Bas'

A new cultural phenomenon, a new style or new art does not suddenly spring up out of the blue. Neither can we explain the new on the basis of a single factor; that would be insufficient for more than a fleeting manifestation. If the new is to be awarded a permanent place in the annals of history it will have to prove itself in depth and breadth – depth, to make a deep impression on the audience, and breadth, to remain solidly founded, even if one contributing factor changes.

The above applies to the birth of jazz in New Orleans around the turn of the twentieth century – it cannot be accounted for by a single factor. It was neither the brothels of this port nor the Storyville bars that led to the birth of jazz. The fact that so many jazz writers get wrapped up in the red-light district of New Orleans can be attributed to a craving for colourful sensation, for lawless sleaze (albeit 'written' sensation and sleaze). Historical truth does not benefit from such cravings and they do not explain anything. Economic and social conditions did sometimes lead to black musicians seeking employment in the brothels, but the very notion that a real jazz band, with music that is so far from sentimental and sweet, would actually have found its niche in a brothel is so obviously misguided that we have to refute it out of hand.

The music flourished and there was a profusion of enthusiastic musicians (often more semi-professional than professional), which can partly be attributed to the fact that instruments could be bought very cheaply from the junk shops in New Orleans. The army, which had fought in Cuba against Spain, had shortly before been disbanded, and with it the military bands. This paved the way for the poor, who in this case were blacks, to get hold of instruments which they otherwise would not have been able to afford. This does not, however, explain the birth of jazz music. Let me explain what happened in New Orleans during the first ten to fifteen years of the twentieth century.

The original name for New Orleans was La Nouvelle-Orléans, and it was the capital of the colony of Louisiana, founded by the French during the reign of Louis XIV. This area was bought by the Yankees at the beginning of the nineteenth century, but it retained its French character for a long time – Roman Catholic and French-speaking. It is remarkable that this city, with one of the key ports for the slave trade, freed blacks long before the Civil War and that there was little racial discrimination. Coloured people were socially divided from whites, belonging to different classes, but that is where the differences ended. After 1865 the coloureds began to fare quite well and the Creoles (of mixed descent) in particular formed a flourishing middle class. The old French families and the well-off Creoles lived in the Vieux Carré, the old city. The culture of the Creoles was French, not only in terms of their language but also in terms of morals and customs.

Those who could afford it sent their children to be educated in France and, even though they were only part-French, they called themselves French and looked to France for their roots. Music played an important part in their lives. French opera held a central place in their culture and both amateur and professional orchestras were of a high standard. Creoles also had a great love for marching music, which had flourished during the Napoleonic era. New Orleans was no different from the French provincial towns in this respect.

The Creoles lived in a part of town called Downtown. To the west, on the other side of the road, lay Uptown, the home of the Anglo-Saxon Americans who had come to live there at a later time. In the poorer neighbourhoods lived blacks who had left their rural homes for the cities, where they hoped to make a living as casual labourers. The musical traditions of these country folk lived on in the blues, string-band music and folk music, but also in the spirituals that were sung in the Baptist Churches.

Both Creoles and blacks had been doing quite well after the Civil War. Access to the higher positions was not closed and many held important positions, right up to the State Parliament. This changed in 1890 when discrimination became harsher, even in these parts.[224] As a consequence both the Creoles and the blacks became impoverished. Creoles were forced out of their positions as a result of boycotts and discrimination, while blacks were increasingly socially and economically deprived. Music formed an escape route with many opportunities to play at parties, weddings, festivals, picnics with dancing, and so on. It was a well-established custom that Downtown Creoles played in Uptown. The number of blacks from rural areas who sought employment from the Uptown whites also kept growing. Competition was born – the contrast was sometimes sharp but it made contact possible – and an exchange took place of their respective heritages.

The Downtown Creoles provided the music strictly according to the French palate – they were technically capable and good at reading scores at parties, while the blacks, possibly in order to honour their own culture as opposed to that of the Creoles, played more American music. They took greater liberties in their interpretation of the printed notes (going so far as to pretend that they could not read music), and there were many features typical of their own tradition that gave the music its own character. Occasionally they played the blues (Bolden apparently being the first to do so in 1896).

The musical flavour that the Creoles introduced to the mixture of styles – the socio-economic situation created a necessity to merge in many areas – was very significant for the new music which was to emerge, namely New Orleans jazz. A typically French playing style can sometimes still be detected in the clarinet pieces – tunes like 'High society' (an old French march) give their origin away. Grace and lightness were generally regarded as the Creole-French contribution, while their extensive knowledge of the theory and technique of music must not be underestimated and will certainly have been important to jazz musicians.

We mentioned that Creole-French elements can sometimes be detected, but besides that some of the old traditions are still alive in New Orleans as well. Kid Ory was able to play old songs like 'Blanche Touquatoux' in 1945, sung in the French dialect Creole patois. Then there is 'Eh La-Bas' ('There downtown'), recorded in New Orleans in 1944,[225] which has a strong flavour of the French chanson. Old French quadrilles are occasionally still danced.[226]

Black music in New Orleans

'219 blues'

African-Americans who came to New Orleans later brought their own traditions with them – including their spirituals, blues, folk songs and work songs. We hear a reverberation of the latter in Oliver's 'Snag it'.[227] Some of the stylistic eccentricities of the trumpet are reminiscent of the way black preachers deliver their sermons; the taste for rendering a melody together, while each one is free to sing his or her own version – not unisonant or homophonic, but with a sort of restrained polyphony – to some extent resembles the way Dr Watts' hymns were (and still are) sung, and dancing songs such as 'Liza Jane' and children's songs such as 'Sally Walker', even though they have been transformed (e.g. Armstrong's 'Georgia grind'[228]), have survived through jazz.

Buddy Bolden occupied a prominent place among blacks. He was a Baptist and a regular churchgoer – though we can hardly call him devout. He was born in New Orleans in 1868, but his family is said to have come from Tunica, a place west of New Orleans known for its brass bands. It is not impossible that he introduced some, if not a considerable amount, of that tradition to New Orleans.[229] Bolden was musically well educated and played the cornet. His musical career began in 1895 as leader of several bands in the parks of Uptown, Johnson Park and Lincoln Park, where people danced in the open air.

Bolden was a very popular musician, but the great influence he had on many young people, including a certain Bunk Johnson, is even more significant. The band in which he played in 1897 consisted of the following instruments: clarinet, cornet, trombone, guitar, double bass and drums. It seems possible that he was the first to have introduced this now traditional formation of New Orleans ensembles.

It is also significant that he was the first, or one of the first, to include music of black origin in his repertoire, in particular the blues, or related music. Bolden's 'Take it away', played later by Jelly Roll Morton,[230] his 'Bucket got a hole in it',[231] and many others, have sixteen bars but the pattern of the melody comes very close to that of the blues and does not have the structural characteristics of ragtime.

There was something else which set the blacks[232] apart from the Creoles. Initially, they would have made it their duty to emphasize the difference between their own style of music and the other, more French, style. That is also the reason why blacks set out to use their instruments in an own special way – to achieve sounds the others were not able to produce. As a result they developed their own taste in instrumental style that was in keeping with their own traditions. We have already mentioned the French clarinet style, which continues to be recognizable. This contrasts starkly with that of black roots which has strong vibrato and a stronger attack of tone. Besides using the normal mutes many more tricks were devised for the trumpet. The use of the mute to create a 'wa-wa' sound was particularly revolutionary. It is said to have been the brainchild of King Oliver. Another trumpet player who has also been credited with the honour of being its inventor is Mutt Carey. He came from New Orleans but later moved to Los Angeles and wrote as follows:

> Joe Oliver and I were the first to use mutes and that sort of thing. We were both freak trumpet men. I have to give Oliver the credit for starting it off. Joe could make his trumpet sound like a holy roller meeting [referring to a sect whose singing was often intense and emotional]. That man could do anything with his horn![233]

To sum up, we can say that the fact that the blacks began to emphasize the characteristic features of their own music, so as not to lose ground in competition with the Creoles, led to a characteristic approach that maximized the potential of the instruments. This use of the instruments found its way into jazz music, which was just developing around that time. Intonation, tone modulation and vibrato are all characteristic non-Western, pure African-American elements in this music. Also phrasing, the pattern of melodies, rhythm and, as we shall see, structure differ in jazz from Western music.[234]

The first Creole musician to play the blues was Jelly Roll Morton. I will come back to him later but he is important to us here because he made a recording of the first blues he ever heard, the '219 blues', sung around 1900 by Mamie Desdoumes, a female vocalist from New Orleans. 219 is the number of a train, also 217 and so on:

> Two nineteen took my babe away, (x2)
> Two seventeen will bring her back some day.

Stood on the corner with her feet just soakin' wet (x2)
Beggin' each and every man that she met.

If you can't give a dollar, give me a lousy dime, (x2)
I wanna feed that hungry man of mine.[235]

Brass bands in New Orleans

'Just a closer walk with Thee'

Buddy Bolden often played in the brass band parades that were so popular in New Orleans. Any excuse was sufficient for staging a parade. These bands, however, also had, and still have, a special task: to play at funerals, a typical custom of New Orleans.[236]

Spirituals were sung in the house of mourning where the deceased lay. When it was time for the funeral, the procession was led by a brass band that usually consisted of an E-flat clarinet, two trumpets, an althorn, a trombone, a tuba, a drum and a bass drum. They played spirituals like 'Nearer my God to Thee', 'Just a closer walk with Thee', and so on, in a slow and stately tempo. On arrival at the graveyard the band stayed outside and the family followed the coffin to the graveside. When the mourners returned, the drum sounded a roll, the band set up and began to play as soon as the party stepped outside. The music was slow till they reached the corner of the graveyard, but then became fast and lively. The 'second line', adults and children who walked alongside the band, followed along the pavement. There were many brass bands that played on this sort of occasion, but the Excelsior Brass Band and the Onward Brass Band were particularly well known. (The Eureka Brass Band and the Young Tuxedo Brass Band still play today.) Many later jazz musicians owe a significant part of their education to these bands, King Oliver being one of them.

Jelly Roll Morton in New Orleans

'King Porter stomp'

Ferdinand La Menthe, also known as Jelly Roll Morton, was born not far from the Vieux Carré in Downtown, New Orleans around 1885. He gave the following account of his roots – like an ancient legend, accompanied by ceremonial piano chords:[237]

> As I can understand, my folks were in the city of New Orleans long before the Louisiana purchase (when the land was bought by the Yankees), and all my folks came directly from the shores of France, that is across the world in the other world, and they landed in the new world years ago.

I can remember the time of my great-grandfather and my great-grandmother. My great-grandfather was Emile Pechet. He was regarded as one of the greatest jewellers of the South. My great-grandmother was Mimi Pechet. She travelled great distances (as a nanny you see), and she died aged about a hundred when I was grown up. As long as I knew them, they were not capable of speaking a single word of American or English.

My grandmother was called Laura. She married a French colonist called Monette, who was a wholesaler of liquor. That was my grandfather – and neither of them spoke American or English.

My grandmother gave birth to Henry, Gus, Neville and Nelusco, her sons, all with French names, and three daughters, Louise, Viola and Margaret ... Louise married F.P. La Menthe, also a colonist and regarded as one of the leading building contractors in all the South. Now Louise was my mother, mother of me – Ferdinand Jelly Roll Morton.

Of course you will be asking yourselves where the name Morton comes from, because it's an English name. Well, I'll tell you. I changed my name for reasons of business when I began travelling around. I didn't want to be called 'Frenchy' ...

My first instrument consisted of two chairs and a tin can. It sounded like a symphony to me, because the only music I heard in those days (around 1890) were classical compositions. The next instrument I tried was the harmonica when I was five ... We always had musical instruments at home, including the guitar, drums, piano, trombone, etc. We had a whole lot and there was always somebody enjoying playing ... When I was seven years old I was regarded as the best guitarist in the neighbourhood, and sometimes I played in a string band – there were a lot of them around at the time. The small combinations of three instruments, consisting of double bass, mandolin and guitar played serenades late in the evening ... Of course my family never imagined they had a musician in their midst. They always thought of a musician as a hobo ... apart from the musicians of the French opera, where they often went. Actually it was at a recital at the French opera that I hit upon the idea of taking up the piano ... One day at a party I saw a gentleman sit down at the piano and I heard him play a good piece of ragtime.[238]

Here you have a glimpse of the beginning of the musical career of the man who was to create the jazz-piano style. His story shows the various factors that played a role. He must have been a good pianist as early as 1900 or thereabouts. Besides a semi-classical style of music he will have been thoroughly acquainted with ragtime. He also made early acquaintance with the blues, as we have seen.

About 1902 he composed the 'King Porter stomp', which has the structure of pure ragtime. We know it only from the many later versions made for the gramophone, so that it is hard to imagine how he would have played it. But the piece as we know it shows clearly how the approach differs from real ragtime; it has a very free left hand, a much freer, less jumpy melody and a more fluent rendition. The structure of the various themes also differs somewhat from that of standard ragtime. The phrases consist of eight bars, repeated, making a total of sixteen bars per theme. Jelly Roll (the American word for 'Swiss roll') Morton even gave a demonstration of the difference between ragtime and jazz – the style of piano playing which he introduced or, at least, developed – using the 'Maple leaf rag'[239] to illustrate his point. This shows the very varied and richer rhythm – although a steady 4/4 time is retained – and the extraordinarily beautifully phrased rendition of the themes.

The tango became popular around the turn of the century. This dance with its characteristic rhythm was conceived either in Havana or in Argentina by black labourers from Central America. In either case it is clearly a mixture of African and Spanish musical heritage: the tangana is an African dance, but the Spanish element dominates the melody. Jelly heard tanganas and later confessed that he found them difficult to play well and that he was not very keen on the tunes. This led him to compose a few of his own, which constitute some of the most beautiful music he has written. They are in fact quasi-tangos, with a jerkiness and excessive dance music quality characteristic of the tango, restructured to produce a fluent beat that is closely linked to the very beautiful melody. The themes themselves are just fascinating. Of these gems – which are even more beautiful than Albeniz's quasi-tangos, and others – 'Mama 'Nita', for example (probably composed on the West Coast where he married Anita), and 'Tia Juana' (a place on the West Coast)[240] are just two examples.

Finally we would like to mention his 'New Orleans blues' from 1904, among the first blues ever to have been played by a Creole. Here too Jelly handles the structure very freely, dividing the twelve-bar strophe into a sort of introduction consisting of four bars and a long phrase of eight bars. There are four themes, of which the first three are vaguely reminiscent of the tangos we have just mentioned, while the last one is played in the more usual jazz rhythm. Each theme is played twice. The structure of the piece, the actual composition, was very important to Jelly. Although variations were permitted within the given framework, there was no essential deviation from the fixed sequence of the themes and their structure. We can best compare this approach, common to all jazz that originated in New Orleans, with the procedure sometimes followed in Europe in the seventeenth century: the composer wrote the themes and supplied the general instructions, while the performer was free to add the embellishments and to choose the instruments. The way Jelly went about it becomes clear if we compare the two recordings of 'New Orleans blues' (under the title of 'New Orleans joys')[241] recorded in quick succession in 1923. Although they differ in detail, the overall structure and the themes remain the same, so that the total impression is very similar. He had to play the piece quite quickly here, or it might not have fitted on the small 78 rpm disc. (Later, in 1935, he played the piece again in essentially the same way, but at a much slower pace.[242])

In 1905 Jelly composed the 'Jelly Roll blues', which was published in 1915 in Chicago[243] where he was then based. Its structure is similar to that of 'New Orleans blues', except that the first four bars of each theme are regarded as a break. This is a typical feature of jazz, which Jelly paid much attention to and valued greatly. The steady rhythm is interrupted for one or two bars in order to allow a free passage to be played with the upper hand. In the band's version of 1926, Morton either leaves the breaks to a solo instrument or he plays them himself on the piano.

Jelly Roll Morton did not have an easy character. Many aspects of his performance can be explained by his high ideals and the great demands he placed on his music (and thus also on other jazz musicians), and by the fact that he refused to acknowledge that he was subject to racial discrimination. He tried to live as if it did not exist, seeking recognition for himself as a Creole. In his study of Morton's background and the childhood influences and memories which moulded his character, Lomax discovered the extent to which his race- and class-consciousness affected his view of the music world.[244]

Jelly Roll Morton was very creative and talented – one of the most important musicians to have shaped jazz and a driving force behind its development. As the creator of the jazz-piano style and composer of countless important pieces of music, it would be impossible to ignore him and we will certainly be coming back to him later.

The development of early jazz

Jack Carey

Jack Carey, Mutt Carey's brother, was a trombonist who founded a band in New Orleans around 1913. It was made up of two clarinets, a trumpet, a trombone, a double bass, a guitar and drums. He composed a number of pieces for his band, the Crescent Orchestra, including a piece which was known to black musicians as 'Jack Carey', and to white musicians as 'Nigger no. 2' (we will come back to this shortly). The composition has been, and still is, widely known and loved as 'Tiger rag'. Jelly Roll Morton claimed to have composed it and it is difficult to confirm or refute this. However, it is undoubtedly difficult to argue with his analysis of the composition, where he shows that the succession of themes is derived from a French dance suite, beginning with a quadrille.[245] Acquaintances of Carey have suggested that Mutt Carey took the themes from an old music book of French dances.

Carey's band was one of the first to have played in New Orleans during the time between 1910 and 1920. Oscar Celestin's and Edward Ory's bands also played there. Members of the latter included Oliver and the clarinettist Johnny Dodds, for a while. Several circles of close friends arose from this time – something which was to be of great significance to the history of jazz. There was Clarence Williams' band, who went on tour in Texas with Sidney Bechet and Freddy Pechard's group, the Olympia Orchestra, which was dominated by a number of Creoles including Alphonse Picou, who devised the clarinet solo in 'High society'. In 1907 the band was still playing a lot of legitimate Western (i.e. French) dance music. Some time later during 1913 Keppard went on a nationwide tour, from San Francisco to New York, with an orchestra called The Original Creole Orchestra which included the clarinettist George Baquet. This band opted for jazz.

Jimmy Noone, Babe Dodds, Johnny St Cyr and Bunk Johnson also played in New Orleans, in various combinations, while after 1915 musicians like Louis Armstrong, Paul Barbarin and many others from the younger generation joined them. (I have mentioned only the names of those who were to become famous.) There was a great surplus of musicians as is often the case when art is flourishing, as for instance during the seventeenth century in the Netherlands. Many of those mentioned were semi-professional and depended on earning their income as labourers or traders; they performed occasionally for a ball, party, picnic or per part-time contract at one of the dance halls, clubs and so on.

What kind of music did the bands play then? Initially it was ragtime, compositions originally written for the piano and subsequently arranged for bands. They were published in *The Red Back Book of Rags*[246] and other publications. It seems that after 1900 this part of the repertoire began to lose its significance. There were also the 'tunes of the day', the popular songs. The New Orleans musicians were primarily concerned with their own interpretation of these songs, which formed a welcome starting point for performances and gave the audience what they wanted. The songs were pleasant enough. A good example of this is 'When you and I were young' and 'Maggy'.[247] Then there was the blues, particularly Jelly Roll Morton's 'Jelly Roll blues', 'New Orleans blues', etc. Original compositions like Bolden's 'Bucket got a hole in it', and 'I wish I could shimmy like my sister Kate' (possibly Louis Armstrong's composition), published by Clarence Williams, were also played in the sixteen-bar structure. Finally, musical compositions based on marches were played, the best known of these being 'High society'.

In all these cases – with the exception of written ragtime – there was a particular melody, or melodies, plus the chords. These constituted the material that each band used for its own arrangement – it was a question of what it did with the material. Most important was the given tune (or tunes); the chords were secondary. Improvisation in the true sense of the word, namely to create a new tune ad lib based on the given chords, was uncommon. What took place was not improvisation, but 'embellishing around the melody',[248] the word improvisation was not even used yet! The musicians often played without the help of sheet music, or without referring to a written score. This was called 'faking'.[249] Still, a definite discipline by way of an agreement as to when the band was to play ensemble, solos, breaks and so on was certainly present. This agreement can also be regarded as a framework, even though everything within it was determined with much more care than in the 'composition' that was the starting point for the performance. A certain amount of freedom was definitely present in the rendition, but only within the given framework or there would have been chaos, or a succession of solos only. This did happen later in jazz music, but it would have been unthinkable for early New Orleans music, which was primarily geared towards ensemble.

What was the quality of the music? Sometimes good, sometimes mediocre, depending on who was playing, of course. Neither would it have been very sophisticated at all times. But we must be careful here because we must not apply Western standards in our assessment of quality. We must not expect to find refined modulations, for example, since there was no demand for it; neither can we expect subtle compositional solutions because this music was not designed for the concert hall, and also because these musicians lacked the relevant education. With such expectations we are barking up the wrong tree. This music was not Western music, played in a rough and crude manner; it was the birth of a new kind of music, African-American music, which bears no historical, spiritual or technical relation to Western classical music (from Mozart to Brahms and César Franck).

It has often been said that this music was loud and wild, but we must try to put this in its proper context. This criticism was expressed by people who had no understanding of these new sounds. The first time I heard Bach's second *Brandenburg Concerto*, the first Bach concerto that I consciously and attentively listened to, I heard only loud and apparently unconnected sounds. This was due to the fact that I did not understand what I was hearing, I did not know when musical sententces started and when they stopped – I had nothing to go by, no grip on it. The same applies to early jazz. To the untrained ear it was incomprehensible. There were no guidelines for arranging the strange and new sounds to make sense, which was why it was called 'wild'. So, was it not hard and loud? Let us agree that a trumpet cannot sound louder than it can be played, and that this maximum volume is more often reached in our concert halls than in performance by a good New Orleans jazz band.

The objections about the music being loud and wild confirm that this was indeed a new type of music – a new style that simply could not be compared with the contemporary dance music of the time or with Western marching music (i.e. the types of music that bore the closest relation to jazz music with regards to theme and structure). It is a remarkable fact that the prominent jazz musicians had enjoyed a good education. They all knew their music through and through, and there is as little truth in the romantic notion that naturally-talented musicians suddenly caused this music to spring into existence out of the blue, as there is in other similar cases.

In case we need to prove our point further, here is a quote from Babe Dodds, the most important drummer in the history of New Orleans jazz. He got his nickname because he was the younger brother (by 12 years) of the clarinettist Johnny Dodds. Babe Dodds said:

> When I was only fourteen, I was obsessed with the idea of playing in my brother Johnny's band ... I had been playing since I was a little lad and I thought I was good. But Johnny's answer was, 'Buzz off, kid! Learn to play percussion first and don't bother me before you can.' I took his advice and went to music school – I called it school – four years long and I soon realized that my drumming had been completely wrong. I had to start all over again and completely unlearn everything I was used to doing. This is how I got the basic rudiments of drumming. When I was nineteen I was quite a well-educated musician, at home in all sorts of drumming techniques. I went back to my brother for a job and he got me my first professional engagement – with King Oliver in the famous King Oliver Band, where Johnny was playing the clarinet. Maybe I should point out something important about my brother for the connoisseurs. Johnny had respect for good musicians and good music, but he loathed musically poor musicians attempting to play jazz.[250]

Early white jazz

'Clarinet marmalade'

It is 1917 and the Original Dixieland Jazz Band plays in New York to great applause. They arrived there after having spent some time in Chicago without much success. They were white boys from New Orleans. Since about 1910, possibly earlier, a number of white bands had been playing the new music or, at least, were trying to produce something which resembled the music of the Uptown blacks. They stayed more with ragtime. However, their tempo was faster and their music was rhythmically weaker – partly due to their white background, no doubt, where rhythm was not a natural part of their cultural heritage.

In 1917 they had so much success that their music was recorded for gramophone records. The first jazz 'on record'. The story goes that Kempler had already been approached by the record companies but that he had turned them down, partly because he was afraid that others would 'steal' their music. In any case, these records are the earliest documentation for us; they give our story a solid foundation so that we do not have to reconstruct it or to form an opinion based on all sorts of assertions. We can hear it for ourselves.[251]

It is immediately evident that this music – even at the time of writing, more than forty years later – still sounds fresh and new. It may come across as wild because we have to get used to the tempo, which is often fast, and because the rhythm is not very marked (we will come back to this in the analysis of the New Orleans jazz of the African-Americans); we somewhat miss the firm structure which, after all, also this music demands.

If we really concentrate, however, we hear that the music is anything but rough and uncontrolled. There are often subtle dynamics, there are accents and contrasts, there is a fixed structure within the given framework and there is polyphony between the clarinet, the trumpet and the trombone. These are all characteristics which we recognize from black New Orleans jazz, though there are differences. Black jazz music is much more tranquil, more distinctive and transparent, with more artistic balance than white jazz. You sometimes get the impression that the white musicians are overdoing it with regard to the tempo or in the fierce attack of the tone, though their music is never out of tune, coarse, chaotic, noisy or unmusical.

The setup was the same as that of the black bands: trumpet (La Rocca), clarinet (Larry Shields), trombone (Ed Edwards), piano (Ragas) and drums (Tony Sbarbaro), but note the absence of the saxophone.

They played ragtime compositions like 'Tiger rag', which we already mentioned, and original compositions in this vein like 'Clarinet marmalade', 'Sensation rag', and so on, and occasionally a blues number like 'Bluin' the blues',[252] which was strongly reminiscent of Morton's 'Jelly Roll blues', and others.

Handy's blues

St Louis blues

'Handy, Father of the Blues'. You may have heard this phrase, or seen it in print, countless times. But what is it? A story? A mistake? A slogan? It is an advertising slogan for a publishing company named Handy!

Handy was born in 1873 in Florence, Alabama. He had a musical education, sang popular songs in a quartet and in 1896 he became the leader of Mahara's Coloured Minstrels. This was a touring band that had a very varied programme – from Shakespeare to the latest hit – including 'coon-songs', the imitation black songs. Handy played the accompanying music in the orchestra pit and also overtures like *William Tell*, selections from operas like *The Mikado*, and pieces such as 'Dichter und Bauer' which was renamed 'Poet and peasant' for this purpose. In 1903 he became the leader of a dance band called The Knights of Pythias Band and Orchestra in Clarksdale, Mississippi.

One evening at a ball, Handy was playing the quadrilles and other contemporary dance music. Then someone requested: 'Play some of your own people's music.' Handy tried a sort of minstrel song but the man was not satisfied. He proceeded to pull in a three-piece string band from outside and it began to play 'rough backstreet music with a lot of repetition, which earned them more than the uniformed band's combined salary for the whole evening'.

This is a quote from Abbe Niles' foreword to Handy's publication, *A Treasury of the Blues*. Niles, acting as W.C. Handy's official historian, writes, 'It was still hard to believe that there would be anything at all of commercial value in that disorganized musical by-product,' and indeed it took about another ten years before Handy was fully convinced.

It is striking that this musician was able to observe and listen to the music of his black counterparts as a complete outsider. He claimed to be very interested in the music, but more as a curiosity – as something fascinating. Only very gradually did he dare to stray from the secure path of light music in the Western vein.

What did he do next? Niles continues the account:

> Then Handy came along, who started to draw inspiration from the folk music he had already heard so often – folk songs that were rough and without much meaning. It required a musician to take responsibility for putting something of lasting value into this music. Without this man, W.C. Handy, the blues would not have permeated the national (American) consciousness so quickly, nor would it ever have formed an integral part of it as is now the case.[253]

That 'lasting value' is chiefly pecuniary, by the way, as there are hundreds of records where the 'ordinary, rough and little significant' blues is sung by folk troubadours with a beauty and quality such as no production of Handy even comes close to approaching. Without Handy the blues would indeed probably not have permeated popular music, but whether his diluted product is indeed worth the effort remains to be seen. 'Handy, Father of the Commercial Blues', that is the truth.

Perhaps he was not even that. It is a fact that the first blues to be published was issued by Stark – Artie Matthew's 'Baby Seal blues' in August 1912; next came Hart A. Wand's 'Dallas blues' in September 1912, and third was Handy's 'Memphis blues', three weeks later. The strange thing is that Handy had already composed the piece three years earlier but apparently could not or did not want to publish it.

At best, Handy is a folklorist, someone who tries to present contemporary folk music in a way that makes it more accessible to a 'better' audience of 'higher cultural standing'. His blues, for example, always has a sixteen-bar introduction, which is in fact given more emphasis than the twelve bars of blues that follow. The type of blues we discussed earlier, however, the living blues of the troubadours, exists as a permanent reminder that there is no need for improvement or refinement of this very subtle and deep folk art, and that its commercialization by a handy and well-trained musician does not automatically imply that the art itself has profited.

Let us consider the full implications of this. Westernization does not necessarily imply improvement, and presenting something in such a way that it becomes socially acceptable does not automatically imply that it has become good and pure and art.

However, this is the impression of Handy that the film *St Louis Blues* presents, historical distortion aside. In the film Handy's father, the preacher who cannot accept his son's career as dance musician, is persuaded that his son is doing something meaningful when his work, the 'St Louis blues', is performed by a big symphony orchestra rather than a jazz or dance band, fit for the best class of people in Washington. This may have contributed to the aspect of social acceptability (albeit a very dubious aspect), but in that sort of setting the blues is twice sold short – first it is commercially westernized and second, 'dignified' as classical! 'Handy – *Stepfather* of the Blues'!

Handy's version of the blues, which was also taken up by others, based on authentic black music or personal inspiration, was identified by its subject matter and titles. In very many instances it uses place names like Memphis, Dallas, St Louis, Beale Street (a street in Memphis), something that seldom occurs in traditional blues. The Handy blues is furthermore far less realistic. With all the sharp edges smoothed the music is also less authentic – less articulate. In spite of the use of the blue note (i.e. a minor third or seventh in a piece which is otherwise major) which is so typical of African-American music, the character of this type of blues (most of which is sheet music) relates more to white popular music than to real African-American music.

4
The 1920s

Post-1918 New Orleans music in Chicago: King Oliver

'Southern stomps'

During the First World War there was a great shortage of industrial workers due to the large numbers of whites serving in the army or navy, while there was an increased need for production. One of the consequences of this was that blacks from the South headed for the industrial centres in the North because there were well-paid jobs to be had in the factories. This provided them with the opportunity to break away from the South, with its apartheid, its nasty 'Jim Crow' attitudes and its impoverished living conditions, for a better future in the North.[254] Chicago was a particularly attractive destination and the black population there doubled from 50,000 to 100,000 during the war years.

It was this fact, rather than the closing down of the red-light district in New Orleans, that encouraged also many musicians to move to the North. They came to offer their music to the blacks who were already resident there and relatively well off. Freddie Keppard, Jelly Roll Morton and many other musicians from New Orleans performed there for varying periods of time between the years 1914 and 1918.

Joe Oliver, whose trumpet-playing in New Orleans had won him the title of 'King', also arrived in 1918. Until 1920 he played in a number of different bands, of which the members were almost exclusively people from New Orleans. He formed his own band in 1920 and played in Los Angeles in 1921–1922 with a slightly different line-up – and his good friend Jelly Roll Morton on the piano. He returned to Chicago in 1922 to form the band with which he was to become famous. It is hard to overestimate the significance of this band, which only made minor changes in the line-up until 1924. Many musicians came to listen to them and gained a thorough knowledge of the content of New Orleans style. Whites came to listen too, and the effect this music had on them requires further discussion. Last but not least, in 1923 they cut a series of gramophone records that will remain significant because of the superior quality of their music. These records have continued to win admirers and still inspire those with a heart for the music of New Orleans. We may be grateful for the first recording of real black music in 1923. Only two such recordings were made prior to this – one by the Ory Band and the other by Johnny Dunn's band. These records immediately sold well and were often played – the original editions are very rare and the fact that they are almost always in bad condition is evidence of this.

The band always featured top musicians with King Oliver and Louis Armstrong on cornet; Johnny Dodds on clarinet; Honore Dutrey on trombone; Lil Hardin on piano; Bud Scott on banjo; Warren 'Babe' Dodds on the drums, and bass saxophonist Charlie Jackson[255] joined in for some numbers, thus doubling the trombone contribution.

In spite of this line-up and in view of later conceptions of jazz, it would be quite wrong to classify Oliver and co. as 'great soloists', as Coeuroy does;[256] it would be even more inappropriate to call them great 'individualists'. Those who take the time to listen to these records[257] will discover that the emphasis falls entirely on ensemble, although there are the odd solos. A significant part of the records consist entirely of ensemble playing.

The majority of the pieces they played were original compositions, written by Oliver, one of the other band members or other African-Americans who were working in the same or a similar style (like Jelly Roll Morton, Richard M. Jones, Thomas A. Dorsey, etc.). They also played cover versions of classics like 'High society', but hardly ever played contemporary popular music and never schmaltz. The extraordinary impact of this band, which is still evident, is indeed partly due to their good choice of repertoire. Their music sounds fresh, even now [at the time of writing], never old-fashioned or outdated.

The themes are usually longer winded than those of the average ragtime with its core of four bars which are continually repeated. Instead, the themes are more often constructed of phrases of eight bars (which are sometimes divided into two sub-phrases of four bars). Thematic units of twelve bars also occur regularly. This adds to the richness and renders this music superior to the schmaltz of those days, which stuck to the time-honoured basic melody of four bars, repeated and embedded in a larger structure of sixteen bars. The fourth theme of the 'Chime blues',[258] to which we will come back later, is a good example of this. Be that as it may, there is a legion of beautiful and elaborate melodies; listing them would serve little purpose.

A comparison of the different recordings of one particular piece, for instance 'Riverside blues', 'Dippermouth blues', 'Snake rag' or 'Mabel's dream' can show us that this band did not improvise; the various versions of each of these pieces hardly differ from each other. Small differences can be attributed to the working method we discussed earlier, in which each musician has some freedom to occasionally play a note differently, within the largely predetermined framework, as long as the arrangement (mostly unwritten) is not affected.

The musicians have their own particular styles of playing. This is one of the reasons for the ease, freedom, suppleness, which yet preserves the purity of style that each of the musicians produces. Individualism, on the other hand, with musicians vying to be 'in front', does not occur. Each individual is completely committed to the rest of the band and tuned in to hear the other members. The starting point of each performance is the melody or melodies, as many compositions consist of several themes. This melody is varied, interpreted, played in the band's own style, but never abandoned in order to improvise on the given chord progression. If there is more than one theme, as is the case in 'Chimes blues', each theme is rendered in a different way, partly to ensure clarity but also to retain the clear structure of the whole. The first theme of 'Chimes blues', for example, is played ensemble and subsequently repeated identically (as always); then the second theme is played homophonically (and repeated); the third theme is played (twice) by the piano; the fourth theme is introduced by the trumpet (the first ever recording of Louis Armstrong playing solo) and then repeated note-by-note, and the rendition is finally concluded by a repeat of the second theme. Compare this recording of Oliver with later versions, e.g. that of 'Mournful serenade' by Jelly Roll Morton's quartet,[259] (the same sequence of themes, each one repeated), and with that of George Lewis and his band who, as late as 1955,[260] played an identical rendition of the different themes. The framework for the authentic New Orleans' compositions seems to be quite tight and any variation in personal style for cover versions remains strictly within that framework, while the melody, which can be clearly followed, is retained.

We have discussed ensemble work several times. It is now time to focus on it, because it is the heart of this New Orleans music. It is pure polyphony. The schematic structure is thus: two trumpets render the theme in unison and in pointed rhythm, the trombone provides the foundation in long, legato phrases while selecting notes from the base chords, while the clarinet ad libs above the trumpets. The clarinet and the trombone also base the structure of their phrases on the given theme. On occasion they may play the theme, while the trumpets depart from the theme both melodically and rhythmically. The clarinet sometimes plays the same rhythm as the trumpet, possibly with a different melody, matching note by note, before releasing itself for a counter-melody that creates a more open polyphony. Part of the theme is sometimes played by the trumpets, while the clarinet and trombone play freely at first before continuing the tune with a few bars together, in parallel, and the trumpets now play a rhythmical counter-melody. It is important to realize that the parts that are played freely, simultaneously with the actual theme, are not just erratic tunes to a haphazard beat (as we so often hear in later Dixieland jazz) but they too are melodically sound. Compare the two different versions of 'Riverside blues' because the recordings differ so much technically. In one case the counter-melody stands out and it becomes apparent that it is just as rich as the main theme, which is more clearly conspicuous in the other case.

The reason we are devoting so much attention to this is to emphasize that this pure polyphony expresses a resourcefulness and ingenuity that cannot possibly be produced by simply playing or improvising. It was at this point that later imitations failed. They took over the pattern we mentioned at the beginning of this discussion and assumed that the rest could be improvised during the performance itself. They underestimated the austerity of the framework and were therefore oblivious to the freedom it provides.

What role do the rhythm instruments – piano, banjo and drums – play? They do not constitute a separate section that thrashes out the beat like a pounding-machine. Instead they join in with the whole, using their varied manner of rendition to support the theme in their own way. Anyone who has heard Babe Dodds' drum solo[261] knows what a rich melody he is able to elicit from his instrument, and those who have heard his discourse about his manner of playing[262] cannot fail to admit that he uses his intelligence in his music, constantly searching for the right way to support his band, selecting just the right tone to provide that firm basis that allows the polyphony even more freedom. There is no tapping out of the beat, although his drumming always retains the strict, strong beat which constitutes the bonding element for the rest of the band. Banjo and piano together support the trombone in laying the harmonic foundation; they too play a very capriciously varied rhythm which nevertheless helps to provide a steady beat.

In searching for other musical equivalents we should not compare this music with the later swing music, with its strong beat, its tight and sometimes sharp rhythm, but rather with the basso continuo as used by Bach. It gives a similar fluent support to the work of the melody instruments – nowhere marking the beat as tightly as a metronome, and always following the melody. It is a lively and warm rhythm, loose and dynamic. The set tempo, like Bach's, almost completely lacks accelerandi and rallentandi, though there is of course a certain rubato in the rendition of the melody instruments, where we find a free rhythm with agogic accents.[263] We have mentioned Bach's name here and, indeed, this music is similar to his; not only in its structure with the emphasis on the polyphony, but particularly in atmosphere and nature. Listen to 'Where did you stay last night?' and compare it with Bach's sixth *Brandenburg Concerto*. The resemblance is remarkable. The same type of polyphony, the same sort of rhythm, but the comparison has to be taken further than establishing a musical resemblance; the atmosphere is similar – the same serenity, the same joy, the same lively sharpness, the same lack of any romanticism or rhetoric, the same fortitude. It is striking that Oliver also feels it necessary to repeat a theme, thus enhancing the solid serenity and flexibility. Finally, common to both there is pure joy, not exuberant, not wild and uncontrolled, but a deeply rooted cheerfulness.

The cheerfulness and openness here is as little superficial as in Bach's music. The view that only the tragic, the serious in the sense of sombre, the sad, is really deep and meaningful is a typical Western,

Romantic mistake. It may be true to those who no longer recognize the Christian beliefs or no longer accept them, but the Bible teaches a different view. A joyful disposition is the fruit of a real understanding of the word of God. Joy is not superficial – on the contrary, it is very deep. It is only to those who find depth and real truth in the tragic, the ruinous, that joy is an escape, a denial of reality; and this type of joy is then expressed in a wild letting go of oneself.

Oliver's joy is deep and real. There is no sign of escapism – just a peaceful solidity for the joy to rest on. Why would that be? What is behind that great inner affinity with Bach's music? How can there be such a conformity of musical structure? These people hardly knew Bach's music, if at all. What they heard of Western music was popular amusement pieces like Suppé's 'Dichter und Bauer', or possibly one or two compositions by other nineteenth-century composers. Dutrey played cello music as part of his practice routine, for instance! This therefore rules out any immediate factor being responsible for this remarkable state of affairs. We believe it can only be explained by a common spiritual background. Bach's was very positively Bible-believing Christianity.

What about these blacks then?[264] Most of them were not churchgoers, nor were they devout. On the other hand, they did not have a negative attitude towards God and his word, nor towards the church; they were not against it, not anti-Christian. Louis Armstrong, not a devout man by any means, still deems it necessary to mention in his autobiography[265] that he enjoys going to church and does so if possible. A few letters Oliver wrote shortly before he died, at an indescribably difficult time, speak for themselves. In 1937 he wrote this to his sister: 'I am still out of work. Since the hotel closed I haven't produced a single note. But there is much to thank God for. Because I have food and can sleep . . . It seems that each time one door closes, God opens another.' Two months before he died, when he was to undergo surgery: 'Perhaps I will never see New York again. Don't think I'm scared because I wrote that. I'm trying to live closer to the Lord than ever. I have a feeling that the good Lord's going to take care of me.'[266] This attitude made it possible for the fruit of the blacks' own Christian culture to leave its mark on the work of these people. We can typify many aspects of this black culture as early Christian; these people too stood alone, with their faith in their hearts and the Bible in their hands, just as the churches in Ephesus or Corinth to whom St Paul wrote.

The African-American culture was characterized by a heavy emphasis on developing its own Christian lifestyle, and real scriptural joy was one of its characteristic traits. If these musicians had been hostile towards Christianity and broken with their roots it would not have been possible for their music to carry this mark of deep joy, often despite their circumstances, the fruit of Christian faith.

This is how their musical affinity with Bach is ultimately to be understood. This is why their rhythm, which we compared to the basso continuo because it serves a similar function, and the polyphonic musical structure, which these blacks had independently rediscovered, bore such resemblance to the music of Bach.

Still, this music remains a miracle. Its high quality, its integrity, its nature we must ultimately simply accept for what it is: partly the result of the genius of these musicians, who put the aspect of playing together as a group before any individualistic presentation of technique and ability, and partly to be attributed to their realization that freedom only exists in alignment to a given structure, to the theme and to the style of the other musicians.

Is there no African element in their music? We think there is very little. We have not been able to trace the roots of this art form in traditional African music, with its characteristic polyrhythm. Indeed, polyrhythm is hardly perceptible anywhere in the USA; it is not a characteristic of African-American music, which is neither Western nor, to be sure, African. African polyrhythms are produced by superimposing a variety of rhythms in different metres. The polyrhythms we sometimes find with Oliver are of a completely different nature. Within the structure of 4/4 time the melodies, which are played by the instruments with their own rhythms (and agogic accents), can develop a polyrhythm because one of the instruments may be slightly 'ahead of' or 'behind' the others. This helps create the lively sense of suppleness in this music. However, it is not typically African in character. Neither can this music be explained in any way in terms of the context in which it was played. It has nothing to do with red lights and gangsters, nor with the nightclub ambience of New Orleans or Chicago.

This section was entitled 'Southern stomps'. It is the title of one of the most beautiful pieces recorded by King Oliver's Creole Orchestra. It also characterizes the significance of this band, who played New Orleans music, devised by African-Americans from the Southern States, particularly from Louisiana. Only when they started to play in Chicago, however, were they able to make an international impression and to become a force in the twentieth century that simply could not be ignored. But even though this music was played in the twentieth century, in the Western world, its nature was determined by factors which in no way reflected the Western world of the twentieth century. New Orleans jazz was born in the same period as Picasso's modern art and the Expressionism of Klee and Mondrian, but the music and the art are in no way connected. There is no line of connection to be found, however thin, between New Orleans music and the modernist Parisian art scene.[267]

The fact that music was played in the Western world which did not belong to the West, was bound to lead to unusual problems. As soon as jazz became influential and was adopted by others, tension arose –

misinterpretations followed, and subsequently a fundamental restructuring of the music into something which could be referred to as Western and contemporary. This process of tailoring it to the world of the day completely determined the development and profound alterations that we shall be analysing next.

Post-1918 New Orleans music in Chicago: other bands, Morton

'New Orleans joys'

Oliver's band was not the only New Orleans ensemble playing in Chicago. As is often the case in times of cultural growth and activity, overproduction was rife in New Orleans. There was an increase in demand for this type of music by the black audiences in the Northern States whose numbers were steadily increasing, so the most obvious solution for the New Orleans musicians was to seek employment in the North. Some of their music has been recorded. 'Play that thing' by Ollie Powers' Harmony Syncopaters is a particularly special recording, featuring Tommie Ladnier's superb trumpeting and Jimmy Noone on the clarinet. Even though the general characteristics of New Orleans jazz are not lacking, this is a group with a completely different style.[268]

Another recording made in 1923 is that of 'Wild cat blues' and 'Kansas City man blues' by a band led by the pianist, composer and publisher Clarence Williams.[269] Thomas Morris played trumpet; Charlie Irvis or John Masefield, trombone; Buddie Christian, banjo; but the leading role was certainly taken up by soprano saxophonist Sidney Bechet. His very dominant style, personal but sometimes too individual and to the fore, partly due to his instrument which in itself produces a dominant sound, was at its best here. This band's jazz closely resembles Oliver's in many respects, but the splendid balance that typifies Oliver's work, which hinged on the fact that all the instruments were of the same calibre, is less perceptible here. Still, it remains joyful, honest music, controlled, and with a great sense of inner calm despite its outward intensity.

Sidney Bechet had not long been back from a tour of Europe, including Paris, before he made this record. Europe had been exposed to jazz earlier, for the Original Dixieland Jazz Band had visited London in 1921 and the Jim Reece Europe band had done a tour of France prior to that. If Morton is right, one of the numbers they played was 'Jelly Roll blues'. What made Bechet's visit memorable was that it gave rise to the first serious review of jazz. It was no one less than Ernest Ansermet, the famous conductor, who in 1919 felt compelled to comment on a concert staged in Paris by the band in which Bechet played.[270] He wrote:

> The first thing that hits one when listening to the Southern Syncopated Orchestra is the surprising perfection, the exceptional taste and the enthusiastic performance of the band ... It is only in the area of harmony that the blacks have not developed their own means of expression ... They seem to have a style of their own and their form is solid, abrupt, rigorous, with an ending as brusque and relentless as that of Bach's second *Brandenburg Concerto*.

Anyone who has heard 'Wild cat blues' referred to above will know how accurately and perceptively Ansermet was listening. He closes his article with a special comment about Bechet:

> Meeting this very black, fat young man with his white teeth and narrow forehead is quite an experience. He is very glad if you appreciate what he does, but he cannot tell you a thing about his music except that he goes his own way. Just think – his own way may be the main road that the whole world will walk along tomorrow.[271]

Jelly Roll Morton was also in Chicago in those days. He recorded a number of his compositions – records that are always worth listening to (there is nothing outdated about this music), in spite of the fact that the difficulties in recording techniques for the piano in those days are clearly audible.

We have already discussed the recordings of 'New Orleans joys'. If we listen to Morton's recordings of 'Froggie Moore' and 'London blues' and then compare them with the rendition of the same pieces by Oliver's band,[272] the importance to the musicians of the structure of the piece and the themes implemented becomes abundantly clear. The latter number in particular is one of the most beautiful that Oliver made and is a typical Morton composition in its curious structure. Each new chorus (a closed part containing the theme or a variation of it) of twelve bars consists of a four-bar break, followed by a four-bar theme and finally by a four-bar refrain, i.e. a recurring short, closing theme. The first two groups of four bars keep on changing themes and each theme is rendered twice.

The performance of these bands was very influential, but it was especially the gramophone that was to play a very important role in the propagation of the music.

White jazz in Chicago

'Tin roof blues'

At the beginning of the 1920s a white group form New Orleans was playing in Chicago. They had taken the place of the Original Dixieland Jazz Band, who had left for New York. They were young people who in

New Orleans had been listening to black music whenever they could. They obviously did not go to the black neighbourhoods, or other places that were accessible to blacks only, but they could hear this music at parades and open-air performances.

The Brunies brothers were the core of this group of enthusiastic youths. Leon Rappolo, of Sicilian origin (at home his family played only the music of their native country), learnt to play the clarinet because it was impossible to gain a place in a brass band with a violin.

After the Dixieland Band, they were the first to record something of the music that could be heard in Chicago. The band was called New Orleans Rhythm Kings. Paul Mares, the trumpeter, later said:

> In 1922 we spent a number of successive weekends in Richmond, Indiana making recordings for Gennett. We were so set on making gramophone records that we accepted the first offer that came our way so as to beat the other bands to it ... The band certainly played good music. We only had two different tempos: 'slow drag' and 2/4 time. We did our best to imitate the black music we had heard at home. We did the best we could, but of course we couldn't play 'real coloured style'.[273]

The records that were made then are still worth listening to.[274] The repertoire seems somewhat more old-fashioned than that of Oliver – more real ragtime (e.g. the 'Maple leaf rag'), and also numbers which are strongly reminiscent of the entertainment music of that time. Nevertheless, their playing was thoroughly musical. They strove for pure polyphony and often achieved it; the solos were tasteful and often captivating. The music sounds different from that of the Dixieland Band, which was more spirited, but also less calm, more jumpy, with a lot of staccato. This music was more fluent, calmer and more tuneful, though that sometimes made it too sweet, too weak. It is as if white musicians face a dilemma in trying to imitate their black counterparts: either wild and turbulent, or calm and then too sweet and, indeed, depending on their taste, either the one or the other manifested itself. These white youths do not seem to have possessed the inner calm that can express itself forcefully in a joyful outburst. Certainly one of their mistakes was to include a tenor saxophone in the band. This particularly affected the quality of the recording – lack of clarity in structure and little clear definition of tone. The instrument, popular among dance bands in those days, was not suited for the New Orleans ensemble. The blacks – who had created this sort of music with their fine taste and intuition, did not include it in their line-up. They opted for clearly contrasting parts: clarinet, trumpet, trombone, so the saxophone was of no use to them.[275]

Their 'Farewell blues' has become famous – it was the theme song of a Dutch dance band for years. Their 'Tin roof blues' also became famous. It was indeed a beautiful composition, which borrowed one of its themes from Oliver's 'Jazzin' babies blues'. Brunies' trombone solo has become a classic; no band would perform the number without including it. Rappolo's solo is also very musically and melodically refined, but this is possibly the very factor that made it less suitable for direct reproduction.

This band's music proves one thing: while they were busy trying to approximate black music, these musicians were not performing wild and uncontrolled improvisation; on the contrary, they were producing a very gentle, fluent basso continuo upon which the music, played in an orderly and calm fashion, was based. This assures us that original New Orleans jazz was not wild or rough; it utterly belies the theory that the music was loud, noisy and without nuance. That view, as we have seen, stems from a lack of understanding and ignorance of the structural laws which apply to this music. As a result people could not make sense of the sounds that reached their ears.

The development of jazz on the white scene

'Riverboat shuffle'

If we investigate the significance of original New Orleans' jazz music in the early 1920s, it becomes apparent that the few records produced at that time made a tremendous impact. A handful of musicians spread over a small number of bands caused almost all dance bands to change their tone within a short space of time.

Listen to the early recordings of the New York dance musicians who called themselves Original Memphis Five.[276] Listen to the very calm music that jazz musicians like Phil Napoleon and Miff Mole were able to produce; it will certainly have been easier on the ears of the audience than the sharp sounds of the Original Dixieland Band. But note too how in the polyphony and strict structure of this music the influence of New Orleans music is unmistakable.

Dance bands that included at least one jazz-oriented musician soon appeared and proceeded to play music which, although it was far from being pure jazz, had very clearly undergone exposure to it. A good example of this would be the California Ramblers.[277] Ted Lewis, besides his own humorous numbers which are also interesting (though not with jazz in mind), also let his band play some pure jazz in the New Orleans Rhythm Kings' tradition, and some of the best white jazz musicians (e.g. Muggsy Spanier and George Brunies) found their niche there. Ted Lewis was perhaps the most musical and as yet unsurpassed American singer of all time.

Paul Whiteman also needs to be mentioned here. He was a successful band leader in the 1920s who managed to equip himself with the aura of someone who had created jazz, and then have people believe that he indeed had done so. How he did it, remains a mystery. The first thing I ever heard about jazz (probably around 1932) was that Whiteman had invented it when the pane of glass from a swing-door shattered. How this myth ever came about is baffling, because if you listen to the recordings by this band their music is the most boring, soulless dance music, though sometimes played in clever arrangements. On the odd occasion you hear a couple of bars of Bix Beiderbecke, the talented white cornettist who spent the last years of his life playing with this big band – bored and in despair.

I want to continue with Bix and other second-generation whites. Firstly, we must mention the Austin High School Gang, a gang of youths from a School of Advanced Vocational Training in Chicago who became so enthusiastic when they heard the New York Rhythm Kings' recording of 'Farewell blues' and other records that they went out and bought the instruments to try and produce similar music. As we shall see, their music was to assume great historical significance. They listened to the records and some of them (still mere boys) soon became professional musicians. From their recordings it becomes very clear that their music is fashioned after the example of the young men from New Orleans, the New Orleans Rhythm Kings, and of the blacks. Muggsy Spanier's music in those days, for example, was decidedly reminiscent of Armstrong's.[278]

Bix Beiderbecke was born in Davenport, Iowa, where as a boy at home he played his cornet along to Original Dixieland Jazz Band gramophone records. He was still young when he arrived in Chicago. He did not stick it out long at school – his time was almost entirely taken up by music. He soon became a serious contender with (and friend to) the boys of Austin High School. His first real contract came at the end of 1923 with the Wolverines, one of the most important bands on the white scene of that period. Bix can be heard playing his remarkable style in recordings by this band,[279] which confirms that those who tell us that he was very good are not making it up.

In 1925 he joined Frank Trumbauer's band, which was in fact nothing more than a dance band. The music they played, as we are now able to hear on the record, was anything but fantastic. On the contrary; it sounds a bit old-fashioned now – a bit sweet, too tame. Still, Bix got the chance to play his own music, inspired by and based on the work of black musicians like Oliver and Armstrong. We can hear this on a number of records made by a small group of musicians from the larger band, and apparently inspired by Armstrong's Hot Five, which we still have to deal with. Bix's personal performance, primarily characterized by a very individual tone and intonation, and a special method of phrasing, stands out very well on these recordings.[280] It is a pity that the other musicians just fall short of his calibre, with the exception of the clarinettist, Don Murray, an otherwise forgotten musician who is certainly worth listening to. The most important recordings of this group are undoubtedly 'Jazz me blues', 'Royal

Garden blues' and particularly the very beautiful 'Riverboat shuffle'.

Bix's music was very significant. He later joined Paul Whiteman's band where he was permitted to play the odd four-bar solo in its over-commercialized performances. Even though the band's arrangements were sometimes clever, there is no way in which they can be regarded as captivating, and Bix came to grief.

His creative ability was repressed, his artistic consciousness was overtaxed and, finding solace in alcohol, he perished. His life was to become a legend, his name one that would inspire countless musicians, his tragic lot a prototype of the fate that awaited (and still awaits) so many jazz musicians; but his music, as we said, made an enormous impact, particularly in the white scene. At this point we must specifically make mention of a circle of New York musicians – Red Nichols, Miff Mole, Joe Venuti, Eddie Lang and others – who, as we have seen, had already been exposed to the influence of the Dixieland Band and other similar bands around 1920. They too made many records under the name of The Five Pennies, Miff Mole's Little Molers, The Louisiana Rhythm Kings, etc. Their music is sometimes purely commercial; sometimes they aim higher and a very special sort of jazz emerges which has unfortunately not been able to endure the test of time. Nevertheless, their main significance is that these recordings heralded the arrival of jazz in Europe and that much early European jazz – from around 1928 until the Second World War – was inspired by these very records.

But with these recordings we have wandered a long way from the early and honest enthusiasm of the Austin High School Gang with talented musicians such as Muggsy Spanier, Jimmy McPartland and Frank Teschemaker – far from their ideal of playing this new music in their own way, seriously and artistically sound. The enthusiasm of the circle of Red Nichols, amongst others, was great and we can soon get carried away writing about these young people, but it must not distract us from the fact that they drew from very different sources than the black music of Oliver and others. Their music emanates from their enthusiasm for it, attempts to grasp and equal it, but ends up being flawed because it strives to grasp something that is not really their own. We miss the inner peace, the naturalness and stylish confidence. Perhaps the most pure is Bix Beiderbecke, for the very reason that he dared to be himself and to play music that did not pretend to be black. His phrasing and his treatment of melody is purely Western.

In any case, these white musicians did work that was pre-eminent in the history of jazz; we shall return to their contribution at length in a future chapter.

Black folk songs in the 1920s

'John Henry'

It is evident that during this time African-Americans in rural areas and in the cities sang folk songs. This sort of music was not performed by artists or blues singers, who rendered their own type of song, so it was seldom or never recorded. It was not until later – in the 1930s – that it was recorded, non-commercially. We do know something of the folk songs of this period, however, because it had been studied for some time. The most important book dedicated to the subject was Odum and Johnson's *Negro Workaday Songs* that was published in 1926 and recorded the results of research in North and South Carolina, Tennessee and Georgia. It included discussions of the Race series recordings, i.e. records played by blacks and exclusively intended for sale to blacks. It was the first time they were given any consideration by researchers, an example that has unfortunately often been ignored.

The famous ballad 'John Henry' is also recorded in the book. It is a typical black song – also with respect to the content – about a railroad worker who was hacking away at the rock to make a tunnel when the steam drill was first introduced. He challenged the drill and won in a contest, but payed for his supernatural effort with his life. It is a song that was sung by blacks everywhere and is also a typical folk song by virtue of the fact that there are many versions of it.[281] We have chosen the version which later appeared in J.A. and A. Lomax's book *American Ballads and Folk Songs*. We have abridged it somewhat by omitting verses.

> John Henry was a li'l baby,
> Sittin' on his mama's knee,
> Said: 'De Big Bend Tunnel on de C & O road
> Gonna cause the death of me,
> Lord Lord, gonna cause the death of me.'
>
> Cap'n said to John Henry:
> 'Gonna bring me a steam drill 'round,
> Gonna take dat steam drill out on the job,
> Gonna whop that steel on down,
> Lord Lord, gonna whop that steel on down.'
>
> John Henry tol' his cap'n
> Lightnin' was in his eye:
> 'Cap'n, bet yo' last red cent on me,
> For I'll beat it to the bottom or I'll die,
> Lord Lord, for I'll beat it to the bottom or I'll die.'
>
> John Henry started on de right hand,
> De steam drill started on the left,
> Before I'd let dis steam drill beat me down,

I'd hammer my fool self to death,
Lord Lord, I'd hammer my fool self to death.

John Henry said to his shaker [a helper]
'Nigger, why don't you sing?
I'm throwin' twelve poun's from my hips on down,
Jes' listen to the cold steel ring,
Lord Lord, just listen to the cold steel ring.'

De man dat invented de steam drill,
Thought he was mighty fine,
John Henry drove his fifteen feet,
And the steam drill only made nine,
Lord Lord, an de steam drill only made nine.

De hammer dat John Henry swung,
It weighed over nine pound,
He broke a rib 'n his left-hand side,
And his intrels fell on the ground,
Lord Lord, his intrels fell on the ground.

John Henry was hammerin' the mountain,
And his hammer was strikin' fire,
He drove so hard till he broke his poor heart,
And he laid down his hammer and he died,
Lord Lord, and he laid down his hammer and he died.

John Henry had a pretty li'l woman,
And the dress that she wore was blue,
And the last words that she said to him:
'John Henry, I've been true to you,
Lord Lord, John Henry I've been true to you.'

Oh, who's gonna shoe yo' li'l feet,
And who's gonna glub your hands,
And who's gonna kiss yo' rosy lips,
And who's gonna be your man,
Lord Lord, who's gonna be your man.

Dey took John Henry to de graveyard,
And dey buried him in de san',
And every locomotive come roarin' by,
Says: 'Dere lays a steel drivin' man,
Lord Lord, there lays a steel drivin' man.'

Church music in the 1920s

'Gospel train is leaving'

The gramophone industry flourished in the 1920s. It was not yet threatened by the radio and shared the general welfare of the economy. There were Race records for the blacks (see the photo insert, which shows the sleeve of a Race record). They now form an almost inexhaustible mine of information on which we can draw to learn about all kinds of black music, including spirituals.

Preach discs were also launched. These were 25 cm records, 78 rpm, with a short sermon on one side preceded by a spiritual. Much of the flip side was filled with singing. These records were made by black preachers who took several members of the congregation with them. The recordings give us a good impression of the ideas, the style of speech and singing in the black churches. The Revd Gates and his associates Weems, Burnett, Moseley, F.W. McGee, E.D. Campbell and many others can be heard on these records.

The sermons were rendered in a typical style that developed in black churches, comparable to a recitative, a sort of musical rhetoric, often of great beauty. The congregation is not wholly silent but supports the rendition by the odd 'Hallelujah', 'Lord have mercy', 'Amen!', and so on, or by forming a humming accompaniment. If we listen to these records it becomes clear that wild ecstasy and unbridled emotionalism are not in any way the hallmark of black religious practices. Yet it is this aspect that has been stressed all too often. The reason for this is the same as in the case of jazz music – much of it stems from a lack of clear understanding of what is happening. The character and rendition are not Western, but neither are they African, primitive or unbiblical! In their assessment some allowed themselves to be compelled by a sort of exaggerated longing to display the spectacular, the foreign, the exotic, the colourful aspects. This is why so much attention was given to what happened in strange sects, where one indeed finds trances and other such phenomena, but they occur equally in white churches of a similar sort.

The rendition is generally calm and collected, as we hear on these recordings,[282] comparable to later recordings of church services.[283] The content is orthodox evangelical and the personal contact between the believers and their Lord and Saviour is strongly emphasized. The language is often rich and expressive, sometimes naïve in the choice of analogy but in all simplicity deep, with biblical wisdom.

We have already said that one side of the record contains a sermon, and we would like to give you the beginning of one by the Revd T.E. Weems that is taken from a Columbia Race record from around 1927. It is entitled 'God Is Mad with Man':

> My brothers and sisters, I'm going to preach to you tonight from a subject from the sixth chapter of Genesis, 6th and 7th verses:

> 'And it repented the Lord that he had made man on the earth, and it grieved him at his heart. And the Lord said, "I will destroy man whom I have created from the face of the earth ... ".' Our subject is: God is enraged by man. That is why every born again child of God will live in such a way that the Lord will not be enraged with him. Because whenever God is enraged there will be problems in the country. God was enraged with people in the days of Sodom and Gomorrah, and the city was destroyed with fire and brimstone. God was enraged with Nebuchadnezzar ... God was enraged with Belshazzar, and he sent a hand to write on the wall. So then, every time God is enraged with somebody, he brings their life to an end. That is why each and every person who is really born of the Spirit, must live as Christian and as a born again Christian, so as not to enrage the Lord. Well now, in the days of Noah there were men and women ... who were very bad ... and nobody would get on their knees and pray.

Many sermons were about the confidence of the believer, resting in the forgiveness of sins in the blood of Jesus Christ, and very often Christian conduct would be the subject. On the flip side we find spirituals. The renditions are strongly reminiscent of the camp meetings: the minister says his lines in a melodious fashion, clearly articulated and rhythmic, and melodically defined, and then the congregation sings the recurring chorus. An image that we often come across is that of the train – a modernization, if we may say so, of the old image of the chariot which we have already come across in 'Swing low, sweet chariot', and which was inspired by the story of Elijah's ascension. The image of the train is sometimes greatly expanded:[284] the ticket is faith, Christ is the engine driver, and this 'gospel train' takes the believer to heaven.

Very beautiful is the song spoken by Revd Burnett and sung by his congregation (represented here by some of them, of course): 'The Gospel Train is Leaving', a sermon with singing, the label tells us.[285] The preacher begins, accompanied by an organ: 'I want you to sing concerning the unconverted Christian', whereupon the congregation joins with a chorus: 'Tell me how long the train has been gone (x 3), People were coming and the train done gone.' Then the minister sings again: 'I looked down the road and saw them coming from the South, East, West and North, each crying: "Tell me how long has the train been gone"' (which would be repeated by the choir). It is a clear warning not to delay, but if God calls, to hear his voice and obey (based on passages like Psalm 32:6, Revelation 2:21, and others).

During the same period there was a sort of literary and cultural revival going on among black intellectuals, known as the Harlem Renaissance. A few important black poets had works published which were worthwhile in every way.[286] Still we must be aware of the fact that only a few blacks were involved, striving for emancipation – complete equality with whites – by means of cultural accommodation (namely proving themselves to be equal to whites in terms of their culture, so as to be accepted by them). By renouncing their own culture, they became alienated from their own people in many respects. This was a small group and we must not treat them as representative of all African-Americans.

One of the most likeable characters from that movement was James Weldon Johnson. He was born in 1871 in Jacksonville, Florida, and graduated from the University of Atlanta, Georgia. He has held many important positions, including that of secretary of the NAACP (National Association for the Advancement of Coloured People) and of Professor of Literature at Fisk University (a black university in Georgia). His first collection of poems was published in 1917, and *God's Trombones* in 1927. The latter collection are sermons by black preachers which he had condensed and turned into poetry. He tried to capture something of the characteristic features of these very rhetorical and often musical preachers using rich metaphorical language. Did we not compare their rendition with a recitative? He aptly called them 'God's trombones'. The following poem is probably the most beautiful one and it contains a rich and deep exegesis of Genesis 1:

> The Creation by James Weldon Johnson
>
> And God stepped out on space,
> And He looked around and said:
> 'I'm lonely – I'll make me a world.'
> And far as the eye of God could see
> Darkness covered everything,
> Blacker than a hundred midnights
> Down in a cypress swamp.
> Then God Smiled, And the light Broke,
> And the darkness rolled up on one side,
> And the light stood shining on the other,
> And God said: 'That's good!'
>
> Then God reached out and took the light in His hands
> And God rolled the light around in His hands
> Until He made the sun;
> And He set that sun a-blazing in the heavens.
> And the light that was left from making the sun
> God gathered up in a shining ball
> And flung against the darkness,
> Spangling the night with the moon and the stars.
> Then down between
> The darkness and the light
> He hurled the world;
> And God said: That's good!

Then God himself stepped down –
And the sun was on His right hand,
And the moon was on His left;
The stars were clustered about His head,
And the earth was under His feet.
And God walked, and where He trod
His footsteps hollowed the valleys out
And bulged the mountains up.

Then He stopped and looked and saw
That the earth was hot and barren.
So God stepped over to the edge of the world
And He spat out the seven seas –
He batted His eyes, and the lightenings flashed –
He clapped His hands, and the thunders rolled –
And the waters above the earth came down,
The cooling waters came down.

Then the green grass sprouted,
And the little flowers blossomed,
The pine tree pointed his finger to the sky,
And the oak spread his arms,
The lakes cuddled down in the hollows of the ground,
And the rivers ran down to the sea;
And God smiled again,
And the rainbow appeared,
And curled itself around His shoulder.

Then God raised His arm and He waved His hand
Over the sea and over the land,
And He said: 'Bring forth! Bring forth!'
And quicker than God could drop His hand,
Fishes and fowls
And beasts and birds
Swam the rivers and the seas,
Roamed the forests and the woods,
And split the air with their wings.
And God said: 'That's good!'

Then God walked around
And God looked around
On all that He had made:
He looked on His world
With all its living things,
And God said: 'I'm lonely still.'

Then God sat down –
On the side of a hill where He could think;
By a deep, wide river He sat down;
With His head in His hands,

God thought and thought,
Till He thought: 'I'll make me a man!'

Up from the bed of the river
God scooped the clay;
And by the bank of the river
He kneeled Him down,
And there the great God Almighty
Who lit the sun and fixed it in the sky,
Who flung the stars to the most far corner of the night,
Who rounded the earth in the middle of His hand,
This Great God,
Like a mammy bending over her baby,
Kneeled down in the dust
Toiling over a lump of clay
Till He shaped it in His own image.
Then into it He breathed the breath of life,
And man became a living soul.
Amen. Amen.

Origin of the commercial spirituals

'Creep along Moses'

James Weldon Johnson also published a book of transcripts of spirituals.[287] In the introduction he tells the reader how he used to sing in a quartet in his youth. It was apparently not an unusual occupation – the number of existing quartets at that time could be calculated by dividing the entire black male population by four. These quartets sang popular songs, sometimes black folk songs but mainly Negro spirituals. They harmonized by ear and often rehearsed while waiting for the barber – hence the name 'barber-shop quartets'.

It seems that this custom was more prevalent among the middle class than among the rural population; it is evidence of the important part music played in the lives of black people. The spirituals would have been regarded (though not by black Christians) mainly as a traditional and trusted form of music – a living legacy. Recordings were made of these quartets, particularly in larger centres with a high concentration of blacks, places like Birmingham, Alabama and Norfolk, Virginia. Their songs were not actually black folk music in the true sense of the word. Rather, their repertoire consisted of spirituals following in the tradition of the Fisk Jubilee Singers, in addition to a more worldly, somewhat popular repertoire, on the whole strongly influenced by whites. These spirituals, just like those that originated in the more academic climate of the black universities, were severed from a direct connection with the church. They provided relaxation for amateurs.

It is difficult to distinguish clearly between these quartets and another kind of quartet which, judging by the number of recordings they made,[288] must have been very popular. The Americans, with their typical realism, christened their music 'religious entertainment', although it almost always referred to quartets who sang spirituals because their audiences enjoyed them and not because of any religious sympathies. They do link with the tradition we have just mentioned, but they are also strongly influenced by the current trends in entertainment music. 'Creep along Moses', sung by the Taskania Four (the name is clearly popular and not religious) in 1925, is based on a rhythm that immediately reminds us of the Charleston, a dance rhythm that was fashionable at the time. This religious entertainment is obviously hardly ever very deep. The lyrics were deliberately chosen to be neutral, chosen with care not to provoke anyone's conscience.

The blues of Bessie Smith

'Young woman's blues'

While Handy was performing his blues against a background of dance-music, 1923 also saw the first recording of blues sung outside this setting. It was Bessie Smith's debut, 'Down hearted blues'. This and subsequent records were bestsellers, though almost exclusively to black customers. Bessie Smith, one of Ma Rainey's pupils, sang primarily in the North, while 'Ma' remained faithful to the South. This is probably why Bessie became better known.

Bessie Smith was an artist. She sang the blues in traditional fashion, striving for great sophistication of rendition and she developed the form from pure folk music to something which, though it cannot be compared with classical music by Western concert standards, is a serious form of artistic expression. She developed the form, while she sometimes added non-twelve-bar strophes, particularly introductions. Accompaniment is often left to a small ensemble consisting of a piano and one or more melody instruments. It is the musical accompaniment that gives away the folk blues background of this music which, although it was influenced by jazz, is certainly not identical to it. When Louis Armstrong accompanied Bessie Smith, his style and the nature of his performance differed from his performance with jazz bands.

A remarkable feature of this genre is that it was performed almost exclusively by women. Besides those already mentioned, there is a long line of female vocalists – almost all altos – who enjoyed success on the black scene and made many recordings (in the Race series). There was Victoria Spivey,[289] Ida Cox, Mamie Smith, Clara Smith, Lillian Glynn and many more besides.

Most of them sang their own versions of the blues – based on original folk blues. They used their own approaches to acquire an own style, both in terms of melody and of lyrics. Even though the titles of the songs might indicate that we are dealing with blues, and though stylistically – in character and nature – almost all their work is blues, the form does sometimes clearly deviate from the twelve-bar scheme. Very different from Handy, who adapted the blues to the world of entertainment music, and from Ravel, who occasionally borrowed the odd element from the blues for a Western composition, here the blues was expanded and developed without violation to the character, taste and tone of the songs.

Below are the lyrics of 'Dyin' by the hour'.[290] Both the wry humour and the way the otherwise traditional theme is interpreted is typical of Bessie Smith's blues. This record, which includes some magnificent trumpet accompaniment by Ladnier, opens with a quote from Chopin's funeral march. This must not be seen as the profane use of a Western theme but rather as a memory of New Orleans funerals, where this music was familiar to the French-speaking population:

> It's an old story, every time it's a doggone man (x 2)
> But when that thing is on you, you just drift from hand to hand.
>
> I'd drink up all this acid, if it wouldn't burn me so (x 2)
> And telephone the devil, that's the only place I'd go.
>
> Once I weighted two hundred, I'm nothing but skin and bones (x 2)
> I've always laughed, but now it's nothing but a moan and a groan.
>
> Lord, if I'm dying by the hour 'bout that doggone man of mine (x 2)
> He said he didn't love me, that's why I'm dyin' and lose my mind.[291]

Folk blues in the 1920s

'You don't know my mind'

There were a few men who, particularly in the Northern cities such as Chicago, enjoyed parity with Bessie Smith and co. such as 'Texas' Alexander[292] and Lonnie Johnson, for instance, but most of the recordings made by men in the 1920s were the work of folk musicians – troubadours. They were recruited by 'talent scouts' in the South and then went to a particular city, e.g. Chicago, where they made recordings for the Race series. Then they usually disappeared again. So all we get to hear of the blues on record is the work of professional artists and never pure folk music, the sort everybody sang.

There are countless singers with whom we can make acquaintance on these records – far too many to name, not even briefly. Many of them cut no more than a few sides before disappearing completely to their Southern homeland again. In some cases these performers were semi-professional, having a different job besides their musical activities. That may be the reason that later on we seldom come across them again.

The blues they sing – accompanied by guitar or piano, or the odd violin or trombone, as an exception – are structurally similar to those we have already analysed, but other forms have also cropped up in the course of time. The twelve-bar construction is retained (unlike the blues of the previous chapter). One of the variations we could call the 'long-lined blues'. Usually in the standard structure of the blues, no more than two of the four bars of each line is sung. In the type we are referring to here, however, the phrase carries on and lasts for seven bars. The eighth bar constitutes a rest and the last four bars are then sung again.

A good example of this, and one which confirms that this genre was developed from the older standard type, is 'Lonesome Atlanta blues' by Bobby Grant:

> I'm so lonesome, I'm so lonesome, hear me crying, baby I ain't lying,
> I'm so lonesome, I'm so lonesome that I've got the blues.
> I'm so sad and lonesome, mamma, I don't know what to do.
>
> When you have a feeling, a mean old feeling, that dirty old feeling, that feeling,
> When you have a feeling that your gal don't want you no more,
> You better take my advice and leave her even if it hurts you so.
>
> I'm gonna walk down the dirt road, that long, long dirt road, that dirty old dirt road, mmm that dirt road,
> I'm gonna walk down the dirt road, 'less somebody let me ride,
> If I can't find my baby, I run away and hide.
>
> I'm going back to Atlanta, I mean down in Georgia, crazy 'bout Atlanta, I mean Atlanta, Georgia,
> I'm going back to Atlanta, down to the Cater Street,
> If I can't find my baby, I believe somebody'll be kind to me.[293]

This song was clearly developed by expanding the ordinary structure of the blues melodically, as it were, with many repetitions.

This type of blues often features a refrain, with the last part of the strophe as a recurring theme. Barbecue Bob's blues is one example, the first two strophes of which are quoted here. The first line is sung completely and the refrain takes up the remaining eight bars:

> You don't know, you don't know, you don't know my mind, cruel gal,
> You don't know, you don't know my mind; when you see me laughing I'm laughing just to keep from crying.

> I asked my brown, can you stand to see me die; she said, man, I can stand to see you die,
> You don't know, you don't know my mind; when you see me laughing I'm laughing just to keep from crying.[294]

There are even more variations and deviations than these, but the original structure always remains discernible. This folk art is, strangely enough, yet to be properly researched and analysed; hardly any work has yet been done.[295]

This type of the blues was sometimes sung by more than one vocalist, by two or three. The tempo was mostly faster in that case and the lyrics then assumed a different character. Instead of meditative it became a sort of satire – the kind of humour that is unique among blacks. A good example of this is the jaunty, satirical little number sung by Walter Vincent with Chatman's Mississippi Hot Footers. He always sings the first line on his own and the refrain is then sung by a number of men together:

> Jack had chickens on the roof, every night he was missing 'bout two,
> Using that too, using that too, you ain't to get mad, your friends gonna use that too.
>
> Jack had biscuits on the shelf, every night he found them gone,
> Using that too, using that too, you ain't to get mad, your friends gonna use that too.[296]

The song continues on the subject of flowers, then a car, whisky, and even his wife. The accompaniment consists of two guitars and a violin – an instrument often played in folk music of this sort. The instruments seem to be perfectly designed for the character of the piece. This sort of derivative of the blues is rare, however, and the original form is far from becoming extinct.[297]

Piano folk music

Boogie-woogie

It is no longer possible to trace the origins of the old piano folk music called boogie-woogie. Some say it originated in Texas at the beginning of the twentieth century, while others mention other places. What is certain is that boogie-woogie flourished in the Northern cities, Chicago in particular, in the 1920s. The structure is almost always the same as the twelve-bar blues, often with a sort of refrain, i.e. the last four bars remain the same in each verse.

The pianistic style of this folk art is lively, the strong, rhythmic bass of the left hand being the most striking feature. Each beat consists of two notes, one of which is played low and the other higher, creating a sort of walking bass. There are many variants however, to avoid monotony. Above the bass, the right hand administers the melody which usually consists of short phrases that are often repeated. Each new strophe usually has a new variation on the basic theme.

It is the art of folk musicians who play in small cafes or at dance parties in (poor) people's own homes. The boogie-woogie is, after all, also a dance. The pianist often assumes the role of dance leader as it were, indicating (in musical fashion) the type of step or dance to be performed. These black dances have to be regarded as real folk dances, performed collectively, (and relatively) unconnected with Western duo-dancing.

A considerable number of recordings of this music were made in the 1920s. Pinetop Smith and in particular Jim Yancey later became famous, both giving exceptionally polished performances, experts at contrasting extremely quiet passages with lively ones.

It took time for this music to gain fame because when these recordings were made, boogie-woogie was virtually unknown beyond the circle of black workers for whom it was intended. In 1928 Meade Lux Lewis made his *Honky Tonk Train Blues* for Paramount, the company exclusively responsible for producing the Race records series.[298] It went bankrupt shortly after and the record became a collector's piece. A copy was later discovered by the jazz critic and connoisseur John Hammond, who subsequently tried to trace the pianist. Many years passed before he succeeded; Lewis turned out to be working in a garage in Chicago. Hammond then had Lewis record his composition once again. The flip side of this recording featured a piano solo by a white jazz pianist who was well known at the time.[299] That is why the record was bought, and it was only later that the purchasers discovered the exceptional recording on the B-side. This is how the 'Honky tonk train blues' – today still one of the most beautiful pieces inspired by riding in a train – became famous overnight. It also heralded the popular boogie-woogie fashion which was predominant for some time in the late 1930s. Boogie-woogie then became quite a wild sort of music with a rhythmically monotonous beat and an extremely fast tempo.

Fortunately there were others who sought real boogie-woogie, and this is how Jim Yancey was rediscovered. He went on to record some particularly beautiful numbers.[300]

Jug bands

'Memphis shake'
The word 'shake' in this title refers to a dance – once again, a type of folk dance. Many of the strange-sounding words we come across like 'strut', 'shimmy', 'grind', 'rock' and so on, refer to types of dancing.

This particular piece, 'Memphis shake', was played by the Dixieland Jug Band,[301] one of the best examples of this strange combination of instruments. Jug bands originally were probably small rural bands, composed in rather random fashion according to the availability of musicians. The few that managed to penetrate the city scene would have been regarded as curiosities; they would also have represented the best of their sort.

These bands were in possession of a variety of home-made instruments, which is hardly surprising considering how poor these folk were. The percussion section consisted of the wife's washboard, simply but very cleverly transformed into a real instrument. The bass section was a jug, a pitcher or small storage tin into which they blew; it was apparently a very useful instrument which produced a sound somewhere inbetween that of a tuba and a bass ('struck' strongly pizzicato, which was a common style among the blacks). The trumpet was replaced by a kazoo, an instrument made by attaching a nozzle to a little toy tin-instrument by means of a membrane. There was also the blue-blowing, a comb with paper stretched across it, which was blown in humming fashion. The harmonica was very common to these bands and very popular among the blacks, who knew exactly how to produce the most beautiful music on it, never needing to work for virtuosity. Finally, a violin was often included. It was probably adopted from white folk music, for a great deal of white folk-dance music (square dances, closely related to cowboy songs, very rarely recorded and now virtually obsolete)[302] was led by the violin. Blacks are very adept at playing it, and their style is very different from the Western style. One of the best examples is 'Hen party blues' by the same Dixieland Jug Band.[303]

This music should not be underestimated. The fact that Johnny Dodds plays in both of the examples mentioned above and, more importantly, is not an odd man out in the ensemble, speaks for itself.

One of the oddest bands in this genre to make recordings was Bobby Leecan's Need More Band, whose 'Apaloosa blues' is particularly noteworthy.[304] The band consists of a banjo, guitar, cello, harmonica, washboard and kazoo. Stylistically, their polyphonic music is very closely related to New Orleans jazz. This is evidence that the essence of the music does not lie in a particular combination of instruments, even if the contrasting timbres of the traditional clarinet-trumpet-trombone group does constitute the ideal synthesis for the purpose.

Jelly Roll Morton's jazz in 1926

'Black bottom stomp'

The 'Memphis shake' we just discussed appeared on the flip side of the original Victor production of 'Doctor Jazz' by Jelly Roll Morton's Red

Hot Peppers, which brings us to a series of records that include some of the best jazz music ever recorded.[305] In September and December of 1926, Jelly Roll Morton made these records together with a group of New Orleans musicians; it was not his band – the group came together just for these recordings – a so-called 'recording combination'. The musicians did know each other, respected each other and were united in their feeling for style and interpretation. Jelly himself had composed a significant number of the pieces they played – 'Dead man's blues', 'Sidewalk blues', 'Cannonball blues', 'Jelly Roll blues' and 'Grandpa's spell' – and he was able to get his musicians to play every nuance that he regarded essential. This becomes evident when we compare his own piano solos with the recordings of the band.

The musicians who made these recordings with Jelly Roll Morton all have strong recollections of them. It was quite extraordinary. The members of the band were George Mitchell, cornet; Kid Ory, trombone; Omer Simeon, clarinet; Johnny St Cyr, banjo; Andrew Lindsay, bass and Andrew Hilaire, drums.

Simeon recalls:

> The people from Victor (the recording company) treated Jelly as somebody special. And that's what he was, considering that he was the best of his sort in the whole country. And they paid us above the normal margin to work with him ... You see, Jelly set high standards when it came to his music, and if the musicians couldn't play real New Orleans style, he went looking for others.

> I'll tell you how the band's rehearsals went. He was very precise. Very bright, always very lively, but also very serious. We mostly rehearsed for about three hours for four sides. And in that time he indicated the effects he was after, like for instance an accompaniment for a solo – he would play that through on the piano with one finger and then the musicians would play it together, making it a three-part.

Johnny St Cyr tells:

> The solos were free. We played as we sensed it. Naturally Jelly had his own ideas; sometimes we listened to him and sometimes we tried to make something better of it. As for me, I just did whatever he asked me to do ... Now Jelly was a very, very nice man to make a record with, and I'll tell you why ... He never told you exactly what you had to play, but left it to your own judgment and said, 'Take a break here' ... and 'the clarinet has to take a break there.' That's the reason why his records show so much variety ... If Jelly asked me 'Can you take a break here?,' I answered, 'OK.' Then he would say, 'Good, let's try it.' And when we got to that place, we took the break; as if you were saying 'OK, let me take that one.' You allowed yourself to be led by your own taste, you see. If it sounded good, then it was alright. If it wasn't so good, he would say, 'Wait a minute, that doesn't sound so good; see if you can't change it a bit.'

> That's the reason why his records are so full of inventions and variations; it was because he gave his people so much freedom. Sometimes we asked him – if we had an idea, you know – and then we would ask him whether we could take a certain break somewhere.

On the subject of New Orleans music in general, Johnny also tells us:

> In New Orleans we had a system of playing which aimed to play music at its most beautiful ... Whatever you did, it had to be good. No playing out of tune. You had to keep within the bounds of the given melody, but we, old hands, were very good at making a number more beautiful.[306]

That is how Jelly got his men to play exactly what he wanted them to play, still allowing them the freedom to follow their own style within the framework of his composition.

Even when Jelly played existing compositions he was able to put his stamp on the rendition to such an extent that it would almost become a Jelly number. This stands out particularly in the 'Black bottom stomp'; he reconstructed the main theme upon which the solos were based, so that the original version, consisting of a short theme of two times four bars, four counter-melody bars (quite tiresome) and four bars repeating the initial theme,[307] became a theme of four bars, the fourth of which was a break, then a repeat of the theme moving into a coda, making a total of ten bars (and the boring connecting piece was excluded).

These records, along with those by Oliver, constitute some of the most beautiful New Orleans jazz ever recorded; they are very different from those by Oliver because Jelly's own trademark is clearly evident, which just goes to show how broad and versatile this black music is – anything but a dead formula. Polyphony and variation – not improvisation – are certainly the main features which incite its striking joy, its openness and suppleness, particularly in the rhythm. These are the very characteristics that the dance music lacked completely in those days before this new music became influential. The dance music of the whites was boring, wishy-washy, superficially bright but essentially uninspiring, cool and tame. That very difference is one of the reasons why jazz, like that on Jelly's records, has been so influential; its success stemmed from the lack of spirit in the Western popular music of the time, and its imitation was an attempt to seize something of it. This would certainly explain the quick spread of the jazz playing-style, though it unfortunately led to a change of jazz character.

White Chicago jazz

'I've found a new baby'

The white boys from Chicago we mentioned earlier (the Austin High School Gang, Bix Beiderdecke), who were moved by the music they heard from Oliver and Morton, Armstrong and Dodds, and others, were the first whites outside New Orleans to seriously attempt to emulate this style. The influence of Louis Armstrong in particular, who performed with various bands as soloist, was enormous.

These boys were certainly talented and very enthusiastic, but it was inevitable that they would interpret the music in their own way. This music was different to anything they already knew – the dance music of those days and the late Romantic style in classical music. This new music seemed to spring spontaneously from the black soul, since the musicians did not play from written notes. Not realizing how traditional and fixed this music was in its structure, they considered it revolutionary.

Their music therefore became founded on an odd mis-interpretation of New Orleans jazz as it was played in Chicago between 1920 and 1925. They considered this music revolutionary because they thought that it was played 'just like that' – directly improvised, conceived, as it were, on the spur of the moment. Was this not part of their spiritual attitude – the desire to express themselves uninhibited, independent of any tradition, independent of any norms – enjoying themselves, just letting themselves go? Jean Jacques Rousseau, the eighteenth-century philosopher, taught that it was the things that came directly from a person, without the veneer of civilization, which were real and relevant and worthwhile. His ideals had dictated the spirit of Western culture for two whole centuries, penetrating deeply, and were adopted by these youngsters too – though they had probably never read Rousseau. This attitude of Western humanism had become generally dominant and, yes, is still dominant across a great part of Western culture.

Oliver, Morton et al., started with the melody, which was then varied. All instruments, harmonically speaking, based their chords on a bass note (usually rendered by the bass but otherwise by the piano) – the chords normally changed after a number of beats, depending on the melody that was being backed up. The 'Chicagoans' (the name by which these white musicians from Chicago became known) based their playing on the chords and not on the given theme – a typically Western way of approaching music. This allowed them the freedom to improvise, to let themselves go. The mutual alliance between soloist and accompaniment remained intact because the musicians adhered to the given harmonic scheme; they were therefore able to deviate from the given musical theme.

Their approach to music was typically individualistic. The emphasis no longer laid on the polyphonically played ensemble (a significant number of Oliver's records are solely given over to ensemble music of this type), but on the freely improvised solos. They abandoned the fixed structure of the pieces with their repeats and diverse themes, and the average Chicagoan rendition opens with a (virtually homophonic) exposition of the melody, followed by a succession of freely improvised solos, bound together by the chord scheme only, and ending in a rather noisy and chaotic tutti. It is, after all, not possible to play polyphonic New Orleans jazz in an individualistic fashion; it would irrevocably lead to chaos and a wild clash of individual styles.

The music of the blacks was rhythmical. In that respect, however, it was anything but African; African polyrhythms do not occur. The best way to understand what the rhythm instruments collectively achieved is to observe the similarity with the Baroque basso continuo, as in the music of Bach. At the same time we must indicate that the rhythm of the melody, with all the agogic accents evoked by melody instruments, plays a significant role in the character of black jazz.

A series of curious associations – rhythm is African, primitive, original, real, primal, free from cultured civilization, the heartbeat of life itself – caused the Chicagoans to interpret rhythm very differently from what it actually was in this music. To them, it became a rigid metre with regular strong beats (and deviant accents like the off-beat, an accentuation of the otherwise unaccentuated beats, the 2nd and the 4th of the bar). The Chicagoans thus became the creators of jazz as we know it: music with an individualistic character, with the accent on freely improvised solos and a rhythm that is powerful and strongly metric in character.

Their music demanded aggressive rendition; this was their way of trying to approach the joyful openness of the black music. That is why their music is often loud, not only in terms of volume but also in atmosphere and character. This vehemence, this dynamism, was achieved by creating a strong tension between the rhythm of the melody (created by agogic accents, rubato, etc.) and the clearly defined metre rendered by the rhythm section. From now on we have to draw a sharp dividing line between the melody and rhythm sections, something which was not necessary in the music of Oliver and Morton. Off-beat rhythms increased the tension. The peace and inner joy of black music have been replaced by fervour, agitation, tension and lack of restraint.

Around 1927 the Chicagoans made an important series of records, with McPartland (trumpet), Teschemaker (clarinet), Spanier (trumpet), Mezz Mezzrow (saxophone), Eddie Condon (banjo) and Gene Krupa (drums). The trombone was often replaced by the tenor sax, which reduced the transparency of the ensemble sections (if they were present at all). Teschemaker was possibly the most clear and distinct exponent of what they were trying to achieve. The way he formed tones suggests strong emotion – a wild letting go, without restraint. 'I've found a new baby'[308] was one of their most characteristic recordings, with its fast tempo, its short-winded phrasing, and a rendition which hardly does justice to the theme upon which it is based. This became jazz as it was later almost always understood to be because, needless to say, the Chicago style made a terrific impact among the white population in America and Europe – and indeed everywhere where 'jazz' was played.

Armstrong's Hot Five and Hot Seven

'Heebee jeebees'

On 12 November 1925 the first recordings by the Hot Five were made, a combination of old friends: Louis Armstrong, trumpet; Johnny Dodds, clarinet; Kid Ory, trombone; Lil Harlin, piano and Johnny St Cyr, banjo. Together they formed another typical recording combination. Since Oliver's old band had broken up, Armstrong had been the star soloist with a number of big bands which were not playing real New Orleans music. Dodds had been playing with all sorts of smaller combinations like the jug bands, but he stuck to the strict idiom of New Orleans. Ory often played in the band that Oliver formed later on (which we shall come back to), while some of the other musicians made music for a living with one particular band, and some with various bands.

Now they had come together and were going to make records in original New Orleans style. They composed much of their music themselves, played in loose arrangements with rich polyphonic ensemble music, solos and breaks with a clear structure, always musically sound. There is no sign of individualism or loose improvisation. The music is lively, cheerful, but never exhilarant; neither is it sentimental, though some pieces like the very beautiful 'You're next', created on 26 February 1926, may be described as tender. There were still more treasures to be unearthed that day: 'Cornet shop suey', 'Muskrat ramble' and also 'Heebee jeebees'.[309] The latter was a fantastic success. Armstrong sang scat – it was the first time a white audience had heard it – a style of singing without words, using the voice as a kind of instrument. The Chicagoans and their friends loved it. As far as they were concerned another tradition had been overthrown: here people let themselves go, free from all the stuffy airs and graces. This was improvisation!

Perhaps the Chicagoans were not far off the mark because, indeed, in the scat chorus solo the seeds of something new had been sown. It should not surprise us that it was Armstrong in particular who would take that road. Was he not the highly acclaimed solo star who put up individual performances? It must have meant everything to this lad from the backstreets of New Orleans to be so popular among whites – whites who said he could improvise so well, whites whose reaction to his sometimes vehement and intense performance betrayed their pleasure, whites who revelled in his ability to handle the prescribed melodic material roughly and freely. The 'new' seeds had originated from the influence of the boys from Chicago (the Chicagoans, their friends and kindred spirits), who had steered Armstrong in that direction. They learnt much form Armstrong, certainly, and all Chicagoans clearly show traces of that influence, but in interpretation and spirit they were themselves in fact – inadvertently and unintentionally – influential.

This is how jazz became 'hot' – fierce, improvisatory, giving an impression of letting go. The Hot Five's records, made a couple of months later in the summer of 1926, already show this trend much more strongly. 'Drop that sack'[310] particularly has a very rough, vehement introduction of a character previously unknown to New Orleans jazz. The link with the melodic theme, which in the past was always respected by the musicians and formed the basis for variation, became increasingly loose, and the music began to resemble that of the Chicagoans, though the rhythm was more fluent, less rigid.

It is interesting that in the process – which is very evident when we listen to the records chronologically – the joy and the bright tone are also lost. The music has become hard, almost relentless. And we come across something else, something we noticed earlier in white music, namely that besides the vehemence there is also another aspect, softer, dreamy, almost sentimental (e.g. 'Melancholy blues' and 'Wild man blues', originally recorded for Brunswick[311]). The original style of New Orleans music was never that fierce, but neither was it sentimental; its rich polymorphism was founded on very different foundations.

This combination which, with the addition of Babe Dodds (drums) and Briggs (tuba), now called itself Hot Seven made a whole series of recordings in 1927, which certainly was not classical jazz in the sense that it can be referred to as a great achievement. It features some beautiful details, very nice solos – in other words this music had not suddenly lost its power and significance, but some of the real serenity, which was anything but lethargic, had been lost. Sometimes you get the impression that the musicians were playing against each other, rather than with each other; Armstrong was powerful and sometimes dominated the band and so was Dodds. In an attempt to salvage the unity, he opposed Armstrong forcefully. Much of the balance was lost in this way. The work of the rhythm section, certainly of very high quality, lost some of its suppleness and melodiousness – its task now became that of marking the beat. Armstrong's solos are classic examples of this sort of jazz – 'hot jazz', which was in fact Chicago jazz. (The trombone solos are sometimes weak; these were not played by Kid Ory, as is often assumed, but by someone else, probably a certain John Thomas.) As we have said, besides the fierce recordings like 'Potato head blues', 'Hotter than that' and 'Alligator crawl', there are also a couple that were suddenly very calm – approaching the sentimental – like 'Melancholy blues', which we have already mentioned, and 'Wild man blues', recorded by Brunswick.[312]

During the session of 16 November 1926 we are clearly still in the transitional phase. Although the music is already showing the new trend more clearly, it has not yet lost the old liveliness and inner peace. Then 'Skid-dad-de-dat'[313] was recorded, which acts as a sort of summary of what we have just been saying. The record may be referred to as a study of contrasts: fierce passages constantly alternating with excessively soft and calm sections. Then there is an abrupt break, followed by everyone joining in for a very quiet homophonic passage, until Armstrong strikes up a fierce trombone and leads a number of polyphonic bars, only to be interrupted by another very abrupt break. In the middle of the record, Armstrong suddenly breaks out in a raucous scat-song passage on top of a sweet theme, whereupon again a familiarly quiet and bright solo by Dodds follows. It is a curious record, captivating and of high quality, full of contradictions that express what was happening during this transitional period.

At this point it would perhaps be best for me to introduce the magnificent set of eight recordings made by the New Orleans Wanderers (or the New Orleans Bootblacks as they were sometimes known). They started up on 14 June 1926 with exactly the same members that made up the Hot Five, but without Armstrong, who was replaced by George Mitchell. These records are also particularly interesting because there is no sign of the problems we hear on the Armstrong Hot Five records from those days (like 'Drop that sack', for example, recorded on 28 May), and neither is there any trace of the hard and fast music that we sometimes find on the Armstrong recordings. It would seem that Armstrong must take the blame for those characteristics. These recordings constitute some of the best New Orleans music ever recorded. If we compare them with the Morton records we mentioned earlier (which were re-recorded shortly afterwards by a band that was again largely composed of the same members), we realize what an impression Morton had made on the music of his peers. It also teaches us how rich and versatile this sort of jazz can be. It is no use mentioning all these recordings separately. Almost every number is brilliant, with 'I can't say'; 'Too tight'; 'Gatemouth' and 'Perdido Street blues' coming tops.[314]

A study of this music illustrates again how it is always based on a given theme, both in ensemble music and in solos. I would particularly like to point out again that there is no way in which the rhythm section can easily be distinguished from the melody section. The work of the melody instruments is in itself strongly rhythmic, full of variety also in that respect, and the so-called rhythm instruments rather join in with the whole than mark the beat. Note George Mitchell's beautifully punctuated playing, and you will see what I mean. It may be that, having heard the records, Morton asked him to play. Finally I have to confess that the alto saxophonist who is introduced here (even though he does understand his job), does not complement the polyphonic passages. The clarity and transparency are clouded, not because of the material he is playing, but because the instrument itself produces a sound which does not actually befit this music.

Back to the Hot Seven: late 1927 sees the process we have been talking about draw to a close; that is when Armstrong blew New Orleans jazz apart by his individualistic, improvisational, fierce interpretations. One of the last recordings the band made, the 'Savoy blues', is admittedly a beautiful piece – especially Armstrong's solo in the middle – but the polyphony had gone and the character of New Orleans jazz had changed irreversibly.

Armstrong subsequently set off again, this time with different musicians. Dodds, Ory and St Cyr were no longer the appropriate musicians for his intentions. They were also too big for him; the records that were to come are almost always Armstrong records. He was the big man and the band permitted to accompany him was much weaker. Its members could sometimes play a short solo, but then only to give Louis another chance to dazzle. 'West End blues',[315] recorded in June 1928, is a good example. It is an almost sentimental number, with some magnificent playing by Armstrong alternating with some weaker solos by others, and concluding with a piece that makes no musical sense and comes dangerously close to musical kitsch, amounting to a failed attempt at a nice ending.

The development of new African-American jazz after about 1927

'Swing out'

The new formula caught on. It promised to be a success with audiences. It gave the musicians the opportunity to forge ahead without too much trouble. Like Armstrong, many blacks will have had little problem accepting this new concept of jazz. Many of them lived in Chicago and were not believers; they were very much related to the white Chicagoans in spirit. Still, the pressure accompanying these musicians must have played a significant role, because if we compare the records that were made for their own black audiences (and were released by recording companies like Paramount, who produced for the black music market) with the sort of jazz we want to discuss next, they were noticeably quieter, more cheery, calm and melodious – this was music from 'South Side Chicago'.[316] Also the records Dodds made at that time are different.[317] They retain the polyphonic element and are less improvisatory and vehement.

The music in which the new principles clearly emerge is possibly best represented by the Luis Russell Band – in essence a band founded by Oliver in 1925, which was now breaking new ground. The arrangements are very concise, limited to an introduction, the odd (homophonic) ensemble and some accompaniment of the solos. The solos certainly became the centre of focus at this point.

The performances of Wat Hogginbotham (trombone), Charlie Holmes (soprano and alto saxophone) and Henry Allen Jr (trumpet) are sometimes well worth listening to (e.g. 'Feeling drowsy'[318]), but they do lack the inherent depth which would give this music lasting value.

They simply do not have the calibre of Oliver's band or of Morton's. This must to some extent be attributed to the fact that the new formula allows itself to be handled so easily. The immediate effect is good; it makes an impression and sweeps you along, rendering the creative effort that produces a top-notch performance unnecessary. Listen to 'Swing out'[319] and you will understand what we mean (and, incidentally, this is not a sub-standard example).

The later jazz of Oliver and Williams

'Red River blues'

The Luis Russell Band we just mentioned performed between 1928 and 1930, at least that was the period they flourished, but now we have to go back a bit in history. The state of affairs in the 1920s was rather complex and many developments took place which are worth looking into.

Oliver lost his famous band in 1924 and the musicians dispersed to various other bands. He formed a new band but for all sort of reasons things did not go very well. After that he played in various other bands, finally forming a band in 1925 which, in spite of regular changes to the line-up, performed successfully for about two years.

Oliver's new band was bigger than his previous Creole Orchestra and roughly looked like this: Oliver and Bob Schoffner, trumpet; Kid Ory or Higginbotham, trombone; Darnell Howard, Barney Bigard and Townes, sax and clarinet; Luis Russell, piano; Bud Scott, banjo; Bert Cobb, tuba; Paul Barbarin, drums. It was not a band capable of playing real New Orleans music.

It is our impression that Oliver, after the disappointment of his first band falling apart, did not attempt more of the same but, conscious that very few of his musicians actually came from New Orleans or felt at home in this genre, deliberately set out on a different route. Still, if you listen to the records this band made – mainly in 1926 – its style is typically Oliver. The affinity with his older music is greater than you may initially think. Polyphonic ensemble choruses occur regularly, although they do not form the heart of the music.

Oliver supervised his music with the greatest of attention. He also began playing many of his own compositions such as 'Snag it',[320] which became very popular. Pieces arranged for sax or clarinet trio alternate with solos, sometimes with a quiet accompaniment, sometimes unaccompanied, arranged choruses for brass and polyphonic passages reminiscent of New Orleans jazz. The polyphony is often also present when a solo instrument is accompanied by an arranged sax ensemble. The music seldom or never degenerates into a straight succession of solos. The transition from one chorus to another, or from one solo to another, is invariably very meticulous and well-considered. There is always the musical finishing touch which time and again makes this music an adventure to listen to.

The quietness and simplicity of Oliver's music is striking. It makes us conscious of our feelings of protest towards the hot jazz trend. The rhythm is discreet, tender without being sentimental, the solos always musically sound and melodious – never violent and wild.

A beautiful and particularly successful recording is that of the 'Dead man blues'[321] of 17 September 1926, recorded during the fruitful months when the Bootblacks, Armstrong's Hot Five and Morton and his group were making the hit records we discussed before. Oliver's music is somewhat incongruous here – less New Orleans in style. However, if we compare this version of 'Dead man blues' with that by Jelly Roll Morton made four days later, the similarities are remarkable and the differences seem not so essential. (Jelly and Oliver had composed 'Dead man blues' together.) It is conspicuous that of the entire rhythm group in Oliver's version, only the tuba plays during solos, keeping time in a loose, variable manner. The solo that Oliver himself plays is a real gem, strong and powerful, never rough; in sharp contrast to the work of Armstrong in 'Drop that sack', for example.

In May 1927 Oliver performed in New York with this band with great success. He made a number of important recordings during that time, in which we hear that his interpretations did not change; to the contrary. It is serenity and melodiousness that is emphasized, and increasingly so. There are some beautiful examples from that period including 'I'm watching the clock' and 'West End blues',[322] one of his own compositions that he recorded in June 1928. A comparison with the Armstrong version, which was recorded four weeks later, shows the difference. It displays serenity versus dreaminess; meticulous musical supervision versus the dominant soloist with some accompaniment and little homogeneity; the equality of the various band members, even during the solos, versus the solo individualist who pushes the others aside; sticking faithfully to the thematic material versus breaking away from material and turning to free improvisation . . . and that is before we have said that Armstrong's 'West End blues' does not even fall in the category of fierce hot jazz. If we were to compare it with the latter, the contrast would be greater still.

Finally we have to point out that also Oliver did leave his own stamp on his musicians, because these records essentially sound much the same, irrespective of the line-up or soloists. Compare 'Black snake blues', for example, from April 1927, in which Ory plays the trombone, with 'I'm watching the clock' from September 1928, in which Higginbotham plays the same instrument. The similarity in style between the trombone parts is, both in terms of interpretation and of rendition, quite remarkable. The difference between Oliver and Morton's music – the stamp of the latter being much more outspoken – lies in their characters. Morton pushed himself strongly to the fore while Oliver remained modestly in the background, but this should not detract from the similarities in their musical ideals and (partly) methods too.

Oliver's influence is evident also in the many records his friend Clarence Williams made, with all sorts of recording combinations. Oliver himself joined in occasionally, but they mainly feature other trumpet players (like Ed Allen and or Anderson) whose style is strongly reminiscent of Oliver's. Williams too strives to make pure music, balanced and unified, melodiously simple, but never at the expense of power and without ever being sentimental. There are many examples of this, but we shall mention only the 'Red River blues'[323] in which Cyrus St Clair's beautiful tuba-playing is the first thing that strikes us, though Ed Allen's trumpet solo is also impressive. Oliver was present during this recording and can be heard contributing to another number recorded later the same day (29 May 1928) called 'I need you', where he plays the high part in the polyphonic ensemble.

What we are dealing with here is not the contrast between big band jazz and the jazz of smaller ensembles, the latter being hot jazz. No, we are dealing here with a concept of jazz that seems quite different from the original New Orleans jazz, but which is in essence more closely related to it than hot jazz is. Do not think that this music was always slow and that it was mainly blues. On the contrary, there are loose, quick numbers of a cheerful and lively character to be heard. One of these was Clarence Williams' 'Cushion foot stomp',[324] a beautiful and joyful piece of music – played partly polyphonically – of which the atmosphere and character is strongly reminiscent of old-time New Orleans music.

Morton's later developments

'Harmony blues'

> Jelly was really ahead of his time. In fact most of what he said was above our heads. So now and then I'm starting to understand what he was getting at. He was always talking about the playing of the melody. But in those days jazz (i.e. hot jazz) was the only thing in the world to me apart from eating and sleeping and I didn't understand what he was talking about.

So spoke a trumpet player who worked with Jelly in 1929–1930.[325] Jelly Roll Morton's position in those years is summarized briefly in those few sentences. He wanted to hang on to his idea of music. He hated the new sort of jazz, 'jig' music, with its free improvisation and badly thought out arrangements. He wanted to keep playing New Orleans jazz, but the musicians did not understand him – they wanted something else.

The conflict between Jelly's ideals and what his musicians wanted or were able to play can be heard clearly on the recordings he made during those years. In 1927 and 1928 he made a number of recordings which retained the same sort of character and quality as the older ones: 'Jungle blues', 'Kansas City stomp', 'Mournful serenade' (which was the same as Oliver's 'Chimes blues') and 'Shoe shiner's drag'.[326]

In December 1928 he recorded the beautiful 'Deep creek blues', one of his best records, which in fact had a less distinct New Orleans character and was closer related to what Oliver or Williams did in those years.

The years 1929 and 1930 saw little in the way of successful recordings, at least not of the whole band playing together. On the other hand there were some exceptionally beautiful trio recordings, such as the 'Turtle twist' from December 1929, with Barney Bigard on the clarinet, Jelly on piano and someone else drumming.[327] The recordings of the whole band often manifest something unbalanced, with the musicians playing roughly and hardly conforming to Jelly's wishes, on the basis of which he had arranged the pieces. Here and there we hear nice passages; the records are not bad, but they lack the qualities that made the earlier Jelly recordings such an experience.

'Jersey Joe' and 'Mississippi Mildred', recorded with members of the Luis Russell Band in November 1929[328] are good examples of what we mean. There are some good solos – it is jazz in the positive sense of the word, certainly – but the balance, the fine musicality and also the unity is markedly lacking.

On occasion they did succeed, only really in the slow numbers when the musicians were not so fiercely jigging and could capture the atmosphere because they were still able to sense it. 'Harmony blues'[329] and 'Pontchartrain blues' spring to mind, good pieces, well arranged, with solos that fit naturally and do not impose themselves upon the listener. It is odd that the clarinettist seems a bit weak in these numbers. The reason is that Jelly was so determined to employ a certain type of clarinettist, and was so insistent that people play *his* music, that once, when there was no clarinettist available to suit his style, he wanted to prove the point to his musicians that jazz was quite capable of being played simply by sticking to the notes. So he wrote out the clarinet part and had it played by a certain Victor Houseman, a musician who was present at the studio and who could play many instruments in case a reserve was needed to cover for sick leave or absence. This anonymous musician's style was too classical really, for he was no jazz clarinettist, with too little vibrato and so on for what Jelly had in mind; still, the result is not unsatisfactory.

Jelly was not able to retain his position however. On one hand there was the black audience, badly affected by the depression which crippled the economy in 1929. They preferred to hear their suffering sung about by the blues singers whose records were still being released regularly by companies like Brunswick. On the other hand the more advanced musicians and the wider white audience no longer wanted this kind of music; they preferred jazz played in the spirit of the Chicagoans or they turned to the more 'respectable' jazz of Ellington or Henderson, a genre to which we will be coming shortly.

So Jelly made his last recording in 1930. At that point the Victor Recording Company dismissed him and began recording vast quantities of Ellington.

As from 1929 or 1930 onwards we no longer hear Johnny Dodds, King Oliver, Morton, Kid Ory and many others on record. The musical ideals of these people were too high; not wanting to set aside their principles, they remained faithful to their own music but ran into difficulties with their supporters. Oliver and Jelly battled on for a few years before ending up dejected; Dodds lived in great poverty, while Kid Ory abandoned music altogether. It was not primarily the economic situation that caused them to disappear from the public arena, though it is true that they could have gathered a few crumbs from under the table if times had been better. The main factor that caused those who clung to their high musical ideals to sink into oblivion and poverty, however talented they were, was the change in taste, the trend towards the new type of jazz which was more permeated by the spirit of the Chicagoans. On top of that, band leaders like Jelly and Oliver hardly succeeded in playing music in the way they wanted, because the musicians no longer understood them and wanted to branch out.

This defeat must have affected Jelly badly. Not only had he aimed for high quality New Orleans jazz with its own character but he had also hoped that white audiences would accept him and his music. He dreamed of emancipation, not by assimilation – adopting the white Western culture – but by being accepted in his own right, with his own music, with its own character.

Much is true in Blesh's verdict:

> While jazz may be regarded as the symbol of struggle and hope, swing can be seen as that of defeat. The success of blacks in America cannot be measured by the phantom of popular acclaim and even less so by the number of dollars they earned – which could not buy equality anyway. Swing – both in terms of style and in terms of the mentality which created it – has heralded the abandonment of the real Negro elements in jazz for the benefit of white elements which are more accessible and acceptable to white society. This swing [which refers to a new kind of jazz that evolved from the music that Oliver and Morton opposed], at first sight a symbol of victory, is in fact one of the failures of emancipation.[330]

The development of jazz in New Orleans in the 1920s

'Short dress gal'

The jazz music we have just been talking about was played in Chicago and New York. That is where the big recording studios were located. New Orleans lay off the beaten track – it was a provincial outback. That is why only little of the music that was played there was recorded, although enough was happening there.[331] There is only a relatively small number of gramophone records to show us that the jazz born in New Orleans itself also continued its development there. If we listen to Celestin's Original Tuxedo Jazz Band, and particularly 'Careless love' from 1925,[332] we can hear that the music they played was in essence no different from that of Oliver. The musicians were not top class – the clarinet is positively weak – but the sound, the emphasis on polyphonic ensemble work, the whole attitude of the music is as we described it when we were dealing with Oliver's Creole Orchestra.

One of the better bands was that of Sam Morgan, a skilled trumpet player, who had assembled a number of musicians capable of producing something worth listening to. Their recordings, made in New Orleans in 1927, are technically very respectable but over-emphasize the saxophone, producing a very strange sound on the recordings. Still, we can hear a very captivating polyphony being performed, the basis of which – almost naturally – is the melodic material being played. It is powerful jazz though we are almost obliged to call it sweetly-flowing.

Strangely enough, and deviating from what New Orleans musicians in the North were used to, a number of Negro spirituals were recorded here – because they formed a permanent part of the performances, no doubt, but possibly also because contact with brass band music was still strong. It is not worth mentioning or examining here the few recordings they made, but I will make an exception for 'Short dress gal'.[333] There is a short vocal part on this record and the refrain goes, 'Don't you like that, everybody lookin', with your dress up to your knee' (no doubt this mockery was directed at the emerging trend for very short skirts). The trombone elaborates on this directly afterwards with a mocking solo – almost tender – but its purpose is to underline the gist of the text. The musician was Jim Robinson, about whom we shall hear much more later. After that comes an ensemble that extends the 'short dress girl' caricature even further, this time in a quasi-sentimental fashion. There was humour in this music of a kind seldom heard before.

Whites were also still playing jazz in New Orleans, as they had been doing for some years. The Halfway House Orchestra, among others, was producing some very good work as descendants of the New Orleans Rhythm Kings. They also made some recordings but these are very rare because they were unfortunately never re-released.

The entrance and development of Ellington

'Creole love song'

'You'd better learn to jazz or you won't make money,'[334] Henderson once said to someone who played only classical trumpet. This sentence is typical of the man. He was the leader of quite a large dance band at the beginning of the 1920s but he soon began to attract real jazz musicians.

They were able to take on the solos, which attracted the audiences; they were able to play 'jazz'.

Fletcher Henderson tried to become Whiteman's black rival and he certainly succeeded, even if it was only because the had Armstrong, Joe Smith (trumpet), Jimmy Harrison (trombone) and Coleman Hawkins (tenor sax) in his band. Perhaps Henderson's success inspired Whiteman to take on better jazz musicians like Beiderbecke too. Anyway, their function remained the same – to be soloists and relieve the heavily arranged pieces with a hot jazz solo here and there. It boiled down to a soloist-individualist exhibition of talent, technique and strength. The arranged parts were often quite monotonous. If you listen to the old recordings you will hear that many of the hits from those days were sweet and boring, with a sudden, fierce solo to liven things up a bit, followed by yet more sax ensemble without any spirit.

When the Oliver records were released, Henderson was working on the East Coast – mainly in New York. Oliver's hits of 1926, like 'Snag it', definitely made a big impression on him. The outcome of this can be heard on Henderson's best recordings, namely 'Stampede' and particularly 'Jackass blues'.[335] The solos are more vehement, for Armstrong had made his mark on the trumpeters; it is not for nothing that he had worked with Henderson for more than a year. The arrangement and interpretation are less 'sweet', less like the style of the average dance band, than previously. This was more like real music.

At the end of 1926, Ellington's star began to rise. He came from Washington, from a completely different scene than musicians like Oliver, Dodds and so on. He came from a well-to-do family whose lifestyle corresponded with that of the higher white middle class. He had attended a School of Higher Vocational Education, taking classical music lessons, and prided himself on his immaculate clothing and fine, cultivated manners.

The following quote gives an insight into his youth: 'Those ragtime pianists sounded very good to my ears. And they looked so fine. Especially when they let their left hand go. I noticed that that left hand gave the effect and that the sound was most influenced by a showy left hand. And that is why I developed a showy left hand myself.'[336]

It was not long before he arrived in New York with a small band. There he made his first recordings, 'Rainy night' being one of them.[337] The line-up was very promising, many of them being the same musicians that appear in the band with which he was to become famous, a couple of years later. What we get, however, is very irritating, sweet dance music without colour or spirit, with a fierce saxophone solo, sticking out like a sore thumb in the midst of all that soft and straight saxophone gurgling.

Ellington learnt his lesson. 'The character of our band changed when Bubber (Miley, a trumpet player in the line of Oliver) joined. He played with all sorts of mutes all evening, in a jazz-like style. That is when we came to the conclusion that we should just forget that "sweet music",' said Ellington himself.[338] He also learnt to make good use of the musicians he had in the band. He must have learnt much from the records of Oliver and Williams (1926–1927). His arrangements became livelier, the content of the thematic material (mostly self-written by this time) improved and the contrast between solos and arranged parts became less sharp, disappearing completely soon after. Ellington was creating a new sort of jazz – his own sort.

Ellington can be compared with someone like Handy in many respects. He too adopted from his fellow blacks any musical or playing style he saw fit; he too approached the music from the outside, as it were, and put it in a different light. It is hard to say exactly what light, because in strictly technical terms there is little difference between the structure of an Ellington composition and a good Oliver record (big band) or a Morton number like 'Harmony blues' – and yet the music does sound different. What Jean de Trazegnies, a strong admirer of Ellington, wrote about him typifies him. He says that Ellington was different from other black musicians; he was a gentleman. It was he who saw the potential for creating an art form from the still somewhat unrefined music that blacks like Armstrong were playing – almost instinctively and for their pleasure – that was to become a credit to his people. He wanted to plane down any rough edges still evident in the music of 1926.[339]

Perhaps Ellington's position can be characterized clearly by 'Creole love call' (recorded in October 1927). 'The Duke had of course never heard a Creole love song, or anything like it. You could have heard Creoles sing out their love in Louisiana, but he had never been to the South. Still the title seemed to suit the soft, languid atmosphere of the music',[340] wrote Ulanov, Ellington's biographer. That is true, but what Ellington had heard was 'Camp meeting blues', one of Oliver's last records with the famous Creole Orchestra. In a beautiful clarinet solo, Jimmy Noone plays the theme that Ellington then proceeds to borrow from Oliver – without so much as an acknowledgment. But the atmosphere and the nature of Ellington's music was also different from that of 'Camp meeting blues', although the influence of Oliver's records from 1926 is very clear here. Again, it is difficult to say why this music is different, but for anyone listening to jazz for the first time it sounds more familiar because it is more Western in spirit and character. That is of itself not necessarily bad, but the striving for effect and respectability, and the fake 'primitiveness', make the music less interesting even though it may possibly be more technically sophisticated than the work of Oliver, Williams or Morton. There are some riveting solos and the work is musically sound; there is really no point saying that this is bad music. To the contrary.

The popularity gained by Ellington and his musicians was immensely important to them, especially when whites, fellow-musicians and audiences were generally so full of admiration for them. This was the way to overcome the racial barrier which had always been so hard to come to terms with, this was the way to gain acceptance. This was also the time of the Harlem Renaissance (which we mentioned earlier) and it certainly did not leave Ellington unmoved. He developed a racial awareness, and Africanisms began to play a conscious role in his music. Ellington was moved to seek 'jungle-istic' effects in the trombone and trumpet parts.[341] Miley showed him the way. Oliver had been the inventor of the 'growling wa-wa' trumpet style – a technique using mutes – but it had never been jungle-istic, not even when his successors in the ranks of Williams took over. It did become so when Ellington went to work on it. More than a mere musical accessory, an extension of the expressive potential of the trumpet, it became an effect intended to evoke associations with Africa.

Mills, the manager of the band, advertised performances of 'primitive rhythms' and Sonny Greer, with his very extensive percussion set, was able to make the slogan seem true. The primitivism of twentieth-century Western culture which around 1905 sent artists in Paris rushing off to admire and pursue African sculpture, assisted this cause. It is all a bit reminiscent of the eighteenth-century slogans of the Rousseau followers who extolled the noble savage, so pure and genuine, as yet unspoilt by civilization.

Such views were all the more acceptable to many listeners who came into contact with Ellington's music, either live or on records, because his clever arrangements and great musical talent seemed to give their hobby – jazz – status and an aura of seriousness. They were oblivious to the fact that they were using the Western elements in Ellington's music as an excuse for their love of African-American music.

It seems to us that Ellington was taken much too seriously here in Europe at that time. The quality of show, the commercial side, the intention to dazzle the audience one way or another, were all overlooked. Everybody was impressed by the typical Ellington tricks when he was on stage: having the band slowly emerge from the darkness into the light while they were very effectively growling out 'East St Louis toodle-oo', their signature tune. The audiences did not realize that these were not authentic African musicians, musicians playing their own folk music, but products of a man who, having discovered what Westerners were after, cut and tailored it to their palate. Ellington later tried to make his music more serious by introducing Western forms and more modern chords. But besides that the schmaltzy pop, the commercial tunes of the day also remained in place. A good example is the recording of one of his concerts from 1952: besides the 'Harlem suite', in spirit a typical albeit a somewhat late product of the Harlem Renaissance, it included the highly commercial theatrics of the drum solo 'Skin deep' which, indeed, can only be described as shallow, as well as a variety of efficacious show solos by different soloists, technically fantastic, and the purely commercial 'Ellington medley' etc.[342]

The music itself fails to move us after we have heard it a few times. As it lacks depth and authenticity, which we need, it leaves a void. We must not forget, however, that this band, with its talented musicians and very gifted leader, produced some nice music which is certainly worth listening to. Even if we only take the recordings made before, say, 1932 into consideration (the band's best period in my opinion), we could mention 'Take it easy', 'Black and tan fantasy', 'Rent party blues', 'Saratoga swing', 'Jungle blues', 'Sloppy Joe', 'Saturday night function' and many others,[343] as well as an unpretentious piece like 'Drop me off at Harlem', with its pure rendition and melodious charm, which is still able to inspire us.

Is it jazz? Why not? It is Ellington's version of jazz. After all, what is jazz? Quarrelling about categories or restricting ourselves to an exact definition will only lead to a futile discussion.

5
The 1930s

Jazz in Kansas City around 1930

'Kansas City breakdown'

Between 1926 and 1930 there were big bands also outside New York and the strict New York scene we have discussed. They occasionally played in New York, but were otherwise busy playing in their hometowns or touring elsewhere. These bands played jazz in their own way – music that was adapted for bigger bands – with simple but strongly rhythmical, arranged parts including many solos, rather free and improvised but not without showing the influence of Oliver and Williams. We are specifically referring to the Missourians who certainly made some good records, like *Scotty Blues*,[344] and particularly Benny Moten's Kansas City Orchestra, a band that became very popular in the city they had included in their name and where they often performed at dance evenings for whites. As a result they started to include more strongly rhythmic music and if we follow the development of their music from 1926 to 1928 or 1929 this can be clearly heard. They began to use riffs – short melodic phrases played very rhythmically and repetitively – which turned the work of the melody section into rhythm, as it were. They also included many solos, virtually continuously.

Nevertheless it has to be said that what they produced was very musical, quiet and lively, without striving for effect, without a show of quasi-depth – direct and bright. The rhythm section of this band was excellent; it is not often one comes across rhythm played so freely, so liberated from a strict beat. Benny Moten's piano-playing was certainly a contributing factor. From 1926 there is the still rather stiff 'Harmony blues' – not to be confused with Jelly Roll Morton's composition of the same name, the lovely 'Hot water blues' from 1928 and 'Kansas City breakdown', which has an unusual tuba passage.[345]

Blind Willie Johnson

'Jesus coming soon'

By the end of the 1920s there was a lot of blues-singing available, particultarly on the Brunswick Race series. It was folk music, sometimes of high quality. Spirituals were sung too, primarily in the church, of course, but also on record. But let us now focus on Blind Willie Johnson, who made a number of beautiful recordings for Columbia in 1927, 1929 and 1930.

Willie Johnson was born around the turn of the century near Temple, Texas. His father was a farmer. When he was seven years old he became blind as the result of an unfortunate combination of events. During the 1920s he became a preacher and street evangelist, which was no unusual occupation in the South. He lived in various places near Dallas, Texas, finally settling in Beaumont, a small place in Texas.

We are very grateful to Columbia for having made more than thirty recordings of him, which is all we have of him because he died of pneumonia in 1949. It enables us to study his rich art. His repertoire was very varied, including white songs like the hymns 'Let Your light shine on me' and 'If it hadn't been for Jesus'. It also included spirituals like 'Nobody's fault but mine', 'Mother's children have a hard time' and 'Bye and bye I'm going to see the King', as they were generally known in the area where he lived. He also sung songs in the drawn-out style, the way Dr Watts' hymns were traditionally sung, notably 'Dark was the night',[346] one of the most beautiful recordings of black music ever made. He hums the whole piece and has the guitar sing along, as it were. It is a beautiful example of the special character of African-American music. Humming is a typical African type of musical expression. Apart from that, the piece really has nothing to do with Africa at all. As explained earlier, this style of singing was both truly African and typically Western-puritanical. The way Blind Willie sings it makes it pure art – one has to hear it to understand just how much depth and beauty a simple folk singer like this was able to produce.

He also did some composing himself – songs that testify to his insight and understanding of biblical preaching. We do not know for certain whether these compositions are his, but if they are not, then the same must be said of Blind Willie *and* the composer, *and* the whole community in which they lived and worked. The following beautiful song 'Jesus coming soon' relates to the serious flu epidemic of 1918:

> In the year of nineteen and eighteen
> God sent a mighty disease.
> It killed men by the thousands,
> Oh, Lord there is none like Thee.

That is the first verse he sings. His rendition of this sort of song is interesting because he tunes his guitar differently from what he does for a more Western song, and that is different again from what he does for traditional spirituals. He sings the latter in deep growling voice, which has a peculiar effect. At first it sounds raw, but once you get used to it you begin to understand its idiosyncratic charm, and also its seriousness and dignity.[347] The refrain is as follows:

> *I have some warning, Jesus coming soon.*

When he sings this his wife joins in. In the next few verses he elaborates his theme, until he continues:

> God is warning the nation,
> You can't go on in that way,
> Don't walk in the ways of the heathen,
> But seek the Lord and pray.

'God moves on the water' is a beautiful song in the same vein. It is about the disastrous sinking of the Titanic. He tells of how the vessel sunk, that proud ship that was supposed to have been unsinkable. The refrain goes: 'God moves on the water.' We would like to transcribe it as 'the Spirit of the Lord moves across the waters,' depicting how God breaks human pride.

In 'Soul of a man' he asks what the soul actually is. Since there is no answer forthcoming, he concludes:

> I read the Bible often,
> I try to read it right,
> And as far as I can understand,
> It always is a burning light.

That is his answer to the question.

It is telling that, while there seemed to be so much demand for black music and spirituals, yet Blind Willie was virtually forgotten – except for a few collectors who valued his records as priceless treasures. In 1954 a man who lived in New Orleans spent two years trying to trace Blind Willie. After the recordings of 1930 no more records were made of his work. Finally he discovered where Blind Willie had lived and learnt a few things about him, which he recorded in a documentary produced by Folkways.[348]

The commercialization and development of jazz

'Hobo, you can't ride this train'

The years 1929, 1930 and 1931 were years of economic crisis. Money was scarce and there was high unemployment. Everyone had to be frugal. It meant a rough ride for professional musicians.

Only those who could satisfy the demand of the greatest number of customers had a chance of making a reasonable living from their music. So, paradoxically, it was not the small (and therefore cheap) groups who were doing well, but the big bands – at least the bands who made it their business to meet the requirements of audiences who were willing and able to spend money. That is why they played entertainment music – music which can be appreciated without any trouble, music lacking content that in no way encourages listeners to think, never confronting people with real issues but instead twittering of sweet moonshine and love stories. Rhythm is something the music does sometimes have, but though it may be exciting, it is not really deeply moving. It is rhythm bereft of real musical sense. In other words, it is music which has sold its soul to Mammon. Let us not forget that all art has an economic aspect – that it costs large sums of money to put up a concert with a solo performance, but that in itself is not a bad thing. Music is not good because concerts are held with empty stomachs and only a large dose of idealism to live from. No, it becomes good when musicians of whatever musical or cultural status can give their best without worrying at every note or change of act whether the level of satisfaction experienced by the audience or the takings at the box office will suffice. Commercial art is not bad because it is commercial, but because profits are regarded as the only relevant criteria.

They were hard times. Johnny Dodds, Kid Ory, Oliver, Jelly Roll Morton – they no longer had a chance, for they did not play according to the requirements of the majority who had money. No, it was not those musicians but the big bands – like the Casa Loma Orchestra, the Dorsey Band and also, with a generous helping of real musical talent, the Ellington Band – that survived or did well, got bookings, made recordings, performed concerts for the radio, and so on.

These were hard times for the talented musicians. You needed strong principles to refuse Mammon and public demand when your stomach was empty, particularly if you had the talent that could get you places. Armstrong was one to retain his popularity during that period. On the basis of the reputation he had established earlier, he was able to keep on performing and making records. Now he sung of the 'Peanut vendor' however, and sentimental songs like 'Confessin' ', a quasi-hot 'Tiger rag', a quasi-tragic 'I'm just a gigolo' and show pieces like 'Hobo, you can't ride this train'.[349]

What came naturally to the real cabaret artist, the singer of entertainment songs, the accordion virtuoso, the musician with a natural talent for performing the type of song that originated from Tin Pan Alley (the aptly named music publisher's world where hits were made and cleverly sold), with verve and pleasure, was an ordeal to musicians like Armstrong. They saw through the emptiness, the sentimentality. They could not believe in the music they were playing. To forget their suffering, their lot, many of them began to drink heavily; it gave them the strength to do what they had to do – keep working and remain popular.

This would explain much of the banter, which was regarded by the audience as highly witty entertainment. When Armstrong sung 'I can't give you anything but love', he could not help but make a silly remark, laugh stupidly or pull a funny face. That is how he coped with the situation, deep down; at least he was still the boss and not a slave to the futile and empty songs with their meaningless lyrics.

We can also understand Fats Waller in this context. He was a very talented pianist from Harlem who followed in the tradition of James P. Johnson, whose roots were in ragtime. Fats Waller was a fine pianist who made some beautiful recordings – 'Numb fumblin' '; 'Alligator crawl'; 'Viper's drag'[350] and more – and who was also a competent composer. If this man had had the chance, we would have been many silly jokes poorer, but much music richer.

Yes, those jokes. Take a completely hollow and fatuous piece of music with third-rate lyrics, like 'Mandy'.[351] It is the epic tale of a certain Mandy who falls in love with a . . . Mr Handy. Well, it does rhyme. The plot unfolds: 'Oh, don't you linger, here's a ring for your finger.' Assuming the singer was an intelligent being, it would be hard not to sympathize with the urge to follow this up with 'Give me a ham dinner,' and then to pepper the rest with all sorts of meaningless shrieks and screams, as these are to be preferred to the nonsensical lyrics. The audience loved having the truth thrown in their faces, while they did not even understand that this was happening. Who is the artistic murderer here? We are afraid that it is Joe Public who is jubilant as long as the material is silly and rhythmic. It is a great tragedy. The musicians are not blameless either because they could have opted for poverty, like Dodds and Morton did, or thrown the towel in as Ory did – but who will dare to throw the first stone?

Beginning to look to the past

'Apologies'

It is understandable that musicians looked back nostalgically to the past, because they found themselves in a situation where making music consisted of a succession of solos only, introduced by the whole band playing a simple little theme. The solos seemed bright and direct, but after a while they were a repetitive continuum of the same ideas. Be that as it may, the alternative was to sell themselves commercially – which amounted to selling their souls.

This is how it came about that a number of musicians, both black and white, came together in 1934 to make a few records. One of the numbers was 'Apologies', the full title being 'Apologies to Oliver and Armstrong', and rightly so because what they were playing was the Oliver number 'Dippermouth blues'. It was a piece that they all remembered from the early years in Chicago, little more than a decade earlier. The recording was not a great success – the members of the group were too diverse – but it was a first attempt.[352]

That same year some white musicians from New Orleans got together. They were the leftovers from The New Orleans Rhythm Kings and a few others who had left for the North. They too played recollections of better times, including 'Tin roof blues'.[353]

It was in this vein that Bob Crosby worked on. In 1935 he formed a band that was to enjoy popularity for several years. It was a large band with a very characteristic sound, which was partly the result of Bob Haggart's special arrangements – tasteful, simple, lively and colourful. They played a sort of jazz that attempted to capture the spirit of the older New Orleans jazz in modern arrangements. The solos were always very skilfully incorporated in the whole. It was never a matter of simply performing individually; the solos always reflected the mood of the piece. Besides new pieces they had composed themselves, they also played some Oliver numbers like 'Riverside blues', which they renamed 'Dixieland shuffle'. Occasionally they even did some polyphonic ensemble work.

All these people, and the Crosby band in particular, paved the way for the 'revival' that was to come – the renewed interest in New Orleans jazz. The audiences were being taught without being crudely subjected to real black jazz – prepared, so that the New Orleans style would not sound unfamiliar to them later. It is therefore justifiable that besides 'Tin roof blues', which we have already mentioned, Kershaw also included 'Five point blues', a piece the Crosby Band played in 1938 on a record he had compiled himself called *An Introduction to Traditional Jazz*. Besides its historic value, it is a number that is certainly worth listening to.[354]

The emergence of the study of folk music: Leadbelly

'Irene'

Around 1933, serious attention was given to real African-American folk music for the first time, not for commercial reasons but out of a historical-scientific interest. That was when Lomax began to make recordings of authentic American folk music for the Library of Congress. He took his recording equipment and workers to a number of locations where he made recordings of anything he considered worthwhile. They recorded[355] songs by real cowboys, work songs by both blacks and whites, Indian music and white folk music. America possessed more of the latter than you might think and Sharp and George Pullen Jackson had already collected much in this area, albeit in the form of text and musical notation.

Black music was also recorded: the sing-song manner the sailor used to convey to the pilot the result of soundings taken, the way the overseer led the workers as they unloaded railway tracks, children's songs, spirituals, sermons, whatever he could find.[356] They also visited penal colonies where blacks were sentenced to forced labour on the plantations under conditions strongly reminiscent of the old days of slavery. They heard exceedingly beautiful workaday songs sung by groups of prisoners, led by a precentor – a prisoner just like the rest.

They heard a group of prisoners in Sugarland, Texas, singing a particular song and recorded it. It was sung while harvesting sugar cane – which was cut down with sharp machetes – while the men were traipsing side by side in a long row through the mud. The precentor sings of 'Shorty George', the train on which the wives travelled to come and visit their husbands, and he asks one of the prisoners for what crime he is there. After each line the others answer in unison with a long, solemn and sad 'Oh...o'.

> What's the matter, something must be wrong
> *Oh...o*
> Keep on a-workin', Shorty George done gone
> *Oh...o*
>
> You ought to come on the river in nineteen-four,
> You could find a dead man on every turn row.
>
> But it ain't no more cane on this Brazis,
> Says they all grind it to molasses.
>
> Little Boy, what'd you do for to get so long?
> Said: 'I killed my rider [loved one] in the high sheriff's arms'.
> Etc.[357]

In a camp in Louisiana, Lomax discovered a black man who turned out to have a fantastic repertoire of folk songs and he also had exceptional talent. Lomax had him sing for the state governor and the singer was released on parole. Lomax subsequently had him perform in many places, in order to allow the Americans to hear the rich wealth of folk music that was there for the asking in the deep South.

Huddie Ledbetter, nicknamed Leadbelly, accompanied himself on the guitar and sung a virtually endless repertoire of work songs and authentic folk songs, some typically white, some typically African-American in character. Leadbelly apparently worked for a while as a sort of apprentice with Blind Lemon Jefferson, the blues singer from the 1920s. It seems that Leadbelly's repertoire embraced much more than the blues we know from Blind Lemon Jefferson. Since the selection of songs by the recording companies was so one-sided, perhaps it would be better to assume that they succumbed to popular demand.

What did Leadbelly sing? He sang a song about the cotton harvest:

> Jump down, turn around, to pick a bale of cotton
> Jump down, turn around, pick a bale a day. (x 2)

He sings of the man working on the land who calls to his wife to bring him water:

> Bring me li'l water Silvy,
> Bring me li'l water now,
> Bring me li'l water, Silvy
> Every li'l once in a while. (x 2)

He also sung a folk song that was to become popular and was later performed by many singers, none of whom equalled Leadbelly's rendition. 'Irene' was originally a white folk song, without a doubt, but there is a black flavour to the arrangement.

> Irene goodnight, Irene goodnight,
> Goodnight Irene, goodnight Irene,
> I kiss you in my dreams.
>
> Sometimes I live in the country,
> Sometimes I live in the town,
> Sometimes I have a great notion
> To jump in the river and drown.

Not surprisingly, Irene is not a lively number. It tells of how he bumped into his true love, Irene, the day after he was married to another woman, and of how he was now separated from her forever by circumstances and age difference.[358]

Lomax also made recordings of singing evangelists, not only accompanied by a guitar, but sometimes by a mouth organ too. This instrument is very popular in the impoverished outback of the South. Not only religious music,[359] but also folk music was often played on this instrument. The best known harmonica player was Sonny Terry. He was born in 1911 in Durham, Georgia. His father also played the mouth organ. Much of his knowledge of technique and repertoire he learned at the dances on Saturday evenings when the jug bands played and harmonica music was performed as well. He was familiar with spirituals from the church, but he played the harmonica like nobody had done before, the way he had taught himself. He had a fantastic technique, which enabled him to sing while accompanying himself, without any breaks – it was unbelievable that an individual could achieve such a feat. He never strove for technique just for the sake of it – his aim was always to play the music as pure and melodical as possible.

Sonny, who was blind, was discovered around 1938 and, like Leadbelly, he performed for all sorts of outfits of educated whites from academic or university background. He also played in some Broadway shows, but whatever he did and wherever he did it, he remained himself, playing only his own music. Sonny is no exception – there are many like him – but musically he is the best and richest by far. He has a varied repertoire: blues, spirituals, folk songs, with 'Locomotive blues' being the icing on the cake. It is a piece which draws its inspiration from the train – an imitation of the sound, if you like – but it is musically so fine, so full of variety, that all other attempts to capture the train in music (with the possible exception of Meade Lux Lewis's 'Honky tonk train blues') pale into insignificance.[360]

Gershwin's opera
Porgy and Bess

If my memory serves me correctly, it is at the opening of the third act that the script of George Gershwin's *Porgy and Bess* describes the scene of the square at Catfish Row: people happily going about their business, someone playing the harmonica and others dancing and singing. The accompanying music is however nothing at all remotely like that of Sonny Terry. No, it is a Franz Lehar-esque overture that opens this part. Neither is there in the whole of this opera a single note of black music to be heard, not even an imitation. There are no real spirituals – not only are there no traditional ones, there is not even a single one that even remotely resembles the spiritual song of the blacks. No blues, no black folk songs – not even in a Western setting or adaptation. *Porgy and Bess* are less black than Bizet's *Carmen* is Spanish or Puccini's *Butterfly* is Japanese. Gershwin's opera is based on the book *Porgy* by Du Bose Heyward which was written in the 1920s. It is a book that was written with a typical Southern approach to blacks. It is full of stereotypical characterization. The life of the blacks is portrayed as idyllic and colourful, but blacks themselves are stupid and actually slightly ridiculous people. As the writer says, 'The strange mixture of comedy and tragedy leaves an unmistakable mark on the life of the Negro in its deepest moments.'[361] The writer regularly lets black people cut a laughable figure at the most serious parts of the book, the climax being Porgy's run from the police. As if there were not enough reasons for their behaviour – reasons the author does take the trouble to show us, though in fact sympathy for the lot of the blacks held ransom by whites is not completely lacking. In the opera these blacks do not speak properly, of course, but utter a sort of childish gibberish. Those who have heard blacks speaking – perhaps on the Folkway documentary recordings; those who have heard the prayer of the raspberry-seller from New Orleans[362] so moving and linguistically beautiful, will know that there is no such thing as an 'inferior black language'. It is part of a stereotypical perception of blacks.

Certainly, blacks have their own dialect, but they do not have this stupid language which sometimes becomes almost nonsensical. Incidentally, their dialect differs little from the dialect of the whites from the South. Did anybody really believe that instead of singing of the 'promised land' in one of their spirituals, they would say 'primus lan' '? Those who have heard the records we mentioned earlier, by rural preachers and musicians, will know better. Infidelity, crime, naïve love, dirt and stench, unbelievable ignorance, faith without a clue as to what it was all about – that describes a typical black persoon as the book would have us believe it.

The libretto does not improve matters – to the contrary. This is a piece that we can classify as one of the last examples of the black-faced minstrel shows: whites with blackened faces impersonating blacks to amuse themselves at the expense of blacks on the one hand, and to perform some of their music butchered to the tastes of the white audience on the other hand. This was then all bundled into an opera tailored to Broadway standards, composed in the veristic tradition of a Mascagni or similar. This was essentially no different from Gershwin's so-called serious jazz compositions of the 1920s – like 'Rhapsody in blue', a rhapsody that resembles a piano concerto by Rachmaninoff – which were played by the so-called 'King of Jazz', Paul Whiteman, with his big band. Their value may be debated, but jazz and black music must be left out of it. Gershwin was a very good composer of songs – very talented. 'Summertime' from *Porgy and Bess* became a popular song, and rightly so because it has many outstanding qualities.

It can only be described as deeply tragic that black singers have become so alienated from their own folk that they will perform a piece like *Porgy and Bess*. Tragic, because they are betraying their own culture and doing so in an opera-type operetta, which can please only at the expense of the unaffected, Southern black whose music, religion, way of life in many respects is much deeper and more beautiful than what is depicted here. Of course, injustice and poverty coupled with its inevitable partner, impoverishment, undeniably exist, but whose fault is that? It would be more appropriate to portray blacks as they really are, to break down that patronizing, denigrating view of them; making a piece like this is no contribution at all.

If it were possible to regard this piece as just a jolly operetta – in the same way as no one expects to find real Japanese people portrayed in *Madame Butterfly* – it would not seem so bleak, but here in Europe it has long been welcomed as a representative piece of black culture. The arrival of this piece of music incited lectures to be held on black music and the nature of blacks. It can only be put down to total ignorance, an absolute lack of any knowledge of real black music and black culture.

Musically, *Porgy and Bess* may be classified on a higher plane than Al Jolson's minstrel performances like 'Mammy' and 'Sonny Boy' and others, but that does not detract from the fundamental similarities.

Jelly Roll Morton's recordings for the Library of Congress

Jazz can be beautiful

> Many people have a mistaken idea of jazz. Somehow it got into the encyclopaedia that jazz should be considered as a load of bleating sounds and poor-sounding noises – something that was even supposed to be painful to the ears. Jazz music is to be played sweet, soft, plenty rhythm. When you have your plenty rhythm with your plenty swing, it becomes beautiful.
>
> For a start, you can't play diminuendos and crescendos if you always play as loud as you can. You have to be able to go down if you want to come up again. If a glass of water is full you can't get any more in it, but if you have half a glass, you have room to add some more water. Jazz music is based on the same principle, because jazz is based on strict musical laws ... Jazz ... you can apply to any sort of melody. It depends entirely on your ability for transformation.[363]

Jelly Roll Morton's lecture on jazz in the Library of Congress was attended by Alan Lomax with his portable recording equipment. Lomax invited him to lecture there and that is what he did, many times. He explained his views on the history of jazz, described pianists from the beginning of the twentieth century, explained how he developed the jazz piano style from ragtime and blues, told of the lives of the musicians, analysed the structure of jazz and demonstrated which music was good and which music was not that good. He imitated pianists he had heard play more than thirty years previously, he gave us a glimpse of his artistic skill, with all his intelligence and feeling for nuance. Lomax later examined everything that Jelly said, the result being the very important book, *Mister Jelly Roll*. A large part of the recordings made was released on record.[364]

Besides his anecdotes and the story of his childhood and education that we quoted extensively in a previous chapter, we can also hear a number of renditions of his compositions, unlike any he had previously been able to record. What we get to hear is a Jelly – purified and deepened. He had been through a lot, but his music had never changed, essentially. Here in the recordings of 'Mama Nita', 'New Orleans blues', 'Jungle blues', 'The crave', 'Fickle Fay Creep' and many others – too many to list – just as in that magnificent series of piano solos he played for commercial recordings,[365] we hear that it is not in the least necessary to give black folk music social status and an artificial character by transposing it into a Western style derived from Romantic music, and arranged in a way that damages the music's own character. On the contrary, just as much as the old band recordings of Oliver and Morton, these records prove that folk music can be developed to a high artistic standard by including all sorts of refinement and nuance, without affecting its African-American character. Jazz can be music that reaches out far beyond the simplicity of folk music, but not at the expense of the typical qualities of that folk music – its unique depth, its own idiom – they must not be denied or swapped for a more socially acceptable, Western style to which it is not suited.

As Westerners we have to accept blacks with this music. They have made an important contribution to the musical culture of this world, but we must not expect them to deny their own past. In fact, doing so would imply that we do not accept black Americans but simply tolerate them once they have sold their souls to our culture. No, the ideal does not mean holding back the blacks, keeping them on the bottom rung of the ladder, because that is when they make such beautiful music. Not only would that be cruel – it would be an absolute mistake. Oliver and Morton and others prove that development and depth are certainly possible, built on the traditions characteristic to the African-American culture, without blacks having to remain paupers.

Ferdinand 'Jelly Roll' Morton died in 1941 in Los Angeles in dire conditions.

The collection of jazz records and the study of the history of jazz

Collector's Item

Teenagers and young adults in America and Europe in the 1930s realized that there was much to be discovered at markets and in junk shops for those who were willing to listen and search: records by absolutely unknown musicians. One of the releases in Europe was the Parlophon New Rhythm Style series (that included many of Armstrong's Hot Seven), which opened up a completely new world. There was also much that was not worth the trouble, of course, and there was also a lot that promised much but turned out to be empty and unmusical.

The first jazz record collectors started up as early as the 1920s, but many fared like me. It was 1936. I was at secondary school. We had a gramophone at home. Once in a while I wanted to buy a record, of course. I bought ... a sentimental song played by a band, of whom I have forgotten the name. I bought another one, but that was disappointing too after only a short time. I had heard Ellington's 'Mood indigo' at a friend's house, so I bought it, only to discover that 'Bundle of blues' on the flip side was actually much nicer. It did not bore me so quickly. Then I bought an issue of *Jazzwereld* ('Jazz World'), one of the magazines of that era which made a serious attempt to get to grips with jazz, even if there was inevitably copious advertising of popular stars. I went to the Dutch Jazz Club *(Nederlandse Jazz Liga)* by myself one evening. It was one of the clubs to be found all over Europe (and also in America), for young people who wanted to know more of the new music. Perhaps I was unlucky, but the speaker failed to convince me of his views, and the jam session afterwards – which consisted of a number of musicians improvising in the sprit of Chicago – seemed chaotic and noisy. Nevertheless, I did meet other young people there, and they already had a couple of records too. We arranged to meet up. I went to them and discovered Armstrong. We swapped. We pillaged the markets, bought some in the shops – increasingly fewer – discovered records by the unknown Luis Russell band, and once came across a very strange record by an absolutely unknown celebrity. It was 'Black bottom stomp' by Jelly Roll Morton's Red Hot Peppers, and it cost 35 cents (10p) at the market! We came in contact with older collectors and, about three years later we were – I was – at home in the world of records. I was familiar with Victor, Okeh, Paramount and, besides the European releases, I managed to get hold of some collector's items – records by little or better known groups which had never been released in Europe. I got to sample and know Red Nicholls, Bix Beiderbecke, and the Chicagoans. Above all I learnt to appreciate Morton and Oliver – through Brunswick's daring release of an Oliver album in 1936 – and soon discovered the blues, Bessie Smith first, and then countless unknown blues singers on the Brunswick Race series. Even a spiritual by the Mitchell's Christian Singers found its way into my collection. I swapped, I bought from people who ordered from American second-hand record shops, such as Orin Blackstone in New Orleans and others.

For others it will have been the same story. Delauney's pioneering *Discography* helped us to learn to identify the musicians. In America people tried to discover something about the history of jazz, to find out who was who. There were a few important books on jazz published during those years. Many of them have already been obscure for a long time. Allan Ramsay and Smith's *Jazzmen* is still valuable today [at time of writing] as a source of information and an introduction to the history of jazz.

All this work has proved to be of tremendous significance. During those years the many committed enthusiasts separated, like wheat from chaff, the material they collected, and the legacy of the past was categorized. People learned to distinguish the different trends and the foundation was laid for further study, lectures, re-issues and many sensible talks given on jazz. The rewards of this, which included many re-issues of old records, were to be reaped after the War.

Spirituals in the 1930s: Rosetta Tharpe

'Rock me'

In the 1930s spirituals were still being sung in the churches and recordings made of quartets. The most important of these was possibly the Mitchell's Christian Singers. The quartet included Brown, a driver;

Davis, a worker in a tobacco factory; David, a coal merchant; and Bryant, a bricklayer. They performed in churches, at evangelistic meetings, and so on. One of their records is called 'Travelin' shoes'.[366]

> They stopped ridin' by the sinner's door,
> They all cried, Sinner, are you ready to go,
> *He said: 'Oh Lordy, no no no no,*
> *Because I ain't got my travellin' shoes.* (i.e. the faith)
> *It's my duty to say no no no no,*
> *Because I ain't got my travellin' shoes.'*

The first few lines are taken up with a succession of solos sung by different voices; the refrain was sung together. Then the wagon – the 'chariot', of course – stops at the door of the gambler, the liar, and finally at the door of the Christian, who is able to answer 'yes yes yes yes'.

This period saw church solos and particularly those by women, who performed spirituals in the same style as Blind Willie Johnson, strongly influenced by the singing style of the blues as it had developed over the previous few decades. Since secular music had progressed so much as a result of the work of Ma Rainey, Bessie Smith and many others, it was inevitable that church music too would be influenced. Some female blues singers became believers and continued their music in the church, now singing spirituals. People were listening to gramophone records. An enrichment and revamping of the style of singing was inevitable. Building on the old traditions, the result of developments in the secular scene was incorporated.

A typical example of this, and one of the best, is Rosetta Tharpe. She sang 'hits' in 1935 as vocalist in a dance band. We did not hear her again until around 1938 when the first records of her as a singer of religious songs were released. She had become a Christian and a member of the Church of God in Christ. She accompanies herself on the guitar. The desire to preach the word of God is very evident in her music, for example in 'God don't like it'. We should mention that orthodox Christians in America do not drink or smoke – the fruit of a Puritan lifestyle. She sings about this too:

> They tell me that this yellow corn
> Will make the very best kind,
> But you better turn that corn into bread,
> And stop that drinking moonshine. ['moonshine' is whisky]

Refrain:
> *Because God don't like it,*
> *I know I am so glad He don't like it,*
> *I know, ain't you glad He don't like it,*
> *I know it's a scandalous and a shame.*

> This ol' race is goin' to be lost,
> If it keeps on like it's goin'
> It's so weak they have a little church,
> But the preacher's drinking moonshine.
>
> Brother when your name is in the church,
> And you drink God's Holy Wine,
> You can't walk those golden streets
> All staggerin' full of moonshine.[367]

The next song, 'Rock me' is beautiful and, like the previous one, probably her own composition:

> Now won't you hear me swinging,
> And the words that I'm singing
> Washed my soul with water from on high.
> Now the world of love is around me,
> Evil sought to bite me,
> Oh, if You leave me, I will die.

Refrain:
> *You just hide me in Thy bosom*
> *Till the storm of life is over,*
> *Oh, rock me, in the greatness of Thy love.*
> *Receive me, and I want no more*
> *Till You take me to You – blessed home above.*
>
> Say, I'm maintaining,
> I just go on uncomplaining,
> But before this time another year:
> My life may all forsaken,
> And death may overtake me,
> But if I'm within Thee I have no need to fear.
>
> Oh, make my journey brighter,
> Make my burden lighter
> Help me to do good wherever I can;
> Oh, let Thy presence thrill me
> let its kindness still me
> When You hold me in the hollow of Thy hand.[368]

Blues after 1935

'Big Moose blues'

In rural areas the blues was still being sung in the original style. The influence of the Race records was certainly perceptible here and there, but essentially nothing changed. It was different in the cities.

Professional singers were having a hard time and more than a few of them began to serve Mammon in their own way – by singing smutty lyrics, by emphasizing all the elements that would attract a certain kind of white audience. There were also some who fared better. After the years of severe crisis had passed, a new generation of singers emerged. The style had changed, the tempo was faster, the tone was lighter, and the accompaniment more rhythmic – like the jazz which had evolved post-1928. Nevertheless, the work of Merline Johnson ('The Yas Yas Girl') is certainly worth listening to. The blues of Big Bill Broonzy, Johnny Temple and Sleepy John Estes was a more direct continuation of the music from prior to 1930 – the work of Leroy Carr, Texas Alexander and others – but we will not be able to check up on it extensively here.[369]

There was also an interesting record of this genre by Sonny Boy and Lonnie, who were unknown artists. It features a blues singer, accompanied by piano and guitar, who sings of his experiences on a naval transport ship in the War. We estimate that the recording was made in 1944 or 1945. *Big Moose* is the name of the ship.

> It was in San Francisco, it was way way out in the bay,
> It was in 1943, way way out in the bay,
> Yes, just a Tuesday morning that old *Big Moose* go roll us away.
>
> We rolled that Pacific, sailed it both day and night, (x 2)
> Yes, some was drinking and gamblin', some was low low on their knees.
>
> Japanese bombs was falling, falling down down from the sky, (x 2)
> Sometimes I wanted to leave that shiphold, but I had no place to go.
>
> We landed in Finch Haven, New Guinea, it was on the twenty-fifth day (x 2)
> And I said: 'Lord Lord have mercy on our poor GI Souls.'[370]

The birth of swing

'In the mood'

The middle of the 1930s saw the gradual emergence of a new style. It was a sort of Chicagoans jazz but then adapted for larger bands. The black bands like Henderson's led the way. They played arrangements that were strongly rhythmically oriented, in which saxophone ensembles alternated with brass ensembles – in unison or harmonized. Solos, free and improvised, were often played and accompanied by riffs (short melodic phrases which were constantly repeated and had a strongly rhythmic effect). Influences from the Benny Moten Band and others were incorporated. The music was 'hotter', and the combined effect was a fluent, strong rhythm, harmonically rendered, peppered with fierce solos, direct, vehement and improvised – at least that was the impression they gave.

Around 1935 the time was ripe. A white band, that of Bennie Goodman, began to use these arrangements – particularly those of Fletcher Henderson, like Morton's 'King Porter stomp' – and played them with machine-like precision on the basis of a rhythm section that strongly marked the beat. They played contemporary hits. It was a great success, and swing was born, the new sort of dance music which was to keep thousands of fans spellbound.

This was par excellence the dance music of the twentieth century. It was music that could capture white audiences in every respect and give them what they demanded. It was jazz, but it was not too challenging, fierce but not too complex, always softened and made pleasing by harmonization or, in the case of solos, by smooth accompaniment. Besides the apparent spontaneity, directness, seemingly primitive release of power, without dinner jackets or tail coats and without the formality of a classical concert, there was the omnipresence of the rhythm. Everyone now had access to the popular tunes rendered in an almost ideal way – 'ideal' in the sense of twentieth-century Western mentality.

Goodman created a formula – at least he was able to suitably apply the formulas the black leaders of big dance bands had worked out. It was a formula that hit the mark so well that not only was it predominant for a whole decade (until 1945) but it is still alive now [at the time of writing]. Turn on your radio and some band somewhere in the world will be playing this sort of music. It has something of the streamlining that affected design and changed the shape of such diverse products as the car, the train, the vacuum cleaner and the iron during those years. It was colourful, vehement, supple, stylized, smooth – it was swing.

Many, many swing bands were able to profit from the craze. It became the era of jazz – the era that jazz was sold using all possible modern sales techniques, with much advertising while it was tailored to the demands of the public. Glenn Miller, Dorsey, Lunceford, Barnet and also Artie Shaw were the manufacturers.

Listen to 'In the mood',[371] the most popular piece at the time. The musical starting point is a riff-like theme that hypnotizes the masses, as it were, and forms the ideal stimulant for Western paired dancing, which is almost a duet in itself, full of vehemence and improvisation – a letting go, a freeing from the conventions, from that which a modern audience might perceive as over-rigid, stylized norms. Loose and direct, rhythmical and fierce, free and carefree – that was the music, that was the dance, that in many ways was the twentieth century.

To the musicians themselves it was often less pleasant; Artie Shaw disappeared suddenly one fine day. He did not arrive for a performance. He could no longer take the pressure. Perhaps he saw what Goodman himself once said: 'Many musicians today don't know any more what they really want, do they? Perhaps I don't know either. But something happens when you realize that what you are doing isn't really music any more – it has become entertainment. It is a fine difference and it determines your playing. Your whole attitude changes.'[372]

The swing of Basie and co.

'One o' clock jump'

The swing music that was played by Goodman and his many more or less original counterparts was an adaptation of black jazz, fashioned to white dance music. When we say black jazz, however, we are chiefly referring to the jazz of Fletcher, Henderson and such – jazz that originated from Western dance music, but was very substantially influenced by authentic black jazz as played by Armstrong, Rex Stuart, Buster Bailey, Joe Smith and others. The blacks had found the formula – the whites applied it. I wonder whether a black band playing the same music as Goodman would have had the same amount of success, though it must be said that Goodman was one of the first to include black musicians in his band – two of them being Lionel Hampton (drums and vibraphone) and Teddy Wilson (piano).

Both black and white elements were very strongly blended in this type of jazz. Blacks contributed their own musical tradition – some of the joy of early jazz also added to the success of this music; the white influence lay in the cultivation of great precision in ensemble playing and, most importantly, in improvisation and in 'hot' and hefty beat accentuating rhythms in the spirit of the jazz inspired by the Chicagoans. Because of the teamwork and their playing together it became increasingly difficult to hear the difference between the black and the white musicians – something that hardly posed any problems in the 1920s, the era of Bix and Teschemaker, Oliver and Morton, Armstrong and Dodds.

Still, it is important to see that the impact made by black musicians remained very great, and indeed, it would be difficult to exaggerate the significance of the Count Basie Band in the era of swing.

Basie and his musicians came from Kansas City. Most of them had been playing there in Bennie Moten's band. When Moten died in 1935, Basie reorganized the band, but musicians from Kansas City still formed the core. We do not want to contend that they were all born there, but they all received their education and began their careers there.

Jam sessions were cultivated extensively in Kansas City. They also occurred elsewhere, but less intensively. For these jam sessions various musicians, who did not otherwise form a band, got together for the purpose of playing music together. It meant that they took turns to play the solo while the other musicians improvised a background of riffs. Thus a real Chicagoan idea became the basic principle of all jazz.

It certainly became the basic structure of all Basie's music, although he could not quite manage to make the music work without any arrangements at all, while in line with other swing bands he increased the saxes to four and included four trumpets, three trombones and, of course, a four-strong rhythm section of bass, guitar, piano (Basie himself) and drums.

Jo Jones, the drummer, tells us a little about their approach to the work:

> The Basie Band gave you the impression of a small band. The arrangements were almost all played from memory and it didn't matter how many of us there were – there was always the freedom and the flexibility of a small band. This was not the case for other bands from that period, however good they were in many respects. [He goes on to talk about a recording.] When we went into the studio we first decided what we were going to play, looked briefly at our notes (with some instructions and agreements about the consecutive choruses), and then there it went. We played once, twice or three times at the most, and the record was made. Some of the best sides we hadn't even discussed beforehand. We just sat there doing something during the break and the recording technicians recorded it.

On the question of whether the band rehearsed he answered:

> I don't know how to explain it, how to tell you how it actually went on. I have never understood how an arrangement like that (i.e. one which came into being simply by virtue of playing and otherwise only consisted of agreements) came about. What I do know is that we were there and we began to play, but we didn't rehearse. It all just went so automatically.[373]

The significance of this band in the evolution of swing and in what was still to come was very great. 'One o'clock jump', the band's signature tune, is a piece of a kind that has been copied and imitated in all sorts of different ways and one that has contributed to Basie's impact.[374]

6
The 1940s

The birth of modern jazz

'Cherokee'

Swing was by definition jazz, at least if you hold that the definition of jazz is rhythm plus improvisation. That was the direction pursued by the big bands. Performances by recording combinations, the (public) jam sessions, anything that could be called jazz and stood out, fitted that definition. The scheme was the same as it had ever been: the short, riff-like theme was played first or, if a popular little tune was being played it was done in strong staccato with the same effect; then solos, one after the other, one much fiercer, heavier and more direct than the other, with the only binding element being the chord scheme and the tempo. The accompaniment was fashioned by drawing out chords or by improvised sax riffs. The whole thing was supported by the constantly pumping, beat accentuating rhythm, decorated by the drum if possible.

The audience got used to it. It had to be constantly fiercer, otherwise it was not authentic and did not keep people entertained. That is why the saxophone began bleating, the clarinet was played hoarsely and the trumpet began to cultivate high tones. It was all for the sake of effect – to suggest heavy emotion, a direct release. Was it musical? Seldom. Perhaps the audience enjoyed hearing the sax produce ugly sounds and being entertained by music that balanced precariously on the edge of its own definition. This is reminiscent of the approval of the violation of norms which the Bible talks about in Romans 1:32. In this case it violates the norm which also applies to art and ultimately determines its value: 'meditating on things true, noble, reputable, authentic, compelling, gracious – the best, not the worst; the beautiful, not the ugly; things to praise, not things to curse' (Philippians 4:8).

Jam sessions were originally intended for the musicians only; it was their chance to enjoy making music after having played empty music in a commercial orchestra, possibly for hours on end. Now it became a compulsory part of performances, an act of letting yourself go with great emotion. It became an empty and futile repetition of tricks which had the appearance of spontaneity; it became the cultivation of non-music to please Mammon or, if Mammon was not involved, a striving for the approval of audiences that yearned for sensation, for a vehemence that crushed the definition of beauty, for increasingly intense stimulation.

To the musicians this became a trial, dull, a self-inflicted void. No wonder they tried to put the soul back into music after 1940, tried to give it meaning, to restore its dignity as music. That is how modern jazz came about. It started with the formula for swing music: solos based on a certain progression of chords remained the basic materials, and the themes remained partially taken from the hits of the day. There was no more reaching for Oliver's (or anybody else's) old music. Nevertheless there was a heartbeat behind the new music – we could perhaps call it an existentialist heartbeat.

This process was described very clearly and concisely by one of the most talented and influential musicians, a man who significantly contributed to the fashioning of modern jazz, Charlie Parker, the saxophonist. He tells of how he first discovered the modern jazz concept:

> It was in December 1939. The stereotypical chord progressions which were used the whole time were boring me terribly and I kept thinking that something else would have to come. I could hear it in my thoughts sometimes, but I couldn't play it. Well, that evening I played 'Cherokee' (a popular swing number) and while I was doing it I discovered that by using the higher intervals of a chord as the melody line, thereby adapting the chord changes, I could play what I had been hearing in my thoughts. I came to life.[375]

Parker, however, was not the only one. There were others – all intelligent young blacks who were looking for a way to fill swing with something other than the endless repetition of a few tricks which had made the music so empty and so infinitely boring. Intensity and spontaneity – fine, they had nothing against it, but they wanted to produce something with meaning, something real; 'real' being an expression of what lived in them.

Kansas City was one of the cities where this sort of sound was being developed. Mary Lou Williams tells the following about the pianist Thelonius Monk:

> He felt that musicians would have to start playing something new and he began to do it. Most of us admired him for it. He was one of the original modernists, a good one, who applied about the same harmonies then as are being played today. But in those days we called it 'zombie music' and waited until only we musicians were left by ourselves and the audience had left. Why 'zombie music'? Because the shrill chords reminded us of the music from Frankenstein or other horror films. I myself was one of the first to produce these frozen sounds and after a whole night of playing a jam session (for an audience), I started playing strange chords, nothing but modulations, together with Dick Wilson, a very progressive tenor saxophonist.[376]

It does not sound as if they were simply looking for new chords, new musical approaches, but as if they were also trying to express something in their music, something that was related to the character of a horror film. The fact that Kansas City led the way was possibly the result of another factor, one that was also responsible for shaping modern jazz, namely that musicians there were striving for individualism more than elsewhere.[377] For modern jazz is individualist, as its proponents loudly reiterate.

A further characteristic of the new jazz was a thirst for freedom – freedom for the musician who was playing. It was realized in improvised solos in which, from then on, even the traditional chord scheme was no longer binding. It was freedom from all bonds. As Dave Brubeck volunteered:

> What is jazz? If the soloist does not have complete freedom, it ceases to be jazz. Jazz is the only form of art that exists today in which freedom exists for the individual without losing contact with the others. If we play arrangements we try to get our freedom in the middle section. We start with an arranged chorus, and then there is complete freedom for as long as the soloist feels like playing, and then it ends with the arrangement again. And if it goes well, the beginning and end are largely ridiculous, because the parts in between have come at the level where you are really busy improvising.[378]

This quote reminds us a bit of the spirit of the greatest philosopher of existentialism, Heidegger. He said that human beings in their ordinary living live in the 'impersonal', an improper form of existence. One is only oneself if one realizes one's own *Dasein* ('existence'), if one places oneself in one's own freedom. That takes place here in the improvised solos.

The catchword has thus become 'individualistic freedom', freedom that wants to have people really free – completely free of any ties; free too from any norms. That is why modern jazz tries to break down the laws of structure which apply to melody, and not only search for the unconventional, but also for the irrational, for elements that demonstrate the freedom of the individual. Stearn, so far the best historian of modern jazz and a person who is positive about its development, puts it like this: 'The bop soloist (bop was the name of the new sort of jazz) now began and ended at odd moments and places by shifting the respiratory pause and so often created a long, unbalanced melodic line which ignored the regular pauses.'[379]

Love does not govern here. Everyone tries to outplay the other, even in the very matter of irrationality. A musician would stop in the middle of the solo and leave it to the following soloist to pick up the pieces; another would leave the stage while somebody else was playing; and for the listeners, the audience, there was not the least bit of interest.[380]

All this was strongest in the 1940s. During the War years this kind of jazz was being developed in New York by Charlie Parker, whom we have already mentioned, by Dizzy Gillespie and by a group of musicians that regularly met together at Minton's, a nightclub in New York. These jam sessions there were decisive. After the War modern jazz soon became widespread and popular, thanks to gramophone recordings and concerts staged by these people. They were all very intelligent and skilled musicians who knew very well what they were doing and, particularly at first, were prepared to give it their all. Commercial success at that point was still more or less a pipe dream because this jazz was no longer dance music. The audience sat motionless at the concerts and there was nothing left of the exuberance that had been so fundamental to swing music.

There are reasons why jazz developed along these lines, at that time and in that scene. The petering out of swing was one reason. The new music was in many respects a backlash against swing because, although it retained many elements of swing, these musicians were looking for something opposite in character and nature. This music became 'cool' – as opposed to 'hot' – which means that any emotion which would otherwise have been released, was repressed or avoided. The rhythm was different – more restless, more nervous, sometimes based directly on African rhythms – in any case there was no 'pumping' as there was in swing.

There were more reasons, however. The position of blacks also played a role. The race issue became very acute because of the war conditions which required them to devote themselves to American civilization. The question was, should they let themselves be used again? Building on the accomplishments of the Harlem Renaissance, blacks were no longer willing to play the entertainer for whites who found them useful when it came to popular music but otherwise gave them the cold shoulder. Blacks wanted to find their own expression in jazz, one which was different from what the whites had made of it. However, the spirit of music that was being produced at the time was, in fact, of pure Western character and was very closely related to the modern art of Picasso, Klee, the abstract painters and the thought of the modern existentialist philosophers.

Freedom, irrationality, individualism – but no joy. On the contrary, this was an escape from reality, a reality that was perceived as a strange power, a prison for those who thirsted after absolute freedom. It was also a prison that resulted from repression. And it was the suffocation of the ever boring, endless repetition of sameness, concretized in the meaningless emptiness of swing's quasi-fierce release of emotion.

This is not joy; this is hatred of the world, of reality, and ultimately of creation itself. It explains the preference for the strange chords, searing and incoherent. As for the harmonies, they were not only a further development of what was already there but they were sought for as an expression of what was on these musicians' hearts, what inspired them: a feeling of alienation, of fear, of emptiness, of their experience of reality as a horror film – 'zombie music'.

From the typically modern aspect of this new sort of jazz, we can also understand why it was so easy for whites to adopt – so easy in fact that they were even able to play an important role in its development. Take Dave Brubeck and Shorty Rogers' group of musicians in the western USA. It is hard, if not downright impossible, to distinguish white from black here.

You could detect now, more so than in the past, that the best and most skilled musicians were playing two different sorts of music. We have seen that this had been the case also with Armstrong and his people in 1928. On one hand there now was the fierce expression of freedom, vehement and, despite all inwardness and being locked up in oneself, extrovert, outward-oriented.[381] On the other hand there was the introversion, the inward reverie, the daydream, unattached and free from reality, quieted and literally 'cool'. The well-known number by Parker, 'Lover man',[382] is a good example. It is music that appears very quiet and calm, missing all the emotion of early jazz; inside it is a direct expression of what moves the musician, his feelings of being abandoned, lonely, alienated from reality, the very consequence of his search for individualist freedom in an existentialist sense.

No, joy and warmth were banished from the lives of these musicians. Parker paid for it with his mental health and ultimately with his self-inflicted death. Others either put water in their wine or sought refuge from the tension and problems in the use of narcotics.

This jazz is a phenomenon that is essentially modern and the product of our Western world. That is why it is so well understood by young people in the West, and why it is so attractive to them. That is also part of the reason why modern Western classical composers, like Schoenberg and Stravinsky, had such a big influence on the musicians of modern jazz. This is not superficial music, not at all. It has an affinity to post-War, Western, modern art – the works of the Experimentals, the Tachists, modernists who also strive for abstraction and the irrational. This can be heard in the characteristic tone forming, cool indeed (the opposite of warm), withdrawn, disconnected form reality, light and not particularly mellifluous. This tone forming alone – both in the brass and the woodwind – distinguishes modern jazz from all earlier forms of jazz. Modern jazz is also not the logical consequence of early jazz. On the contrary, it is a new form of music with a completely different content, a new spirit and a new structure, and the only thing it has in common with early jazz is its origin, in that it evolved from the jazz scene.

Grossman described one of the characteristics of modern jazz as 'playfulness'.[383] What he means is that these musicians sometimes do not seem to take their music seriously, but that they appear to play with it. It does not mean that they *are* not serious. Modern jazz musicians are dead serious; they know what they want, they are very conscientious artists, and they strive to develop their music. In that respect their music is a far cry from folk music. The playfulness however points to something else, an attitude, an attitude to life that will not allow itself to be tied to anything, that always wants to remain free, to treat things without strings attached, to 'play' with them. What comes to the fore here is nihilism, a lack of ability to commit oneself to anything, to be bonded and, instead, to adopt a 'free of obligations' attitude that covers an inability to believe in anything, a struggle to retain personal freedom at whatever cost.

This becomes particularly clear if we bear in mind the cultural history of these blacks or, rather, that which still determines the lives of many blacks both in terms of sprit and culture, namely Christianity – the biblical message. This music is a clear refutation of it. While performing 'Swing low, sweet chariot', Gillespie sang 'Swing low, sweet Cadillac'.

This is no naïve black faith, but something that verges on blasphemy. So he frees himself 'playfully' from 'that old time religion' sung of by churchgoers. Another musician changed the title of the well-known spiritual about Moses to 'Let my fingers go'.[384]

All this is not unconnected with what is going on at present. The attitude of many students today is one of playing around, with 'no strings attached', a general lack of interest and a certain unwillingness to devote themselves to anything. It is an international phenomenon that is seen in an extreme form among the 'nozems', forerunners of the hippies in the Netherlands. On one hand these young people are dangerous anarchists who, given the chance, will sometimes commit themselves to a cause with valour that verges on the romantic and with a contempt for life that is real and deep, as for example during the Hungarian insurrection (in which young students often played such an important role). On the other hand they can be apathetic individuals who care little or nothing for anything and remain unmoved by any ideal. Boredom, counterbalanced by an impatient need to rush along – these are the symptoms of the empty spirit syndrome, sometimes with explosive nihilism, boredom in the sense of *nausée*, as Sartre called it, an aversion to all being.

All this is part of our culture, certainly, in the same way that this music, which is anything but commercial, is part of our culture, but that does not mean that only those who live and behave likewise are really 'in touch with the times', the only ones who really live, who understand their age. It is as meaningless as the allegation that only those who vote communist really understand contemporary politics. In culture as well as in politics many persuasions exist side by side and everyone uses their own criteria to tackle the issues of the day. The persuasions may be dignified by age, like liberalism or Christianity, or they may be more recent trends like socialism and communism; likewise, in other areas of human culture all sorts of schools of thought are found to exist alongside each other and in opposition to each other. Abstract art can exist alongside art that is Impressionist in spirit, alongside art that is related in spirit, not necessarily in form, to seventeenth-century art. Provided that these trends do not get bogged down in the repetition and imitation of earlier forms but are sustained by a living spirit that engages with the issues of our time, provided that they are tuned in to the reality of today, that they are 'in touch with their time' and, as such, culturally meaningful. Whether their aspirations and their presuppositions are right is the next question, and these will have to be tested. This pursuit of the truth, however, must be based on the Truth of the living God, being God today just as he was at the time he first revealed himself to us through Scripture, and who therefore manifests himself just as substantially in his work today. The categorical rejection of everything that is produced by the secular world as inhuman, meaningless and not worthy of anything is just as foolishly dogmatic as the verdict of the moderns who hold that only modern jazz, abstract art and communism are 'of our time'. The latter is a violation of living reality; the former will lead to neglect of spiritual warfare and the testing of the spirits while everything is deemed to be worthless and empty anyway.

I am writing this because modern jazz as an expression of a twentieth-century existential attitude is very important and its quality and meaning as a cultural phenomenon may not be underestimated. I am also writing it to show that there may be other trends today, also in jazz, each of which will have to be tested individually as to its value, but under no circumstances should they simply be written off as old hat in the way the haughty proponents of modern jazz have done to other trends. Next we shall look at some of these other trends.

The rediscovery of New Orleans jazz

'Burgundy Street blues'

> I enjoy playing for people that are happy. I enjoy seeing people happy. If everyone is in a lively mood, I get the spirit and I can make my trombone sing. If my music makes the people happy, I will try and do more. It's like a challenge for me. I like to see people around me. It makes me warm inside, and that comes out in my music. When I play melodious music, I try to convey my feelings to my fellow audience. I always have that in my thoughts.[385]

That was the voice of Jim Robinson in one of the nicest statements ever made about New Orleans jazz. It makes the contrast in spirit between modern jazz as described in the previous chapter and this New Orleans jazz abundantly clear. It is the latter that we are going to discuss now.

As mentioned before, the book *Jazzmen* appeared in 1939. It was an important book and indicated a trend that sought to put new life into the old jazz of the 1930s which had become intolerable. Just prior to that, Panassié had produced a few recordings on which Mezz Mezrow and Bechet played alongside an almost forgotten Tommy Ladnier. He had tried to establish the whereabouts of the musicians who had made recordings ten or fifteen years earlier. It transpired that they were largely living and working in poor conditions or that they had bid their music farewell and gone looking for other jobs. George Mitchell had become a postal worker in Chicago, for example. Jimmy Noone, Johnny Dodds and various others had made a few recordings just before the War.

The research that preceded the writing of *Jazzmen* included a series of interviews with the musicians themselves in order to gather information about the early history of jazz (prior to 1920 and before the first recordings were made). It turned out that much had happened in New Orleans and that many obviously important musicians had never been recorded.

The research team consequently took the train to New Orleans to carry out further investigations. They discovered that many of the pioneers – who had been paraded as almost mythical personalities in stories about New Orleans – were still alive and were playing as semi-professionals[386] or had chosen a different trade.

The first recordings of the older of these musicians were made in 1940, under the name of Kid Rena's Delta Jazz Band which consisted of Rena (trumpet), Jim Robinson (trombone), and two clarinettists who had regularly featured in the New Orleans stories: Alphonse Picou and Louis Nelson. The recordings were not brilliant, but they served the purpose of reconstructing the past.[387]

It soon became evident however that there was also a young reserve force living and working in New Orleans – musicians who had missed the developments which had taken place in the North and who were still playing straightforward old-style New Orleans music. It was jazz as it had sounded before Oliver went North.

On 16 May 1943 a recording was made of a group of New Orleans musicians. It comprised of people of Louis Armstrong's age who had remained steadfast in the New Orleans tradition. Around ten recordings were made and they belong to the best of this genre: George Lewis, who could play his clarinet so beautifully, performed his almost seraphic, lyrical music, rich in variation, musical to the very core, and of great beauty; Jim Robinson turned out to be a trombonist who was able to combine melodic invention with rhythmic accentuation in an entirely characteristic style; the trumpet player Kid Howard played a style slightly reminiscent of Armstrong's around 1925 (around that time they had played together on a riverboat that did excursions from New Orleans up the Mississippi); the rhythm section was also very competent and maintained a rhythm that was completely free of any swing influence.

It was a curious series of records. No two are the same – not in mood nor in structure. New Orleans style is richly versatile – anything but a restricted formula. Lively ragtimes like 'Fidgety feet' and 'Climax rag' stand alongside quieter pieces like 'Deep Bayou blues', and there are also lyrical numbers with a beautiful melody, warm and charming, like the spiritual 'Just a little while to stay here'.[388]

The records were recorded in an unusual way. The musicians, who had little knowledge of recording procedures, were told that the first few attempts would just be experiments and that the actual recording would take place the next day. Their performance was therefore completely relaxed – purely for pleasure, while the recordings were in fact being made. That is why some of the numbers begin in the middle of a chorus or the recording finishes before the musicians did. It is New Orleans music at its best. The structure consisted, as we described earlier, of variations on one or more themes, polyphonic ensemble choruses alternating with solos, ensemble-playing based on the themes in a melodic rather than a harmonic sense.

At the same time, however, the contrast with the New Orleans jazz of Oliver, Morton and others, was also clear. In general it were the best educated, most intelligent and most enterprising of the musicians that left in the 1920s. Those who stayed behind knew little or nothing of music theory and, in contrast to Oliver and others, were not familiar with Western harmony and pure intonation within the well-tempered music system. This explains why they sometimes intonate differently and to our ears, when we have not yet understood how this music is put together, sound out of tune. If we listen closely, however, it appears to be a question of taste – a difference in musical thinking. They put melody and sound before harmonic purity. George Lewis always played the clarinet so as to produce the best sound, even when he had to squeeze his instrument somewhat in order to produce a well-tempered, pure tone. Neither do these musicians imitate the famous musicians of older recordings (for they did not know them); they have their own style. The result is fresh, New Orleans music with its own character and content. It is different from that of Oliver and such, possibly less refined, though it is not rough or uncivilized and never barbaric or primitive. It is less Western in tone and harmony but pure and of great beauty, rich in variation and melody. Most importantly, it is not over-exuberant and does not unleash itself in an uncontrolled fashion – it is music of great joy, of elation, almost. They make the odd mistake here or there, but their enormous enthusiasm and pure musicality more than compensate for that.

In researching for the book *Jazzmen*, the name Bunk Johnson kept cropping up. He was a trumpet player who was said to have influenced Louis Armstrong greatly and was supposed to have been a musician of extraordinary quality. Eventually he was traced to Louisiana, where he was living an impoverished life in a small town. He was given new dentures, a new trumpet, and he played. First he did a number of recordings in New Orleans on 11 June 1942. It turned out to be something quite special, different from the Kid Rena Band. In spite of the fact that he had never made a public appearance outside his hometown and had not been active for years for all sorts of reasons, this proved to be a musician with very special talent. The recordings made a few months later with George Lewis and Jim Robinson's group[389] allow us to enjoy the extraordinary qualities of the other musicians whom we have just mentioned, and admire Bunk's playing in particular. His music was a revelation – beautiful in tone, calm, with superb phrasing, rich in melodic invention and skill of variation. 'Thriller rag' and 'Franklin Street blues' were supreme numbers, but we could quote many more.

In 1943 Bunk Johnson played with the Yerba Bueno Jazz Band in San Francisco for a while, and I will come back to that. Then in 1944 he was back in New Orleans and played with the George Lewis Group. They made a series of beautiful recordings in the summer of 1944, all under the American Music label and unfortunately very difficult to get hold of [in the Netherlands] now. They played ragtimes, old New Orleans schmaltz hits like 'When you wore a tulip', very lyrical versions of spirituals like 'Walk through the streets of the city', in which the melody itself is repeated without variation, and a number of blues.

There is little point in analysing all these records, but there is one that stands out as the most beautiful recording of New Orleans style made after the 1923 to 1927 period. It is a beautiful live recording of blues without a specific title.[390] Various themes are used; a particular theme of twelve bars is played polyphonically and then varied in the next chorus of twelve bars. Then comes a new theme, repeated in the following chorus in a different variation. Next there is a succession of solos (clarinet, trombone, and trumpet) based on the last polyphonically played theme. It is followed by new themes and variations, always in twos. As a binding element there is a refrain, for all choruses end with the same motif in the last four bars.

There is something else that gives all these recordings such a special character and that is Babe Dodds' drumming. He had played with Oliver previously but he comes over better here thanks to the quality of the recordings. There were also a few records made of Dodds speaking and demonstrating how his music is structured – how the tone changes from high to low, how his support of a polyphonic ensemble is different from that of a solo, and how he also allows himself to be guided by his instrument. He ends his discourse with a useful remark aimed at drummers who think that they can just sit there and beat something out. 'No,' he says, 'you have to use your head. What else is it there for?'[391]

'Burgundy Street blues', a solo by George Lewis, was also recorded on the American Music label.[392] Later again Lewis played this piece several times on record, providing us with a good point of comparison that teaches us much about his method. At first it sounds like pure, free improvisation on a blues chord scheme, with a set refrain in the last four bars. If we compare it with the other recordings, however, the successive improvisation pieces turn out to be new themes which are always played in the same order. There is much more structure and coherence, consideration and musical composition in this piece than is immediately obvious. It is not a succession of improvised pieces but a fixed framework of themes, which are coherently linked with each other and are also linked by a similar sounding refrain. He once recorded this piece on a 45 rpm disc, which allows more recording space, and there this pattern becomes particularly evident. As soon as his composition has ended, he stops playing and the surplus recording space is devoted to a piano solo which indeed sticks out like a sore thumb.[393]

The Lewis-Robinson Band made many other recordings, sometimes with different trumpet players and sometimes without a trumpet player at all. In 1945 they went to New York with Bunk Johnson where they surprised the jazz enthusiasts with their lively performances of

New Orleans music. They made a few recordings there including the beautiful and sharply played 'Tishomingo blues', for Brunswick,[394] and a series for Victor (released on HMV in the Netherlands), which is far less satisfactory than the American Music recordings we mentioned. It sounds as if the musicians have been wrenched from their roots, for they use a loud and heavy style – quite inappropriate in relation to their own lyrical style – to let us hear that they can indeed produce something like Armstrong's Hot Five. It was a temptation, one which for Bunk – constantly confronted with the notion that he was the great teacher of Louis Armstrong – must have been particularly hard to resist. The band split up after that, homesickness and other problems being the reason. Bunk then tried again with another group and produced interesting results. Musically however, these recordings are far below the standard of the older recordings made in New Orleans.[395]

The end came soon afterwards for Bunk, while George Lewis and his band are still playing [at the time of writing]. Bunk was still making nice recordings but in the 1950s his playing deteriorated and became too comfortable and mechanical, while he tried to conform to the demands (of the audience) for a well-tempered intonation at the cost of some of the lyrical purity of tone. Nevertheless, several numbers were fine, like those he recorded for Riverside.[396]

New Orleans style turned out not to be obsolete, not by any means a thing of the past but alive and kicking. Now that doors had opened again, many of the old guard began playing again. The trombonist Kid Ory – one of those who went looking for another job in the 1930s – also took up his instrument again. Although subsequently many recordings were made of these musicians, we shall not be following their progress further, to avoid getting bogged down in a rather dry summary.

White revival and Dixieland jazz

'Far away blues'
The renewed interest in New Orleans jazz reached young people all over the world who then tried to copy the style. Indeed, after 1945 in almost every city in the USA, Western Europe, Australia and where, Dixieland groups, mostly amateur ones, were set up. We call this music Dixieland so as not to confuse it with the real New Orleans music we dealt with in the last chapter, and which was nothing but the old music emerging from the darkness of obscurity into the limelight.

In moving on I do not want to reject the work of a few very good bands like that of Claude Lutter in France (approx. 1947-1948), Humphrey Lyttleton's band in England and our own [Dutch] Erik Krans' Dixieland Pipers, even if some of the traits we are going to talk about were evident in their music.

In social and artistic terms Dixieland is not such a bad phenomenon. It shows that young people want to make music themselves. It gives them opportunities and no doubt much pleasure. It stimulates working together in groups and is certainly anything but a pernicious pastime. Whether they always understand the music they want to play is quite a different matter. They model their music on the gramophone records of New Orleans jazz that we have discussed in this book. Nevertheless, their interpretation of the music often comes much closer to Chicago jazz than to the real New Orleans style. This can be demonstrated if we compare a direct imitation of Oliver with the original:[397] the rhythm seems to be closely related to that of swing and has none of the basso continuo that Oliver has; at the same time they are busy improvising instead of playing variations within the melodic and compository structure. Their definition of jazz is vehemence and letting go. As far as Oliver was concerned, a break was a rest filled by an instrument; to the Chicagoans it was an excuse for another fierce outburst. The theory of jazz in the spirit of the Chicagoans – jazz equals rhythm plus improvisation – dominates their artistic commitment.

Naturally they also want to play polyphonically, but they think they are supposed to be improvising and usually shun careful practice. If they are to avoid chaos they can do little but stick strictly to the formula: the trumpet renders the melody, the clarinet 'saws' away above it, the trombone slides up and down a bit and provides a few rhythmic accents. This formula, endlessly repeated, makes each number sound just like the others without any variation in mood or expression. That makes the music boring after a while. Perhaps it is pleasant to listen to for a time but it lacks real depth and invention. Dixieland jazz might be described as New Orleans music played to a set formula, according to the spirit of the Chicagoans, which nullifies the excellent qualities of freedom and spontaneity.

There are others however. As early as the 1930s, a group of musicians conducted by Lu Watters and Turk Murphy were experimenting in San Francisco. Around 1940 they emerged as the Yerba Buena Jazz Band. Their aim was to study New Orleans jazz, to play in that vein again, to breathe new life into it and to carry it on as a living tradition. The result was good, though it was a bit stiff, not very smooth and little differentiated at first. But they stuck to it and some of their music became more interesting and rewarding.[398]

One LP particularly worth mentioning features New York trumpeter Everett Farey.[399] It was recorded in New York in 1954 by a recording syndicate led by Bob Helm, the clarinettist from Turk Murphy's band. The small band – clarinet, trumpet, piano, washboard and bass (or tuba) – performed to an unprecedentedly high standard – one of the best records of New Orleans style music ever made by whites – with a pure peacefulness, a joyful liveliness, original themes which betray a finely-tuned feeling for style and perfect polyphonic ensemble playing.

Play this record and then any modern jazz record – a good one – straight afterwards. The contrast is striking. The joyful liveliness of the one compared with the tension – the malaise – of the other; the inner peace – anything but lethargic – compared with the nervous restlessness, the inner lack of restraint and defiance; the warm openness compared with the abstract remoteness. Two worlds are expressed, neither of them superficial, both sustained by a spirit that consciously strives for the pure expression of that which moves people deep down, but what a difference in their approaches to reality. It is not a matter of old-fashioned versus modern, old versus new, but of a spirit which openly and warmly tries to work in a way intrinsically similar to that of African-Americans in their own music, as opposed to a spirit of existentialist *nausée* and alienation.

In England, Ken Coyler came close to the ideal. He was a sailor and made a trip to New Orleans where he had the chance to play with George Lewis, among others. Back in England he held tightly to the character and spirit of the music he had become acquainted with. He began his musical career with Chris Barber. When Barber developed a taste for Dixieland jazz Coyler broke with him. He went on to form his own band, whose rhythm section might be described as too stiff and monotonous but whose music is pure and fresh. One of their successes was 'Far away blues'[400] and its title seems appropriate to the content of this chapter. After all, we are talking about the search by musicians and connoisseurs for the spirit of New Orleans jazz – lively, joyful, with unity in diversity, individuality within a collective, inner peace and vitality, freedom within the confine of a set musical structure. They dreamed of matching that beauty, which was a rich fruit of black Christian culture. Perhaps the dream is so elusive because while the fruits are so desirable, the faith that generated them is often lacking.

The last remark would also explain why possibly a greater number of the combos that one finds all over the place playing modern jazz and the Dixieland bands reach a higher standard. It really is not so much a question of talent or of the technical development of these amateurs but of having a deeper understanding of what one is playing – of more deeply empathizing with the music one is performing. This will be obvious when we look around a bit. In the area of modern jazz, whites everywhere – in America and in Europe – have clearly attained a standard which revival bands, in their endeavour to reproduce the nature and character of New Orleans jazz, seldom or never manage.

The same remark would also explain why, with the exception of a few real New Orleans bands like that of George Lewis, music of a high standard and of a quality that is comparable to that of the old jazz of New Orleans is played only in the form of spiritual songs in church these days [around 1960]. That is our next focus in the next chapter.

Commercial spirituals since approximately 1940

'The wheel in a wheel'

Earlier in this book we spoke of the development of a genre of commercial spirituals of the 1920s – religious entertainment that existed alongside real church spirituals and the westernized spirituals styled on the ideal of Romantic concert singing. This genre continued to exist through the years, its nature allowing itself to pursue the trends in dance music as they came and went.

It is therefore logical that swing would influence these quartets and small choirs at the end of the 1930s. A new technique was developed for this: the rhythmic element was more strongly emphasized and riffs were implemented. The so-called short refrain (a short phrase sung ensemble at the end of each line, after every two bars) was designated a place 'under' the music as it were, and was then repeated throughout. The rendition of the precentor was more drawn out – more rubato – and more typical swing phrasing was introduced. The so-called long refrain or chorus of eight bars was often dropped or included only incidentally, and then it was sung in an equally light rhythmic manner with accents typical for this type of music.

The nature of these ensembles was often reflected in their flowery names, like the Dixiaires, the Sensational Nightingales, the Southern Sons, the Swan Silverstone Singers and the Dixie Hummingbirds. Just occasionally we hear more serious names like the Selah Jubilee Singers, the Golden Gate Quartet and so on. As choir music this is not technically bad, but it is sweet, light, rhythmically playful, mellifluous with many jazzy effects and, as a result of the infinitely repeated phrase that serves as a riff, eventually monotonous and boring. The lyrics often have little content and are mainly traditional, for you cannot confront people who might enjoy listening to the music with harsh biblical truth. They might be open to a bit of edification but they do not want depth and height, and neither do they want to be confronted with admonitions or unpleasant thoughts. In fact the audience wants to 'suit their own desires', to hear 'what their itching ears want to hear' (2 Timothy 4:3).

This genre is still very popular in the USA today[401] and can perhaps be attributed to the great revival of interest in religious matters. It is a fascination that the Americans themselves have described with the pithy expression 'a religious boom', though no one would dare to measure its depth or to guess how serious it is. The music makes it clear that while there is real conversion, there is also much chaff under the wheat.

New church choral song

'On Calvary'

We have just mentioned that, aside of the spiritual singing in church, the 1940s saw the emergence of a new kind of spirituals as far as technique was concerned. It was admittedly completely removed from the church environment, but churchgoers inevitably became acquainted with the new form of quartet singing through gramophone records, radio broadcasts and perhaps because a singer from one of these 'religious entertainment' choirs had become a Christian and started attending church. Whatever the reason, by the end of the 1940s the new style of spiritual was being sung by quartets in churches all around. But here the innovations were grafted onto the old living tradition of church song; more importantly, this music rediscovered its soul: those who sang it also meant what they sang.

This is already evident when we look at the texts. 'Religious entertainment' would produce songs that were not unpleasant for the audiences, with more or less neutral lyrics, those that made general reference only to love or heaven. In the case of the church quartets the lyrics would stay much closer to the sometimes pointed truth of the gospel – the word of God is, after all, a double-edged sword.

As a result, the nature of the music changed as well. While the commercial spiritual was often light and rhythmically strong, it also became monotonous in its endless repetition of the same rhythmic motifs (riffs). This technique was ultimately rather limited. The church quartets, however, immediately strove for greater freedom and movement, to bring more variation into the music, to do justice to the lyrics and to let the melody speak. The result was, to put it briefly, that a completely new art form emerged, much richer than the music from which it originated. We call it a new art form, because we are dealing here with quartets and small choirs that never improvise but sing well thought-out arrangements (rendering 'framework compositions', as was the case in New Orleans jazz) that disclose a wide range of possibilities. It is an art form which, having arisen from their own traditions, was in no way westernized but rather deepened and developed what had remained largely dormant in black culture up to that time. This new development, which began to flourish in the 1950s, produced music of a quality that could compete favourably with the best black music ever produced. The character of this music is very closely related to New Orleans jazz, which should not surprise us if we consider how Christian traditions as to lifestyle and attitude made itself felt in this jazz.

In examining the technique of singing the new style of spiritual – sometimes called 'gospel singing' – we shall begin with the use of the voice. It falls back on the old traditions of hymn singing – of Dr Watts – and of the hollers and the blues. This very characteristic use of the voice is sometimes called 'crying' or 'shouting'. In Rosetta Tharpe's method of singing, for example, this synthesis of older singing techniques was already evident. It is a very clear sound that is produced, a sort of calling or even screaming, though it is anything but that because it can also be heard in the softer and even in the pianissimo passages. The rich, full sound is certainly linked to the way it is produced, by no means similar to classical or opera singing, but more the full application of all the properties of the human voice. If you want to call it unnatural, then that is fine, but it would be wise to take into consideration that the Western manner of classical singing is much further removed from the natural use of the voice. What actually happens here is a sort of cultivation of the natural voice. Training certainly plays a part – there is no greater misunderstanding than the idea that this sort of music emerges of its own accord, without practice or study.

In the structure of the music the main principle is that one solo voice is accompanied by the rest of the quartet, who sing rhythmic phrases in full harmony. We call them phrases, because in contrast to the commercial spiritual it is not a short motif that is taken, but a longer phrase that is performed with strong rhythm. By analogy with older jazz we have to say that this is more a matter of 'stomping' than of 'riffs'. Above this fabric of sound there is also often another voice, which in quick passages outlines the text of the next line in a way that reminds us of the recitative-like manner in which sermons are recited by black preachers. This means we can always hear beforehand what is about to be sung. It is a method that is vaguely reminiscent of what happens when Dr Watts' hymns are sung in the old familiar way.

With what I have just described I had in mind a beautiful song called 'On Calvary' by undoubtedly the best group of this genre, The Spirit of Memphis Quartet.[402] If we listen to them more closely on their LP[403] that was released in 1958, it strikes us that we are far from having exhausted the subject. All a small choir (there are about seven vocalists) is capable of is utilized here to the full: polyphony, homophonic singing in unison or in chords, solo voice with rhythmic accompaniment, and solo voice accompanied by the other voices singing a longer phrase slowly. The melodic given is always respected, although it is varied by rubato passages (stretching the melodic line or accelerating phrases), while everything is rendered on the fixed basis of a rhythm, marked almost continuously by clapping hands or by a low voice that may also be varied in all sorts of ways.

Just listen to one of their loveliest pieces, 'Toll the bells easy'.[404] It is a familiar spiritual type of song with eight bars of verse and eight bars of chorus. They start by singing the chorus three times:

> *Toll the bells easy, (x 3)*
> *Jesus going to make up my dying bed.*

Their ability is amply evident here. This simple theme is rendered in very different ways, with syncopation, with apparent reductions and accelerations of tempo – 'apparent' because the joyful, steady rhythm, made very quietly audible by the handclapping, binds all together into one entity and is never abandoned. The words tell us: just let the (funeral) bells ring cheerfully, for the Lord himself will be at my deathbed. The verse that is sung after that with low voices rendering a rhythmic accompaniment, goes on to tell us of the firmly-rooted belief that the Lord will take us to be with him in his future.

On the same record they sing 'That awful day', a song that is rendered in exactly the same way as the old Dr Watts' hymns (it originated from his music no doubt), but it is sung here really artistically. Another beautiful one is 'Blessed are the dead', a song in which the alternation of recitative voice and ensemble calls to mind the music of Schütz (as we hear it in his *Musikalische Exequien*; the lyrics are incidentally also related).This last relationship may be described as strange, though less so if only we understand how similar attitudes to life lead to related expressions of it. Incidentally, this development is related in all sorts of ways to what is going on in the Protestant choral music of Distler and others in Germany in particular in the first half of the twentieth century: the same shying away from solo performances, from continuing the Romantic concert tradition (which otherwise still reigns supreme); a free singing-style; the use of logically rounded off melodies and of a polyphony that is harmonically sound, etc. One thing is certain – there can be absolutely no question of contact or influence between the two movements.

Back to the African-American church-choir song. There are more elements we can mention that typify this music. Something that the Spirit of Memphis seldom used, but many other groups did, The Christian Travellers[405] for instance, was to open with a long and slow solo introduction, with structure and melodies strongly reminiscent of those of a Dr Watts song or a holler – a practice that certainly stems from this tradition. We hear it too at the beginning of the Davis Sisters'[406] rendition of the well-known spiritual 'Go down Moses, tell old Pharaoh to let my people go'.

This music is not always straightforward. Those who think that the Spirit of Memphis Quartet, which belongs to a Baptist church in that city, sing light music that can be completely understood and assessed the first time it is heard, are much mistaken. When hearing it for the first time, there is the problem that the use of the voice here takes some getting used to. Only then does it become clear how peaceful and controlled this music is. There is no question at all of trance, theatrics, of letting go or improvising. There is admittedly sometimes a trace of over-expressiveness, a sort of fervour that is vaguely reminiscent of the style of swing, as in the case of the Davis Sisters, for instance. It is possible that swing did have some effect here or acted as a stimulus. The sense of over-emotionality is however very different from that of swing, which was all about letting yourself go. In this case it is more about expressing a certain mystical trait that is characteristic of black American Protestants. There was a desire to testify to the personal relationship with God, to a strong personal experience of faith. Fortunately this is not the norm, but it makes it harder to differentiate between the serious and the commercial spirituals of this genre. The latter are on occasion prone to excessive vehemence; more in the spirit of swing, true, but it does make it hard to tell the music apart from what the more church-oriented small choirs sometimes produced.

Black folk music after about 1940

'We call 'em reels'

We must not think that real black folk music disappeared around 1950 under pressure from later developments. Quite the opposite. Much of the music we discussed in the first few chapters was recorded only recently. That is quite simply due to the fact that the folk music of that ilk is only now being recorded for the first time. By way of illustration, real hollers can be heard on a recording of Lomax made in 1947.[407] That LP also features 'Whoa black', the holler we discussed earlier.

The Folkways releases must be commended. It is a label that specializes in folk music from all around the world, providing an invaluable service to jazz lovers and others who want to hear more of this music. Take the series of beautiful recordings made in Alabama by Harold Courlander and released on a double LP in 1950.[408] We would particularly like to draw your attention to the captivating spirituals sung by Doc Reed together with Vera Hall Ward, which were also released on a record[409] that is both interesting and especially lovely.

A set of nine LPs of beautiful and very important recordings by Frederic Ramsay Jr., made during a special expedition to the Southern States in 1954, was also released by Folkways. We hear what a farmer sings and what an old preacher sings; we hear the latest developments in rural church song, which did not escape the influences we mentioned in the previous chapter. We hear the song of a sect and a beautiful prayer by a female berry-seller in New Orleans, in the poetic language of the King James Version of the Bible. We hear evangelists, a string band, blues songs and guitar playing by a certain Scott Dunbar, of wonderfully good quality, and much more. An informative booklet is supplied with each record. Sometimes they are mainly interesting, other times they are movingly beautiful – but these records have become an essential source of information in the study of North American black music. This book would never have been possible without them.[410]

An interesting phenomenon is that one person almost never sings both blues and spirituals. No Christian is heard singing the blues, and no non-Christian is heard singing spirituals. The dividing line between Christian and non-Christian is very distinct in African-American society. I mentioned blues, but we should really call them hollers and other secular songs, because there is little evidence of the blues as such. That music is apparently the property of artists – the troubadours we talked about earlier.

Horace Sprott was a very poor farmhand who lived in rural Alabama. His mother was a Christian, his father a non-Christian. That is why he is familiar with both types of music. He is not particularly intelligent and he is slow, but he knows many folk songs and is able to tell us, light-heartedly, a bit about them in his own way. A few fragments of interviews with him have been included on the Ramsay LPs I have just mentioned. So, after he has sung one spiritual, he tells us that he learnt it from a woman who was dying. He was the only one at the funeral who knew that song and for that reason would sing it:

> They wanted it sung over her body. Couldn't a one sing it? So I told 'em I'd sing it. Told 'em, yes I can, I can sing it like she sung. Say: 'If you sing it, I'm going to have the undertaker to call you.' So, at the moment before the sermon began they told me to stand up to sing that song for sister Sarah. I stood up ... but when I was stood up I began to speak. I told them I wished they'd let me stay sitting. Because when I sit, my spirit goes high ... but as soon as I stand up, my spirit [as it were] goes and sits down ... And so they didn't let me sing that song. I couldn't sing it like I wanted, because they wouldn't let me do my own thing. They shouted and sang and spoke, and I couldn't do it while everyone was making such a racket. But they say that I did sing it. That I sung it and another one too, I was glad about that. The Lord gave me that talent. I didn't get it from myself, and it isn't from myself. It's from Him. That's why I don't sing many reels ... naturally I sing them once in a while ... about as often as church songs – By 'reels', do you mean blues, or ... – That is correct. We call them reels.[411]

Blues and spirituals among the working class after about 1940

'I can't make this journey by myself'

Make no mistake; the spiritual song in the old tradition is sung not only in the rural areas of Alabama. If you were walking around Harlem, the black neighbourhood of New York, you might well bump into Blind Gary Davis, a singer just like Blind Willie Johnson. Blind Gary Davis is sixty and comes from South Carolina. While singing he accompanies himself on the guitar. Perhaps he would speak and sing like this:

This is the song, friends, I want you all to understand, is the song that I sing whenever I get to the place where I can't pray. I begin to let this song answer for prayer when it gets so that I can sing – you know the time comes when you can sing, but you can't pray – I begin to let this song answer for prayer:

> Lord, I can't make this journey by myself, oh, Lord, (x 2)
> On the land, on the sea,
> I want Jesus to come and go with me;
> Oh, Lord, I can't make this journey by myself.

Then he continues with the next verses:

> I can't bear this heavy burden by myself
> I can't go in this dark valley by myself. Etc.[412]

In this personal way, he sings many other spirituals, both traditional and newly composed ones like 'Say to the Devil, say no'. In Atlanta, Georgia, you may come across the Two Gospel Keys, Mother Jones and Emma Daniel singing in the street. They go around together, accompanying themselves on guitar and tambourine. They might sing a song like this:

> Oh, Lord, You know, I have no friend like You,
> If heaven's not my home, oh, Lord, what shall I do,
> No one to kick me from heaven's welcome door,
> I can't feel at home in this world anymore.[413]

We could tell of many more. As for boogie-woogie, it is still played as a living folk art. Ordinary folk playing for ordinary folk. In the same way the blues is around as well, sung by itinerant troubadours as of old. Lightnin' Hopkins,[414] for one, is a singer like that who started his career after the War. There are others – Muddy Waters Morganfield, Jesse Fuller and so on. Some of the older singers like Big Bill Broonzy, who died a short time ago, carried on playing also after the War.

It is not only in underdeveloped areas that we find black folk music – it can still be heard all over the USA. The traditions are not kept alive artificially by folklorists – they simply are alive, just as alive as spirituals are in the churches.

7
The 1950s and Beyond

Jazz in the 1950s

'March of the Charcoal Greys'

Besides the music we dealt with in the last few chapters, all kinds of jazz music were being played in the mid-1950s. The Dixieland bands were there, of course, as was the music of Turk Murphy and co. – white New Orleans jazz. There were blacks in New Orleans who kept up the old traditions[415] – George Lewis being one of them. There were brass bands playing the music of old;[416] there were swing bands of various types and quality; there were groups of every category and grade of white Chicago-style, especially the ones led by Eddie Condon.[417] Then there was Ellington and his music which, on the one hand, was becoming increasingly ambitious and, on the other hand, sometimes dropped right down to the level of mood music.[418] There was Wilbur de Paris with his New New Orleans jazz and – we have by no means reached the end of our list – there was modern jazz of many kinds, ranks and stations. Sometimes it was music of high quality, alive and real, and at other times it was straightforward dance or entertainment music with modern influences (sometimes really quite enjoyable because the sharp modern spirit was absent and the expression toned down, more human. We are thinking here of the pianist Oscar Peterson, for instance). There was also rock-and-roll. In other words, even if we remain within the confines of the definition of jazz and forget all sorts of entertainment and dance music (for instance, Victor Sylvester's Metropole Orkest), there was such an abundance of trends and sorts, which clearly shows that we are not dealing with one single, straightforward development.

Fans of a particular musical preference, in general, and adherents of modern jazz, in particular, very often postulate that their music is the only really contemporary sort. They consider those who are still playing Chicago style, or worse, New Orleans or Dixieland style, as doing nothing more than imitate what has already been done – merely reproducing or imitating old music. But this assessment is fundamentally flawed because those who play Chicago jazz or New Orleans style are not concerned to establish a living museum in any shape or form. They are rather fighting in their own way for something they find more meaningful and useful than so-called modern jazz. They are not trying to evoke the past but are fighting for the future, and whichever side you are fighting on, you will not be able to predict the outcome.

The progress of history is at stake here – the formation of style and culture. Make no mistake; what the best connoisseurs of modern jazz say, and what the advocates of modern abstract art (from Miro and Klee to the Tachists, Experimentals etc.) say is true – namely that their new art form implies a new lifestyle and a new perspective on reality, and that those who really want to appreciate this new music must be modern, namely people who are inspired, or who at least are moved, by the same spirit. Precisely for this reason they should not be allowed to force a dilemma on us: to have to choose to live either with the times or in the past. In fact, the Chicago tradition is alive and kicking, but so is the real blues, for each of these musical trends, though they may to a certain extent be determined by circumstances, is primarily the fruit of the spirit and attitude of the musicians who choose to play it, and of their audience.

The opinion that only one type of jazz can be real – 'real' in the sense of being 'with the times', artistically and culturally meaningful – is a grave fallacy. Rather, it appears that those who favour the latest movement as the only valid one are ascribing victory to themselves before the battle has even been fought. It is very easy to regard with suspicion those who behave differently, to label them as 'conventional', not 'with it', mere imitators, but that is not fair and neither is it right.

No, if musical expression is also a representation of a person's view of the world, and people have different world views, there will be many different trends. Folk music, as well as the marches from New Orleans or the blues, will live on in similar forms, as long as they satisfy a genuine demand. The different sorts of jazz will continue to exist as long as some remain unconvinced that the modern, more or less existentialist world view, is the only possible and right one.

Wilbur de Paris's New New Orleans' Band[419] shows us that these problems are not as straightforward as the modernists think. The musicians who, one way or another, had kept a close track of developments were Wilbur de Paris (trombone), who played with Ellington for a while, his brother Sidney (trumpet), who played swing and had already produced an updated version of the New Orleans style around 1942[420] – he was an advocate of this renaissance – and Omer Simeon (clarinet), who had made an early debut with Jelly Roll Morton but was hardly conspicuous since the 1930s. They came together in the 1950s to play New Orleans jazz, without imitating what had already been done and without compromising their knowledge of later developments, or their training and experience. Sometimes, as in the 'March of the Charcoal Greys', it seems that they are telling us, with a smile, of the good old times. At other times they may play one of Morton's pieces or a slow rag, rhythmically and melodically first class. These are not people who continuously worked in a living New Orleans tradition; they are people with years of experience in the world of swing and the later type of jazz, who are attempting to win back something. The modern sound of the rhythm section, manifest in the drummer's continuous use of the cymbals in a swing-style steady beat, is interesting. We can also detect other elements redolent of swing – long solos, for example, though they do stick to the thematic given and vary rather than improvise.

Listening to this music conjures up associations with *The Family of Man* photographic exhibition, which used 500 photographs, chosen from many thousands, to illustrate the lives of people. The particular choice of photographs was guided by a vitalistic view of people and their lives: life goes on in its own biotic way, through birth, childhood, love, marriage, having children, getting old and dying. That is life. On this basis there is a place for culture, religion and so forth. This is the essence of human life. When we listen to the music of de Paris we sometimes get the same idea: the rhythm, continuous and unrelenting, is not an expression of great certainty and serenity as with Bach or Oliver but expresses the rhythm of life as the vital basis for everything. On the foundation of this rhythm, determined and as it were rocked by it, we hear the play of the melodies and variations as a representation of the cultural, the typically human aspects of human life which are limited and determined, but also driven, by the vital and biotic.

Thus there is a rich diversity of music, even if we remain within the confines of what we can call jazz, not to mention the many sorts of popular and dance music, some quite strongly influenced by jazz, others less so. Each sort of music has its limitations, its weak points and its peculiarities, and the good examples frequently show positive qualities, which make it worth listening to them. Not in order just to like everything. Those who like everything apparently are not moved by anything and can not get past a clinical assessment of technique. Our generation will have to learn discernment, to recognize deceptive qualities, to gauge emptiness, to appreciate real beauty, to reject effect for the sake of effect, to test principles as to their values and consequences, to reject and resist music that seems unhealthy, mechanical or boring, and to accept richness with gratitude. We must not deceive the next generation by keeping alive the myth that contemporary has to mean 'modern'; rather, we should offer them an informed assessment of that which has been produced, giving real values the credit they deserve and pointing out the unartistic or unacceptable principles, after first having banished to the scrapyard all that is inferior, directed at money more than at beauty.

It is now time to look more closely at so-called modern jazz.

The development of modern jazz

'Fontessa'
Ever since its birth and particularly since it became more popular during the War years, modern jazz has been evolving. New stars came, old stars went, bands and particularly smaller combinations got together and split up again. The importance of being 'cool' increased, especially

through the work of Miles Davis. There was experimentation with new types of rhythm, like the rhythms of Cuba. Improvisation remained the focus but here and there people were experimenting with arrangements. Stan Kenton ventured to have a large, strong, disciplined band perform this jazz, featuring some important jazz musicians. The result was music that resembled modern jazz in appearance only and not in spirit, except for the passages in which he allows one of his soloists a rare free hand. Perhaps Stan Kenton was the Paul Whiteman of modern jazz?

We could go into the progress of modern jazz in detail, but after the new developments of the 1940s there is nothing of much significance to mention. Modern jazz had made its mark and even if we account for all the individual differences there remains much unity in form and method. In other words, modern jazz has become a well-defined style. Incidentally, this remark is intended in support of modern jazz rather than against it. Trends and whims are, of course, present but these can be attributed to marketing hype rather than to essential changes.

Modern jazz became enormously popular in the 1950s, not in the sense that everyone appreciated it and that the schmaltz – the top hits of the day – were modernized, though a certain amount of modernism was present in strictly commercial jazz. Rather, modern jazz became popular in the sense that a great number of people – particularly young people – became interested in it and were taken with it. As a result gramophone record sales of modern jazz increased considerably at the expense of old jazz.

How did this popularity come about? I think it was because the music expressed not only something that appealed to young people but also something that was connected with their own self. It gave expression to familiar emotions, even if often they were unable to put these emotions into words. We will return to this later on.

Another proof that this music made a connection with young people was the extent to which they accepted and swallowed it, even though it was quite predictable, with little in the way of variation. That can be partly attributed to its method – a short theme, more or less in riff form, played ensemble, followed by long solos and then by a repeat of the short theme – but mainly it is to be attributed to the emphasis on a feeling of emptiness, meaninglessness, hyper-individualism, 'playing God' and an aversion to reality. These things are expressed in a certain abstraction of tone and a strong irrationalism, whereas warm, caring humanness is all too often absent.

The last of these things is perhaps the most objectionable. Those who are down, going through an existential crisis, aware of their *nausée*, feeling rejected, uprooted, and regarding their life void of ideals, empty, a sort of inevitable, unpleasant reality, need not pull others down with them. The highest and most fundamental norm – love – applies also to art and music. We have to love our neighbours by giving them joy and beauty, and not by confronting them with the epitome of hopeless human misery without pointing out the good things. The norm for art, which Philippians 4:8 formulates as 'meditating on things true, noble, reputable, authentic, compelling, gracious – the best, not the worst; the beautiful, not the ugly; things to praise, not things to curse' is violated all too often. That does not mean that there are no very talented modern jazz musicians. It is not a question of being talented but of putting one's talents to good use. Our brief profile may have included too many generalizations, because there sometimes also is, almost contrary to its basic principles, a genial, warm sound to modern jazz, with some sense of rest and melodiousness.

Modern jazz, if at least it is really modern, emanates from inner tension, or rather, from acute inner tension. Some artists experience this to such an extent that they are in danger of falling apart and therefore may yield to the use of narcotics. In fact, this demonstrates the very existential, very heart-rending reality of this music; it is anything but superficial entertainment. It is deeply rooted in a view of life and the world.

If we look around in the 1950s,[421] we discover all sorts of combos (a small band that plays modern jazz) each of which has its own type of music. There are the Jazz Messengers, who became the Horace Silver Quintet after their drummer was replaced, a combo that plays a consistent style of nervous jazz music. There is the J.J. Johnson Quintet, which is a bit mellower in its musical expression. There are various combinations which, even though they apply very modern influences, in fact perform a sort of music that is closely related to swing – Ruby Braff's band, for instance. As far as I am concerned, the Miles Davis Quintet is the best. They play consistently modern, highly tense, outwardly restrained but inwardly very emotional music with an irrational melody. This music is of a very high quality that makes the contestable elements all the clearer. In other words, this is the best music of its kind and therefore it should be the focus of our debate, because there is no point in quarrelling about third-rate music by musicians who are not capable of better.

We shall not be participating in the discussion jazz enthusiasts often engage in, as to whether 'West Coast jazz' is a useful term to describe the sort of jazz that is associated with California. What is certainly true is that modern jazz there, possibly more than other types, attracted bigger and more serious audiences. Dave Brubeck and his band was the most successful, which is not surprising because while technically very clever, their music almost always lacked real depth and meaning, an easily digestible, uncomplicated product. When we listen more closely, the constant evocation of an atmosphere that can almost be described as mild desperation, the inability to keep up a real atmosphere of tension, empty meaninglessness, *Geworfenheit* and *nausée*, becomes very, very tedious at a certain point. It is not only because the musicians do not quite manage to convince us that they *are* really struggling with deep issues of being human, but also because it becomes tedious when someone keeps making the same old negative claims.

We also find West Coast jazz[422] played by the group of musicians among whom Shorty Rogers and Jimmy Giuffre assumed an important and influential position. Musical arrangements played a bigger role here than elsewhere in modern jazz and musicians were more absorbed by music-technical problems, consciously focusing on contemporary, Western music by Bartok, Stravinsky, Milhaud, Honegger, Schoenberg and such. This should come as no great surprise to us. The spiritual background to modern jazz and to modern Western classical music is virtually the same; the difference lies in their historical backgrounds, either swing or Romantic music.

These developments may have strange consequences. It is not impossible that in the not too distant future a clever musician at home in both types of music will combine them. (John Lewis, whom we will be talking about shortly, went a long way towards achieving this.) That would mean that large audiences, who are now followers of jazz, would have to be moved to the large concert halls. In terms of cultural history it would mean that a larger group of people who had lost touch with the pursuit of Western music for all sorts of reasons would find their way back to the concert hall. This would heal the rift in our Western world between art and the public. It would also serve to give the number of admirers and lovers of modern art a strong boost. Strange visions. We will just have to wait and see if that happens, and only when it does will we be required to form an opinion about it. Even the question of whether it would be gain or loss, whether we should applaud it or not, is a question which cannot easily be answered.

We would like to mention one other ensemble, The Modern Jazz Quartet.[423] It is indeed modern jazz in the sense that it uses a combination of instruments of which the sounds and playing methods do not contrast but are closely related, like the piano and the vibraphone, the bass and the drums. Those who listen to the music carefully will understand why we group these instruments together like this. The band and its music are in many ways inspired by Western music: old forms like the fugue and Western harmony from Debussy onwards are implemented time and again. Although its music can certainly still be classified as jazz, of all the bands I have dealt with this one comes closest to playing contemporary Western music, not only in sound and timbre but also in its whole approach to art and music and the sort of musical problems they pose themselves. It will therefore come as no surprise that downright lovers and connoisseurs of Western music who have never had a good word to say about jazz show positive interest in this band.

Possibly their most characteristic piece is 'Fontessa'.[424] An interesting aspect is the assertion of their leader that the various parts might be typified by names of clowns. It is interesting in the sense that clowns have been prevalent in Western modern art since Picasso's blue period (around 1900). The appearance of a clown creates jollity and fun and though their behaviour is extrovert they are inwardly melancholic – focused on the problem of their own existence. The clown reflects modern society where people don a mask to face the world, go along with it, while they are inwardly a long way off, like gnostics, turning away in a sense from this wretched and, in principle, bad world.

Listen to what Lewis writes about 'Fontessa':

> 'Fontessa' is a small suite based on the *Commedia dell'arte* [a sort of (Italian) play in which the same character (Harlequin, Columbine, Pantalone, etc.) always performed in rather improvised roles] from the sixteenth and seventeenth centuries. I was particularly thinking of their plays that consisted of a very sketchy intrigue whereby the details, the dialogues, etc., were improvised. This suite consists of a short prelude to open the curtains and to denote the subject. The first piece after this prelude has the character of older jazz (swing) and the vibraphone plays the improvised parts. You might well say that this part has the character of Harlequin. The second part has the nature of more recent jazz, and the improvised parts are for the piano. The character of Pierrot typifies it best. The third part has the character of even more recent jazz and reveals the principal motif. The rhythm section plays the improvised parts. Its character is possibly that of Pantalone [the old man, who is usually deceived in love]. The prelude is repeated at the end. 'Fontessa' is the principal motif of the suite consisting of three notes, and may be a description of the character of Columbine.

The drum solo mentioned is indeed the culmination of the piece which here, more than elsewhere, evokes a Debussy-like atmosphere that can best be described with the words 'we are floating in an empty space'.

Swing ad absurdum

Rock-and-roll

You might be surprised that we have included rock-and-roll in our synopsis, but this type of music is too closely related to jazz to ignore it.

Technically speaking, this music is swing ad absurdum. Only a fierce and over-simplified rhythm remains. As far as melody, everything is kept as simple as possible and the harmonic schemes are of the least complicated sort. In other words, it is music that has been stripped of everything that makes it interesting. Only the heavily stamping beat is omnipresent. The idea is to strive for a fast release of emotion – very sensual, but without an iota of nuance, no sophistication; on the contrary, it is as crude and direct as possible. It is music exploited by clever and unscrupulous people. It is music that is consciously empty and hollow and simplistic – music created for the modern youth culture.

What is the sense of it? Is it proof that the Western public lacks any taste at all? Let us not jump to conclusions too quickly. For those who are said to lack the gift of discernment are also those whose fine intuition enables them to identify exactly what they want to hear and accept, therefore they definitely do have taste. No, the meaning of this music is its meaninglessness – its lack of content and eloquence. It is music that allows its audience to dance exuberantly on the edge of the abyss, driven by an intense longing to let go and live it up, all founded on the well thought-out logic: 'Let's eat and drink and be merry for tomorrow we die.' Heidegger described it as 'living to death' – *sein zum Tode* – but here there is no recognition of existential angst; there is no attempt to look for depth because that would mean looking into the abyss – the abyss that is illustrated to some extent by the drum solo in 'Fontessa', the abyss the Surrealists paint, the modern poets describe, and modern jazz expresses in sound. It sometimes resembles a hell and at other times it *is* hell. You only have to take a sincere look at modern poetry or to check what kindred spirits have to say about the interpretation of modern art to understand how true this is.

It is on the edge of hell that people want to dance, live it up and let go. They find no real joy there, only a grim struggle to hold on to something, life itself, freedom, happiness, knowing that all of it constantly eludes them. Everything is meaningless, so dance, live it up and let go, but do not look into the abyss . . . because the abyss may open up.

Rock-and-roll is the flip side of the modernist record.

The problem of jazz in our world

'Mamma don't allow'
'Mamma don't allow no drummer man in here,' is how one of the lines from a popular song from the 1930s goes. It is an American song. The problem turns out to be in no way representative of Europe, or the Netherlands, alone.

'No jazz in my house,' the parents say. The children, teenagers, do not know why. They ask themselves why jazz should be inferior to Beethoven, and . . . continue listening in secret. That is often how it goes.

'Mamma don't allow no drummer man in here.' Much of this trouble with jazz has more of a social than artistic character. Parents are not concerned about jazz as music. Perhaps they more than once forgot to switch off the radio in time when something jazzy was broadcast without prior warning. It is often a strange association of ideas that is the real reason behind the rejection of jazz. Jazz is associated with the jungle – primitive – uncultured – the pub – superficial – ugly – blacks – trance – sexuality – dancing – entertainment – low – bad. It is a strange sequence of ideas. They could of course be classified into all sorts of groups, but one thing is clear – jazz is wrong because it is music that belongs to a socially lower world, that of the 'dirty blacks' who do not know how to behave and therefore live it up in a trance. It smacks of racism, snobbery, bourgeois mentality, fear of being shaken out of one's lethargy and of unfamiliar urges suspected there.

We say that the verdict is socially qualified because it is seldom based on the music itself, or on a real examination of the matter at hand. Beethoven is certainly held in esteem as the counterpart of jazz, but this implies nothing more than esteem of a time-honoured Western concert tradition, and it can hardly be said of many of those who hold this esteem that they have a real love of Romantic or classical music.

There is also another argument: jazz is entertainment. That may certainly be true, because if we speak of jazz in this way, we are referring to jazz as an absolutely straightforward cocktail of any music that is based on a 4/4 beat, uses trumpets and possibly saxophones, and has lyrics in English. Since an awful lot of popular music (indeed, not without the influence of jazz) satisfies this definition, the verdict seems just. Nevertheless we must ask the question: Is the Romantic concert tradition and its music the highest standard? Should we demand that youngsters partake of this lofty fruit and look to it for their entertainment?

Please let us understand that popular music – a new Western substitute for folk music – also satisfies a need, in the same way that Beethoven, Bach and Mozart do. This music has a function, not so much as spiritual food or as something to be enjoyed, but much rather as a social binding agent – something that supports social contact. That is why young people need it. Is it entertainment? Yes, certainly. At the same time we must remember that there is good popular music and bad popular music. You now know that I give rock-and-roll a place in the latter category, but I cannot and do not want to put all the different styles into neat little boxes.

Jazz too is the music of the youth. Certainly. Because young people are exposed to this music via popular music and also because it is burdened with a social taboo. The latter is one of the very strong attractions it has for teenagers. If we were to give jazz social status by donning evening dress to attend jazz concerts, it would stop being the music of teenagers before very long. But, do these arguments really relate to the jazz we have been talking about in this book? Sales of serious jazz records is proportionally negligible: for old jazz it is less than 1 per cent, for modern jazz it is higher but by no means approaches the figures for classical music (i.e. Western classical) or any other socially accepted types of music, like French chansons, for example. Jazz is sometimes entertainment – as is a French chanson and a German song from a Lehar operetta – and we can distinguish between good and bad jazz, as well as all the intermediate stages. If, however, we want to use the word jazz to define black folk music and what evolved from it – well, then we have to distinguish carefully.

Do you not want your children to listen to modern jazz? Then withhold modern Western music from them too, and modern Western literature, and modern visual art, because the content in all these things is related.

Young people want Dixieland jazz. Certainly, because they can play it themselves. It gives them the opportunity to make music without having to lug the heavy burden of the Romantic music tradition around with them. Do you not want them to play jazz? Then turn to the direction that contemporary German church music is taking. There may be some good opportunities there. But maybe there is a lot to be said for playing collectively in the spirit of New Orleans and for exploring its art and life as well. There are many possibilities.

So what are the consequences for a young person who enjoys listening to modern jazz? We mean real, serious jazz and not the different forms of (possibly better) popular music in which there is only a slight influence of the new sounds and forms. There are in principle two possibilities: either he or she is just following the trend that appeals to his or her age group, without real interest in the essence, the content of the music, in which case it will be a phase that will pass without a trace; or she or he understands this music very well and can relate to the emotiveness of the music that expresses her or his own feelings (even if she or he cannot express that in words). In the latter case you will either have to submit to the idea that each new generation establishes its own attitude to life, or you will have to attempt to point the way to something you consider more positive. For Christians the Bible is there as a rich source of wisdom and joy, as a radical remedy for any negative attitude to life, but that means using it, reading it and studying it. Not just for the sake of doing so, but sustained by and aligned to the love of our Saviour, Jesus Christ, and in the knowledge that God, the Creator of heaven and earth and our Father in heaven, if we believe in him, will sustain our lives, even now, so that a quiet, joyful, firm certainty may be ours, even in this world where sin has sometimes brought such misery. Faith in the God of Carmel means death to all nihilism, gnosticism, existentialism and the hopelessness that ultimately regards death as the only absolute end and purpose.

What we want to say is that the problem of modern jazz has a spiritual and a social side, and that the most dangerous aspect of this is that people often do not get round to facing up to the spiritual problems, writing the music off as that of 'blacks and brothels and people who are out for kicks'. Whatever our attitude to these questions, one thing is clear to us: jazz in whatever form does not belong in church. That would only be expedient if almost everyone understood and accepted the music – and not even then. Bach's *Brandenburg Concertos* are not played during church services either, nor are quartets by Beethoven, irrespective of what we regard the music to be and even if we could defend the former as being Christian music. As for spirituals, they fall more into the category of hymns, but even then it is my opinion that these songs should first become generally accepted. That might happen if they were to be included in the repertoire of Christians – at home or in small choirs. These songs must first become familiar to us – become our own idiom. This, however, will take a long time. And should we even be looking in this direction? Why should we want to do that? Because of our own spiritual poverty perhaps?

Whatever our position, we have to watch out for the misleading associations: jazz and spirituals – black music – primitive – barbaric – wild – unchristian – ugly. Let us be fair in our judgment; black music, in its many varieties, is certainly worthwhile and sometimes is a clearer fruit of Christian civilization than a lot of Western music is. We should also consider that the later genres of jazz – swing and modern jazz – are fruits of white civilization rather than something blacks can be held responsible for.

We have to be honest and not allow ourselves to be distracted by unfounded prejudices. Black music it is not by definition bad music. Holding this view is no better than the attitude that led to the recent refusal by a white school in Little Rock, to the great indignation of the general population, to allow a number of black children to attend.

We should also take the following song by an African-American to heart. Would we be able to sing like this in similar circumstances, without a feeling of revolutionary defiance? The facts that are exposed in this song are, unfortunately, all too true. The same mentality is still found here in the Netherlands too, otherwise we would not have felt it necessary to write this chapter.

We are referring to Big Bill Broonzy's 'Black, brown and white':

> This little song that I'm singing about,
> People you know it's true,
> If you're black and got to work for a living,
> This is what they will say to you.
>
> *They say if you's white, you's all right,*
> *If you's brown, stick around,*
> *But as you're black,*
> *Mmm, brother, get back, get back, get back.*
>
> I was in a place one night,
> They was all having fun,
> They was all buying beer and wine,
> But they wouldn't sell me none.
>   *Refrain.*
>
> Me and a man were working side by side,
> This is what it meant,
> They was paying him a dollar an hour,
> And they was paying me fifty cents.
>   *Refrain.*

I went to an employment office,
Got a number and I got in line,
They called everybody's number,
But they never did call mine.
  Refrain.

I helped to win sweet victory,
With my little plough and hoe,
Now I want you to tell me brother,
What you gonna do 'bout the old Jim Crow.
  Refrain.[425]

Tragedy threatens in the development of gospel songs

'Didn't it rain'

One of the greatest tragedies of African-American music is that it is a living folk art within a Western world where folk music has all but died out, and its character is distinctly joyful and good-humoured. Western civilization knows only a very refined, erudite art music, on the one hand, and entertainment music, which has been taken over completely by commercial managers and artists, on the other hand. The tragedy is that this living, black folk art might easily be exploited by shrewd business people who, in doing so, may also hope to breathe some new life into the otherwise soulless entertainment music. Dance music of our generation is very strongly rooted in black jazz. That is not bad in itself, but attempts are then made to have blacks sacrifice themselves to Mammon. It is easily done, because money and fame lead to social recognition, and blacks in their difficult position are understandably happy to acquire it. Only those of strongest character, people with the most deep-seated convictions, are capable of resisting it.

Alongside a great deal of black music, adapted and customized for the Western consumer of popular music, we still do find some real black folk music and serious jazz of all kinds. The Negro spiritual world has, however, managed best to steer clear of all this. The danger of commercialization is, after all, not so great if the songs are only sung in churches and by practising Christians. We then have to exclude music of the well-established genre of 'religious entertainment', by which we mean the small bands like the Five Blind Boys, the Golden Gate Quartet and others who made jazzed-up versions of westernized concert spirituals (in the vein of the Fisk Jubilee Singers or artists like Marion Anderson, Roland Hayes and Paul Robeson) fit for general consumption.

An important development in the area of Christian music has been taking place in churches during the last twenty years or so. This includes the emergence of females who sing gospel songs or spirituals, solo or accompanied by small choirs, during fellowship meetings or services.

Most recently, however, the work of Mahalia Jackson and others has attracted attention from outside the circle of black churches, and that created a particular problem for these people. It was a blessing on one hand but, on the other hand, they were inclined, not as a result of commercial exploitation this time but with a view to confronting the audience with the gospel, to give in to the taste of the public in the hope of reaching a wider audience. This did not so much affect the lyrics as the performance of the music. Musically speaking this can have the same effect as commercialization.

An active faith, deep joy, a pure attitude keep things healthy and prevent excesses, but without them danger lurks. The reason we are taking up the subject here is that it helps explain some aspects of the performances of, for instance, Clara Ward at a gospel concert in New York in 1958 or 1959.[426] A few of the numbers she sings, like 'Didn't it rain' and 'The old landmark' (which did not just happen to be lyrics that are quite hollow when rendered this way) were definitely performed for effect and are actually pure swing music. Clara Ward hoped to use these pieces to attract her audience and to make the listeners receptive to her more serious numbers, some of which were good and pure, though we are not terribly impressed with the technique used on the Hammond organ.

The account on the sleeve testifies to the great success of this sort of music: people are fed up with modern jazz, with its tenseness, its super-individualistic mood, its refined effects, its monotony and emptiness; they are looking for something real, fresh and alive. This music has those qualities, sustained by an open attitude to reality, founded in a biblical faith in and love for the Father in heaven. It is music that has remained fresh, unspoilt and oblivious to alienation from reality. This essentially healthier sort of music is a breath of fresh air to adherents of contemporary jazz.

If we listen to Clara Ward, we find that her intentions are good, but here and there she makes concessions that are dangerous in that they affect the character of this church music. Fortunately a lot of her music is soundly rooted in the tradition and therefore remains beautiful and fascinating. It is certainly worth listening to. Nevertheless, we must keep our ears open and test the spirits, soberly and without contempt, with comprehension and prayers that it will not lead to this type of black music becoming denaturalized by Mammon, the greedy Moloch of our day.

We would like to point out that the sometimes dubious practices of the recording companies too may force some musicians along a road that is lucrative but hardly culturally responsible. Even some of the Spirit of Memphis Quartet records[427] are clearly commercially motivated. Hollow lyrics, soulless music with the emphasis on effect – rhythmic or sentimental – characterizes such renditions, which are best forgotten and can open our eyes to the tragedy we have discussed.

Spiritual solos: Mahalia Jackson

'I'm going to move on a little higher'

We have already mentioned the fact that some spirituals and gospel songs were also sung solely by women. By 1940, Sister Rosetta Tharpe had already incorporated all manner of jazz and blues influences into this genre of spiritual, particularly in rendition and style of singing. There were many others besides Sister Rosetta: Lottie Peavey, Jessie Mae Renfro, Mary Knight, Georgia Peach (one of the first to pursue this genre, having given many concerts at Christian gatherings all over America as early as 1930), Clara Ward and so on. A refreshing aspect of this music is that alongside the 4/4 beat, we find 6/8 or 5/6. As for harmony it is the common chords that are played, not those which we would describe as 'modern'.

Alongside the development of the small choir, the significance of this genre on the Christian scene has increased greatly since the Second World War. In the larger black churches, at least, the liturgical emphasis is increasingly falling on solo singing and choir, and the song of the congregation has taken on a secondary role. The possible causes and consequences of this are not yet clear.

Over the last few years there have been some recordings made of parts of church services. Recordings made of smaller churches in Harlem show us that the congregation there still wholeheartedly joins in the singing.[428] On the other hand, recordings of Sister Ernestine B. Washington's rendition of all sorts of spirituals and hymns, solo or accompanied by the choir, conjures up pictures of a big church. The congregation is left merely to express their approval of what is sung.[249] Many churches have replaced their harmonium with a Hammond organ. While it certainly has its drawbacks, we must remember that it is relatively cheap and still very versatile, and is being used in almost all churches in the USA.

I will now conclude by telling you a bit about Mahalia Jackson, undoubtedly one of the most important female solo singers of spirituals. She was born in New Orleans in 1911 and is presently singing in Chicago. The song 'I'm going to live the life I sing about in my song'[430] is an artistic testimony of her faith. In it she makes clear that song and lifestyle have to correspond. It would be inconsistent to sing spirituals in the church on Sunday and then to give yourself over to rock-and-roll on Monday. It is a paradox to walk as a child of God in the daytime and to have the 'devil on the cover' at night. 'Make no mistake, don't underestimate me,' she sings, 'I want to follow the right path and walk in the light, even if people scoff at me for it.' It is good to bear this in mind when listening to her music. She is not primarily an artist – someone who wants to serve art, someone who searches for beauty and focuses everything on it. Her priority is to serve the Lord and bring people into contact with the gospel or to strengthen them in their faith. As she sings in another song,

> Out of the depths of my soul I cry,
> Jesus draw nigh, Jesus draw nigh.
> Lord lend an ear to my whole honest plea,
> Jesus draw nearer to me.
> Oh, Lord, I want to labour,
> Faithful each day, walking in your true way,
> Telling the world what a Saviour I found,
> Spreading the gospel all around.[431]

If we bear these words in mind, it helps us understand why she sometimes does things that are not entirely representative of good taste or pure artistic skill, like the songs of Western origin that she sings, even though they do not really suit her style, partly because they do not belong to her own African-American tradition. She does it because she sees it as a way of reaching audiences that might otherwise not listen to her message. It is for the same reason that she allows herself to be accompanied by a band that is not really suited to her style.[432]

There is, incidentally, more to say about the accompaniment because even where these objections do not apply, we cannot say that the band that accompanies her is particularly proficient. It is not difficult to determine the reason for this. It would be ideal if she had a New Orleans ensemble. That this is not wholly inconceivable we can see by a few recordings made in that way. We refer to two beautiful little tracks sung by Lottie Peavey in San Francisco in 1944. She was accompanied by a New Orleans-style band, namely the Yerba Buena Band, with Bunk Johnson on trumpet. They sounded good together, forming a stylistic unity. 'When I move to the sky' is particularly beautiful, a very solemn piece in which the bowed bass strongly adds to the character. They hum one of the choruses completely, while the trumpet plays a polyphonic counter-melody. It is an extraordinary record if we consider that it features a very good and typically black rendition of a traditional Negro spiritual, accompanied by a largely white New Orleans band whose trumpet player is a black man from New Orleans. It can be described as a combination of the best aspects of the African-American tradition.[433] We know of one other exceptional example, namely the four tracks that Ernestine B. Washington recorded, accompanied by Bunk Johnson and George Lewis's band. Her voice is not as good as Lottie Peavey's, but *Does Jesus care?* still turned out to be a very special record that is certainly worth listening to.[434]

However, these are rare exceptions, for there are not so many New Orleans bands around any more. The black religious music that we are hearing now has come into blossom after the era of New Orleans jazz which, for all sorts of reasons, started to die out. There is however a much more compelling argument which explains why solo gospel songs are seldom accompanied by New Orleans ensembles: the average black Christian feels roughly the same about jazz as the elder of a Reformed church in the Netherlands, partly because jazz musicians are often unbelievers – or non-churchgoing people – but mainly because it is not church music. Puritan tradition demands that only religious music be sung and approves of music only if it is explicitly Christian. New Orleans music would hardly fit into this category, the very nature of modern jazz would preclude it and a modern combo supporting a singer like Mahalia Jackson or Lottie Peavey would indeed be a curse.

There is little choice left than a more or less neutral ensemble that plays with a mere whiff of jazz – to put it very unkindly, a sort of café palm-court orchestra.

The band that accompanies Mahalia Jackson is fortunately so unobtrusive, and she is so good herself that it does not matter. The best recordings naturally are gospel songs – songs in her own tradition.[435]

The following song gives us a clear impression of Mahalia's faith and knowledge of the Bible. It is a song that tells of going to heaven, heaven being comprehensively illustrated for us using biblical terms. It is inevitable – and highly scriptural – that most of the words in fact refer to the new earth, after the Last Day, which is also referred to. Almost every line in the song refers to a biblical text. I have noted them at the end of the text and will thus conclude this book with a recent piece of work of pure African-American tradition, in a genre that is completely new within the tradition. Mahalia does not sing as black people used to sing [in solo performances]. Blacks who think that to be the case should consider their alienation from their own culture; if they are still singing spirituals, then they would be sung in the well-worn style of the Fisk Jubilee Singers.

This song is an expression of a living, developing church art. It is a truly Christian song, one of the most beautiful products of twentieth-century Christian art:[436]

> One day a morning, soon one morning,[437]
> I'm going to lay down my cross, get me a crown.[438]
> Soon one evening, right in the evening,[439]
> Right in the evening, I'm going home[440] to live on high.
>
> As soon as my feet strike Zion,[441] lay down my heavy burden
> Put on my robe in glory,[442] going home one day and tell my story.
> I have been coming over hills and mountains,
> Gonna drink from the Christian fountain[443]
> You know all, God shut the door that morning,[444]
> We will drink form that all-healing water.
> And we gonna live on the river[445]>
> We gonna live on forever,
> We gonna live in glory, glory.

O, Lord, I am going out sightseeing Beulah,[446]
March all around by the altar,[447]
Gonna walk and never get tired,
No blight, Lord, never falter.
I'm going to move on a little higher, Gonna meet old man Daniel,[448]
I'm going to move on a little higher, Gonna meet the Hebrew children,[449]
I'm going to move on a little higher, Gonna meet Paul and Silas,
I'm going to move on a little higher, Gonna meet my friends and kindred,
I'm going to move on a little higher, Gonna meet my loving mother,
I'm going to move on a little higher, Gonna meet the Lily of the Valley.[450]

I am going to feast with the Rose of Sharon[451]
It will always be howdy howdy
And never goodbye.

O, will you be there early one morning,
Will you be there somewhere around the altar,
Will you be there when the angels shall call the roll?[452]
God knows I'll be waiting, yes I'll be watching somewhere at the altar,
I'll be waiting at the beautiful (yes) Golden Gate.[453]

Meet me there early one morning,
Meet me there somewhere around the altar,
Meet me there when the angels shall call all God's roll

Selected Bibliography to the First Edition

I would like to mention a number of books here. I have included a short summary of each:

J. Baldwin, *Go Tell It On The Mountain*. New York, 1954. A novel which gives an excellent picture of the life of members of a sect in Harlem.

J.E. Berendt, *Das Jazzbuch*. Frankfurt, 1953. The history of jazz written from the standpoint of an adherent of modern jazz.

Rudy Blesh, *Shining Trumpets, a History of Jazz*. New York, 1946. This is one of the best surveys of the history of jazz (including a summary of spirituals and the blues), written by a devotee of Jelly Roll Morton, etc. There is also a later British edition.

R. Bless and H. Janis, *They All Played Ragtime*. New York, 1950. Ragtime and its impact. A new edition was published in 1959.

W.L. Grossman and J.W. Farrell, *The Heart of Jazz*. New York, 1956. A good book that concentrates particularly on the background and significance of New Orleans jazz as opposed to modern jazz. The second half is a detailed description of Dixieland and New Orleans bands that were playing in the USA at that time.

Rex Harris, *Jazz*. Pelican, 1952. A good introduction to the history of traditional jazz.

Rex Harris and Brian Rust, *Recorded Jazz, A Critical Guide*. Pelican, 1958. A good guide to the best records and a rundown on the musicians. Traditional jazz only.

J.W. Johnson, *The Books of American Negro Spirituals*. New York, 1940. Interesting introduction to the spirituals, which are primarily dealt with through the eyes of the black intellectual.

Lomax, *Mr. Jelly Roll*. London, 1952. Jelly Roll Morton's biography. It provides some very important insight into the birth and development of jazz against a background of social problems.

J.A. and A. Lomax, *Folk songs: USA*. New York, 1947. An interesting collection in which all genres are represented.

R.W. Logan, *The Negro in the United States – A Brief History*. Princeton, 1957. An excellent sketch.

J.W. Schulte Norholt, *Het Volk Dat In Duisternis Wandelt.* Arnhem, 1957. A good book about the history and problems of black North Americans. The black intellectual viewpoint may be somewhat overemphasized.

H.W. Odum and G.B. Johnson, *Negro Workaday Songs.* Chapel Hill, 1926. Folk songs. Includes a lot of lyrics.

F. Ramsay and C.E. Smith, *Jazzmen.* New York, 1939. One of the first books about jazz that is devoted to historical research and knowledge of the facts. Still important.

N. Shapiro and N. Hentoff, *Heah Me Talkin' To Ya.* London, 1955. A collection of the reflections of jazz musicians. An important source of information and insight into what inspires these people.

M.W. Stearns, *The Story of Jazz.* London 1957. A rich source of information on the lead up to the birth of jazz, and a detailed study of the development of jazz. The author also focuses on problems 'around' jazz. A very good bibliography.

I also want to mention two gramophone records with recordings of lectures on jazz, with musical excerpts:

Leonard Bernstein, *What Is Jazz?* Col. (Am.) CL 919. Excellent analysis of musical elements given by an educated musician, with well-chosen examples.

Langston Hughes, *The Story of Jazz.* Folkways FP 712. Pleasant, rather traditional introduction, with good excerpts.

Updated Discography and Resources

Most of the music discussed in this book has been re-released on CD. It may however require a lot of research to track recordings down. In order to help you find CDs here follows a short list of guides, websites, compilation CDs and recommended CDs by particular artists.

Guides:

Richard Cook and Brian Morton (eds.), *Penguin Guide to Jazz on CD*. London: Penguin, 2000, 5th editon. The merit of recordings rated by stars.

John Cowley and Paul Oliver, *The New Blackwell Guide to Recorded Blues*. Oxford: Blackwell, 1997.

Barry Kernfeld (ed.), *New Grove Dictionary of Jazz*. London: The Macmillan Press Limited, 1994, 2nd edition. The most important reference work for jazz with an extensive selection of the most important releases.

Colin Larkin (ed.), *The Virgin Encyclopedia of the Blues*. London: Virgin Books, 1998.

Websites

On the site <www.allmusic.com> one can search for information about releases of particular artists.

Jazz: <www.allaboutjazz.com>

Gospel: <www.blackgospel.com>

Blues: <www.realblues.com>; <www.bluesworld.com>

Smithsonian Folkways: <www.si.edu/folkways> contains information about 2300 LPs/CDs on the Smithsonian Folkways labels.

Compilations jazz

Ken Burns Jazz: The Story of America's Music (Sony/Columbia, 5-CD box). Spans nearly a century of jazz styles.

New Orleans Traditional Jazz Legends (Mardi Gras, 6-CD set).

Jazz bands and soloists

Louis Armstrong: *The Hot Fives and Hot Sevens* (CBS). Armstrong before 1940.

Johnny Dodds: *The Chronical Johnny Dodds*, Volumes 1-3 (Classics). The most creative moments of this leading clarinettist of the New Orleans jazz in small as well as big ensembles.

Jelly Roll Morton: *The Complete Jelly Roll Morton 1926-1930* (RCA, 5-CD box).

King Oliver: *Volume 1, 1923-1929* (BBC). Ten tracks of Oliver with the Creole Jazz band, and recordings of the Dixie Syncopaters, Oliver's second band.

Compilations gospel

All of My Appointed Time (Stash/Jass). Forty years of a capella gospel by groups like the Golden Gate Jubilee Quartet and The Soul Stirrers, and female vocalists like Georgia Peach and Marion Williams.

Jubilation Volume 1: Great Gospel Performances (Rhino). Featuring tracks from Mahalia Jackson, The Soul Stirrers, Aretha Franklin, Shirley Caesar, and more.

Oh Happy Day (New Cross, 4-CDs). A compilation of 80 tracks from the golden age of gospel. Great recordings from the Chess and Veejay vaults, including the Five Blind Boys, the Staple Singers, and more.

Gospel singers and groups, recommended CDs

Blind Gary Davis: *Blind Gary Davis Complete Recorded Works 1935-1949* (Document DC 5060).

Mahalia Jackson: *Gospels, Spirituals and Hymns* (CBS). Beware of Mahalia re-issues – many are of dubious quality. This, however, is the very best available, featuring Mahalia at her peak in the 1950s and 1960s.

Blind Willie Johnson: *The Complete Blind Willie Johnson* (Columbia/Epic). Double-CD of this great gospel blues artist.

Spirit of Memphis Quartet: *Travelling On* (Hightone).

Negro Religious Field Recordings, Volume 1 (Document DC 5312).

The Staples Singers: *Great Day* (Milestone). A fine selection of the Staples' early 1960s recordings.

Compilations blues

Southern Journey, Volume 3 (Rounder). 61 Highway Mississippi-Delta country blues, spirituals, work songs and dance music. Field recordings by Alan Lomax.

The Best Blues Album in the World ... Ever (Emd/Virgin). A good mix of old school and new school blues.

Blues soloists

Big Bill Broonzy: *Trouble in Mind* (Smithonian/Folkways 40131). With topical songs, rural blues and spirituals.

Ida Cox: *Ida Cox*, Volumes 1-5 (Document).

Blind Lemon Jefferson: *King of the Country Blues* (Yazoo); *The Best of Blind Lemon Jefferson* (Yazoo 2057).

Leadbelly: *Leadbelly, King of the 12-String Guitar* (Sony/Legacy 46776).

Bessie Smith: *Bessie Smith: Empress of the Blues*, Volumes 1-4 (Sony/Legacy).

Part III

MUSIC ARTICLES

African and African-American Music

•African music as it really is: disenchantment and confirmation of a romantic dream[454]

Africa, the Congo, music . . . those words are sufficient to conjure up images of impenetrable jungles housing fearsome and highly dangerous wild animals, sun-baked clearings in the middle of African settlements, where wild dances are performed to the sound of tom-toms and drums and spine-chilling war-whoops. One is also persuaded to think of crocodile-infested waters, miles wide, where from their tapered canoes 'aborigines' render their songs, perhaps slightly more romantic and sweet but just as impassioned and just as much 'a call of the jungle'.

It would be interesting to find out how these images ever originated and better still, how true they are to reality. The latter is a real possibility now that the potential of the gramophone is increasingly being exploited, making even music like this accessible to us. Now that we can make acquaintance with this phenomenon we discover to our surprise that there is more than we dared dream of, possibly less fearsome and inaccessible than we thought, and much richer, more varied, more multiform than we suspected.

'Drums', yes they are there, and if one listens to the royal drums of the Watusi – as they can be heard in our living rooms on Decca's excellent African music series – one discovers that this art form, while its main focus is rhythm, is surprisingly more varied, rich and melodious than one ever thought possible. This really is royal music – very, very impressive. The wild dancing, yes it exists, and it can now be heard on a record in the same series devoted to dances of the Congo – and perhaps we have here the prototype of the image we associate with Africa, because this indeed resembles it somewhat. Yet what we do not expect is to hear sublime and very modest music played on the chromatic harp, or the almost fugacious music played on a quartet of xylophone-like instruments from Tanganyika [Tanzania]. And then there is also the sung rendition of old sagas and legends – like those of Ganda, the old hero of Uganda, and the stately song of a chief, sung by a male-voice choir.

But the exciting voyage of discovery, with the help of the gramophone, is not yet over. From the region of Uganda where the Nile originates we hear instruments that are identical to the instruments portrayed in ancient Egyptian frescos. And if one recalls that it was not uncommon to find a Negro slave among the Egyptian musicians, one begins to suspect that the ancient Egyptians may have been very different from the stately and emotionless image created by the sculptures of their Pharaohs.

The Africa one gets to know on the Decca series and on other records (Pathé and Contrepoint) is very different from that the Africa of romantic dreams: it is a continent, now for the most part accessible to the recording instrument, of which the music turns out to be that of peaceful and musical people. A great diversity of music, not only as to genre but also as to character, can be heard: authentic folk music alongside regal art performed by professional musicians; refined playing of solo instruments alongside the less perfected and refined songs of the ordinary people; exuberant liveliness, yes, elation, alongside tender love songs and melancholic elegies.

We are not sure whether to call it fortunate or unfortunate, but alongside the recording instrument also the record, with even greater ease, has penetrated to the furthest corners of the globe. As a result, new music emerged in Africa, inspired by the South American guitar and singing tradition, which already contained strong African elements and therefore did not sound out of place there.

Also South African songs and Portugese folk music, from the time before the gramophone had made its entrance, had an influence and produced endlessly repetitive krontjong-like music. This music is poor and monotonous compared with the earlier traditional polyrhythms; it is also superficial, with the original artistic tension sadly missing. This can be heard clearly on a record from the series. There are many more facets to these newer developments; their complexity will become apparent when one listens to the Philips records that were released specially for native African listeners, records with an emphasis on choral song.

Besides music that is mainly interesting – to our ears, at least – there is also music of real beauty. Alongside deep passion there is the sheer banal. In any case, this remains a fascinating area to broaden our musical horizons. The music that has not yet been spoilt by modern developments will be of help to scholars studying the African-American music of the USA and South America, to learn how 'African' it really is. Although it is sad that we have not yet found any music of the same quality as the Negro spiritual or good jazz (it is a pity that the latest influences mostly tend to be of a popular kind), somebody, someday, may well still be able to make a surprise discovery.

•From Eliza to Odetta[455]

Who does not know the story of valiant Eliza, who, with her child in her arms, fled to freedom over an iced river? Another person in the famous book *Uncle Tom's Cabin* was just as brave, keeping his will and soul intact even though he did bow outwardly to a cruel master. This was Uncle Tom himself who really was a Christian hero. For slaves like him there was no conjecture about being black. They simply were, and bore the curse of it.

But freedom came, in 1864. Not a time of ease and prosperity, though. There is a spiritual testifying to this, which says:

> Ever since I've been free (3x)
> Nobody knows the troubles I've seen.

Different openings were available to the freed blacks, who were uneducated, without work, and without anything to call their own. They could try to find work as share-croppers, field-hands, or in other kinds of menial work; or they could go to the cities, which seemed to offer them an easy life, even if it turned out that they had to work there as skilled or unskilled labourers. If they were lucky, they found opportunities to study and climb the social ladder. Without going too deeply into the innumerable subtleties of the resultant social framework, we can say that, culturally speaking, the black population was eventually divided into two camps: those of low social standing who had a culture of their own; and those, a happy few, who had some social status. The latter tried to integrate themselves into the white society.

The latter achieved their aim first of all by following the ways of the whites: playing classical music, reading European literature and adopting good manners. They were never 'raucous' in their singing, and they did not clap their hands during church services. If they sang songs from their own cultural past, it was Negro spirituals in a Europeanized, Schubertian style. Their own contribution, an unwitting one perhaps, was to make these spirituals known to the Western world: the songs that everybody knows, the songs sung by Burleigh, Marion Anderson, Paul Robeson, all of whom are good representatives of this side of African-American culture. As a whole these people tried to forget their past, and to unlearn everything that had a specific 'black' tinge to it.

Later, in the 1920s, they became more conscious of their position as black people and began to speak more openly about the hard road to recognition, also acknowledging their oneness with the mass of black people. This was the time of the Harlem Renaissance, and the fine poets and writers that must be mentioned here are James Weldon Johnson, Sterling Brown, County Cullen, Fenton J. Johnson, Arna Bontemps and also Langston Hughes. These writers were race conscious, much interested in black folklore and in the plight of their fellow blacks. In their literature they avoided presenting blacks in a stereotypical way. They wrote in normal English, bringing a sharp end to stylized 'Negro'-talk – the 'nebber' and 'de' type of pronunciation that till that time had invariably represented the speech-habits of African-American characters in books, and which was associated with their presumed naïvety.

In addition, a few white people began to write about African-Americans in a more sympathetic way, for example Du Bose Heyward in his novel *Mamba's Daughter*. The main character is a girl, Mamba's grand-daughter Lissa who, by Mamba's sheer energy and self-denial, is able to rise from the low stratum of black life to a higher one. In the end she appears in the Metropolitan Opera House in the leading role in a black musical play, a kind of black opera with an African-American cast. At the end of the performance, this girl Lissa steps forward and recites one of James Weldon Johnson's famous poems.

She does not try to conceal the fact that she is black but rather stresses it. She is the true embodiment of what the black renaissance strove to achieve. One has the impression that the opera, which is not named, is meant to be none other than *Porgy and Bess*, based on Du Bose Heyward's own novel *Porgy*.

However, *Porgy* is far inferior to *Mamba's Daughter*. In it we find rather too many of the old stereotypes. The main character, for instance, is an ignorant black who, even when he sings spirituals, sometimes makes the audience laugh because he does not seem to understand what he is singing – a fact that is clearly controverted by the many field recordings made since the 1930s by Courlander, Frederick Ramsay and the Lomaxes. *Porgy and Bess*, as such, is really one of the last black-faced minstrel shows. It is in the tradition of a genre which has prospered since the 1930s in which white actors with blackened faces ridiculed black folk music and missed all its depth and sincerity. In Gershwin's music not one real blues number, not one real spiritual is to be found. When the script tells us we are in a square in Charleston where black folk are assembled and are playing mouth-organs and similar instruments, we do not hear one note of real folk music, not even an echo of it, but only music in the characteristic style of the Broadway musical.

What is this black music we have referred to? It is the music of the black labourers, farmhands and longshoremen and, of course, of the black women in their cabins or their kitchenettes in the big cities. Within its scope we find many styles and types. First, there is the sharp division between the secular song and the spiritual. The latter, which is sung in churches, is strong and rhythmical, accompanied by hand-clapping or, according to a tradition that goes back to the seventeenth century, chanted in long-drawn phrases. Among the performers of this music are the itinerant street evangelists like Blind Willie Johnson, the quartets, the choirs and the (female) soloists who perform at meetings.

There has also been, since the 1930s, the gospel song, developed and promoted by Thomas A. Dorsey, a former blues singer and composer. It has given a new impetus to an already rich black musical tradition. And there is black secular music: the folk songs, the work songs, the hollers and all the other Southern backwood genres, the 'backwood' often ending at the city boundaries. Out of all of these, African-American musicians developed a highly imaginative kind of song, a truly original creation: the blues. The blues was a product of the Mississippi region, where it was sung and probably also created by itinerant artists, troubadours who, with their guitars or mouth organs, performed for an eager public, in the roadhouses, soda fountains, rural drugstores or just in front of any cabin. They provided dance music or the sad and moaning blues, in which they gave poetic expression to the hardship and plight of the their people. On the surface these songs deal with broken love but at a deeper level they are about the black people's unending struggle for due recognition by the whites and for proper human treatment instead of being thrown back 'to their own place'.

In the cities up North this blues took on another slant. Here they became nostalgic reminiscences of the South, for which the many blacks who had gone North in search of a better place felt homesick, or they became an expression of their new life, faster, more easygoing on the one hand, but on the other as sordid and poor as it ever had been.

At the end of the nineteenth century a new music emerged. For the African-American people music became a new way to acquire position, to earn money and maybe gain some recognition. But their highly original creations – ragtime first, and then, a decade later, New Orleans jazz – only made it to the slippery dives, the redlight districts or the low-down honky-tonk bars, catering to the unlicensed world of vice, cheap pleasure and lust. The very best place they could aspire to play in was a dance-hall, for other venues were denied to them. The cultured world ignored them since their music was not classical and, after all, was 'as low as the world where it was born'; respectable society seldom called for this music's natural, cheerful sounds, often because it was felt that the musicians themselves were not fit to appear in decent company.

The musicians, more often than not decent middle-class people, worked hard in their quest for a respectable life and a reasonable place under the sun. This meant that many of them, consciously or unconsciously, strove for recognition, as black artists amongst whites for a better and more equal position. And in a way they succeeded. Not only was their music recorded, since the early 1920s, but it certainly promoted their position and, because many a young white musician or jazz lover admired their skill and talents, it did much to break down the race barriers.

After a while a larger world opened up for black musicians, even if it seldom led higher than the entertainment world. In this field they began to take an important place. Yet there was another side to the coin: they had to commercialize their style, play music less alien to Western traditions, blend their own vigour with the hip, heavily-arranged dance music their customers were used to. Their rhythmical sense and their ability to make variations on a theme were misunderstood by their audiences, who found something primitive, associated with natural freshness and vitalistic energy in the rhythm, free exuberance, a kind of uninhibited outpouring of the subjective self. All this was thought to be founded on extemporization.

In this way orginal jazz grew into hot jazz and swing, music based on beat and on improvisation. Worse than anything was the never-ending pressure on the musicians to go commercial and to cater to the taste of the masses. To do so could mean riches, but these were won only at the cost of self respect. This is the tragedy of many a black musician's life, often drowned in heavy drinking.

This tragedy was repeated later on in the blues field with the commercialization of rock-and-roll, and it may be repeated again by a craze for gospel music, polished and 'civilized', for this field has been opened to white ears by the well-deserved success of Mahalia Jackson and a few vocal groups like the Staple Singers. 'Success' here implies success among white people, of course, because long before these figures were hailed by white audiences they were famous among their own people.

Out of this situation of frustration, of feeling that they were obliged to play the clown for a white public, with the added typical twentieth-century *Lebensgefühl*, there grew in the 1940s a new music, modern jazz, which, just because it was really modern in its expression of anxiety and despondency, spoke to the hearts of cultured modern Western people, in the USA as well as in Europe. So, rather paradoxically, this music of protest and frustration became much applauded and helped, in its own way, to promote the social progress of African-Americans.

The race barriers still exist, and equality is as yet a dream. But blacks have gained strength from their successes and have learned to be proud of their own achievements. They have outgrown the 'Uncle Tom's' attitude, and now dare to enter the world with their own heritage, their own 'colour', culturally speaking. So an Odetta, who thirty years ago might have become another Marion Anderson, has turned to the best of her own people's traditions, to the music of Ma Rainey, using her rich voice to revive the great performances of this gifted blues singer of the 1920s.

But despite all social iniquity, racial bias, and all the problems that people 'from the Redwood Forest to the New York islands' wrestle with, there is the legacy of the musical past of these people, for whom music means so much as to be almost their life. This is a legacy of music and song often of great beauty, depth and originality, handed down for listeners on the many old (sometimes much-battered) records. Folk music of a high artistic standard or art of a low social class, whatever it may be, it is a genuine expression of all the sorrows and joys of a musically highly gifted people, music with a message for everybody, for they are human just like us.

•American folk music at its best[456]

It is some time ago now that a representative from Philips came to see me about releasing some old and rare jazz records. Our conversation led to a plan that meant spreading our wings a bit wider and focusing on blues and spirituals alongside early jazz – after all, a lot of work has already been done in the area of jazz. As little has been done with spirituals, in particular, this offered new possibilities. We also agreed that special effort would be put into the presentation of the sleeves and into the text of the accompanying notes. One important aspect, as far as I was concerned, was that the lyrics should be printed in full – this is sadly and all too often an area of neglect.

The result of our deliberations can now be sampled in *Treasures of North-American Negro Music*, the title of a series not dedicated to jazz only. The original intention was for me to write an introduction that would apply to all the records in the series. After many attempts to write a concise summary of the special character of the music I came to the conclusion that this was bound to fail, either for being too superficial or too detailed. So you will understand my delight at stumbling upon a poem that perfectly matched the requirements for my introduction. It was promptly printed on the inside of the sleeve:

> There is music in me, the music of the peasant people.
> I wander through the levee, picking my banjo and singing my songs of the cabin and the field. At the *Last Chance Saloon* I am as welcome as the violets in March. There is always food and drink for me there, and the dimes of those who love honest music.
> Behind the railroad tracks the little children clap their hands and love me as they love Kris Kringle.
>
> But I fear I am a failure.
> Last night a woman called me a troubadour.
>
> What is a troubadour?

This poem conveys some of the characteristic mood of the best African-American folk music. That is just what we were looking for in the old recordings.

All the records are 45 rpm, containing four sides of original 78 rpm (25 cm) recordings. The first record is dedicated to Leroy Carr, one of the most outstanding folkblues singers. These recordings represent some of his best blues numbers, with very original lyrics – gentle, subtle in rendition, direct and yet very poetic. *The Midnight Hour Blues*, a record that I have regarded for many years as one of the cream of my collection, is a jewel that has to be listened to and studied again and again. The authentic atmosphere of the blues – very well finished and well balanced – is captured here as it has seldom been captured before.

The record of spirituals is dedicated to Blind Willie Johnson, one of the greatest artists of this genre. If we compare this record with the one already mentioned it becomes clear how completely blues and spirituals differ from each other in mood, expression and meaning. This record too represents artistry of the highest quality. The music will sound strange to an unaccustomed ear, but those who make the effort to immerse themselves in this specific world of neither African nor Western music, nourished by a mature Christian faith, will certainly discover much beauty of lasting value.

The jazz record was perhaps the most daunting to compile. So much work had already been done in the area of jazz re-releases that we decided not to include anything which had already been released in Europe on other main labels. In retrospect it was easier than we had anticipated, and the discovery that whole areas had been neglected in the re-releases surpassed all our expectations. This was partly because these records are so rare but also because the history of jazz has almost always been viewed from only one angle, namely that of fierce, hot jazz – which is best represented by Armstrong. But at the end of the 1920s, pure jazz of a completely different character was being played, particularly by musicians led by King Oliver, who looked for a quiet balance – pure musicality, pure control. It may have been a response to the development of jazz under Armstrong and co. We were grateful to come across two beautiful examples – four sides played by bands under Clarence Williams. This is jazz music of the highest quality, significant and of lasting importance.

I recently met Bryan Rust – the collector who wrote Oliver's discography – in England and he told me that it was King Oliver himself who was playing alongside Allen in 'Red river blues' and 'I need you'. Apparently Clarence Williams had written it down in the notebook he used to keep account of his activities. The beautiful solo on the A-side is played by Allen, but Oliver can be heard in good form in the ensembles; his clear, sharp tone comes out very distinctly in these magnificent recordings.

Yes, and this is what we will end with: please note what good recordings these are, also from a technical perspective. Seldom has such good balance between instruments been achieved, seldom such transparency, enabling the instruments to be heard individually while the homogeneity is retained. These recordings are technically almost peerless – even today.

Blues

• Poetic fiction in the blues[457]

Travelling musicians have been around for a long time. They were already in business during Roman times, when they were called a 'joculators'. The French word *jongleur* is a derivation of that. The art of the *jongleur* flourished in southern France during the twelfth century. It was also appreciated in the courts of the nobility. Noble ladies, in particular, needed their services to help while away the hours, and the subject of their songs was love, handled in a distinct and new way.

Thus a new genre, the Provençal chanson, originated, probably under the influence of the Moors.[458] In any case, its attraction came from its poetic fiction. After all, the songs were invariably directed at an eminent lady, who was married and had to remain anonymous. They always focused on the object of love, her charm, the pain of being away from her, her refusal to return the love, the hope of winning her and plighting troth. In view of the way these chansons emerged and the society in which they flourished, it is probable that the songs reflected a reality of life, albeit in a very stylized form. The lady of the manor, who had often been married for the sole purpose of sustaining the dynasty, would quite likely have entertained liaisons, a practice that was not uncommon in an area that at that time honoured anything but a Christian lifestyle.

The reason for mentioning this is because the blues prompts associations of more than one kind. They are not songs sung by any black person from the rural areas of the Southern States of the USA, even though the hollers and field blues are in many ways related to blues in the true sense of the word and are almost certainly the prototype for this genre. The blues is par excellence the music of the travelling musician, and various sorts of folk song shaped the specific details of this skilful art form. Precisely where its final form was established and codified and by whom, will remain a mystery, but it is clear that its development must have been complete around 1890–1900, for by then blues was a mature art form. The geographical location of its origin was certainly the Mississippi basin, and we can possibly narrow it down to Georgia, Alabama and Louisiana. Since this art form was created by troubadours, 'at home' across a wide area and without social distinction, it remains impossible and futile to attempt pinpointing the exact location where blues originated.

Like Provençal chansons, the blues are based on poetic fiction: the unfaithfulness of a lover, or the threat of unfaithfulness if the subject's situation does not improve. Like Provençal chansons, these songs too reflect a social reality. The marriage relations among blacks were indeed very loose (a legacy going back to the days of slavery, when a husband

and wife were allowed to be sold separately by the slave owner), while the ever recurring 'I'm going away' theme was reflected in the reality of a migratory lifestyle – poor rural folk kept moving from one job to another, sometimes to faraway places. At least, that is how it was for those blacks who did not belong to the class of strict, churchgoing believers, for the blues is a distinctly 'worldly' music, radically different from the spirituals in its view of life. The mood, which is strongly meditative and melancholic, beautifully evoked by the artistic, wonderfully ingenious form with its rules for phrasing and strophe formation, is very different from the mood of the authentic spirituals sung by believers from the same social class.

We have written all this in response to the release of the London LP *Backwoods Blues*, in which we hear the art of four of these troubadours, selected from the hundreds available. Because of his skill and possibly also because he spent a long time in Chicago, one of them became better known, namely Big Bill Broonzy. On this record he plays two blues numbers from 1932 under the pseudonym Johnson. The two numbers from 1927 by Bobby Grant are the most beautiful. These performers all sing their own compositions, remaining faithful to the poetic fiction we mentioned earlier: you can sing the blues, even if you are not in the predicament about which you are singing – indeed, that will seldom be the case. They also abide by the rather strict rules of the blues in terms of musical structure. Just one of the eight numbers deviates from this structure, with a sixteen-bar scheme, though the technique and the mood are typically blues. These simple, uneducated musicians who learned their art from a generation of blues singers that preceded them, accompany their renditions on guitar in their own individual style, each devising their own effects. Although this is very different from the music of the female blues singers who performed in the cities, like Ma Rainey, this is not in the least primitive, unsophisticated folk music; it is art in the true tradition of the troubadour, art that no lover of 'folklore' should disregard.

• Blind Lemon Jefferson[459]

The blues that emerged in the last quarter of the nineteenth century is the song of the African-Americans, the unforgettable song of their plight. It built on the cry by which slaves used to pass messages down the gang line, and as such retained, musically speaking, a great deal of African characteristics, and on the slow, melancholic work songs, and especially on the personal songs of sorrow that came into being after emancipation and which expressed deeply troubled hearts. These are the roots of the blues, but how and through whom the music developed will remain a secret. The melodic structure and content of the music in its early form was already quite similar to the blues that became prevalent across the Southern States around 1900. Although we cannot say exactly where the blues originated, the music does presuppose a certain artistic development in order to have arrived at the typical twelve-bar strophe with its definite harmonic pattern, which reminds one of a figured bass, too balanced, too ingenious to be equated with the earlier types of song.

The only way of getting behind the history of the music is to compare the little verbal and written information we have available with the available gramophone records. The first of these recordings, dating back to 1923, featured the great blues singers; but in the 1930s there was a more deliberate, scientific attempt to record in remote locations the songs of blacks who were still familiar with the old forms. If we listen carefully to these ear-witness recordings, released in America on Library of Congress albums, it is evident that these country blues represent either an earlier form of blues or that they were derived from commercial recordings of the better known blues singers. The conclusion, albeit a hypothesis, is that the balanced twelve-bar form of the blues is the work of a number of artists who used the rudiments, developed them and artistically united them. This conclusion is not backed up by traditional accounts, for there is no mention of any such key musicians. But Gertrude 'Ma' Rainey began her artistic career as early as 1900 and it is possible that she reflects in her music the tradition of her own predecessors, who are unknown to us.

It is odd that the great musicians of this genre, those who made the blues a serious medium of artistic expression, are women. There is not a soul who can remotely compare with Ma Rainey or Bessie Smith, not even among the other female blues singers of their ilk. Apart from them there is a number of male blues singers from the same period, but their music conveys a completely different character. The blues of these male singers, performing in exactly the same period as their female counterparts (if we may refer to them as such), seems more archaic, less sophisticated and less individual. One of them, and certainly the most important one, was Blind Lemon Jefferson. He too was greatly respected among the black population and until his death, around 1930, his work in Texas, and later in Chicago, certainly did have an influence on other musicians. While the women performed in black theatres and their performances were to some extent comparable with recitals, he sang in pubs and on street corners, moving from one place to another. His music was therefore more closely and more directly related to the black proletariat; his music was more folksy and, in a sense, less artistically driven.

None of that alters the fact that his work, recently released on the London label, is the work of a real artist. His singing is reminiscent of a recitative style – almost without a trace of vibrato and often sliding down when singing the third and the seventh of a key, which is a typical characteristic of blues singing. His own guitar accompaniment is particularly beautiful. At first hearing it sounds so simple, but this is a simplicity achieved by an artist who skilfully transforms sounds by a few means into fullness. The music may be called 'archaic' but only if the word is used as a compliment. It is rudimentary, certainly, but full of promise, with direct expression rather than artistic accomplishment as the goal.

This music is not spontaneously easy to listen to, one of the biggest hindrances being the very poor quality of the recording, but if one perseveres, this blues music from the mid-1920s reveals a primal force that makes all later blues seem like pure hype and stylism. It is real, living folk art, top quality and full of unexpected beauty.

• Ida Cox[460]

As yet, nobody has been able to state for certain how or where the blues originated, although it is very probable that this music had its roots among the African-American population of the Mississippi basin. Was it originally authentic folk music or was it derived from the music of professional singers who performed for black audiences in the theatres? Whichever way, for as long as we have been able to bear witness – and the first recording was released as early as 1923 – the blues has manifested a typical urban character that reflects the poor social standing of the blacks. It is to be noted that there seems to have been hardly any male singers prior to 1925.

From a musical point of view there are undoubtedly also all sorts of typically African muscial characteristics to be discovered, for instance, the practice of humming a verse (or part of it). Humming does not feature in the Western mode of artistic expression. The owners of blues records from the early 1920s will no doubt rate Ma Rainey top, followed by her pupil, Bessie Smith. Ma, in particular, demonstrates a directness and allegiance to her people that confers to her music, exemplary in its unity of content and musical expression, an unmistakable stamp of authenticity.

There were also other artists who did not have to work their way up 'from the bottom' and whose position is comparable with that of contemporary singers like Ella Fitzgerald. Unlike Ma Rainey and others who were forced by social deprivation and racial discrimination to sing on cabaret-like stages of all kinds, they are artists who by the nature of their work and their artistic approach really belong there. These singers were later to borrow their repertoires from Broadway songs. Their material was very inferior, their lyrics had little content or meaning, being flippant love songs, sentimental and superficial. It is one of the consequences of black emancipation that they were afforded an important position in the 'entertainment business' with its pseudo-jazz and suchlike. In the early days, however, those opportunities were not available to blacks, so that they had to focus on black audiences. This is one of the reasons why the early singers were more aware of their own culture. An authentic black inspiration was most important to them and the nature and quality of their cabaret was strongly influenced and determined by the art of well-known artists like Ma Rainey.

Perhaps this is the best perspective from which to view the work of Ida Cox. Her inspiration is less direct, less linked to her roots, more geared to an attractive rendition. Yet the source of her inspiration is so powerful, the tradition still so alive, the taste still so pure that we encounter not a trace of tasteless superficiality, and the expression remains unaffected black music in a pure way. A song like 'Coffin blues' could so easily have become sentimental, although these days you can hardly imagine a song being written with such words:

> I rubbed my hands over your head and whispered in your ear
> And I wonder if you know that your mamma is near.

It would be far too serious and dramatic, and yet it is anything but that. This beautiful and magnificently accompanied song has become a work of art of great value. The central theme of this music, the self-pity, the satire, reflects purely black invention and tradition. It is a background that contrasts strongly with the commercial slant of the Broadway songs, which aim particularly to satisfy a demand for entertainment.

Words like those of the contemplative 'Misery blues', where she recalls how her husband said:

> I'm leaving mama and your crying won't make me stay
> The more you cry, the further I'm going away.

would be quite out of place in music of the later, entertainment genre; certainly when sung in this way – with real raw emotion.

Ida Cox was fortunate to often have had excellent accompanists. Those who have heard her recently released record on London, with its eight blues tracks, will have to admit that the mood and character of this music owes as much to the accompaniment as to the singing of Ida Cox herself. The great black trumpet player Tommy Ladnier turns out to be exceptional here. His solo in 'Ramblin' blues' is beautiful, with fine phrasing, inspired and free of all theatrics. In that regard every single one of these numbers is a worthy example of the classical period of black music. Charlie Green too, who won fame for his accompaniments to Bessie Smith, shows his artistic taste and strength here. As far as we have been able to establish, his solo in 'Misery blues' is unique – the only true solo by him on record.

Cabaret? Maybe, but then so pure, so musical, so averse to superficiality and cheap effects, that the use of the word seems misplaced when we think of what we often classify as cabaret today.

• Folk songs of black Americans[461]

Art, be it folk art or an example of the most refined, technically perfect expression of an advanced civilization, always has many aspects. This enables us to approach a work of art from many different angles. The odd thing is, though, that very many artists themselves pay precious little attention to matters of form, technical structure, and so on, and this is especially true of folk artists. They are not interested in sophistication or balance but only care about content and meaning, very much like orators who, when questioned about their speeches, will not open a discussion on their linguistic choices or styles of rhetoric but will refer to what they said and why they said it.

This is something we may not forget when listening to how blacks, lacking any kind of education (which by no means implies that they also lack intelligence and insight), talk about their art form – the blues. We can enjoy listening to just this on a beautifully presented record released by Alan Lomax on the Nixa label. It is a collection of recordings made in 1940 somewhere along the Mississippi and features the voices of three blues singers who talk about and demonstrate their music. Lomax regularly interjects with a word of clarification or by giving musical illustrations of what has been said about a work song, church song and so on.

Their music obviously is a direct expression of what moves these people, what impassions them:

> I want to get to think plainly that the blues is something that's from the heart – I know that, and whenever you hear fellows singing the blues, I always believed it was a really heart thing. Things that have really happened to you, you know what I mean? – That's right, that's the blues. When I have troubles, Blues's the only thing that helps me. I mean that's the only way to kind of ease my situation.

The last of these remarks, particularly, betrays the emotion involved in the music; the songwriting itself becomes a means of moulding thoughts and feelings and putting them into perspective. What we have to understand, however, is that while an awareness of and direct inner contact with the circumstances that is sung about is essential (they themselves hold that those who do not share their plight cannot sing the blues), these musicians do not necessarily sing only of their own present predicament. So, for instance, they may sing about a childhood memory that has no direct significance for them anymore. Art has its own means by which to sing the world we know and live in, and poetic fiction is one of them (which is not necessarily the same as direct experience). Just as a singer of Schubert's songs about the pretty millerwoman (*die schöne Müllerin*) need not necessarily be in love, let alone with a millerwoman, so blues singers do not always experience the plight they are singing about. What the discussion with these black singers does make clear is that their art is a reflection of experiences, feelings, thoughts, pleasures and pains that are real for the community to which they belong. That is why we recognize the blues as an expression of all the trouble and strife of the blacks in the Southern States of the USA, and for the same reason we also recognize what one of the three men expresses in the words: 'We coloured people have had so much trouble (but) we try to be happy anyway.'

In any case, this record has turned out to be an incredibly fascinating and interesting discussion about this folk art and it is beautifully illustrated with examples. Lomax's words (on the sleeve) are indeed apt when he writes that also illiterate people are quite capable of analysing a complex situation and expounding their insight. This record is therefore essential and very instructive to anyone researching the racial issues in the USA. Our insight into this original black creation, the blues, can be considerably enriched by listening to this recording. It helps us understand why the music – pure folk art without a sign of commercial degeneration – is so profound, and remains so universally fascinating.

A second record, also on the Nixa label, is a beautiful selection of labour camp songs sung by prisoners. These songs take up most of the record, but there are also a few blues numbers and a ballad ('Stackolee') to enjoy. The music was recorded by Lomax in 1947 in the Mississippi State Penitentiary, which in fact was a very big plantation. This is live folk art of great beauty and depth, with splendid melodies and harmonious part-song. It is remarkable that the music of these simple songs never becomes coarse, sentimental or shallow. The emotion is too real for that. Note how the reality of their troubles is never sidestepped, in contrast to the content of songs that appeal to the masses. Indeed, the first track on the blues record sounds to me as if it could have been an 'adaptation' of a theme song from a film of the 1930s (which in itself is a rarity), but the corny love song was transformed into:

> Sometimes you'll be held up, sometimes held down,
> Sometimes your friends even don't want you around
> There's some things you gotta keep, some things you gotta repeat
> People, happiness, well, is never complete, you know.

And the chorus:

> *O, life is like that, well, and that's what you've got to do,*
> *Well, and if you don't understand, people, I'm sorry for you.*

•African-American music as a source of beauty and of historical information[462]

The 1920s produced African-American music at its best: blues, as sung by male and female singers, and New Orleans jazz. Incredibly much was recorded during this time, though only performances by professional musicians. Recordings of sermons and spirituals sung by ordinary members of the congregation are the only examples of authentic folk music. Inevitably collectors got up and dived into this inexhaustible source of surprising discoveries. Their work in sifting through the material has turned out to be very important and has laid the foundation for a discography which for the most part must now be regarded as complete. It forms the essential background to any further study of this area of music. It was not until the end of the 1930s that a more thetical study, based on true knowledge and insight, emerged. It came in the form of *Jazzmen*, a pioneering book by F. Ramsey and C.E. Smith. Its scope was limited, with the focus still exclusively directed at jazz and its development. A few years later Rudy Blesh took a step further with his *Shining Trumpets* whose research included authentic folk music as recorded by the Library of Congress.

Serious gaps in our knowledge and insight of the development of spirituals, blues and jazz remained, however. Courlander, who made a number of recordings in the west of Alabama in 1951, addressed this problem superbly. Most of this music was released on two indispensable Folkways LPs: *Negro Folk Music from Alabama, Secular and Religious*. As is customary with records bearing this label, it appeared complete with photographic material and all lyrics included! Many notions held by serious researchers were confirmed or refuted and the scope of the area to be covered greatly increased. Also the nature of the questions became clearer and in fact only now could they be correctly formulated. Further, as a result of this, the missing links could be demonstrated, and one began to feel that the singers of authentic folk music might hold the key to an invaluable wealth of historical information. What made these recordings of untrained folk singers so special was the fact that they were collected beyond the reach of the 'civilized' world and therefore reflected the circumstances that had elsewhere died out. Besides its scientific value, we must not ignore the musical significance of these recordings. Those who listen to the recent release on Folkways of spirituals sung by Doc Reed and Vera Hall will hear songs of inconceivable beauty. Their lyrics and presentation far surpass anything that might be expected of 'just untrained common singers', and Reed's warm baritone, in particular, puts such words of contempt to shame.

But there remained more missing links and many unanswered questions. Frederick Ramsey – the once celebrated author of *Jazzmen* – has once again done invaluable service by searching the furthest corners of the Southern States for singers or bands that would shed more light on many of these matters. His first discovery was the rural brass bands which, though the quality of their music may not have been very high, helped us identify one of the pre-New Orleans jazz phases and also laid bare a whole new field in African-American music. Then came the three records by Horace Sprott, released as part of the *Music from the South* series on Folkways labels and accompanied by an excellent insert with photographs, lyrics and commentary. Sprott was a singer with good qualities and while he might have been just a farmer, it was his very naïvety that also protected him from outside influences. It enabled him to tell us an incredible amount about the emergence of the blues and the social background and meaning of these secular songs. This way a comparison can be made with spirituals, of which he sings a few very beautiful and absolutely unknown examples. It is not only the songs that are important and of musical interest, however. There are interviews recorded too, quite simply, on Sprott's doorstep, in which he tells of the holler and cornfield songs, of work songs and spirituals and how they came about. Particularly interesting and surprising is the fact that this man seems to know nothing of the real blues – at least, he does not sing them himself. He sticks closely to its forerunner – the holler – and sings several beautiful numbers. Their lyrics and content are not unlike that of the blues sung by professionals, but their rendition and musical structure is quite different. Especially curious is the blues he claims to have learned from Blind Lemon Jefferson – the 'Black snake blues'. If we compare the blues we are familiar with from Jefferson's record with the song Sprott dug up from memory, it seems that he has re-translated the song back to its previous form, as it were – the holler!

Do not be misled: these records are not only interesting and important to the academic – the musicologes – but are also essential for any serious African-American music enthusiast. This is the way to learn to understand and get a feeling for the music that fascinates one. Further, these Folkways records include material that, besides being interesting, is also surprising and surprisingly beautiful. Surely this is the main source that drives any study of music, or any search for knowledge: to be captivated by something which through inspiration, content and form fascinates us because of that ultimately indefinable quality – beauty.

• Hollerin' and cryin' the blues[463]

Big Bill Broonzy
It is said that music evokes emotion, but this is true only in a very strict sense. For feelings, as a function of the human psyche, may be very diverse and as such they are not yet artistically differentiated. Sorrow, joy and many other emotions are general human emotions, but not variable; indeed they are subject to psychological laws. If, however, we inspect the great variety of emotions, of atmosphere and mood – the wealth of expression realized in the diversity of styles over the course of time – it is an entirely different matter. The joy expressed in Bach's *Brandenburg Concertos* is very different from that of Beethoven's

Eighth Symphony. The melancholy mood of Schubert's 'Death and the maiden' is very different from the peculiar but definitely also melancholic mood rendered in Josquin des Préz's 'Je ne puis tenir d'aimer'. In each piece of music, atmosphere, mood, emotion display a different hue, an individual sound, and therefore they cannot be perceived just as a psychological phenomenon but rather as an artistic expression – aesthetic emotion. The blues as sung by the African-Americans depicts matters relevant to all ages and all peoples – broken hearts, struggles and anxieties, floods and disasters, and so on – but it is done in a very characteristic way.

The mood of the blues as a purely stylistic phenomenon is something unique. Just as we may be moved by the special mood of one of Mozart's piano concertos and feel more affinity with the character of his music each time we listen to it, once we have heard the blues – not only as sound but also as a spiritual mood – we will not want to abandon it again. So, let us welcome with open arms the new Vogue LP *Big Bill Broonzy, Blues singer, Vol. 1.*

The fact that we are able to listen with pleasure to this recording is proof that there is more to a melancholic mood of this sort than just being moved psychologically. If it is true, and we do not deny it, that music conveys feelings, then it would seem logical that no one would enjoy listening to the blues, for no one grieves for the fun of it and certainly no one will go looking for it. It follows that the blues is a form of expression that must be understood artistically. Do not think that when Broonzy sings of his sorrow because his loved one is lost and he is having to leave home and hearth because of flooding, that at that moment he is literally experiencing this sorrow himself. Art shapes human feelings and experiences as they occur in a particular period or in a particular milieu. The art of the blues came about against the social background of the American blacks, their spiritual and material distress and their repudiation by whites (though the latter is seldom expressed in black music).

Big Bill Broonzy, a huge black man from Missouri, made his first records in 1926. He was one of Blind Lemon Jefferson's pupils. Don't be misled into thinking that using the 'natural voice' in singing comes automatically to anyone. Even Broonzy trained his voice, albeit in a non-Western fashion. He has kept on developing and refining his means of expression, the highlights of which we undoubtedly hear in this music recorded in Paris in 1951 on the Vogue label. In stark contrast to the blues as sung by his female predecessors of the 1920s, we encounter here, possibly for the first time, male-voice blues that can be equated with the music of those predecessors. Form and content are in perfect balance and Broonzy has not fallen into mannerism, whereby the form overtakes the content, as some of his contemporaries did, for instance Leadbelly during his later period. The blues has a meditative character;

the songs are not ballads but nevertheless reflections, sometimes with a hint of satire, sometimes aimed at the audience and sometimes very introspective, defiant or resigned – often quite simply an expression of suffering, as in the following:

> I've been hollerin', hollerin' and cryin', cryin' the whole night long,
> Baby, I've been hollerin' and cryin', cryin' the whole night long,
> The woman that I'm cryin' about,
> Oh, I don't know where she's gone.

We find satire – self-ridicule – in the words:

> Please don't mistreat me, you know Big Bill's a motherless child,

The poetic structure that embodies the thoughts arouses wonder and admiration in us, again and again. Take this for instance:

> In the evening, in the evening mamma, when the sun goes down,
> In the evening darling, I declare when the sun goes down,
> Yes it's so lonesome, so lonesome, I declare when your love is not around.

One side of this record containing four blues tracks serves as a résumé of everything the blues expresses – in song and word. What the technically perfect guitarwork can add to this is a matter for the listeners to discover for themselves. The other side with its 'Blues in 1892' gives a poetic vision of the emergence of the blues. The diction and narrative style of the spoken part are beautiful – even musical. Then there is the 'Moppin' blues', a very old blues, also in its form, and the beautiful meditative blues to which the title of this article owes its name. The blues as meditation and mood, without beginning and without end, is inadvertently symbolized here by the fact that the record ends in the middle of a stanza. Big Bill was too much 'into' it to be bothered by technical hitches. Each era, each style has in its own way given form to the expression of suffering, melancholy, grief. Let us not ignore this music just because the singer is dark-skinned; this happens far too often. Broonzy himself expressed it beautifully in his unforgettable 'White, brown and black' with the refrain:

> If you're white, it's alright,
> But if you're brown you can get around,
> But if you're black, oh brother, get back, get back.

• Nothin' but the blues[464]

The folk music of the African-Americans is a curious phenomenon. It has made a huge impact, it is sometimes highly revered and yet it has remained relatively unknown. Negro spirituals: one of the greatest creations of the African-American slaves – a gift to the whole world. That is how they are spoken of, but usually with reference to very westernized forms only or commercial versions, like the streamlined performances by many small choirs that are mistaken for authentic spirituals.

Another surprising feature is that, with the exception of my own work and a few short paragraphs in books on jazz, no study on the development of the Negro spiritual after about 1870 has ever been published. The blues has scarcely fared better. A few extensive studies recently appeared in publications solely dedicated to the subject. But because blues music itself is foreign territory to the readers, many will find the books virtually incomprehensible. It is the same old story: dozens of commercial offshoots and by-products. Then there is Bessie Smith's work which, although it may be very good, can only provide a one-sided view of the music. Likewise, the mood and nature of blues music that has been grafted onto all manner of jazz is hardly recognizable as such in most cases.

Alongside a number of EPs on Fontana devoted to various blues singers, I have attempted to capture the versatility of the real blues on a LP on the same label.[465] I have tried to highlight in a comprehensive way the great diversity of the blues. The blues is a very strangely balanced and exceptionally beautiful form of folk song. The twelve-bar scheme arranged as three musical phrases of four bars, the second line of the text being a repetition of the first line, with a conclusion in the last line, built on a very simple progression of chords, gives a wealth of possibilities. The rural blues, the urban blues, the jazzier blues of Bessie Smith, Clara Smith, Ruby Smith and others, each has its own character and style, and in each genre the singer can apply a personal style to the rendition of the blues.

As to its content, which is nurtured by the lyrics and refined by rendition and instrumentation, the blues is anything but a superficial sort of folk music. Its depth, its multi-level content, the strange cocktail of melancholy, humour, pessimism and optimism, and its simplicity which is not the result of poverty, fascinates and surprises the listener again and again. Lack of space prevents me from elaborating on the blues, its musical structure, its content and style; listening to the music will be more effective.

This record is compiled as follows: I have devoted one side to vocal blues whereby the various genres are as well represented as possible. That was not so difficult since a great number of recordings have been released in a series for merchandising within the black communities, of which little was obtainable through the usual channels. Some of it was re-released, but a great deal is known only to specialist collectors. The flip side of the record is devoted entirely to instrumental blues, namely blues played by jazz bands. This side turned out to be much harder to compile. What I had in mind was to include only the records that have never before been released in Europe, and particularly those that were both musically accomplished and reflected the authentic mood of the blues as closely as possible. We have also tried to give the side a certain musical unity. It is a frequent criticism of compilation records that the pieces are so diverse in character that it becomes a sort of random mishmash. It is up to the listener to decide whether our plan has succeeded; we were certainly grateful for some positive reviews.

Fontana has created a beautiful sleeve: the introductory text is generously spaced giving the whole album a handsome appearance, and the technical skill with which the recordings have been copied is almost ideal.

Spirituals and Gospel

- **Let's sing the old Dr Watts: a chapter in the history of Negro spirituals**[466]

African-American music has been the subject of more books and articles than any other type of folk music. Apart from its intrinsic quality this is mainly to be attributed to the simple fact that this music has had a major influence on entertainment music in the white world of Western[467] culture, beginning in the nineteenth century with the kind of minstrel music Stephen Foster used to compose, through ragtime to swing and modern jazz. As anyone knows who has some knowledge of real jazz and blues, there is often behind this coarse and superficial adaptation of some aspects of true African-American music that very music itself, and this has inspired many persons to undertake a thorough study of its history and background. Here we must stress the reality of its intrinsic qualities, since without these the real and sustained interest in the often old and sometimes very poorly recorded music of the African-Americans would be unintelligible.

The religious songs of the blacks have not been accorded this wide interest. Some of the older forms have inspired musicologists to look for the sources of this type of music, searching out the African and Western influences. But, surprisingly, they have often neglected to look at the recorded music and have confined themselves to scored songs – and scores, as might be obvious to anyone who has heard this music on record or 'live', do not give any real knowledge of the true nature of this music. This may be a mistake that is inherent in many a folk music study made in the past. Thus George Pullen Jackson in his *White Spirituals in the Southern Uplands*[468] claims to have discovered the 'sacred harp' type of religious white singing, of which no student of white folk songs had seemed to be aware, although there were already many records of this type of singing to be found if one cared to look for them. It was not before the justly famous series of recordings made by John and Alan Lomax in the 1930s for the Library of Congress that recordings began to play a part in the study of the less obvious types of black songs and music in the USA.

Still, the spirituals and gospel songs seem to have been largely neglected. This is the more surprising when one realizes that not only in the last century but up till today they were and are sung in all black churches in the United States by the congregation, and also by professional groups at all kinds of meetings; since the early 1920s literally thousands of records of spirituals, gospel songs and even sermons have been issued in the so-called Race series to be distributed and sold in black quarters. Yet the paragraphs concerning black religious songs which one does frequently encounter in books on African-Americans are very often nothing more than passing comments on the early forms; in the major studies devoted to the history of jazz and blues one finds also this type of comment, as religious music is seen only in relation to the early history of these secular types of music. It seems that almost everybody is ignorant of (or wants to ignore) what goes on in the black churches or in the religious life of the African-American people.

Thus when I named my book on American black music *Jazz, Blues and Spirituals*,[469] many critics thought this an embarrassment. But I chose the title with a purpose: it has a better ring to it than any other sequence of the nouns would have, and I wanted to attract attention to the fact that I had looked for the history of American black music in the interrelation of these three main types (and some minor ones), believing that the religious type is just now, in our own time, at its peak. Spirituals and gospel songs are not relics of the past; precisely their present development is in many respects the most interesting, and certainly so from the point of view of quality and enjoyable listening.

Apart from the reasons stated above that gave rise to many misunderstandings of the true import of the black religious songs, it must be noted that for many people, especially for musicologists, Negro spirituals were almost always identical with those spirituals sung by choirs like the Fisk Jubilee Singers and a few individual singers trained in the Western tradition such as Marian Anderson and Roland Hayes. Such an identification mistakenly equates their renderings of the above with true black religious songs, thereby missing the original traditions.

What must be stressed here is that the type of music we are talking about cannot be evaluated without a wide knowledge of jazz, blues and folk songs and their history, and without listening to often rather rare recordings. Since the 1930s, through the work of historians such as Ramsey and Smith, Blesh[470] and others, and of critics and discophiles writing in many jazz magazines, the great bulk of recorded jazz (or what goes under that name) has been critically sifted, making the whole activity of re-issuing and studying old recordings possible. The same has still to he done, however, with recorded spirituals and gospel songs.

One of the truly surprising but very rewarding aspects of African-American music is found in the fact that almost all facets of its long history can be heard on record – genuine instrumental ragtime, for example, can be studied from the Riverside *(379)* recording by the Love-Jiles Ragtime Orchestra in 1960, although this music belongs historically to 1900. The same applies to religious music, and we are able to hear on record even the oldest types.

As a historian and a lover of the music involved, I will take the historical approach in preference to the musicological one. I shall, therefore, avoid discussions of scales, meters and such technical musical aspects. Rather, I shall try to set forth some general historical observations, leaving much further study, of course, to be done.

In seventeenth-century New England there was a great immigration of Europeans, mostly nonconformist English who, like the Pilgrim Fathers, settled there because they had not felt secure and happy under the religious pressures put on them by the English monarchy. They were Puritans, 'independent' in their church governmental theories but having a general theological tradition which revealed the influence of the Genevan Reformation. Basic to their religious outlook however was a mysticism that goes back to the late Middle Ages.[471]

What interests us most is the type of song they used. The standard picture of the gloomy and ultra-solemn Puritan, abstaining from all music, joy or humour has been proved to be entirely wrong;[472] actually much of English folksong was imported to New England through them. However, they had some peculiar inhibitions concerning church music, which, according to their opinion, had to be plain and solemn.

The psalms were imported to England by the Calvinists in the second half of the sixteenth century. Calvin had taken great pains to have the psalms made available for church singing, and the Calvinist Reformation won many a friend through this new and lively, joyful way of singing together. These psalms were scorned by the Anglican party as 'Geneva jigs' or 'Beza ballads'. Many English adaptations were made of the Genevan Psalter, notably the *Ainsworth Psalter*, printed in Amsterdam in 1612 on behalf of those who later were known as the Pilgrim Fathers. Very well known also was the *Bay Psalm Book*, published in 1640 in Cambridge, Massachusetts, of which the music was set by Ravenscroft.

But the typical Puritan mysticism that demanded holiness in all matters concerning faith and church life, meaning by 'holiness' a character that was the opposite of 'worldly', made these believers somewhat suspicious towards art and beauty. So they started to sing the psalms slower and slower, until they were sung extremely slowly – so slowly that it was almost impossible for the singers to sing the note to the full lengh of the syllable. Hence they added little 'grace notes', a kind of embellishment to make the very slow singing possible – in a sense they returned to the melismatic practices of the late Middle Ages. But, since people added these notes in their own peculiar ways, congregational singing acquired thereby a curiously ragged quality; the slowly moving melodic line of the chant was sung as if it had torn edges.

Another peculiarity of this early type of psalm singing was 'lining out'. Each line was first said by the precentor and then sung by the congregation. So one would hear alternately a solo voice saying the line and then, slowly and falteringly, the same line sung all together. As far as I know, though this type of singing still takes place in some churches holding to Puritan traditions, it has never been recorded by a regular record company for ordinary sale. The only recorded example I know of was made in 1959 by Alan Lomax in the Mount Olive Regular Baptist Church, Blackey, Kentucky – 'Primitive old Regular Baptists'[473] – whose members are called 'hard shell' by the locals. Noteworthy, also in this recording, is the way in which the sermon is shouted, sung, moaned, groaned, with rhetorical outbursts that lend this type of preaching a musical twist, almost certainly beyond any conscious intentions of the preacher. Although it lacks something of the fine rhythmic feeling that makes itself felt in many black sermons, in rhetorical make-up and passionate flow of words it is representative.

In addition to the above-mentioned features of Puritan singing, the legacy of African music has been also of great importance for the formation of the African-American song. African music is not always accompanied by drums, tom-toms, and so on. On the contrary, one can almost say that only music of a solemn nature, with a religious or 'official' purpose, has this polyrhythmic accompaniment. Songs sung as magical incantations at religious meetings with dancing and other ceremonies normally are accompanied; thus we can appreciate the fine rhythm orchestra of the royal chapel of the king of the Abatutsis.[474] Many other folk songs go unaccompanied, as anyone knows who has heard recordings of African music.

The songs sung at the religious ceremonies are usually slow and solemn, such as 'Orin Muritali Alhaji' from Nigeria.[475] Listening to this music we become aware of the fact that it is not strange to our ears, quite unlike Chinese or Arabian music which sounds unfamiliar and can be rather difficult to understand for Western ears. African music in its scales and general melodic structure is quite close to the older types of European folk music – for example, one finds pentatonic scales in both African and Scottish music. However, there is one general feature of African music that is seldom found in European singing: responsive singing, as heard in the 'Nago dance'[476] wherein the priestess sings her part alone, answered by the whole group singing the second part of the song together as a kind of refrain.

Keeping all the foregoing in mind we can easily understand what happened to the blacks when they were brought to North America in the seventeenth century, where they entered a dominantly Protestant society strongly influenced by the Puritan ethos emanating from the New England colonies, and where their owners took much concern for their spiritual welfare. They became Christians and entered the churches.

In Central and South America the blacks came to large plantations, owned for the most part by French or Spanish absentee landlords. Roman Catholic missionary work affected their religious life very superficially, so that here African cults in the form of Voodoo and African music and folklore persisted more strongly. The history of the spirituals we are relating is almost exclusively a North-American and a Protestant phenomenon.

When blacks entered Puritan churches in the seventeenth century they heard psalms being sung, lined out and very slowly. To the Africans they sounded less strange, however, than they sound to us today. The 'lining-out' they understood as responsive singing of a slow, solemn melody, alternating between soloist and group, not unlike their own songs at serious occasions. The scales were, if not very familiar, at least not strange or entirely foreign to their ears. That the drums were inactive would seem to be quite natural, for these songs were addressed to God, quite different from the deities or powers which they had tried to overpower magically by their chants in Africa. Thus, however surprising to us, Puritan psalmody was readily adapted for the African ear. They assimilated the psalms so eagerly that, even today, one can hear these songs sung in this way when one enters a black church in the United States; and the influence of these songs cannot be overestimated, as we shall see presently.

Frequently these songs are announced as 'the old Dr Watts'. And so Dr Isaac Watts, an outstanding hymnodist of the nonconformist churches in England in the early eighteenth century, enters our picture. As will be recalled, he was very discontent with the way congregations sang, and in order to improve this he cast the psalms in new metrical versions and wrote quite a few hymns and spiritual songs as well as a number of treatises on congregational singing and on other theological issues. His success was enormous, as witnessed by the widespread acceptance of his compositions in the English-speaking world.[477]

However, the American Puritans kept to their old style of singing although they did accept Watts' hymns. In this respect Watts' intentions were fruitless. When a black preacher says 'Let's sing the old Dr Watts' in his introduction to a hymn, one can be certain to hear singing in the old style described above. It is not inevitable that the songs referred to by such an announcement among black churchgoers will be the actual songs written by Watts himself, but one can be sure that the song is old. For example, in a recording by H. Courlander in 1950 in a Baptist Church in Bogue Chitto, Alabama, wrongly called a prayer meeting, the fragment we hear is actually from Charles Wesley's 'A charge to keep I have'[478] wherein we hear lined out 'To serve the present age, my calling to fulfil'.[479] In the Greater Salem Baptist Church in Chicago (the church attended by Mahalia Jackson) I heard in 1961 a rendering of 'Rock of ages', sung five times as slow as by any white church congregation. Hymns sung in this 'Dr Watts' style can often be heard on Race records,[480] very often as an introduction to a sermon.[481]

As we have said before, these songs are sung in a slow, chanted way, with people frequently adding little notes to the long sustained syllables in order to be able to sing them. We can hear this more clearly when we listen to one person singing alone, a situation which is not at all strange or rare; church people often sing church songs alone at home while working just to make themselves feel happy. We can hear this on a record from Ramsay's Folkways series in which Mary Price sings 'Dark was the night'.[482] The song is hymn no. 250 (Common Meter, Canterbury) in the 1851 edition of Watts' songs cited. It is not at all sure that she used music; more probably she was singing it from memory. Quite often some changes occur in the texts of songs like these because they have become part of an oral tradlition. Mary Price sings this song lining out each new line, adding grace notes in a very fine way. The result is that we hear something that seems to be new; something that has nothing to do with European music. Often this newness has been traced to an African style of singing, but without any examples from Africa being advanced. The weird and wavering melody, weaving up and down, is actually nothing but the old melody sung very slow, although to us it does not sound slow because of the added grace notes.[483]

From this point we can pursue two possible directions. The first we shall only indicate: studying the importance of this type of spiritual song in the development of secular song. We guess that at least one of the major sources of the peculiar way of singing 'hollers' is the 'old Dr Watts' songs. Listen, for example, to Rich Amerson's 'Black woman'.[484] Not only does the quavering melodly remind us of the way Mary Price sings, but there is also a likeness in the way there is a stop in the flow of the melody when something is said in spoken words, not sung, precisely in the way lining out occurs in Dr Watts songs.

Another example in this connection is to be found on the Lomax's record *Murderer's Home*.[485] the holler 'Whoa black' (although here we must attribute the melody not to Dr Watts but rather to some hillbilly source, either white or black). The singer often stops to speak a line in a way appropriate to the performance, which indicates that the stopping is not simply at random but belongs to the 'order' of the holler as such. On the same record we could single out 'Tangle eye blues', a very fine holler of high musical qualities.

These hollers, less African in origin than people may often think, have perhaps been an important contributing factor in shaping the style of the blues. Blind Lemon Jefferson's singing suggests this in many instances, as does Big Bill Broonzy in his 'Hollerin' and cryin' the blues'.[486]

However, returning to the history of religious song, we must note the deep and wide influence of singing 'the old Dr Watts'. We should remind ourselves of the way the lines are sung in a Watts hymn – slowly, with flowing sliding figures upwards and downwards. Taking this melodic line as the key we can make some surprising discoveries. Thus we can more readily understand the very fine rendering of 'Dark was the night' by Blind Willie Johnson (1927).[487] Not only does this song belong in this context because of its title, the same as Mary Price's – nor are we surprised to find that the melody is carried forward in the same way – but we may further note that the way in which the guitar plays an independent, interweaving melody derives from the odd manner in which Watts' hymns are sung. Compare this also with the singing of this same song by Lewis Jackson and Charlotte Rucell:[488] the way these two voices each make their own line, each adding grace notes in their own way to the basic slow melody, yet blending together so well. It is reminiscent of what Blind Willie Johnson does, although admittedly his is good music and theirs is simply coarse religious singing of historical interest only. The only 'African' element in Blind Willie's rendering is his humming – Western tradition does not have this, but it is a quite common way of expression in black music both in Africa and in the United States.

The crude way of singing the hymns called 'Dr Watts', though rightly scorned by Watts himself, can make marvellously fine music when executed by true musicians. Listening to Mahalia Jackson's rendering of 'Amazing grace',[489] an eighteenth-century song, we may from what we have discovered above readily understand the background for her fine and to our unaccustomed ears sometimes fantastic figurations in the melodic flow. Many other church singers have sung in a similar vein: Sister Ernestine B. Washington sings 'The Lord is my shepherd' on a recording made in the Washington Temple in Brooklyn.[490] On the same LP she sings 'I trust in God' in this decorated style directly after the sermon. However, the recording engineer evidently did not understand the Dr Watts character of this performance, since he subdued the minister's voice that was lining out every sentence, so that now it can be heard only faintly. Cleophus Robinson often sings hymns very slowly and with a 'Dr Watts' phrasing.[491] Also Alex Bradford, known for his part in the show *Black Nativity*, often sings in this way.[492]

Among the rather infrequent renderings by gospel choirs or groups of a song in a genuine Dr Watts style is 'That awful day' sung by the Spirit of Memphis Quartet.[493] Here the lines are first 'shouted' by the soloist and then sung by the whole group of about seven men with some occasional free-flowing parts by one voice. They bring melody and harmony as well as structure and clarity to the whole rendering of the old hymn – about the finest performance in this style known to me.

But apart from such examples of 'Dr Watts' singing by gospel singers and groups of today in a more artful way we ought also to note the deep influence of this tradition upon all gospel singing. Quite often a rendering begins with a slow and forceful solo part, as in 'Go down Moses' by the Davis Sisters[494] or in 'Only a pilgrim' by the Christian Travelers,[495] the source of which lies undoubtedly in this tradition. Without taking account of its influence one cannot understand one of the main distinctive features of the art of gospel singing today.

We started by quoting an example of a white backwoods sermon in the South.[496] What seems now to be an odd and queer way of preaching was once rather normal and widespread. And it cannot be doubted that the peculiar way black preachers deliver their speeches, with rhetorical passages that are almost musically phrased, was patterned after these. The only important change that can be noted is the musicality and rhythmic feeling inherent in these sermons and prayers, qualities that can be noted on many Race records made in the 1920s or later; indeed recording of sermons has continued until the present so that today there are many LPs that give complete sermons, just as spoken at a church sevice. I speak here not of the folkloristic white recordings made for curiosity's sake, but of releases made for the black market, as on the labels Battle or Nashboro.

This preaching style has influenced the performance of many gospel songs that include spoken passages. Examples are the beginning of 'Walk on' by the Pilgrim Jubilee Singers[497] and the middle part of 'On Calvary' by the Spirit of Memphis Quartet.[498] But many more examples could be quoted. In fact, examples of the things dealt with here abound and can be heard on almost every recording of gospel singing.

Thus, while admitting Watts was right in thinking that the way of singing named, oddly enough, after himself was crude and quite unmusical, we must acknowledge that its influence on all types of black singing has been deep and has often led to results of moving beauty. This influence continues to be reinforced as these hymns are still sung in black churches, where their origin in the mystical tradition (not in the words, but in the way of performing) is remembered. It comes as a surprise, but is understandable in the light of is history, to find that in many black churches it is not so much the quick and forceful, rhythmic songs but rather the extremely slow singing of these old hymns that leads to a kind of 'going crazy' in the Spirit, and all that goes with that.[499]

• The Negro spiritual in church[500]

Although African-Americans were introduced to the gospel by Westerners, they developed their own, un-Western form of worship service. Songs sung in their own African-American style, neither Western nor African, have played a big role. Besides the more recent recordings of church services made for the purpose of research, hundreds of church-service recordings were made in the 1920s in series produced particularly for the African-American market. These gramophone records were intended to serve a purpose similar to that of (radio) broadcasts of church services today, namely evangelistic purposes. The sermons are of course brief and were recorded in the studio – the LP was to make its appearance only much later.

The first of the musical examples I will play in the broadcast is the recording of a church service in which the Revd McGee is preaching on Joshua 2–18. He begins by reading the text: 'Behold, when we come into the land, thou shalt bind this line of scarlet thread in the window, which thou let us down by.' Then he goes on to tell of the capture of Jericho using, almost exclusively, words taken from Scripture (Joshua 2–6):

> And Joshua the son of Nun sent out of Sittim two men to spy secretly, saying, Go view the land, even Jericho. And they went, and came into a harlot's house, named Rahab, and lodged there (Joshua 2:1) ... And the Lord said unto Joshua, See I have given into thine hand Jericho, and the king thereof, and the mighty men of valour. And ye shall compass the city, all ye men of war, and go round the city once. Thus thou shalt do six days. And the seven priests shall bear before the ark seven trumpets of ram's horns: And the seventh day ye shall compass the city seven times and the priests shall blow with the trumpets.

Next he tells of the effect of the screams of Israel's children: 'The walls came tumbling down.' Then a spiritual is sung with the following refrain:

> *Joshua fought the battle of Jericho, Jericho, Jericho* (x2)
> *And the walls came tumbling down.*

Note how musically the preacher's rendition is – almost a recitative. The members of the congregation are not sitting still while this is going on, but support him musically. While the sermons are not always as straightforward as this, pieces of Scripture are often retold exegetically. This can clearly be traced back to the times of slavery when it was forbidden to learn to read and write. The next church service starts with this spiritual:

> I shall not, I shall not be moved (x2)
> On my way to heaven I shall not be moved (x2)
> Just like a tree standing by the water,
> I shall not be moved.
> Jesus is my Captain, I shall not be moved (x2)
> Just like a tree standing by the water,
> I shall not be moved.

This is followed by the sermon and we hear the opening words: 'Glory, Hallelujah Amen. This morning my subject will be how God is using his power. And my text will be "the main key to heaven", and you will find my text in Hebrews, 11th chapter, 3rd verse. And we find that faith is the main key ...'

Not all these are recordings of real sermons. We often hear a lot of singing of authentic Negro spirituals, with a few exegetical remarks by the minister, like this one by the Revd Gates:

> There's one thing I know, once I was blind, but now I see. You sinners try to know too much. You can't know everything. I don't try to know everything. I don't know why a black cow gives white milk. I don't investigate, I just drink the milk. So you sinners, believe in Jesus Christ and be saved. Believe and be saved. I want to ask the congregation, everybody, to help me sing this song:
>
>> Lord, Lord, I done left this world behind,
>> I done crossed the separation-line and left the world behind.

Then the minister interjects once or twice with an adapted version of the refrain:

> Sometimes your soul gets happy and you feel like shouting, and you don't care what the world says. Oh, when you crossed the separation-line, and left the world behind, you want everybody to know how glad you are. Pray on, pray on, please do.

Musically speaking, this is not part of our (white) Western world, but although the form of their services is different and the Baptist or Methodist influence is sometimes quite evident, we still recognize that these are our brothers and sisters in the Lord. They are not ashamed of their faith and, above all, they give the Lord due praise in their song.

• Spirituals in concert form[501]

Directly after the American Civil War, universities were built to give 'liberated' black slaves the education that would enable them to sustain their new position. This is how the Fisk University (among others) originated and that university employed a music lecturer by the name of White. He instructed his students in a Western way. Their own folk songs and in particular the Negro spirituals, which were their own Christian songs, were too primitive and uncivilized for his liking. So he taught them to sing these in a Western fashion. In order to do this, the Western harmonic system had to be adopted. However, this turned out to be more complicated than White had anticipated, since black music was based on a more or less pure pentatonic scale and was directly linked to speech melody. It became necessary to adapt the melodies to Western harmonic requirements and in order to do so to introduce foreign elements into these songs. Black vocal music does not, for example, make a distinction between a major and minor third, and it lacks the seventh, which as the leading tone is so important to the Western system. So the original Negro spiritual had to undergo quite an overhaul before it could fulfil the demands of westernization. Also the polyrhythm, inherent to black music, seemed impossible to write down. It is much more complex than just syncopation, often placing accents in a very un-Western way and readily combining contrasting melody rhythms. So the harmony was given a much greater role than in the authentic songs, while rhythms were often simplified.

The Fisk Jubilee Singers took these adapted Negro spirituals across the USA and Europe and used their earnings to fund the building of their university. Thousands of people were thus introduced to the marvellous treasure of the songs of the African-Americans. The interest of the listener had been aroused and it would stay that way. Many serious musicians and music lovers – like Dvorak during his stay in the USA –

became engrossed in it. The appreciation of authentic African-American music in its natural – original and unrefined – form was to take much longer to develop, and even now it is not as popular as one would expect, given the growing interest in folk music.

As we have mentioned, the adaptation of the Negro spiritual by the students of Fisk University was just the beginning of a far-reaching movement. Educated blacks in particular dedicated themselves to the cause and we would like to put one of them, Roland Hayes, at the top of the list. The highlights of his work have now been brought together beautifully on a LP that has recently been released. This tenor, who has a beautiful voice, has immersed himself for years in the music of his people and, unlike Marion Anderson, has concentrated all his artistic skill on it. If we could compare him with anyone it would be with Benjamin Britten who likewise adapted the treasure of Anglo-Saxon folk songs to suit the concert hall. You can judge the nature and scope of that work by comparing Hayes' interpretation of 'Little boy, how old are you?' with the much more authentically black version by Revd Kelsey and his congregation.

The record is not a loose collection of songs but has been arranged to form a summary of the life and works of Jesus Christ – a sort of Passion, if you like. One realizes what beautiful songs these are and, although sometimes far-removed from the authentic folk music, how sensitive and moving this music with its discerning piano accompaniment actually is. The characteristic poetry used by blacks to express the biblical message suddenly becomes accessible to the Western ear. There is no point in disparaging the music vis-à-vis folk music. We must bear in mind that the rendition is of a very high quality and well considered and it does not treat the spiritual as a merely sentimental encore to a recital of Western classical music.

The logical sequence of the songs in their historical setting sometimes gives an extra dimension to their content. The song about Peter's commission, however, should have come after the Passion and Resurrection. Incidentally, that song is also one of the most striking and outstanding, in which Roland Hayes sings:

> You hear the lambs a-cryin'
> Oh, shepherd feed my sheep.
> My Saviour spoke these words so sweet.
> 'Peter, if you love me, feed my sheep'
> 'Lord, I love Thee, Thou dost know:
> Oh give me grace to love Thee more.'
> You hear the lambs a-cryin'
> Oh, shepherd feed my sheep.

• Voices of victory[502]

Is this music authentic? Are these real Negro spirituals? These are questions that almost immediately spring to mind when we listen to the record of spirituals sung by the choir of the Victory Baptist Church in Los Angeles, California.

A possible counter question would be, What is 'authentic'? Does authentic music include only that music which is sung now in the same way as it was a century ago? Does amateurism and lack of practice have to become apparent before we may use the term? Does it always have to be old, undeveloped, spontaneous and direct in order to warrant being called 'authentic'? Indeed, the use of the term with respect to folk music often gives sufficient fuel for debate. It is particularly so when we speak of the music of African-Americans, who have gone through so much and have been subjected to so many great changes and spiritual displacements that have left their marks.

In any case, the choral singing on this record is not authentic, if by authentic you mean that this music came into being all by itself and that it was preserved in embryonic form from time immemorial, aside from any cultural development. But why should we not use the word authentic here? After all, this record is a real act of cultural achievement – a pure reflection of what moved the soul. On this record we hear a few newly contrived spirituals that still remain completely faithful to the traditional context. Most of the spirituals however are old and developed long ago when blacks created their own musical culture, in conformity with a strong faith in the God of the Bible and his Son, as an expression of their faith, hope and love, in a biblical sense.

Since the emergence of these songs, much has happened however. Liberation came, followed anew by much trouble and oppression. Both continue to exist, but blacks were increasingly able to find their own space and secure their social status. Blacks were encouraged when they discovered that whites greatly admired their bounty of songs. They noticed that adjusting to Western cultural norms meant a step towards emancipation and social equality. They began to refine their spirituals, which were neither African nor Western, so that they would sound better to the ears of the whites. The songs certainly lost some of their typical black character, yes, their essence. Songs of faith became nice songs, music that brought social recognition and appreciation. Blacks sought civilization and development in the Western sense, and where biblical faith did not really affect the hearts of people they happily adopted a liberal faith for the sake of being in touch and up to date. Elsewhere, though we will not discuss that in detail here, a completely modern Western spirit in an existentialistic sense took hold of many of them, and that found expression in modern jazz, bop and cool.

So, alongside those who stayed with the old legacy and the ancestral faith, whose song for that reason may be called authentic, like the Spirit of Memphis Quartet, came others who were more progressive in the sense that they were actively seeking emancipation – and equality with whites. If necessary they would have gone as far as denying their cultural past. But they did not need to do this, as it was their own treasury of songs that brought them recognition all over the world. Was that not why Roland Hayes and Marion Anderson were so admired? Yes, was it not jazz and black music that conquered the world? To deny that tradition would also deprive them of a powerful ally that could help them seize their own space. It is not so easy to set aside all that their ancestors brought – and the communities that held on to the old ways because they adhered to the biblical faith were protective of it, and thus kept alive (the memories of) their own culture.

We have taken up this discussion because it explains the record of the Voices of Victory. Listen to the poetry that is recited in 'I am somebody': 'I am somebody, I won a place for myself, because just listen, are Roland Hayes and Marion Anderson not black too, and Joe Louis and the comedian Bert Williams, and that world champion and that popular cabaret artist?' All kinds of celebrities are mentioned, who would be utterly foreign to orthodox black Christians in their lifestyle and social environment. For it seems to me that this church is not founded and built on biblical faith in God and Christ, but on the pursuit of emancipation. The sermon is traditional, but its content is without question moralistically liberal.

From this point of view and from the point of view of the cultural situation however, this music is authentic – a true expression of what moves these black people. Fortunately they are aware of the character of the spirituals to the extent that they do not strive to romanticize it, and we are spared pathos, with all that rallentando etc. It is a wonderful choir – and sing they can; musically speaking this is alive and real. The wealth of songs that is drawn upon is rich and versatile. Alongside the music by the Spirit of Memphis Quartet, for example, and alongside the songs we hear on Folkways records, recorded in the outback of Alabama, this too is an expression of what lives in the African-American soul – as long as we remember that we are dealing here with very different people, people who seek their faith and their hope in emancipation and are in pursuit of social recognition and equality with whites.

Researching American black music is rich, not only because there is so much of beauty to be heard but also because by listening to it, with a wealth of recorded examples, we can keep track of how social and religious differences express themselves directly in the music itself. This music is authentic and plays an integral role in any attempt to form a true picture of the music of the African-Americans.

• Two church services in Harlem[503]

Around 1870 the Fisk Jubilee Singers performed Negro spirituals in front of mixed audiences in Europe and the USA. They were so successful that the songs have attracted a great deal of interest ever since. The interest often was not bereft of sentimentality, however, and seldom it developed into a real love for the music of the blacks; it was generally a case of a random encounter without any serious attempt to understand the music.

There has always been a small circle of dedicated collectors interested in the rare gramophone records of the 1920s and early 1930s that were released in the Race series and sold exclusively in black neighbourhoods. The last few decades, however, has seen the re-release of some of this authentic music on London, for instance, and as educational recordings like those on Folkways. Gradually the music has been reaching a wider audience. Though this audience still consists primarily of jazz lovers and connoisseurs, it has become apparent that real black music is quite different from the familiar renditions by Marian Anderson or Ronald Hayes, not to mention Robeson. The popular choirs and vocalists might have been well trained, but they sound positively Schubertian. As with the folk music of other races, listeners have learned to appreciate this folk music for its own merits.

Now there is a new acquisition in this slowly expanding area: the Ducretet-Thomson release of two church services in Harlem recorded on respectively Christmas Day and New Year's Eve in 1955. In marked contrast to almost all the earlier forms, this singing does not in any way strive to comply with the norms of Western concert music and singing. All pretence is shunned. We hear a church service, unarranged, untouched by the hand of a director. The authentic black song never gives any satisfaction to those who long for sentimentality – to the contrary. 'My Lord is my shepherd' for example, is a clear and spiritedly rendered song, and its joyful exuberance, which remains controlled, will in no way induce the shedding of that obligatory tear, as for instance in 'Nobody knows the trouble I have seen'. This record will not satisfy those looking for such a sort of Negro spiritual. Rather, this is for lovers of folk music – for those enthusiasts and connoisseurs looking for the authentic, without a trace of commercial or propagandistic flavour. Indeed, these church services have nothing artificial about them. They have nothing to do with art at all. The only essential difference between this and any other church service anywhere else in the world is that the American blacks enjoy their singing and sing very well, in natural harmony.

The church service is held in a small, storefront church and the sermon is already in progress when our recording begins. We hear a sort of parable with practical instructions. It would have been called an *exempla* in the Middle Ages. This method of preaching is quite common in the USA (and in England). Then comes a gospel song with piano accompaniment – a contemporary black composition following the pattern of Anglo-American hymns. A member of the congregation then tells of his or her conversion. Indeed, there is little to set this church service apart from any other. Another gospel song is sung, this time one with a stronger Negro-spiritual character, followed by a full-blooded Western hymn 'Blest be the tie that binds', music by Fawcett (1740-1817) and words by H.G. Nägeli (1768-1836), which is apparently a popular hymn because we came across it in the *Song and Service Book for Ship and Field* (no. 99) published by the American Government in 1942. After a short prayer of thanks comes the 'Amen'.

On the flip side we hear a New Year's Eve service from a similar sort of church. It is strange that there is virtually no difference in song, liturgy and sermon between the churches in Harlem and those in the South, be they urban or rural. The recording begins with a particularly well-sung spiritual, 'My Lord is my Shepherd'. Its structure conforms to that of an authentic Negro spiritual, i.e. the religious or sacred song created by indigenous African-Americans in the nineteenth century. The structure and composition of both words and music of these songs are very different from that of gospel songs and white hymns, though the content is closely related or similar. This becomes apparent when we compare this song with its fierce rendition with the white hymn that follows, which is of a much softer nature – a typical example. We hear a short sermon, followed by a prayer softly cued in by the organ. Unfortunately the minister was out of range of the microphone so that it is hard to make out what he is saying, and the voices of some members of the congregation agreeing with him – 'that's the truth', and similar exclamations – dominate and sometimes drown him out. The service concludes with a gospel song.

All in all, this record gives a good representation of the sort of church service, as described by many a travelogue or tourist who have visited the USA. In terms of time, much more is spent on singing than on preaching. To reiterate, this singing is not art, but the very absence of the artificial (or contrived) makes it more real and stirring than the works of large, trained choirs which sing so 'nicely'.

• The African-American church service in the USA[504]

Writing on this subject in brief is no easy matter. First and foremost we have to realize that there are vast differences between one black church and the next, between a rural church and an urban church, as we find in New York, Chicago or Washington, between churches attended by poor labourers and cleaners and churches consisting of educated members – with their solemn hymns – who try to mimic the 'dignified' singing of the whites. On the other hand, perhaps there really is such thing as a typical black church, a church in which you can sense that blacks have their own culture, and that black culture is different from white culture. In trying to identify what it is that is different we can disregard dogmas; most of these churches are orthodox with some degree of Pentecostalism. Neither do we need to examine the liturgical differences. The declamatory sermons – more like eulogies than exegeses – are equally a feature of some white churches. We are just as unlikely to find it in the nature of the hymns, which are not really that different from what you might hear in white circles. In fact, the characteristic feature of these churches lies exclusively in their great musicality, both the exceptional sense of rhythm and the melodic qualities.

During my stay in the USA I was privileged to attend several services in otherwise exclusively black churches. Let me tell you about my experience by describing one of these services. It started at around 10 a.m. with Sunday school. The men sat together in small groups, as did the women, the boys, the girls, and the small children. The groups read and discussed a passage from the Bible, and this concluded at 10.50 a.m. The service itself began at around 11 o'clock with the congregation singing 'Amen, Amen' slowly and rhythmically. One of the elders prayed aloud. Next the choir entered, men and women dressed in long, coloured robes, strutting rhythmically as they made their way to the front and seated themselves on either side of the pulpit. One or two songs were sung, a soloist sang, another prayer was said, the collection was held, visitors were welcomed and the week's agenda was announced, all interspersed by choral song. Sometimes the congregation joined in and sometimes the choir sang alone, but if the song sounded good many members of the congregation would stand up and start clapping to the rhythm. It was all part and parcel of the service, for how else does one praise the Lord? That is their motivation and in support they quote Psalm 47. Incidentally we never managed to clap along because they clap on the second and fourth beats and not on the first and third ones as we are accustomed to.

• Visiting Mahalia Jackson[505]

In October last year I spent a week lecturing at Calvin College in Grand Rapids. The final Saturday I was to travel to Chicago, so I phoned Mahalia Jackson and asked which church she attended and what time their service began. She was not at home, but someone else gave me the information I needed. That Sunday morning I went to her church, the Greater Salem Baptist Church, a large church in the middle of a black area of South Chicago. Chicago is an enormous city that covers an area possibly as large as the province of South Holland. My friend, a professor from Trinity College in Worth (a suburb of Chicago), and I were the only whites in the church. The service began at 11 a.m. and finished at 2 p.m. As we were leaving the church, a woman suddenly appeared next to me and announced, 'I'm Mahalia.' Then she asked me who I was and I had to introduce myself.

Afterwards I asked her whether I might take a couple of photos of her in front of the church. So as to avoid any misunderstanding we posed in front of the board upon which the name of the church is written – a typical feature of American churches. When my American friend had taken the photos, Mahalia invited me to visit her. I asked whether my friend – for whom even though he was American all this was as new as it would be to most Dutch people – might accompany me.

So that is how we came to be at her house the next evening. She lived at 8358 South Indiana, one of the big roads running from north to south. (The numbering of each block begins with the consecutive hundred – hence the high number.) Since there were eight blocks to a mile, one can work out that her house lay exactly 10 miles from Madison Street, the road running east to west that starts at nought and marks the divide between North and South Chicago. One can also figure out that her house is situated close to the corner of the 83rd street because, with the exception of a few city-centre streets, all east-west streets are numbered.) Her house is situated in a good neighbourhood in the black area of South Side Chicago, where there is a lot of detached property.

The house is a bit old-fashioned – conventional, you might say, with many bric-a-brac. But that seems to be part of their culture and nothing extraordinary. The house was neat and tidy. As soon as I walked in, Mahalia asked whether I wanted to interview her. I explained that I was not a journalist and that I did not intend to interview her. And before long we were chatting away. I asked all sorts of questions about the services in her church, such as why there were several choirs, one behind the pulpit and two more, one along each side of the church. She told me that the first choir sang traditional spirituals while the other ones sang the newer sort of gospel songs.

I asked her about her relationship with the blues as sung by Bessie Smith. She told me that there were strange stories going around, claiming that she had been one of Bessie Smith's pupils, but nothing was further from the truth. But in her youth in the New Orleans of the 1920s it would have been impossible not to hear Bessie Smith regularly, for many people were playing her music on their gramophones.

We proceeded to discuss at length the bands that accompanied her on her records. She herself preferred a simple piano accompaniment and/or organ – the usual accompaniment for female vocalists. She said that all the elaborate and jazzy accompaniments on her records were in fact the work of the recording companies. We then listened to a couple of her records.

Later I showed her my book and she checked the lyrics I had selected as examples. Fortunately they were correct. Then she autographed her photo in my book.

She also told me about a new tour (of the USA), soon to start. I would like to mention this here. We must understand that there are hordes of singers like her in the black churches in the USA. She is not a unique or novel phenomenon. What is strange, however, is that even in America white audiences seem completely oblivious to this thriving gospel singing in black churches. They simply do not know the first thing about it. It may be as a result of the exceptional quality of her voice and rendition – she is certainly a class apart – that she has traversed across the boundaries separating the world of the blacks from that of the whites, and she now sings almost exclusively for white audiences. This demands quite a different approach, namely a controlled performance with little movement, quite different from what black audiences want. Black female singers are very uninhibited in front of their own audiences, not so much musically – that is not what I am getting at. A black singer might perform as follows: she begins by talking a bit and then starts singing, sometimes leaving the stage and wandering around the floor, while the black audience also express their approval of the texts – something that is very important to them – by clapping along, standing up when they are enjoying it and sometimes even joining in with parts of the song or forming a sort of accompaniment. A female singer singing to a black audience would find it very odd and irritating if everybody kept quiet. That would be interpreted as criticism – a sign of disinterest. Because Mahalia has adjusted to the behaviour of white audiences and performs with distinguished restraint, black audiences do not favour her so much anymore. Mahalia has thankfully made no concessions in her style of singing.

Mahalia Jackson and the many other female vocalists along with larger and smaller choirs represent a living church music tradition that is still unfolding. It has nothing at all to do with evangelism – it is simply church art in the form of music, just like that of Schütz and Bach and so many others. It is music to the glory of God, to sing his praise and testify to what he has done for his people.

A few days after I had visited Mahalia, I was invited to visit Thomas A. Dorsey, an old black man who once was a blues singer. Since 1930 – when he became a Christian – he has turned to composing church music. This man is the leader of the National Convention of Gospel Choirs and has played such an important role in developing modern gospel that he may be called the creator of it. He composed many of the songs Mahalia sings. Like Mahalia, he too lives on South Indiana Avenue in Chicago, just 10 blocks away from her. He publishes his compositions in manuscript form and they are available in gospel stores or black bookshops selling Christian literature and music. He is a very important man in this world, which is much greater and more extensive than is often supposed.

• USA 1961 [506]

September 1961. 'Hello, you are speaking with Rookmaaker from the Netherlands.' 'Well, why don't you come over tonight?' answers Len Kunstadt from Brooklyn, the famous collector and the publisher of *Record Research*.

After a long journey I finally arrived at Grand Avenue (though there is nothing very grand about it) where Len, an incredibly enthusiastic young man of about thirty, completely aware of all that is and has been going on in NYC, apologized with, 'I'm terribly sorry. I forgot I had another appointment, but do come along with me.'

That is how, ten minutes later, I came to be sitting in Victoria Spivey's home. She is a well-known blues singer who has been working hard at her comeback. The three of us left for Central Plaza, where a band was playing including musicians Wingy Mannone, Toni Parenti, Gene Sedric, Zutty Singleton and the very good trombonist Conrad Janis. Len made sure that I was introduced to everyone and so, a few days after seeing the Manhattan skyline for the first time, there I was amongst musicians. The music was good, with a sort of Dixielandish Chicago style.

I have met Victoria Spivey several times since. Shortly after our first meeting she gave her first concert for several years, together with Lonnie Johnson at the Gerdes Folk Music Centre in 4th Street. Lonnie was also making his second debut there. His style and voice have not changed since the 1930s. The audience was very enthusiastic. Those who want to hear what I experienced there should listen to the Prestige Bluesville 1044 recording of Lonnie with Victoria. What struck me was the pleasant atmosphere between the musicians. Ellington helped Lonnie to make his comeback with a guest appearance that November in New York. The place was full of friends of Lonnie's, all of them musicians. He was very nervous at first but once he got going he was his old self and was able to convince each member of the audience that he was still in complete control of his guitar and voice.

These sort of encounters are curious. Up till then Lonnie had been to me a sort of mythical figure that could be heard on a number of rare recordings from a colourful though very distant past. And then, suddenly, one is standing next to the very man, chatting away.

America is a wealthy country but the black neighbourhoods are not much better than the 'Jordaan' area in Amsterdam (or the Brixton area in East Ham). Victoria Spivey lives on the third floor of a rear block in a humbly furnished room that did not even contain a piano; how she is able to manage the keys so skillfully is a mystery. But recordings of her work are being released regularly now and *Record Research* advertises them, so perhaps things are improving for her. Decent housing for blacks is rare and expensive. The well-known poet and writer, Langston Hughes (whose successes include *Tambourines to Glory*), lives in Harlem in anything but a villa. Even more so, the warm-heartedness of these people, their lively interest and the intensity of their lives bely their outward circumstances.

In Chicago I had a stroke of luck. I had phoned Mahalia Jackson beforehand to find out which church she attended. After the service she came to meet me and invited me to her home. She lived in one of the best neighbourhoods of the South Side of Chicago, in a detached house, very neat and tidy though somewhat old-fashioned by our tastes. We talked mostly about the church services and the place of music in church, also about the accompaniment to her recordings. She was not very happy with the latter, as she felt the producers at Columbia compelled her to have a jazzy backing while she preferred much simpler piano accompaniments, as she had when she was on tour in the Netherlands.

I also met John Steiner, the great Chicago-jazz expert. It is a pity he has never written a book since he has extensive historical knowledge and also knows all the musicians personally. While visiting I listened to some of his fantastic collection of tapes and records. He took me to a performance by Franz Jackson's band where Bob Schoffner, the trumpet player, was particularly exceptional; he had previously played with Oliver in the time of the Dixie Syncopators and told me that he had not been able to play for two years round 1927 as a result of a lip ailment and had remained unknown for that reason. Those were, after all, decisive years in the history of jazz. The Frank Jackson's band also made a number of records (on Pinnacle, for instance) but not as impressive as what I heard that evening. In any case, they give us an idea of what Schoffner is capable of. He is not unlike a young Armstrong .

In Chicago I also heard Revd Cobb's congregation sing. That was really quite an experience. Three choirs, each numbering a hundred men and women, sang with great composure and tremendous enthusiasm the one well-rehearsed number after the other – at least that is how it was in this church concert. I spent most of my time investigating the living church music, the singing of bands like the Staple Singers, the Davis Sisters, and many, many more. Much is happening in this area; the music is alive and constantly evolving. Not only do new songs keep on emerging but the style, too, is changing fast. The vocal style is firmly rooted in tradition but not traditionalist. There is an incredible number of bands and church choirs around – almost every large church has at least three. It is odd that most of this development has passed the Netherlands by. We need not feel too ashamed, however, as few white Americans know anything about it. One has to go to the churches and to the gospel concerts that are held in black neighbourhoods where there is hardly a white to be seen. The records too are sold almost exclusively in the black neighbourhoods.

On my final days in the USA (December 1961) I watched the premiere of *Black Nativity*, which has since been performed and televized in the Netherlands. It was something completely novel for that sort of play to be shown on Broadway, even by New York standards, and the *New York Times'* critic did not know what to do with it either. But it is no wonder this music is coming to the fore. It is like a river of song and singing bursting its banks and washing into the white world. Mahalia Jackson was the first, but there is a vast amount of this type of music, much of which is good. There is also commercial music of this sort circulating (but only for black audiences in the USA) and this is the type of music that is easiest to hear and come by, for instance the records of the Golden Gate Quartet. This is an area that requires weighing up and sifting through just as has been done with jazz and dance music, to enable us to distinguish what is good and to record it in writing as well. I must say that I was pleased not to have to alter my views that I set forth in my book *Jazz, Blues and Spirituals* too much. That does not, of course, alter the fact that experiencing the live music and coming into contact with those who contribute to it (like Thomas A. Dorsey, to whom I may come back at another time) has bestowed reality and richness to my views.

In conclusion I would like to comment on two things. A big surprise was to befall me upon my first visit to Rudi Blesh, famous for his beautiful *Shining Trumpets*. A photo of a dark man, still quite young, is printed on the sleeve, but he turned out to be quite old and completely grey, though nevertheless a very pleasant host with a fantastic collection of records. On a subsequent visit he played me the tapes of recordings he had made on Solo Art of Don Lambert, a pianist from the Jelly Roll Morton era and a very imposing one. The recordings were made in a beautiful wing of New York's best studio – in other words, under ideal conditions. Solo Art subsequently released a record of this music and this is now available. Don Lambert died at the beginning of 1962 and these are now the only recordings that bear witness to his talents.

Then there are the records. The size of shops like Goody in New York is unbelievable, though once you leave New York it gets harder to find them. There are many discount shops in New York where almost all records are priced at $2.00 (rather than the usual $4.00). It is a quest to find good and cheap sales outlets in other towns but they are there, if you persist. In the USA music is recorded and brought on the market much quicker than in the Netherlands. Good and bad can be had in plenty, once you know your way around. But watch your budget, otherwise you will need to take an earlier flight home.

Jazz

• Listening to jazz[507]

Something very strange has been taking place over the course of the centuries of which the cause is not easy to establish. During the Middle Ages and after that, people determined the value of a work of art was partly determined on the basis of the time and skill it took to create it and the cost of the materials used (gold, silver, precious stones). The Renaissance marked a change. People started to call it primitive to value art in this way. Artists were praised who knew how to make a room with plain white walls look interesting. In painting all the emphasis shifted to the artistic intention, and the execution of it – the actual painting itself was considered incidental. In sculpture artisans often executed the design of the master. This has now been taken even further in works of art fashioned not from precious materials but from rust, waste paper or other things that one would not spare a second glance in everyday life. Not only that, but the construction is sometimes so botched that viewers get the impression they could do it themselves, in a very short space of time.

Here the emphasis is placed on the purely artistic aspect of the work to such an extent that neither the materials used nor the labour put into it is of any further consequence.

Music has fared a bit differently. It too had its 'stamps of merit'. Good music was what musicians in smart clothes produced in concert halls. The proper way to listen to it was attentively and in silence, and any noise was considered annoying – a kind of insult to the music. Good music was always heavy, not music to sing along to, and an important aspect was that listeners had to take trouble to work out what it means. Music performed in a place lacking that aura of serenity (such as a restaurant or a park) was therefore by definition considered inferior. Besides, music that became popular raised the suspicion that it had to be superficial and not of great value. Whatever would happen if orchestras were to play dressed in casual clothes? Would it not be an insult to the music, or to the audience, and would it indeed mean that the music need not be taken seriously? Jazz music is such music, often played in shirtsleeves to a noisy audience. Some may get up and dance to it and it does not matter a bit if they clap along to the music. Is that not one of the reasons why many think jazz has little substance and is of no great artistic significance?

Indeed, there is an offshoot of jazz music that is played in the very concert halls that we would associate with classical concerts. It is called modern jazz and it has incorporated many European influences. It is jazz that suits the palate of those who otherwise appreciated only classical music but it is not the sort of jazz I wish to pursue here.

I do not think that the concomitant circumstances that give the music an aura are a fair gauge of the value of the music. Let us recognize that there also is second rate, poor, even boring and lame 'classical' music that does not gain in merit because we listen to it seriously. Similarly, we cannot say that quality depends on the form: a musical piece is not beautiful because it is a symphony. Neither does it depend on the choice of instruments: the fact that a composition was written for violin, grand piano or clarinet does not automatically make it a masterpiece. Yet the loss of these external distinguishing features constitutes for many a stumbling block in judging jazz honestly. Let us see how we can reach a better verdict.

For music to be worthwhile there are a number of prerequisites. Firstly the music has to be worthwhile to listen to, i.e. it has to be artistically sound, and have something (beautiful) to say. Secondly, the listener has to listen with understanding. Never believe the suggestion that the beauty of music will be apparent to us just like that, or that it speaks a universal language that everyone will understand immediately. Just try listening to a piece of Indian or Arabian music and 'appreciate its beauty'. You soon realize how hard this is, and the first thing you will say if you are really serious about trying to enjoy it is, 'I wish someone would tell me how this works and what it means.' We are not even able to discern whether we are listening to flat, empty, commercial music or to real classical music. Our Western music is familiar to us and that is why it seems to us that we are able to understand it automatically. But even then we sometimes have difficulty with certain types of modern or old music. We also have to be prepared to persevere, even if we do not 'get it' straightaway. All these conditions apply also to learning to appreciate jazz music. With the following remarks I hope to help the listener determine the 'value' of jazz music.

It is important to realize that the word jazz embraces many genres of music. This is partly due to the history of this music. Sometimes the name jazz is given to the instrumental folk music of African-Americans. It is seldom heard here in Europe and can only be heard on records (themselves rare). These blacks are very musical and making music is far more part of their daily lives than it is of ours. Sometimes they play the mouth organ and, where we might expect a bass, they accompany it with a jug – a sort of bottle they blow on. This is not because they are trying to be funny but because they are too poor to afford 'real' instruments. Yet the music is sometimes amazingly deep and beautiful. There are of course also superficial and idle examples. Blacks are not all musical geniuses who always get it right; one muscian will manage better than another. Any singing in this genre is generally of the folk blues type.

The beginning of the twentieth century in New Orleans saw the emergence of a special sort of black instrumental music that was called jazz. This music has nothing to do with our Western classical music. It is a new musical concept that incorporates many elements in a highly inventive way. A band is generally made up of one or two trumpets, a trombone, a clarinet, piano, guitar or banjo, bass and drums. The instruments are usually played slightly differently from the way in which they are taught at European music schools, but that is partly because the desired effect is different. One characteristic is that this music has not been composed like our classical music. Instead, this is music is just a combination of a number of themes in a particular way. Each band has its own arrangement of these themes, with all sorts of variations on the given themes. The music has little or no improvisation. Riverside will shortly be re-releasing King Oliver and the records of his band made in 1923. When one studies these, they give some understanding of the beauty and depth of this sort of jazz.

Improvisation, namely making music spontaneously on the basis of the given progression of chords, actually emerged somewhat later in the form of so-called Chicago jazz. This is in fact a white variation of authentic black music with some novel elements added. Black jazz too was influenced by the new concept of improvisation combined with a strong, simple rhythm. Louis Armstrong's records after about 1928 and those of Luis Russell's band in later years serve as good examples.

In the 1930s swing music was developed as a sort of jazz played by large bands. The ensemble passages were of course arranged, but in between a lot of room was left for soloists to improvise. This sort of music has a strongly accentuated beat. Benny Goodman and Count Basie set the trend for a formula that is so well suited as contemporary dance music that we can still hear this sort of music.

Modern jazz emerged in the 1940s. Improvisation was central here as well but the spirit was different, less commercial and less geared to dancing audiences than swing was. Modern jazz gives spiritual expression to modern existentialist philosophies.

It would be a mistake to suggest that jazz has developed in a straight line, from a pristine stage to a highly developed modern stage, for also the route from Bach to Stravinsky was not one simply from a less to a more developed form. It is rather a matter of changes determined by shifts in the spiritual climate. Take the position of blacks in America for example, which has now changed. But at the heart of the matter lies different attitudes to life. In the case of New Orleans jazz it is an open, positive attitude to others, a willingness to work with others on equal footing, whereas a lot of modern jazz emanates from individualism, a negative attitude to society that is the result of a sense of inner discontent.

We have not discussed mainstream jazz in these brief notes. This is music that expresses itself in a less extreme way and pursues certain stylistic characteristics rather than depth. Neither have we mentioned Dixieland, a poor imitation of New Orleans jazz, which misses the essence of the original. There are also all sorts of commercial forms that have taken various jazz elements, which they tailored for their own purposes before introducing them into entertainment music.

It is very difficult for the lay listeners (i.e. those who have never made an effort to listen to jazz seriously) to distinguish real jazz from the commercial imitations; it can be done, however. The difference is best parallelled by comparing Beethoven with Franz Lehar, for instance, or with Richard Strauss.

• 'Jazz', jazz and classical[508]

One of the types of music commonly called jazz is that American and English music that is in fact exclusively intended for dance and entertainment. It is music that has incorporated more old traditions than is apparent at first hearing. One could say that old Anglo-Saxon folk music – the ballads that were sung also in America by the first European immigrants – lives on in this music. Folk music (and folk art) hardly has a place in our twentieth-century world; it has become folklore, something of a museum piece that at best leads a depressed life. So it is understandable that the old Anglo-Saxon song lives on embalmed, even though it has remained what it was: music for the people.

The cultural development in the West has no room for folk music; worse still, Western culture has developed a sharp division between popular and entertainment music, on the one hand, and classical music, on the other. (For the sake of clarity, 'classical' music here means all Western classical music, including modern classical and pre-classical.) This division has become so sharp that the two types exist as if in two separate worlds. Classical music is referred to as truly cultured, sublime, high, deep, beautiful, and the only type actually worthy of the name music. Folk music, on the other hand, which can live on only as entertainment and dance music, is certainly regarded as an inferior kind. But, such a view is little more than a sort of accepted snobbery. After all, who does not occasionally enjoy listening to a nice song or a lively little tune? It is patently obvious that Bing Crosby pales into insignificance besides Panzera, and likewise Doris Day besides Kathleen Ferrier. But such a comparison is unfair because the rejected party completely lacks pretension: his or her music has an entirely different function and position in society. It may not have the depth and beauty or permanent value and significance, but it does offer joy, lively entertainment, a sentimental tear and the pleasure of singing along to it while shaving or doing the washing . . . music that is no more than an adornment to life. But neither does it attempt to be anything else.

Furthermore, in spite of all the differences in value and content and place and function there is only one real difference between all these types of music: the difference between good and bad music. This division cuts across all that is referred to as 'classical' as well as all that is referred to as 'popular'. Kitsch is certainly present in music – yes, but not all popular music is kitsch; there is deep and sublime beauty, but not all classical music can pride itself on that. However, we are not trying to write a defence of entertainment music – the 'covered-up' continuation of folk music, which is very diverse in quality; the question we are asking is rather why all black jazz is simply dumped into the category of 'low' entertainment music by so-called lovers of classical music. It is, after all, a category that the real jazz connoisseurs regard with as much contempt as lovers of classical music do. Any quest to find it in their discotheques would be in vain.

Firstly, let us ask how this modern entertainment music has come to be called jazz, while jazz is actually black music. We have to look for the reason in the fact that this music, made by people who possess few creative qualities, went to look for inspiration in black music. That already happened during the first half of the nineteenth century when the songs of the Negro slaves made an impression on the likes of the rather talented Stephen Foster. Numbers not unfamiliar to us, such as campfire songs 'My old Kentucky home' and 'Oh Susanna' are examples of this. The ragtime piano style that emerged around 1900 had strong black influences. As a matter of fact, the best composers, such as Scott Joplin, were black. But, particularly after New Orleans jazz began to attract the attention of audiences, the record companies were trying to breathe life into their own often inanimate products by borrowing elements from black music. This purely Western entertainment music, in order to give it some credibility, was now also crowned with the name of jazz.

So the main answer to the question we posed can be found in this misnomer. The shrewd sellers of dance and entertainment music used the word 'jazz' to refer to a type of music that was seperated by a deep chasm from Negro folk music. The one thing they had in common was that both were far removed from classical music.

Old jazz, i.e. music worthy of the name in its actual and original sense, is a type of music that has nothing to do with Western twentieth-century culture. It is the folk music of black Americans, fashioned by social and cultural circumstances that made Western influence impossible to escape – think for example of the tonal system and the instruments used – but it is a completely homegrown folk art that emerged with its own hallmark. It had a completely new style and was to have its own tradition. This is well illustrated by its use of instruments. A trumpet, a clarinet, a trombone, piano and bass – these are Western instruments but they were used in an entirely new way. We have to recognize that whereas strings take the lead in our music, in black music wind instruments are most important. A violin to us is equivalent to a trumpet for them!

The method of playing was often different too, for many blacks took up their instruments without knowing anything about traditional Western techniques. In jazz the clarinet is played with vibrato. Sometimes Africanisms were introduced, such as the way a black musician would use the bass as a rhythm instrument by plucking it – pizzicato – in the same way a musician would have plucked a single-stringed calabash.

The African-American folk music of today can be understood in terms of its origin and structure only as a development within the specific black culture in New Orleans between 1890 and 1920. It is an entirely individual art form that cannot be ascribed to any Western development. The social circumstances surrounding that culture help us to see why the technical means upon which the blacks and Creoles founded their music were derived from Western culture. However, the fact that they were able to detach themselves stylistically and in terms of their own artistic expression from white music is a testimony to the artistic self-respect and significance of their music. Yes, that is where the real wonder of New Orleans jazz lies.

This music, while not of the Western world, was in it. It required its own space within the existing social and cultural order, of which black musicians were also part. But – and this may be key to understand the misnomers and misunderstandings – space was nowhere available except within the contemptible confines of dance and entertainment music, however uncomfortably the musicians sometimes fitted there.

In our Western world there is on the one hand classical music, which can be enjoyed only in perfect silence, almost reverence, while the listener is dressed in sober and dignified attire. On the other hand there is light music that gurgles away in the background while one is chatting or amusing oneself casually in leisure dress. There is no place for real and authentic folk music, and no concept of its unique position, an art that is alive and real and not to be reduced to the annals of folklore where it languishes as a relic. The wonder of New Orleans jazz is that very simple and illiterate people created it – musicians who made their living as furniture makers, dockers, barber's assistants or grocers if they were not able to make a living as professional musicians. They were too conscientious to compromise by playing 'jazz'. They would rather die of hunger, like Johnny Dodds, their greatest clarinettist. Since our composers and musicians are among the highest purveyors of culture, Westerners find it downright incomprehensible that the social environment of these uneducated, illiterate and simplest of middle- and working-class people could produce music like that of King Oliver's Creole Orchestra or Jelly Roll Morton's band. Their music exudes pure, balanced polyphony, calmness and control, an exceptionally subtle art of variation, 'abstraction' as in a *Musikalisches Opfer* by Bach, with clarity and style of high quality. But they all played in shirtsleeves and with a joy in playing that makes classical concerts seem uninspired and cold. Listen to the first few stanzas of Morton's 'Kansas City stomps' with its lively musical humour. This music is not classical, as we understand it, but neither is it schmaltzy, like pseudo-jazz. On the contrary, it is real folk music that is sustained by the entire black population of the USA, and it expresses all the joys and sorrows of their existence. It is anything but superficial, but seldom as complex as the music of Brückner or Debussy.

This music is like a displaced person – a foreign body – in our culture. That is why lovers of classical music will have to break down their walls of prejudice, misunderstanding and lack of orientation. Only then will they be able to understand this music and its significance. This, incidentally, applies also to schmaltz or popular music lovers, who will find this sort of jazz equally hard to take.

Make no mistake: real jazz is not 'popular'. Even in America the percentage of real jazz music released on gramophone records represents barely more than 1 percent of the entire market. The music is too subtle, too complex in melodic and rhythmic variation and in its idiom too foreign to the ear of the Western listener to be attractive to the lover of entertainment music. Jazz music, music 'in shirtsleeves', was and is real folk music, and just one simple set of categories is appropriate: there is good jazz music and there is bad jazz music!

'Was and is' are the words we have just used, for New Orleans jazz, which reached its climax in 1925-1926 is indeed anything but dead. To the contrary. This music is experiencing a revival at the moment, partly in reaction to the direction taken by swing music, a derivative of jazz that has for a long time made the subsistence of real jazz economically unviable.

In order to be able to understand the emergence and the development of the music we refer to here as 'swing',[509] we have to realize that the emancipation issue was and is to the American Negro a matter of life and death. For this reason blacks turned to swing when they realized just how popular entertainment music had become. It was played by a large number of brass instruments and saxophones (an instrument seldom used in early jazz). The black musicians also recognized that its success could partly be attributed to elements that had been derived from their own music. Henderson was the first to form a substantial band consisting of black musicians, of which Louis Armstrong, the famous black trumpet player, was one of the soloists who at first managed to combine this with work in smaller New Orleans jazz bands. Especially after 1928 this trend to play swing became more widespread. Later on Louis Armstrong was not strong enough to resist the temptation of fame and fortune and began to concentrate all his artistic skill on this sort of pseudo-jazz. Ellington's music too can only be understood on this premise: he became the prime agent in making jazz *salonfähig*, i.e. presentable, by introducing the principle of programme music. Those black musicians who really loved their music and were too veracious to adapt readily to the Western taste, were ousted and faded into obscurity, having been left in dire straits financially. The same fate met the greatest of black musicians, Ferdinand Jelly Roll Morton.[510]

Whether all of this really furthered the cause of emancipation is debatable.

> While jazz is a symbol of struggle and hope, swing is one of defeat. The success of blacks in America cannot be measured by the illusion of popular admiration; neither can it be counted in dollars that can never buy equality. Swing music as a form and a complete trend is the abandonment of the real Negroid elements of jazz for the benefit of Western elements that are more comprehensible and acceptable to the white community. Swing would appear to be a symbol of victory but in reality is the failure of emancipation.[511]

While it cannot be denied that the anaemic entertainment music prevalent in the America of the day gained much vitality and life thanks to the sometimes very gifted musicians who were forced by economic necessity to turn to swing, neither can we deny that around 1936 this music degenerated into a monotonous rhythm and an equally monotonous repetition of simple little rhythmic figures, interspersed now and then with a solo that displayed clichés. But because so many talented musicians had to play this music, things were bound to change: the gradual renewal was wholly directed towards the further development of harmony in the spirit of modern Western music, and a remodelling of the melody while digressing further and further from the original black traits. The music that emerged, called bebop, progressive jazz or cool, was not only completely westernized in technical features, but also in spirit closely related to surrealism and existentialism – i.e. modern Western movements. It is played most creatively by young, highly intellectual blacks, who created a truly modern twentieth-century form of music. It would be premature to make an assessment of this music at this stage. As we have already mentioned, the old New Orleans jazz began to push its way through to the fore again as a reaction to these developments. For it can not be denied that this new type of music (progressive jazz) has many decadent elements to it and regards new effects and technical intricacies as progress, while it loses cultural ground and musical value by persisting to base its melodies on diluted Western entertainment music.[512]

The development the hymn form of the blacks – the Negro spiritual – can be afforded a similar analysis. Here too we see Western influences affecting the melody and tonal system, but how was it that this music managed to incorporate all these influences in such a way that the song we can call the authentic Negro spiritual – the religious song of Christians, sung in church – is and remains a manifestation of pure black origin? Here too we have westernization, also often with emancipation as its motive, resulting in hybrids. Think of Marion Anderson et al. who sings these songs with a beautiful voice, but with a musical setting and accompaniment à la Schubert. Paul Robeson too sings Negro spirituals with his phenomenal bass in an entertainment-song style, and he is not bothered about violating the songs by giving the lyrics a communist flavour. Fortunately the authentic tradition of Negro spirituals manages to live on among blacks, never static, ever progressive. We are fortunate to be able to get to know this music, just as with real jazz, through listening to gramophone records, at least those of us who take the trouble to seek advice from experts.

So black music joins the musical life of the twentieth century alongside the old music of our own culture, also the newly opened-up music of the centuries before Bach and the contemporary modern music that still sometimes sounds a bit foreign to us. It is not only those with authority on music that are able to recognize the merit of this art form once they have been helped over the mountain of misconceptions and misunderstandings. More and more people feel they must grasp the opportunities jazz has created for them to be creatively involved with music; even in the Netherlands the number of amateur jazz bands of all shapes and sizes should really not be underestimated. Then, besides all that, there is a (negative) product characteristic of our own culture, namely entertainment music. It was given the name 'jazz' and, although it bears only a superficial resemblance to jazz, that was enough to ensure that real, authentic black music is often condemned as inferior.

• Original Dixieland jazz band[513]

Art mirrors its time and bears the stamp of the social and spiritual attitudes of the world in which it was conceived. So goes the presupposition behind all cultural-historical contemplations that appear in print today. Although this proposition has proved to be a very fertile working hypothesis, the connection is not always obvious or straightforward. The emergence of Dadaism for instance is understandable. From the years of the World War that shocked the soul so deeply, it formed an expression of the feeling of disruption and futility of contemporary cultural ambition. And it is not difficult to understand that the very same spiritual crisis acted as a catalyst for the expansion and development of the modern art forms of Expressionism and Cubism, which are such strong protests against the past and sometimes seek so passionately for new forms and new values. The connection with jazz music, however, is far less direct.

While it is true that jazz music did not emerge from the Western cultural climate of the first two decades of the twentieth century, it did win an instant audience during and after World War I. Suddenly people started responding to this completely new language of sound. What was it about the music that seemed to cater to a need that the audiences themselves were unaware of? Perhaps it was the exuberance, without sentimental superficiality, or perhaps the absence of Western cultural problems. Was it because world developments made everything sound trite and empty that this music was able to give something that the older dance and entertainment music could not give? Ragtime had certainly paved the way, but it was jazz music that communicated something more varied and richer than that piano music, particularly when the music of the Original Dixieland Jazz Band (ODJB) is compared with the second-rate imitations of the black ragtime of Joplin et al., which was what audiences understood as 'ragtime'.

Perhaps that would help us understand the sudden success of the ODJB. Had Keppard and his Creole Orchestra not already played in New York, Chicago and elsewhere outside New Orleans prior to 1910? Were there not already a lot of New Orleans bands playing this kind of music far away from their hometown? It is certainly not impossible that the sudden interest was stimulated by the fact that this New Orleans music was now being played by whites. Blacks and their music only gradually worked their way to the fore during the 1920s.

Indeed, as we have just said, the music of the ODJB comes from New Orleans and if we listen to the music they made in 1917 and 1918 for Victor – now released by HMV on an LP – we are listening to the reaction of a group of whites to the music of the black people of that city. Typical 'white' features are the somewhat hurried rhythm, the rhythmically indistinct melodies and the lack of inner rhythms and cross rhythms, which in black music secure a unity in subtle ensemble whereby the melody instruments also have a rhythmic function and the so-called rhythm instruments also contribute to the polyphonic melodic fabric. However, the polyphony, the application of breaks – in short, the entire outward form of this music – comes from the blacks.

If we listen to this music, or rather study it by playing it over and again, we come to understand why it was that this particular jazz band was the first to win audiences outside New Orleans, thereby playing such an influential role. Did a very musical Bix Beiderbecke in the years of his youth not play these very records, and do we not find back a lot of its characteristic turns of phrases and melodies in the music of the later bands – chiefly white, of course? And does the background to the music of Bob Crosby's band from the 1930s not become clearer when we listen to 'Bluin' the blues', perhaps the best of the eight numbers played on this record? The great and lasting influence that makes possible this re-release – it is not only the historical significance that causes this music to keep attracting audiences – lies in the indisputable qualities, the musicality, the vitality, the controlled pleasure of playing the music, the originality of these musicians who, inspired by what they had heard from blacks in New Orleans where they had played together since 1908, nevertheless in no way just soullessly imitated them. Second-rate art will never be more than a passing trend, like the top hit or schmaltz. Even though the greatness of Oliver, Armstrong and Morton was necessary to strengthen and fortify the first impulse of the ODJB, the mere fact that jazz is such a permanent feature of our century, truly international and universal, may also be evidence of the value of the music of the ODJB. It was the band that was the first to attract the attention of audiences outside New Orleans to what was originally a strictly local phenomenon.

The records that have now been so superbly re-released have in this respect no doubt played a role that would be hard to overrate.

•Jelly Roll Morton[514]

The appreciation of the great pianist and band leader Jelly Roll Morton certainly has a very curious history. Although other musicians recognized his talents and he was one of the greatest players at the beginning of the twentieth century, yet, as a musician, he was greatly underestimated. He was certainly actively involved in the development of jazz music from the beginning and he was often consulted and quoted as a respected figure in the jazz world. However, only seldom did he get the credit he deserved for his own work, which was of the highest standard.

In the 1930s a listener in France, the Netherlands or the USA would occasionally hear one of Morton's extremely rare recordings, study it and recognize that Jelly Roll Morton was producing jazz at its best. In 1939, when this *genius manqué* was getting on in years, he was given his first opportunity since 1930 to be recorded. In September 1939 he made a number of records with a band and some of these recordings are now available in the Netherlands. The members of this band were: Morton himself on piano, Sidney de Paris and Jones on trombone, Albert Nicholas and Sidney Bechet on clarinet and soprano, Couldwell on tenor, Wellman Braud on bass, Lawrence Lucie on guitar and Zutie Singleton on drums. They give a magnificent rendering of the classic number from around 1900, 'I thought I heard Buddy Bolden say', which is equally an account of Jelly's own life. 'Climax rag' shows that he has not forgotten how to play the piano, while 'Oh, didn't he ramble', gives us an insider view of a New Orleans funeral, and we could mention more. These were also Bechet's first recordings (besides those he did with Mezzrow) since the earlier days when he played some beautiful numbers with Clarence Williams and Armstrong.

The piano solos that Jelly plays are clear evidence of his skill. Vocals were added to some of the solos recorded later in December, on General. Let us hope that these highlights, representing the best of all black music that was ever recorded, may soon be available in the Netherlands too. Fortunately we will not have to wait till then to hear Jelly Roll Morton, as a number of his older records are available.

When we listen to his older recordings we really have to ask ourselves how a man of his calibre could ever be forgotten or repudiated. The most beautiful of all is 'Deep Creek blues', recorded on 6 December 1928. It is simply one of the very best. This masterpiece may stand alongside 'West End blues', 'Armstrong's muskrat ramble' – and any of your most favourite numbers. Strangely enough, the band with which Jelly recorded this number consisted entirely of unknown musicians. The way Jelly was able to leave his stamp on this band and soloists and made even obscure musicians shine, is truly remarkable. The band members were: Edwin Swayzee, Ed Anderson and possibly Lee Collins on trumpet, Billy Cato on trombone, Russell Procope, Joe Garland and Paul Barnes on sax, Bass Moore on bass, Lee Blair on guitar and Mainzee Johnson on drums. After the fantastic opening introduction we hear a legato trumpet solo accompanied by sustained notes from the band. Then we hear the trombone in a magnificent solo, before losing ourselves completely in Barnes' perfect soprano solo. We had already heard Jelly now and again in the accompaniment but next he plays a solo by himself, the true value of which can only be assessed once it has been listened to a few times, for each time there are new elements of beauty to be discovered. A clarinet solo with a striking tuba accompaniment and a tenor solo accompanied by the band transport us to the final, light conclusion that Jelly himself plays. Those who deliberately omit this record from their collection cannot be called serious collectors of jazz!

Doctor Jazz and *Original Jelly Roll Blues*, both recorded on 16 December 1926, also belong to the first-rate records. Indeed, Jelly has one great soloist after the other at his disposal: George Mitchell, the trumpet player who deserves more acclaim, Omer Simeon, a man with a genuinely classic style, Kid Ory who hardly needs introduction, John Lindsay on bass and Johnny St. Cyr on banjo. On *Doctor Jazz* the maestro himself plays the piano and sings 'Hello Central, give me Doctor Jazz'. The playing instructions for these are: again and again!

Jelly Roll Morton died in 1942 and there remains just one concluding remark: may Jelly receive the general acclaim he deserves from those who listen to these records, as jazz lovers have already afforded him. As exponent of a special genre alongside Armstrong's Hot Seven and Hot Five, he may certainly never be forgotten. Jelly – the Mozart of jazz!

• Ory's Creole trombone[515]

At the turn of the century, black music took on a new character with the emergence of the New Orleans style. During that period it was the Creoles who helped transform the music, and one of them was the great trombonist, Kid Ory. As early as 1910, Ory had led his own band, Ory's Brownskin Band. Oliver played with them for a while and was later succeeded by a still very young Louis Armstrong. Ory took his band on tour all over the United States although they often stayed on the West Coast. That is where he was in 1921 when he made his first recordings in Los Angeles on the very obscure Sunshine label. One of these recordings, recently re-released by Jazz Collector, was his own composition 'Ory's Creole trombone', in which his trombone plays a very important role. For this version, he was joined by Mutt Carey on trumpet, among others. The number has something strangely archaic about it, a strange imbalance that takes us back to the years when jazz was emerging. The execution with its rather weak clarinet is further evidence that jazz was still waiting for its stylistic completion. Oliver's Creole Jazz Band was to achieve this a few years later by taking the New Orleans style to unprecedented heights and giving it its well-defined characteristics.

Kid Ory did not sit still during the 1920s. He made his best music with Jelly Roll Morton and with the Bootblacks. On the records he made with the Armstrong Hot Seven or Five he does not always stand out as well as he could have. Perhaps the disquiet that often pervades his playing here is the result of psychological tension between him and the much younger Armstrong, who had once played in his band, and to whom he was now playing second fiddle. Anyway, the version of 'Ory's Creole trombone' that he recorded with the Hot Sevens in 1927 is quite some performance. It displays some beautiful teamwork and good solos although the strangely archaic character can still be heard clearly – even now – in a number of passages typical to this number.

Kid Ory kept on playing, even through the years of the Depression when no records were being made and he, like so many other grand old-timers, became obscure. Whether the few records the Ory Creole Jazz Band made on 8 September 1945 constitutes a revival, is therefore questionable. The recordings, now released on a Blue Star EP, show us that Kid Ory remained faithful to himself and to the New Orleans style. At the same time, there is evidence of substantial developments and exposure to the swing of the 1930s. Listen to Ory's playing and to the rhythm section, for example, and compare the way they play and the overall sound they produce on this record with that of the old New Orleans records. The rhythm and melody section used to form a unity, whereas here they stand more or less alongside each other. We hear Mutt Carey again, who had once played trumpet with Ory twenty years earlier, and Darnell Howard on clarinet, who had worked with Kid Ory in the years 1925–1927 when Oliver was making records with a big band. Howard shows evidence of swing influences too but, without a doubt, here the music did remained full-blooded New Orleans jazz. Of the ten numbers on his LP the most beautiful are possibly 'Down home rag' and '1919', but for the sake of comparison 'Ory's Creole trombone' is the most interesting. The composition has not lost any of its archaic traits, which contradict its by now very experienced rendition. But, let us close with the words from one of the tracks:

> Do you know what Ory says
> If you don't like the way I do,
> It will be for me no harm.

• Jazz on the riverboats[516]

> Mister Jelly Lord
> He's simply royal at the old keyboard ...
> He plays his music as his rule
> While he sits upon his throne,
> That old piano stool ...
> ... his melodies
> Have made him Lord of the ivories ...
> Just a simple little chord
> Now at home as well as abroad
> They call him Mister Jelly Lord.

That is how Jelly Morton sang of himself on the record that has just been re-released on Brunswick. Modest he was not, to be sure, and yet was he not right? Is this simply advertising for his own music, as if it were a product, or did this Creole musician really think his music was that significant? In other words, was he a purveyor of dance and light music or a real artist? It is not easy to give a straightforward answer to this question. What is the difference between art and entertainment? Either way the musician has to earn a living and carry out a contractual obligation, and in both cases the objective is to bring pleasure – to create something to be enjoyed. Perhaps there is ultimately only one difference – disposition. In art it is the artist's intention to convey higher values, to create beauty in sound, to express deeper emotions, while in entertainment the artist strives to provide diversion, pleasure, fun without requiring any intellectual effort on the part of the listener.

This distinction keeps cropping up in relation to jazz music. For musicians and connoisseurs always make the same distinction between 'commercial' and 'authentic'. 'Commercial' music looks the audience in the eye and gives them what they want, while real musical values are at stake in 'authentic' music. It is an unmistakable fact that we can indeed often decide after a couple of bars whether a piece of music is 'authentic' or 'commercial' on the basis of the musician's disposition. There is generally no difference in the composition of the band and the music is for dancing and/or entertainment purposes in both cases. Oddly enough, this often means that 'real' jazz is dished up to an audience that is there to dance or to be entertained. This music is by no means adapted to their ears, is not easy listening and carries high artistic quality afforded by very talented musicians who give of their best.

It might only be possible to clarify this strange situation by the strange circumstances in which jazz emerged, as the instrumental music of a very musical people – the African-Americans. Given their situation and social position it is understandable that they started out with musical groups that resembled the Western brass band. Their repertoire consisted of spirituals and music derived from Western entertainment music. To them the music had a very different meaning from what we would attach to brass band or popular music. This was their own music, their folk music, and they put everything into giving it its own style and making it their own cultural heritage. They did not have to wait long for opportunities. In New Orleans, the centre of black culture, there was great demand for light music and they were be able to meet that demand since their music was, to the untrained ear, in many respects similar to entertainment music. This also provided an opportunity for black and Creole musicians to climb the social ladder and earn recognition. As a rule, this was more important to them than the fact that there was good money to be earned, though the two are not unrelated.

So New Orleans jazz came into being with the inherent paradox of being art to black culture and entertainment to the audience. If they remained faithful to their own idiom, to their own highly original style, then we have 'authentic' jazz – black folk music. If they watch the audience and conform to the norms of Western entertainment music, then it becomes 'commercial' jazz. The strange thing is that between 1910 and 1930 blacks were given the chance to play authentic jazz, even though it was anything but easy to listen to with its polyphony and developed diversity of form, so different from entertainment music. One of the places where this music was played was on the pleasure boats that cruised the Mississippi, and in 1926 and 1928 this music was recorded on an LP called *Riverboat Jazz* on the Brunswick label. Even today it does not sound outdated, and it is worth playing some entertainment music from that period (which is as boring and trite as one can get) just to appreciate the difference between the two. The first two numbers by Morton are musical masterpieces, of exceptional quality, and by no means easy listening. Then there is 'Snag it', by Oliver (who, together with Jelly Roll Morton, spearheaded the development and refinement of black music), an engaging number full of surprises. On the flip side we make the acquaintance of the trumpeter and singer Punch Miller. He too is able to show us why this music still manages to occupy the minds of so many people to this day, 'Gates blues' and 'Down by the Levee' being two prime examples. The music might be dated, in the same way that the music of any other past composer is dated, but it is still fascinating and alive. The very fact that the music is still worth listening to, even outside its original milieu and aside from its use for dance and entertainment, may be proof that this is art with intrinsic musical qualities.

• A New Orleans suite[517]

When Jelly Roll Morton more or less by accident made his recordings for the Library of Congress collection, it signalled the comeback of the old traditions of the music from New Orleans. Jelly himself initiated this revival with his unrivalled series of piano solos, which are now almost all available on record, I am pleased to say.

These recordings, which date back to 1939, constitute the highlights of the musical career of the greatest Creole pianist – a man who not only could play music but also thought about his music and was able to communicate these thoughts. This is evident in some of the instruction he gives on the Library of Congress records. He says, for instance, that one of the misconceptions of many so-called jazz bands is their belief that everything has to be played fast and loud – without diminuendo whatsoever and with no nuances.

New Orleans music does indeed recognize nuance, and the recordings of George Lewis Stompers are now available to illustrate this in the form of a series of ten sides recorded on 16 May 1943, released on Vogue. This is the cream of real Jazz!

We may well refer to George Lewis – and we must not forget the trombonist Jim Robinson – as the greatest finds of this revival. Up to this time they had never made any gramophone records since they lived quietly in New Orleans. We are grateful that the new interest in this music, due to Morton's recordings, helped preserve the pure style of their playing for us to enjoy.

George Lewis was born in 1900 and is the greatest New Orleans clarinettist after Dodds. He is possibly even more accomplished than Dodds, certainly if we concentrate on his almost seraphic tone. If we can fault him on anything, it is that his melodious and rhythmic inventiveness sometimes ignores the harmonic chords. This poses a real problem for us, however: can it really be true that the musicians who made these first-class recordings were so naïve that they had never heard of harmonic schemes and suchlike? Rudi Blesh thinks that we are dealing here with a natural tendency towards polytonality, and it is indeed the case that the rhythm section sometimes follows a simpler pattern than the melody group or the soloist. Two things are certain, however. First, this polytonality is not related to that of our modern music – it is not modern, Western or twentieth-century at all. Second, if these musicians thought that the question of polytonality was merely irrelevant, they were correct, for one does not notice it when listening to the recordings many times. The music is not off-key. Indeed it would be impossible to imagine the music without its polytonality.

The band includes Kid Howard on trumpet – a fine stylist and a good lead; Jim Robinson, who plays a very free, New Orleans-style trombone – very melodious, to the extent that he sometimes even carries the melody; George Lewis; and a rhythm group (Marero – banjo, Zardis – bass and Mosley – drums) working as a gentle and solid backing without unseemly intrusion, and no piano. Note Mosely's well-timed supporting ruffles.

All the sides are played ensemble (polyphonically) in a spirit of unity, without being disturbed by the individualism that brought this music to a premature conclusion around 1928. The polyphony is interspersed with solos by Lewis, a few times by Robinson and Howard, and occasionally someone joins Lewis in a duet. In the ensemble passages we hear how, just as in the old King Oliver numbers, the clarinet almost becomes dominant, while the trombone gives a quiet and melodic backing and the trumpet, through short phrases, gives George Lewis the necessary 'drive', while he plays continuously without ever falling into repetition or losing inspiration.

These are remarkable recordings. They are not easy to follow and and one has to listen to them many times in order to hear all that is going on. 'Climax rag', for example, sounds at first hearing like a sea of sound – as if the musicians were in a trance – until one suddenly grasps how controlled and perfectly balanced and composed this beautiful piece of music is. We could review these records one by one, for they are all different. Each track has its own characteristic mood – its own characteristic stamp. One can listen to all ten sides without once hearing a repetition. First the music is gentle, then it is playful, then exuberant, then unpretentiously withdrawn or melancholic. The ten sides form a suite of high quality – a wealth of sound that demands but also rewards our undivided attention, again and again.

• Johnny Dodds: a great and modest musician[518]

Those lucky enough to have witnessed New Orleans jazz at the height of its success around 1926 certainly knew that the music had special qualities, but they were not aware of how unique it was or how short-lived it would be. Suddenly, for reasons that we will not go into here, it had come to an end and the economic reality denied even a short-lived aftergrowth.

Instead, jazz lovers turned to their records, casually purchased, and played them again and again for the sake of reminiscence. That is how the next generation came to hear the music and appreciate its beauty.

This is also how collectors came into being. During the crisis years (between 1930 and 1940), re-pressing gramophone records was not, of course, the recording companies' primary concern. The group of collectors and connoisseurs was as yet much too small and the object of their desire still too uncharted to make it worthwhile. But that small circle was searching in markets and junk shops, and old records were bought for a song, played, assessed, swapped and discussed. The musicians that had made those hundreds and thousands of records had little idea of the importance of their work. This left the collectors standing in the midst of a mishmash of names, codes and labels, with little to guide them. Once it had been established who were the best and once the style of the most important musicians was identified, the task began of tracking them down on other records, together with other musicians with unknown names – often pseudonyms – purely on the basis of their styles.

Some of the collectors from that era were ardent specialists that concentrated on one particular soloist, a particular band, or a particular type. We cannot thank them enough for their dogged determination in finding out everything there was to know about their protagonist and obtaining the relevant memorabilia. They sifted out everything that could be classified as worthless dance music to retain the 'real' music, thereby laying the foundation for all future discographical works.

The Johnny Dodds records, which have now been released on a double LP on London, will have been collected in this same way. Yes, as Armstrong's great counterpart on the Hot Five and Hot Seven recordings, Johnny Dodds was familiar enough. You can picture the look on the faces of Dodds collectors upon inspecting their purchases after a day scouring town and market, to find confirmation that along with the Ragamuffins on Paramount (a black label), it is indeed Dodds playing. Alternatively, how they would do their best to wrench that Paramount Pickers' record from someone else and, in doing so, get to hear the characteristic sound of Dodds once again. Trying to establish which musicians are featured in a band is usually a complex task, but this is not the case when one tries to verify the presence of Johnny Dodds, for his personality, endless inspiration, fantastic technique, particularly full tone, confidence and taste always stand out clearly. His clarinet playing is not obtrusive, however. Johnny Dodds was far too modest a person and a musician to be accused of posing as a great soloist.

Although the record we hear on London was not electrically recorded (at Paramount an electrical recording meant nothing more than that the studio was equipped with electric lighting!), Dodds' playing is so powerful and rounded that even here the beauty of sound, phrasing and rendition certainly become evident after only a few hearings. His imagination is infinitely rich and likewise his taste, which makes him sound different each time and ensures that he always tunes in to the mood and nature of the piece at hand. There is supreme variety in his art. Is jazz the art of improvisation? No, it is rather the art of variation! Listen to 'Loveless love', so highly commended on the sleeve, in which he plays so many variations to a simple sixteen-bar popular theme, that of an eighteenth-century American ballad. Time and again he finds new means of expression, new turns, with the sequence-of-breaks variation as the climax.

Dodds respected New Orleans jazz too much to go along with its inevitable commercialization after 1930. Consequently he went through years of bitter poverty and illness which, after an ambivalent comeback reception, led to his death in 1941. When anyone made an honest appeal to him, he was much too self-effacing to refuse it. This may be why we sometimes hear him playing in bands which, however honest and commercially untouched they may be, were far below his standard. But he succeeds by unwittingly stirring the other musicians up and by outdoing them, without obtrusion, by his pure musicality. These are all pure examples of Dodds' great music. Re-releasing these hitherto very rare records is a worthy tribute to a great, though because of his modesty too little commended, musician: the clarinettist, Johnny Dodds.

Rock

• The background to modern music: an interview[519]

Rock music has swept through our society. There was nothing to stop it after rock-and-roll. Now garages, workshops and offices have it blaring out to staff, customers and visitors every day, and millions of gramophone records are finding a way through to families – and into teenagers' rooms.

These facts demand that we stop and think. What is the background to the world of modern jazz and rock? Are these types of music a reflection of the modern understanding of life? What are we to make of it? Should we appreciate it or condemn it? We put these questions to Dr H.R. Rookmaaker, Professor of Art History at the University of Amsterdam, who has won acclaim for his writing on contemporary art and music. He is one of a very small number to use the Bible as the basis for analysing and judging modern art. We are therefore very grateful that he immediately agreed to this interview.

First about jazz, which emerged at the beginning of the twentieth century and paved the way for further developments in popular music:

Why do you think jazz music received such a generous reception in our Western culture?
   The first thing we have to consider is that the entertainment music that was dominant at the time, in the 1920s, was so empty, so very superficial that a good shot of something was necessary. The solution turned out to be black music. From the African-American point of view it is tragic in a way that everything they do is used by whites for the purpose of entertainment.
   Jazz also gave Westerners the opportunity to protest – protest at the middle-class with their bourgeois lifestyle. I'll define it more accurately: the bourgeoisie are those who attempt to build a decent little life for themselves even though they lack the necessary ideological base. That protest did not last long however, because the market pounced on jazz and prepared it for mass consumption. The musicians themselves responded to that with protest. Which takes us to modern jazz and other developments that sprang up after World War II.

Do you see a relationship between modern jazz and the present view of the world, as Sartre and others interpreted it in existentialism?
   The music emerged in the 1940s among intellectual musicians who had thought long and hard about the key questions of our society and the meaning of being human. Indeed, I think that a fundamental link exists between what someone like Sartre holds and this type of music. In a way you could call it existentialist music. There are parallels. The

postwar mood of despair provided fertile ground for the music. It was fashionable in a way to listen to this music in that mood of despair. This jazz that was breaching musical norms had its parallel in the beat generation, who were setting the tone in literature at that time. In the music a sort of snowball effect took place. Once the listeners had grown accustomed to the fierce sounds, it left them with a desire for more fierce stimuli. The outcome of this development was free jazz, which was bereft of any prescript. Of course you can say in retrospect that there were rules and that they were adhered to, but each time those rules were stretched so that it became more and more anarchistic.

Are there differences between rock-and-roll and the beat and rock music of the 1960s, and can you outline their background?

I don't think you have to look for any really profound meaning in the different names. They represent variation within one collective trend. The rock-and-roll genre is a bit older. The music fits perfectly into the rebelliousness that we have been experiencing over the last few years. However, the roots of this phenomenon lie in the Age of Enlightenment – i.e. in the eighteenth century. That is when the ideological revolution took place that is continuing to affect our present society. Just think of Groen van Prinsterer's book *Unbelief and Revolution* that was published in the mid-nineteenth century. It gives an analysis of the revolutionary ideas of that time, but is a book that everybody today should read for its prophetic insight. You could say that the 1960s have seen the Enlightenment reach the person in the street. The same kind of ideas come to the fore in the world of rock. I often use one of Bob Dylan's songs to illustrate the point. He sings of times gone by when he used to know well what was good and bad, but that the new world of which he has become a part no longer has norms. I was recently talking to a student who told me he didn't think shoplifting was a bad thing. He could back this up with all sorts of sociological explanations, and he would not accept that shoplifting in itself was a sin. This is the loss of norms that we see around us. Thousands are crossing over from a world-with-norms to a world-without-norms. That is not a question of a new generation. Many young people are crossing that threshold but a lot of the older generation are doing it as well.

How is it that that rock music presupposes enough noise to wake the dead? Why the maximum sound output?

That is a difficult question. I don't know whether anyone would be able to answer it. The concept of cool communication certainly has a role to play. One used to try and understand music by listening to it. Part of the enjoyment was analytic reflection, though it was not only an intellectual occupation. That is not the case with the new music. The listener becomes immersed in it, becomes part of it. It is a sort of trip. You can do it with drugs, but also with music. You more or less lose yourself in it and that is the very thing the music strives to do. It is not about analysis of the music at all. That is also why lighting effects, which prevent the audience from seeing the performers properly, are used. Yet this music does convey something. There is 'cool' communication – the term coined by MacLuhan – whereby all the senses are stimulated. The communication does not work by persuasion but by taking part in it.

Which direction is this music taking at the moment?
It has all become a bit softer the last few years. There are songs with serious intentions, those making a real stand, but there is a lot of money to be made and there is inevitably commercial exploitation. There is the odd good song. There's the hard trip music we've already mentioned, but there's also a lot of lively and sentimental stuff. There's usually a bit more to pop than to the older entertainment music, which was plainly banal and fatuous.

I often hear people ask whether we, as Christians, can accept this modern music that so often conveys misery, despair or revolution?
I find this formulation of the problem unacceptable. If my neighbour, Mr Peters, is a communist, is he any less my neighbour? I have to accept him as my neighbour because he is a person and created by God. That does not mean that I have to agree with him or become a close friend, but I must not forget his needs. I have to make friends with him, otherwise we will be joining the priest and the Levite in the parable in ignoring the wounded. That is the very reason we are called to be aware of what is going on in the world. Take existentialist music. You could compare it with the beginning of our catechism: the scream of desperation. The deception is that there is only despair and no redemption, no answer. Christians can and should give the answer.

Isn't it a bit much to contend that every Christian should know everything about everything?
That is not what I mean, I mean that the body of Christians – the church – needs to be thinking about these things, one person grappling with this issue, the other with that, otherwise we miss the boat, and we will have to relinquish one domain after the other, head over heels, to unbelief. Why were we [as Christians] not the first to talk about the threat to our environment? We should have been at the forefront saying: 'This is God's creation. We shouldn't be damaging it!' Why did we reject the original black jazz years ago, without ever bothering to listen and ask ourselves whether it might help to rejuvenate Christian music? Have we really understood our calling?

Has no authentic Christian music emerged this [twentieth] century?
The only meaningful Christian music comes in the form of the gospel songs of Mahalia Jackson et al. A lot of new music of this genre

was made in the 1950s. Besides that [in the Netherlands] there are only our psalms and hymns, which are good as regards content but with a form, language and style that are old. Apart from black gospel there is no contemporary [Christian] music of any value or significance.

While we're on the subject of gospel I would like to go back to the previous question for a moment. In the 1950s I often heard people say, 'Those Negro spirituals are really beautiful, aren't they?' If you mentioned Mahalia Jackson, however, the reaction was completely negative: 'So rhythmic – heathen.' What had happened? People were 'enjoying' the completely romanticized and secular version of the black gospel. That's what happens when we're not keeping track of things. when we leave the good stuff and latch on to the bad. We trail along behind the world at a (safe) distance and neglect our own task.

What is your approach to youngsters who have become captivated by modern music?

I don't think that simply forbidding them to listen to it is the right way. If God doesn't prohibit it in the Bible, then we mustn't do it either. It is clear that adultery is a sin. That is clearly written in God's Law, but we may not impose new embargoes in order to stop people listening to music. One has to teach youngsters that music is not a neutral thing, that there is content and meaning that need be identified. Then you should say, 'Listen to this. Listen to that. Look at this point. Look at that aspect.' That is fighting the good fight – the spiritual battle – also in the area of popular music.

Recently I read this comment by Mahalia Jackson: 'It is impossible to sing spirituals in the church on Sunday and then give yourself to rock-and-roll on Monday.'

I agree hundred per cent. Making music of the rock type is out of the question because there is a big difference between doing it and listening to it. Jesus didn't say, 'what goes in corrupts' but he said, 'what comes out corrupts.' You must not submit to music that is by nature unchristian. Neither should you adopt rock by retaining its form and giving it new words. The content of rock is not in its words but in its form. The music has conveyed something before you have heard the words. 'Christened rock' is an utter contradiction in terms. Love of God and our neighbour is our basic norm. That means that we have to keep ourselves clean, but this implies that we have to be fully aware of what is going on. That's the only way we can help others.

What if you don't know anything about the background to modern music?

In that case you have to start by accepting the troubles and shortcomings of these times. Parents who are not able to give guidance to their children shouldn't oppose them without explaining why they are doing so. We can't change the fact that we are in the middle of a corrupt and broken world. One can't expect it to change in the twinkling of an eye with a minimum of effort. Let's start by admitting our own guilt, and by guilt I mean the full gravity of guilt. What has any of the last generations done for the cause of good music? What have we done to contribute? Once we have confessed we need to get working – and pray for God's blessing.

Can you elaborate on the task in practical terms?

We will have to start working together as Christians to make really new things. Renewal is possible if we make a concerted effort to separate the good from the bad, incorporating the good things and purging the bad. Our own works will have to be checked against Philippians 4:8 though we must not suppose that the text is referring solely to the sweet and charming. For we do need to recognize the trouble and strife in the world. It is going to take a lot of work to bring about change. When the spiritual reformation we pray for comes, when the Spirit really starts working, there must be followers ready to throw themselves into the task also in the area of music. This asks for preparation. A man like Dürer was a truly Reformed artist who was already active when Luther arrived.

A lot of people at the moment are arguing for upfront testimonies and for social isolation.

I know, but I don't believe that shunning the world has ever been the answer. Testimonies always involve struggling in this world. If there is no struggle, if we reach a stage where we are no longer active, we have become saltless salt – worthy of being discarded.

Can you fully identify with Luther's words, 'If I knew the world was going to end tomorrow I would plant a tree today?'

Yes, but also with Jeremiah and Isaiah who continued testifying to the Lord against the tide of their own culture. It's not a choice between withdrawing or participating, but we are called to 'prophesy'. That means standing by the grace of God in this world and saying, 'Look folks, the world is falling apart,' not in the superficial sense of 'you are bad and worldly' but with thought and discretion. We have to identify what exactly is good and what exactly is bad, otherwise no one will listen to us, otherwise our evangelization will be futile because we are unable to answer the questions of those who have become alienated from God. I believe that our calling is a prophetic attitude in the world of today. Is there an end to that calling? You have reached that point when you are pushed into a concentration camp. It's not up to us to decide when there is no room left for anything besides a straight testimony. That is decided by the God-led circumstances. If I am burned at the stake – yes, then I have to stop.

Classical Music

• Old music[520]

Have you ever looked at seventeenth-century paintings, like those of Vermeer? Did you notice how often they portray musicians? Indeed, people used to make a lot of music, particularly at home. Although concerts as we know them did not yet exist, and the Romantic phenomenon of the 'great soloist' had fortunately not yet emerged, musical performance itself was at a level of high quality. That was certainly the case, otherwise the composers of that period would never have attempted to write what they did, for this music is seldom easy. Still, it is very different from the later classical music. It is a world away from the individualistic assertion of technical virtuosity. We therefore also miss, fortunately, the museum-like quality that classical concerts sometimes have, when we feel obliged to bow down before the grandeur, sophistication and sublimity. As if it is not the primary purpose of music to give us pleasure. This also explains why we do not come across the bombast that sometimes makes nineteenth-century music so unpalatable – the so-called profound, the problematic, the crusade, the 'struggle' of the 'heroic' but 'oh so tragic' human being. The seventeenth century is more down to earth and at the same time much richer, because in its joyful directness it dares to express all sorts of moods – all aspects of life, even those less grand ones – humour, excitement, joy, but also sorrow, yearning, and so on. Nevertheless, it is never pretentiously sophisticated, never sentimental, never driven by mood alone – this music is deeper, and it reflects the breadth of human experience rather than only the emotional side.

While I realize that much of what I have written here is not that easy to pinpoint, we do recommend making a deep and serious attempt to understand seventeenth- and early eighteenth-century music. You will soon discover that there is far more music of that period worth listening to than only that of the musical giant, Bach.

This is also music that the jazz lover will be able to appreciate for here we find polyphony (the intertwinement of different parts), a steady rhythm and the same joy that characterizes good old New Orleans jazz. Modern jazz has learned a lot from the forms of this old music, but has embraced little or nothing of its character: where modern jazz is melancholic, bitter, abstract – alienated from reality – this music is open, joyful, and directly in touch with all aspects of everyday reality.

We may be very grateful that this sort of music is so easily accessible nowadays, particularly when we hear such magnificent recordings as the one discussed. It includes pieces by Pachelbel and Rosenmuller played by two violins and basso continuo (cello and harpsichord). There are also a number of pieces by Telemann and Buxtehude for harpsichord (a beautiful instrument that you could fall in love with), and a number of pieces by Telemann in which the flute plays an important role.

The information on the sleeve is clear and enlightening. Sylvie Spycket, the French ensemble that is featured on this record, plays with fantastic colour and verve – I could also call it 'swing'. It is obvious that this record, called *Les Maîtres allemands des XVIIe et XVIIIe siècles*, was played with much joy. I hope that many of you will listen to it and find it so.

• Bach and Mozart[521]

This time I have been asked to review two records, so that I was more than usually tempted to compare them. The first is an excellent performance of Bach's Cantata No. 12, *Weinen, Klagen, Zorgen, Zagen.* The second is an equally good performance of a mass by Mozart sung by the Viennese Sängerknaben and Symphoniker, directed by Rudolf Moralt. It is authentic in its use of a boys' choir.

Bach has a heavily laden text that talks of the suffering of Christians who have to bear the cross of Christ and, based on Romans 8, looks forward to future glory. The mass is also a heavy text, scriptural in content, talking of the work of our Lord. Like the Bach text it is a eulogy to Christ. Both works were written in the composers' early days – Bach's in 1714 and Mozart's in 1779 – but what a difference: not in the musicality of the performance, nor in the talent of the composers, for that is beyond discussion.

Bach's work is based on a solid and strong rhythm. It is heavy of tone – it is not a cheerful text – but not melancholic or tragic. On the contrary, a peaceful, certain joy that suffering does not have to have the last word pervades his music and makes it a Christian testimony – a call to a Christian acceptance of life.

A strong rhythm also permeates Mozart's work, but what a difference in tone – much lighter, more playful, more elegant. It is as if we had just entered an eighteenth-century Baroque church in Austria, in reality closer to Rococo than Baroque, of which the sensual and elegant adornments strike us as wordly. There is also a direct connection here, since this mass was written to mark the crowning of a statue of the Virgin Mary.

It is important to follow the text and it is a pity that it has not been printed on the sleeve. Nevertheless, it can be found in Höweler's *XYZ der Muziek* or in a similar encyclopedia. It will then become clearer that this music does not really fit the text at all. I am not talking about the form here, as the important passages are emphasized and, in view of the ceremony for which the mass was written, the part that refers to Mary – namely that Christ was born of the Virgin – is treated elaborately. Mozart also has not violated the text and has kept to the orthodox Christian understanding of it. But this is our complaint: the light, playful tone, the fact that there is nowhere any real expression of depth and that the work seems more like an opera than a mass, mutilates the dignity of the subject. In some of the solos, in the instrumental introductions and interludes, we are repeatedly reminded of the *Magic Flute*, for instance. However, what we find pleasing in the *Magic Flute*, transforming the music into a sparkling fairyland, suddenly becomes patently worldy in its superficiality here. It is refined humanism that is expressed, which does bow to the tradition in which the text is anchored but does not express it convincingly from within. Different values, different sentiments from those rooted in the text, find their expression here. We are not accusing Mozart of playing a cynical game, but we do not think that it is traditional faith – not even Roman Catholicism – that is being pronounced here.

If we want to study Mozart and the elegant world of Louis XVI, in which he lived and flourished – the world of the Enlightenment and of the gallant Rococo – then a work like this is very educational. All at once we can see where the weak spots are in the refined purity of Mozart's art – from an orthodox Christian viewpoint. It helps us understand Mozart's greatness in his *Figaro* or *Magic Flute*. We also see the positive side of his art in his elegant and apperceived ceremoniousness that almost makes Bach seem crude and coarse. But with Bach's supreme music we hear the voice of sober reality, cast in a well-defined form by a steady hand. Mozart flits through the heavy bits; Bach stands in the midst of the suffering and strife of daily life and is able to speak of real biblical joy, as in the bass aria that speaks of God taking away all pain.

These records are both strictly biblical in word, but they represent two different worlds. Scripture, to Mozart, is a piece of traditionalism; the core of the music and its rendition lies elsewhere. With Bach there is a sober directness that makes clear that his music does not honour tradition but rather speaks of personally experienced realities.

To use the phrases of the popular record review, with respect to Bach: play it often and be edified; with respect to Mozart: play it often and enjoy it but you might as well forget the text.

Notes to Volume 2

Part I: Philosophy and Aesthetics

1 *Gereformeerd Jongelingsblad* 6 (1947) p.54; 12:p.102; 20: pp.174–175; 38: pp.322-323
2 *Mededelingen van de Vereniging voor Calvinistische Wijsbegeerte* ('Proceedings of the Society for Calvinistic Philosophy') June 1967.
3 *Stijl* 2,3 (1953) pp.72–75; 4,4: pp.102–105.
4 *Oorsprong en Toekomst van de Creatieve Mens* (Amsterdam:Buijten en Schipperheijn, 1965).
5 First published in two parts in the Calvinist philosophical journal *Philosophia Reformata* (1946–47).
6 Cf. Dooyeweerd, *Encyclopedie der Rechtswetenschappen* II, p.139.
7 See Dooyeweerd, *New Critique of Theoretical Thought* II, pp.127–129, in the following we will abbreviate this title with *NCTT* (*Wijsbegeerte der Wetsidee* II, p.87; in the following abbreviated with: *W.d.W.*).
8 We will talk about culture later, see p.43 of this volume.
9 Also see Vestdijk, *Verwey en de Idee*, pp.102, 103.
10 See p.33 below.
11 For rhythm see the arithmetic analogy below.
12 See the biotic analogy.
13 Depth in a painting is also suggested 'in the movement of thought' by perspective. Perspective also falls within this analogy!
14 See 2B, #1, p.63.
15 Cf. Dooyeweerd, *Enyclopedie der Rechtswetenschappen* II, p.139.
16 Also see the same *Encyclopedie* II, p.13.
17 The meaning nucleus of the economic aspect is after all 'frugality' or 'saving' (cf. *NCTT* II, pp.66–67).
18 This anticipation expresses itself in music in the dynamics (diminuendo and crescendo), while sometimes one or more instruments play louder than others, so that they stand out, while the others in that case form a background or accompaniment. This seldom if ever appears in older music and in primitive music.
19 Cf. Korevaar-Hesseling, *Kunstgeschiedenis* (1923), p.20.
20 And neither may we draw the conclusion here that Rembrandt was a greater artist than van Eyck!
21 People often deny the relationship between beauty and the ethical aspect. With this they really never get any further than proving that love does not appear originally in the aesthetic sphere of meaning, and that therefore beauty and love are two law spheres differing in meaning. The connection between the two is always laid directly in naïve experience, which shows even more clearly that the denial in question has a purely theoretical character that falsifies reality.
22 See e.g. the compilation: *Drie op Een Perron* by Van Hoornik, Den Brabander and van Hattem.

23 *NCCT* II, p.347; *W.d.W.* II, p.278.
24 Economic retrocipation.
25 Social retrocipation.
26 See thing-causality *NCTT* III, p.64; *W.d.W.* III, p.44.
27 In this discussion of style we have limited ourselves mainly to the aesthetically qualified structures. For non-aesthetically qualified structures, this and the following paragraphs do not apply or apply to a lesser extent. The element of style does remain important, as we will discuss in more depth, see p.47, but the intermodal meaning coherence is then not led by the aesthetic aspect.
28 This is the historical structure function. Cf. 2B, #3, p.65.
29 Cf. Dr P.J. Bouman, *Van renaissance tot wereldoorlog* (1937), pp.39 ff., 52 ff.
30 Or rather, 'the norms, as they had wanted to positivize them, in view of their basic assumptions (religion)'. See also #4 below, p.39.
31 Refer also to my article on 'Style and World View', p.80 ff.
32 A negative answer to this question leads to the levelling, characterless 'internationalism' that had, and still has, a great influence, especially in architecture. It is human pride, hubris, which thinks it is able to ignore the influence of the integrating factors and of external limitations.
33 Cf. *NCTT* III, pp.496-498; *W.d.W.* III, p.436.
34 An anticipation to the social aspect.
35 See Burckhardt, *Kultur der Renaissance*, chapter 5.
36 An anticipatory moment to the logical.
37 Cf. NCTT III, p.590; *W.d.W.* III, p.530.
38 In the same way one currently speaks of 'abstract' art, while abstraction is not something of naïve experience and also not an act that belongs to concrete activities, such as the creation of works of art, but a method of science. 'Abstract art' is thus the consequence of not distinguishing the activities of the artist from those of the scientist. This is because one denies the existence of naïve experience. Abstract art is therefore a *contradictio in terminis*, since something concrete can never be abstract!
39 Amsterdam: Kosmos, 1935. See e.g. the Goetheneanum of anthroposophy.
40 See also Vriend, p.56.
41 Rotterdam: Brusse, 1940; p.200.
42 See *NCTT* III, pp.115–117; *W.d.W.* III, pp.83–85.
43 Whether one can also speak of inspiration outside of the aesthetic meaning we will leave aside.
44 Cf. *NCTT* II, p.472 ff.; *W.d.W.* II, p.407 ff.
45 Art is thus never literally an imitation of nature. Even those artists who support the statement that 'art is an imitation of nature' do not act according to it. For if they did, their work would not be able to reveal any style: nature is 'styleless', cf. #10, p.47.
46 Technique is a moment in the meaning of controlling formation.
47 See *NCTT* II, pp.176–178; *W.d.W.* II, p.122.
48 Here we might expect two cultures alongside each other, a Christian one and one in antithesis. But Christians and non-Christians do not live in isolation from each other; they influence each other and cooperate in the development of civilization. It is possible within a non-Christian society

for a Christian or a group of Christians to form a (partial) Christian art, and that in all sorts of contexts, such as the church, family or economic enterprise, the visible church will be revealed – but not as separate from the world, since in structures of state and economic enterprise Christians have to cooperate with others.

49 Cf. also in this regard #10 below.

50 *NCTT* III, p.114 (*W.d.W.* III, pp. 82, 83).

51 What is meant here is that the subjectivist in principle can say nothing else. We will also say: 'I find ... ', because we are amenable to revision and continue to be open to discussion. We too do not have a monopoly on wisdom and truth.

52 Cf. J. Maritain, *L'art et scolastique*, translated into Dutch by Terburg; see the chapter on 'Christian art'.

53 Ibid. p.99, cf. Pieter van de Meer de Walcheren, *Mijn Dagboek*, pp.66, 67, 75, 80, 84, 138, 146 (Utrecht: Spectrum, 5th ed.). See also #3, p.33 above.

54 The disclosure towards the juridical meaning is then naturally not normatively correct, whereby beauty is affected as a whole.

55 One can also read in this regard *NCTT* III, p.523 ff., p.534; *W.d.W.* III, p.467 ff., p.479.

56 Primitive in the sense of not disclosed, not differentiated.

57 See *W. d. W.* III, p.297 and *W. d. W.* II; meaning of history.

58 See *W. d. W.* II, p.297 ff.

59 In #11, p.49 ff. we will see an example of handling a young culture such as this.

60 Autonomous art is not as yet 'l'art pour l'art'!!

61 Cf. *W. d. W.* III, bottom of p.111.

62 'Styleless' is not used depreciatively here, as is obvious indeed. The term 'styleless' applied to works of art and other cultural forms is depreciating, however, since in that case it indicates that one of the aesthetic retrocipations has not been done justice to in the correct manner and that the norm for beauty is therefore not being satisfied.

63 Gates, lamps, ashtrays, etc.

64 'Streamline' is less an economic than a stylistic requirement.

65 Cf. Dr. K.J. Popma, *De vrijheid der exegese*, p.30, where among other things one reads, 'but there is for the man of sin no longer a place in history. The wicked are rejected from the earth.' It is obvious that with this the historical function has not vanished, that the normative aspect of our cosmos has not been affected.

66 For an extensive discussion of these matters, see *NCTT* III, p.346 ff. and *NCTT* II, p.312 ff.; *W.d.W.* III, p.295 ff. and *W.d.W.* II, p.240 ff.

67 See *Mens en Melodie* (1946) 2 and 4, where the texts are discussed more extensively by the expert Casper Höweler.

68 One can obviously never speak of free art in connection with the spiritual song, since in this case one is dealing with a form of enkapsis.

69 While black Americans dance to instrumental jazz music, we need to indicate that they do not dance to vocal blues. And yet the latter does not on that account manifest a less undifferentiated character. Blues songs are real folk songs.

70 Let us be thankful that in spite of the fact that in history little positive Christian art has been produced, not even in Western Europe, there is still so much beauty to be enjoyed. In this respect it becomes very clear what 'common grace' means.

71 See #8, p.45 ff.

72 The subjective actualization of not-permanently-actualizable structures is an exceptional case of this actualization-relationship.

73 *NCTT* III, pp.146–147; *W.d.W.* III, p.119–121.

74 See p.33.

75 The internal structural principle is therefore not affected. Cf. *NCTT* III, pp.637–638; *W.d.W.* III, p.561.

76 Writing in 1947, Hans Rookmaaker reflects here the view of political parties presented by Dooyeweerd in the original 1936 Dutch edition of *A New Critique*. Dooyeweerd later adopted the view that a political party is qualified as a moral, not pistical community. See L. Kalsbeek, *Contours of a Christian Philosophy* (Amsterdam, 1975) pp.255-258.

77 We can classify cinema as belonging to the genotype of drama.

78 See *NCTT* III, pp.139–140; *W.d.W.* III, p.111.

79 When we use the term 'bound to', we mean that the structure to which the others are bound is the leading structure. Thus if we say: 'Structure A is bound to structure B', then A is the guided structure and B is the guiding structure in the interlacement coherence.

80 We need to see architecture as one of the socially qualified structures, as we already discussed earlier.

81 Cf. *NCTT* III, p.565; *W.d.W.* III, p.510.

82 That 'abstract art' is a contradiction in terms we already discussed in note 38.

83 One finds this 'abstract' sculpture portrayed in Hamann, *Geschichte der Kunst*. See also the work of Barbara Hepworth in *Studio*, October 1946.

84 Thus one can appreciate different 'paintings' of e.g. Mondrian as designs for a stained glass window, for the decoration of a wall in a modern building, etc., but not as free works of art!

85 See the previously quoted book of Maritain, note 52.

86 See also chapter I, # 6, pp.43 ff.

87 In the first instance, a disclosure through the historical function.

88 Harmony in the music-technical sense of the word.

89 As I see it, rhythm holds a similar place in literary art. We would like to assign the so-called melody rhythm the same role as rhythm in expressive art and so on, namely as a retrocipation of the aesthetical in the numerical meaning (this melody rhythm is therefore a moment within the aesthetical meaning-individuality of the melody).

90 See *NCTT* III, p.637; *W.d.W.* III, p.561.

91 We will not investigate the post-psychical functions.

92 This is thus an aesthetically qualified imaginative image that is founded in the psychical aspect.

93 Frugality or 'saving' is the meaning nucleus of the economic aspect, which entails the 'balancing of needs according to a plan' (cf. *NCTT* II, pp.66–67).

94 Cf. *NCTT* II, p.238; *W.d.W.* II, p.176: 'Every positivizing formation of the modal norms of these later (i.e. later than the historical) law spheres is founded in the original formation of the cultural principles.'

95 The number of people who are discussed in literature, etc.

96 Taste is, as has already been discussed, a social analogy within the aesthetical. The intermodal relationship of meaning is again apparent here.

97 A. Smijers, *Algemene Muziekgeschiedenis*, p.288.

98 Cf. *NCTT* III, pp.117–120; *W.d.W.* III, pp.86–90.

99 Cf. *NCTT* III, p.419; *W.d.W.* III, p.374.

100 Cf. *NCTT* III, p.134; *W.d.W.* III, p.104 and *NCTT* II, p.390; *W.d.W.* II, p.322.

101 Many aestheticists struggle with the problem: how can art that reproduces something ugly be beautiful? This question usually comes up because they are creating a psychical aesthetics in which the meaning-boundaries between the beautiful and the psychical are erased. The answer must then also be that the work of art is (aesthetically) beautiful but has a (psychically) repulsive effect on us. In music, for example, dissonants are used to portray hair-raising moments, while dissonance as such do not strike us as pleasant. Psychically they evoke 'feelings of uneasiness' in us, but aesthetically they have to be justifiable, otherwise we are not dealing with a true work of art.

102 See social function.

103 *NCTT* III, p.121; *W.d.W.* III, p.91.

104 That a statement (of faith) that stems from human hubris, such as 'die Natur sich der Kunst unterwerfen muss, dass nur der das Bild zu geniessen vermag, der den Respekt vor den Natur verloren' (about Neo-Impressionism, in Hamann, *Geschichte der Kunst*, p.651) expresses itself in art is obvious.

105 At school we learn to think scientifically. Cf. Brunner, *Offenbarung und Vernunft* (Zürich, 1941) p.5.

106 Cf. P. van der Meer de Walcheren, *Mijn Dagboek*, pp.138, 84. (Utrecht: Spectrum, 5th ed.). Here 'apprehend' or 'experience' is preferable to 'sense' since, given our upbringing, 'sense' misleads us by connoting a psychology that violates all the meaning-boundaries.

107 See 2A, #1, p.56.

108 This also applies to paintings. We can see only a limited number of paintings in a museum during a particular interval of time, since we need to walk past them in order to look at them!

109 Cf. also the remark at the end of 2B, #2, p.65.

110 See 1, #6 of this article, p.43.

111 An anticipation to the social.

112 See #6 of this chapter, p.73.

113 See *NCTT* II, pp.127–128; *W.d.W.* II, p.87.

114 Cf. the definition of community, *NCTT* III, p.157; *W.d.W.* III, p.131. That the authoritative relationship also occurs in the orchestra or choir is directly apparent when we think of the position of the conductor.

115 It is very clear that this enkapsis expresses itself in the form. It is apparent that composers often put tremendous effort into it – Beethoven, for example, wrote three *Eleonore* overtures and finally composed the overture *Fidelio* as the definitive introduction to this opera.

116 Think of Ivone Georgi's ballet troupe, who, amongst others, danced the *Phantastique* of Berlioz, about which art critics had nothing good to say.
117 See also 'The relationship of actualization in the symbolic meaning-aspect', p.71.
118 We want to see the brass band too as a case of enkapsis with a social interlinkage.
119 Upon closer analysis one recognizes a state of affairs corresponding with that of painting: the close enkapsis paper-ink, in which the objective structure of the visual image of letters and notes is founded.
120 See *NCTT* III, p.151; *W.d.W.* III, p.125.
121 For an analogy see *NCTT* III, pp.150–153; *W.d.W.* III, pp.125–128.
122 Cf. *NCTT* III, pp.92-32; *W.d.W.* III, p.59.
123 See *NCTT* II, pp.573, 575; *W.d.W.* II, pp.506, 509.
124 See *NCTT* II, p.487; *W.d.W.* II, p.422.
125 *Nieuw Nederland 1* (1946), 49, p.7; 51, p.5–6; 52, p.10–11; 53, p.6
126 The word 'positivize' was used originally in the field of legal formation, where legal norms are given shape in the so-called positive law. This concept is now also applied to other fields.
127 The current article was published in *Correspondentiebladen van de Vereniging voor Calvinistische Wijsbegeerte*, c. 1948, pp.11–14.
128 *Tydskrif vir Wetenskap en Kuns* (Journal of the South African Academy of Science and the Arts') October 1949.
129 *NCTT* I, p.171.
130 In their individual founding relationship, going from the bottom to the top: numerical, spatial/kinematic, physical, biotic, sensitive (psychic), logical, historical, lingual/symbolic, social, economic, aesthetic, juridical, ethical and pistical.
131 Cf. *A New Critique of Theoretical Thought* III, p.479–480.
132 Published in *Correspondentiebladen van de Vereniging voor Calvinistische Wijsbegeerte* ['Newsletters of the Association of Calvinistic Pilosophy'] 17 (1953) 1, pp.16–18
133 Cf. my article 'Sketch for an Aesthetic Theory based on the Philosophy of the Cosmonomic Idea', p.62 above.
134 Originally published in *Stijl*, February 1953; an English translation appears in volume 4 of the *Complete Works*.
135 Published in *Correspondentiebladen van de Vereniging voor Calvinistische Wijsbegeerte* 31 (1967) 1: pp.8–15; 2: pp.9–19.
136 All historians agree that during the eighteenth century a deep break occurred with the past. This is certainly clear also in the history of art. Much has been written on this subject. To mention just a few works: R. Williams, *Culture and Society 1780 – 1950* (London, 1958); T. Hetzer, *F. Goya und die Krise der Kunst um 1800*, *Wiener Jahrbuch für Kunstgeschichte* XIV (1950), p.7-22; A. Hauser, 'Die Romantik und der Verlust der Realität', in *Philosophie der Kunstgeschichte* (München, 1958) p.56 ff.; W. Hofman, *Das irdische Paradies* (Munich, 1960); H. Ulmann, *Der Weg des 19. Jahrhunderts am Abgrund der Ersatzreligion* (München, 1949); S. Spender, *The Struggle of the Modern* (London, 1963); G. Groen van Prinsterer, *Ongeloof en Revolutie* (Kampen, 1904/1848).

137 Cf. J.H. van den Berg, *Leven in meervoud* (Nijkerk, 1964, 3) p.140.

138 Cf. ibid., p.140 ff.

139 'L'art primitif procède de l'esprit et emploie la nature. L'art soi-disnat raffiné procède de la sensualité er sert la nature. La nature est la servante du premier et la maîtresse du second. Mais la servante ne peut pas oublier son origine; elle avilit l'esprit en se laissant adorer par lui. C'est ainsi que nous sommes tombés dans l'abominable erreur du naturalisme.' As quoted in my *Synthetist Art Theories*, cf. notes 507 and 655 in volume 1 of the *Complete Works*.

140 Cf. my 'The Artist a Prophet' in *Art and the Public Today* (Huémoz, 1969).

141 J. Klapwijk, *Tussen Historisme en Relativisme* (Assen, 1970), with German summary; T. Lessing, *Geschichte als Sinngebung des Sinnlosen* (1919); M.C. Smit, 'Historisme en antihistorisme', in *Wetenschappelijke bijdragen, opgedragen aan Prof. Dr D.H.Th. Vollenhoven* (Kampen: Kok, 1951) p.153 ff.; E. Rothacker, *Die dogmatische Denkform in den Geisteswissenschaften und das Problem des Historismus* (Wiesbaden, 1954); E. Troeltsch, *Der Historismus und seine Probleme* (1922); E. Troeltsch, *Der Historismus und seine Überwindung* (1924); K. Heussi, *Die Krisis des Historismus* (1932); Popper's idea of historicism is maybe related, but not quite what is meant here.

142 A. Malraux, *Le musée imaginaire ... La métamorphose des Dieux* (Paris, 1957); cf. W. Richter, *The Rhetorical Hero, an Essay on the Aesthetics of A. Malraux* (London, 1964).

143 See J.M.M. Aler et al., *De Functie van de Kunst in onze Tijd* (The Hague, 1962). My contribution is an attempt to describe this function as simply and concisely as possible. However, there too I became convinced that I was not actually dealing with the work of art.

144 See also my article 'The Artist a Prophet?' (*Art and the Public Today*, Huémoz, 1969) in volume 5 of the *Complete Works*.

145 I also wrote about the structure of a work of art in my *Art and Entertainment*, see volume 3 of the *Complete Works*.

146 Three entries in Baker's *Dictionary of Christian Ethics* by Carl F. H. Henry ed. (1973).

147 For further reading, see Gilson, *Painting and Reality* (London, 1957); R. Berger, *Decouverte de La peinture* (Lausanne, 1958); R. Huyghe, *Dialogue avec le visible* (Paris, 1955); F. Wurtemberger, *Weltbild und Bilderwelt* (Vienna, 1958); H. Sedlmayr, *Kunst und Wahrheit* (Hamburg, 1958); E. Panofsky, *Meaning in the Visual Arts* (Garden City N. Y.: Anchor- Doubleday, 1955); J. Hospers, *Meaning and Truth in the Arts* (Chapel Hill: University of North Carolina, 1946); H. Read, *The Meaning of Art* (Baltimore: Penguin, 1949); H. Read, *Icon and Idea* (London, 1955); E. H. Gombrich, *Art and Illusion* (Princeton: Princeton University, 1960); R. Arnheim, *Art and Visual Perception* (London, 1956); K. Boulding, *The Image* (Ann Arbor: University of Michigan, 1956); W. Schone, *Über das Licht in der Malerei* (Berlin, 1954); H.R. Rookmaaker, *Kunst en Amusement* (Kampen, 1962); H.R. Rookmaaker, *Modern Art and the Death of a Culture* (Inter-Varsity Press, 1970); Lawrence Lipking, *The Ordering of the Arts in Eighteenth-century England* (Princeton: Princeton University, 1970).

148 For further reading see *Encyclopedia of World Art* (New York: McGraw-Hill, 1961) IV: 'Criticism'; V: 'Aesthetics'; and extensive bibliographies; H.R. Rookmaaker, *Synthetist Art Theories* (Amsterdam, 1959 / *Complete Works* 1; H. Osborne, *Aesthetics and Art Theory, a Historical Introduction* (New York: E.P. Dutton, 1970).

149 Originallly published as 'De werklijkheid, Wijsbegeerte, Kunst en Wij' in *Beweging* 40 1 (1976).

150 E. Panofsky, *Die Perspektive als Symbolische Form, Afsatze zu Grundfragen der Kunstwissenschaft* (Berlin, 1964) pp.99–168.

151 This article was published in *Philosophia Reformata* 41, 1–2 (1976) pp. 77–79; *Turnabout in Aesthetics to Understanding* was published by the Insitute for Christian Studies, Toronto (1972).

Part II: Jazz, Blues and Spirituals

The books referred to by shortened titles are listed in the Selected Bibliography to the First Edition on page 310. The recordings listed in these endnotes pertain to those mentioned throughout the book. In order to help the reader/listener, I have also given the records ratings according to my opinion of their importance. [Note that an Updated Discography has been included in this volume, p. 312.] Records have not primarily been rated according to their quality but according to how interesting they might be to the jazz novice. Four stars mean that the recording makes for essential listening – worth getting hold of; three stars, less so, and so on.

Where a record is hard to obtain, it is indicated with one cross, and if it is very rare, two crosses. The records are, as far as possible, samplers, i.e. multi-track recordings that feature various good examples of different genres. Two of these are mentioned several times and have been abbreviated and the crosses omitted. They are:

ITJ **** Brunswick 87003 LPBM, *New Orleans, Dixieland, Chicago: An Introduction To Traditional Jazz.*
HJC ***† *History Of Classic Jazz:* a collection of five LPs, bound, with introduction. Riverside SDP 11 (RLP 12-112/116).

Besides the standard abbreviations of the well-known labels, the following abbreviations have been used:

FoW – Folkways
FoW MS – Folkways' *Music from the South* series, nine records, also available separately. FP 650/658, indicated here as I-IX.
LiC – A Library of Congress recording of US folk music. (The Library of Congress is a large scientific institute in Washington.) With the exception of a few other recordings, it is primarily these albums of black folk music which interest us. (There are also recordings of Indian music and white folk music.) After 'LiC', I have indicated with a roman numeral the number of the album which includes that particular track. These albums have also been released as LPs and are available on order.

Note: London records mentioned here are also available on the Riverside label.

152 Originally published in Dutch by Zomer en Keunings (Wageningen, the Netherlands, 1960).
153 ** FoW P 500 B (together with B, two records, series *Negro Folk Music of Africa and America*).
154 HCJ.
155 O. Downes, E. Siegmeister: *A Treasury of American Song* (New York, 1943, second edition) p.90.
156 LiC VIII No. 40.
157 ** FoW P 500 B.
158 Ibid.
159 Ibid.
160 Note that in the lyrics a refrain printed in italics means it is sung by the choir. Also, we have used standard and not phonetic spellings in the lyrics.
161 *** *Murderer's Home*, Nixa NJL 11.
162 I traced the melody from a similar Dutch song called 'In Holland staat een huis', back to a spiritual. Perhaps it was derived from Dutch children's games – on the record *He Shut the Lion's Mouth*, Vi 38507, Elder Richard Bryant, vocals and orchestra.
163 ** FoW EFL 1417, *Negro Folk Music of Alabama*, secular. For children's songs also: *Ring Games*, FoW FP 704.
164 Ibid.
165 *Celestin's Tuxedo Jazz Band*, Storyville SEP 308 (EP).
166 Natalie Curtis-Burlin, *Negro Folk Songs*, Hampton series IV, New York, 1919.
167 See leaflet with FoW EFL 1417.
168 Dr. J.W. Schulte Northolt, *Het volk dat in duisternis wandelt* (Arnhem, 1957) p.163.
169 A.o. on FoW EFL 1417.
170 J. Chandler Harris: *Uncle Remus* (New York, 1933) p.7 ff.
171 This adaptation by J. Harris of the stories in which Brer Rabbit plays the leading role was used by Walt Disney for the cartoon film based on the story.
172 ** FoW MS VI
173 M. Mark Fisher, *Negro Slave Songs in the U.S.* (Ithaca, N.Y., 1953) p.30.
174 M.A. Grissom, *The Negro Sings a New Heaven* (Chapel Hill, 1930) p.69.
175 G.P. Jackson, *Spiritual Folk-Songs of Early America* (New York, 1937) p.193, no. 184; Idem, *White Spirituals*, p.264.
176 Many versions including Mahalia Jackson (Vogue 103); a church, Dr Watts-type songs, **FoW EFL 1418 (*Negro Folk Music of Alabama*, religious); †† Rev. J.M. Gates (Victor 20216; ca. 1925).
177 H.A.L. Jefferson, *Hymns in Christian Worship* (London, 1950); S.R. Cowell, 'The "Shaped-Note Singers" and their Music', *The Score* (London, June 1955); G. Woodcock, 'The English Hymn', *Folk I* (London, 1945); G.P. Jackson, *White and Negro-Spirituals* (New York, 1943) and the literature mentioned in note 174.

178 See introduction J.W. Johnson, *Books of American Negro-Spirituals*, (New York, 1940).
179 Several renditions, a.o. by the Davis Sisters, **† Savoy Mg 14014.
180 Doc Reed, ** FoW EFL 1418.
181 Georgia Peach, † Classic Editions 5001.
182 J.B.T. Marsh, *The Story of the Fisk Jubilee Singers* (Boston); G.D. Pike, *The Jubilee Singers and their Campaign for Twenty Thousand Dollars* (Boston, 1873).
183 Fisk University Jubilee Quartet, †† Victor 16453; ca. 1910.
184 Rev. T.E. Weems and congregation, †† Col. 14254-D; ca. 1926–1927.
185 Rev. J.C. Burnett, **** Fontana 467064 TE.
186 E.g. *Noël à Harlem*, ** Ducretet-Thomson 260V069.
187 LiC X, by Doc Reed.
188 *** FoW MS V.
189 LiC VIII by Moses Platt.
190 Mississippi John Hurt, †† Okeh 8654, 1928; and Woody Guthrie a.o., ***† 'Stain Gang' Stinson SL 87.
191 ** FoW MS VI.
192 *** *Murderer's Home*, Nixa NJL 11.
193 ** FoW EFL 1417 – Ruby Pickins Tartt discovered the singer Rich Amerson.
194 LiC VIII.
195 Langston Hughes, Arna Bontemps, *The Poetry of the Negro 1746–1949* (Garden City, N.Y., 1953).
196 Cf. e.g. LiC IV, McKinley Morganfield (and text on leaflet).
197 **† Jazz Society AA 513 (78 r.p.m.); London AL 3508 (small LP).
198 * FoW MS IV.
199 E.g. 'Another man done gone down', by Vera Hall, LiC IV; Joe Williams, 'Baby please don't go', †† Bluebird B 6200, 1934.
200 **** Fontana 462021 TE. In this analysis I have borrowed a lot from an unpublished study about the blues of the late Drs F.G. Boom. Cf. the LP *Nothing but the Blues* that I compiled: **** Fontana 682073 TL.
201 †† Bluebird B 5877, 1935
202 **** Vogue LD030; ** Philips B08102L.
203 See note 200.
204 Anonymous, *Belle Bradley: her Story* (New York, 1953).
205 Barbecue Bob (= Robert Hicks), †† Col. 14331-D.
206 LiC III.
207 **** FoW FP 38, Doc Reed and Vera Hall Ward.
208 Snitcher Roberts, *Snitcher's Blues*, †† Okeh 8781, 1930; and the Fontana record mentioned in note 198.
209 Idem.
210 **** Vogue LD030.
211 Cf. M.W. Stearns, *The Story of Jazz* (London, 1957) p.276.
212 Sterling Brown, *Ma Rainey*, *Southern Road* (New York, 1932) pp.62-64.
213 Records of Ma Rainey reissued on London, a.o. **** London AL 3502.

214 FoW MS I.
215 † Traditional Recordings, (Col.), TPL 1007.
216 *** FoW MS V.
217 *** FoW FP53 (Jazz, vol I, the South).
218 Cf. R.W. Logan, *The Negro in the United States* (Princeton, N.Y., 1957) p.39 ff.
219 A late example from before 1920 is HCJ – Fred van Eps, *Ragtime Creole*.
220 *** London AL 3515 and HCJ.
221 Literature about ragtime: R. Blesh and H. Janis, *They All Played Ragtime* (New York, 1950; second ed. 1959); G. Waterman, 'A Survey of Ragtime', *Record Changer* XIV:7 (New York, 1956); G. Waterman, 'Joplin's Late Rags', *Record Changer* XIV: 8 (1956). These articles have been reprinted in M.T. Williams, *The Art of Jazz* (New York, 1959).
222 G. Waterman, 'Joplin's Late Rags', *Record Changer* XIV: 8 (1956) p.5.
223 R. Blesh and H. Janis, *They All Played Ragtime* (New York, 1950; second ed. 1959) pp.253, 254.
224 See note 218 and also S.B. Charters, *Jazz: New Orleans 1885–1957* (N.Y.: Belleville 1958) p.3.
225 † American Music 513
226 S.B. Charters, *Jazz: New Orleans 1885-1957* (N.Y.: Belleville 1958) p.22
227 ITJ.
228 † Odeon 279.790, recording of 1926. Various reissues.
229 Leaflet FoW MS I.
230 * HMV B 9216 (and reissues) (tape recording 1939); **** General 589, piano solo (reissues on LP by Vogue and M.M.S.).
231 A rendition by George Lewis Orchestra: ** Blue Note BLP 7027, 1955.
232 We use the word blacks to distinguish them from the French-oriented Creoles, although many of these English-speaking Protestants were also black people.
233 *Heah Me Talkin' To Ya*, p. 50 (see bibliography on p.311 for full title).
234 Cf. Winthrop Sargeant, *Jazz: Hot and Hybrid* (New York, 1946).
235 **** Vogue V 2119 (and reissue on LP of Vogue).
236 ***† American Music: *Babe Dodds No. 1*; Young Tuxedo Brass Band, *** Atlantic 1297, 1958; Eureka Brass Band, ** FoW FA2462, 1956.
237 Originally LiC, reissue on ****† Circle LP (L14001), recently another reissue: **** Riverside 9001.
238 Text printed in Lomax, *Mister Jelly Roll*, p.3 ff.
239 Same series as in note 237, ****† Riverside 9003.
240 Recordings of piano solo's of 1923: **** London L 3559; recordings of 1937 on LiC, same series as note 77, ****† Riverside 9004.
241 **** London AL 3559 and ****† AFCDJ A09.
242 See note 240.
243 Piano solo 1923 **** London AL 3559, tape recording **** RCA LPM-1649-C.
244 As described in his book, *Mister Jelly Roll*.
245 **** Riverside 9001.

246 Compare Scott Joplin's *Entertainer* (*** London AL 3515) and Bunk Johnson's rendition of the same piece on the basis of such an arrangement (* Philips B O7009 L).

247 ***† American Music LP645.

248 *Heah Me Talkin' To Ya*, p.77.

249 Cf. Ramsey & Smith, *Jazzmen*, p.v.

250 *Heah Me Talkin' To Ya*, p.37.

251 ** HMV DLP 1065.

252 See note 251; cf. **** RCA LPM-1649-C.

253 W.C. Handy, *A Treasury of the Blues* (New York, 1949; second edition) p.18; see also W.C. Handy, *Father of the Blues, an Autobiography* (New York, 1947).

254 H.C. Cayton & St. Clair Drake, *Black Metropolis*, London, 1946.

255 About the recordings, where they have been issued and the musicians involved, very accurate information is to be found in W.C. Allen and Brian A.L. Rust, *King Joe Oliver* (N.Y.: Belleville, 1955).

256 A. Coeuroy, *Histoire générale du jazz* (Paris, 1942).

257 **** Philips B O7435L, **** Col. 1065, and Riverside 12–101.

258 **** London AL 3504.

259 **** HMV B9221.

260 ITJ.

261 ***† Blue Star BS95 (1946) and other issues.

262 ***† American Music, *Baby Dodds Album No.1*.

263 Accelerando means an increase in tempo. Rallentando means a decrease in tempo. Rubato denotes that part of the melody is to be slightly overstretched or played slightly too quickly. Agogic accent is a subtle extension of the note in order to emphasize it within the melody.

264 Also compare Grossman & Farrell, *The Heart of Jazz.*

265 Louis Armstrong, *Satchmo, my Life in New Orleans* (New York, 1954).

266 Ramsay & Smith, *Jazzmen*, pp.89, 91; idem., *Heah Me Talkin' To Ya*, p.169.

267 So we do not agree with C. Delaunay, *De la vie et du jazz* (Lausanne, 1946).

268 †† Anthologie du jazz AFG 7, *** London AL 3524.

269 †† Okeh 4925, 1923. *** Fontana 682.055 TL (*Bechet Memorial Album*).

270 Bechet, who recently died, had been recorded many times. His best, apart from the ones already mentioned, are the recordings from 1925 together with Armstrong under leadership of Clarence Williams. See the Fontana LP, note 269.

271 This whole article has been incorporated in M.T. Williams, *The Art of Jazz* (New York, 1959) p.3 ff.

272 Morton's piano solos on **** London AL 3559; Oliver's band on **** Philips B 07435L and HCJ.

273 *Heah Me Talkin' To Ya*, p.116.

274 ** London AL3536.

275 The bass sax from Oliver's band served to double the trombone contribution and Bechet employed his soprano sax as a clarinet. The alto and tenor saxes are the very instruments that obscure the sound in this sort of band.

276 HCJ.

277 Ibid.

278 Ibid.

279 Ibid.

280 * Philips B 07020, *The Bix Beiderbecke Story*; * Philips BO7226L (only 'Goose pimples').

281 Recordings on the record: LiC VIII (Arthur Bell, 1939); *† Asch 343-3 (Leadbelly, 1943); *** Vogue V 2074 (Broonzy, 1951), etc.

282 **** Fontana 467064 TE; HCJ; for the rest this kind of recordings are very rare.

283 E.g. * Ducretet-Thomson 260 V 069, 1955.

284 It is curious that the image of a train was already used on a gravestone in Ely (England) dating from 1845.

285 **** Fontana 467064 TE; †† Col. 14180, 1926.

286 See Langston Hughes and Arna Bontemps, *The Poetry of the Negro 1746-1949* (Garden City, 1953); the anthology edited by Rosey E. Pool and P. Breman, *Ik zag hoe zwart ik was* (The Hague, 1958); Dr. J.W. Schulte Northolt, *Het volk dat in duisternis wandelt* (Arnhem, 1957) p.218 ff.

287 J.W. Johnson: *Books of American Negro Spirituals* (New York, 1940).

288 Of both kinds, though many records were made they were not reissued and these recordings are now very rare. For that reason I will not list any record numbers.

289 *** Fontana 467063 TE. Cf. also **** Fontana 682073 TL.

290 ***† Col. DZ 346; Philips issued a whole series of LP's of Bessie (B)7002L/B O7005L, of which in my opinion *** B O7002L is the best.

291 **** Fontana 682073 TL

292 ** Fontana 467136 TE.

293 *** London AL 3535 (*Backwood Blues*).

294 †† Col. 14246-D, 1927–1928.

295 We already mentioned the unpublished study of the late Drs. F.G. Boom and Iain Lang, 'Jazz in Perspective, the Background of the Blues' (London, n.d.). Also very important is the recording of a conversation between three blues singers: *Blues in the Mississippi Night*, ** Nixa NJL 8.

296 †† Br. 7126, 1929.

297 **† Score SLP 4022 (Lightnin' Hopkins) and also many records of Big Bill Broonzy, recorded after the War.

298 ** London AL 3506.

299 ***† Parlophon R 2187: Jess Stacy.

300 *** London AL 3525; *** HMV. DLP 1048; *** Riverside 1028. And boogie-woogie recordings on HCJ and ** Br. BL 54014.

301 †† Victor 20415.

302 FoW FP1.

303 **† HMV JK 2773.

304 **† HMV B 5430, 1927.

305 **** RCA LPM-1649-C.

306 Lomax, *Mister Jelly Roll*, pp.192, 193 and 102.

307 †† HMV B 5173 (Johnny Hamp's Kentucky Serenaders, a dance band ca.

1925/1926.
308 ITJ; also *Dazzling Jazz, Traditional,* ** Philips B 07226L ('China Boy').
309 Many reissues of these records, such as **** Col. 3 SX 1029; **** Philips B O7181L.
310 ** Coral 94040 EPC, ITJ.
311 Ibid.
312 ITJ; of these Hot Seven there are many reissues, a.o. *** Col. 33s 1041; *** Philips B O7237 L.
313 See note 309.
314 **** Philips B O7428L.
315 **† Parlo R448 and reissues.
316 HCJ and ** London AL 3505, etc.
317 See previous note; also *** HMV DPL 1073; ** Vogue-Coral LRA 10025.
318 **† HMV B4970 and reissues of music by this orchestra.
319 Ibid.
320 ITJ; **** Vogue-Coral LRA 10020.
321 ****† Jazz Society AA 539; for other releases of this orchestra see previous note.
322 Ibid.
323 **** Fontana 462023TE; compare also **** Fontana 682073 TL, on which there are also two pieces of Williams.
324 ** Col.33s 1067.
325 *Heah Me Talkin' To Ya*, p.167.
326 **** RCA LPM-1649-C.
327 * HMV DLP 1044.
328 Ibid.
329 ** HMV B 10683 and other reissues.
330 Blesh, *Shining Trumpets*, p.262.
331 S.B. Charters, *Jazz, New Orleans 1885–1957* (N.Y.: Belleville, 1958).
332 ** FoW FP 55.
333 *** Fontana 467137 TE.
334 *Heah Me Talkin' To Ya*, p.198.
335 † Col. MZ 336. No reissues known to me. Another version on **** Fontana 682073 TL. Other recordings of this orchestra: London AL 3547 and HCJ.
336 B. Ulanov, *Duke Ellington* (New York, 1946) p.14.
337 London AL 3551, HCJ.
338 *Heah Me Talkin' To Ya*, p.209.
339 J. de Trazegnies, *Duke Ellington* (Brussels, 1946) p.7, 8.
340 Ulanov, *Duke Ellington*, p.64.
341 Ibid. p.45, 73.
342 RCA L 20099.
343 Reissued on ** Philips and ** HMV DLP 1094.
344 †† Bluebird B 6084.

345 ** HMV DLP 1067.

346 **** Fontana 462022TE.

347 *** FoW FG 3585.

348 Ibid. Unfortunately not much has been reissued here. Records are very rare and almost always in poor condition, proof of the fact that they were played a lot by the African-Americans who possessed them.

349 HMV DLP 1105.

350 ** HMV CLP 1035.

351 †† HMV JF 11.

352 † HMV B8408 (reissue on RCA).

353 ITJ.

354 Ibid.

355 They were (partly) issued on albums (later on LP's).

356 We have already often quoted this series, LiC.

357 LiC III.

358 Many recordings exist. Leadbelly is very well represented on releases of FoW, such as ** FP 14, ** FP 4, ** FP 24, etc.

359 LiC X (Turner Junior Johnson, 1942).

360 *** FoW 35 (recording ca. 1950).

361 On p. 33 of the 1930 edition.

362 *** FoW MS IX.

363 Lomax, *Mister Jelly Roll*, pp.64-66.

364 On **** Circle 14001-14012. Recently a new issue of this series came out: **** Riverside 9001-9012.

365 For General, reissued on **** Vogue LD 100, **** Vogue LDE080, and by M.M.S.

366 †† Perfect 0298 (also other recordings are very rare. Unfortunately no reissues).

367 ****† Decca M 30270.

368 ****† Decca BM 02737.

369 Br. 87054 LPBM, *Bad Luck Blues*, a collection album on which a number of this kind of records were brought together. Cf. also **** Fontana 682073 TL.

370 **† Continental C-6053.

371 RCA A 130212 (Artie Shaw). Recordings of swing bands also on *Dazzling Jazz, Big Sound,* * Philips B 07228L.

372 *Heah Me Talkin' To Ya*, p.282.

373 Ibid., pp.273, 275.

374 See the Philips record in note 360.

375 *Heah Me Talkin' To Ya*, p. 315.

376 Ibid., p.280.

377 Ibid.

378 Ibid. p. 361.

379 Stearns, *Story of Jazz*, p.230.

380 Ibid. pp.223-4.
381 E.g. Charlie Parker on * Savoy G 12000.
382 * Vogue EPL 7036.
383 Grossman & Farrell, *The Heart of Jazz*, p.114 ff.
384 Ibid., p.122. Modern jazz is well summarized on the LP *Dazzling Jazz, Modern*, * Philips B 07227L.
385 *Heah Me Talkin' To Ya*, p.362.
386 As mentioned earlier, semi-professional is someone who has another job alongside their musical activities and whose income does not depend on playing music.
387 † Esquire 10-111 and 10-112.
388 **** Blue Note 1206 (LP).
389 Releases on Jazzman and Jazz Information. Reissues e.g. *** Commodore CEP 79.
390 ****† American music 638.
391 ****† American Music Baby Dodds No. 1.
392 ****† American Music 531.
393 ** Br. EPB 10006.
394 ITJ.
395 Philips B O7009L.
396 HCJ. Also, for example, ** Blue note BLP7027; *** Riverside 207.
397 E.g. Oliver's 'Sobbin' blues' with the rendition of the Down Town Jazz Band, RCA 75.159.
398 HCJ and *Dazzling Jazz, Traditional*, * Philips B O7226.
399 **** London H-APB 1039: *Riverside Roustabouts*.
400 ** Decca LF 1196.
401 Part of * Vogue 30.056, for the rest e.g. Fontana 462047, etc.
402 **** Vogue LD073.
403 **** Parlophon PMD 1070.
404 Ibid.
405 *** Vogue LDM 10008.
406 ***† Savoy MG 14014
407 *Murderer's Home*, *** Nixa NJL 11.
408 ** FoW EFL 1417-1418
409 **** FoW FP38.
410 FoW MS.
411 FoW MS IV
412 ***† Stinson SLP56 (recorded in 1954).
413 FoW FP53 (with several other recordings, also by Leadbelly).
414 † Score SLP 4022.
415 FoW FA 2463.
416 Eureka Brass Band. * FoW FA 2462; Young Tuxedo Brass Band, *** Atlantic 1297; Original Zenith Brass Band, * Riverside 283.
417 'Dazzling jazz, traditional', ** Philips B07226L.

418 'Solitude', Philips B 07302L.
419 *** London LTZ-K15024.
420 ITJ.
421 'Dazzlin jazz, modern', * Philips B07227L.
422 Many recordings including RCA A130222.
423 ** London LTZ-K 15022.
424 Ibid.
425 **** Vogue V134 (recorded in 1951).
426 London LTZ-D15168.
427 Vogue EPL 7538 and on Vogue 30.056.
428 ** Ducretet-Thomson 260 VB 069 (1955).
429 *** Westminster WP6089.
430 **** Philips B 07077L.
431 Ibid.
432 Philips 429177 BE.
433 **** *Good Time Jazz* JS 845 and re-releases on EP.
434 **† Melodisc, 1102 Disc 7110 (of which there are also more recent releases).
435 **** Philips B O7077L and other releases on Philips and on Vogue.
436 **** Philips B O7077L.
437 Referring to the day she dies (or Judgment Day).
438 2 Timothy 4:8; Revelation 2:10; 4:4.
439 See note 437.
440 John 14:2; 2 Corinthians 5:1.
441 The new, heavenly Jerusalem; Hebrews 12:22.
442 Zechariah 3:4; Revelation 1:13; 7:9–17.
443 Revelation 21:6; John 4:14; Isaiah 12:3.
444 Matthew 25:10; cf. Revelation 3:7.
445 Ezekiel 47.
446 A name for the land of Israel in Isaiah 62:4, referring here to heaven.
447 Revelation 9:13; 11:1.
448 In heaven or on the new earth she will meet Daniel.
449 Refering to the three Hebrew youngsters in the furnace, Daniel 3.
450 Christ, cf. Song of Solomon 2:1.
451 Ibid.
452 'Roll' refers to the Book of Life, cf. Revelation 20:12; 21:27.
453 Revelation 21:18-21; 22:14; 21:12.

Part III: Music Articles

454 *Gramofoon*, November, 1954.
455 Originally published in *Philips Music Herald* (1964/65) pp. 17-20.
456 *Gramofoon*, November 1958. Series discussed: *Treasures of North American Negro*

Music, including records (45 rpm): *Leroy Carr*: Fontana TE 462021 (45); *Blind Willie Johnson*: Fontana TE 462022 (45); *Clarence Williams' Jazz Kings*: Fontana TE 462023 (45).

457 *Gramofoon*, March 1956. Record discussed: *Backwoods Blues*, London.

458 Cf. 'Les Troubadours et le Sentiment Romanesque' by R. Briffault (1945) on *Backwoods Blues*, London.

459 *Gramofoon*, March 1955. Record discussed: *The Folk Blues of Blind Lemon Jefferson*, London AL 3506.

460 *Gramofoon*, July 1955. Record discussed: *Ida Cox Sings the Blues*, London AL 3517.

461 *Gramofoon*, January 1958. Records discussed: *Blues in the Mississippi Night*, Nixa NJL 8; *Prison Songs – Murderer's Home*, Nixa NJL 11.

462 *Gramofoon*, April 1956. Record discussed: *Music from the South: Field recordings taken in Alabama, Louisiana and Mississippi*, by Frederick Ramsey Jr., Guggenheim Fellow, Vol. 1: *Country Brass Bands* (FP 650), Vol. 2–4: *Horace Sprott 1–3* (FP 651/652/653).

463 *Gramofoon*, September 1955. Record discussed: *Big Bill Broonzy, Blues Singer*, Vol. 1: *Vocal and guitar*, Vogue LD 030.

464 *Gramofoon*, January 1961. Record discussed: *Nothin' but the Blues*, Fontana TL 682073.

465 *Nothin' but the Blues*, Fontana TL 682073.

466 Published in *The Gordon Review*, Vol IX, 2–3, 1966.

467 I use this term 'Western' to denote white European culture, often on the level of folk song and the like, as found in the United States. Thus we do not mean 'Western' in the sense of hillbillies, etc.

468 Published by Chapel Hill, 1933.

469 Wageningen: N. V. Gebr. Zomer & Keunings Uitgeversmaatschappij, 1960 (in Dutch).

470 F. Ramsay and C. E. Smith, *Jazzmen* (New York, 1939); R. Blesh, *Shining Trumpets: A History of Jazz* (New York, 1946).

471 I shall not go into details here, but hope in a forthcoming book to analyze this Puritan trend that has been of great influence upon orthodox Protestant life, especially in the attitude towards cultural activities and art.

472 See P. A. Scholes, *The Oxford Companion to Music* (London, 1947) s.v. 'Puritans and Music'.

473 Atlantic 1349, in the Southern Folk Heritage series, the album *White Spirituals* (recorded in 1959).

474 Riverside RLP 12-112, *History of Classic Jazz* I.

475 Ed. H. Courlander, Negro Folk Music from Africa and America, Folkways P 500 A. See also in the same album "Jesha for Oshun' from Brazil or the 'Nago dance' from Haiti on P 500 B.

476 Folkways P 500 B.

477 See also from America *The Psalms, Hymns and Spiritual Songs of the Rev. Isaac Watts, D.D.*, edited by Samuel Worcester, D.D., new edition by Samuel Worcester, AM. (Boston, 1851), and H.A.L. Jefferson, *Hymns in Christian Worship* (London, 1950), pp. 42-49, chapter title 'The Victory of Isaac Watts' (although the latter writer cannot refrain from voicing his anti-Calvinistic bias on every page).

478 Folkways PP 658, recorded by Fred Ramsay in 1954, in the album *Song and Worship* (*Music from the South* IX).

479 Folkways EFL 1418.

480 Race-records are records issued for and sold in Negro quarters. The older ones are quite rare. (Until a few years ago records of this type were still pressed in the old way, on '78 r.p.m.).

481 Some examples from the 1920s are Revd J.M. Gates, 'Amazing grace', Victor 20216, and 'Need of prayer', Columbia 14145; many sermons of Revd Burnett on Columbia; and Revd E. D. Campbell's 'Come let us eat together', and 'Let's go to my Father', Victor 35824. Even quite recently Race records of this type existed, such as Deacon L. Shinault (from Chicago), 'Lord I come to Thee, and I cannot Live in Sin' (Dr Watts) Ping 1005. About 1961 an LP recording of congregational singing in the Bethlehem Missionary Baptist Church of St. Louis, Missouri, included 'Amazing grace' sung in the Dr Watts manner: Rev. Cleophus Robinson and Sister Josephine James and Congregation, *Pray for me*, Peacock PLP 107 (Peacock is also a Race record company). Also A. Lomax's *Negro Church Music*, Atlantic 1351, records a hymn in this style by the Rev. R.C. Crenshaw, Memphis, Tennessee.

482 *Music From the South: Elder Songsters* II, Folkways FP 656.

483 Compare this with another example of solitary singing in the Dr Watts style by Suddie Griffins, Folkways PP 655, *Elder Songsters* I.

484 H. Courlander in his Negro Folk Music From Alabama, Folkways EFL 1417.

485 Nixa NJL 11.

486 Vogue LD 030.

487 Originally Columbia 145320, reissued several times: Folkways 55; Folkways FG 3585 (Blind Willie Johnson, ed. S. Charters); and by myself on Fontana 462022 TB.

488 Folkways FP 656, as quoted above in note 480.

489 Vogue 103.

490 Westminster WP 6089.

491 Cf. his performance of the eighteenth-century hymn 'A Charge to Keep I Have' about 1953, Vogue LDM 10008, remastered from Peacock, and some of the numbers on the LP Battle BM 6116 recorded about 1960.

492 Cf. Choice MG-507.

493 About 1953, King 577 LP.

494 Savoy MG 14014, ca. 1956.

495 Vogue LDM 10008, ca. 1952.

496 Above, note 473.

497 Peacock PLP 105, circa 1961.

498 King 573, Vogue LP 073, circa 1953.

499 We can hear this on Columbia CL 1548, Abyssinian Baptist Gospel Choir recorded in 1961 in a church in Newark, N. J. V

500 NCRV *Omroepgids* ('Broadcasting Guide') 32, 1956 – this was an introduction to a broadcast by the NCRV.

501 *Gramofoon*, December 1955. Record discussed: *Roland Hayes Sings*.

502 *Gramofoon*, February 1957.

503 *Gramofoon*, November 1957. Record discussed: *Two church services in Harlem: Christmas Day and New Year's Eve*, Ducretet-Thomson 260V069.
504 *Signaal* 4, 4, February 1962.
505 *Signaal*, April 1962.
506 *Doctor Jazz*, January 1963.
507 *Jong Gereformeerd* 8, March 1965.
508 *Ruimte* 1, 14, April 1955.
509 This is the term often given to modern dance music.
510 See A. Lomax's excellent biography, *Mister Jelly Roll* (London, 1952), which is also an excellent introduction to the history of jazz music.
511 Rudi Blesh, *Shining Trumpets, A History of Jazz* (New York, 1946) p.262.
512 R. Pryor Dodge, *Jazz, Its Rise and Decline*, Record Changu XIV, 3, 1955.
513 *Gramofoon*, April 1955. Record discussed: *Original Dixieland Jazz Band: Historic recordings of the first recorded jazz music*, HMV, 1955.
514 *Glorieuze Klanken* 6, 1950.
515 *Glorieuze Klanken* 12, 1953.
516 *Gramofoon*, May 1956.
517 *Glorieuze Klanken* 2, 1953. Record discussed: *George Lewis New Orleans Stompers*, Vogue.
518 *Gramofoon*, June 1956. Record discussed: *Johnny Dodds with the Dixieland Thumpers*, London AL 3505.
519 *Daniël* 27, # 9, 1972. Interview conducted by M. Golverdingen.
520 *Signaal* 2, 4, January 1960. Record discussed: *Les Maîtres allemands des XVIIe et XVIIIe siècles*, Sylvie Spycket ensemble, BAM LD 035.
521 *Signaal* 3, 7, May 1961. Records discussed: Bach Cantata No. 12, *Weinen, Klagen, Zorgen, Zagen*, and a mass by Mozart sung by the Viennese Sängerknaben and Symphoniker, directed by Rudolf Moralt, on Philips G 05403 R.

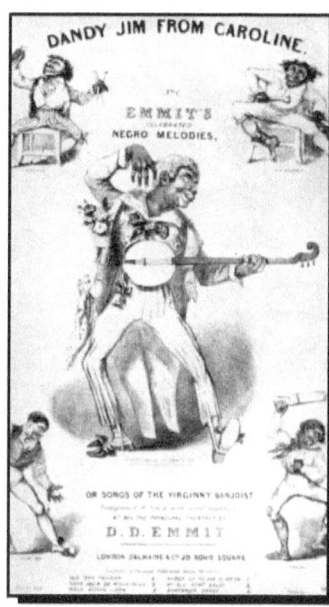

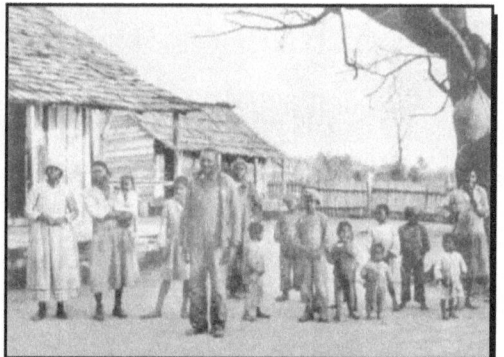

1. A manuscript edition of minstrel music. It shows how blacks were consciously subjected to parody (p.18).

2. A glimpse of a black village in the South. These people own a wealth of folk songs, often musically resplendent.

3. A chain gang. Black convicts at work in penal colonies in the 1960s still sang work songs as they were sung in the days of slavery (p.162).

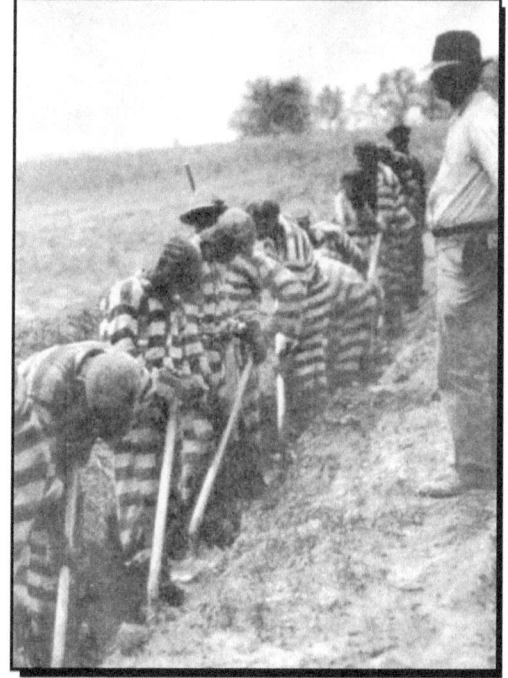

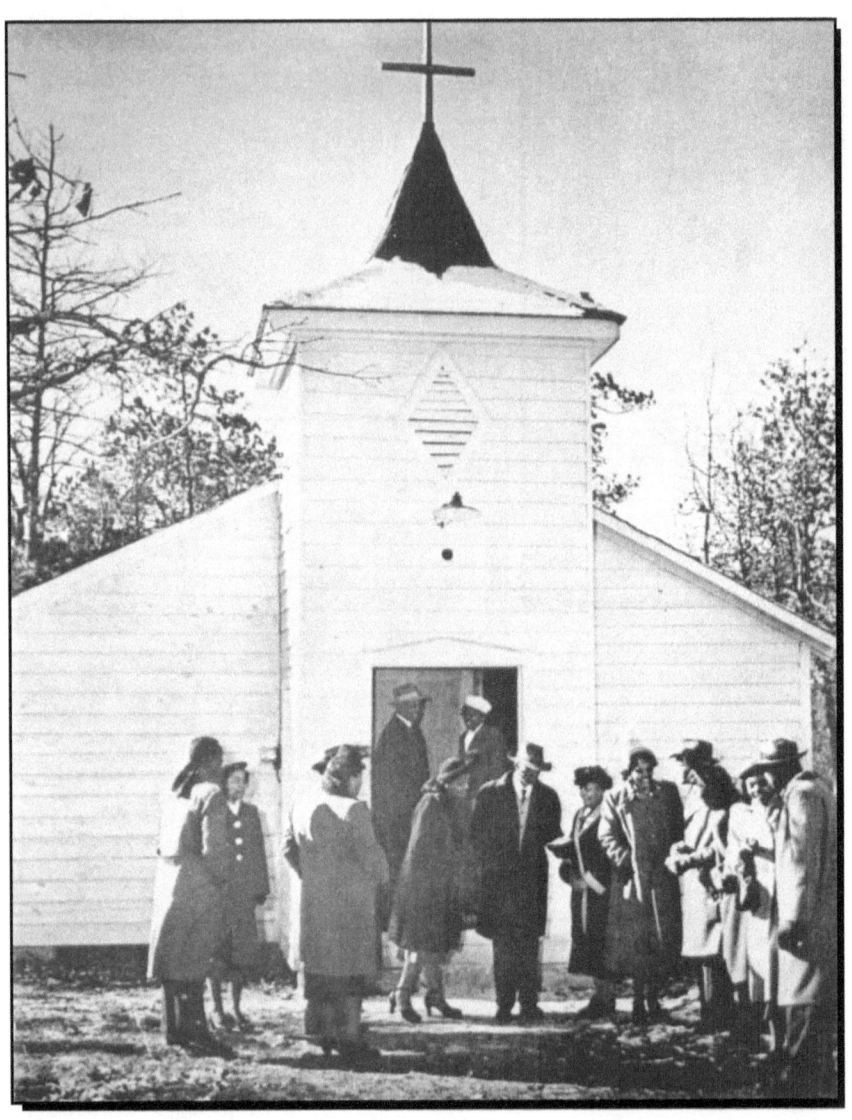

4. A typical wooden church common to the rural South (this one, in Virginia).

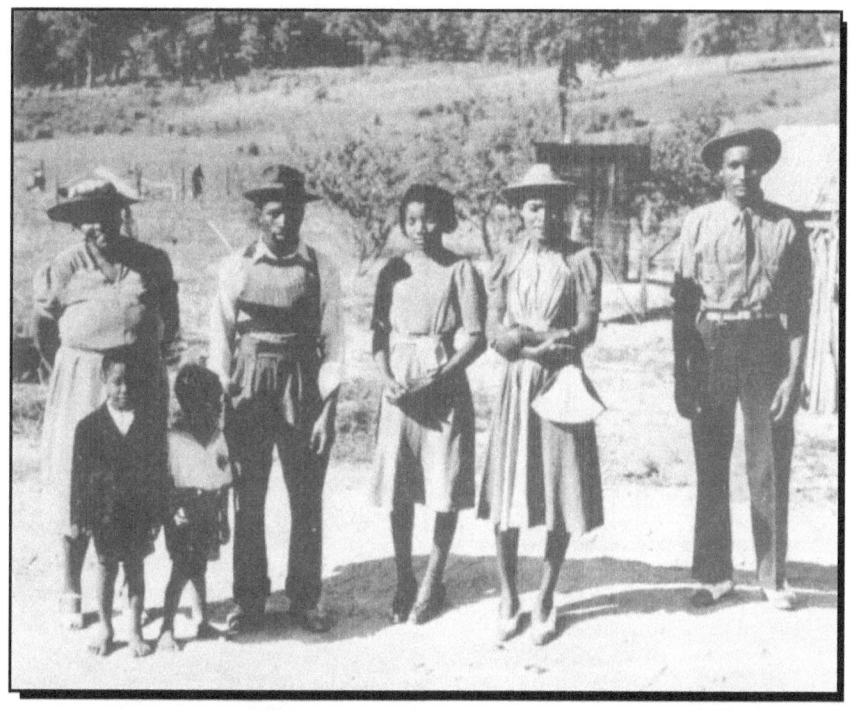

5. People going to church in their Sunday best (photo, around 1960).

6. A glimpse of the congregation during a service (photo, around 1960).

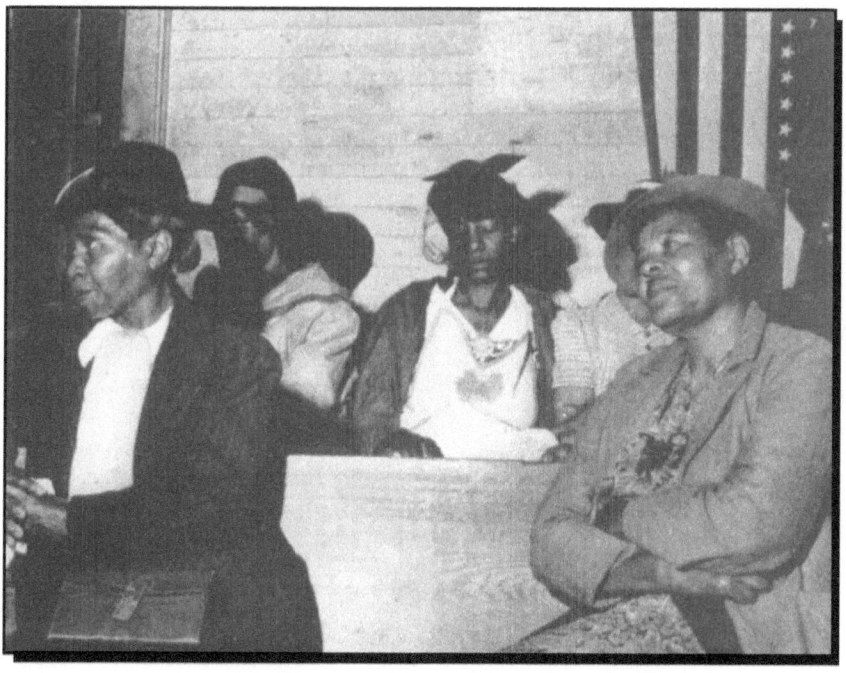

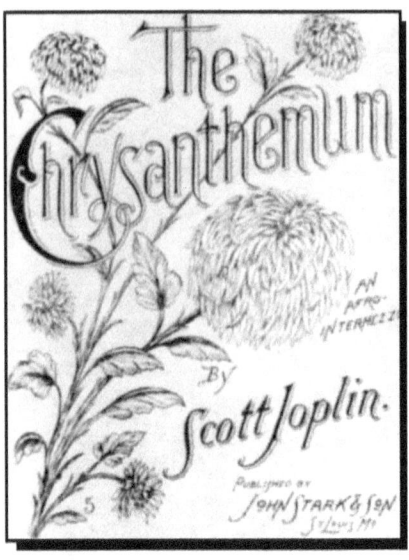

7. Front page of an issue of one of Scott Joplin's ragtimes (p.195).

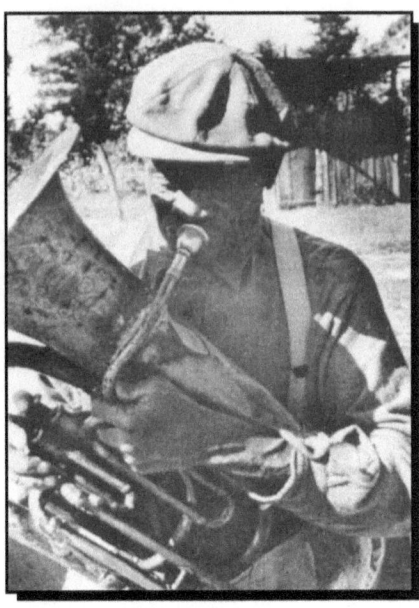

8. Jack Wimes, a euphonium player in one of the brass bands seldom seen in rural areas nowadays (p.193).

9. Scott and Celeste Dunbar while recording on Ramsey's tape-recorder (Mississippi, 1954). They were typical representatives of an active folk-music culture (p.290).

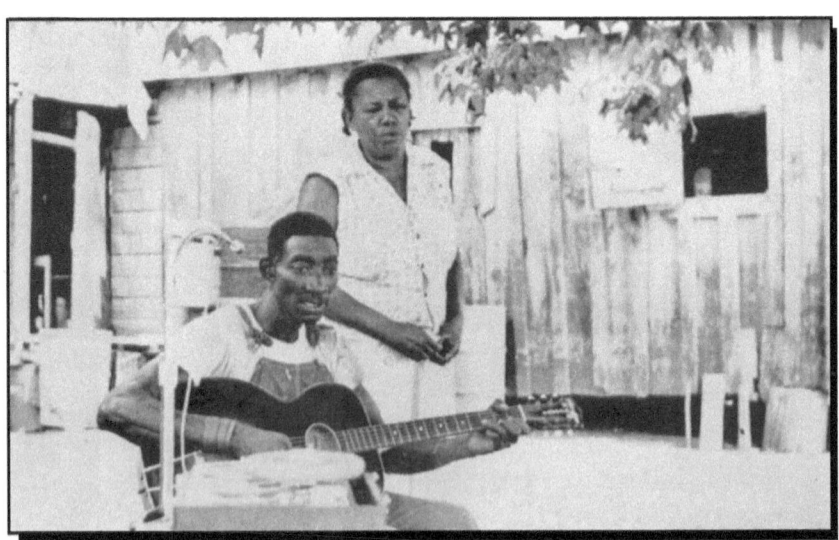

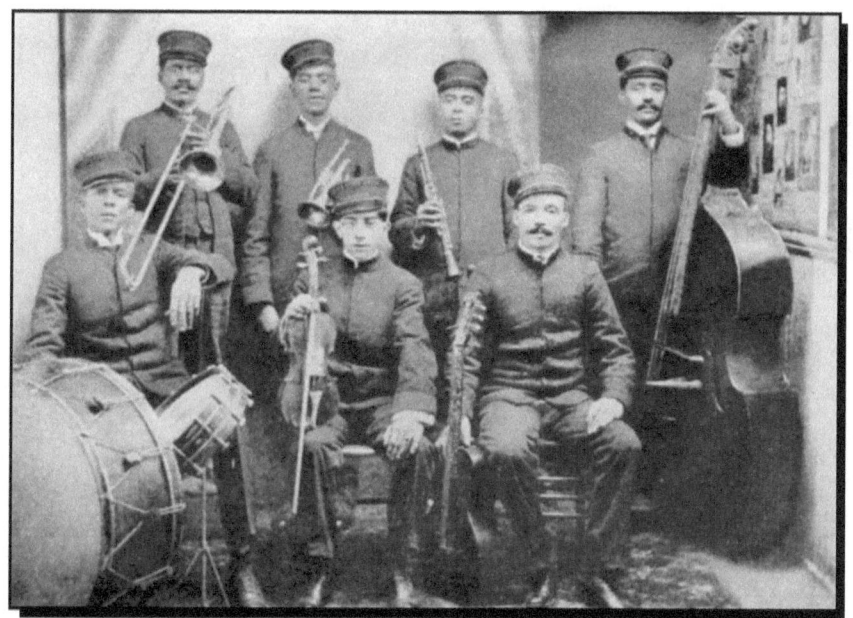

10. One of the first jazz-bands in New Orleans, the Superior Band photographed shortly after 1900. From Left to right: Buddy Johnson, Bunk Johnson, Big Eye Louis Nelson, and Billy Marrero. Seated: Walter Brundy, Peter Bocage, Richard Payne (see p. 204).

11. The famous King Oliver's Creole Jazz Band, whose performances and recordings made such a great impact – unparalleled. From left to right: Baby Dodds, Honoré Dutrey, Bill Johnson, Louis Armstrong, Johnny Dodds, Lilian Hardin, King Oliver (seated) (see p. 211 ff.).

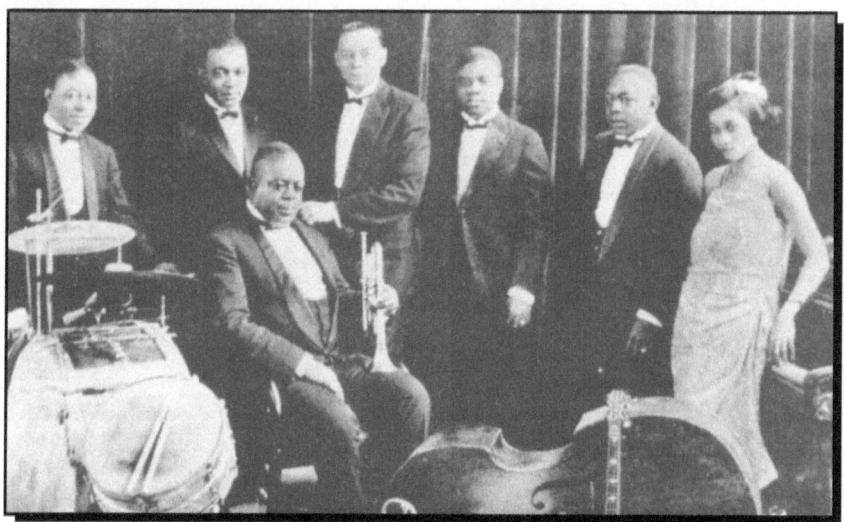

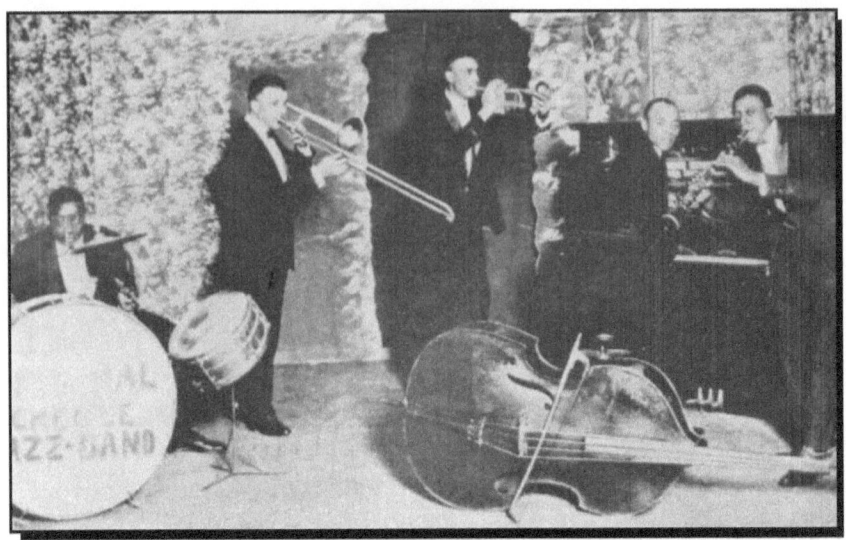

12. Kid Ory's band in which he played in San Francisco in 1921. From left to right: Minor Hall, Kid Ory, Mutt Carey, Fred Washington, Dink Johnson. Ed Garland, double bass, was absent.

13. Kid Ory and his band after 1945, playing on the West Coast once again. From left to right: Minor Hall, drums; Kid Ory, trombone; Lloyd Glenn, piano; John Buckner, trumpet; Joe Darensbourg, clarinet; Ed Garland, double bass (see p.283).

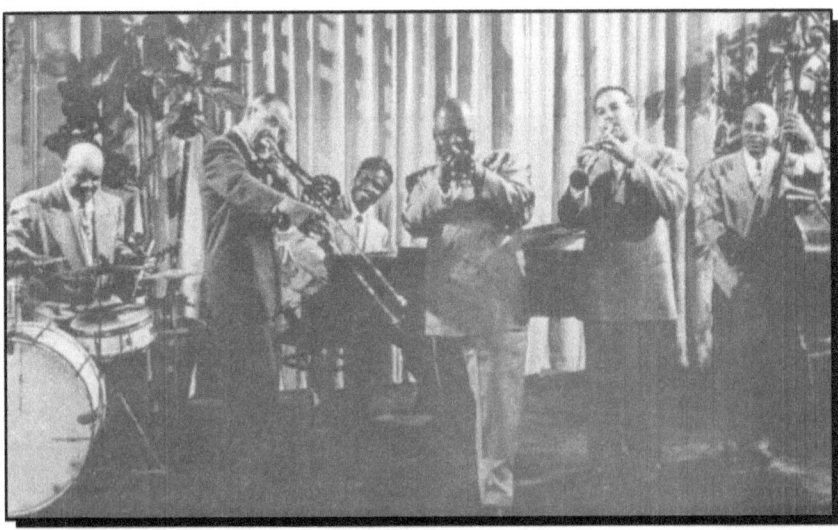

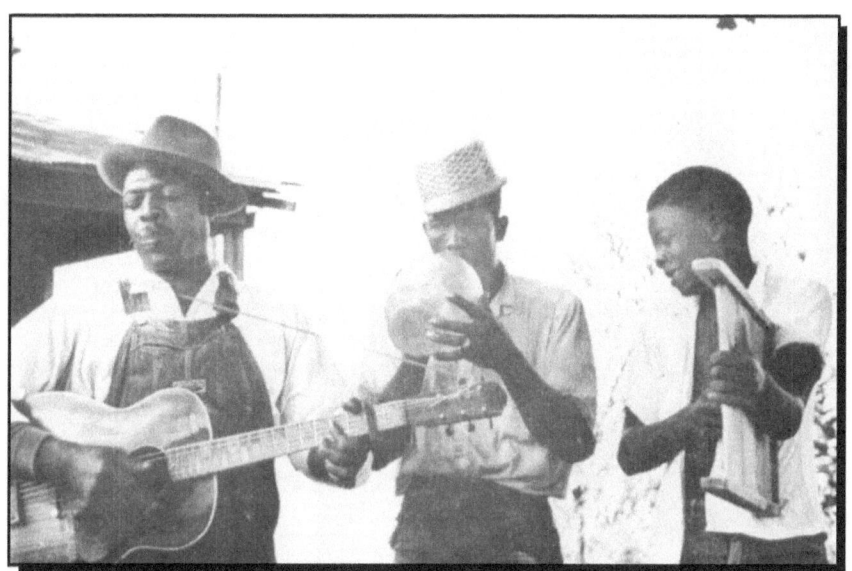

14. A band typical of those (still) found in rural areas. All the instruments used by this jug band were either home made or bought very cheaply. Pictured here are a guitar, a jug and a washboard. From left to right: Philip Ramsey Sr.:, Mozelle Moore, Philip Ramsey Jr. (p.234).

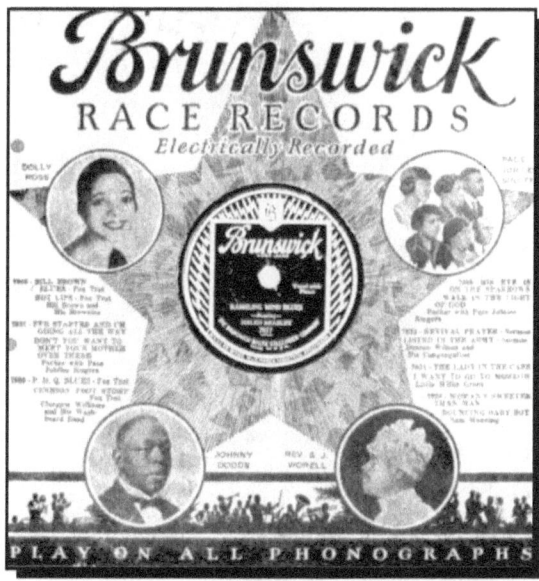

15. A Race record sleeve. This sort of record was exclusively reserved for black music played by blacks, and were sold in black neighbourhoods. They have preserved a great deal of valuable black music, jazz, blues and spirituals. The photograph on the sleeve includes a shot of Johnny Dodds and notice of a Clarence Williams record. There is also a preacher and a small choir which sung spirituals (ca. 1928–1929).

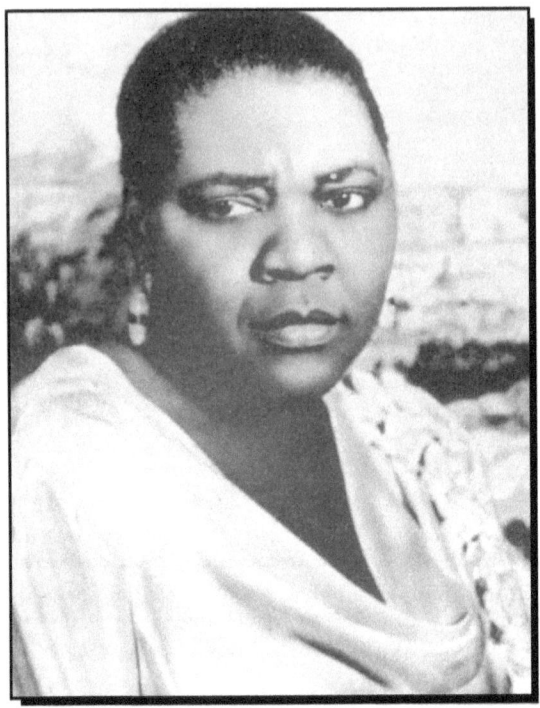

16. Bessie Smith. She sung the blues in an inimitable and very refined style. She was a real artist who performed all over the USA for very enthusiastic black audiences. Many recordings of her music were made and sold (p.230).

17. Gertrude 'Ma' Rainey, who performed mainly in the South, also for blacks. She may even have been a greater artist than Bessie Smith, her pupil. She was closer to her own folk, and she perceived the spirit of the blues as folk music better than the urban Bessie Smith, who was influenced by jazz (p.191).

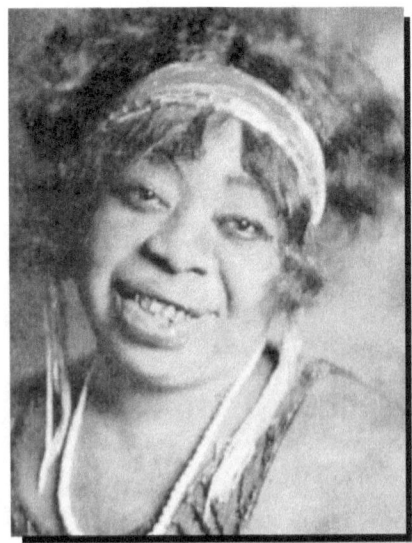

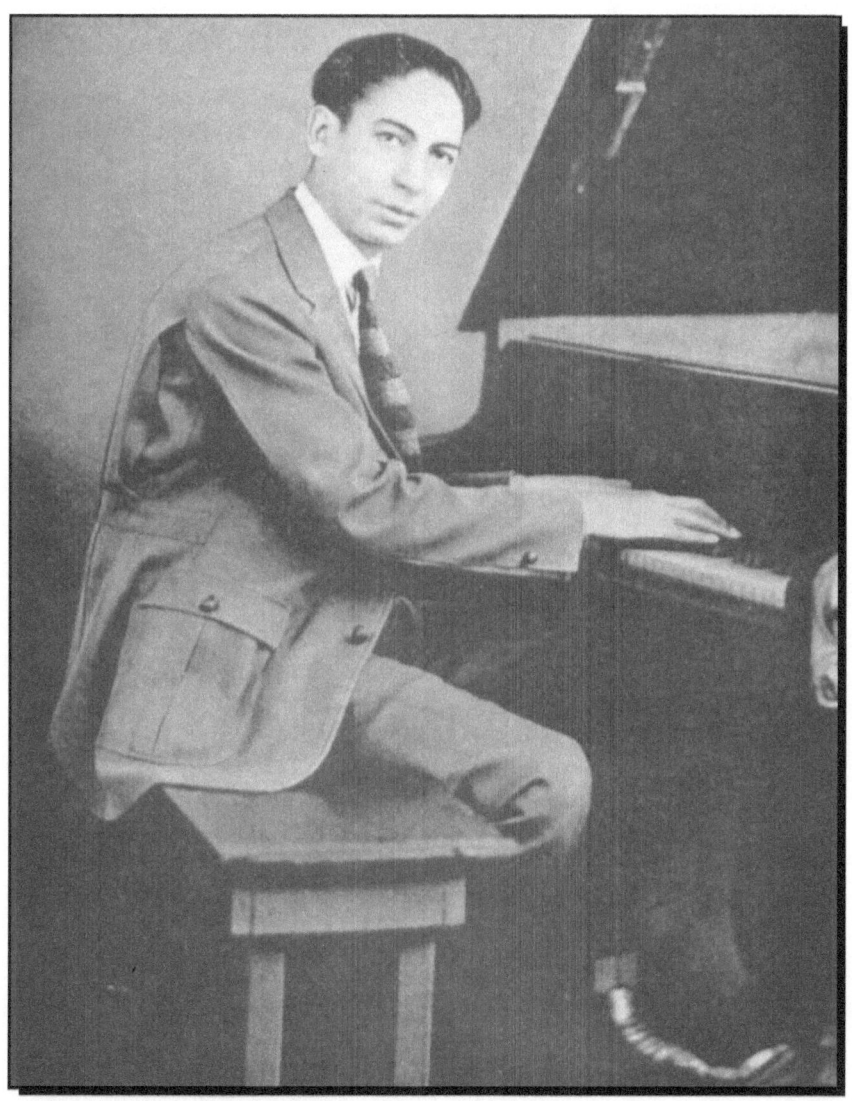

18. Jelly Roll Morton, the man who created and developed the jazz-piano style. He was a very intelligent and conscientious musician whose principles, which were very important to him, were of great significance in the evolution of New Orleans jazz. This photo dates back to the years he worked in Chicago, shortly after 1920 (p.218).

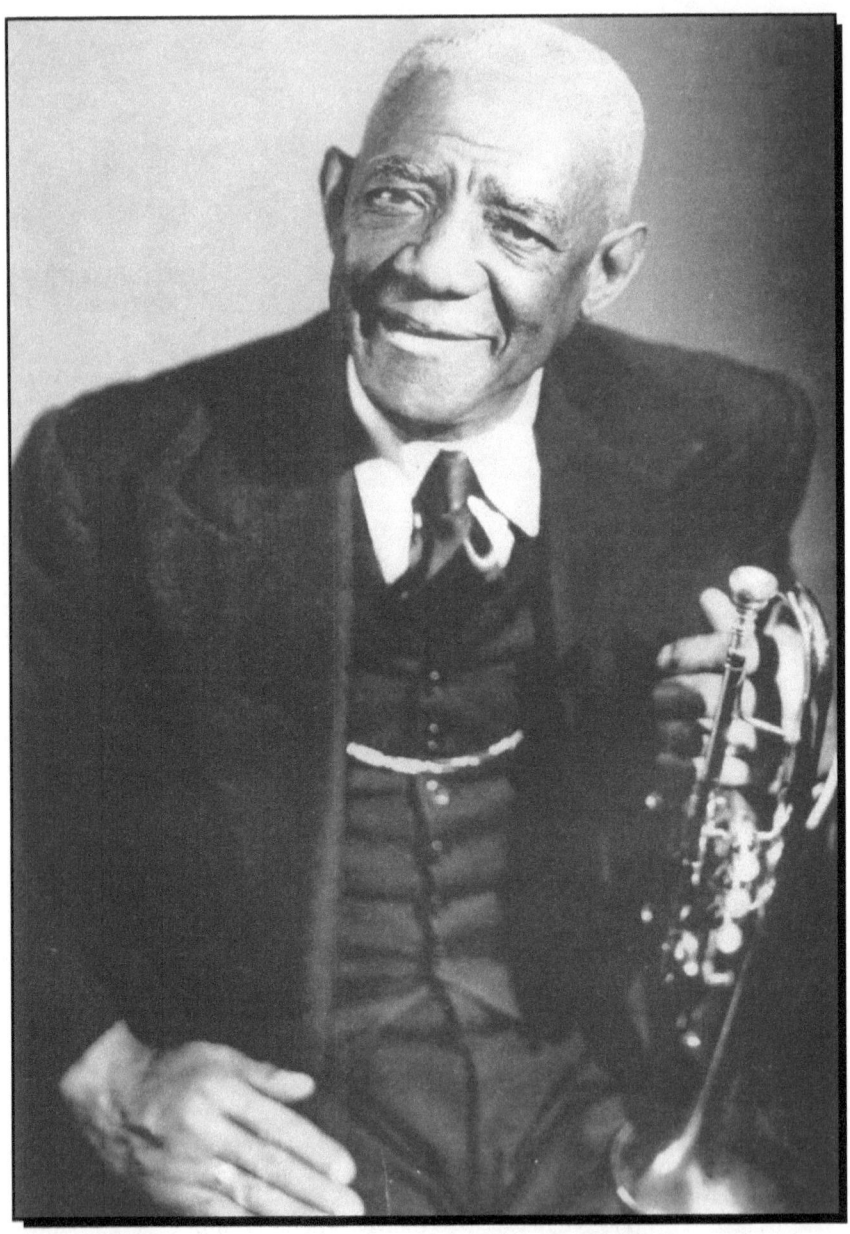

19. Bunk Johnson, one of the older trumpet players to have played a role in the creation of New Orleans' jazz at the beginning of the 20th century. The photo was taken in 1946 (p.281 ff.).

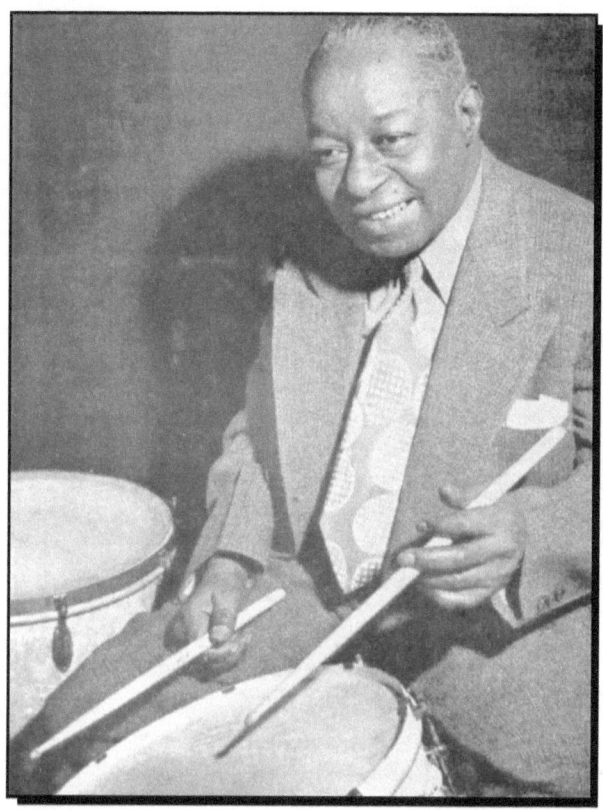

20. 'Babe' Dodds, Johnny Dodds' younger brother and the greatest drummer in the history of New Orleans jazz (pp.207, 282). He played with the King Oliver Band from 1923–1924 and from 1944–1945 in Bunk Johnson's band.

21. The Lewis-Robinson Band during a recording, with George Lewis on clarinet and Jim Robinson on trombone (p.283).

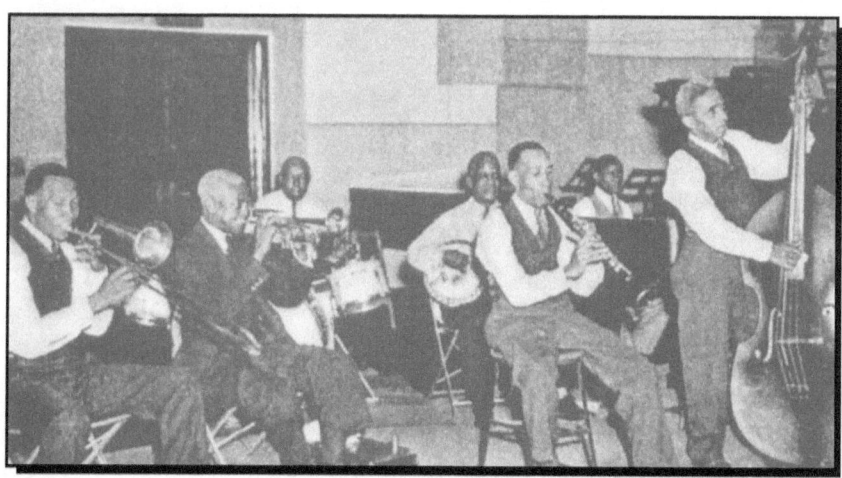

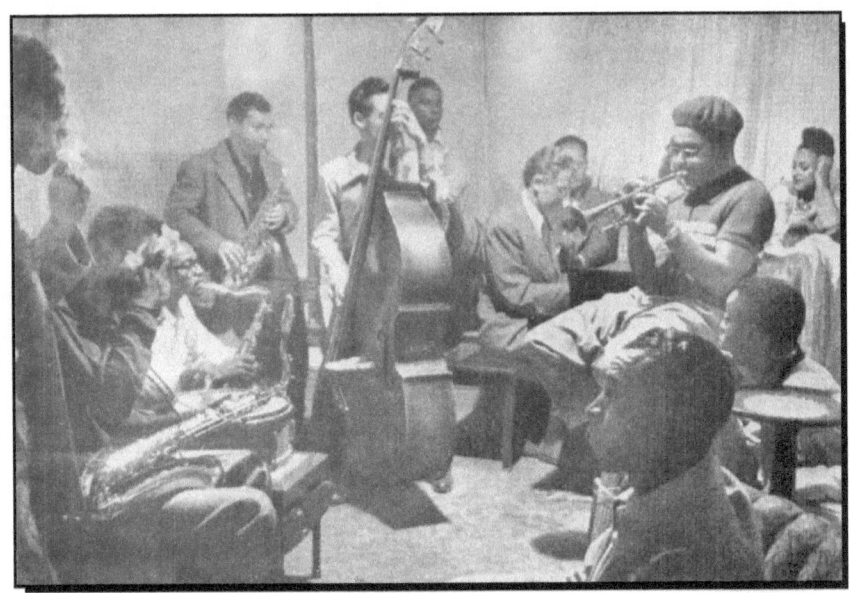

22. A jam session. Modern jazz was created at this kind of informal get-together in New York during the war years. Here we see Dizzy Gillespie (wearing a beret), who played a leading role in the shaping of it (p.275).

23. The Spirit of Memphis Quartet, one of the best ensembles in the field of contemporary church choir singing. For many years the ensemble consisted of the seven men, here from left to right: Jet Bledsoe (lead), Fred Howard (baritone), Earl Malone (bass) and below from left to right, Silas Steele (lead) and Robert Reed (tenor) (p.288).

24. The Dixie Hummingbirds. Although they too sing spirituals, both their name and their pose betray their commercial slant (p.286).

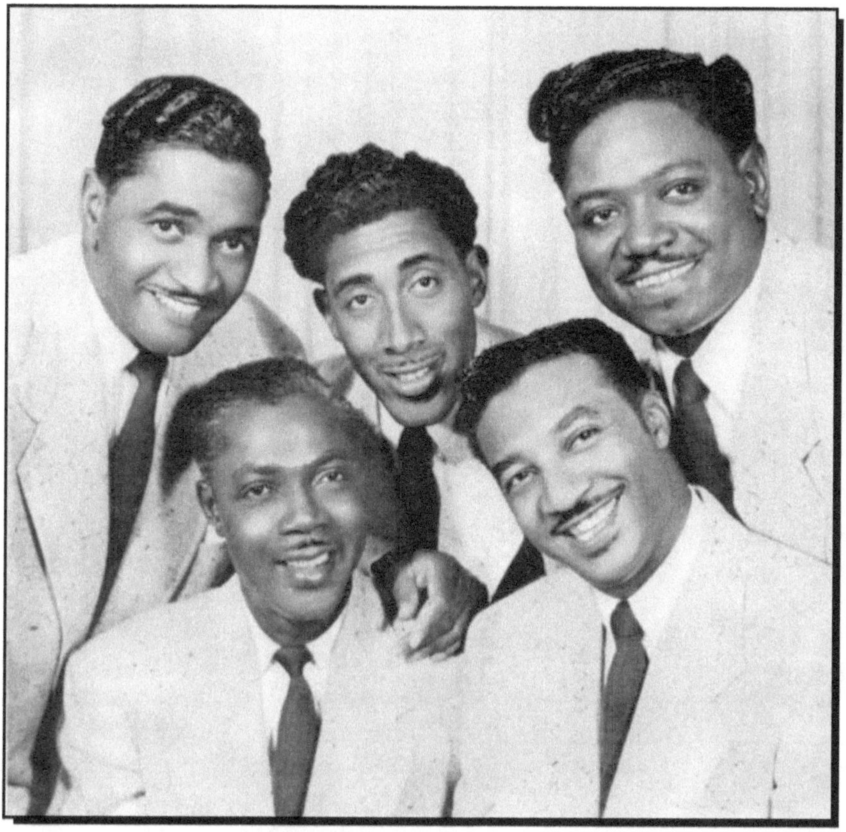

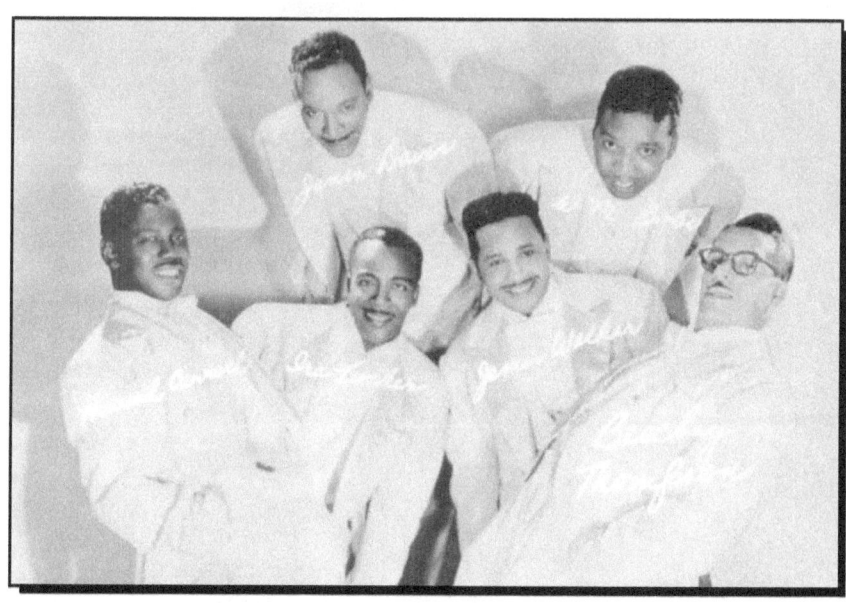

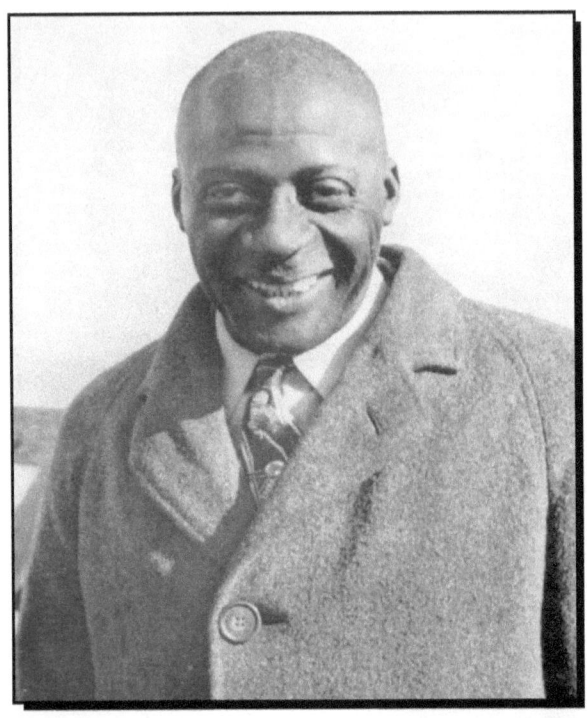

25. Doc Reed, a farmer whose extraordinarily beautiful singing of spirituals was discovered by Ruby Pickens Tartt from Livingston, Alabama, near where he lived. John A. Lomax made recordings of him for the Library of Congress and Courlander for Folkways (p.290).

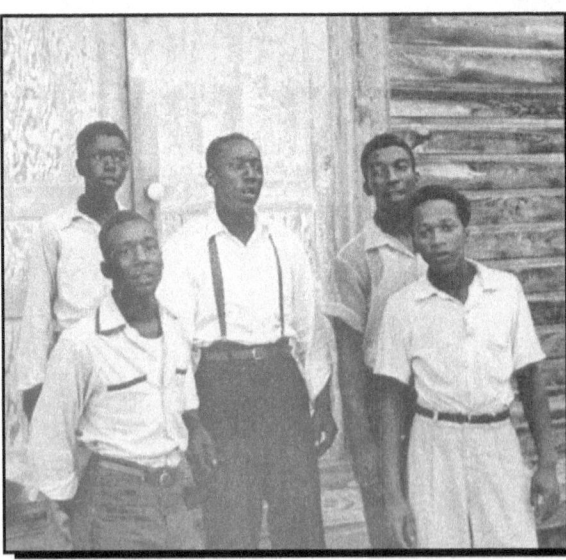

26. For many years small choirs that tried to imitate the Spirit of Memphis Quartet or sometimes the more commercial groups have been popping up throughout rural areas. They sung their spirituals in churches. These are the Starlight Gospel Singers, of whom Ramsey made recordings for Folkways in 1954 (p.290).

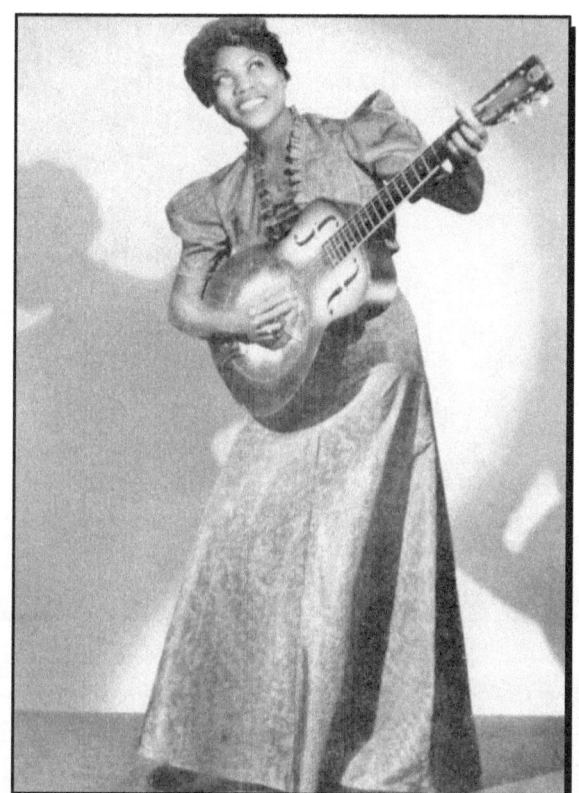

27. Sister Rosetta Tharpe, originally a 'crooner' with a big swing band, who after 1938 became one of the most prominent solo interpreters of black Christian church songs. Her style has been influenced by blues and jazz, although she joined in with the tradition of the spirituals of Blind Willie Johnson, Georgia Peach and others (p.267).

28. A storefront church in one of the big cities of the North. It was one of many small black churches housed in what had once been a shop, and where we can often hear beautiful spirituals being sung.

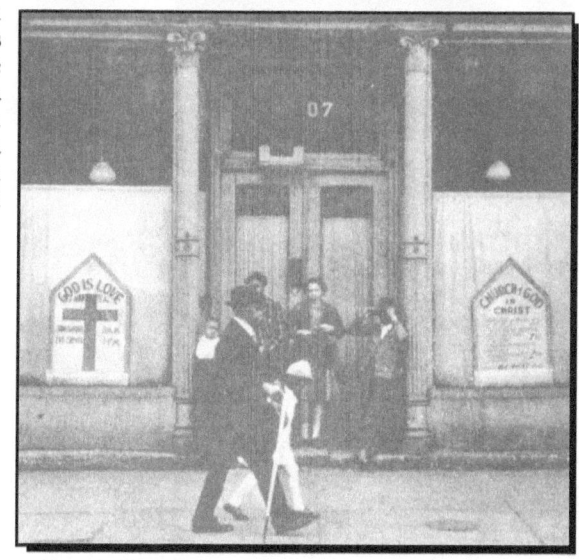

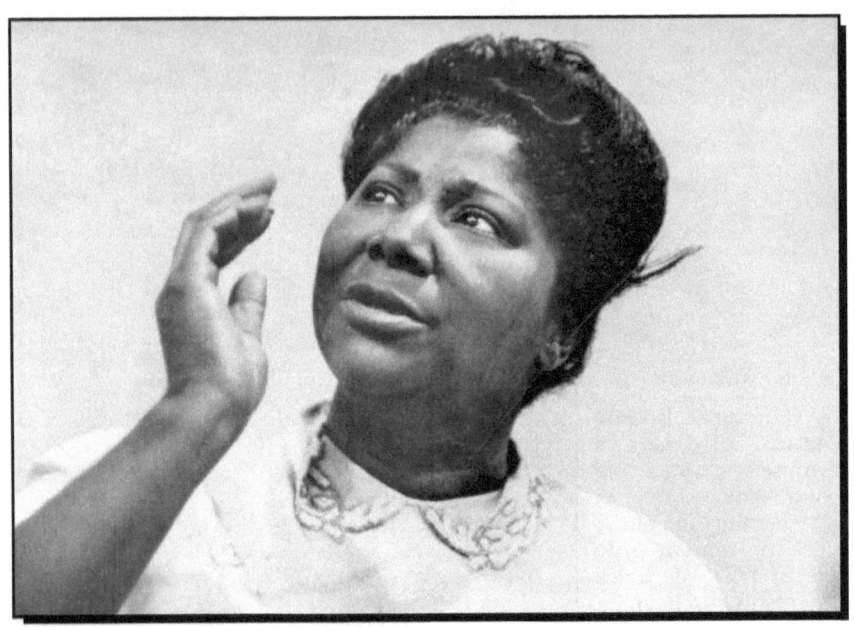

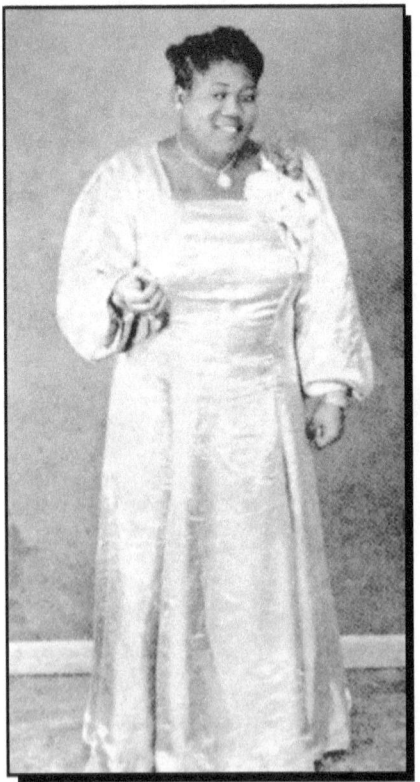

29. Mahalia Jackson during a performance – the most important ambassador of solo spiritual singing (i.e. gospel singing), who achieved great fame through her gramophone records (p.306 ff.).

30. Georgia Peach (Clara Gholson Brock) was already singing gospel songs in the 1930s, performing at church concerts all over the USA (p.306).

www.ingramcontent.com/pod-product-compliance
Lightning Source LLC
Chambersburg PA
CBHW031603210526
45464CB00004B/1414